Opening the Bible

Selected Writings of Antony Campbell, SJ

Opening the Bible

Selected Writings of Antony Campbell, SJ

ATF Theology
Adelaide

2014

Text copyright © 2014 remains with the author for all papers in this collection. All rights reserved. Except for any fair dealing permitted under the Copyright Act, no part of this book may be reproduced by any means without prior permission. Inquiries should be made to the publisher.

Unless noted otherwise, the Scripture quotations contained herein are from the New Revised Standard Version of the Bible, copyright © 1989, and 1993 by the Division of Chrisian Education of the National Council of the Churches of Christ in the United States of America, and are used by permission. All rights reserved.

National Library of Australia Cataloguing-in-Publication entry

Author: Campbell, Antony F., author.

Title: Opening the Bible : selected writings of Antony Campbell SJ /

            Antony Campbell.

ISBN: 9781922239808 (paperback)
ISBN: 9781922239815 (hardback)
ISBN: 9781922239822 (ebook)
ISBN: 9781922239839 (ebook ; pdf)

Notes: Includes bibliographical references and index.
Subjects: Campbell, Antony F.
            Bible. Old Testament--Commentaries.
            Priests' writings.

Dewey Number: 221

Cover design by Astrid Sengkey
Layout/Artwork by Anna Dimasi

Text Minion Pro Size 11

Published by:

An imprint of the ATF Ltd.
PO Box 504
Hindmarsh, SA 5007
ABN 90 116 359 963
www.atfpress.com

CONTENTS

Abbreviations (for the Contents only)
ABR	*Australian Biblical Review*
ACBA	Australian Catholic Biblical Association
ATF	Australian Theological Foundation
BETL	*Bibliotheca Ephemeridum Theologicarum Lovaniensium*
CBQ	*Catholic Biblical Quarterly*
CBQMS	*Catholic Biblical Quarterly* Monograph Series
Dtr	*The Deuteronomist*
FOTL	*The Forms of the Old Testament Literature*
MCD	Melbourne College of Divinity
WJKP	Westminster John Knox Press

Introduction
Page xi

Summaries Of What Is To Come
Page xvii

The Book of Job

Life and Job
Original: *God and Bible* (New York: Paulist, 2008), 115–20
Page 3

Job: Case Study or Theology
Original: *Psychiatry and Religion: Proceedings of 1987 Conference, pp. 38–44*
Page 9

God and Suffering—'It Happens': Job's Silent Solution
Original: *American Theological Inquiry* 3/1 (on-line)
Page 17

The Book of Job: Two Questions, One Answer
Original: *ABR* 51 (2003) 15–25
Page 31

Recommended reading:
Gustavo Gutiérrez, *On Job: God-talk and the Suffering of the Innocent* (Maryknoll, NY: Orbis, 1985).
Edwin M Good. *In Turns of Tempest: A Reading of Job* (Stanford, CA: Stanford University Press, 1990.)
Carol A Newsom, *The Book of Job: A Contest of Moral Imaginations* (Oxford: Oxford University Press, 2003).

The Books of Samuel

Synchrony and the Storyteller
Original: *David und Saul im Widerstreit: Diachronie und Synchronie im Wettstreit. Beiträge zur Auslegung des ersten Samuelbuches*, edited by W Dietrich, OBO 206; (Fribourg: Academic Press, 2004), 66–73
Page 47

Diachrony and Synchrony: 1Sam 24 and 26
Original: *David und Saul im Widerstreit: Diachronie und Synchronie im Wettstreit. Beiträge zur Auslegung des ersten Samuelbuches*. W Dietrich (ed). OBO 206; (Fribourg: Academic Press, 2004), 226–31
Page 57

From Philistine to Throne (1 Sam 16:14-18:16)
Original: *ABR 34* (1986): 35–41
Page 63

Who Dares Wins: Reflections on the Story of David and Goliath and the Understanding of Human Freedom
Original: *Psychiatry and Religion. Proceedings of 1986 Conference*, 49–66
Page 73

2 Samuel 21-24: The Enigma Factor
Original: *For and Against David: Story and History in the Books of Samuel*, edited by G Auld and E Eynikel, BETL 232 (2010): 347–58
Page 83

Associated books:
A Campbell, *1 Samuel:*   (FOTL, Eerdmans, 2003)
A Campbell, *2 Samuel:*   (FOTL, Eerdmans, 2005)

Narrative and Storytelling

Pentateuch Beyond Sources: A New Paradigm
(= PBS Introd + example: Gen 30:25–31:18)
Original: *ABR* 61 (2013): 18–29
Page 99

The Nature of Biblical Narrative
Original: previous use not able to be located
Page 119

The Storyteller's Role:
Reported Story and Biblical Text
Original: *CBQ* 64 (2002): 427–41
Page 133

Women Storytellers in Ancient Israel
Original: *ABR* 48 (2000): 72–73
Page 153

Child Sacrifice and God Wrestling:
Genesis 22 and 32
Original: Adapted from *Genesis Revisited: A New Reading–Beyond Sources* [in preparation])
Page 157

Preparatory Issues in Approaching Biblical Text
Original: *The Blackwell Companion to the Hebrew Bible*
Page 161

Associated books:
A Campbell, *Of Prophets and Kings:*   (CBQMS 17, 1986)
A Campbell, *Joshua to Chronicles*   (WJKP, 2004)

Form Criticism (OT)

The Emergence of the Form-critical and Traditio-historical Approaches
Original: *Hebrew Bible / Old Testament: The History of Its Interpretation.* Volume 3, Part 2, Chapter 31 (Göttingen: Vandenhoeck & Ruprecht, [planned for 2010; announced for October, 2014])
Page 185

Form Criticism's Future
Original: MA Sweeney and E Ben Zvi, editors, *The Changing Face of Form Criticism for the Twenty-First Century* (Grand Rapids, MI: Eerdmans, 2003), 15–31.
Page 219

Structure Analysis and the Art of Exegesis (1 Samuel 16:14–18:30)
Original: *Problems in Biblical Theology: Essays in Honor of Rolf Knierim.* Henry Sun, *et al*, editors, (Grand Rapids, MI: Eerdmans, 1997), 76–103
Page 239

Associated books:
A Campbell, *God and Bible* (Paulist, 2008)
A Campbell, *Experiencing Scripture* (ATF Press, 2012)

Nature of the Bible

Creationism! Utterly Unbiblical
Original: *Eureka Street,* 7 (1997): 30–34
Page 277

The Bible's Basic Role
Original: Paper read to the general meeting of ACBA, 2003
Page 287

Word of God or Word of God's People: The Bible's View
Original: adapted from the Epilogue in *Experiencing Scripture*
Page 301

The Pentateuch: Guard's Van or Engine
Original: paper read at MCD Centenary Conference, and the general meeting of ACBA, 2010
Page 313

Martin Noth and the Deuteronomistic History
Original: *The History of Israel's Traditions: The Heritage of Martin Noth.* S.L McKenzie and MP Graham, editors, JSOTS 182 (Sheffield: Sheffield Academic, 1994), 31–62
Page 319

Rethinking Revelation: The Priority of the Present over the Past
Original: previous use not able to be located
Page 353

The Reported Story: Midway Between Oral Performance and Literary Art
Original: *Semeia* 46 (1989): 77-85
Page 365

Past History and Present Text: The Clash of Classical and Post-Critical Approaches to Biblical Text
Original: *ABR*, 1991, 1–18
Page 377

Associated books:
A Campbell and M O'Brien, *Sources of the Pentateuch* (Fortress, 1993)
A Campbell and M O'Brien, *Unfolding the Deuteronomistic History* (Fortress, 2000)
A Campbell and M O'Brien, *Rethinking the Pentateuch* (WJKP, 2005)

Relationship to God

St. Ignatius Loyola and God's Unconditional Love
Original: *The Way* 43 (2004): 31-42
Page 399

God: Judge or Lover?
Original: *The Way* 30 (1990): 92–102
Page 411

The Growth of Joshua 1–12 and The Theology of Extermination
Original: *Reading the Hebrew Bible for A New Millennium: Form, Concept, and Theological Perspective,* W Kim, et al. (eds) (Harrisburg, PA: Trinity International, 2000), 72–88
Page 423

God, Anger, and the Old Testament
Original: *Psychiatry and Religion. Proceedings of 1988 Conference,* 15-19
Page 443

Dei Verbum:
Literary Forms and Vatican II—
an Old Testament Perspective
Original: *God's Word and the Church's Council: Vatican II on Divine Revelation* (Adelaide: ATF Press: 2014)
Page 451

The Good News and The Year for Priests
Original: *The Summit* 37, 2010: 8 & 10
Page 465

Qohelet the Wise
Original: previous use not able to be located
Page 471

Reflections Around Frank Gil's
Have Life Abundantly: Grass Roots First
Original: *InterfaceTheology* Volume 1 Number 1 2014
Page 473

**Some Thoughts for a Theologically Fuller
Eucharistic Prayer**
Original: Frank Gil, *Have Life Abundantly: Grass Roots First* (Adelaide: ATF Press, 2013), 103–6
Page 485

Associated books:
A Campbell, *God First Loved Us* (Paulist, 2000)
A Campbell, *The Whisper of Spirit: A Believable God Today* (Eerdmans, 2008)
Frank Gil, *Have Life Abundantly: Grass Roots First* (ATF, 2013)

Index of Biblical References
Page 489

Introduction

The beauty of a volume like this for someone like myself, whether collected essays or selected writings, is to see the struggle unfolding over a lifetime with fundamental issues of Christian faith and issues of the Older Testament, driven by the pressure of the biblical text.[1] Perhaps the younger me is best characterised by the reaction of the assembled students of the United Faculty of Theology to my self-description as a 'simple Bible Christian', a statement that was greeted with a wave of spontaneous laughter. Apparently students were not convinced; but I was sincere. I certainly held to the Bible as the 'word of God', however understood but understood by me in a fairly black and white way. Over the years, the biblical text has hammered at me to the point where the 'word of God's people' seems more appropriate and significant awareness is required in its use.

In this volume, the early part of the piece on the emergence of form criticism, in the five volume *Hebrew Bible/Old Testament* (HBOT; volume 3/2, chapter 31) reflects on this move with traditional academic distance. More technically, the major move for me was the realisation that the nature of the Bible was not to be learned from books about the Bible (not even 2 Timothy), not from Church pronouncements and teaching, and not from learned theologians. The nature of the Bible, what it was, was to be learned from close observation of the Bible itself, how it functioned and what it did. That is summed up for me in this volume in the article 'Word of God or Word of God's People: The Bible's View'. What the Bible did was frequently retain contradictory

---

1. None of the terms for Old Testament, Hebrew Bible, First Testament, or even Older Testament are fully satisfactory. Older and Newer Testament are more ecumenical than most (for more see at the start of *Making Sense of the Bible Difficult Texts and Modern Faith* [New York/Mahwah, NJ: Paulist, 2010], 2).

views. How it functioned, often enough, was to invite us to 'go think'. While that could be Word of God or Word of God's People, it is a long way from the black and white position of my earlier days.

I am not the sort of person who has long conceptualised and clarified smaller fragments or building blocks of our tradition which, because small, can be relatively complete and achieved. My restlessness has drawn me in other directions. The unfolding of it all over a lifetime can be glimpsed in these selected writings. Convictions in some areas are very long lived; that is as it ought to be. This issue of an understanding of the Bible is definitely one of those areas, an area where convictions are very slow to change. Many traditionalist folk will die traditionalist; many of the liberally inclined will die liberally inclined. All that any of us can do is simply plot as best we can the forces that motivate our views. All we can ask of others is that they look as openly as is possible at those motivating forces and go where they are led—wherever they are led.

Some figures joust; others quest. Jousters seek to prevail, that accuracy and clarity may triumph. Questers seek to pursue their task so that accuracy and clarity may shine a light into dark and obscure areas where accuracy and clarity may contribute to understanding. I hope to have always engaged in a quest for greater understanding. I distrust those who seek to prevail. It is not our human lot. My hope is that my view contributes. That is the hope of this volume.

The term 'Selected Writings' rather than 'Collected Essays' has been deliberately chosen since this volume represents about sixty to seventy percent of the material that was worth presenting here. The principles of selection are regrettably most pragmatic. Some texts that ought to be here are not to be found here simply because their documents were not to be found on my computer. Repetition has not been avoided; the evolution of an idea is important as are the multiple forces piled up in various ways that drive the evolution. Other texts are sometimes repetitive because the struggle with the nature of the Bible will often return to principal key passages in the Bible. It is appropriate here to admit that no one is totally unaffected by the spirit of the times and the quirks and fads that flesh is heir to. Nevertheless, it is my claim that the positions held here are driven by the biblical text first and foremost.

The pieces selected for this volume are grouped in half a dozen categories, some more obviously, some less so. First among them is the book of Job. It struggles, as do we all, with the issue of God and of evil in our world. The appeal to free will is too facile and too partial an answer; it has little to do with earthquakes and tsunamis, with plagues and famines, with droughts and floods, with hurricanes and cyclones, to say nothing of the inequality of the human lot across our globe. The book of Job struggles frankly and fearlessly with the issue; it has no answer, besides legitimating the struggle and scathingly rejecting some traditional approaches. At one stage, it offers a 'silent solution', the possibility of a category mistake, challenging Job to look at life in the animal world. It is a 'silent solution'; Job is not asked whether suffering in the human world is so different from that of the animal world, whether even human suffering is amoral, not caused by morality? It is left to us to wonder what these thirty or so verses mean within the book and within our lives.

The second category contains studies around the books of Samuel. 1–2 Samuel have been at the core of my life as a student of the Older Testament, involving two commentaries (*1 Samuel* and *2 Samuel*, FOTL 7 and 8). They are critical for an understanding of the confusion of story with history in some form or other. We may reflect on the media's claim that a TV presentation, a novel, or a film is based on 'a true story'. It may indeed be based on a true story; it may be a most biased portrayal of that story. Our courts of law reveal how differently reality may be remembered and portrayed. The unified block 2 Samuel 13–20 (too extensive to be treated here) can so easily be passed off as history, as best Israel's past could produce it. Examined more closely and more critically, it is a profound exploration of ruthless power and its capacity to corrupt—even Davidic power.

Naturally all of this concerns narrative and storytelling and so a third category was clear. It is often said that a picture is worth a thousand words. It is equally true that a story can communicate a message better than a theological or historical discourse. Israel probably handled its storytelling more professionally than we do. It may well be that Israel's narrative texts are better understood as bases from which storytelling begins rather than as reflections of the final form of stories. The storyteller's role was critical.

Academically, I come out of a form-critical stable; I claim myself as third generation von Rad. For my generation, form-criticism was a strong liberating force in the approach to biblical text. The attempt to pin this down in academic categories has, in my judgment, failed.

A central question must be asked, and too often is not: what kind of a text is this? The follow-up question is: what does this matter for its meaning? So there had to be a fourth category on form criticism. The HBOT chapter ('The Emergence of Form-critical and Traditio-historical Approaches') is certainly the most recent and probably the fullest and most objective of what I have written on the theme.

What is a constant in all of these concerns is the nature of the biblical text and that has to be the fifth category. One cannot constantly ask the question, 'What kind of a text is this?' without asking the question: 'What kind of a book is this in which these texts are accumulated?' We don't discover the answers in a treatise of dogmatic theology. We discover the answers in pondering the biblical text. So the probability of a Pentateuch had to be pondered. Some think of a Tetrateuch or less (stopping at Numbers or well before); others want a Hexateuch (going to Joshua) or even an Enneateuch (going to 2 Kings). The Deuteronomistic History deserved a fat book all of its own; the Chronicler's History, focused intensively on the Jerusalem Temple, got its share of a thinner book. The issues of revelation, storytelling, and the interplay of past and present all claimed their share of attention.

Finally, all of this made no sense without constant attention to the relationship with God, so that was the sixth category. It is a bit of a catch-all, but the issue of God, as one who exclusively loves or ultimately judges is central to Christianity and has its bearing on the issue of God's anger. Vatican II has a document on divine revelation and it needs to be put in perspective. Full Christian theology is best expressed in a eucharistic prayer, which legitimates where the collection ends.

It is neither possible nor desirable to provide a list of all the abbreviations used. Those who need to know will know where to look for these. Equally, original pagination is not provided and spelling, punctuation preferences, and such-like matters have not been unified. The listing of associated books is not so much tooting my own bassoon, but an indication of where smaller studies lead, or of broader investigations that are the background to these smaller studies. It is hoped that the collection will be of value to the many who treasure the biblical word.

POSTSCRIPT: shortly after I had finished this Introduction, I learned that Jesuit Theological College (JTC) would cease functioning as a theological institution at the end of 2014. In many ways, the material gathered here is a tribute to a forty-year generation of theological endeavour. I am deeply grateful to JTC, its faculty and students and the Jesuit Order that supported it, for what they made possible in that generation. Aspects of my understanding of Church and faith emerging from those years are expressed by Frank Gil in *Have Life Abundantly: Grass Roots First* (ATF, 2013).

Summaries Of What Is To Come

At this point, we offer a series of short summaries, one for each piece in the body of the book. They take the place of an index of subjects at the end of the book which, in a book like this, would be unwieldy and unhelpful. The summaries should help a reader find what they want to read and avoid what they don't want to. If bogged down in reading a piece, the summary may help answer the question: what on earth am I doing reading this? Placed separately, current thinking does not contaminate past thought.

The Book of Job

Life and Job
Summary

The book of Job is a study in human suffering. This piece addresses two issues from the book. First, can there be an altruistic worship of God or do we worship God for what we hope to get out of it? Second, when people suffer, what is going on and where is God. In the words of a recent book, Where the hell is God?[1] The book of Job's answer to the first question is: YES. On the second question, the traditional answers given by the friends are dismissed, but a straightforward answer is not forthcoming. The book settles for mystery; a reality not imprisoned in words but left mysterious yet life-giving. A comprehensive answer

---
1. Richard Leonard, *Where the Hell is God?* (Mahwah, NJ: Paulist, 2010).

to the issues associated with suffering is not within human reach. The pain associated with suffering does not reflect estrangement from God.

Job: Case Study or Theology
Summary

If the book of Job is presenting a case study, then the reader's approach must be pastoral. What can be said to someone in such suffering? What help is most effective? If the book of Job is a theological study of suffering in relationship to God, our approach to it must be totally different. There is a very delicate flower in the turf of Job's text and it would be a great pity to trample on it without being fully aware of what we are doing. If the analysis of Job presents him as a flawed and obsessive personality, then the endeavour to explore the condition of the sufferer before God in a limit case of the perfect human being whose suffering cannot be attributed to sin or human imperfection is destroyed. Job's blamelessness is critical to the whole enterprise of the book. The central message of the book of Job is that the origin of human suffering is not to be found in the malice of God or in the fault of the human sufferer. We can suffer without having brought it on ourselves and without being estranged from God.

God And Suffering—'It Happens':
Job's Silent Solution
Summary

John McKenzie, an honest exegete if ever there was one, settles on an 'experience of God' as the ultimate answer to human suffering theologically. Some such experience has to be the answer; there is no other. This piece, however, looks at the second section of God's first address (Job 38:39–39:30) as offering to move the whole issue to a quite different context. The experience of God is still crucial, but the context is radically other than generally allowed for in studies of the book of Job. It is possible that part of the text of Job allows for a context that is amoral. 'Amoral': where success or suffering depends on Nature's lottery of talent, energy, or luck—above all, luck. Human suffering is not exclusively associated with the moral quality of human living, with goodness and badness. Space must be allowed for the amoral. The first part of the speech given God is all about matters beyond the envelope of the earth—and beyond the grasp of Job. The matters of the second part are all within the envelope of our earthly world. They are about what Job *does not do*, rather than what Job *cannot do*. The realm of this second part is amoral, realm without the involvement of moral causes, a realm where what happens happens. The final verse in the book is important. It has long been known to scholars that, without changing the text, the verse cannot be understood along the traditional lines of 'I despise myself'. Job 42:6 is better understood as an exit line: 'I have had enough of this lamentation stuff'.

The Book of Job: Two Questions, One Answer
Summary

The first issue is about religious altruism; the second about the question why life is given to 'the bitter in soul'. To this second question, no answer is given. Job is said to have spoken rightly of God and Job's only utterance has been 42:5 when, in the book, Job has not seen anything at all. The logic of legal debate does not bring clarity to the issue. Job's attitude is portrayed coming out of a profoundly personal experience. What did the friends say? What was it that God condemned? When one turns to what Job said, an answer has not been found in words. By its very definition, an answer without words must be left in silence.

The Books of Samuel

Synchrony and the Storyteller
Summary

The next two pieces were presentations to Samuel specialists at a conference in Basle, Switzerland. A synchronic approach deals with the biblical text as we have it now. A diachronic approach deals with the biblical text through the lens of the historical trajectory assumed for it. It is a matter of product for the synchronic and process for the diachronic. In my judgement, instead of the Documentary Hypothesis with its intertwined sources (J, E, P, D; now with Blum, KP and KD), it is important to recognize three things. First, our biblical narrative texts are the base from which a storyteller might operate; they are not the finished product. Second, on occasion they make variant versions available to the storyteller, understanding that only one version would be used in a given telling. Third, aspects of the base text need to be filled out by the storyteller. Myth-making is important. Myth-makers are the historians and the storytellers who can make their beliefs plausible and widely accepted. The Pentateuch may be considered the originating myth of ancient Israel.

Diachrony and Synchrony: 1 Samuel 24 and 26
Summary

The comments from the previous piece are illustrated in the text of 1 Samuel 24 and 26. In the first passage, Saul, in pursuit of David, has retired to a cave to ease nature and David and his men are concealed in the back of the cave. Three versions are contained within half a dozen verses. Outside the cave, some interpretation by the storyteller is essential. In a synchronic telling of the story, choices have to be made for the events within the cave; outside the cave the storyteller's skills need to be allowed for. Works of art today can illustrate both approaches. They can be subject to microscopic analysis in the ateliers of specialists. The same paintings can be hung appropriately and viewed from respectful distances. As for paintings, so for texts.

From Philistine to Throne (1 Sam 16:14–18:16)
Summary

This piece is an address delivered to people interested in psychiatry and religion. Its basic concern was to counter the popular view of poor little David up against the mighty Goliath—a situation where God had to do the job for David. Instead it argues that according to the biblical text David was the right man for the job with the right tools—God's task was to enable David to have the courage to do what David knew he could do. Two texts are preserved separately in Hebrew and Greek; we will base our treatment on the Greek. In the Hebrew text, where it is different from the Greek, David's motivation is ambition: what will be done for the man who kills this Philistine? In the second variant, preserved in both Hebrew and Greek, David's motivation is his trust in Yahweh. The preservation of two variants, which are not mutually exclusive (ambition and faith), leaves readers with a task: go think. Which is the better motivation? Equally, which is the better approach: belief in a God who does the job for you or belief in a God who enables you to do what you know you can?

Who Dares Wins: Reflections on the Story of David and Goliath and the Understanding of Human Freedom
Summary

Like its predecessor, this is an address that was delivered to people interested in psychiatry and religion. As will be clear, the David and Goliath story is far more than a piece of Davidic propaganda as to how David rose to prominence in ancient Israel. A major issue is raised for us to think about. How does God work in our midst? The previous piece dealt with this and the issue of motivation by ambition or faith. This piece focuses on the issue: do we in prayer ask God to do things for us or do we ask God to empower us to use our human talents and prowess and therefore act with courage and the readiness to risk our best? The story is all about divine action and human freedom. What God did for David was to enable David to do what he could do for himself. In such theology, God is a companion and a partner.

2 Samuel 21–24: The Enigma Factor
Summary

This paper was originally delivered to a conference of Samuel specialists in Nijmegen, Holland. There are six elements in these four chapters. Traditionally they have been distributed across the books of Samuel where modern scholars judged they best belonged. Recent scholarly work has shown that the concentric structure of these materials must be preserved. The paper argues that there are three waves in the traditions of David that have come down to us. The first wave reflects David's coming to power; it is substantially favourable. The second wave reflects David's middle years, in power in Israel; it is reflectively neutral, both admiring and critical. The third wave, 2 Samuel 21–24, surprisingly brings a critical edge to the picture of David. Ambivalence (innocent and not-so-innocent readings) is present in this third wave and must be respected.

Narrative and Storytelling

Pentateuch Beyond Sources: A New Paradigm
Abstract[2]

The Documentary Hypothesis has lost its dominant position in current pentateuchal studies. A new paradigm has not yet emerged to take its place. Two factors, one economic (the cost of hand-copied manuscripts) and the other textual (the brevity and often incompleteness of textual units), suggest a new paradigm, the text as 'user-base'—the text as a base from which an intermediary (probably among 'the wise') would lead into a theological reflection, or the telling of a story, or whatever was appropriate to the occasion. Such intermediaries would expand a text as needed, would supply whatever supplementary information was needed, and would expand the telling appropriately. The so-called pentateuchal sources are by-and-large compiled chronologically. Three traps of this procedure related to the grasp of meaning are outlined.

The Nature of Biblical Narrative
Summary

Something of a paradigm shift has been in the making for a while in biblical studies. A resolution of tensions between critical and

---

2. This ABSTRACT, in contrast to the summaries, was part of the original publication.

literary approaches is still to be achieved. The focus of this piece is the relationship between oral performance and written text. Central to it is the notion of the 'reported story'—the outcome of reporting what a story is about. Associated with this is the idea of written biblical text serving as base for oral performance. Many biblical texts look in two directions. Rearward, they look back to the storytelling traditions involved; forward, they look to the stories to be told in the future. The reported story is a base for the storyteller whose job is to retell the story. The reported story preserves the past while preparing for a future telling. The move is from oral (past story) to written (reported story) to oral (future story). A high tradition of storytelling leads to a high tradition of reporting, and serves to foster equally high standards in the future.

The Storyteller's Role: Reported Story and Biblical Text
Summary

While the preceding piece treats of both the reported story and the biblical text as base for storytelling, this present piece focuses more on the reported story. In large part, the Pentateuch, the Deuteronomistic History, and the Chronicler's History are composed of smaller story units. It is these smaller units on which attention is focused, with a priority given to the notion of reported story. The key question to be answered is whether the practice of the reported story existed in ancient Israel and therefore may be visible among our texts. The attribution of a role to the storyteller resolves significant problems in many storytelling texts. For the most part, the difficulties involved in many biblical story-based texts can be entrusted to the good sense of the skilled storyteller.

Women Storytellers in Ancient Israel
Summary

The previous piece dealt with two assumptions: first, that narrative text need not be a story as performed but might be a report of the story; second, that narrative texts were often not a storyteller's final production but rather a base from which storytelling would begin.

This short little piece takes up another assumption: the widespread view that storytellers were usually men. It contains an assumption itself: I assume that palace singers were among the storytellers of ancient Israel. Stories would have been sung rather than not.

Child Sacrifice and God Wrestling: Genesis 22 and 32
Summary

This piece makes the enormously significant distinction between stories told in mythic time and stories told in historic time. Taken in historic time, the story of Abraham's being commanded to sacrifice Isaac and the story of God's wrestling all night with Jacob are correctly called 'outrageous'. Both two stories are situated in mythic time and that the participants in both are the same, God and Israel. Von Rad's words about the wrestling story, 'It contains experiences that extend from the most ancient period down to the time of the narrator,' are true of both stories. There are times when von Rad's Lutheran piety can lead him astray. There are times when his instinct is spot on. In this judgement, I believe his instinct was spot on. Trust in God's commitment is fine, and religious believers entrust themselves to that divine commitment; but we have no idea what it might look like and neither did Israel. For Christians, it is associated in some way with Jesus Christ.

Preparatory Issues in Approaching Biblical Text
Summary

This piece was originally written for a general handbook on Old Testament studies.[3] Some 'how to' articles are controlled by theory rather than practice. My aim was to avoid this trap. What is written here may initiate people into what this practitioner believes are among the central preparatory tasks of biblical interpretation. 'Critical' is the element that separates moderns from their predecessors. The nature of the text (as God's word?) can be a massive issue; both divine and

---

3. *The Blackwell Companion to the Hebrew Bible,* edited by Leo G Perdue (Oxford: Blackwell, 2001).

human texts can claim to impose thought or to invite to it. The nature of the biblical text can only be determined by close observation of the text itself. The biblical text tends to amalgamate, not to adjudicate. It is helpful to realize that we approach texts in much the same way that we approach people. In this context, we need to be aware of the difference between us meeting people and medical professionals meeting patients. It is akin to the difference between *reading* a text and *studying* a text. A good model for approaching the study of a text is that of a worker approaching a job. First the worker studies the job: what needs to be done? where is the best place to start? what questions need to be answered and what can be said about the job overall? Then the toolbox is opened and the worker reflects on what tools are likely to be most useful and what order to use them in? After that, it is up to a good worker to get good results. The insights of biblical criticism have been validated over a long period of time. The awareness flowing from these insights and questions will in varying ways shape part of the context within which any interpretation of biblical text proceeds.

Form Criticism (OT)

The Emergence of the Form-critical and Traditio-historical Approaches
Summary

This piece was commissioned for a five volume encyclopedia of biblical studies covering biblical interpretation from the year dot to the present day.[4] Authors for the five volumes have been recruited from all over the world. I am particularly proud to have been invited, as a non-German, to do this article on form criticism and tradition history. Despite coming out of a strong form-critical stable (above all, Gerhard von Rad and Rolf Knierim), I am sceptical of the role form criticism has been asked to play in much recent biblical scholarship.

---

4. *Hebrew Bible / Old Testament: the History of its Interpretation*, edited by Magne Saebø (Göttingen: Vandenhoeck & Ruprecht, 1996–2014).

The article basically traces form criticism from its beginnings with Hermann Gunkel selectively to the present day with Rolf Knierim. Form criticism has its origins in the conviction that the analysis of sources was a job splendidly well done, which had had its day. Whatever else has been done, the central question of form criticism remains, a question that must always be asked and answered: what sort of text is this? The attempts to move form criticism from an informed intuition to an academic discipline are manifold. If they succeed, the future will not lack for work.

Form-Criticism's Future
Summary

Form criticism had a meteoric rise in the early part of the twentieth century and fell from favour at its end. If it embodies an essential insight, it will have a future. If form criticism is to regain a place in the armoury of the interpretative arts it needs to be refocused on the lasting insight and value that once contributed to firing enthusiasm for it. For Gunkel, the move to the distant and often non-Israelite oral past may have been liberating, despite its highly hypothetical quality and deep uncertainty; it offered an opening to literary appreciation. The focus away from the present text into a surmised past did not generate enough value for those focused on the final text. Intrinsic to form criticism is a focus on the itself text before undertaking any analysis of the event contained within the text. The second wave of twentieth century form criticism was headed by von Rad and Noth. The task of systematizing OT form criticism was taken up in their different ways by Klaus Koch and Rolf Knierim. Looking back, Gunkel turned to form criticism because, for him, the source criticism (*Literarkritik*) of his time lacked any meaningful attraction. A later generation turned away from form criticism because, for many, it had been refined to the point of losing all meaningful attraction. If form criticism is to have a future, it will have to focus on two key areas in the study of biblical text. First, what is the nature of this text? Second, what is the shape or structure of this text, its basic components, and their relationship to each other.

Structure Analysis and the Art of Exegesis (1 Samuel 16:14–18:30)
Summary

A central feature of Rolf Knierim's teaching was the establishment of a Structure Analysis of any text being closely considered. What are the main blocks making up the texts? How do the elements under consideration relate to the other parts of the text? How does meaning flow from all this? Not a list of contents (He entered the room and spoke) but an assessment of formal elements (Introduction to a speech). The problem in this case is that the text in question is a combination of two quite different stories: David, man of faith (God is with me); David, man of ambition (what's in it for me?). The two, ambition and faith, are potentially compatible; in the text they are not. Would it be respectful of the text to make compatible what the text does not make compatible. So I put one story in roman type (main story and the other in italic (variant). So what is nature of the text? The story of David's rise to prominence? But there are two stories! Perhaps it has to be: legends of David's rise to prominence. As such, the biblical text is a base from which the storyteller begins, offering the choices that a storyteller must make in presenting such a story.

Nature of the Bible

Creationism! Utterly Unbiblical
Summary

This piece arose out of a moment of outrage at some claim made for creationism. The complexity of the biblical handling of creation was to the fore. It is quite clear that Israel believed in a creator God, but Israel also had multiple presentations of how that creation was brought about. Israel used its belief in creation to maximum theological effect. Belief in God as creator was a resource for life and prayer. Creationism as a literal interpretation of the Bible is bunk.

Literalism can be a bit of a red herring. I take the Bible as literally as it wants to be taken—but it is not always easy to determine how literally it wants to be taken. It is a sad day for us when we allow ourselves to be persuaded to abandon all the theological wealth of the Bible on creation and to believe that when we take the Bible literally we find so insipid a message as creationism.

The Bible's Basic Role
Summary

We begin with the outcome of a life devoted to the study of the Bible. It may not be a mine of information or instruction, but it may be an invitation to reflection and response. There are two quite different approaches to biblical text. A *spiritual* approach focuses on reading rather than study, looking primarily to spirituality, prayer, preaching, and so on. A *critical* approach focuses on study rather than reading, explores the incarnational, probes the foundational, and risks the interpretational. The biblical text does not impose thought on us from outside; it invites us inside ourselves and calls us to reflection. I do not want neon lights, but the soft uncertain illumination that filters through so much of human living. I have a very strong religious faith and I have very deep doubts. I do not find the fact of doubt to be in conflict with the act of faith. I do not look for modern science in biblical texts; I do not look for insights into the meaning of life in recent science. The discoveries and theories of science are fascinating and illuminating. They do not diminish our sense that we and our universe are insufficient. So we seek a cause that is sufficient; the sense of spirit validates our search.

Word of God or Word of God's People: The Bible's View
Abstract[5]

There is no question that the Bible is the Sacred Scripture of the Jewish faith and the Christian faith. There is the question Why? An

---
5. This ABSTRACT, in contrast to the summaries, was part of the original publication.

obvious answer would begin that the Older Testament is concerned with the origins of the Jewish people, of much of their law, and wise reflections on their lives, besides being the Word of God. The faith of Christian people embraces that and goes on in the Newer Testament to the life, death, and resurrection of Jesus Christ—the story of it in the Gospels and reflection on the meaning of it in much of the rest of the Newer Testament.[6] Is that the whole story or is there more to it? 'The word of the Lord' or 'the word of God' (*debar yhwh*) has a lot to do with it, but there is an enormous amount of thinking that has to go into that. There is also the fact that verses of the Bible often differ from or contradict one another (my mantra: the Bible often amalgamates, it seldom adjudicates). That involves the invitation 'Go think' and that invitation can be offered by our God or by the wise among God's people. What does that say about the nature of at least substantial parts of our Bible?

The Pentateuch: Guard's Van or Engine?
Summary

This piece takes the position that the Pentateuch is best understood as the guard's van rather than the engine in the train of Israel's traditions. Looking over the Pentateuch's traditions, right at the beginning there is the massive difference between act and consequence (do the deed, experience the consequence, as a hand placed on a hot stove), which needs no God, no umpire, as in Genesis 3:7, and crime and punishment which needs a God, a judge, as in Genesis 3:14-19. There are so many other things: three locations for Abraham; two for Isaac; Jacob with conflicts all over the place. Things get no better in Egypt. The Sinai traditions are rich in tension. The great Julius Wellhausen in the nineteenth century and Gerhard von Rad both argued that the Sinai traditions were late. But their views did not prevail. A giveaway is that these traditions are about 'all Israel' and all Israel cannot be

---

6. For reflection on the terms Older and Newer Testament see the box on page 2 of AF Campbell, *Making Sense of the Bible: Difficult Texts and Modern Faith* (New York/Mahwah, NJ: Paulist, 2010). While no terminology is fully satisfactory, Older and Newer indicates sensitivity to Jewish sensibilities and may not pose insuperable problems to many NT scholars.

early. Christians can be grateful that the infancy narratives (Matt 1–2 and Luke 1–2) have recently been seen as written after the gospels, presenting in story the understanding portrayed in the gospels. So too for the Pentateuch. The fact of our understanding ourselves and our situation better reveals to us something of who we are—and also something of who our God is and aspects of the story of God's relationship with us. Seen as Israel looking back on its experiences, the Pentateuch has surprising depth.

Martin Noth and the Deuteronomistic History
Summary

Martin Noth was the father of the Deuteronomistic History, proposing that subject to certain modifications of the text, there was a single unified text from Deuteronomy to Second Kings. An overview presents the unified structure. This unified structure, the house that Noth built, has been subject to the attentions of restorers, rebuilders, and redecorators. An appendix provides the text of the Deuteronomistic History as identified by Noth, with a layout that allows the reader to see the text assumed to be original (aligned left), the deuteronomistic material added to it (indented and italicised), and texts assumed by Noth to be later (aligned right and also italicised).

Rethinking Revelation: The Priority of the Present Over the Past
Abstract[7]

In most circles it has long been taken for granted that the composition of priestly material (P) in the Pentateuch dates to around the time of Israel's exile. With the more recent disintegration of the claim for a Yahwist (J), the trend in biblical circles is to see that the composition of non-priestly material in Genesis 1–11 and beyond could well have come from about the same time. It is difficult to date the composition of most ancestral texts much earlier than the book of Deuteronomy,

---

7. This ABSTRACT, in contrast to the summaries, was part of the original publication.

around the late seventh century (see A Campbell and M O'Brien, *Rethinking the Pentateuch*, especially page 22, Table 1). Close examination of two texts, Genesis 6:5–9:17 (the Flood) and Exodus 25–Numbers 10 (the Sinai sanctuary), allows the argument to be made that such texts do not portray how it was thought to have been back then, long ago, but rather how God is to be understood in the authors' day, the time of composition. The experience of their present determines how texts were written for ancient Israel. The experience of the present determines which texts are read by us today. Where revelation is concerned, because the practice of selective reading has existed for a long time, we change nothing in what we *do*. On the other hand, it may be necessary for much to change in what we *say* and *think*.

The Reported Story: Midway Between Oral Performance and Literary Art
Abstract[8]

This paper sets out to argue the beginnings of a case for the possibility that some of the Old Testament narrative texts contain neither the record of the oral telling of a story, nor the skilled fashioning of a story as a work of literary art, but, instead, provide the report of a story. Such a reported story would contains the basic elements of character and plot as well as key details, but would pass over much that could be easily supplied from the storyteller's imagination. Beyond the theoretical possibility, the case has to be argued for the existence of such reported stories in the Old Testament text. To escape the subjectivity of intuitive judgment, argument is based particularly on the absence of elements necessary to the proper unfolding of the plot, elements which are significant but easily supplied or developed. Examples discussed are 1 Sam 18:20–27; 19:11–17; 22:6–19; 2 Sam 3:12–16. The possible recording, in such reports, of variant ways of telling the same basic story is also noted. Examples discussed are 1 Sam 19:1–7; 20:1–42; 24:1–22 (*RSV*). A particularly evident setting

---

8. This ABSTRACT, in contrast to the summaries, was part of the original publication.

for the reported story would be a major written narrative composed of a considerable number of stories which needed to be condensed from their full oral potential (for example, the Story of David's Rise). Another setting would be as aide-mémoire for other storytellers. The intention of the reported story, as literary genre, would be to communicate the gist of a story so that it might be recalled or retold.

Past History and Present Text: The Clash of Classical and Post-Critical Approaches to Biblical Text
Summary

Toward the end of the twentieth century, William Johnston wrote:

> It is now clear to everybody that the historical-critical approach, however valuable, is woefully insufficient. It alone will not put us in touch with the underlying mystery; it alone will not bring us to those eternal realities towards which the Scriptures point; it alone will not enrich our lives with mysticism.[9]

The key here is the phrase, 'it alone'. The historical-critical approach is valuable and often indispensable. It is not the be-all and end-all of biblical study. The historical or incarnational quality of God's word is essential to most Christian and Jewish belief. It is ultimately an issue of the nature of God's word. On the one hand, is it written in clear or in code; on the other, is it free of the trammels of human ambiguity or is it richly enmeshed in them?

Relationship to God

St. Ignatius Loyola and God's Unconditional Love
Summary

I have long been uneasy with faith's claim of God's unconditional love for us. Love, yes; unconditional, there's my unease. Parental

---

9. William Johnstone, *The Wounded Stag* (London: Fount Paperbacks, 1985), 25.

love can manage the unconditional. Beside that, whatever we can do, God can do better. Many of us are blessed with unconditional love. Jesus' love points to the Father's unconditional love for us. Certainly, the language of an unconditionally loving God is absent from the *Spiritual Exercises* of St Ignatius Loyola. For feudal soldiers, loyalty was paramount. What does it mean then to say God loves us? How do we talk of love where mutuality is so stretched, where the disparity is as wide as creator and creature? The 'Principle and Foundation' at the beginning of the *Exercises* is surprisingly loveless—devoid of any mention of the word. At the end of the *Exercises*, there is a final contemplation *'para alcanzar amor'*. The usual English translation was: a contemplation for *obtaining* love—clearly wrong. More recent translations omit the verb. The meaning in the text is clear: to get a grip on, to grasp the reality of God's love for us. Primary is God's love for us; secondary is our response. We do not *obtain* love; it has been given us. The contemplation invites us to contemplate and realize the love of God that has been given us, not as reward but as free gift—like the sun from above and the waters from a spring (not a trickle but a torrent, like the Jordan at Banias).

God: Judge or Lover?
Summary

There is no more challenging theme in contemporary faith's struggle for understanding than that of God's unconditional love for us and its relation to issues of divine justice, anger, and punishment. If God's love is unconditional, is human life belittled and deprived of worth? We need to look at anger in God and anger at God. Biblical passages include the flood, the desert generation, and Israel's prophets. Beyond the Bible, for us the question remains whether, if tongue-tied and silent before such mystery, we must also stammer, while aware of the inadequacy of our stammering. The safeguard, both for human honesty and respect for our God, is constantly to be aware of the inadequacy of any language we may use. But speak we must; we can no other. There is anger at God. How dare God be powerless in appalling situations? Theologically appropriate or not, such anger is there. In the silence of mystery, the place for anger at God is ambiguous. The core of Christian faith has always opted for the primacy of the metaphor of God as lover. But the trappings of religious practice have all too often brought the metaphor of God as judge to the fore. To be unconditionally loved by God is no license for lesser living or evil-doing, unless the shallowness of one's understanding of love is intolerably thin. There is no greater bond than love that knows no bounds.

The Growth of Joshua 1—12 and The Theology of Extermination
Summary

The extermination texts are appalling, but that is not the end of the question. The narrative begun in Joshua 2 offers a presentation in which Joshua's Israel occupies much of the south by military or political action—with a little bit of help from God. Further developments change this presentation to one in which God's action gives the whole land to Joshua's Israel—with a little bit of help from them. The concern of the piece is to explore text, not to eliminate shameful theology. A definitive interpretation is not claimed; possibilities are signalled. One possibility is that an earlier text can be pointed to that is coherent with Joshua 2 and might generate the same level of outrage as the late ninth century Mesha stele from Moab. A second possibility relates to the issue of the extermination texts (Josh 10:28–41 and 11:8b–15). A similar concern (*herem*, the ban) is clearly expressed in Deuteronomy—but not in terms of extermination. It is possible that extermination is later. The origins of the theology of extermination remain obscure. Why for God's sake, in Deuteronomy of all places, are the heights and depths so dangerously close?

God, Anger, and The Old Testament
Summary

The God of wrath is an all-too-common stereotype for the God of the Old Testament. The Old Testament's witness to an unshakably committed God, an unconditionally loving God, is frequently overlooked. Of course, if we believe in a loving God, we can scarcely avoid belief in an angry God. Belief in God's love for every human being, a love not easily annulled by infidelity, has to go hand in hand with belief in God's powerful anger. When people anywhere live in poverty or oppression because of the apathy, greed, or prejudice of others, how can one think of God as genuinely loving these people and not think of God as grieved and angered? How much more when people are destroyed by what is evil? It is important to give due place to this anger in God. If we shrink from using the language of God's anger, we run the twin risks of belittling God's love and burdening God with responsibility for all that befalls us. In my understanding, love excludes coercion and the perfect love of God is powerless to coerce. Despite Leibniz, we have no guarantee that the world brought into being by God was the best of all possible worlds; we also have no way of knowing whether it was possible to bring into being a better one.

Dei Verbum: Literary Forms and Vatican II— an Old Testament Perspective
Summary

It is the responsibility of historians to determine whether Council documents are a base from which the future might be developed or a culminating crown summing up the preceding developments or a stopgap while a process of theological reflection continued. Which was *Dei Verbum* and how does it look fifty years later? Most of the documents of Vatican II sought to address the world; those of its predecessors addressed the Church. The 'pastoral' qualities of the Vatican II documents means that quite opposed positions can be found within the same document because quite opposed positions could be found within the same Church. Close inspection makes clear that Dei Verbum affirms an overall image of the past and encourages a sure march into the future. An ecumenical Council is not a gathering of learned theologians; it is not a gathering of naïve believers; it is not a gathering of specialist guides to lead the faithful to the future. Far from it. A Council is a mirror of the Church it represents. Where is revelation to be sought? Inside the bureaucracy of the Church or outside the bureaucracy among the believing faithful. *Dei Verbum* quietly insists on the reverence owed to tradition and equally quietly insists on the openness to the future owed to biblical studies. More than what is said what is not said can be so very revealing. Familiarity with the Council leaves no doubt that battle raged on many fronts between the Curia and the Ecclesia. Echoing Paul VI's 'Jamais plus la guerre' (no more war), the Curia should never again be at war with the Ecclesia. It may take a century of two to work out the balance, but the balance between centre and periphery is essential to the leadership of the Church.

The Good News and The Year for Priests
Summary

In this Year for Priests it is particularly appropriate to reflect on the Good News of Jesus Christ, the unshakeable evidence of God's love for us, as experienced in the lives of ordinary people, ordained people and priestly people. The core belief of Christianity is that Jesus Christ is God's presence to the human race, not in the luxury of rulers or the rich, but in an ordinary life, ending in the ordinariness of a Roman cross, the gallows of the day—followed by a most unordinary resurrection. At stake is the understanding of love. Love used of God must be transcendent love, love that transcends all that we know about love in order to be love that is truly God's. To have meaning for us, however, it cannot betray our human experience of love. The love we experience among humans is love for people who are flawed. That God's love for us should not be different in this respect is good news indeed. That the God of all our universe should be believed to love each one of us in the ordinariness of our lives is unbelievable good news, unbelievable but not beyond belief—we believe, we rejoice, and we have cause to be so deeply glad. The joy of the priest is to be particularly concerned with a constant witness to that love.

Qohelet the Wise
Summary

The summary of Qohelet's message was: I've tried royalty and religion and neither help; to sum it up: eat, drink, and be merry. Modern translations are more nuanced. But they speak of 'toil', as the Hebrew does. Qohelet is addressing an agricultural society where most people's work was toil, work in the fields. Most of western society is no longer agricultural. Toil has become for us 'work'. Qohelet's words, in modern dress, must be: eat, drink, and see the good in what you do. Interpreting slightly, we have: live your life and see the value in what you do. Wise advice surely, and a good mantra for human living.

Reflections Around Frank Gil's
Have Life Abundantly: Grass Roots First
Summary

Earlier in 2014 ATF Press published a book by Frank Gil (a pseudonym), *Have Life Abundantly: Grass Roots First,* in which Gil abandons the idea of proving God's existence and seriously challenges two core aspects of the current Roman Church. What is reasonable but cannot be proved can be believed. In the first part of his book, Gil pictures four situations that can support people in their belief (associated with context, instinct, emotion, and reason). What Gil proposes is a view of Christianity that for many of us turns on its head the Christianity we have inherited (and maybe rejected). No more guilt and punishment, no more sacrifice and redemption. In their place, a God who loves, who has chosen to become one of the humans whom God loves—not so much to redeem them as out of love for them. The two core aspects of the Roman Church which he challenges as cancers in the body of the institution are its clericalism and its monarchism (unwieldy word). Clericalism is more widespread than often thought. Clericalism embraces popes, archbishops, bishops, priests—and beyond to the people of God. Gil takes a wholesale approach to clericalism, with moves that are global, simple, and breathtaking: the people of God should seize their part (five sevenths) in the sacramental structure of the Church. Monarchism, with regard to the pope, is dominated by two issues: life tenure and absolute power. Gil has simple suggestions for both. Gil writes wisely about the potential shapes of a future Church. He leaves the details to those whose Church it will be. His emphasis is indeed wise: the 'grass roots' (people of God) must grab what can be theirs. It would be unholy folly to wait to be given it.

Some Thoughts for a Theologically Fuller Eucharistic Prayer

Summary

A eucharistic prayer is an odd place for extensive theology, but Frank Gil's prayer is worth a place in this collection. It echoes threefold gratitude: to our creator, our saviour, and our sanctifier. The creator allows outreach to the universe; the saviour places major emphasis on the Incarnation, God's becoming human; the sanctifier touches on God's presence in our midst now. The lead-up to the consecration of bread and wine explores in detail the life of Jesus Christ, from infancy to the final events at Jerusalem. What follows the consecration is the traditional triad of prayers for leaders of the Church, for other people around the globe, and for those praying this eucharist. A final reflection is appropriate.

The core of the core: why did Jesus Christ die on the cross? To live a very ordinary life to the full, in those Roman days with the principles that were his. And why that? Well that raises the biggest, most unbelievable mystery of all—reason enough to water down if not reject Christian faith and reason enough to involve sin by us, so much more tangible than love by God for us. The best available reason I know for the life, death, and resurrection of Jesus Christ: to show us the unbelievable value that God sets on an ordinary human life, shown by living one, and the commitment that God has to us ordinary humans, the love God has for us (see Psalm 8). From the gospel: 'no one has greater love than this, to lay down one's life for one's friends' (John 15:13). 'Whoever has seen me has seen the Father' (John 14:9).

The Book of Job

Life and Job
(original: *God and Bible*)

The book of Job is legendary as a study in human suffering before God. It deals with two questions. *First*: do people worship God unselfishly, or only for the benefits they believe in or hope for? *Second*: when people suffer, what is going on and where is God? I believe these questions are best kept separate.

The *first* question is handled in prose over a couple of chapters at the start of the book and about half a chapter at the end. God is portrayed in it behaving badly; Job comes out of it with flying colors (1:20 – 22; 2:10). The *second* question is handled in poetry, as there is great feeling to be expressed; it stretches over almost forty chapters as the core of the book. Retribution theology (the good rewarded, the wicked punished) is assumed by the characters in the book. It is not the central question of the book; held by the friends, it is dismissed by God.

The *first* of the two questions is asked by the satan. Says God: 'Have you seen Job? Splendid chap.' Says the satan-figure: 'Does Job fear God for nothing?' (Less formally: does all right out of it, don't he?) The passage is often described as archaic, an old and traditional tale. The way it is told, it is clearly set in a stylised and archaic setting. But the question is painfully real for any of us today: do we love God unselfishly, or because one way or another we do well out of it—or hope to?

The *second* question is asked by Job. The first part of the text provides the setting: Job is on his rubbish heap, feeling thoroughly sorry for himself. So his question: 'Why did I not die at birth? . . . Why is light given to one in misery, and life to the bitter in soul?' (3:11, 20). In various forms, it has been asked by thinkers through the ages.

The book gives a clear answer to the *first* question: 'Yes, we humans can love God unselfishly.' Would that the book gave an equally straightforward answer to the *second* question, but it does not. It settles for the claim of mystery, without blame or hostility; it banishes some common and unhelpful answers. The response of mystery is in speeches given to God and addressed directly to Job (38:1–41:34). The unhelpful answers are banished in a short speech given to God and addressed to Eliphaz on behalf of the three: they were wrong and Job was not (42:7–9).

Following Job's passionate lament (chapter 3), the three trot out the traditional answers that are still around today and that don't help us at all. 'None of us is perfect, Job; you've surely done something to deserve it.' You are surely to blame. 'Hang in there, Job; it will be all right in the end. In the meantime, put your trust in God.' Ironic, when we think that in the story it was God who gave the satan-figure a free hand. 'The wicked always get their come-uppance; that's the way it is, Job. If you're not wicked, you'll be OK in the end.' If you are not to blame, then be grateful because it will all come out well in the end. 'Don't blame God for it'; count on it, 'you deserved much worse'. No harm in having that lot given the flick. Job resists them vehemently. A poem on wisdom closes off the exchanges (chapter 28). A final discourse from Job himself brings his words to an end (29:1 – 31:40).

Elihu comes on the scene without prior introduction. He angrily lambastes both Job and the three (which may be why he does not feature in the final adjudication). His is a response from the human plane. Basically, he lauds the greatness and transcendence of God; whatever detracts from God is wrong.

The response given God, from the whirlwind or stormwind, takes a different tack (38:1–41:34). Its opening, 'Who is this that darkens counsel by words without knowledge?', implies criticism ('darkens', 'without knowledge') and addresses Job alone ('this' is singular; 38:2). The speeches deal with what God does and Job cannot do—'Job, where were you? . . . Have you done? . . . Do you know?' Basically, Job is out of his depth in his search for clarity (cf especially 31:35–37). Blame or hostility are absent. At the end, Job accepts the criticism: 'I have uttered what I did not understand, things too wonderful for me which I did not know' (42:3). The response given God is from the divine plane. Unlike Elihu, it is not about God; it is about human limitedness.

The tone of the divine speeches (38:1–41:34) is inescapably ambiguous—whether omnipotent/transcendent, or overwhelming/bullying, or insight-generating/caring, etc. In many ways, how readers hear Job's final words will depend on how they have experienced the tone of these speeches. Their inherent openness as to tone means readers' experience of them is likely to be influenced by factors beyond the text itself. The understanding of God that Job may have come to (as is perhaps the case for Jonah also), if it were touching on the sublime, may perhaps be better not imprisoned in words—left mysterious yet life-giving.

In his conclusion to the exchange with God (42:1–6), Job says: 'Now my eye sees you' (42:5). In the book, he hasn't seen anyone, not since Elihu lapsed into silence. The text has had God speak, not appear; 'the LORD answered Job out of the whirlwind and said [= Hebrew]' (38:1). Job has just been listening to about four chapters of divine discourse. What is this sight? What might this mean? The physicality of 'my eye' does not sit well with insight alone. The text, like its topic, is obscure; it conceals rather than reveals. Avenues toward an understanding include (a) accepting an appearance (or equivalent) as part of God's speaking from the storm, or (b) accepting the incomprehensible vastness of God accountable for so much beyond the vagaries of human life, or (c) accepting a move for Job's experience of God from mediated (indirect; via another) to unmediated (direct; personal). 'Hearing of the ear' [literal Hebrew] would normally imply a report of someone else's experience, while seeing with 'my eye' would definitely imply one's own experience. As avenues, they are possible; in the context, they are perhaps the best we can do.

The end of the book has God say to Eliphaz, as representative of the three: 'You have not spoken of me what is right, as my servant Job has' (42:7, 8). We can be comfortable that the friends were wrong we may be puzzled as to where Job spoke about God what was right; it is more what Job said about himself that was right. The views held by the friends, justifying God and demeaning Job, are deemed wrong. Job's rightness must be contrasted here with the error of the friends. God's judgment that Job spoke rightly reflects Job's exchanges with the three; it is not about Job's response to God. It relates best to Job's integrity and his refusal to accept the views about God implicit in what is expressed by the three.

The complexity associated with the meaning of the text may mirror the complexity associated with the understanding of the issue. God's discourse, with the wide sweep of its issues and concerns, claims mystery beyond the human capacity to grasp. In a brief adjudication given God (42:7–9), the views of the three are dismissed, baloney unfit for human consumption; the stance of Job is endorsed.

Structurally, 42:1–6 concludes the exchange with God, accepting mystery and situating Job in relationship with God; 42:7–9 concludes the exchanges with the three, having God adjudicate clearly in Job's favor. Beyond doubt: first, against the three, Job holds to his innocence and integrity; second, God declares for Job.

The three have produced explanations for Job's suffering; basically they have blamed Job for it, a view vigorously rejected by Job. The discourse given God emphasizes human limitation. Job admits this limitedness (42:3) and the text reports a changed situation (42:5; for 42:6, see the final note below). Job's 'and now' or 'but now' implies something new, a change. Job's 'my eye sees you' implies a relationship—and spells out nothing. The nature of Job's seeing may escape readers' interpretation of the text; something of the kind may not be out of reach of believers' own experience of life. In the text, without a specific theophany, Job's encounter with God does not claim an experience that is peculiar to Job; it does not exclude the possibility for others of some such perception, seeing God differently. The three, who defended God by blaming Job, are declared not to have spoken rightly of God. Job, who rejected the friends' view of God and who refused to accept blame for his situation, is declared to have spoken rightly. Inadequate theology is inadequate. Relationship with God in suffering is possible.

God is given two responses, at quite different levels: one of more than four chapters, addressed to Job; one of three verses, addressed to Eliphaz. *At a primary level*, in two speeches—spoken to Job, reflecting his complaints about his suffering—Job is corrected by God (38:2) and the correction is accepted by Job (42:3). The first speech given God (38:1–39:30) emphasizes divine transcendence over against human limitedness, personified in Job. The second speech (40:6–41:34) addresses the folly of achieving an esteem for human worth by disparaging God (40:8). *At another level*, a second short response—spoken to Eliphaz, reflecting the exchanges between Job and the three friends—has God reject the views of the three and strongly affirm the stance of Job (42:7–9). The ending of the book, troubling in itself, portrays Job in favorable relationship with God (42:10–17). A comprehensive answer to the issues associated with suffering is not within human reach; the pain of personal suffering does not reflect estrangement from God.

(Note: readers need to be aware of the rich ambiguity of both verses 42:5 and 42:6. *Without acknowledging it,* most translations give an 'emended' version of 42:6. It has long been known that—without emendation, without input from elsewhere, such as context or tradition etc—the first part of the verse *cannot* mean 'I despise myself', 'I disown what I have said', or some such equivalent. Modern studies increasingly recognise that the two verbs in the first part of the verse may both bear on the two objects in the second part. So it is possible that the translation may be along the lines of literally 'I repudiate and am of changed mind about dust and ashes'; as an exit line, more freely, 'I back off and I've had enough of all this ash-heap stuff'. It is highly unlikely that—with the possible exception of Job's demand for clear explanation—the tenor of an entire book, especially this one, would be reversed in one obscure final verse.)

Job: Case Study or Theology
(original: *Psychiatry and Religion*)

It was a friend who practises both as psychologist and biblical scholar who pointed out to me that the encounter with a text proceeds on much the same lines as the encounter with a person. I suspect an academic approaches a book in much the same way that a psychiatrist approaches a client. You want a history from a client. So do we from a book. Where did the author study and under what scholars? What is the background to the book: doctoral dissertation or years of mature study? What problem is the client presenting? What insight or impulse drove the author to write this book? What are the client's circumstances and resources? Who has the author been reading, talking to, working with? The comparison can be pushed quite a bit further, but that is enough for present purposes.

It was a psychiatrist friend who first loaned me a recent book in the Gaskell Psychiatry Series, entitled Job's Illness: Loss, Grief and Integration. A Psychological Interpretation, by Dr Jack Kahn.[1] A glance at the Introduction showed training in medicine and psychiatry. A glance at the Bibliography showed half a dozen translations of the Bible, four entries under Bible Commentaries, nineteen entries on matters Literary, Philosophical and Historical (none of which were seriously biblical), and fifty-seven entries on matters Medical, Psychiatric and Psychological. I restrained my initial impulse to condemn Jack Kahn for hubris, reflecting that what matters is not how many books you read but how well you choose what you read. Had he chosen his commentaries well?

---

1. Jack Kahn with Hester Solomon, *Job's Illness: Loss, Grief and Integration: A Psychological Interpretation*. Gaskell Psychiatry Series (London: The Royal College of Psychiatrists, 1986).

The titles were not encouraging. Bible Commentaries and an Encyclopedia, but no commentaries specifically on the Book of Job. The dates were even less encouraging: 1839, 1902, 1919, and—a little more up-to-date—1947. Regrettably, as far as the date was concerned, the 1947 offering turned out to be that great classic, *The Guide for the Perplexed*, by Moses Maimonides, dating from 1168. With some indignation, I then wondered what utterly unenlightened press might, in this twentieth century, have published a book on Job, garnished with some of the trimmings of an academic bibliography, but with practically no consultation of any worth-while scholarship on the Book of Job since Maimonides in the twelfth century. Imagine my shock to discover that my unenlightened publisher was no less august a body than the Royal College of Psychiatrists.

There is a value in being open to surprise, as well as to others' eccentricities. Who knows, freedom from knowledge might generate freedom for helpful insights. But I was not immediately attracted to explore Dr. Kahn's contribution. There was not even a disclaimer somewhere to indicate that he was aware of the importance of what he was ignoring. Ah well, his book could wait for some unlikely moment of idle leisure. But the fates were against me. A second psychiatrist friend gave me a copy. My reaction—gratitude apart, of course—was one of mild horror: My God, psychiatrists are buying this! They may even read it! Then came Dr Chiu's invitation to present a paper to this conference. So that did it. My paper had to address the question whether Jack Kahn's exploration of the Book of Job was legitimate.

The basic issue
I do not want to cast myself in the role of the professional scholar jealously defending specialist territory against the intrusions of well-meaning amateurs. The Book of Job is a work of literature and a classic. It is not burdened with the peculiarities of history and composition which can make some biblical books minefields for the uninitiated. So why should I entertain reserves simply because Jack Kahn's bibliography is hugely out of balance? In this paper, I am waving a yellow flag of caution about a particular book by a particular psychiatrist who is trespassing on my professional turf. I do so because there is a very delicate flower concealed in that turf, and it would be a great pity to trample on it without being fully aware of what we are doing.

The basic problem inherent in Kahn's undertaking is reflected in the conflict between the beginning and the end of his first chapter. At the beginning, he quotes from Maimonides, who refers to:

> the strange and wonderful Book of Job [whose] basis is a fiction, conceived for the purpose of explaining the different opinions which people hold on Divine Providence... This fiction, however, is in so far different from other fictions that it includes profound ideas and great mysteries, removes great doubts, and reveals the most important truths.[2]

The chapter concludes:

> From a purely psychiatric point of view, it is possible to find in the Book of Job a sensitive and detailed account of the onset, course, and treatment of a mental disorder in which the most prominent feature is depression...
>
> The purpose of this book is to study the illness and the events surrounding it, and to find in the Bible story an account of some of the universal problems of mankind as revealed through critical events in the life of one individual. It is also concerned with the progression of ideas of human identity and the way in which human beings have searched for a harmony between experience of the self and experience of the universe.[3]

There are two things seriously wrong here, and Jack Kahn skates far too lightly around one and does not seem to be aware of the other.

If Maimonides is right that the Book of Job is a fiction—and modern scholarship would agree with him—and if we take seriously that it presents itself as a third-person narrative about Job, the bulk of which is high flown poetry presented as the speeches of Job, then we must be cautious about finding in it 'a sensitive and detailed account of the onset, course, and treatment of a mental disorder'.

---

2. Kahn, *Job's Illness*, 1–2, quoting from Moses Maimonides (1168), *The Guide for the Perplexed*, translated by M Friedlander (London: George Routledge & Sons, 1947), 296.
3. Kahn, *Job's Illness*, 12.

Firstly, the account is not from the patient, but from an author—and a poet to boot. Dr Kahn does not have access to 'critical events in the life of one individual'. He has access to a third party's poetry. Surely this is significant for the legitimacy of using this ancient text as a subject for psychiatric analysis. If what we have are the words of a person describing their own experience, some validity would have to be allowed to attempts at interpretation or analysis. But when the words are put in a character's mouth by an author, we have only the product of creative imagination; there is not the control of present or remembered personal experience. One might always argue that an author must build on some analogous experience—but surely the process is fraught with difficulties and dangers. The risk of using such second-hand expression for diagnostic purposes seems to me to become overwhelming when the text being created is poetry. The whole procedure becomes vastly more insecure when we recognise that it cannot be simply assumed that the author's intention is to provide 'a sensitive and detailed account of the onset, course, and treatment of a mental disorder'.

This is the difficulty which I consider Kahn skates all too lightly around. He writes:

> For the purpose of this chapter, the Bible text will be considered as recording the words of a living person, and we shall look upon these words as being Job's own communications about his feelings and experiences.[4]

In my judgement this is a totally illegitimate procedure. Maimonides said the Book of Job was a fiction; I know of no competent biblical scholar who would disagree. Can we dismiss the reality of the text to say that 'for the purpose of this chapter' the Bible text will be considered to be something that it is not.[5]

---

4. Kahn, *Job's Illness*, 24.
5. I fear that at the base of Kahn's approach is a conviction not uncommon among those who have not had some experience of serious biblical scholarship. Put brutally, the conviction is that any event mentioned in the text happened, even if perhaps the record of it has suffered some distortion. The question is not seriously entertained as to whether the text intends the event as real, or intends to portray the 'how' of its happening. There are other pointers to this elsewhere in Kahn's book.

These considerations so far concern what might be called the practical difficulties of using a text like the Book of Job for psychiatric diagnosis. There is a theoretical difficulty which is far more serious. If the purpose of the Book of Job is to explore the situation of the sufferer before God by deliberately setting up a limit case of the perfect human being whose suffering cannot be attributed to sin or human imperfection, then the entire endeavour is destroyed by the psychiatric analysis of Job as a flawed and obsessive personality.

This limit case of the totally innocent sufferer is precisely what I understand to be the central purpose of the Book of Job. The figure of Job is set up as one who is completely sinless. The book opens with the description of Job as 'blameless and upright, one who feared God and turned away from evil' (Job 1:1). This description is from the author. The taint of evil is kept so far from Job that he is portrayed even offering sacrifice for the possible sins of his children. Notice that this is the point seized on by Kahn to diagnose Job as obsessively scrupulous. But this is the precise opposite of the author's intention. The author has God repeat the description of Job as 'blameless and upright, one who fears God and turns away from evil' (1:8). Even Satan accepts the description, only impugning Job's motivation. For the author, Job is blameless. Chapter 31, the end of Job's speeches, is a massive re-emphasis of this point.

Job's blamelessness is critical to the whole enterprise of the book. The purpose of the book is to explore the situation of the sufferer before God. Job consistently affirms his innocence. His friends equally consistently and ever more scathingly deny it. In a key passage, Job affirms it against them:

    For example, when he comes to the question of treatment, Kahn writes: 'In order to consider Job's illness in terms of therapy, we must bring in a dimension other than the one in which the story is told. The original framework is the cultural and religious one, and, ostensibly, it concerns a man who was tested by God in a wager with Satan, who survived the test (at least in the first place), and who later rebelled . . . We shall alter this framework by giving a naturalistic explanation of Job's experiences, and, for this purpose, we shall treat the religious framework as only part—although a very important part—of the influences which impinge upon the mind of an individual.' (Kahn, *Job's Illness*, 51). But we do not have access to Job's experiences or Job's mind, but only to the poetry of the author who situated that poetry within this religious framework.

> Far be it from me to say that you are right;
> till I die I will not put away my integrity from me.
> I hold fast my righteousness, and will not let it go;
> my heart does not reproach me for any of my days
> (27:5–6).

While God is portrayed reproving Job—'Will you even put me in the wrong? Will you condemn me that you may be justified?' (40:8)—which is presumably the reference of Job's 'I despise myself and repent' (42:6), it is quite central to the book to realise that God is portrayed condemning the views of the friends as wrong, while maintaining Job as right.[6] God says to Eliphaz:

> My wrath is kindled against you and against your two friends; for you have not spoken of me what is right, as my servant Job has . . . I will accept his prayer not to deal with you according to your folly; for you have not spoken of me what is right, as my servant Job has (42:7–8).

The central message of the Book of Job is that the origin of human suffering is not to be found in the malice of God or in the fault of the human sufferer.

This is the point that Jack Kahn misses. For example, early in the piece, he writes:

> Possessions contribute to the image of the self, and when the possessions include family members, obsessional processes may be used in order to preserve their lives and control their fate. The obsessional activity provides a safeguard for the well-being of those who figure closely in the obsessional individual's life.
>
> Job's greatness and his perfection are thus connected with his possessions and the lives of his children. The

---

6. Note that Job's 'I despise myself and repent' (42:6) cannot be understood as a retraction of the constant affirmations of his innocence. Any attempt to interpret it as such a retraction is negated by the emphatic condemnation of the three friends.

> breakdown of his physical and mental integration is associated with the loss of his children and his wealth. Far from being perfect, Job's personality contained features which in our own culture might be considered to be the precursor of mental breakdown.[7]

In Kahn's presentation, Job is the source of his own troubles. He has cracked under the pressure of his own obsessions. As a figure in literature, he is of no help to us in exploring the situation of innocent suffering before God. Instead Job becomes a paradigm of the patient in need of therapy.

The message of the Book of Job
In brief, the message of the book of Job is: there is suffering which occurs in situations where neither God nor the human sufferer is responsible. Job is portrayed as attributing his suffering to God's hostility towards him and blaming God for it—and Job is portrayed as wrong. God's hostility, God's punishment, was not the source of Job's suffering.[8] The friends are portrayed as attributing Job's suffering to Job's sin—and they are portrayed as wrong. Job's sin was not the source of Job's suffering.

With these two blind alleys eliminated, in the context of the Book of Job there is only one possibility left. We can suffer without having brought it on ourselves by sin and without being estranged from God.

It would be a disaster if we lost the Book of Job as one of the greatest defences of human integrity before God, maintaining the right of the innocent sufferer to be innocent. I fear that Jack Kahn in transforming Job from perfect figure to obsessive perfectionist loses that defender of our integrity.

---

7. Kahn, *Job's Illness*, 15–16.
8. One could argue that the prologue presents God as testing Job, or at least permitting Satan to test him. But to attribute Job's suffering to divine testing would be to agree with the three friends (for example Job 5:17–18)—and the epilogue declares they are wrong. There is a tension between the prologue and the poetry. The prologue permits Job's suffering to result from God's pride, wounded by Satan's jibe. There is a sense in which this creates space to allow for the strength of the poetry's language against God. It is an unresolved tension between prologue and poetry, and it must remain unresolved. To resolve it in favour of the prologue would be to destroy the balance and purpose of the Book of Job.

God And Suffering—'It Happens': Job's Silent Solution

(original: *American Theological Inquiry*, 3/1)

Part one: solutions

When looking at suffering intellectually, JL McKenzie concludes with characteristic honesty: 'We have no answer to the problem.' He settles as such on 'an experience of God' as the ultimate answer (*Two-Edged Sword*, 237). Some such experience has to be the ultimate answer; there is no other. Nevertheless, I propose that the second section of the initial divine speech (Job 38:39–39:30, some thirty-three verses), may invite us or allow us to move 'the problem' to a quite different context. The experience of God is still crucial, but the context is radically other than generally allowed for in the book of Job.

Issues of the shape of the book of Job can wait till Part Two of this article. It is enough for now to say that the speeches given by God (in Job 38–41) are the culmination of the book. There is a strong sense in these speeches, above all concerning creation and the associated material (Job 38:4–38), that Job is not in the same dimension of being as God, that Job has indeed uttered what he did not understand—things too wonderful for him that he did not know (see Job 42:3). However, following these verses there is a major section that may deserve more scrutiny than is usually given (that is, Job 38:39–39:30).

At the end of a course on the book of Job, Hamish Graham, a young doctor about to leave for six months or so in Darfur, drew my attention to this section. His question: Why is so much text given to the animal kingdom? His thought: Is it because the animal kingdom is an *amoral* realm, one where moral goodness and badness (righteousness and wickedness) play no role? Could this be the case with human suffering—at least occasionally? Is this passage suggesting that, in the exchanges with his interlocutors, Job might be situating his suffering in the wrong context?

The purpose of this paper, then, is to point out that a good case can be made for the possibility that part of the text of Job subtly invites its readers to imagine an alternative context for human suffering, an *amoral* context, one where the reality of human success or failure, joy or sorrow, is not exclusively associated with the moral quality of human living, with goodness or badness. Space must be allowed for the amoral, for Nature's lottery of talent, energy, and luck; above all, luck! Where human suffering or success is concerned, it is possible that 'it happens'; moral causation need not be alleged.

Those who spend time studying the book of Job usually come to the speeches given by God in the final chapters with an expectation that the tensions which have been steadily building will at last be resolved. Initially, Job's defense of himself matched with his three interlocutors' defenses of tradition; then Elihu's defense of God; finally, word from God. The expectation, alas, will not be fulfilled. Few would disagree with McKenzie that the divine speeches are 'magnificent poetry, but not altogether relevant to the discussion' (*Two-Edged Sword*, 236). Finding the wisdom we expect requires serious exploration.[1]

The opening speech from the storm, attributed to God, is an evident unity. God's speaking is announced in 38:1, 'the LORD answered Job'. Job's reply does not begin until 40:3, 'then Job answered the LORD'. Reinforcing the strong sense of unity is God's line of questioning that extends through both chapters 38 and 39. As a concluding coda, God's speaking is articulated again at the end, 'and the LORD said to Job' (40:1).

This evident unity may prevent the reader from seeing that the divine speech is built out of two quite different panels. It comes as a surprise to realise that they are equally balanced in extent, even if the cosmic concerns of the first panel palpably outweigh the zoological concerns of the second.

---

1. Recent helpful studies on the book of Job include: Clines, DJA *Job 1–20* and *Job 21–37*. WBC. (Dallas, TX: Word, 1989, 2006); Good, EM *In Turns of Tempest*. (Stanford, CA: Stanford University Press, 1990); Greenberg, M 'Job', in R Alter and F Kermode, *The Literary Guide to the Bible* (London: Collins, 1987) 283–304; Gutierrez, Gustavo. *On God: God-Talk and the Suffering of the Innocent* (Maryknoll, NY: Orbis, 1987); Habel, NC *The Book of Job*, OTL (London: SCM, 1985); Miles, J *God: A Biography* (New York: Knopf, 1995), 308–28 and notes; Newsom, Carol A *The Book of Job: A Contest of Moral Imaginations* (Oxford: Oxford University Press, 2003); Penchansky, David, *The Betrayal of God: Ideological Conflict in Job*. (Louisville, KY: Westminster/John Knox, 1990).

Despite the balance in extent, the two panels are remarkably different. The first panel has all the weight, first, of creation itself, second, the stabilisation of the ocean, and then associated material of cosmic dimension: dawn; springs of the sea, with death, dark, and the expanse of the earth; light and dark; snow and hail; rain and ice; stars and constellations; the weather in all its mystery. These are all beyond the envelope of this earth—and beyond the grasp of Job.

The change from one panel to the next is sudden: from 'the waterskins of the heavens' to prey for beast and bird, lion and raven (Job 38:37–41). The mystery world of the cosmos is left behind and the discourse traipses through the length and breadth of the animal world.

The second panel contains the prey of predators, the birthing of goats and deer, the freedom of wild ass and ox, the thoughtless speed of the ostrich that leaves its eggs unprotected, and the fearsome might of the warhorse. Creating an envelope, highlighting the unity of the panel, it ends with the prey of hawk and eagle. All these are found within the envelope of our earthly world. The hawk may fly high and the ass roam far; all belong with our earth.

The balance needs to be seen. Despite appearances, the gravity of matters cosmic does not receive more treatment than the reality of matters worldly. The difference is surprising. First we will look at the balance; then we will turn to the difference.

Balance
The first element of balance is quite clear. Practically the same number of verses is given to the first panel as to the second. Laying the foundation of the earth extends for four verses (38:4–7). Stabilising the sea extends for another four verses (38:8–11). The associated matters take up another twenty-six verses (38:12–38). The grand total is thirty-four verses. The second panel, the zoological catalog, has thirty-three verses (38:39–39:30).

There is perhaps something perverse in readers (or this reader at least) that creates the impression of greater weight and substance for matters that are largely unseeable and certainly unknowable. The tangible and knowable of the animal realm somehow seems almost trivial by comparison. Frankly, who bothers about ravens and ostriches? Oh, the folly of ignoring what is almost under one's nose while being vastly impressed by what is thoroughly out of reach.

The number of items constituting the two panels is fluid; for both, the items can be counted in various ways. Allowing for this however, the count is surprisingly similar. In tabular form, it can look like this:

Cosmic:	Zoological:
1) the foundation of the earth	1) the prey for lion and raven
2) the stabilising of the sea	2) the birthing of goats and deer
3) the dawn	3) the freedom of the wild ass
4) the recesses of the deep	4) the liberty of the wild ox
5) the dwellings of light and darkness	5) the ostrich
6) the storehouses of snow and hail	6) the warhorse
7) the torrents of rain	7) the hawk
8) the constellation	8) the eagle
9) the weather	

The parity is far from perfect, but the balance is inescapably there. The panels have to be seen as two, within the one speech. Neither can be ignored.

Difference
The difference between the two panels is evident in three aspects: first, as already mentioned, the cosmic is outside the envelope of this earth while the zoological is firmly within it; second, the questions addressed to Job are significantly more aggressive in the first panel than in the second; third, Job's potential in relation to these questions is essentially different.

The first aspect hardly needs further mention. Creative activity, the dwellings of light and dark, the mysteries of snow and hail, rain and ice, the movements of the stars, all these are in the lofty realm that surrounds the earth. They may bring it light and dark, ice and snow, rain and hail, but these elements are brought to the earth—they are not perceived as there already, belonging as part of it.

To the contrary, the animal kingdom is of the earth—even the soaring hawk and eagle. Ass and ox, ostrich and warhorse may be beyond Job's control, but asses and oxen can be domesticated; the warhorse is under the control of its rider. They are part of the phenomena of the world; they belong on earth.

The second aspect needs attention. It is not a matter of whether the questions put in the speech given by God are heard either as 'in some way caring' or alternatively as 'rather crushing' (the Hebrew is somewhat less emphatic than the NRSV translation). It is that the first panel's questions have among them elements that belittle Job. 'Tell me, if you have understanding' (v 4). 'Surely you know' (v 5). 'Declare if you know all this' (v 18). 'Surely you know, for you were born then' (v 21). They are found at the beginning of the panel and in the middle, but there is a sense in which they set a tone for the whole. In the second panel, that tone is not repeated; it is not present.

The third aspect correlates with the preceding two. The questions in the first panel are quite clearly beyond any capacity that Job might dream of. He was not there when God laid the foundation of the earth (38:4). He could not possibly know such mysteries as the springs of the sea, the recesses of the deep, or the gates of death. Control of the dawn, of light and darkness, of the weather in all its variety, or the stars and their ordinances are well and truly beyond the limits of human capacity (at the time of Job and still in ours).

The same cannot be said of the questions in the second panel. These questions, in the main, concern what Job *does not do* and, as matters stand, *cannot do*. But the key phrase is 'as matters stand'. Most of them are not in the category of what Job unquestionably *could not do*. In this, they differ from the cosmic questions of the first panel.

Job does not hunt prey for the lions or provide the raven with prey for its young (38:39–41). But it would not be beyond Job to provide such food if needed. He could always tether a poor beast where the lion would find it or lay out food where the raven would see it. Careful observation would reveal when mountain goats give birth or deer calve. Wild asses and wild oxen can be domesticated. Warhorses have riders. Hawks and eagles have their nests in the lofty fastness of the rocky crag, but their food needs can be provided for.

What has been spelled out here in detail was potentially clear at a first reading. The speech given by God (Job 38:1 – 40:2) is made up of two panels—and they are different.

The meaning of the first panel is articulated in its own text: Job is not in the same dimension of being with God; Job is not in God's league. 'If you have understanding' (38:4). Clearly Job does not have understanding equal to the task. 'Surely you know' (38:5, 21). Equally clearly, Job does not know in either case. Both tasks are well and truly beyond this mere man. The other issues in the first panel are in the same category: well and truly beyond Job.

Power is not the issue in panel one. Job has conceded that already and has complained about it from early on in the book (for example, Job 9:4–19). The issue is ultimately one of being. God and Job exist in different dimensions of being (ontologically). What is natural for God is impossible for Job. What is wisdom for God is quintessentially out of reach for Job.

We have seen an essential difference between the first and second panel. The first panel concerns matters that Job *could* not do in *any* circumstances. The second panel, however, concerns matters that Job *cannot* do in the *present* circumstances. We need to explore whether the difference between the two panels is significant for a fruitful interpretation of the relevant text.

To facilitate imagination and to highlight what is particular to the second panel, it is helpful to envision other forms that the panel might have taken. It is perfectly possible, for example, that after the cosmic realm in the first panel a second panel continued in the earthly realm with issues that lay well and truly beyond Job, with matters that Job *could not* do in *any* circumstances.

Numerous examples are available from prophetic texts where actions are claimed for God. Could Job bring about a plague, a groundwater drought, or the destruction of a temple (Amos 7–9)? Could Job claim responsibility for the gift of Israel's grain, wine, and oil, silver and gold, wool and flax (Hosea 2)? Could Job make the threat to strip Israel of its protective defenses and withhold rain from it (Isaiah 5)? Could Job bring a nation from far away against Israel or be responsible for famine, war, and pestilence (Jeremiah 5 and 28)? Such a second panel in the divine speech is perfectly possible. It would shift from the cosmic to the earthly realm. It would propose issues, as in the first panel, that Job *could not do in any* circumstances. Within the patterns of Hebrew thought and language it is perfectly possible. What we have in the second panel is by no means the only possibility; it could have been otherwise.

In the divine speech we have, the second panel is not of the same kind as the first; it is not simply a continuation of the first panel of the speech. It is different enough to merit consideration in its own right.

Does the difference have meaning?

From the history of the interpretation of the book of Job, it is clear that the second panel can be read as a continuation and reinforcement of the first, developing the same message beyond the realm of panel one. This should be unarguably clear. Competent scholars have read it in that way; so, it can be read in that way. The question is whether 'that way' is the *only* reading.

The questions in the second panel focus attention on the animal realm, akin to the human realm but different from it. The questions 'Do you know?' and 'Can you do?' focus attention on this other world, a world that is not Job's. It is a world with suffering and death, with success and failure, with hunger and plenty. But it is an *amoral* world. The freedom of the ass or the liberty of the ox, the success or failure of the hunting lion or questing eagle are in no way correlated with moral qualities such as goodness and badness.

It is a realm adjacent to the human. It is a realm without the involvement of moral causes, where what happens happens. Does this zoological catalog, drawing Job's attention to a realm adjacent to his own, suggest a possible reading that Job's arguments about the justice and injustice of human suffering and pain are being mounted in the wrong context? *Then*, in the time of the book, we might have suggested the 'wrong context' as a possible reading; *now*, in our own time, we might propose it as a valid reading.

Brought by the catalog to contemplate the animal realm, where the amoral holds sway, is Job invited to contemplate the possibility of an amoral context for human suffering? Goodness or badness does not cause an animal's fate. Is the possibility to be contemplated that goodness or badness do not always cause a human's fate, that goodness or badness may not be the sole cause of human suffering or well-being? For completeness' sake, we might add that the book of Job entertains a third cause: suffering appropriately endured can purify.

In much modern thinking, morality may not affect human fate or human suffering. The possibility is there that 'it happens'; it is not caused on moral grounds. The question posed to the interpreter of Job is whether the marked difference between the two parts of the divine speech could have been interpreted then, or can be interpreted now, in the direction just indicated.

Two interpretations at least are possible. In the first, panel two reinforces panel one. In the second, panel two adds another perspective to panel one. Panel one is clear; Job is not in the same league as God. Panel two is less clear, but may suggest the thought that, as in the animal world, suffering in the human world may be amoral, divorced from the moral qualities of goodness or badness.

A third reading is also possible: both of the above. The two interpretations complement each other. First, panel two reinforces panel one. Both panels make clear that Job is not in God's league: for panel one, not in the same dimension of being as God; for panel two, not in the same situation that can be claimed for God. At the same time, however, panel two adds another perspective to that of panel one in adding the potentially amoral aspect of some human suffering, analogous to the animal kingdom.

Two hermeneutical options are present. Might the text have been open to an amoral interpretation in ancient times? Might the text be open to an amoral interpretation in modern times?

That Job is not in the same dimension of being as God is *certain*; it was certain then and it is certain now. God is not to be thought of within the reduced limits of human capacity or imprisoned within the constraints of human imagination. God's actions are not to be assessed within the terms of human courts of law (Job's error!).

Though not certain, it is *possible* that the human suffering Job argues about with such intensity may, at least on occasion, stem from an amoral context ('it happens') rather than a moral one. It may have been possible to conceive of it as possible then, in the time of Job. It is certainly possible to conceive of it as possible now, in our time.

The text that follows in the book of Job does not advocate or give an opening to an understanding of the cause of some human suffering as amoral. Hence the subtitle of this article: 'Job's silent solution'.

Job's reply is general: 'I am of small account; what shall I answer you?' (40:4). His second statement is ambiguous: 'I know that you can do all things, and that no purpose of yours can be thwarted' (42:2). It can be a confession of difference in the dimensions of being. On the other hand, 'you can do all things ... no purpose of yours can be thwarted' is readily understood as a confession of divine power. Given Job's earlier views about divine power (for example, 'who has resisted him and succeeded?' [9:4]), this points to silence and submission rather than insight and inner progress. 'I have uttered what I did not understand, things too wonderful for me, which I did not know' (42:3) is a direct response to the first panel of the divine speech and does suggest insight and inner progress. However, it is only indirectly relevant to the second panel. In what is to come (Job 40:6–41:4, above all Behemoth and Leviathan), the issue of power is primary: 'Have you an arm like God, and can you thunder with a voice like his?' (40:8). Insight and inner progress have little place.

What is clear in the responses noted here (40:4; 42:2, 3) is that the possible role of the amoral in regard to some human suffering is left untouched and undeveloped. Given the climate of the time, it is not surprising that it was left unspoken—if it was understood as a possible solution in the first place. Given the considerations we have discussed, it appears to have been available as an understanding of the text *then*. It is certainly available as an understanding of the text *now*. Job does not appeal to this solution; today, however, it may appeal to many.

Part two: structures
Prose begins and ends the Book of Job (prologue and epilogue), while the middle is poetry. A lament by Job gets the poetry under way (Job 3), followed by three rounds of speeches between Job and each of the three 'friends' or interlocutors (with the third round incomplete); a poem on wisdom marks the closure of these exchanges (Job 28). After that, three chapters are given to Job himself (Job 29–31); a new figure on the scene, Elihu, is given six chapters (Job 32–37); then YHWH himself (that is, God) is presented speaking to Job from the storm wind (Job 38–41). Job replies, God speaks again and Job replies again. Finally, YHWH adjudicates, and the epilogue ends the book.

In the mid-twentieth century, the book of Job was often seen as a magnificent but mangled piece of literature. The prologue-epilogue was archaic and at variance with the whole. Job 28 and the Elihu material were secondary. The third round of exchanges was incomplete, involving textual disruption and loss, and the Behemoth and Leviathan material was secondary, involving disruption of Job's single reply to a single divine speech. Over the years since, a strong sense of unity and purpose has been restored to the book. Brief discussion of some aspects is important.

Prologue
Independently of issues of origin, a couple of points are important regarding the prologue-epilogue section of the book. First, the story that is now distributed over the prologue and the epilogue has nothing to do with the central issue of the poetry of the book of Job. It explores the issue whether religious faith can be free of self-interest. The question raised in the story by the Satan-figure is: 'Does Job fear God for nothing?' (1:9). Job is wealthy, thanks to the God Job worships. Strip Job of his wealth and he will curse God (the Hebrew euphemism is 'bless God' but the meaning is clear). A second time round, the Satan-figure's claim is that, stripped of his health, Job will surely curse God. The double climax of the story: in neither case does Job curse God (1:20–22; 2:10). Job's faith is not motivated by self-interest. End of argument; end of story.[2]

The restoration of the unjustifiably disturbed balance of human order is left to the epilogue (42:10–17). Human suffering is involved in the story; Job is stripped of his wealth, his children's lives, and his personal health. This suffering, nevertheless, is not the point of the story. The story is about human religious faith and human self-interest.

The human suffering inflicted on Job creates a perfect setting for the poetry of the book, focused on the issue of suffering. Nevertheless, the suffering in the prologue can be a distraction from the suffering in the poetry.

The importance of the issue in the prologue's story is easily overlooked. Perhaps the question it poses to those of religious faith is too painful for commentators to bring it to the fore. Perhaps the behavior narrated of God is deemed too shameful to be attended to. Whatever the reasons, the importance of the story should not be downplayed.

Second, the narrative presentation of the story highlights the unreality of this trial situation. Leaving other elements aside, the sequence of mishaps is massively unreal. 'I alone have escaped to tell you. While he was still speaking, another came and said . . .' (1:15–16, 16–17, 17–18, 19). Reality has never been so unreal. Readers may be grateful.

---

2. Antony F Campbell, 'The Book of Job: Two Questions, One Answer', in *ABR* 51 (2003): 15–25.

Prose/Poetry; Prologue/Epilogue Boundaries
The standard division between the story (prologue and epilogue) and the central core of the book has usually been along the lines of prose and poetry. So the prologue is seen as Job 1:1–2:13 (prose) and the epilogue as 42:11–17 (prose); the central core is then 3:1–41:9 (almost entirely poetry).

Job 42:7–9 is essential to the central core but creates two problems for the prose/poetry division of material. First, the three verses are prose. Second, they involve Eliphaz, Bildad, and Zophar whose arrival was narrated in 2:11–13. The problem is solved by recognising that the prologue (and its story) ends with 2:10 and the central core begins in prose with 2:11–13; it also ends in prose, 42:7–9, thus introducing and dismissing the three, Eliphaz, Bildad, and Zophar, without whom there would be no central core.[3]

It is also important to recognise that the epilogue is to be understood as restoration of the disturbed balance and not as reward for Job's piety. The language of reward is absent from the epilogue. 'The LORD restored the fortunes of Job . . . The LORD blessed the latter days of Job . . .' (42:10, 12). The language and conceptualisation of reward is not present. The balance was disturbed in the prologue—improperly; it is restored in the epilogue—equally improperly.

Job 28
Job 28 is a poem about wisdom; it has no links into the book of Job. Whether it comes from the author of Job or not is unimportant. Its function in the text is important. It marks the end of the series of exchanges between Job and the three. After it, the three are not heard from again. Job has three chapters to himself, Elihu has six, and the exchanges between God and Job all but wrap it up. Job 28 matters as a marker. At the same time, reflection on wisdom in this context is not out of place.

Elihu
The Elihu material is widely regarded as a later addition to the book. Elihu is not named with the three at the beginning, nor is he present at the end (perhaps having spoken negatively of both Job and the three,

---

3. Campbell, 'Book of Job'.

he has no place in God's adjudication between them). A compelling reason to view the Elihu chapters as later additions is that in 38:1, after six chapters of Elihu, the text has 'the LORD answered Job'. It is unlikely that Elihu would have been passed over so lightly.

However, the Elihu speeches take an approach that is otherwise largely absent from the book of Job. Job has defended himself and accused God. The three have defended God from their own understanding of experience, from their inherited tradition, and from their personal conviction. Different from these, Elihu exalts God from the point of view of human perception. This is quite different from God's inviting Job to see himself from the point of view of divine perception. Elihu's speeches are variously assessed; however, they add a perception that is otherwise missing.

Behemoth/Leviathan

A standard position in the past was to end the original poetry of Job (prescinding from 42:7–17) with *one* divine speech (38:1–40:2) and *one* reply from Job (made up of parts from 40:1–5 and 42:1–6). The material associated with Behemoth and Leviathan (40:6–41:34) was assessed as secondary. More recent studies have moved away from this position, focusing on the present text and evaluating the Behemoth and Leviathan material positively.[4] However, the issue of God's overwhelming power renders this material problematic. The solution to Job's problem proposed in it is that of God's superior power rather than that of the difference in dimension of being.

The power theme is introduced at the start: 'Have you an arm like God, and can you thunder with a voice like his?' (40:9). It is continued in God's challenge (40:10–14), in the portrayal of Behemoth ('its strength is in its loins and its power in the muscles of its belly' [40:16]), and of the portrayal of Leviathan (especially 41:1–11 [Heb 40:25–41:3]; other examples include such declarations as 'I will not keep silence concerning its limbs, or its mighty strength' [41:12; Heb 41:4] and 'On earth it has no equal, a creature without fear' [41:33; Heb 41:25]).

The origin of this block of text is immaterial. The assumed dislocation of Job's sole reply to God is possible. What is troubling,

---

4. See especially Robert Alter, *The Art of Biblical Poetry* (New York: Basic Books, 1985), 85–110.

however, is that what is being proposed at the end of the book as part of the *solution* is precisely what was highlighted by Job earlier in the book as a significant part of the *problem*—the overwhelming power of God. 'He snatches away; who can stop him? Who will say to him, "What are you doing?"' (9:12). 'The thunder of his power who can understand?' (26:14). The emphasis on God's overwhelming power as a solution to Job's problem—which it is not—appears to be based on a misunderstanding of the initial divine speech, coupled with an inappropriate development of the passage on the warhorse (39:19-25). In this sense, whatever its origin, this block is of secondary value.

Job 42:5
It is symbolically appropriate that this verse is wide open to various translations.[5] Its final phrase, however, is crystal clear: 'but now my eye sees you [NAB: has seen you].' The difficulty with it is equally clear: nowhere in the text of the book has Job seen God. Job has just *listened* to a lengthy discourse from God. God spoke to Job: 'then the LORD answered Job out of the whirlwind' (38:1; the Hebrew adds, 'saying', the equivalent in Hebrew of quotation marks). It would have been so simple to formulate the text as: 'the LORD *appeared* to Job in the whirlwind and said'. But the text does not have that.

An appeal to Job's growth in insight and inner understanding, in the light of all that has just been said, is most attractive. Against this, the corporeality of 'my eye sees you' seems to demand something more physical. For lack of something better (*faute de mieux*), we are left to assume that God appeared to Job and spoke. It is symbolically appropriate that the *seeing* is unclear. Human seeing of God is seldom clear. Yet the human experience of God is the only ultimate answer for the suffering in human life.

Job 42:6
It is again appropriate that the poetry's final verse should be opaque. The first part of the verse has two verbs and no object; the second part of the verse has two objects and no verb.[6] To the best of my knowledge, the syntactical structure of the verse is unique in the Hebrew Bible.

---

5. See especially EM Good, *In Turns of Tempest* (Stanford, CA: Stanford University Press, 1990), 370-78.
6. For more detail, see Antony F Campbell, *God and Bible: Exploring Stories from Genesis to Job* (New York/Mahwah, NJ: Paulist), 120.

It has long been known to scholars that, without emendation, the verse cannot bear the meaning usually found in modern translations or even commentaries (that is, 'I despise myself' or equivalent).[7] It is highly unlikely that Job's stance should be changed so radically in the profound uncertainty of one opaque verse. It is more likely that, taking the two verbs together and the two objects together, 42:6 is an exit line: 'I have had enough of this lamentation stuff.'

It is dishonest to translate the verse in the traditional fashion without a note to say that an emendation, a change, has been made to the text. John McKenzie resisted dishonesty fiercely. So should we.

---

7. Above all, see SR Driver and GB Gray, *The Book of Job* (ICC; Edinburgh: T&T Clark, 1921), Part One, 373 ('The v is probably corrupt'); Part Two, 347–48 ('The v. seems to be defective ... if correctly read, an obj. has dropped out ... it is better to restore a suitable object by emendation'). Also, Good, *Turns of Tempest*, 25–26, 170, as well as 375–78 and Habel, *Book of Job*, 576, noting the contributions of Moses Maimonides (twelfth century) and Dale Patrick (1976). Clines takes a different and not indefensible tack: 'Therefore I melt in reverence before you, and I have received my comfort, even while sitting in dust and ashes' (*Job 1–20*, xlvi).

The Book of Job:
Two Questions, One Answer *
(original: *ABR* 51, 2003)

The book of Job asks two questions, but it only answers one. Once we see this and accept it, the structure of the book becomes clear. Once the refusal to answer the second question is recognised, the integrity of the book can be preserved.

The first question is asked by the Accuser (the satan; ha-satan): 'Does Job fear God for nothing?' (1:9). The same favourable answer is given twice: 'In all this Job did not sin' (1:22; 2:10). The text involved is not coextensive with the prose; the issue is ended with 2:10, but the prose continues to 2:13. The treatment of the first question is restricted to 1:1–2:10 along with 42:10b–17—a move away from the traditional approach.

The prose text reporting the arrival of the friends, like that giving the LORD's judgement on them, belongs to the central core of the book (chapters 3–41, more or less). The friends are not associated with the first question; their concern is with the second one. Nothing from an older story need be assumed to have been suppressed.

The second question is asked by Job: 'Why is light given to one in misery, and life to the bitter in soul?' (3:20). The book's refusal to answer this question is clearest at the end: 'I had heard of you by the hearing of the ear, but now my eye sees you' (42:5)—when, in the text, Job has not seen anything at all. However this sentence is to be translated (and many options are open—see below) one thing is abundantly clear: in the book, Job has not seen anything at all. The text focused on this second question includes some of the

---

*I am grateful to several colleagues who read through this in draft and whose comments have been most helpful.

prose, beginning with the arrival of the friends and ending with the dismissal of their answers, 2:11–42:9.

The structure of the book emerges as follows: a framing story, dealing with the first question (1:1–2:10; 42:10b–17); embedded within it, the core of the book dealing with the second question (2:11–42:9).

The first issue addressed is that of religious altruism; do God-fearers relate to God because it is right to do so or in the hope of reward for doing so? YHWH points to Job's goodness (1:8); the satan points to Job's prosperity (1:9).[1] In the satan's view, Job will be a God-fearer while he is prosperous. Take away the prosperity and the truth will emerge; 'he will curse you to your face' (1:11). YHWH shamefully—but this is theology by storytelling—gives in and gives the satan his head. Goaded, Job refuses to curse God, does not charge God with wrong-doing (1:22), and does not sin with his lips (2:10). The issue is resolved; the satan is proved wrong. Religious faith is possible for the rightness of it rather than for reward—because it is right, not because it is rewarded. Faith that has integrity is possible. The fact that it is possible does not mean that many of us, if indeed any, live our faith that way. What it does mean is that such faith in God is not an impossible goal to aim for.

Within this framing story, YHWH allows the satan first to strip Job of everything except what pertained to his own person; it included the lives of his children. Then YHWH allows the satan to move on Job's person, with the sole exception of sparing his life. It may be storytelling, but any sense of human decency is outraged by it. Life may do these things to people, but a half-way decent God should not. Possibly the only excuse for the story is that such things happen. A story, allowing for an all-powerful God, can hardly explore the issue without allowing for the horrors that do happen. At the end, the story has YHWH attempt to make amends for what had been done: 'the LORD gave Job twice as much as he had before' (42:10b). For many, this compounds what was shocking enough at the beginning. For the story, it brings to a close the unfortunate episode with which the story began.

---

1. YHWH will be used here as a reminder that the personal divine name is hardly used outside this story. Within the core (after 2:10 until 42:6), it is almost entirely absent, occurring only at 12:9; 38:1; and 40:1, 3, 6. This phenomenon has long been observed and has contributed to the claim of a prose story framing the poetic core.

The source of such revulsion needs to be made clear. In human experience, lives and fortunes can be lost. The loss needs to be grieved (which the text of Job does not allude to in the framing story but, at another level, embodies in the book's core). It may be that, in due course, fortunes are restored and other children born. That life does this to people is a source of grief and pain; it is also a fact of life that such things happen. What is shocking is that God should be presented as responsible for such fate, apparently motivated by pride, and inflicting such disaster on a faithful follower. Even in the unreality of the story-world, such behaviour appears appalling. The only possible excuse for such storytelling is its goal, the affirmation of the possible integrity of religious belief.

It is unwise to dismiss the framing story as 'this ancient folk tale' which presents 'the traditional pious and patient saint', reflecting an authentic 'patriarchal background'.[2] The antiquity of the figure of Job (cf Ezek 14:14, 20) says nothing of the time of composition of this text. The issue of the integrity of religious belief is disturbingly serious. St Teresa of Avila's claim, 'though you damn me, I will love you still', is shared by few. To explore the issue in story may unfortunately but necessarily involve stripping a faithful God-fearer of their prosperity and wellbeing. The stylisation of the story is not foreign to the stylised series of exchanges between Job and the three. The framing story may be of a piece with the rest of the book (so Habel, Janzen); it may be a little earlier or a lot earlier. A link is there in 42:10a, perhaps no more than the three words in Hebrew, 'when he had prayed for his friends'.

The story provides the perfect setting for the central section or core of the book. According to the story, Job is sitting among the ashes, with a potsherd to scrape himself, covered with loathsome sores (2:7–8). So the core begins with Job's three friends hearing of his trouble and coming to commiserate with him. One has to admire their tact. They are said to have sat with him seven days and seven nights 'and no one spoke a word to him, for they saw that his suffering was very great' (2:13). The core has its brief prose introduction and its equally brief prose conclusion (in 42:7–9).[3]

---

2. Norman C Habel, *The Book of Job* (OTL; London: SCM, 1985) 576.
3. 42:7–9 uses YHWH (twice each in vv. 7 and 9). This detracts from the mechanical rightness of the structure proposed here. However, if the divine speech is presented as from YHWH (38:1; 40:1, 3, 6), it is appropriate that the divine rebuke ('you have not spoken of me what is right') should also come from

After seven days, the question is put in Job's agonised cry:

Why is light given to one in misery,
and life to the bitter in soul? . . .
Why is light given to one who cannot see the way,
whom God has fenced in? (3:20, 23).

After a life of affluence and respect, Job on his dunghill with his potsherd is in misery; no one denies that. Ironically, his misery results from 'acts of God' in both senses of the term. Some human suffering can be attributed to the effects of human freedom, but certainly not all. Like hurricanes, earthquakes, and plagues, what happened to Job, war and weather, were the events of nature, 'acts of God', that are independent of human freedom.

For forty chapters the understanding of human life is pondered and plumbed, in all its aspects of misery, bitterness, and meaninglessness. No answer is given. Job is said to have spoken rightly of God, and Job's only answer is 42:5—but in the book Job has not seen anything at all. The three friends, putting forward the standard apologetics of what was orthodox theology, are declared not to have spoken rightly of God. But no answer is given to the issue that has been raised and discussed for forty chapters.

To accept this, we need to look closely at the two verses that bring the poetry to a close, 42:5–6.

We may begin with 42:6. Many a translation is a classic case of church tradition winning out over syntax and grammar. The NRSV renders it: 'Therefore I despise myself, and repent in dust and ashes.' Norman Habel remarks that 'the meaning of the verse depends on the object supplied'.[4] So much for clarity when we need it.[5] No object

---

YHWH. In the final analysis, the book of Job is in Israel's canon of scripture and speaks of Israel's God. If the book is delphic in not saying what is right, it is theologically appropriate to put on YHWH's lips the condemnation of what is theologically wrong.

4. Norman C Habel, *The Book of Job* (OTL; London: SCM, 1985) 576.
5. Two of the great figures from a classical past, SR Driver and GB Gray, comment simply: 'The v. seems to be defective' (*The Book of Job* [ICC; Edinburgh: T&T Clark, 1921] 347). In Job 7:16 (NRSV, 'I loathe my life'), the Hebrew has no object for the verb; the context is unassailable in the direction of its meaning. Such is not the case with 42:6.

is provided nearby for this first verb.⁶ Habel has to go to Job 31:13 to find a suitable one. Edwin Good is unsurprisingly blunt: 'The reflexive sense "despise myself" is impossible.'⁷ Ink could well be spilled for ever. Gerald Janzen's comment would be disputed by no one: 'The translation "I loathe myself" is interpretive.'⁸ To reverse the direction of the principal character in an entire book on the grounds of a single uncertain verse is risky and suspect interpretation—especially a book which has the three other major players declared by God to have been in error.

The verdict on 'repent in dust and ashes' is even more forcefully dismissive. From Maimonides in the twelfth century to Patrick and others in the twentieth, 'in dust and ashes' is out.⁹ Says Janzen: 'If usage determines meaning, then general usage is all against the meaning "repent in dust and ashes" and in favor of "repent concerning . . .".'¹⁰ Good gives the analysis of the syntax: '"Dust and ashes", then, does double duty as the accusative of both "I despise" (*em'as*) and "I repent" (*nhmty*).'¹¹ His translation is adequate: 'Therefore I despise and repent of dust and ashes'.¹² The interpretative debate then turns to the meaning of 'dust and ashes'.

For Habel, it is Job's position of lamentation among the dust and ashes. Following Patrick, he says: 'Thus the text ought to be rendered "I repent/relent of dust and ashes", meaning that he forsakes his position of lamentation among the dust and ashes and forswears remorse.'¹³

---

6. An object, 'dust and ashes', is provided nearby for the two verbs, taken as a pair; see below. In this case, a translation such as 'I despise myself' is out of the question.
7. Edwin M Good, *In Turns of Tempest: A Reading of Job* (Stanford: Stanford Univ. Press, 1990) 26. He is consistent; he renders 7:16a as 'I refuse! I won't live forever' (67). Driver and Gray: 'I refuse (it)!' (72).
8. J Gerald Janzen, *Job* (Interpretation; Atlanta: John Knox, 1985), 254.
9. See Dale Patrick, 'The Translation of Job XLII 6', in *VT* 26 (1976): 369–71; also LJ Kaplan, 'Maimonides, Dale Patrick, and Job XLII 6', in *VT* 28 (1978): 356–58; John Briggs Curtis, 'On Job's Response to Yahweh', in *JBL* 98 (1979): 497–511.
10. Janzen, *Job*, 256.
11. Good, *In Turns of Tempest*, 376.
12. Good, *In Turns of Tempest*, 26 and 375. Curtis, after full analysis of the verb, rejects 'repent' as its meaning and advocates 'I am sorry for' ('Job's Response', 499–500). 'Repent concerning' and 'be sorry about' are not far apart. A 'change of mind' is often central to the meaning of the verb.
13. Habel, *Job*, 576.

Habel assumes that 'God has actually appeared and Job has "seen" God.'[14] In my judgment, the text does not support this assumption. Habel suggests that Job's final reply is deliberately ambiguous. 'While the language suggests a mood of submission, the text functions as a formal retraction of Job's suit against his adversary and a public announcement that his role as a lamenting litigant among the ashes has terminated.'[15] For Janzen, 'dust and ashes are an apt figure for human destiny.'[16] For Good, '"dust and ashes" has to do with lowliness and mourning, with death and with sin'.[17] He agrees with Habel and goes beyond him to assert that '"to repent of dust and ashes" is to give up the religious structure that construes the world in terms of guilt and innocence. It is to repent of repentance.' [18]

These observations are selective; but there is little point in being comprehensively exhaustive. Two conclusions emerge with clarity. First, the openness to interpretation of 42:6 allows adequate scope to the interests of its interpreters. Second, little or no scope is allowed for Job to reverse his claim of innocence and its consequences. The weight of the book is not to be overturned by the unusual and uncertain syntax of a single verse.

The Hebrew of Job 42:6 has a pair of verbs in its first part (despise, repent) and a pair of substantives in its second part (dust, ashes). The preposition linking the two parts is, in such a context, to be rendered 'concerning'. If, with Habel and Good, 'dust and ashes' can be understood in relation to the 'lowliness and mourning', the misery that goes with Job's 'position of lamentation', then the verse asserts Job's putting an end to the debate. It is possible but not necessary to see this (with Habel) as a retraction of Job's suit against God, or see this understanding as an anticlimax (with Good). It can be understood simply as an exit line; as far as Job is concerned, the debate is at an end.

It is not possible, therefore, to read some defence of traditional orthodoxy into 42:6. If it is an exit line, attention turns to 42:5. The syntax of 42:5 is clear; its meaning is certainly not. The NRSV translates

---

14. Habel, *Job*, 579.
15. Habel, *Job*, 579.
16. Janzen, *Job*, 208. In the context of 42:6, dust and ashes are said to be 'not incompatible with royal status' (Habel, *Job*, 257). This understanding of human vocation differs from the 'frail man' of Briggs's translation ('Job's Response', 505).
17. Good, *In Turns of Tempest*, 377.
18. Good, *In Turns of Tempest*, 377.

it with a pluperfect verb and an adversative conjunction: 'I had heard of you by the hearing of the ear, but now my eye sees you.' Three elements are well known and, to my knowledge, disputed by nobody.

i) The verbs of hearing and seeing are in the same tense (*qatal*).
ii) The conjunction (Hebrew: *we-*) derives its meaning of 'and', 'but', etc. from its context.
iii) The verb of hearing can mean either 'to hear' or 'to hear about/to hear of'. The syntax, therefore, allows for a wide range of meanings. Four examples will be enough:
—My ear hears you **and** now my eye sees you.
—My ear hears you **but** now my eye sees you.
—My ear **heard** you **and** now my eye **sees** you.
—My ear **heard about** you **but** now my eye **sees** you.

Two observations need to be made forcefully. First, it cannot be taken for granted that a past situation is being contrasted with a different present (that is, 'I had heard about you, but now I have seen you'). Such an understanding is syntactically possible, but it must be legitimated from the context. Second, in the text there is absolutely no statement of seeing. In the text God does not actually appear. God speaks (cf 38:1; 40:1, 6) and God questions (cf 42:4), but in the text God does not appear. There have been words in plenty to hear; there has been no report of vision.

> It is a new activity . . . Job's claim that his eye sees Yahweh is startling, to say the least. Given the strictures against seeing the divine, many scholars argue that his seeing must be metaphorical: Job is now convinced (Pope); he has direct experience in contrast to secondhand (Driver and Gray, Dhorme); his consciousness of the god comes directly from the god and not from his own musing upon experience (Terrien). There are, however, enough instances in the Hebrew Bible of people who see the god that I do not feel the compulsion of metaphor.[19]

The text's references to the ear and the eye do not suggest metaphor. While the metaphorical is tempting, it may be better to resist

---
19. Good, *In Turns of Tempest*, 373–74.

temptation and refrain from indulgence. After all, what emerges is not what the text demands but what the interpreter believes.

Habel assumes that Job did see God. The assumption facilitates making sense of the text. But it is an assumption and it runs counter to the text. The basis for the assumption is the statement in the text: 'now my eye sees you'. The reader is confronted with this statement and has to come to terms with it. The 'now' moves beyond the activity of hearing. For Habel, the seeing remains within the argument of the book: '*In response to Job's earlier demand*, God has actually appeared and Job has "seen" God.'[20] Given the absence of any report of vision in the text, and resisting a retreat to the metaphorical, the possibility needs to be entertained that Job's claim is to something outside the text.

To move outside a text is something no interpreter likes to do; it is close to an admission of defeat. Yet the statement is there; 'now my eye sees you' says Job, and the seeing is not in the text. With Habel, it can be assumed and correlated with the argument of the book. Alternatively, because the seeing is not in the text, it is a legitimate possibility to assume that the reference is to activity outside the text, to something of the experience of life. The text has been about words—from Job, the friends, Elihu, and God. To move beyond these words ('and now'), it may be necessary to look to a way of knowing without words.

Today's therapists might speak of balancing the logic of the head with the insight of the heart. In ancient Israel, such language does not seem to have been readily available. Certainly, with Habel, it has become clear that the logic of legal debate does not bring clarity to the issue. Equally certainly, if Job adds vision to hearing, he adds nothing to indicate its potential. The text provides only the statement: 'now my eye sees you'. The claim that the next verse, 42:6, is 'the punch line of the Book of Job'[21] reveals not the meaning of the verse but the interpreter's need for something other than what the verse plainly is: an exit line, an end to the discussion. We may want an answer. The text does not provide a verbal one; it may have already pointed in a different direction.

---

20. Habel, *Job*, 579 (emphasis added).
21. Good, *In Turns of Tempest*, 375.

The text has been preparing for an abdication of further speech; it will shortly negate the value of much that has already been said. As far back as 40:3–4, Job is portrayed as determined to refrain from further speech: 'I lay my hand on my mouth . . . I will proceed no further.' This is repeated in 42:3, with the reason for it spelled out: 'I have uttered what I did not understand, things too wonderful for me, which I did not know.' It should not be surprising that the book moves away from words to seeing. The traditional words of the friends are given short shrift. Says the Lord: 'you have not spoken of me what is right, as my servant Job has' (42:7). We may be left unsure as to what Job has spoken that was right; it is quite clear that what the friends have spoken was not right. Job's attitude is presented coming out of a profoundly personal experience. The friends are presented imposing on Job attitudes universalised from what was purportedly the experience of others.

A surfeit of scholarly detail may sometimes obscure central truths; the wood cannot be seen for the trees. The outcome needs to be clear for these final verses in the poetry of the book of Job (42:5–6). Job 42:6 is at base an exit line: it is time to put an end to all that has gone on; for now, the discussion is over. An interpretation that has Job regret what he has said ('I despise myself') can only be achieved by violating the canons of Hebrew grammar and syntax. Interpretations in other directions can be built on the verse, but need not be. As for Job 42:5, seeing by the eye is affirmed in the verse; because it is not explicit in the preceding text, it can either be assumed as somehow within the text or assumed as a reference to life outside the text. In either case, no conclusion is articulated from it. It is left pointing in a new direction—and that is all. Neither of these positions come as bolts from the blue. They are prepared for in the text and they are followed up in the text. Basically, therefore, 42:5 does not contribute to the preceding argument but may point the way to a new direction— without developing it; 42:6 also does not contribute to the preceding argument but brings it to a close. The debate—with friends, Elihu, and God—is at an end.

Having noted the text's presentation of the Lord's verdict on the friends ('you have not spoken of me what is right'), it is appropriate to look at what they did say—what it was that God condemned.

Eliphaz is secure within the conviction that the traditional teaching was right.

> Think now, who that was innocent ever perished?
>> Or where were the upright cut off? (4:7)

He is comforted by the certainty of personal revelation, personal insight.

>> Can mortals be righteous before God?
>>> Can human beings be pure before their Maker? (4:17)

The sound advice he gives Job is cruel in its irony:

> As for me, I would seek God
>> and to God I would commit my cause (5:8).

The sentiment is pious and beautiful. Unfortunately, readers of the text know that it is from God precisely that Job's misfortunes come. From being sensitive initially, Eliphaz moves in the context to a position of painful smugness:

> How happy is the one whom God reproves ...
> For he [God] wounds, but he binds up;
>> he strikes, but his hands heal (5:17–18).

Bildad is no less certain than Eliphaz; it is difficult to find compassion in his words. Where Eliphaz appealed to personal revelation, Bildad turns rather to the long-held truths of tradition.

> For inquire now of bygone generations,
>> and consider what their ancestors have found (8:8).
> Does God pervert justice?
>> Or does the Almighty pervert the right? (8:3).

Once again, the readers of the text are well aware that God has perverted justice and handed over his faithful servant Job to the torments of the satan. What Bildad says holds small comfort for Job. He begins with Job's children; he ends with Job himself, hedged with the condition, if Job is 'pure and upright' (8:6).

As to Job's children:

> If your children sinned against him,
>> he delivered them into the power of their transgression (8:4).

As to Job himself:

> See, God will not reject a blameless person,
>> nor take the hand of evildoers.
>
> He will yet fill your mouth with laughter,
>> and your lips with shouts of joy (8:20–21).

Zophar lays aside any semblance of care and goes straight for the jugular. Eliphaz began by affirming Job's fear of God and the integrity of Job's ways (4:6). Bildad moved to the conditional: 'If your children sinned . . . if you are pure and upright . . .' (8:4, 6). Zophar is outraged enough not to be limited by such delicacy.

> For you say, 'My conduct is pure,
>> and I am clean in God's sight.'
>
> But, oh that God would speak,
>> and open his lips to you . . .
>
> Know then that God exacts of you less than your guilt deserves (11:4, 6).

The fault for human suffering is with humans (Eliphaz). The fault is not with God (Bildad). In particular, the suffering of the 'blameless and upright' Job is less than Job's putative guilt deserves (Zophar). This is the beginning; it gets worse as the exchanges unfold and argument degenerates into abuse. Job gives as good as he gets and provokes the outrage of the insulted wise. Emotion is given full expression; experience and empathy hardly enter the equation.

Job is dismissive of the three.

> What you know, I also know;
>> I am not inferior to you (13:2).

The friends are dismissive of Job.

> Should your babble put others to silence,
> and when you mock, shall no one shame you? (11:3)

A fundamental attitude toward the sufferer is shared by the friends. 'How can a mortal be righteous before God? . . . . A mortal is a maggot and a human being a worm' (Bildad, 25:4, 6). A fundamental trust is given to God. 'He saves the humble. He will deliver even those who are guilty . . .' (Eliphaz, 22:29–30). The fate of the wicked inexorably awaits them. 'Do you not know . . . that the exulting of the wicked is short, and the joy of the godless is but for a moment?' (Zophar, 20:4–5).

Job accuses the three of the ultimate sin that any theologian must fear:

> Will you speak falsely for God,
> and speak deceitfully for him? (13:7)

God turns the accusation on Job:

> Will you even put me in the wrong?
> Will you condemn me that you may be justified? (40:8)

The final verdict in the text favours Job and condemns the friends:

> For you have not spoken of me what is right, as my servant Job has (42:7).

Humankind can stand before God. God can stand before humankind. A relationship is possible. The logic of language does not make all clear. Where there is misery in life, there may also be mystery.

Whether God bullies Job in the divine speeches is largely a matter of interpretation, the text allowing for different overtones to be given to specific texts—that is, the compassionate and caring or the hectoring and angry. There is a place for retaliatory anger; Job has scarcely been presented as polite toward God—for example, 'he [God] destroys both the blameless and the wicked . . . if it is not he, who then is it?' (9:22, 24). In the end, it is not important to the argument. The vastness of the created universe was—and is—mystery enough to have been out of Job's league.

What has been said can be summed up around two issues:

1) the structure of the book of Job;
2) the meaning of the book of Job.

Where the structure is concerned, it may be more helpful to divide the book of Job by the criterion of theme rather than that of prose and poetry. The first theme deals with the question: 'Does Job fear God for nothing?' It occupies 1:1–2:10 and 42:10b–17. The section is self-contained, with its own issue and an answer to it. The second theme is sounded by Job's question: 'Why is light given to one in misery?' It occupies the bulk of the book, from 2:11–42:9. It opens with the coming of the friends and ends with the dismissal of their contribution.

Where the meaning of the book is concerned, an answer is given for the first theme and it is positive. The answer affirms the integrity of religious belief; Job's fidelity to God is not dependent on his prosperity.

An answer is not given to the question at the core of the second theme. Job 42:6 puts an end to the discussion. Job 42:5 claims a seeing by the eye that goes beyond the hearing of the ear and the words involved in hearing. It may be a pointer to a way of knowing without words, but any potential is left unspoken. Words given Job have prepared the way for this refusal of an answer: 'I have uttered what I did not understand, things too wonderful for me, which I did not know' (42:3). Words presented as the LORD's verdict on the friends confirm this refusal. The answers that they advocated so vigorously are deemed by the LORD to have been in error: 'you have not spoken of me what is right'. An answer has not been found in words. By its very definition, an answer without words must be left in silence.

While the book may not offer an answer in words, it is important that certain answers are dismissed. Elihu is ignored, and three traditional bits of baloney are declared unfit for human consumption. When the traditional answers put forward by the friends have been dismissed by God, the silent answer of 42:5's wordless seeing can satisfy more safely.

Associated books:

Gustavo Gutiérrez. *On Job: God-talk and the Suffering of the Innocent* (Maryknoll, NY: Orbis, 1985).

Edwin M Good. *In Turns of Tempest: A Reading of Job* (Stanford, CA: Stanford University Press, 1990).

Carol A Newsom. *The Book of Job: A Contest of Moral Imaginations* (Oxford: Oxford University Press, 2003).

The Books of Samuel

Synchrony and the Storyteller

(original: *David und Saul im Widerstreit: Diachronie und Synchronie im Wettstreit*)

As recently as some thirty years ago, an influential scholar, a member of the western biblical establishment, published comments suggesting a redactor might have 'mindlessly mutilated' a text and referring to 'the more or less mechanical piecework of a redactor'. Such remarks may betray what Robert Polzin has pilloried as a view of ancient editing involving the 'damned hands' of 'inept redactors'.[1] Where this view exists, any attempt at serious synchronic study would be dishonest and a waste of time. I fear that it has been around for a long time and in some quarters has not yet vanished. When experience of the biblical text has led to the conviction that its ancient editors were skilful and intelligent, openness to synchronic study is a matter of honesty and respect. Thanks to the last couple of centuries, the diachronic lives with us now as an opening to the human context out of which the scriptures developed, without involving some ungodly divine ghost-writer for whose existence there is no evidence.

I suspect that the above needs to be said by way of introduction to any discussion of the synchronic/diachronic issue. Both approaches are legitimate; both approaches are necessary. 'A treatment of the product that is incompatible with the nature of the process is likely to be flawed. A treatment of the process that invalidates the product is equally suspect.'[2] Process implies the diachronic, product the synchronic.

For some time, I have been advocating recognition of what I call 'reported story' as the appropriate generic description of a number

---

1. Polzin, *Samuel and the Deuteronomist*. Part Two: 1 Samuel, 2.
2. Campbell, *1 Samuel*, xvi.

of narrative passages of biblical text.[3] First in *Semeia* (1989): 'such a reported story would contain the basic elements of character and plot as well as key details but would pass over much that could be easily supplied from the storyteller's imagination.'[4] Two arguments predominated: the absence of elements necessary to the proper unfolding of the plot; the presence of various ways of telling the same basic story.

In a more recent *CBQ* article (2002), I advanced this discussion a step further, influenced by increasing familiarity with the story texts of the Pentateuch and the Deuteronomistic History.[5] I was impressed by three factors: limited distribution, due to copying by hand; limited literacy, restricting use; limited length of the smaller story units. I discussed three further factors in identifying story texts in need of a storyteller. One of these is significant for the synchronic/diachronic issue: where a text runs different scenarios for the same story; that is, cases where one and the same biblical text contains pointers to more than one version of a story (version = whole story) or more than one option for a story (option = aspect or part within a story).

The only reason for bringing up the 'reported story' question is its relevance for the present discussion. If we accept that certain narrative passages are 'reported story', then we are recognising that they are not the record of past storytelling performance but, drawing on the past, they provide a base from which to launch storytelling in the future. Two features matter in the present context: on occasion, reported stories make variant versions available to the storyteller; on occasion, aspects of the text need to be filled out by the storyteller. 1 Samuel 24 provides a good example of both. For inside the cave, more than one version is made available; for outside the cave, some filling out is essential.

The 'filling out' should not come as a surprise; the presence of variant versions may. Some examples will help to illustrate what is meant. The crossing of the Jordan: it is portrayed as both liturgical and leisured and also military and hurried; the capture of Jericho:

---

3. See particularly my 'Reported Story', 'Storyteller's Role', and, especially for the use of the idea and its genre definition, *1 Samuel*, passim.
4. Campbell, 'Reported Story', 77.
5. For Pentateuch and Deuteronomistic History, see Campbell and O'Brien, *Sources of the Pentateuch* and *Unfolding the Deuteronomistic History*.

it is portrayed as liturgical procession and also military siege; the capture of Ai: day-time ambush or night-time ambush; kingship in Israel: given when requested, for the sake of justice or offered spontaneously, for the sake of defence; David's single combat with the Philistine, Goliath: undertaken when David was present as a matter of duty, being the king's armour-bearer or undertaken when David was present as a matter of chance, bringing supplies for his brothers.[6] Something similar appeals to Claus Westermann in making meaning of the twin motifs of the tree in the middle of the garden and the tree of life there too (Gen 2–3).[7]

It is obvious, I believe, that the telling of a story, the performance, is a synchronic activity. Once a story's telling has been begun, the past is either incorporated in it or is left aside; once a story's telling is ended, what might have been is left for another time. Many thoughts by would-be authors and editors may come together in the single

---

6. It is helpful to have a slightly wider, illustrative but not exhaustive, list of places in Joshua to Kings where major choice between versions or options is needed in storytelling.
   Joshua
   chapters 3–4: *inter alia,* a leisurely crossing with strong liturgical emphasis or a hurried crossing with military force
   chapter 6: military siege or processional circumambulation; silent march or sounding procession
   chapter 8: an ambush established during the day on the eve of battle or established during the night before the battle
   chapter 10: a short campaign (with the camp at Gilgal, 10:15) or a more extended campaign (with the camp at Makkedah, 10:25)
   Judges
   chapter 1: the partial conquest portrayed or the total conquest portrayed in Joshua
   chapter 21: women from Jabesh-gilead or women from Shiloh (MT 21,14b ≠ LXX)
   1 Samuel
   chapters 7–12: king needed for internal justice or king needed for external defence
   chapters 16–18: David's moment, as established member of Saul's court or David's moment of entry into Saul's court
   chapter 20: Jonathan's communication with David: by prearranged signal or by coded message or by personal meeting
   2 Samuel
   chapter 24: pestilence stayed by YHWH's action in spontaneously relenting or by David's action in building an altar
   2 Kings
   chapter 1: Elijah met on the way or Elijah sitting on the hilltop.
7. Westermann, *Genesis 1–11*, 212–13 ['a second voice as it were together with the melody']. German, 289–91.

telling of a story; many may be waiting to be involved in the future. In any single performance, the past may be incorporated; the future will have to wait its turn. The live telling of a story by a live storyteller to a live audience is necessarily synchronic. Not all discourse need be storytelling; the telling of a story, in oral performance, however, is synchronic.

If a story was to be told, based on biblical text, certain actions were essential. We may signal three.

> i) expansion: in the vast majority of biblical storytelling texts, the storyteller has to expand on the text; most biblical texts are too short for sustained stories.
> ii) choice: on occasion, the storyteller may have to choose between versions to actualize or options to profit from.
> iii) gaps: in certain cases, the storyteller will have to decide whether gaps in the text need to be filled or are best left as gaps.

If we attend to the second, the matter of choice, a storyteller could face two different situations. First, in some texts, a single story is reported, without pointers to alternative versions or options. Second, in other texts, pointers to alternative versions or options are present. In the first case, without alternatives present, adherence to the text required a storyteller to reproduce in performance whatever revisions and editorial nuances were represented in the text (two examples: I Sam 9:1–10:16, where the prophet is Samuel and no longer an anonymous seer; I Sam 15:1–35, where Samuel rejects Saul and no longer merely rebukes him). In the second case, where pointers to alternative versions or options were present, a storyteller had to decide which version of a story to tell and which options to exploit (for example: is the Jordan to be crossed in military haste or liturgical stateliness).

Modern interpreters face similar situations and similar decisions. It may be that a modern exposition compares and contrasts two versions of a story (for example: David's emergence on the public scene in Israel). To my mind, this is not the telling of a story or the exploring of the meaning of a story; rather, it is the exploration of what it means that there are two or more possible versions of a story. Modern interpreters face discernment and decision. Discernment:

are there pointers to alternatives in this text? Decision: if so, what is the most appropriate way of proceeding to explore the meaning of the text? The key issue here may be acceptance that some biblical texts reflect more than one version of a story.

The social context is important. Unfortunately, we know all too little of the processes for the production of literature in ancient Israel or of the functions that such literature fulfilled.[8]

We have the analogy of legal texts and ritual texts. We do not have data on the compiling and maintaining of legal codes. We can assume centres of deposit; we can also assume that law scrolls were unlikely to have been taken to 'the gate' regularly. Confirmation for this may be found in the observation that the law codes tend to deal rather more with the special cases than the common and ordinary. One may assume that texts regulating rituals were preserved at temples and sanctuaries. Neither the legal nor the ritual texts are particularly helpful to us in determining the settings for narrative texts.

The origin of prophetic books is more helpful. We have a clear enough picture of the movement from prophetic oracles to collections to books. The committing of oracles to writing is not very different from the committing of stories to writing. The establishment of collections of oracles might well be paralleled by the compiling of series of stories. Many of the stories associated with David's rise to power in Israel may have been grouped in such series. We presume the collections were preserved among disciples (cf Isa 8:16; also Jer 36); something analogous is likely for ancient Israel's stories. We know little enough about the preparation and preservation of the prophetic books; in many ways, the same applies to the great narrative compilations.

There is a widely held view in our discipline that narrative texts were used for storytelling. It is an assumption; beyond the existence of the texts themselves, we have little evidence of stories being told. Gerhard von Rad notes: 'we do not know either the representatives of this high achievement in narrative or the audience to whom they principally addressed themselves.'[9] Assuming storytelling took place, what function did it serve in society? Von Rad again: 'more difficult still to answer is the question as to the relationship of these story-

---

8. Helpful in this context is Niditch, *Oral World and Written Word*.
9. G von Rad, *Old Testament Theology*, 1.55; German, 1.69.

tellers to the world of the cult.'[10] In my judgement, at best only a few of the stories preserved in 1–2 Samuel, for example, would be in any way suitable for use in worship—unless it was for the cult of King David.

Certain factors are safely beyond dispute. Without printing, limited distribution was a fact of life. Literacy for complex and sophisticated documents would not have been greater then than it is now. Given their limited length, most narrative texts could not have been the record of storytelling performance.[11] Liturgical reading, such as is customary today, would seem highly unlikely. Synagogues came on the scene too late; liturgies were focused, as far as we know, on sacrifice, prayer, and tradition rather than on 'the liturgy of the word'; furthermore, few of the narratives that have come down to us seem suitable for liturgical use.

Function is important and too little explored. Without wanting to limit possibilities, education and entertainment are likely to have bulked large for stories. Education is an obvious possibility, although we do not hear of it; entertainment is more likely, but beyond the texts themselves the evidence for it is scant. For the longer compilations, again without wanting to be exclusive, I would single out myth making and policy making as possibilities. As an example of myth making there is the Pentateuch; for policy making an example would be the Deuteronomistic History.

I do not take myth making lightly. Almost every people has one or more originating myths, the British, French, and Germans, for example, the Americans and Australians beyond doubt. Myth makers are those who hold the keys to the past or have a grip on the imaginations of the present. They are the historians and the storytellers, all those who can make their beliefs plausible and widely accepted. The probability of a plurality of such myths in any given people is likely to be high. An originating myth does not have to offer a historically balanced and factually accurate picture of a people's origins; it has to offer a plausible picture that gives meaning to the people it serves.[12] In ancient Israel, for example, there is the Pentateuch.

---

10. *Old Testament Theology*, 56; German, 69.
11. For fuller discussion, see Campbell, 'Storyteller's Role'.
12. For example, 'The 'Pilgrim Fathers' who landed at Cape Cod in 1620 were not rediscovered or inserted in their prominent place in the national mythology [of the United States] until the end of the eighteenth century' (Roberts, *Penguin History of the World*, 628–29).

The Pentateuch can be considered the originating myth of ancient Israel; for Israel, the Bible offers no other equivalent. An originating myth is the account that myth makers caused to be believed as to what constituted a people, giving them identity and destiny, their place and role in the world. An originating myth offers an answer to the question, 'Who are we?', often by reflecting the questions, 'What have we come out of?' and 'What is the future we are going into?'

There is more to myth than originating myths. Beyond myth, within the historical realm of time and space, there is also legend and much more. Tomorrow, we can look synchronically at the contribution of I Samuel 24–26 to the legend of King David.

If apparently the function of stories was often different from that of longer compilations, the approach to them by users was probably often different as well. In the case of stories, when a storyteller looked at a text with more than one version of a story in it or offering more than one option on details, a choice had to be made as to which version to actualise or which options to follow. As we noted earlier, a similar choice confronts the modern interpreter. Where a biblical text contains more than one version of a story, a frequent enough occurrence, it is not unlikely that the modern interpreter is unfaithful to the text in endeavouring to harmonise the two versions into one story. Versions are preserved in text; options are preserved in text. No storyteller would try to actualise more than one version of the story or try to adopt more than one option. Modern interpreters may need to take account of this. It may well be a matter of paying honour and respect to the skill and intelligence of those responsible for our biblical texts.

One example will do, from I Samuel 16–18, the story of David and the Philistine, Goliath. In the Hebrew (MT), the longer text, in my judgement two stories are evidently present. In one, preceded by I Samuel 16:14–23, David was at the battlefield as a matter of duty, as armour-bearer to King Saul. In the other, beginning at I Samuel 17:12, David was at the battlefield as a matter of chance. In the first, David is portrayed as a man of faith, stepping into the void left by the dispirited Saul and in kingly fashion liberating Israel from the Philistine threat. In the second, David is portrayed as a man of ambition, seeking to know 'What shall be done for the man who kills this Philistine, and takes away the reproach from Israel?' (17:26); by boldly seizing his chance and achieving victory, David is portrayed winning entry into the court of Saul.¹³ These are two stories. The realities of faith and ambition can be harmonised; despite verses like 17:15–16. and 31, the biblical text does not harmonise the stories. To my mind, it is highly questionable for a modern interpreter to endeavour to harmonise what the text does not. According to the first story, David has been attached to Saul's court and, as his lyre-player and armour-bearer, would be well known to Saul. According to the second story, David entered Saul's court as a result of his military success and therefore was not previously known to Saul. Hence Saul's question to David: 'Whose son are you, young man?' (17:58). With apologies to a respected scholar, Robert Polzin's attempt to harmonise these two stories and entertain the possibility that this question might be understood, among other things, as asking David 'formally to renounce Jesse's paternity in favor of his own' is laughable—at least, confronted with it, Polzin laughed.¹⁴ Diachronic study has shown clearly enough that text does not have one origin or one literary type simply because it is found on one page.

When users come to deal with myth or policy, most often the originators of the myth or policy fade into the background; what matters is the myth or the policy. This reality resonates with Jon Levenson's description of synchronic or holistic analysis as presupposing an 'authorless' text.¹⁵ My suggestion would be that, with texts which go beyond the story category, interpreters would be wise to refrain from reference to authors and restrict themselves to the one evident fact, occurrence within the text.¹⁶

To summarise. Biblical narrative texts on occasion contain pointers to alternative versions or options. In performance, necessarily synchronic, ancient storytellers would not normally have actualised more than one version. Modern interpreters need to follow suit,

---

13. For full discussion, see Campbell, *1 Samuel*, 169–93.
14. *Samuel and the Deuteronomist*, 174–75.
15. 'My point is that the authorless text presupposed by a synchronic, or holistic, mode of analysis has certain affinities with the divinely authored text of pre-modern Jewish tradition' (Levenson, 'Eighth Principle of Judaism', 221).
16. Robert Gordon, for example, speaks of 'the narrator' applying his skills 'to the development of his all-important theme'. It would be less presumptuous to speak of the text's development of this all-important theme ('David's Rise and Saul's Demise', 322. In today's context, Gordon's appeal to Hans Frei on 'authorial intention' (fn 34) is misplaced and inappropriate.

exercise their judgement on the presence of alternatives, and treat separate stories separately. Where longer compilations are concerned, serving the making of myth, policy, legend, or other functions, it would be appropriate not to refer to authors but to focus reference on the phenomena occurring in the text.

Works cited: listing with appropriate details

Campbell, AF. *1 Samuel.* FOTL 7 (Grand Rapids: Eerdmans, 2003).

———. 'The Reported Story: Midway Between Oral Performance and Literary Art', in *Semeia* 46 (1989) 77–85

———. 'The Storyteller's Role: Reported Story and Biblical Text', in *CBQ* 64 (2002) 427–41.

Campbell, Antony F and Mark A O'Brien. *Sources of the Pentateuch: Texts, Introductions, Annotations* (Minneapolis: Fortress, 1993).

———. *Unfolding the Deuteronomistic History: Origins, Upgrades, Present Text* (Minneapolis: Fortress, 2000).

Gordon, Robert P. 'David's Rise and Saul's Demise: Narrative Analogy in 1 Samuel 24–26', 319-39 in *Reconsidering Israel and Judah: Recent Studies on the Deuteronomistic History,* edited by GN Knoppers and JG McConville (Winona Lake, Ind: Eisenbrauns, 2000), 313–339.

Levenson, Jon D. 'The Eighth Principle of Judaism and the Literary Simultaneity of Scripture', in *JR* 68 (1988): 205–25.

Niditch, Susan. *Oral World and Written Word; Ancient Israelite Literature.* Library of Ancient Israel (Louisville: Westminster John Knox, 1996).

Polzin, R. *Samuel and the Deuteronomist: A Literary Study of the Deuteronomic History.* Part Two: 1 Samuel. San Francisco: Harper & Row, 1989.

Rad, G von. *Old Testament Theology.* Volume I: The Theology of Israel's Historical Traditions. Edinburgh: Oliver and Boyd, 1962. German original, 1960.

Roberts, JM. *The Penguin History of the World* (London: Penguin, 1976).

Westermann, Claus. *Genesis 1–11: A Commentary* (Minneapolis: Augsburg, 1984). German original, 1970.

Diachrony and Synchrony: 1 Samuel 24 and 26
(original: *David und Saul im Widerstreit: Diachronie und Synchronie im Wettstreit*)

An introduction to the diachronic and synchronic approaches to I Samuel 24 and 26 needs to begin with close focus on the texts in their individuality and broad focus on their combination and context. Close focus on I Samuel 24 reveals the presence in the text of more than one version of the moment inside the cave and the need for filling out the text once Saul is outside the cave. As far as I am aware, similar concerns do not exist for I Samuel 26.

Close Focus

Inside the cave (24:3–8, MT; NRSV, 24:2–7)
The general scene is well known. Saul entered a desert cave, west of the Dead Sea, to ease nature. David and his men were in the back of the cave. Hardly the most noble circumstances, however David had the chance to kill Saul and did not do so. So far, so good.

The order or sequence of the verses has been widely recognised as troubled. Commentators used to reorganise them; more recently, commentators have refrained from doing so—not because the order was not troublesome, but, *inter alia*, because good reasons could not be offered for how the text had got that way.[1] Yet the order is relatively typical for Hebrew narrative: an action is first reported and then unfolded in speech. The action is reported in v 5b (Heb; NRSV, v

---

1. Among recent studies: Stoebe, *Das erste Buch Samuelis*—'Abgesehen davon . . . kann auch die Entstehung eines solchen Fehlers nur schwer verständlich gemacht werden' (439); McCarter, *I Samuel*—'It is difficult . . . to explain how such a displacement could have come into the text' (384); also Gordon, 'Word-Play and Verse-Order'. The hypothesis of an offer of options to the storyteller then may offer a way out of the impasse now.

4b); David stealthily cut off a corner of Saul's cloak. The description of this as 'action' is muddied by v 5a (NRSV, v 4a), where David's men incite him to the deed, quoting an otherwise unknown word from the LORD. The words preceding the action are hardly a problem. More interesting is the open quality of the YHWH-word: 'do to him as it seems good to you.'

In what follows, unfolding the action, a difference is present that is often not taken into account. In v 7 (NRSV, v 6), David speaks of action on his own part, God forbid 'that I should do this thing ... to raise my hand against him'. But in v 8 (NRSV, v 7), it is action by David's men that is spoken of, and David 'did not permit them to attack Saul'. The responsibility of the commander for the actions of those commanded is, of course, valid doctrine, but it does not fit this text.

If the text records options for the storyteller's choice, three may be present:

>	i. David may be portrayed demonstrating his respect for the king. It was in his power to do Saul a mischief (which is surely what his men intended in v 5a [NRSV, v 4a]) and he did not do so, but merely cut off a corner of Saul's cloak. This is what David claims in his speech outside the cave (cf vv 11–12 [NRSV, vv 10–11]). The text for this version of the cave incident ends with v 5 (NRSV, v 4).
>	ii. With v 6 (NRSV, v 5), repentance enters in—'David was stricken to the heart'. The clipping of the royal cloak can be construed as an evil in itself, but that is not the understanding in David's speech outside the cave. A preferable understanding is that the part is being used to signify the whole (understandably): urged by his men, David intended to kill Saul, but had a change of heart and clipped Saul's cloak instead. The intent to kill accounts for David's repentance and his speech to his men in v 7 (NRSV, v 6).[2]
>	iii. The men's view of what should seem good to David is that they move to attack Saul. In v 8 (NRSV, v 7), David

---

2. This introduces an understanding of 24:6 (NRSV, v 5) that is not present in my *1 Samuel*.

'did not permit them to attack Saul'. Either before or after this, David would need to snip Saul's cloak, if the motif is to be used in the scene outside (cf v 12 [Heb; NRSV, v 11]).

It would have been easy enough to combine the versions. The biblical text does not do so. I think it fair to say that a harmonising combination would neither represent nor respect the biblical text. The text points to more than one version of the story inside the cave. The storyteller was invited to choose.

Outside the cave (24:9-23, MT; NRSV, 8-22)
Saul left the cave; David too rose, went out, and called to Saul. Two difficulties need to be addressed; a little 'filling out' is quite easy, but quite essential. First, three thousand of Saul's finest are under the king's command, in search of David. David is hardly likely to walk out into the trap; the troops are hardly likely to stand rooted to the spot, staring myopically in the wrong direction. Second, Saul's first words are: 'Is that your voice, my son David?' Assuming broad daylight (otherwise, why the cave and why the corner of the cloak?), the question needs a context to make it appropriate.

The three thousand would be easy to handle in storytelling. A gesture or a command from Saul would take care of them. The question is more difficult to handle. If the storyteller has David leave the cave out of sight of Saul and the soldiers and then climb to a safe spot in the hills from where he can wave the corner of the cloak without risk, both difficulties are resolved. David leaves the cave unseen and so escapes seizure; initially, at least, David remains unseen and so allows Saul's question.

The biblical text does not make this move; a storyteller easily could. Is this in any way disrespectful of the text? I do not believe so. The brevity of the biblical text requires its expansion. The brevity of the biblical text calls for the storyteller's skill and imagination in embroidering it appropriately. Expanding the text does not disrespect it; changing it does.

Broad Focus

The broader context of chapters 24 and 26 repays attention. At the start of chapter 26, the Ziphites bring information to Saul about

David's whereabouts. 'David is in hiding on the hill of Hachilah, which is opposite Jeshimon.' This is exactly the information that they brought to Saul in 23:19, with the added precision there specifying 'the strongholds of Horesh' on the hill of Hachilah (23:19). In the narrative, Saul sends them for more information; "find out exactly where he is' (v 22). At 26:1–2, given the same information, without the precision present in 23:19, Saul is said to have set off in search of David.

The narrative is not following chronological sequence or the unfolding of events, at least it need not be. The Ziphite offer in chapter 23 with Saul's temporising and Saul's positive response to the same offer in chapter 26 without temporising invites users of the text to see the intervening narrative within a single frame.

After the detour, chasing David on the mountain (23:24b–28), the narrative has three encounters: of David with Saul, of David with Abigail, of David with Saul again for the last time—all three figures being in danger at David's hands, although we may not recognise it so readily for Abigail (but see v 17, 'all his house'; v 22 is formulaic). From all three—Saul I, Abigail, Saul II—David receives commendations that are remarkable.

From Saul, the first time: 'You are more righteous than I . . . You did not kill me when the LORD put me into your hands. . . . You shall surely be king' (24:18–21 [Heb.; NRSV, 24:17–20]). From Abigail: 'The LORD has restrained you from blood-guilt and from taking vengeance. … Evil shall not be found in you so long as you live. . . . My lord shall have no cause of grief, or pangs of conscience, for having shed blood without cause' (25:26–31). From Saul, the second time: 'I have done wrong . . . My life was precious in your sight today; I have been a fool, and have made a great mistake . . . Blessed be you, my son David! You will do many things and will succeed in them' (26:21–25). For a David who wanted to be seen as free from blood-guilt and certainly wanted to succeed, this is high praise indeed. Synchronically, it is brilliant.

Diachrony

From a storytelling point of view, diachronic issues are only obtrusive in the opening verses of chapter 24, 'inside the cave'. The diachronic approach is one way in which a text perceived as intractable is accounted for intelligibly and made available for appropriate synchronic interpretation. In chapter 24, a role for the storyteller is evident. An ancient storyteller had to choose; a modern interpreter must allow for this.

From a technical point of view, other issues are available for study. The question of dependence has been raised. Is there dependence and, if so, in which direction does it flow? The question of editing and the presence of later concerns has been raised. How such issues relate to interpretation and the search for meaning goes beyond our present concern.

Synchrony

From the point of view of synchrony, if we have claimed skill and intelligence for ancient editors and compilers, these chapters are eloquent witness to the rightness of the claim. The task of synchronic interpretation is to interpret the existing text intelligibly. For the scene within the cave, the storyteller's options need to be acknowledged; for the scene outside the cave, the storyteller's skill needs to be allowed for.

It is of added importance to situate these chapters in the narrative sweep of the ending of 1 Samuel. David has been portrayed on the run from Saul. He is about to be run out of the country. He is about to be absent from the battle in which Saul will die. Here he receives Saul's praise and blessing. From Abigail he receives the assurance that he 'shall have no cause of grief, or pangs of conscience, for having shed blood without cause'. The narrative handles this phase of the tension between David and Saul with consummate skill—from David's point of view. God could not have done it better.

Conclusion

An analogy may make a suitable focus for discussion at this point.

If the text is regarded as a work of art, a painting, we know that paintings can be subjected to microscopic inspection in the ateliers of specialists; we know too that paintings can be hung on appropriate walls and viewed from respectful distances. For me, there is an echo here of the diachronic and the synchronic. Where it is warranted, a painting needs to be subjected to microscopic inspection. It may be for restoration, to identify the painter, or for some other purpose. Often, the diachronic approach to a biblical text is necessary, whether for restoration, attribution, or some other purpose.

As well as being enjoyed, a painting can still be studied and appreciated when it is hung. But that is not the same thing as putting it under a microscope. As well as being enjoyed, a text can be studied and appreciated when it is approached synchronically. As literary critics and art critics proclaim, good criticism can heighten appreciation and enjoyment. As for paintings, so for texts.

Details abound, of course; but I believe this covers the main thrust, for introductory purposes. An aspect that fascinates me is the observation that in chapter 24 Saul moves into David's territory while in chapter 26 David moves into Saul's. What does the text mean by having David enter Saul's camp? The question of literary type is involved. If the text is a report, the text has David enter Saul's camp because David did enter it. On the other hand, however, if the text relates to a story, why did the storyteller have David enter Saul's camp. Certainly not with murderous intent, with a view to killing Saul. No Davidic storyteller would have wanted to imply that. In the text, Abishai alone wants to kill Saul; in that, he is David's foil. A Davidic storyteller probably wanted to demonstrate David's innocence of blood-guilt and show David receiving Saul's blessing. The combination of the chapters is fascinating.

In all this, I see two things as key and crucial: (i) recognition that ancient editors were skilful and intelligent; (ii) recognition that some biblical story texts contain pointers to more than one version of the story.

Works cited: listing with appropriate details

Campbell, Antony F. *1 Samuel*, FOTL 7 (Grand Rapids: Eerdmans, 2003).

Gordon, Robert P. 'Word-Play and Verse-Order in 1 Samuel XXIV 5–8', in *VT* 40 (1990): 139–44.

McCarter, P Kyle, Jr. *I Samuel*. AB 8 (Garden City: Doubleday, 1980).

Stoebe, Hans Joachim. *Das erste Buch Samuelis*. KAT VIII 1 (Gütersloh: Mohn, 1973).

From Philistine to Throne (1 Sam 16:14–18:16)
(original: *ABR* 34, 1986)

The story of David and Goliath is a widely known Bible story; without doubt, it is also often a misunderstood one. The all-too-frequent tenor of its telling is the triumph of the bare-footed shepherd boy over the mighty Philistine warrior, through sheer trust in the power of God. Yet the description of himself given by David does not fit this picture. And besides this, any Israelite with minimal experience of military matters knew that a slinger was a dangerously accurate marksman (see Judg 20:16, also 2 Chron 26:14). An astonishing victory over the Philistine is not the primary concern. Instead, the narrative sets up a contrast between the dismayed and fearful Saul, who has been abandoned by God, and the courageous, resolute David whose trust in God brings victory. Set in its context, the story makes clear that David is destined for the throne of Israel. A study of the origins of the present text throws valuable light on this understanding.

The combination of traditions around the emergence of David at Saul's court is well-known. So is the fact that chapters 16 – 18 of 1 Samuel are preserved in quite different versions in the Hebrew and the Greek. The combination of two stories, of different genres, has contributed to obscuring the structure and meaning of both. Our task in this paper is to identify these two stories clearly and to bring out the communication that is carefully crafted into one of them, and which is still present in the combined text.

The variety of traditions involved is worth sketching briefly. Samuel is sent to anoint a king in place of the rejected Saul, and he anoints David, son of Jesse (16:1–13); there is no further mention of this anointing until a veiled reference to it in 2 Sam 5:2b.[1] 1 Sam

---

1. The account of David's anointing by Samuel is to be attributed to prophetic

16:14–23 recounts a rather accomplished David's coming to the court of Saul, as a skilled lyre player, to free Saul from the evil spirit which tormented him.[2] Then, in 1 Samuel 17, David appears as the young shepherd, bringing provisions to his elder brothers in the army (17:12–31). Brought before Saul, he professes his readiness to fight Goliath, and he prevails over Saul's misgivings (17:32–40). He also prevails over Goliath. Returning from his victory, with the spoils of his foe, Saul inquires about his identity, as though David were quite unknown to him (17:55–58). David and Jonathan begin their friendship (18:1–5); the singing women trigger Saul's jealousy (18:6–9); Saul attempts to pin David with his spear (18:10–11), and finally has two tries at having the Philistines end his life instead, using as bait the hand in marriage of first Merab then Michal (18:17–29). The variety of traditions is considerable.

Within the story of single combat with the Philistine champion, Goliath, there are a number of difficulties with the present text, which argue against its unity. Briefly, these are: 1) 17:12 gives the impression of being the beginning of a new story;[3] 2) 17:15 gives the impression of being a harmonising addition, holding together differing traditions of David at Saul's camp and David back at the family farm; 3) 17:16 is inconsistent with its context which implies surprise and consternation at the appearance of the Philistine champion (17:24–25); 4) 17:19 repeats details about the locality already supplied in 17:2; 5) 17:23 repeats a full identification of the Philistine champion,

---

    redaction, and should be seen within the wider context of the document created by these prophetic redactors; see my *Of Prophets and Kings: A Late Ninth-Century Document (1 Samuel 1-2 Kings 10)* (CBQMS 17; Washington: Catholic Biblical Association of America, 1986).

2. In fact, 16:18 describes David as a very accomplished young man. Six attributes are listed, each succinctly expressed in two words, very much like a list of the qualities required in a young courtier. Among them is 'skilled in war'. Since David is not named in the verse—simply 'a son of Jesse the Bethlehemite'—it may have replaced an earlier and less formal description. The purpose of the addition would have been to establish David as the model courtier (cf, G von Rad, *Der Heilige Krieg im alten Israel* [fifth ed; Göttingen: Vandenhoeck & Ruprecht, 1969] 41).

    David was made Saul's armour-bearer (16:21); given the rather rudimentary nature of Sauls' court, this need not imply particular military training and experience.

3. The intrusive 'this' (hazzê) for Jesse, 'this Ephrathite' suggests prior knowledge.

already supplied in 17:4; 6) the mass flight and fear suggests that this is intended as the first appearance of the Philistine (see also v 20b), despite the harmonisation in v 23, 'he spoke the same words as before'; 7) 17:50 has the Philistine killed by the slingstone, while in v 51 David takes the Philistine's sword, kills him with it, and cuts off his head; 8) 17:55 gives no indication of Saul's already having had a conversation with David (cf vv 32-39)—it is not merely a question of not knowing his name; 9) 17:57b is in conflict with 17:54a, at least in the narrative sequence; 10) 18:5 is a conclusion, with a perspective extending beyond the events of the day; 18:6, on the other hand, relates immediately to the combat with the Philistine; 11) 18:10–11 is a doublet of 19:9–10 and appears better placed in the context of chapter 19.

It is rare that literary critical problems can be solved along the lines of different traditions preserved in the textual transmission. But that is precisely the case here. When the text which is common to both MT and LXXB (that is, 17:1–11, 32–40, 42–48a, 49, 51–54; 18:6a*–9, 12a, 13) is separated from the text which is preserved in MT but not in LXXB (that is, 17:12–31, 41, 48b, 50, 55–18:6aα, 18:10-11, 12b, 17–19, 21b, 29b–30) all the literary critical problems noted above are resolved.[4] Furthermore, two adequate and coherent narratives emerge, of different genres, but each integral within their respective horizons.

We may note briefly the story contained in the MT additions, only to set it aside. As P Kyle McCarter correctly observes these materials, when collected by themselves, can be seen to form a more or less complete narrative of their own.[5] The story tends toward the folktale

---

4. For recent discussions of the textual situation, see P Kyle McCarter, Jr, *I Samuel* (AB 8; Garden City: Doubleday, 1980), 284-309; Ralph W Klein, *1 Samuel* (WBC 10; Waco: Word Books, 1983), 173-74, 187; and HJ Stoebe, *Das erste Buch Samuelis* (KAT 8/1; Gütersloh: Gerd Mohn, 1973), 312-15. Also Stoebe, 'Die Goliathperikope 1 Sam. XVII 1-XVIII 5 und die Textform der Septuaginta', in *VT* 6 (1956): 397–413; SJ De Vries, 'David's Victory over the Philistine as Saga and as Legend', in *JBL* 92 (1973): 23–36.

5. McCarter, *I Samuel*, 307. McCarter continues: 'This strongly suggests that they represent the bulk of a full alternative account of David's arrival and early days at court that was interpolated in toto into the primary narrative at some time subsequent to the divergence of the ancestral textual traditions that lie behind MT and LXX' (McCarter, *I Samuel*, 307.). Klein prefers redactional additions to an independent account (1 Samuel, 173–74, 187). The text I

form of the young man who, by deeds of derring-do, wins the hand of a princess in marriage and half of her father's kingdom. So, stripped of minor bits of harmonisation, 17:12–31 depict the young shepherd, left at home with the flock when his elder brothers go off to the war, who is sent to the military camp with provisions for his brothers and a gift to their commander. He arrives at the camp as the battle is about to begin and witnesses the challenge of the awesome Philistine champion. He hears the soldiers around him saying, 'The man who kills him, the king will enrich with great riches, and will give him his daughter, and make his father's house free in Israel' (v 25). He hears the same thing being said by other soldiers (v 30). In the light of 18:55–58, it is clear that v 31 is a harmonising link to the other story; in this story, there is no commissioning by Saul. If one assumes the text to be complete at this point, which is possible, the understanding would be that the Philistine drew near to where David was (v 41), and David then dashed out at him (v 48b). The combat is rapidly sketched: the Philistine advanced and drew near to David, (v 41, with the note that his shield-bearer was before him); David ran quickly toward him (v 48b, possibly indicating a surprise attack, while the shield was still in the hands of the shield-bearer); and David prevailed over the Philistine, using his sling to strike and kill the Philistine, without a sword (v 50).[6] David is then summoned before the king, and is attached to his court, becoming firm friends with the crown prince; and he has great success as a military leader (17:55–18:5). His success may motivate Saul's jealousy. He is offered the hand of the princess Merab, with an incitement to further military valour, in the hope that he might die of an overdose of bravery. When this fails, he is at first passed over (vv 17–19). Then he is offered another daughter's hand in marriage (v 21b). His winning of Michal has probably been suppressed in favour of the story from the other version. So the story ends with the note that Saul remained hostile to David, and David remained more successful than all Saul's commanders (vv 29b–30).

---

follow here is substantially that of the MT additions; the sole exceptions are minor harmonisations (for example, 17:15–16, 31; 18:6a*), the omission of 18:10–11, 12b since they reflect the lyre-playing tradition, and the probability of a suppressed story between 18:21b and 29b–30. The minor differences from McCarter cannot be discussed here.

6. The *RSV* correctly begins v 50 with 'So', but this is translating the present combined text; the Hebrew, of course, has 'And'.

As far as the general picture of David's emergence at Saul's court is concerned, this story has much in common with the other. Its fundamental difference is in the motivation attributed to David. While there is a cursory nod to theology in 17:26, the basic motivation in the story is riches and marriage to the king's daughter; the story is developed along the lines of success being too successful.

The second story is the central interest of this paper; it is the one represented in LXXB, that is, without the additional material in MT. This story has its beginning in 16:14–23, which brings David to the court of Saul, as lyre–player and as armour–bearer (v 21). Beginning the story at 16:14 is legitimate. 16:1–13 is the work of later prophetic redaction, part of a much broader context.[7] At its earlier level, 1 Samuel 15 probably contained Samuel's rebuke of Saul, rather than outright rejection.[8] This provides the context for the departure of the spirit of the Lord from Saul; it is clear, though, that 16:14 is the start of a new unit.

16:14–23, then, brings David to the court of Saul, as lyre–player and as armour–bearer; it is the first appearance of David on the scene.[9] Promptly, the narrative moves to the gathering for battle between the Philistines and Israel (17:1–11). Once 17:12–31 has been recognised as belonging to another tradition, the narrative

---

7. For this broader context, see *Of Prophets and Kings*. Chapter 4 deals with the text of 1 Samuel 9 – 15 prior to this prophetic redaction.
8. For the details of the analysis, see *Of Prophets and Kings*, 132-36.
9. It is often believed that the accomplished David of 16:14–23 is in tension with the shepherd of chapter 17. The tension comes from falsely intensifying the extremes. Two points need comment. In 17:33, the contrast is not between the boy and the man, but between the inexperienced soldier (na'ar) and the experienced challenger who has been a warrior from his youth. Na'ar here has its frequent sense of young soldier, capable of killing (2 Sam 2:12-16) and of intercourse (1 Sam 21:5). H-P Stähli, in his monograph on the term (*Knabe-Jüngling-Knecht* [BET 7; Frankfurt a. M: Peter Lang, 1978]), shows the range of its meanings from newborn child (1 Sam 1:22) to royal overseer (1 Kgs 11:28), as well as the two basic senses underlying these; the precise nuance is determined by the context. Here, in 1 Sam 17:33, Stähli gives it the sense of 'half-grown youth', without a full discussion (*Knabe-Jüngling-Knecht*, 91–92), rejecting HJ Stoebe's juxtaposition of 1 Sam 16:14-23 with 17:1-11, 32-54 ('Goliathperikope', 405-10; *Das erste Buch Samuelis*, 335) which is assumed here.
In 17:40, the shepherd's bag is a gloss for the unusual term translated pouch or wallet (*yalqut*), and not the other way round (McCarter, *I Samuel*, 288; Klein, *1 Samuel*, 179). It may derive from the use of *hakeli* [in v 49].

receives very significant shape. The Philistine champion comes to the fore and puts a challenge which threatens the independence and freedom of Israel: 'then you shall be our servants and serve us' (v 9).[10] Confronted with this threat, Saul and all Israel were 'dismayed and greatly afraid' (v 11). In what is now the very next verse, David, who is standing beside Saul as his armour-bearer, immediately presents a diametrically opposed attitude: 'Let no man's heart fail because of him; your servant will go and fight with this Philistine' (v 32).

This is a crucial moment for Israel; it is also a crucial moment in the story, and a turning point in the lives of Saul and David. Here they are presented side by side, Saul dismayed by unkingly fear and David bearing himself in thoroughly kingly fashion. It is the king's role to be military leader and deliverer of his people, but Saul is depicted as unmanned by fear; the deliverer role passes to David. The contrast is central to the whole portrayal of David's rise to power in Israel. As the tribes said at Hebron: 'In times past, when Saul was king over us, it was you that led out and brought in Israel' (2 Sam 5:2a). Saul ceased to be effective in the role of deliverer and protector; the defeat on Mt Gilboa was the final climax of this failure. By contrast, David became increasingly effective as guerilla leader against the Philistines.

The story continues the contrast. Saul opposes David (v 33); David maintains his willingness (vv 34–37). It is not merely the opposing attitudes which are contrasted, but more importantly the motivation behind them. Saul argues from military wisdom: David is inexperienced (a youth); the Philistine is an experienced warrior (from his youth). In theological terms, Saul's judgement is based on trust in arms. David is portrayed as putting his trust in Yahweh (v 37). He begins with his own experience: as a shepherd, faced with a marauding lion or bear plundering a lamb from the flock, he has had the experience of pursuing the predator and forcing it to release its prey; if it turned on him, he caught it by the beard and killed it. He is ready to treat the uncircumcised Philistine in the same way. The conclusions from his experience are given a theological colour:

---

10. It is worth noting here that the mention of Goliath of Gath's name is clearly intrusive in 17:23, and probably so in 17:4. The original story most probably featured an unnamed Philistine champion. The identification with Goliath resulted from the transfer of the heroic deed of one of David's men to David himself (cf 2 Sam 21:19, 22) and its association with this battle story

'this uncircumcised Philistine shall be like one of them, seeing he has defied the armies of the living God' (v 36). This aspect is then made explicit; David's confidence is based on trust in Yahweh (v 37a).[11] So the contrast is advanced: Saul trusts in arms, but David trusts in Yahweh; Saul is doomed to failure, but David will succeed.

This theological contrast should not blind us to the picture of David presented in his description of his experience as shepherd. Faced by a lion or a bear, he went after it—so he is brave. He could catch up with it and force it to release its prey—so he is fast and tough. And if the beast turned on him, he could grab it under the jaw as a prelude to killing it—so he is not only tough, but his reflexes are very good. A little reflection on this autobiographical passage shows why David was, in fact, the ideal person to take up the Philistine's challenge. Instead of man-to-man combat with the huge warrior, skilled in the use of his own weapons, David will use the tactics of speed and surprise. His speed is able to get him within slingshot range before the Philistine realises his danger and takes cover behind his shield; the quality of his reflexes will ensure that his sling-stone does not miss. His demonstrated courage and toughness will enable him to carry it off. But we anticipate. The storyteller is not yet finished with the contrast between Saul and David.

Saul is portrayed putting his armour on David—trust in arms again. David is portrayed taking it off—excellent tactics, as well as a mark of his inexperience, but also narratively symbolic of not putting his trust in arms.[12] The Philistine is depicted taking the same tack as

---

11. With the repetition of the introduction, 'And David said', it is possible to see v 37a as an addition, emphasising this aspect of trust in Yahweh. The presence of the motif of v 36 in the other version of the story (v 26) might be seen as supporting this possibility. If v 37a were an addition, it emphasises what is already in the story, and it is impossible to say when it would have been added. But it is not at all sure that it is an addition. The same would then have to be said of v 10, which has the same repeated introduction. Yet there it seems more likely to be a stylistic trick to highlight the summary and conclusion of the challenger's speech. If so there, it may equally be a stylistic trick in v 37a where it has the same function. Rather similar repetition is present in vv 43-44. See the discussion by McCarter, *I Samuel*, 287-88.

12. The story does not go into detail here, and the text is uncertain (see McCarter, *I Samuel*, 288). In terms of the realities of the combat, two things need to be remembered. Tradition has it Saul was a very big man (1 Sam 10:23), and we may assume that the king's armour was more elaborate than most. More significantly,

Saul, hardly to Saul's credit; he despises David's youthful appearance and his equipment, a stick.[13] This is trust in arms. David replies with a long speech, emphatically trusting in Yahweh. And, of course, when battle is joined, David emerges victorious.

The primary contrast in the story is not between the inexperienced David and the massive Philistine, but between the unmanned Saul and the spirited David. The narrative of LXXB continues this direction. After the rout of the Philistines (17:51–54), there follows the victory song of the women, again contrasting Saul and David. Saul's reaction is depicted as angry and jealous: 'What more can he have but the kingdom?' (18:8). In reality, it is outrageous overreaction; in the context of the narrative, it points in precisely the right direction. David is headed toward kingship. He has demonstrated his ability as deliverer.

The narrative is brought to an end by 18:12a, 13–16. Saul was afraid of David (v 12a) and gave him a military command to get him away from the court. The result was to increase his leadership role: 'he went out and came in before the people' (v 13b). Once again, both in v 13b and v 16b, there is an echo of the tribes at Hebron (2 Sam 5:2a).

Between these two echoes of the end, there are three highly stylized sentences. David had success, and Yahweh was with him (v 14). Saul saw this success, and stood in awe of him (v 15). All Israel and Judah loved David, because he provided leadership (v 16). These are not the sentences of storytelling; they are summary statements. They describe the three players in the Story of David's Rise: David, Saul, and the people. Sandwiched between the echoes of 2 Samuel 5:2a, here at the beginning they anticipate the end. Saul has failed to deliver Israel in its hour of need, for the spirit of Yahweh had left him. David has risen to the occasion and provided that deliverance; he has continued to provide leadership in Israel. The people have recognised this, and their allegiance is with David.

---

perhaps, in a combat between the slinger and the heavily armed warrior, David had to be ready to rely on speed and agility, both for attack and defence. In terms of the narrative in this version, these tactics are not to the fore; the Philistine comes toward David (vv 48a, 49, as against v 48b). The symbolism of not trusting in arms may predominate

13. The tactical value of the stick in the story is worth noting. For the storyteller's sense of verisimilitude, it can help keep the Philistine unaware till too late that he has to defend himself against a sling.

The narrative from 16:14–18:16, without the MT additions which are not in LXXB, is a rounded and compact whole. The talented David leaves his father's farm to go to Saul's court as lyre-player and armour-bearer to the king. In a moment of critical challenge to Israel, David displays the spirited courage which wins victory and deliverance, while Saul quails in fear and dismay. David's qualities are recognised and his success overshadows Saul, for Yahweh is with him; and all the people are well aware of this.

Here, in a microcosm, is the whole of the story of David's rise to power. Placed here in the text, this narrative sets the tone for the extensive collection of stories which follows, ending in David's kingship. As Saul left his oxen to deliver Israel, so here David left his sheep to deliver Israel. Abandoned by Yahweh, Saul could no longer deliver Israel; it became increasingly evident that David had taken over the role of deliverer in Israel, and 'the Lord was with him' (18:14b). Whatever the historical and political reality may have been, the perception of this narrative is that this is the quality which carried David to victory over the Philistine and eventually brought him to the throne, to reign over all Israel.[14]

---

14. The two theological positions latent in these materials are worth highlighting. In the principal story, as discussed here, God's role is to empower David to use his human talents and prowess in a courageous and daring act. With the shift in emphasis toward David as the little shepherd boy—not necessarily present in 17:12-31, where the youngest son need not be so little (cf, 18:1-5), but already present in the Septuagint (paidarion)—there is a shift in God's role. God is no longer portrayed enabling full human potential to be realised, but substituting divine wonder for human weakness. The theological implications invite reflection, but cannot be pursued here.

Who Dares Wins: Reflections on the Story of David and Goliath and the Understanding of Human Freedom

(original: *Psychiatry and Religion*)

This paper really begins where an article of mine in this year's *Australian Biblical Review* ended. The article discusses the story of David and Goliath in the books of Samuel, and in its last footnote refers to the two theological positions latent in interpretations of this story. In one understanding, God's role is to empower David to use his human talents and prowess in a courageous and daring act. But, in the more common interpretation, when the emphasis is shifted toward David as the little shepherd boy, God is no longer portrayed enabling full human potential to be realised, but instead is portrayed substituting divine wonder for human weakness.

Among the questions I wanted to ask was what do interpretations of such a story betray of our attitudes toward God and God's involvement in human existence? Why is it that the story of David and Goliath is so often told in a way that puts God in the role of parent rather than of partner? It occurred to me that it might not be hugely helpful to ask a conference on psychiatry and religion why God keeps getting cast in the parent role—there have been views on this among Freudians, which are not exactly what I want to explore. In this paper, my interest is to explore the story of David and Goliath as a model of divine-human interaction with God in the partner role, by which I mean God's role of empowering human beings to use their talents and prowess in courageous and full living rather than that of replacing human weakness with divine power. It is a feature that is strong in the stories of David as a whole, and it puts a healthy emphasis on human freedom in the relationship with God. For the story of David and Goliath, it could be summed up by using as a subtitle the SAS motto: Who dares wins!

There is no doubt that the story of David and Goliath, as it has come down to us in the present biblical text, is a highly complicated one. Equally though, there is no doubt that in the popular perception its interpretation is quite simple: it is a case of the little fellow against the massive warrior, of the underdog toppling the very definitely top dog, of weakness triumphing over power through divine grace. A recent scholarly commentary speaks of the story as follows:

> Of all David's exploits the one that is best known is the first. The story of the shepherd lad who by courage, cunning, and faith overcomes the gigantic champion of the enemy and brings victory to his people has all the elemental appeal of a fairy tale. The plot is uncomplicated and forceful, the characters almost archetypal . . . Here is David, small, apparently defenseless, with none of the bearing or equipment of a trained soldier . . . David has no real hope in force of arms, and despite his courage and wit he finally must rely on the one good hope that Judah, too, had in times of danger.[1]

Two things are really quite radically wrong with this, and yet they constantly escape notice. The first radical error is the conviction that David had no real hope in force of arms. In the passage quoted, Kyle McCarter rightly pays due tribute to David's courage, cunning, and wit. And it is true that the best equipment in the world is no use at all without the courage, cunning, and wit to operate it properly. But it is quite wrong to say that David had no real hope in force of arms: he had good standard military equipment, and in fact he had the most appropriate equipment for the occasion.

He had good standard military equipment. Slingstones are listed among the items in the ordinary military arsenal of the time. King Uzziah of Judah, for example, 'prepared for all the army shields, spears, helmets, coats of mail, bows, and stones for slinging' (2 Chron 26:14). When troops are assembled, slingers are reckoned among the specialist elite. In inter-tribal conflict, early in Israel's history, when the Benjaminites mustered their forces against the rest of Israel, it is noted that 'among all these were seven hundred picked men who were left-handed; every one could sling a stone at a hair, and not miss' (Judg 20:16). The sling is clearly singled out as a specialist weapon of remarkable accuracy.

---

1. P Kyle McCarter, Jr, *I Samuel*, AB 8 (Garden City: Doubleday, 1980) 295 and 297.

He had the most appropriate equipment for the occasion. Goliath is portrayed as big and heavily armed; he is awesome enough to panic the whole army of Israel. As the story tells it, one may expect that on his own terms, with sword and spear, he is unbeatable. The best military manuals know, surely, that the only way to win in such a situation is not to meet the man on his own terms. The bigger his spear and the heavier his armour, the more likely he is to be a slow mover. The tactics needed to defeat him call for speed, surprise, and a long-range weapon. For David's purposes, the sling was the ideal weapon.

It is important to emphasise that the interpretation of a story comes from the text of the story, not from the historical detail we may be able to recover about it. The text does not make any comment on the aptness of the sling, neither to belittle it nor to approve of it. In the absence of contrary indications, it is legitimate to assume the ordinary expectations of the time: that the sling is to be understood as standard and appropriate equipment.

The second radical error in reading the David and Goliath story as a triumph of weakness over power through divine grace lies in the image of David as 'small and apparently defenseless'.[2] In the text of the story, this is quite definitely not the picture David paints of himself. David speaks of his own experience, when keeping his father's flocks. Faced by a lion or a bear, he went after it—so he is brave. He could catch up with it and force it to release its prey—so he is fast and tough. And if the beast turned on him, he could grab it under the jaw as a prelude to killing it—so he is not only tough, but his reflexes are very good (1 Sam 17:34–35).[3] A little reflection on this autobiographical

---

2. This image has a very long history behind it. It is invited by the Septuagint, the ancient Greek translation, which refers to David in this story with a diminutive, *paidarion*, little boy. In fact, *paidarion* is the most common translation for the Hebrew word *na'ar*, very often rendered 'youth', but having a wide gamut of meanings (see note 6, below). But unless one were very familiar with the text of Samuel, the use of the diminutive would be an invitation to picture David as the little shepherd boy. Josephus, the first-century Jewish historian, in his paraphrase of the biblical text, has: 'Saul admired the lad's daring and courage, but could not place full confidence in him by reason of his years, because of which, he said, he was too feeble to fight with a skilled warrior' (*Jewish Antiquities*, VI, 181). This is remarkable, when we consider that a little earlier Josephus, rendering 1 Sam 16:18, referred to David as 'an excellent soldier' (*Jewish Antiquities* 167).
3. A recent article by a young German scholar simply asserts that a redactor

passage shows why David was, in fact, the ideal person to take up the Philistine's challenge. Instead of man-to-man combat with the huge warrior, skilled in the use of his own weapons, David will use the tactics of the unexpected. Speed and surprise may get him within slingshot range before the Philistine realises his danger and takes cover behind his shield; the quality of his reflexes will ensure that his slingstone does not miss. His demonstrated courage and toughness will enable him to carry it off. This is not a small and apparently defenceless little shepherd boy. He may be the youngest of his father's sons, but that does not say anything about his size or age. If he were meant to be thought of as small, would the storyteller have made so incongruous a move as to have Saul, who towered head and shoulders over Israel, offer David his armour?

So, even on the evidence of the text as we have it now, the archetypal image of the underdog facing hopeless odds is quite misleading. David is the right man for the job, and he has the right weapon for the job.

When the history of the text is explored further, this understanding becomes even more evident. As we noted at the beginning, the text of this story is highly complicated; there are strong grounds for arguing against its unity. This is not the place to go through the exegetical examination of the text in detail.[4] We may just indicate the main

---

attempted to lessen the tension between David as man of war and the child as peaceful shepherd by inserting 17:33-35 (Theodor Seidl, 'David statt Saul: Göttliche Legitimation und menschliche Kompetenz des Königs als Motive der Redaktion von I Sam 16-18', in *ZAW* 98 [1986]: 39-55, see 42). No evidence is adduced to support the suggestion, and in fact there is none available. It appears to be another example of the conviction that the youngest son and shepherd has to be 'small and apparently defenseless'.

4. I have gone into these issues in more detail in the *Australian Biblical Review* article referred to ('From Philistine to Throne', in *AusBR* 34 [1986]), some of which is repeated here. Briefly, the difficulties are:
1) 1 Sam 17:12 gives the impression of being the beginning of a new story.
2) 17:15 gives the impression of being a harmonising addition, holding together differing traditions of David at Saul's camp and David back at the family farm.
3) 17:16 is inconsistent with its context which implies surprise and consternation at the appearance of the Philistine champion (17:24-25).
4) 17:19 repeats details about the locality already supplied in 17:2.
5) 17:23 repeats a full identification of the Philistine champion, already supplied in 17:4.
6) the mass flight and fear suggests that this is intended as the first appearance of

points. David is introduced in the middle of the story (v 12) rather as though it were the beginning; the confrontation with the Philistines and the appearance of Goliath on the scene is repeated rather as though it had not been told before (vv 19-24); one verse has Goliath killed by the slingstone (v 50), while in the next verse David takes Goliath's own sword and kills him with it; finally, after Saul has sent David out with his blessing (v 37), he is portrayed as surprised to see him and knowing nothing about him (vv 55-58).

To jump from evidence to conclusions, without passing through a full discussion of the arguments, here, as often in biblical narratives, we have two stories combined into one. What is most unusual, however, is that the text of one of the two stories is preserved intact in the Greek translation of the Bible, the Septuagint.[5] When the stories are separated, all the difficulties about unity disappear.

In the version which has been preserved intact in the Greek, which omits vv 12-31, David is standing at Saul's side, as his armour-bearer (cf, 1 Sam 16:14-23). When Saul and all Israel are portrayed as 'dismayed and greatly afraid' (17:11), David is right there beside him—in the story and in the text, since vv 12-31 are omitted—to say, 'Let no man's heart fail because of him; your servant will go and fight with this Philistine' (v 32). The story unfolds as a contrast between

---

the Philistine (see also v 20b), despite the harmonisation in v 23, 'he spoke the same words as before'.

7) 17:50 has the Philistine killed by the sling-stone, while in v 51 David takes the Philistine's sword, kills him with it, and cuts off his head.

8) 17:55 gives no indication of Saul's already having had a conversation with David (cf vv 32-39)—it is not merely a question of not knowing his name.

9) 17:57b is in conflict with 17:54a, at least in the narrative sequence;

10) 18:5 is a conclusion, with a perspective extending beyond the events of the day; 18:6, on the other hand, relates immediately to the combat with the Philistine.

11) 18:10-11 is a doublet of 19:9-10 and appears better placed in the context of chapter 19.

5. More accurately, in one manuscript tradition of the Septuagint. The story which is preserved intact in the Greek (while combined with the other in the Hebrew) is contained in 1 Sam 17:1-11, 32-40, 42-48a, 49, 51-54; 18:6a*-9, 12a, 13. The other story, not represented in this Greek manuscript tradition, is contained in 1 Samuel 17:12-31, 41, 48b, 50, 55-18:6a*, 18:10-11, 12b, 17-19, 21b, 29b-30. For further details, see 'From Philistine to Throne'. This latter story tends toward the folktale form of the young man who, by deeds of derring-do, wins the hand of a princess in marriage and half of her father's kingdom.

Saul and David. This is a crucial moment for Israel; it is also a crucial moment in the story, and a turning point in the lives of Saul and David. Here they are presented side by side, Saul dismayed by unkingly fear and David bearing himself in thoroughly kingly fashion. It is the king's role to be military leader and deliverer of his people, but Saul is depicted as unmanned by fear; the deliverer role passes to David. The story continues the contrast. Saul is portrayed as making his judgement on grounds of military appearances (there is no discussion of the sling here), and David is portrayed trusting in God. Even the brief exchange over the armour points in this direction. Goliath bases his confidence on the same grounds as Saul—hardly flattering to the latter.

The primary contrast in this version of the story is between Saul, dismayed, afraid, and unmanned, and David, spirited, courageous, and confident. Saul had been anointed king to deliver Israel. Bereft of God's spirit (16:14), he is unable to deliver his people; instead, he quivers in fear. It is David who will demonstrate his leadership qualities, who will deliver Israel from this Philistine threat, and who will show that God is with him. The victory over the Philistine is the beginning of David's move toward the throne over Israel. The storyteller saw it that way and told the story in order that we would see it the same way.

We should not be led astray by the dialogue with Saul. Saul says, 'You are not able to go against this Philistine to fight with him; for **you are but a youth, and he has been a man of war from his youth**' (v 33). The meaning should be quite clear: you are but a beginner, while he is a very experienced campaigner.[6] Interestingly,

---

6. The language needs comment. In 17:33, the contrast is not between the boy and the man, but between the inexperienced soldier (youth) and the experienced challenger who has been a warrior from his youth. The Hebrew word for 'youth' here has its frequent sense of young soldier, capable of killing (2 Sam 2:12–16) and of intercourse (1 Sam 21:5). H-P Stähli, in his monograph on the term (*Knabe-Jüngling-Knecht* [BET 7; Frankfurt a. M: Peter Lang, 1978]), shows the range of its meanings from newborn child (1 Sam 1:22) to royal overseer (1 Kgs 11:28), as well as the two basic senses underlying these; the precise nuance is determined by the context. Here, in 1 Sam 17:33, in my judgement quite wrongly, Stähli gives it the sense of 'half-grown youth', without a full discussion (*Knabe-Jüngling-Knecht*, 91–92), rejecting HJ Stoebe's juxtaposition of 1 Sam 16:14–23 with 17:1–11, 32–54 ('Goliathperikope', 405–10, *Das erste Buch Samuelis*, 335) which is assumed here.

Saul does not ask David how he proposes to defeat the Philistine. For the storyteller, at one level, Saul is to be seen as a dismayed, despairing man; and, at another level altogether, it would spoil the story to unveil the ending too soon.

There is also the potential trap that in order to depict the despairing king in contrast to his spirited successor, the storyteller has to have Saul insisting that David's situation is hopeless and that he has no chance. Why do we walk into that trap by assuming that Saul's judgement is motivated by the physical stature of puny David instead of by the dispirited despair of a king abandoned by God's spirit? David's description of himself should have made the matter clear.[7]

My suspicion is that people interpret the David and Goliath story in the usual way because people like to envisage God in that way; that there is a tendency in many people to look to God to do the impossible, to expect God to slay all their Goliaths for them. Which leads to my theological concern: which is the more helpful way to envisage divine-human relations? Is it more helpful to conceive of God supporting us by filling in the gaps left by human weakness? Or is it more helpful to see God empowering us in the use of our talents and strengths?

I find it useful to reflect on the two images presented by the differing interpretations of the David and Goliath story. If David is seen as the defenceless little shepherd boy, then what reveals—to all those assembled and to us—that God saves not with sword or spear but will give Goliath into David's hand (v 47) is the fact that such an unlikely weapon as a slingstone finds its way from the shepherd's sling into the Philistine's forehead. On the other hand, if David is seen as tough and strong, with excellent reflexes, and equipped with a dangerously accurate weapon, then the evidence of God's saving power is that this man had the courage to risk facing a fearsome foe when everyone else was desperate with fear.[8]

---

7. Another misleading factor comes from the combination with the other story. There David is explicitly portrayed as a shepherd, who goes directly from the family farm to the military camp (vv 12–30). It is probably the influence of this picture which accounts for the occurrence, in 17:40, of the usual words for shepherd's bag as a gloss for the very unusual term translated pouch or wallet. It is unlikely that it was the other way round.
8. Heavily embellished by novellistic imagination, this is the version portrayed in irreverent detail by Joseph Heller, in chapter 3 of *God Knows* (New York: Alfred

The 'thoroughgoing worldliness' of the Succession Narrative, or Story of David's Later Years (2 Samuel 9–20; 1 Kings1 – 2), has long been noted. There is a similarly secular streak in the stories of David's rise to power in Israel which follow his career from his victory over Goliath to his accession to the throne over all Israel. This is all the more remarkable when we consider that these stories were told with the evident intention of saying that David got to the throne of Israel because God was with him—yet God is never given a principal role in the action.[9] Direct divine intervention is basically restricted to the anointings by Samuel, and these are a century or so later than the original stories.[10] So, the interpretation of the story of David and Goliath given here can be seen as paradigmatic for the other Davidic stories.

In my judgement, the story of David and Goliath is also a helpful model for talking about divine action and human freedom. It is far easier to tell a story than to spell out such matters in cold discourse. What I believe is important to us, in this present context, is conviction about general attitudes. The systematic treatment, which hammers

---

A Knopf, 1984).

9. There are only three explicit references to God by the narrator: 2 Sam 11:27; 12:24; 17:14; see Gerhard von Rad, *Old Testament Theology* (2 volumes; Edinburgh: Oliver and Boyd, 1962–65) 1.312–17.

10. For example: according to the text, it is David's quick reflexes which save him from Saul's spear-cast, not God's intervening hand (1 Sam 19:9–10). It is Michal's intuition and not God's revelation which warns David to save his life by climbing out the window and escaping into the night (19:11–17). It is David and Jonathan's careful checking out of Saul's intentions which later saves David's skin, not any information from the Almighty (20:1–42). Even in a fascinating case where there is the explicit use of divination to inquire of God, in the anecdote about the Philistine siege of Keilah, while God is reported saying, 'Go, do it!', the battle is reported as David's, not God's. Subsequently, when divination reveals that the townsfolk of Keilah are going to betray their deliverer to Saul, there is no question of divine wrath or divine protection—David and his men simply melt into the mountains (23:1–14). The killing which clears the way for David is done by purely human means: the Philistines kill Saul and his sons (31:1–7); a vengeance-seeking brother kills Saul's general (2 Sam 2:18–23; 3:22–30); a couple of disloyal mercenaries kill Saul's successor (4:5–12). In all this, God is not explicitly involved at all. And yet the narrator's judgement on all these stories was, 'And David had success in all his undertakings, for the LORD was with him' (1 Sam 18:14).
See my *Of Prophets and Kings: A Late Ninth-Century Document* (1 Samuel 1–2 Kings 10) (CBQMS 17; Washington: Catholic Biblical Association of America, 1986).

out details of expression and explores all the implications and ramifications, is for professional theologians to elaborate. The task of reconciling God's attributes and human freedom is notoriously difficult. At this conference last year, I admitted to a preference for preserving, as far as possible, the intelligibility of human freedom and reserving mystery to the sphere of the divine, where it most appropriately belongs.

In the interpretation of the David and Goliath story in which David is the small and defenceless little shepherd, God is in an obviously parent-type role. It is a theology which I find uncongenial and unsatisfactory. It generates expectations of God which are demeaning for the creature and unfair for the Creator. It frequently leaves the image of God in considerable need of redemption. I have strong preference for the sort of theology which is able to recognise that David was the right person with the right equipment for the task. In this model of God as partner, what God did for David was to enable David to do what he could do for himself. In the metaphor of the David and Goliath story, David got his start in public life not through the equivalent of a divine thunderbolt but through a well-aimed sling-stone and the strength of his own nerve.

To put a little flesh on God's activity as enabling human beings in their living, I would point to three areas of significance to life. One is that of basic trust. I would hope for a theology that could speak of a God who is worthy of our trust. Another is that of fundamental love. I would hope for a theology that could speak of a God who is capable of unconditional love for us. Thirdly, there is the question of the articulation of ideals. I would hope for a theology that could present a God whose being and love challenges us to the highest ideals of human living. The combination of basic trust and unconditional love with the challenge of high ideals is surely enabling and empowering for rich human living.

As counterpoint to these reflections on two images of God, there are two versions of a saying, popularly attributed to St. Ignatius Loyola, the founder of the Jesuits. The usual version of the saying runs: pray as if everything depended on God and work as if everything depended on you. In the formality of prayer, at least, God is portrayed as the doer on whom all depends. The other version, found in Jesuit documents, is exactly the opposite: pray as if everything depended on you and work as if everything depended on God.[11] In such a spirituality, God is a companion and a partner, but not a substitute or a replacement.

---

11. The Latin reads: *Haec prima sit agendorum regula: sic Deo fide, quasi rerum successus omnis a te, nihil a Deo penderet: ita tamen iis operam omnem admove, quasi tu nihil, Deus omnia solus sit facturus* (Thesaurus Spiritualis Societatis Jesu, 1948, 480). More adequately translated: 'Let this be the first rule of action—so trust in God as if success depended entirely on you, and not on God at all; but so give yourself to the task as if you were doing nothing and God alone were to do it all.' Regrettably, I am told that the attribution of either version to Ignatius remains unsubstantiated; I suspect the one given here would have received his preference.
Which leads to my theological concern: it is far easier to tell a story than to spell out theological matters in cold discourse.

2 Samuel 21–24:
The Enigma Factor
(original: *For and Against David*)

The collection constituted by these four chapters (2 Samuel 21–24) offers a particular contribution to our understanding of the conference theme: Story or History in the book of Samuel. The issue of story or history, of story or report, is form-critically extremely challenging and theologically extremely important. As any reader of Mark O'Brien and my recent *Rethinking the Pentateuch* will know, it is an issue that extends well beyond Israel's 'Former Prophets'[1]. The enigma of this 'special collection' (chapters 21–24) and the enigma of its components both have considerable bearing on the understanding of the Davidic traditions in relation to this issue of Story or History. As present text, structurally the collection is a unit, it lies outside the sweep of Davidic traditions, and none of its six component elements is previously known to us from them.

I have described these chapters as a third wave in the traditions that have come to us about David.[2] The first wave comprises the materials that are associated, in one way or another, with David's coming to power; they are substantially favourable propaganda. The second wave comprises the materials that are associated with David's middle years, in power in Israel; they are reflectively neutral, both admiring and critical. The traditions of this third wave, 2 Samuel 21–24, bring a critical edge to the picture of David. The narrative

---

1. Campbell and O'Brien, *Rethinking the Pentateuch*.
2. Campbell, *2 Samuel*, 185. Carlson makes a move in this direction with his designation of 2 Sam 9–24 as 'David under the Curse', especially if one notes his insistence that the 'darker side of the picture' is balanced by 'more positive aspects' (*David, the Chosen King*, 137). Unfortunately, this question of balance is not pursued in relation to the ambivalent quality of the prose traditions in 2 Sam 21–24.

traditions—stories, reports, lists—have a remarkable and unavoidable ambivalence. The military traditions can be interpreted to portray a David who was less glorious and was supported by a larger military structure than earlier traditions mentioned. The sacral traditions (21:1–14 and 24:1–25) can be interpreted to portray David in a far from glorious light, potentially ruthless and uncaring in the case of the Gibeonites (21:1–14) and guilty of gross imprudence in the case of the national census (24:1–25).

Before scrutinising the text in detail, it may help to express a note of caution and to point to a stylistic possibility with major hermeneutic implications. First, the note of caution: these texts are ambivalent. We must remain open to that ambivalence. We cannot know with what intention the texts were written. We cannot exclude the possibility of simple straightforward commitment to David—an 'innocent' interpretation. Given the continued existence of supporters of Saul (Shimei ben Gera [2 Sam 16:5–13] was hardly alone in Israel), we cannot exclude the possibility of an ironic or sceptical reading—a 'not-so-innocent' interpretation. Second, the stylistic possibility. The shape of the present text we have is undeniably chiastic. Four of the passages are narrative (stories, reports, lists) and narrative moves in linear fashion from a beginning, through a middle, to an end (true to a degree even of the reports and lists; story moves from beginning to end powered by plot, report does the same without the plot, and even lists in fact move from beginning to end). The two poems are static, at the centre of the chiasm.[3] Stylistically, we are confronted by a tension between the end-directed narratives and the centre-located poems. Hermeneutically, this stylistic tension may mirror the tension in the portrayal of David, less than glorious in the narratives, sustained by God in the poems.[4]

---

3. It is regrettable that JP Fokkelman treats the two poems out of sequence, with 2 Sam 23:8–39 in his chapter 8 following 2 Samuel 21, and 2 Sam 24 in his earlier chapter 7, instead of at the centre where they are in the text (*Throne and City*, 10-14, 333–63). As 'the last words of David' 2 Sam 23:1–7 belongs chronologically at the end of David's life (so already Karl Budde, *Richter und Samuel*, 259-60, 'auch an unrichtiger Stelle'). Stylistically, of course, the song is where it is and its location may not be without significance for the interpretation of the whole.
4. In 1890, after listing the six elements that are the components of the chapters, Budde notes the following: 24:1 was linked to 21:14; then 21:15ff and 23:8ff were inserted between them; finally, 22 and 23:1–7 were inserted between these

We all know something of the history of interpretation. It is worth noting that Karl Budde, whose analyses (in 1890 and 1902) have been influential for a century, took for granted that these narrative texts in 2 Samuel 21–24 were history, dislocated from their original place around 2 Samuel 5 and 9. Chronicles agrees. Once a more nuanced view is taken of the traditions in the book of Samuel, new avenues of interpretation open up that were not available a century ago.[5]

The use of this material in Chronicles is instructive, but cannot be adequately explored here. Chronicles has only three of the six component elements in 2 Samuel 21–24. The sequence in Samuel equivalent to that in Chronicles would be, as reconstructed in 1890 by Budde: 2 Samuel 5:1-3, 6-10; 23:8-39; 6:1-11; 5:11-25; 6:12–16:17-20a; chapters 7, 8, 10; 11:1 and 12:29-31; 21:18-22; 24:1-25. Out of consideration for David's reputation, in Budde's judgment, Chronicles does not have: 6:20-23, the whole story of David's family, and 21:1-14; similarly, 21:15-17 is absent, reflecting an all-too-human David. 2 Samuel 9 is absent, the house of Saul being of no interest to the Chronicler. 2 Samuel 5:4-5 would improperly anticipate 1 Kings 2:11. Also absent are the two songs (22:1-51 and 23:1-7), according

---

(*Richter und Samuel*, 256). No argument is given. Budde locates 21:1-14 after 2 Sam 8 and before 2 Sam 9 (Shimei in 16:7-8 and Meribaal in 19:29 look back on this). 2 Sam 24 also had to be located early in David's rule over a united kingdom (*Richter und Samuel*, 256). Budde links 21:15ff. with 2 Sam 5 and the fate of the Philistines there; 23:8ff may belong there too, or in association with 2 Sam 8; celebrating David's victories over the Philistines, 2 Sam 22 could fit in well enough with these, and the 'last words' (otherwise out of place) would follow 2 Sam 22:2 Sam 22 is not from David, but a lot later (*Richter und Samuel*, 259-61). The original order of the text units was: 2 Sam 6:2-23; 21:1-14; 24:1-25; 9:1 – 20:22; 3:2-6a; 5:13-16; 8:16-18 (= 20:23-26)—then 1 Kgs 1-2. The only bits left homeless are the two songs, 22:1-51 and 23:1-7 (*Richter und Samuel*, 264-65).

In 1902, the original sequence was proposed as following 2 Sam 6 and before 2 Sam 9, with 24:1-25 probably before 21:1-14. Budde sees as problematic the three-day plague in 24:10-14 in conjunction with the three-year famine in 21:1-14, to say nothing of the flight before enemies in 2 Sam 15 ff. So 24:1a is introduced, but with a degree of uncertainty. With 2 Sam 24 where it is, David's story ends on a happier note than 21:1-14 and the location of the temple is close to the account of its building (*Bücher Samuel*, 304; see also XI).

5. For Budde, in 1890, the sequence from 21:14 to 24:1 was straightforward (*Richter und Samuel*, 256); in 1902, the sequence was open to variation, with consequences for the placement of 24:1a (*Samuel*, 327–28). For HP Smith, 24:1 must refer back to the famine of 21:1-14; 'There seems to be no other instance of Yahweh's wrath against Israel in our present history of David' (*Samuel*, 388).

to Budde inserted later than Chronicles 6⁶. Faithful to his time, Budde is content to discuss an original sequence and how it may have come to be dislocated. He does not undertake to discuss a possible meaning for the present sequence in Samuel and does not comment on the text's notable differences from other traditions.

The texts

2 Samuel 21:1–14
The four chapters, 2 Samuel 21–24, begin and end with two unusual passages, 21:1–14 and 24:1–25. Both concern the restoring of right relationship between YHWH and the land, a relationship disturbed by the sacral offence of a king. In the first case, 21,1-14, the offence was King Saul's, killings allegedly part of a planned extermination of the Gibeonites. In the second case, 24:1–25, the offence was King David's, taking a census of Israel at YHWH's instigation. In both cases, the relationship was restored as a result of actions by David (cf 21:14 [*wayye'ater elohim la'ares*] and 24:25 [*wayye'ater yhwh la'ares*]). The two phrases noting this restoration are unique, occurring only here; the verb itself is rare, with only eight occurrences in the niphal (Gen 25:21; Isa 19:22; Ezra 8:23; 1 Chron 5:20; 2 Chron 33:3–19).[7] Whatever function the tradition may have served earlier, it is possible that the phrases point to a concern in the final stage of the composition. A similar pointer, in this case to literary genre, is provided in English folk literature by the phrase that often finishes a fairy tale, 'and they all lived happily ever after'.

Whatever the age of the respective traditions, the two passages may have been given their final shape as companion pieces around the theme of restoring God's relationship with the land. The key verb in the phrase (niphal: '-t-r) appears in predominantly late texts. In the past, the historical association of the two passages as part of one document was argued on the grounds of 24:1a ('Again [*wayyosep*] the anger of the LORD was kindled against Israel').[8] Even so, not much

---

6. Budde, *Richter und Samuel*, 267–68.
7. It is important to realise that Chronicles has neither clause. It does not have the Gibeon story (2 Sam 21:1–14) at all; it does not include the clause in its version of the Jerusalem census story.
8. For Budde, in 1890, the sequence from 21:14 to 24:1 was straightforward (*Richter und Samuel*, 256); in 1902, the sequence was open to variation, with

is explained. Association with chapter 21 provides Saul's offence as an explanation for God's anger in chapter 24, but it does not explain the form this anger took, that is, inciting David to do wrong. The two passages may well be 'companion pieces'; this does not require that they were originally part of a single document. In both cases, the restoration of the relationship is David's doing.

Recognising the structure of the two passages, from royal offence (Saul and David) to royal restoration (David in both), requires that in 21:1–14 attention is paid to two actions: the execution of Saul's descendants; the reburial of the bones of Saul and Jonathan.

An 'innocent' reading is clear: David did the right thing and provided the necessary atonement for bloodguilt. Inspired by Rizpah's example, David provided appropriately for the bones of Saul and Jonathan. As David's supporters might have said, how fortunate that a faithful king consulted YHWH in the first instance and acted wisely in the second.

A 'not-so-innocent' reading is equally clear. David took the occasion to eliminate any potential rivals, no matter how remote; rather too late, David came around to the idea of treating with honour the bones of Saul and Jonathan. As Saul's supporters might have said (for example, Shimei ben Gera), how convenient for David in the first instance and how inappropriate for the king to be so slow in doing the right thing by Saul and Jonathan.

Stoebe rightly points out that politically these seven are not significant enough to be rivals to David.[9] A Saul supporter such as Shimei might point to the presumed insignificance of the seventy sons of Jerubbaal, whom Abimelech had killed (Judg 9:1–5), the seventy sons of Ahab, whom Jehu had killed (2 Kgs 10:1–7), the royal family of Ahaziah, whom Athaliah had killed (2 Kgs 11:1), or those killed by Baasha (1 Kgs 15:29) and Zimri (1 Kgs 16:11). The issue of bloodguilt was raised by Abigail (1 Sam 25:30–35) and carefully avoided by David (2 Sam 1:14–16 for Saul's killer; 4:9–12 for the killers of Ishbaal). Interestingly, here in 21:1–14 there is no such protestation of innocence by David.

---

consequences for the placement of 24:1a (*Samuel*, 327-28). For HP Smith, 24:1 must refer back to the famine of 21:1–14; 'There seems to be no other instance of Yahweh's wrath against Israel in our present history of David' (*Samuel*, 388).

9. Stoebe, *Zweite Buch Samuelis*, 459.

We know nothing of the three-year famine or its extent.[10] We know nothing of the process by which David communicated with YHWH. We are told nothing of the context for Rizpah's action in protecting the bodies, day and night, 'until rain fell on them'. What is clear from the text is that Rizpah's example triggered David's attention to the bones of Saul and Jonathan. What complicates matters is that the bones of only one son are noted as brought back, but three sons were involved (cf 1 Sam 31:2–12). Other minor variations: according to 1 Samuel 31:12–13, the bodies were taken from the wall at Beth-shan, were burned, and then buried; 2 Samuel 21:12 refers to their having been stolen from the public square at Beth-shan, and does not mention the burning11.[11] David's earlier embassy to Jabesh-gilead, as recorded in 2 Samuel 2:4–7, expressed his gratitude but moved promptly enough to solicit support for himself. An 'innocent' reading and a 'not-so-innocent' reading are both possible. Neither is excluded by the text.

2 Samuel 21:15–22
A series of four brief reports detail the killing of four significant figures, presumably elite warriors.[12] The first, Ishbi-benob, nearly killed David before being despatched by Abishai13.[13] The summary verse has these four fall 'by the hands of David and his servants' (21:22). An 'innocent' reading is clear: David was a leader who inspired the devotion and loyal service of warriors who did loyal service for him in eliminating the enemies of Israel.

A 'not-so-innocent' reading is equally clear. David may have been a great leader and strategist, but he lacked the stamina of a warrior

---

10. We are also uninformed of the alleged slaughter by Saul of Gibeonites. Hertzberg envisages some association with the massacre of priests noted in 1 Sam 22:6–23 (*1&2 Samuel*, 382–83); Arnold Anderson disagrees, 'It is unlikely that this slaughter of the Gibeonites is to be associated with the massacre of the priests of Nob (contra Hertzberg, 382)' (Anderson, *2 Samuel*, 249).
11. Budde harmonises, *Bücher Samuel*, 308–9.
12. For a discussion of the literature and the possibilities for understanding a difficult phrase, see P Kyle McCarter, Jr *II Samuel*, 449–50. McCarter opts for 'votaries of Rapha' (with C L'Heureux); I lean to members of an elite Philistine corps associated with the symbol of the scimitar (with F Willesen).
13. The Philistine's name is reconstructed in various forms by various translations and commentators. Among them: as here: JPS, NJPS, NIV, RSV and NRSV; Benob, NEB; Dadu, NAB; Dodo son of Joash, JB; McCarter, Dodo son of Joash; Smith, 'the name is now lost'.

and was in great enough danger of his life that his men decided 'you shall not go out with us to battle any longer' (2 Sam 21:17). This is early in the piece; these stories derive from the early days of the Philistine wars and David was in his prime. A later recognition of the same liability occurs in the crushing of Absalom's revolt (2 Sam 18:2–4). Furthermore, the killing of these enemies was achieved by David's men; it was not done by the legendary David. An 'innocent' reading and a 'not-so-innocent' reading are both possible. Neither is excluded by the text.

Two songs at the centre: 2 Samuel 22:1–23:7
The two psalms at the core of this Special Collection clearly praise the king and are supportive of the monarchy. However, they do not look at the king as an isolated political figure in the structure that governs a nation; they both place the king in the context of the nation's God, in Israel's case, YHWH. From the point of view of this paper, it will be important to keep in mind the emphasis given to this context: the king and his debt to his God.

Ostensibly, the first song looks back over the sweep of David's active years, at a time when the LORD had delivered him from the hand of all his enemies (22:1); the second is headlined as David's last words (23:1). In other words, both are surveying David's reign as a whole, the ideal model of kingship in ancient Israel.

2 Samuel 22:1–51
The tenor of the piece shifts in mid-song from the celebration of individual deliverance to the celebration of royal dominance. As is well known, David is not mentioned beyond the first and last verse (both 3rd person). In fact, it has to be said that the first part of the song does not necessarily have to do with a king and the second part does not necessarily have to do with David.

The emphasis on reliance upon God for deliverance and empowerment is strong and clear. The relationship with God receives constant attention in the Davidic traditions (for example, 1 Sam 26:19–20; 2 Sam 16:11–12). It is rather the emphasis on deliverance that seems quite out of place for David; the affirmation of dominance over foreign nations receives more verses in the song than it does in the sweep of Davidic traditions. The emphasis sits better with the ideal for kingship in ancient Israel.

Because of the limited evidence that the text offers, it is difficult to argue convincingly for the presence of deuteronomistic influence in vv 21–31, although the deuteronomistic movement can be counted among the supporters of a reformed Davidic monarchy. For all that, the affirmation of innocence—

> I was blameless before him,
> and I kept myself from guilt.
> Therefore the LORD has recompensed me according to my righteousness,
> according to my cleanness in his sight (vv 24–25).

—would be embarrassing to any Davidic chronicler and runs counter to the image of Psalm 51, 'Have mercy on me O God . . . for I know my transgressions, and my sin is ever before me' (vv 3–5, Heb; NRSV vv 1–3).

The song is a stark reminder to all who hear it that kings rule at God's pleasure and the success of their achievement is God's gift. No model king, no matter how exalted, can dispense with God.

2 Samuel 23:1–7
The song in 23:1–7 is puzzling if applied to David. The 'God of Jacob' is not mentioned in the book of Samuel; the balancing term (literally: 'the pleasant one of the songs of Israel') is unheard of elsewhere (v 1). The imagery reflecting the just ruler is entrancing: the light of morning . . . the sun rising . . . cloudless morning . . . moist and gleaming grass (v 4). Despite 2 Samuel 7 in its most exalted form, the claim 'Is not my house like this with God?' (v 5) would rightly bring a blush to the Davidic cheek. Absalom's revolt was based on the popular perception of David's injustice (2 Sam 15:3–4). The security of David's rule rested on the military prowess of Joab (2 Sam 20:22).

The song exalts royal justice as the base of royal rule. To be praised, the king rules people justly and rules in awe of God (v 3b). No model king, no matter how exalted, can dispense with justice.

2 Samuel 23:8–39
The issues associated with 23:8–39 are many and I will only attend to one here: the Three and the Thirty. Both the Three and the Thirty come as a shock to us; despite all the material on David's early guerrilla

years, prior to this we have never heard of them.[14] We have not heard of the Three as a group; the names of its members are new to us. We have heard of only five names of those listed in the Thirty. Joab, about whom we have heard so much, is not listed as a member of either group. We are told that David's band numbered some four hundred discontented men (1 Sam 22:2); we are later told that the number had subsequently risen to six hundred (27:2). Of the Three and the Thirty we have been told nothing until now.

As with the other passages, an 'innocent' reading is possible: David as charismatic leader of genius attracted loyal support from warriors of the highest calibre.

A 'not-so-innocent' reading is equally possible. The extensive traditions supporting David failed to mention that his military success owed a great deal to a well-developed command structure and highly respected warriors.

Neither reading is excluded by the text.

2 Samuel 24:1–25

If, as an earlier scholarship assumed, 2 Samuel 24:1a formed the link from 21:1–14, then it must be admitted that either 21:14b (cf 24:25) is revealed as an optimistic mistake or David's atoning action was ineffective as a permanent measure. With or without the association, the reality remains that we do not know why YHWH should have remained angry or become angry—or anything else about that anger beyond the census it provoked. As Hertzberg quotes Caspari, it is 'anger for an unknown reason'.[15] What we do know is that in the text, David takes on himself responsibility for the consequences; 'I have sinned greatly . . . I have done very foolishly' (24:10); 'I alone have sinned, and I alone have done wickedly' (24:17).

Once again, an 'innocent' reading is possible. To use McCarter's words, David can be seen 'as a king who had saved them [the people] from grief'.[16]

---

14. The textual difficulties with the two terms are well known (see McCarter, *II Samuel*, 489-91, 499-500). Surprised unfamiliarity may explain some of the uncertainties; interpreters are unanimous, however, on the presence of the two groups, the Three and the Thirty, in the text here.
15. Hertzberg, *I&II Samuel*, 411. Caspari cites as other cases of 'Zorn aus unbekannten Grunde', 1 Sam 2:25; 2 Sam 15:25–26; 16:10-12 (*Samuelbücher*, 662); earlier, see Budde, *Bücher Samuel*, 328, who includes 1 Sam 26:19.
16. 'Thus David was presented not as a king who had brought grief to the people,

Once again, a 'not-so-innocent' reading is equally possible. McCarter again: David can be seen 'as a king who had brought grief to the people'.[17] After all, according to 24:15, seventy thousand people died and the plague ran its appointed course (MT).

Both are possible; neither is excluded by the text.

Artistic form

Interpretation cannot escape the artistic form of these chapters. Within the Hebrew Bible, it is unique. As Brueggemann says: 'It is commonly thought that this arrangement cannot be accidental'.[18] For all the associations that can be made between the two sacral passages (21:1–14; 24:1–25) or between the two military collections (21:15–22; 23:8–39), their chiastic balance and the presence of the two psalms at the centre is too schematic to be an accident and demands explanation—an explanation that exegesis has long been unable to provide.[19]

Furthermore, as we have seen, the four narrative passages are all open to an innocent and a not-so-innocent explanation. This ambivalence is untypical of the Davidic traditions. In the (questioning) stories of David's middle years (2 Sam 11–20), it is often possible to propose a highly negative understanding of what is narrated. For example: did David set up the rape of Tamar by Amnon? Did David set up the killing of Absalom by Joab? The text does not inculpate David. An interpreter may; the text does not. In the case of Absalom's death, the text vigorously exculpates David.

---

but, on the contrary, as a king who had saved them from grief' (McCarter, II Samuel, 518). David is, in fact, presented as a king who had done both. The issue of emphasis is an issue of interpretation.

17. McCarter, *II Samuel*, 518.
18. Brueggemann, *Samuel*, 335.
19. The inclusion of 21:8–22 and 23:1–7 heightens the issue of symmetry. Both are short (eight and seven verses respectively); neither is indispensable. David as liability (21:17) is known from the more auspicious 18:3; the killing of elite Philistines mirrors David's coming on the national scene killing Goliath (1 Sam 17; note the probable insertion of Goliath's name at vv 4 and 23). 23:1–7 is elegant and the justice role of the king is central; the figure of David hardly demanded its inclusion (his legendary reputation was for 'doing right in the eyes of the LORD'; a reputation for the enforcement of justice is not the same thing). The symmetry appears important for the overall communication.

The four narrative passages in these chapters present traditions that are intrinsically ambivalent. It had to be Saul's descendants who were executed, but how convenient; David acted promptly on the report of Rizpah's action, but the reburial of Saul and Jonathan had not been done earlier. It was heroic of Abishai loyally to save the life of David, but it was David who grew tired; it was David's men, not David, who killed the fearsome four. It was a superb military organization of loyal warriors who served David, but the reality of support from the Three and the Thirty changes the image of the sole heroic leader. It was a great-hearted king who could admit his mistake and save his people, but it was David who was the cause of it all, against his top general's advice. In the traditions of David's early years, the period where much of this is most at home, such ambivalence is hard to find. That this level of ambivalence here permeates all the nonpoetic text is most unlikely to be accidental.

We may go a step further. The poetic texts, too, involve God in ways that detract from the sole glory of the king. It is hard to disagree with Brueggemann when he notes: 'The two poems stand together at the center of the appendices and serve as a critical summary of royal ideology . . . It is God who gives victory. It is God who brings low and lifts high. It is God (not David) who has wrought the great victories.'[20] The narrators of the Davidic traditions agree; the LORD was with him. The emphasis in the poetry, however, is dense. David's 'last words', as we have observed, speak powerfully of the fruitfulness of life under a just king. Without going to the extremes affirmed by Baruch Halpern,[21] we are still obliged to admit with Brueggemann again, 'It is evident that the historical reality of David stands in considerable tension with this magisterial assertion'.[22] The poetic texts do not apply particularly well to David; their emphasis sits better with the ideal for kingship in ancient Israel.

Function and setting

The function of the texts in these chapters has to be looked at carefully and discerningly. The chiastic structure of the composition cautions

---

20. Brueggemann, *Samuel*, 344–45.
21. Halpern, *David's Secret Demons*, especially 73–103.
22. Brueggemann, *Samuel*, 347.

against an assumption that otherwise overlooked traditions are being preserved for the sake of their historical value. Each of the four prose blocks can be given an innocent or a not-so-innocent interpretation. The presence of this ambivalence in all four, coupled with its absence to the same degree elsewhere, suggests a bias in favour of a not-so-innocent interpretation. In this understanding, the four prose sections contribute to a down-grading of the nature of David's leadership role. Its legendary quality is subtly lessened. At the same time, items of military history and command structure are given that were hitherto unknown. The two songs, on the other hand, do not have this ambivalence and do emphasise God's role in the success of a king and the importance of justice in the eyes of God.

If we are looking for a setting that gives some sense to all of this, we want one where monarchy is favoured, where God's support is with the king and justice is central, and where the king is not set on too exalted a pedestal. This is where I speak of the 'third wave' of Davidic tradition. Dating is, as so often, uncertain. Whatever the age of the Davidic traditions or segments of the songs, the date of the final composition is not likely to be early. Apart from the restoration of a disturbed equilibrium and the issue of supplication (21:14; 24:25) bracketing the narratives, a couple of aspects in the songs do not favour an early date. First, the third person reference to David's descendants forever (22:51), while possible early is more probably late. Second, the self-description of David as the anointed of the God of Jacob (23:1) is most unlikely to be early. For a Judean king, of David's dynasty in Jerusalem, some time later than the collapse of the northern kingdom in 722 is most likely.

With the uncertainty of a function for this collection and in the absence of an assured setting, it is fair to say that 2 Samuel 21–24 remains an enigma. However, as an independent special collection, it allows the preceding Davidic traditions to end with Joab's return to Jerusalem to the king (20:22)—as is totally appropriate. The little list of David's functionaries at this point wraps it up.

Conclusion

Three areas need to be noted.
First, as 'third wave' in the Davidic traditions, this collection removes some of the shine from the image of King David as the heroic figure of legend. The 'model' David of the book of Kings shows how the

need for such a step could be felt. Jeremiah's attack on Shallum (King Jehoahaz, Jer 23:11–17) shows the concern with justice, but then so does Hammurabi so there is little help with dating or setting there.

Second, the narratives, especially the reports and lists, make clear to us that the Davidic traditions preserved in the book of Samuel cannot be treated as complete history nor as necessarily reliable. Like any documents, they are available for historical purposes. Like any documents, before being used they must be evaluated and their nature (literary genre) established. Above all, the existence of the Three and the Thirty come as a surprise; we are entitled to believe we should have been told.

Third, the literary structure, the chiastic arrangement, is before us in the present text. We may hypothesize but we cannot know what this structure meant in ancient times. We can and should reflect on what it means to us in our times. Thanks to László Simon, the narrative material can be characterized by mobility, seen as moving in linear fashion, in tension with the poetic stability at the centre of the concentric structure.[23] The narrative material tends to diminish the legendary status of David; by contrast, at the middle of the concentric structure are two poems extolling Israel's king supported by YHWH, Israel's God. This tension between linear flowing prose and stable central poetry, between the flawed king and the committed God, may be a significant key to understanding this composition. In broadest terms, today, the imperfect flux of life is tolerable enough when stabilized around God and good government. The two literary features of narrative form and concentric structure may be an essential aid for us, alerting us to the text's communication.

Works cited: listing with appropriate details

Anderson, AA. 2 *Samuel*, WBC 11, (Dallas, TX, Word, 1989).

Brueggemann, Walter. *First and Second Samuel*, Interpretation, (Louisville, KY: John Knox, 1982).

Budde, Karl. *Die Bücher Richter und Samuel, ihre Quellen und ihr Aufbau* (Giessen, Ricker, 1890).

---

23. 'The repetition perceived in the chiastic arrangement of the six pericopes visualises circularity that competes with the sequential reading that moves forward' (Simon, *Identity and Identification*, 312; cf especially 309–22).

———, *Die Bücher Samuel*, KHC 7, (Tübingen, Mohr, 1902).

Campbell, Antony F. *2 Samuel*, FOTL 8, (Grand Rapids, MI, Eerdmans, 2005).

Campbell, Antony F, and Mark A O'Brien. *Rethinking the Pentateuch: Prolegomena to the Theology of Ancient Israel*, Louisville, KY, Westminster John Knox, 2005.

Carlson, RA. *David, the Chosen King: A Traditio-Historical Approach to the Second Book of Samuel* (Stockholm, Almqvist & Wiksell, 1964).

Caspari, Wilhelm. *Die Samuelbücher*, KAT 7 (Leipzig: Deichert, 1926).

Fokkelmann, JP. *Throne and City* (II Sam 2–8 & 21–24), volume 3 of *Narrative Art and Poetry in the Books of Samuel: A Full Interpretation Based on Stylistic and Structural Analyses* (Assen/Maastricht: Van Gorcum, 1990).

Halpern, Baruch. *David's Secret Demons: Messiah, Murderer, Traitor, King* (Grand Rapids, MI, Eerdmans, 2001).

Hertzberg, Hans Wilhelm. *I & II Samuel* (London, SCM, 1964).

McCarter, P Kyle. Jr, *II Samuel*, AB 9 (Garden City, NY, Doubleday, 1984).

Simon, László. *Identity and Identification: An Exegetical and Theological Study of 2Sam 21–24*, Tesi Gregoriana, Serie Teologia 64 (Roma, Pontificia Università Gregoriana, 2000).

Smith, Henry Preserved. *The Books of Samuel*, ICC (Edinburgh, T&T Clark, 1899).

Stoebe, Hans Joachim, *Das zweite Buch Samuelis*, KAT 8/2 (Gütersloh, Gütersloher Verlagshaus, 1994).

Associated books:
A Campbell. *1 Samuel:* (FOTL, Eerdmans, 2003)
A Campbell. *2 Samuel:* (FOTL, Eerdmans. 2005)
A Campbell. *Of Prophets and Kings: A Late Ninth-Century Document (1 Samuel 1—2 Kings 10)*. CBQMS 17 (Washington, DC: Catholic Biblical Association of America, 1986)

Narrative and Storytelling

Pentateuch Beyond Sources: A New Paradigm
(Original: *ABR* 61, 2013)

Abstract

The Documentary Hypothesis has lost its dominant position in current pentateuchal studies. A new paradigm has not yet emerged to take its place. Two factors, one economic (the cost of hand-copied manuscripts) and the other textual (the brevity and often incompleteness of textual units), suggest a new paradigm, the text as 'user-base'—the text as a base from which an intermediary (probably among 'the wise') would lead into a theological reflection, or the telling of a story, or whatever was appropriate to the occasion. Such intermediaries would expand a text as needed, would supply whatever supplementary information was needed, and would expand the telling appropriately. The so-called pentateuchal sources are by-and-large compiled chronologically. Three traps of this procedure related to the grasp of meaning are outlined.

For some time now there has been controversy surrounding the academic understanding of the Pentateuch (Genesis to Deuteronomy) which for a couple of centuries or more has been dominated by the Documentary Hypothesis. In the intensity of study exploring specific texts and seeking some kind of consensus as to what might replace the Documentary Hypothesis, two factors have remained constant.[1]

---

1. *The Pentateuch: International Perspectives on Current Research* (edited by Thomas B Dozeman *et al*. FAT 78. [Tübingen: Mohr Siebeck, 2011]) gives the proceedings of a 2010 conference in Zurich and offers a wide-area approach to these studies—

First, the widespread availability of biblical text is taken for granted. Second, concepts central to the hypothesis have been retained.

Among the factors that bear most weight in the demise of the hypothesis, a couple are of particular significance. The first is the relaxation among Bible users of a tight focus on history. Once it was taken for granted that the goal of biblical writing was the preservation of biblical history; correspondingly, the goal of biblical scholarship was to get the history from the text. Today, other possibilities (theology, literature, entertainment, etc) are to the fore. The second is the very sensitive issue of the word of God. Desacralisation (regarding as profane what was previously held to be sacred) is a feature of much of the developed world at the moment; while the words are often simple the reality is often not. In the *New Jerome Biblical Commentary*, Msgr Raymond Collins writes: 'This traditional formula [the Scriptures are the word of God], apparently simple, is extremely complex and polyvalent'.[2] The impact of cultural desacralisation on biblical studies is, without doubt, extremely complex and polyvalent.

The differences and fractures within the biblical text of the Pentateuch are still there, better known than before. A consensus as to how to understand them is needed; it is yet to emerge; a new paradigm is overdue. The paradigm proposed here offers an understanding of some of the processes that gave us our pentateuchal text. It could provide the basis for the consensus we need now, offering a new paradigm for understanding the Pentateuch.

The need for an intermediary
Right now, we need to recognise that both the larger text and elements of tradition which went into its making demanded the services of an intermediary. The larger text needed an intermediary because a text to be read was available to very few. The elements of tradition demanded the services of an intermediary because they were mostly too short, too fragmentary, too disordered to be communicated without further attention. They were a basis to be used, not the end-product of that use.

The first fact to be aware of is that the need for an intermediary for the larger text—later the present text, today's Holy Bible for Jews and

---

European, Israeli, and American.
2. Collins, 'Inspiration', 1023–33 in *New Jerome Biblical Commentary,* edited by Raymond Brown, *et al* (Englewood Cliffs, NJ: Prentice Hall, 1990), 1033.

Christians—has nothing to do with ancient literacy and everything to do with the cost of copying texts by hand. This is absolutely certain. It is not a question of literacy; it is a question of wealth. The beginning of modern printing began, for Europe, in the fifteenth century. The Gutenberg Bible, the first in the field, dates to 1455. It is reported that at the abbey of Lindisfarne, off the east coast of England, a copy of the Bible required the skins of some sixteen hundred lambs. That is a great deal of money.

In Israel, there was the major institution of the monastery at Qumran, with many significant parchment scrolls. The monastery had its own scriptorium for copying texts. A few kilometres down the road, there was a tannery to provide parchment for the scrolls. High in the rugged hills behind the monastery there was once a dam to provide water for the multiple needs of the monastery. Otherwise, to my knowledge, we have nothing substantial from ancient Israel. The site at Wadi Murabba'at was occupied only sporadically; we have nothing from temples or wealthy families (such as the Shaphan's in Jerusalem). Of course, as is well-known, parchment is fragile, easily subject to destruction by fire or moisture; the clay tablets of cuneiform Assyria are more resistant by far.

A closer model of what may have been available is provided by the Lachish Letters, eighteen relatively short communications between two military commanders, written probably in the early sixth century, painted in a fine script on the fragments of a broken pot.

A second fact that present-day thinkers about the Bible need to be aware of is the brevity of many units of tradition in the larger text. It is relatively rare for these to be of more than ten to fifteen verses. This is an ideal length for a scripture passage, read before a modern sermon. Instinctively, it could be seen to be appropriate as the lead-in for sermons in ancient synagogues (see Luke 4:16–21). The fact to be aware of is the probability that such a practice did not exist in the synagogues of ancient Israel until a century or two before Christ. We know so little about early synagogal practice.

The brevity of such units of tradition still needs to be explained. Gunkel's attempt to do so failed for two reasons. First, a major error in calculating the time taken up by such a unit (not thirty minutes, as he first thought, not the fifteen minutes he changed it to, but more like five minutes). Second, a most unfortunate anti-Semitic justification for the brevity: 'like our children', after a quarter hour, 'the imagination of the hearer is sated and his powers of comprehension are exhausted'.³ The folly of the observation is evident. High class literature is not produced for an audience incapable of appreciating it. So the brevity of many of these units of tradition still needs to be explained.⁴

These two reasons (availability of copied text and brevity of most units) need attention in understanding elements of the larger text, the forerunner of today's Bible, today's present text. Alongside these issues, there are others that need attention (= that need the services of an intermediary, probably someone from the circles of the wise) in understanding the units of tradition that have been integrated into the larger text.

My first insight into these issues came with writing commentaries on the books of Samuel.⁵ In Samuel, they are quite clear; in the Pentateuch, they are not always as clear, but they are there. Such units may contain gaps that need to be filled.⁶ They will often report competing traditions that may be conflicting or contradicting. Frequently, information will be omitted that is reported elsewhere.

All these qualities allow for the creation of the hypothesis of pentateuchal sources over two or three centuries of modern biblical scholarship. The principal problem with this creation is not so much the fragmentation of the larger text, unnecessary or ugly as that can sometimes be. The principal problem is that the sources, to which text is allocated, are in themselves unsatisfactory. They can be skimpy

---

3. Gunkel, *Genesis*, XXXIV, §7, third edition (Göttingen: Vandenhoeck & Ruprecht, 1910) ET: (Macon GA: Mercer University Press, 1997).
4. The question is not new. In 1974, Jay Wilcoxen disputed Gunkel's comments on the brevity of the texts, seeing them instead as basic plots: 'The individual stories are not brief because ancient narrations were brief, but because these texts only present basic plots which in any actual narration would be expanded and elaborated according to the skill of the storyteller and the occasion of his performance', 'Narrative Structure', 57-98 in *Old Testament Form Criticism*, edited by Hayes (San Antonio, TX: Trinity University Press, 1974), 65.
5. *1 Samuel*, FOTL 7; *2 Samuel*, FOTL 8, Forms of Old Testament Literature (Grand Rapids, MI: Eerdmans, 2003 and 2005). In the Glossary to these, see Reported Story. See also Campbell, 'The Storyteller's Role', in *CBQ* 64 (2002): 427-41.
6. These gaps are not to be confused with the gaps essential to Sternberg's understanding of narrative (Meir Sternberg, *The Poetics of Biblical Narrative* [Bloomington, IN: Indiana University Press, 1985]); on the other hand, they are totally coherent with Erich Auerbach's understanding of Israelite narrative, in his *Mimesis* (Princeton, NJ: Princeton University Press, 1953), 23.

where they are needed to be fuller. Above all, they can only be understood as history. Reflective theology has little place in them, despite attempts to achieve it. Entertainment has to be relegated to the possibilities of the past. The upshot of all this is that the problems in the larger text are still there; scholarship's solutions of these problems is looking increasingly unsatisfactory.

A new paradigm
In *Rethinking the Pentateuch*, Mark O'Brien and I wrote a detailed but largely inaccessible book in which we proposed a substantially new model for approaching the Pentateuch, applying a more flexible approach than that of previous generations, involving less fragmentation of the biblical text and greater respect for the capacities of its users (see below).[7] The view advocated there is wholly compatible with a recent description of biblical text given by systematic theologian James Alison. For Alison, in the Bible,

> we are not dealing with texts which were written as 'completed books' for people to buy, take home and read, as we might do with the latest Grisham or Scarpetta. What we have instead is, often enough, something much more like a mixture between preacher's manuals and orchestral scores: the former in the sense that what is being provided is a series of paths, guides and stories by which a master expositor is to make alive the event that is being celebrated, the feast that is being rehearsed; and the latter in the sense that each performance is unique, that there is real skill, accomplishment, practise and judgment required in rendering the silent annotations into the audible form that is their realisation, and that the meaning of the score is only to be sensed in the performance.[8]

Two hundred or more years of industrious scholarship are not to be set aside. The phenomena in the biblical text that were identified so long ago are still there now. What has changed is that, where in

---
7. Campbell and O'Brien, *Rethinking the Pentateuch*.
8. Alison, *Broken Hearts & New Creations* (New York, NY: Continuum, 2010), 241.

the past these phenomena were seen as identifying traces of ancient sources, now in the present these phenomena are seen as pointers indicating to users of the texts how they might also use variants for storytelling, for theological reflection, and so on. In the past, these pentateuchal sources were seen largely as an end product providing, above all, some understanding of the history of ancient Israel, even if problems suggest characterisation as 'salvation history'. In a user-base hypothesis, differences such as the use of divine names and so on need not be residual traces of the hypothetical sources but pointers to different versions or different ways to tell the stories that are there in the text in one fairly complete form and other less complete forms, as reminders of other traditions.

In *Rethinking the Pentateuch*, Mark O'Brien and I wrote:

> Users today normally read the canonical text as end-text, to be *expounded*. Users in ancient days, in contrast, may have used the precanonical text as a base-text, to be *expanded*. The condensed text reported on the substance of past performances of a story; it could have served as a base for reflection and for further storytelling. In other words, in a precanon world, users came to some texts as beginning points, expecting to find choices to make; with the canonical text, in contrast, users come to some texts as fixed points, expecting to find information to receive.
>
> From this, we identify the paradigm shift that can account for the brevity and layered quality of much narrative biblical text: ancient narrative texts were often written initially to be *used by ancient storytellers and others*; they were not written with a view to being *read by moderns* as Bible. Is it unthinkable? (17).

The core insight of this 'text-as-base-for-user' understanding involves a threefold shift of focus:

from

> (a) the ability of a modern reader (b) analysing and dissecting (c) a dense final text

to

(a) the ability of an ancient user (b) to selecting from and expanding (c) a condensed base text.

This paradigm shift in the understanding of the nature and function of some biblical narrative text is the foundation of much that we do in this book. In practice, that 'use' included expanding and selecting. The implication for ancient users is twofold:

1) Narrative text often required expansion to be turned into the telling of a story.
2) Narrative text often preserved variant versions or optional details, therefore requiring choice on the part of the storyteller or other user.[9]

As has been noted, much of the experience of biblical text powering this hypothesis came initially from 1 – 2 Samuel. The paradigm shift is verified in much of the Pentateuch.

The aim of this present article is to indicate aspects of this 'user-base' approach in interpreting early texts, so making them accessible to ordinary Bible users today. For example: episodes in the text may need to be freed from the imagined context of a hypothetical pentateuchal source; attention may need to be focused on the principal story being told, without being distracted by options or alternatives or pointers to other traditions to come, enhancements or supplements, or whatever else; extras in the text, beyond the main story, may need to be explained.

When we are talking about texts that are 'user-base', it is a discussion about the use of the text rather than the shape and size of the text. Nevertheless, there are some largely intuitive perceptions that it helps to keep in mind. What is short can easily be thought of as an oral aide mémoire. What is brought together in a compiled text (so here, main traditions and variant traditions) may well have been preserved separately prior to that compilation. Many questions remain; some written texts existed, where were they kept: with private owners, as the assets of groups or guilds, in temples or sanctuaries? As of now, we do not know.

---

9. *Rethinking the Pentateuch* (Louisville, KY: Westminster John Knox, 2005), 17–18.

Among our texts, we do not have the initial stages of Israel's sacred books. On the other hand, we do have the final form of those books now, which are without doubt the sacred books of Judaism (Hebrew alone) and Christianity (Hebrew and Greek). Courtesy of the discoveries from Qumran etc, the closest we can approximate to the biblical originals, at the present time, is one lengthy continuous scroll (Isaiah), holding fifty or so chapters, relatively fragmentary passages, and mere fragments. The shape of what existed before that we simply do not know; we are entitled to assume that something did. Three issues matter for us here: (i) oral or written; (ii) long or short; (iii) compiled or separate. Today's intermediaries—storytellers, 'ponderers', and others—can operate from memory (oral) or use written notes for backup; presumably both were possible in the past.[10] 'Long or short' can clearly be relative, for either oral or written versions. It would seem likely that in many cases traditions were preserved separately, whether orally or in writing. Compilation of such traditions is likely to have belonged to a final stage, concerned with preservation; before that, separateness seems more likely.

Questions may remain unanswered, awaiting answers. While compilation of such traditions is likely to have belonged to a final stage, the process of compilation involved some inevitable traps and it is important for us to be aware of those traps. Three can be singled out here.

Trap: from diversity to unity
A key feature of the understanding of biblical text as user-base, as functioning as a base for users, primarily from among the circles of the wise, is the assumption that each block of tradition has an independence that is its own. Nothing need precede it; nothing need follow it. Naturally enough, birth normally precedes death and so on. There is no reason, however, why chronological sequence is required for the telling of stories; it may be desired within a story,

---

10. A similar understanding is advocated by Stephanie Dalley for some of the great Mesopotamian myths: 'We should probably understand some of the abrupt changes of theme as bare skeletons which were fleshed out in practice by skilled narrators' (*Myths from Mesopotamia* [Oxford: Oxford University Press, 1989], xvi). It is appropriate to note here the view of some specialists that the fragments from Mesopotamian myths may represent variant versions and should not be combined as though to form a single version.

but not between stories. Similarly, there is no prohibition against the same event being recalled in different traditions, and perhaps recalled differently. For example, is Abraham best associated with Kadesh and Shur, in the south, or with Mamre outside Hebron, where the family tomb was, or with Beersheba, where the most prominent of his wells was? Or, in a later generation, did Jacob leave Canaan because his defrauded brother, Esau, was planning to kill him or because his mother, Rebekah, could not cope with the local women as daughters-in-law, or because the two men's wealth made coexistence intolerable? With the traditions separate and independent, such differences could be easily tolerated. The shift of mindset we discussed earlier may play a role here: prior to compilation, traditions may have been contemplated rather than compared, accepted rather than assessed.

With the compiling of these different traditions into one single flowing narrative a major change could not be avoided. The same differing explanations had to come together for the same events. Unsurprisingly, this led to things being believed to belong together rather than the reality of their differing quite radically. Because they were brought together, they must belong together. The fact that they were apparently different could be submerged under the evident reality that they were recorded together. Any previous tendency to focus on their difference, although they were words that came from God, was replaced in the act of compilation by a tendency to focus on their association with one and the same event, because after all they were indeed words that came from God.

What had passed unnoticed for centuries was brought into the light when source-critical analysis brought separation to the fore. With some rare exceptions, the weight of tradition initially hindered special attention being given to these differences. The challenge of source-critical analysis coincided with the rise of the desacralisation of the world in recent times and allowed the serious questions raised in the ancient past to come back into focus, if only implicitly, raising questions about the word of God. 'This traditional formula [the Scriptures are the word of God], apparently simple, is extremely complex and polyvalent.'[11]

---

11. Collins, 'Inspiration', in *NJBC*, 1033.

Trap: from chronology to history
A further consequence of compilation needs to be put under the microscope. The long text that we recognise as the Pentateuch begins with creation and ends on the brink of Canaan. Much the same was true of the pentateuchal sources (postulated by the Documentary Hypothesis) that were compositions put together by compilers who at some time or other saw the need to preserve Israel's traditions. The big two, J and P, began with creation and ended at Canaan; fragments of E were thought to be present, beginning with Genesis 15 and ending at Canaan; Deuteronomy, of course, began after Sinai and ended at Canaan. When the compilation of the traditions to form these compositions was going on, they were organised in more or less chronological sequence. Traditions about parents preceded traditions about children, for example. This was both natural and relatively easy to do. Compilers could have worked with motifs, such as neighbouring nations (family but distanced), or a focus on individuals, family groupings, tribal concerns, even geographical locations. Instead, they chose chronology—understandable, natural, and as choices go relatively easy. But it was dangerous because of a built-in trap; the generations that followed from ancient times until recently fell into that trap. The trap: to mistake chronology for history. The trap involves what has been called 'one of the deepest instincts in the civilised mind' and it is 'the need to establish a principle of causality in human experience'.[12] The human need for causality inevitably mistakes chronology for history time and again.

Compilation can create the mirage of history. Any approach, user-base or other, that treats each passage for itself, independently of its setting in chronology, has the potential to collapse this mirage. With the assumption of history, the divergences can be judged less significant; with the assumption of independence, the divergences can seem more striking.

Beyond healing the classic flaws found in the Documentary Hypothesis, this 'user-base' approach has three further advantages. First, the brevity of many narrative biblical texts is accounted for. Second, the complexity of many texts is accounted for. Third, the

---

12. Lawrence Langer, *Versions of Survival*, ix, (Albany, NY: State University of New York Press, 1982) quoted from historian Inga Clendinnen, *Reading the Holocaust*. (Melbourne, Australia: Text Publishing, 1998), 45.

industry of interpreters is freed to focus on the meaning of a given text.

The brevity of a particular text is no problem. It is not the final story; it is a base from which the story can be developed and unfolded. The advantage for the story is evident enough. Explanations that have been omitted for the text can be given in full in the telling. Options that are offered in the text do not cause confusion in the telling. One option only would normally be chosen for one telling. What is true of storytellers can be valid for teachers, for theologians. Theologians and teachers build on experience; base texts for storytelling give witness often to the manifold quality of experience.

The complexity (or unevenness) of many texts is often caused by the absence of causes or the confusing presence of options and explanations. Causes are a simple part of the telling of a story. Multiple options are not a problem for the telling of a story where it is understood that only one will be chosen. Explanations are a great help when they are necessary for a given occasion.

Trap: the pentateuchal sources

The issue of meaning is what matters in any biblical storytelling or theologising. Being part of a creation-to-Canaan source immediately imposes constraints on the meaning of a story. Where more than one option is available for the telling of a story, more than one meaning is possible. If a scholar's mind is focused on identifying duplications and distributing these over the various sources, other possibilities for meaning can be overlooked.

Beyond the book of Deuteronomy, the Documentary Hypothesis proposed at least two other sources (Yahwist and Priestly) assumed to have stretched from Creation to Canaan. The Elohist, the fourth source, was tentatively understood to have its beginning in Genesis 15, continuing to the end of Deuteronomy—until discarded, it was a substantial stretch of history. As a result, any story or block of text in such a source was preceded and followed by other text belonging to the source and was understood to portray the emergence of humanity and of Israel in the past. In its final form the Documentary Hypothesis held sway for a century or so (late19th to late 20th). With the demise of the Documentary Hypothesis, the stories or blocks of text are set free. They do not have to be part of finished texts, blended together to inform readers or hearers of a distant past. They are free to be the bases from which storytellers, teachers, or theologians began their work. They are free to be interpreted in their own right and not to be imprisoned in a totally hypothetical documentary structure. An updated understanding of the nature of many biblical texts sets pentateuchal texts free from the difficulties of an outdated hypothesis. Important too is the realisation that these bases may have been created not in the early days of Israel's existence but rather in the period associated with the Babylonian exile and its aftermath, when Israel needed mature reflection on itself, its God, and the meaning of its existence.

Certain rules of thumb can be recommended to authors (and *mutatis mutandis* to readers as well, such as what authors should have left out, readers should ignore). Three may be emphasised where academic study is concerned.

> (1) Where a certain analysis adds meaning to the text, discuss it in full.
> (2) Where a particular analysis seems possibly valid but does not appear to add meaning to the text, set it aside in storage until meaning emerges in connection with it; if it doesn't, note it for others for later and forget it for now.
> (3) Where a particular analysis has the sole merit of demonstrating how eminently smart the writer is, scrub it promptly.

Possibility does not generate necessity; what is possible need not ever have happened. The control question on all such occasions is: in what way does the operation proposed enhance the meaning of the text?

An anxiety may often be present for readers but remain unexpressed: if a text is not the final story but is a base from which the story can be developed and unfolded, does that leave either the ancient or modern user of this text free to unfold and develop the story as the user thinks fit? The answer is a most emphatic negative—'No, it does not'. Most initial encounters with texts, above all for academic purposes, will involve perhaps a teacher, a preacher, or a commentator. These specialist interpreters are not controlled by the unlimited freedom of their imaginations. Their imaginations are controlled by the text they encounter. The ancient users of a text (probably from among the wise), understood their text as user-base, and were controlled by the 'user-base' text they were unfolding or developing. This may seem vague; in concrete detail it is real. Because of potential misunderstanding, it is worth insisting on.

Much the same is true of 'reader response' in the interpretation of texts. Each reader brings to a text what no other reader can; but each reader brings what is theirs to the same text, to the same set of marks on paper. The marks on paper exercise their control on the imaginations that encounter them. As anyone knows who has looked into it closely, the issue today is extremely complex. It always has been. The understanding of text as user-base changes nothing in that complexity. Israel's thinkers in the distant past were suitably controlled by even minimally detailed text. Our thinkers, in today's present, are similarly under the control of the text. The issue has been widely debated in association with reader-response criticism. The meaning of the text, in any given circumstance, is necessarily the outcome of 'the conversation that takes place at the boundary between text and reader'.[13] The text can exercise control over the reader; the text can, in certain areas, leave the reader free. It is the skill of the trained reader or interpreter to know the difference and abide by it.

The question whether such user-bases were initially oral before becoming written is one we cannot answer at this time. We have reference to the existence of male and female singers in ancient Israel (not temple singers; quite possibly storytellers, certainly entertainers. 2 Sam 19:36, Heb; NRSV, 19:35; Qoh 2:8; 2 Chron 35:25); we do not have their texts. Traditional materials may well have been sung to make them more attractive or more easy to remember.[14] We would be unwise to underestimate the sophistication of certain sectors of the ancient past.[15] It is probable that, at certain stages, learners committed to memory material handed on by experienced practitioners, to unfold or develop as needed. We do not at present have any examples of what such material looked like. Before 1947 and the Dead Sea

---

13. Roland Boer, *Symposia* (London: Equinox, 2007), 75.
14. For the illiterate Yugoslav singers of the recent past, see AB Lord, *The Singer of Tales* (Cambridge, MA: Harvard University Press, 1960).
15. See David Carr, *Writing On the Tablet of the Heart* (New York, NY: Oxford University Press, 2005).

discoveries, we had no significant OT scroll fragments from biblical times. The Aleppo codex and the Leningrad codex took us back to around the year 1000, a bare millennium ago; we had nothing earlier that was of any moment. The Qumran discoveries were needed to see the significance of the material from the Cairo genizah. While we have considerable information from ancient Israel, there is still so much we do not know.

All of this may seem somewhat abstract, even while drawing on story-texts from Genesis to Kings. Much will fall into place when specific texts from Genesis to Deuteronomy are being examined. Discussion of the distant past and ancient Israel's use of texts for storytelling, reflective pondering, and theology may seem abstract and remote. It comes much closer to home when we realise that what we are discussing is the nature of the biblical texts and that what is said about Israel's distant past is equally true of our own present now. Modern storytellers have to enlarge on the biblical text, choose between variant options that are offered in the text, and so on. Modern theologians have to explore texts for their implications and assess the contribution of given texts for the formulation of a given theology.

Genesis 30:25–31:18

It will help to have an example of the approach advocated here, particularly in the case of an otherwise difficult text.

Summary of compositional aspects

> *One version (without fragmentation):*
> Genesis 30:25–34; 31:1–2, 17–18, separation done 'today'—breeding already done.
> *A variant version (equally without fragmentation):*
> Genesis 30:35–42, the separation of the flock is in the future—yet to breed
> *Enhancement:*
> Genesis 31:3–16, Jacob's exchange with his wives
> *Supplements:*
> Genesis 30:43
> [43]Thus the man grew exceedingly rich, and had large flocks, and male and female slaves, and camels and donkeys.

Blending:
Nil

The traditions associated with the division of the flock (= wealth) between Laban and Jacob have always posed insuperable problems for commentators. Traditionally, it has been distributed between J and E (so, for example, Wellhausen, Gunkel, von Rad, Noth) without satisfactory results. The documentary hypothesis required a text reflecting versions of one and the same story—which this text does not provide. Westermann concludes that source division won't do and claims one document with revisions and additions. But, in a key verse he adds a significant clause in his interpretation that is not there in the biblical text. The clause (in 30:32) is: 'After the agreed time has run its course'. 'After the agreed time has run its course' helps considerably to create a tolerable text but is in flat contradiction with the biblical text which says: 'I will go through all your flocks TODAY'. The specific 'today' cannot be ignored; the speaker of course is Jacob. For Westermann, 'the variant words in vv 32–33 and the variations in the execution in vv 35–40 belong to one and the same expansion which was handed on in an incomplete state because herdsmen's skills of this sort were no longer understood or of interest'.[16] Unfortunately, no suggestions are given to justify the inclusion of these incomplete variants. The not uncommon appeal to specialist herdmen's skills in these complicated matters needs to be justified and is not.

Preceding Westermann, von Rad had indulged a similar stratagem: introducing into the interpretation what is not there in the text. Laban agrees 'but not without first inserting a safety clause for himself. He himself (and not Jacob) separates all spotted and striped animals from the flocks'.[17] That is in flat contradiction with the biblical text that, as von Rad is well aware, has Jacob propose to 'pass through all your flock today' (30:32). The alleged 'safety clause' is quite out of the question in the present context.

The problem was seen long ago by no other than Julius Wellhausen, who wrote: 'the contradiction of verses 32–34 with what precedes and follows is total ('ein ganz completer'); it is the cause of interpreters

---

16. Westermann, *Genesis 12–36*, 480.
17. von Rad, *Genesis*, 301.

having misunderstood the entire passage.'[18] For Wellhausen, the verses are from E, made possible by the accusation in Genesis 31:7. Incoherences remain.

The blending has been well done. What must be understood is that what the biblical text presents us with is not two echoes of one story, but aspects of two different stories, both incomplete but with more than enough material to complete them. In the first, the division is in the present, with the separation done by Jacob *on that day*. The motivation for Jacob's departure is provided by Laban's sons, not by any deceit on Laban's part. The text associated with the two different stories would be as follows.

> One version: Genesis 30:25-34; 31:1-2, 17-18, the separation of the flock is today—already bred.
>
> 30:25 When Rachel had borne Joseph, Jacob said to Laban, 'Send me away, that I may go to my own home and country. [26]Give me my wives and my children for whom I have served you, and let me go; for you know very well the service I have given you.' [27]But Laban said to him, 'If you will allow me to say so, I have learned by divination that the LORD has blessed me because of you; [28]name your wages, and I will give them.' [29]Jacob said to him, 'You yourself know how I have served you, and how your cattle have fared with me. [30]For you had little before I came, and it has increased abundantly; and the LORD has blessed you wherever I turned. But now when shall I provide for my own household also?' [31]He said, 'What shall I give you?' Jacob said, 'You shall not give me anything; if you will do this for me, I will again feed your flock and keep it: [32]let me pass through all your flock today, removing from it every speckled and spotted sheep and every black lamb, and the spotted and speckled among the goats; and such shall be my wages. [33]So my honesty will answer for me later, when you come to look into my wages with you. Every one that

---

18. Wellhausen, *Composition des Hexateuchs*, 39: 'Der Widerspruch der Verse 32-34 zu Vorhergehendem and Folgendem ist somit ein ganz completer; er hat es verschuldet, dass die Ausleger die ganze Stelle nicht recht verstanden haben.'

is not speckled and spotted among the goats and black among the lambs, if found with me, shall be counted stolen.' ³⁴Laban said, 'Good! Let it be as you have said.'

31:1 Now Jacob heard that the sons of Laban were saying, 'Jacob has taken all that was our father's; he has gained all this wealth from what belonged to our father.' ²And Jacob saw that Laban did not regard him as favorably as he did before.

17 So Jacob arose, and set his children and his wives on camels; ¹⁸and he drove away all his livestock, all the property that he had gained, the livestock in his possession that he had acquired in Paddan-aram, to go to his father Isaac in the land of Canaan.

A variant version: Genesis 30:35–42, the separation of the flock is in the future—yet to breed.

³⁵But that day Laban removed the male goats that were striped and spotted, and all the female goats that were speckled and spotted, every one that had white on it, and every lamb that was black, and put them in charge of his sons; ³⁶and he set a distance of three days' journey between himself and Jacob, while Jacob was pasturing the rest of Laban's flock.

37 Then Jacob took fresh rods of poplar and almond and plane, and peeled white streaks in them, exposing the white of the rods. ³⁸He set the rods that he had peeled in front of the flocks in the troughs, that is, the watering-places, where the flocks came to drink. And since they bred when they came to drink, ³⁹the flocks bred in front of the rods, and so the flocks produced young that were striped, speckled, and spotted. ⁴⁰Jacob separated the lambs, and set the faces of the flocks toward the striped and the completely black animals in the flock of Laban; and he put his own droves apart, and did not put them with Laban's flock. ⁴¹Whenever the stronger of the flock were breeding, Jacob laid the rods in the troughs before the eyes of the flock, that they might breed among the rods, ⁴²but for the feebler of the flock he did not lay them there; so the feebler were Laban's, and the stronger Jacob's.

The introduction of Jacob's exchange with his wives, possible as an enhancement in either version, allows for the introduction of several new elements if desired. They include: the return instigated by God rather than Jacob (Gen 30:25); the accusation of Laban's changes of wages (not in the earlier text); the assertion of God's protection of Jacob; the report of a dream in which the mating behavior of the goats is observed (not sheep and goats as earlier, Gen 30:32); the reference to Bethel and the divine order to return home; the full agreement of both wives; the reference to money paid for the wives and now spent (not in the earlier text where the issue is service for both brides, not money that can be spent); the transfer of property is above all God's doing. Narrators are enabled to omit these or expand them as they judge appropriate.

Beyond the two versions of the separation of the flocks, there is what can only be considered an enhancement, Jacob's exchange with his wives (Gen 31:3–16). It contains a number to details that could be used to flesh out the story, all grist to the storyteller's mill. The text is:

> [3]Then the Lord said to Jacob, 'Return to the land of your ancestors and to your kindred, and I will be with you.' [4]So Jacob sent and called Rachel and Leah into the field where his flock was, [5]and said to them, 'I see that your father does not regard me as favorably as he did before. But the God of my father has been with me. [6]You know that I have served your father with all my strength; [7]yet your father has cheated me and changed my wages ten times, but God did not permit him to harm me. [8]If he said, 'The speckled shall be your wages', then all the flock bore speckled; and if he said, 'The striped shall be your wages', then all the flock bore striped. [9]Thus God has taken away the livestock of your father, and given them to me.
> 10 During the mating of the flock I once had a dream in which I looked up and saw that the male goats that leaped upon the flock were striped, speckled, and mottled. [11]Then the angel of God said to me in the dream, 'Jacob', and I said, 'Here I am!' [12]And he said, 'Look up and see that all the goats that leap on the flock

are striped, speckled, and mottled; for I have seen all that Laban is doing to you. ¹³I am the God of Bethel, where you anointed a pillar and made a vow to me. Now leave this land at once and return to the land of your birth.' ¹⁴Then Rachel and Leah answered him, 'Is there any portion or inheritance left to us in our father's house? ¹⁵Are we not regarded by him as foreigners? For he has sold us, and he has been using up the money given for us. ¹⁶All the property that God has taken away from our father belongs to us and to our children; now then, do whatever God has said to you.'

The intermediary's part
An intermediary, whether one of the storytellers or an advisor to storytellers, might have much to say on telling stories drawn from these traditions. For openers, there would be the decision whether to base a story on the 'already bred' (separation today) tradition or whether to base one on the 'yet-to-breed' (separation in the future) tradition. Associated with this would be, among other things, the issue of integrity (NRSV, 'honesty') insisted on in 30:33 and the question whether the unusually colored from the flock remained with Jacob (30:32-33) or with Laban (30:40, aspects of the Hebrew are abstruse.)[19]

A further issue would be that of completing the stories beyond what is given in the textual base. In the 'already bred' tradition, there is a need for follow-up: the fact of the separation, the observation of the separation, the size of the flocks involved and the wealth embodied in them—all matters that lie comfortably within the competence of an experienced storyteller. In the 'yet-to-breed' tradition, there is the easy task of putting together the initial agreement between the two men. Laban's removal of the unusually coloured animals helps place God solidly on the side of Jacob.

The enhancement, with Jacob's exchange with his wives, is particularly interesting. It contains elements that are not explicit in either of the other traditions. As noted above, the return home is instigated by God not by Jacob. The accusation of Laban's changing of the conditions of the agreement is not noted elsewhere. The assertion

---

19. Westermann, 'It is difficult to understand the text', *Genesis 12–36*, 483.

of God's protection is explicit here, but only implicit elsewhere. Even the stratagem to ensure unusually colored births is attributed to the angel of God in a dream rather than to Jacob's somewhat devious cunning. There is the reference to Bethel that occurs nowhere else in this passage. There is the justification for Jacob's action provided by the two wives. Added to this is the issue of money given for the brides and already spent by Laban. In earlier texts, there is no mention of money being paid but of service being given. The acquisition of property is attributed explicitly to God.

What is clear is that the use of the traditions within this enhancement would have to be done carefully and selectively. Some could be used within the present context; some, if included, would require alterations to the telling of earlier text.

Many commentators will appeal to the specialised and professional knowledge involved in authoring or understanding this difficult text. There is regrettably no evidence for this, beyond the difficulties of the text. The realisation that the text is to be base for two different stories removes the majority of these difficulties. Some difficulties of language (striped, speckled, spotted, and mottled or completely black) or even of species (sheep and goats) are unlikely to reflect sources but more likely to reflect the understandings of different regions and audiences.

The Nature of Biblical Narrative
(Original: not located)

Something of a paradigm shift has been in the making for a while in biblical studies. A future shape has yet to jell. The old historical-critical analysis has not been generating new life for a long time.[1] Other approaches have not so far struck lasting root. The interaction of developmental (cf diachronic) reading and interpretational (cf synchronic) reading is under way, but far from any agreed integration. A resolution of tensions between critical and literary approaches is still to be achieved. The factors involved in any shift are complex; among them, the often competing needs of faith communities, university communities, and so many competent individuals. One element in the total equation may be scholarly assumptions about the nature of much biblical narrative text.

Assumptions are unavoidable. We live with them all the time. Like routines, they help simplify life and eliminate the overburden of decisions to be faced at every turn. Like routines, assumptions can be dangerous; they can trap us in ruts we do not even realise. Those we are least aware of can be the most dangerous. Assumptions must be re-examined regularly; the outgrown need to be replaced.[2]

---

1. Herbert Hahn's comment was made over half a century ago: 'The conclusion seems to be unavoidable that the higher criticism has long since passed the age of constructive achievement' (*The Old Testament in Modern Research* [Philadelphia: Fortress, 1966; original, 1954] 41).
2. One of the great values of Susan Niditch's *Oral World and Written Word: Ancient Israelite Literature* (Louisville: Westminster John Knox, 1996) is that it seeks to bring to the surface some of our unconscious assumptions about literature and ancient Israel. Undoubtedly, some will feel that assumptions of little importance have been caricatured. Yet even caricature serves to challenge; and given what we know today of ancient Israel, it is time to reexamine and challenge assumptions. A recent study building on Niditch's work is Raymond F Person, Jr, 'The Ancient

This article is about an assumption current in biblical studies that is a candidate for re-examination and replacement. The assumption concerns the texts of stories told in ancient Israel—the relationship between oral performance and written text.

Performance and narrative text

Appalling assumptions can sneak up on the greatest of scholars. Susan Niditch opens by upbraiding Hermann Gunkel for portraying a naive, child-like, rural simplicity as the culture from which the Bible emerged.[3] Alas, the same Gunkel did not do much better on the timing of biblical storytelling; it was much the same assumption that got him in trouble. In the introduction to his Genesis commentary, Gunkel seriously overestimated the time for the average biblical text. He notes that most of the Genesis stories comprise ten verses or so and they last, according to the first edition of the commentary, 'not much over half an hour'; in the third edition, this is reduced to 'scarcely a short quarter hour' (die kaum ein Viertelstündchen ausfüllen).[4] Unfortunately, Gunkel cannot have been driven by a desire for experimental accuracy. The Hebrew texts he mentions can mostly be read aloud slowly in two to three minutes each—a quarter hour is quite unnecessary and a half hour is an absurd overestimate (see below). It is all the more surprising, then, that Gunkel commented: the stories are strikingly short (*auffallend kurz*).

A couple of errors are running here for Gunkel. The first was factual: the length of the stories. The second is cultural: the people of ancient times were like our children. The factual error most

---

Israelite Scribe as Performer', in *JBL* 117 (1998): 601–9.
3. *Oral Word and Written Word*, 2.
4. The introduction to the first edition of Gunkel's *Genesis* (Göttingen: Vandenhoeck & Ruprecht, 1901) has been translated by WH Carruth, *The Legends of Genesis* (New York: Schocken, 1964; first published in 1901). It has the following: 'the older legends are absolutely abrupt to modern taste' and goes on to say that 'primitive times were satisfied with quite brief productions which required not much over half an hour' (47; 'etwa ein halbes Stündchen ausfüllen). This was corrected to a quarter hour in the second edition, 1902, noted by Jay A Wilcoxen ('Narrative', 57–98 in *Old Testament Form Criticism*, edited by John H Hayes [San Antonio: Trinity Univ. Press, 1974] see 64). The third edition reference, 'die kaum ein Viertelstündchen ausfüllen' is Gunkel, *Genesis* (Göttingen: Vandenhoeck & Ruprecht, 1910), xxxiv.

probably indicates an underlying assumption: the stories in the written texts either record or approximate to the stories as they were orally performed. The cultural prejudice allows the factual error to be accepted and the assumption to go unchallenged: ancient storytellers were not up to more complex stories and ancient audiences would not have sustained the listening needed. So the conclusion: the shorter a story is, the more likely it is to have kept its older form.[5]

To be fair to Gunkel, we need to be clear on the factual error. According to Gunkel, many of the Genesis stories hardly extended over more than ten verses. These are the stories that scarcely filled out a quarter hour.[6] What led one of the senior and highly respected exegetes of recent times into such a crass error? The most plausible explanation is that Gunkel worked with the assumption that the written text represented a record of the oral performance or a close approximation to it. No worthwhile story would be told in under thirty minutes; with Gunkel's view of an ancient Israelite audience, perhaps in around fifteen minutes—but no less. Yet the empirical evidence is that the 'telling' of ten verses of the biblical text takes on average less than three minutes.

Gunkel's failure to spot so egregious an error can be explained by the cultural prejudice. Gunkel attributes the shortness of the stories to the brevity of the attention span of ancient Israelite audiences. According to Gunkel, the stories are short because the attention span of the Israelite audiences was short. The truly patronising part is the assumption that the ancient Israelites were like our children (*so wie unsere Kinder*). A short piece was enough; after that, their capacity to listen was exhausted.[7] Today, I doubt that we have any difficulty in finding Gunkel's explanation totally unacceptable. He massively underestimated the abilities of an ancient Israelite audience. If the stories are as sophisticated as we have every reason to believe them to be, the audience is unlikely to have been less sophisticated.

Niditch is concerned with the reassessment of assumptions. She offers four scenarios for the relationship of text to performance.[8] They are:

---

5. 'Je knapper eine Sage ist, um so wahrscheinlicher ist es, daß sie in alter Gestalt erhalten ist' (*Genesis*, third edition, xxxiv).
6. *Genesis*, third edition, xxxiii-xxxiv.
7. *Genesis*, third edition, xxxiv.
8. *Oral World and Written Word*, 117–30.

i. performance dictated and copied;
ii. tradition written down by a gifted writer;
iii. literary imitation of oral style;
iv. written composition from written sources.

Niditch highlights 'performance dictated and copied' for the classical prophetic corpus. 'Dictated and copied' may work for some prophetic passages; it does not work for narrative. The texts are too short; it would be Gunkel's fallacy all over again. Three minutes do not a story make. In Niditch's second scenario, the tradition has been formed by multiple performances and the possibility is allowed that 'written notes or abstracts aided the more elaborate performances'.[9] 'Notes or abstracts' may put us on track toward our present texts.

Almost seventy years passed before Gunkel's attitude was challenged by Alexander Rofé; even then, it was less the assumptions than the condescension that was objectionable. Without naming Gunkel, Rofé was justifiably indignant about a patronising attitude toward Israelite storytellers and listeners.[10] Around the assumption that the text records the performance, one sentence is key: 'The oral stage must have been longer, much longer, than the version we have now in scripture'.[11] According to Rofé, to look at the present written form of the stories as representing their form in oral performance would be the same as saying that the longest tale (of those he discusses) was narrated in about seventy seconds. When he went on a little later to discuss 'a very different type of story', one that was 'much

---

9. *Oral World and Written Word*, 120.
10. Alexander Rofé, 'The Classification of the Prophetical Stories', in *JBL* 89 (1970) 427–40. His indignation needs to be heard (432–33).

    Yet are we allowed to consider the present form of the stories as their original oral form? This would amount to saying that the longest tale was narrated in about seventy seconds, implying that the storyteller could not entertain his audience any longer than that and that the audience itself would be satisfied with such a short, concise, matter-of-fact account. This, however, is highly improbable. The Israelite storyteller was not a primitive who could not even master his language, and the Israelite public was not so backwards as not to be able to sustain a story which lasted more than one minute. The oral stage must have been longer, much longer, than the version we have now in scripture. The conciseness of the present stories rather reveals the opposite: the man who reduced these narratives to writing took the pains, and had the skill, to condense them.
11. Rofé, 'The Classification of the Prophetical Stories', 432.

longer (30 verses)', Rofé passed over the significance of what he had been saying, although much more than length was at issue.[12] Thirty verses might occupy about ten minutes, in serious storytelling terms about as inadequate as seventy seconds.

Almost in passing, Gunkel's error was targeted a little later by Jay Wilcoxen, but without noticeable impact on subsequent scholarship.[13] Wilcoxen suggests

> that Gunkel may have missed the point of the brevity of the present texts. The individual stories are not brief because ancient narrations were brief, but because these texts only present basic plots which in any actual narration would be expanded and elaborated according to the skill of the storyteller and the occasion of his performance.[14]

In an article a few years earlier, Wilcoxen had argued that Joshua 6 preserved three forms of ritual, merged to retain the legitimacy of all three. He comments: 'On any single occasion, however, only one of the forms must have been selected.'[15]

Without reference to the work of Rofé and Wilcoxen, Antony Campbell argued in 1989 for understanding some texts as reported story, 'the outcome of reporting what a story is about'. A reported story would provide 'the basic elements from which the full narrative of a story can be developed but would fall short of actually telling the story'.[16] The idea has been taken up subsequently by Campbell and O'Brien.[17] Their emphasis was on the text as base for later storytelling.

---

12. Rofé, 'The Classification of the Prophetical Stories', 433.
13. Wilcoxen, 'Narrative', 64–66.
14. 'Narrative', 65.
15. Jay A Wilcoxen, 'Narrative Structure and Cult Legend: A Study of Joshua 1–6', 43–70 in *Transitions in Biblical Scholarship*, edited by JC Rylaarsdam (Chicago: University of Chicago Press, 1968), 53.
16. Antony F Campbell, 'The Reported Story: Midway Between Oral Performance and Literary Art', in *Semeia* 46 (1989): 77–85, 78.
17. Antony F Campbell and Mark A O'Brien, *Sources of the Pentateuch: Texts, Introductions, Annotations* (Minneapolis: Fortress, 1993) and *idem*, '1–2 Samuel' and '1–2 Kings' in *The International Bible Commentary*, edited by WR Farmer, *et al* (Collegeville: Liturgical Press, 1998), 580–81; restated in *idem*, *Unfolding the Deuteronomistic History: Origins, Upgrades, Present Text* (Minneapolis: Fortress, 2000) 6-7.

Niditch's second scenario, the tradition written down by a gifted writer, points to a correlative aspect of such reported stories—they emerge from the tradition of Israel's storytelling.

Past traditions and future telling
As a result of these observations, another scenario needs to be added to the four proposed by Niditch. Many of the narrative texts we have in the Bible stand in an indirect relationship to the performance of storytelling. They are too short to be stories as performed; beyond that, many of them are not appropriate for that purpose. Instead, these biblical texts look in two directions: one is rearward, back to the storytelling tradition that they report; the other is forward, to the stories to be told in the future.

The rearward glance, the report of storytelling tradition, is close to the second scenario depicted by Niditch (with the added aspect of reporting and reduction).[18] We know the texts we have and the high quality of their literary style; it is a tribute to the quality of ancient Israel's storytelling. Those who told the stories told them well; those who reported the stories reported them well. The plot structure is there. The gems of dialogue are there. The details that go to make a good story are there. There is enough stuff there to hold a report together. The trimmings that any good storyteller can generate are not there. Variant versions are there, even if only briefly noted. A storyteller may choose to use one; no good storyteller would actualise conflicting ones. Contradictory traditions are sometimes noted. Good storytellers knew how to handle them. Fundamentally, a good report preserved whatever possibilities the tradition contained. The aim of a reported story is to recapitulate the story—not to retell it but to recapitulate it.

The reported story is then a base for the storyteller whose task is to retell the story. Choices may be made from that base: which variants to tell, which details to include. A good storyteller will know, on any given occasion, which details to provide and which to withhold, which gaps to fill and which to leave as gaps. A good storyteller will know when to extend a story and when to shorten it. The base may

---

18. The emphasis on the rearward aspect, the derivation of the reported stories from the practice of Israel's storytelling, emerged for me from discussions with Professor Marvin Sweeney.

contain several variants; the good storyteller will only actualise one and will know which is the right one to actualise for the particular audience. It is not a matter of being bound to a text but being bound to a story. The reported story preserves a past tradition, rehearsed in the telling of the story, and prepares for a future rehearsal of the tradition, in the retelling of the story. There is a structured move here from the oral into the written with a view to returning to the oral.[19]

We have no certainty that reported stories functioned as bases for storytelling. That is an assumption, although it is an assumption that is grounded in verifiable argument, is respectful of ancient writers, and is free from patronising elements. The principal grounds of argument for regarding certain texts as reported stories may be summarised under three heads:

   i. the brevity of the texts, as discussed above;
   ii. the details omitted, requiring a fuller discussion than space allows for here;[20]
   iii. the variants included, often to be accounted for as elements or traditions preserved for the consideration of later storytellers and later generations.[21]

The story texts we now have belong mainly in the Pentateuch, the Deuteronomistic History, the Chronicler's history, and some in the prophetic books. Calculating on the average of three minutes or so for ten verses, the record of an hour-long performance of a story would require a couple of hundred verses. The narrative texts of the Bible would be some twenty times more extensive than they are. Not twenty Bibles, but quite a number. Some reduction of the traditional performances of stories was needed to give us the extended texts we

---

19. This reinforces Niditch's important insistence on the influence of oral culture in a world of limited literacy.
20. To cull three examples from one chapter: messages are acted on without being delivered (1 Sam 19:14); people are present in a place without having gone there (19:17); elements of a story are not plausible without a level of explanation that is not given (19:15–16, where the dummy is used too late).
21. The space available does not allow for full discussion. Among other research, these observations are based on preparation of the *First Samuel* and *Second Samuel* volumes for the Forms of the Old Testament Literature series (forthcoming with Eerdmans, Grand Rapids) and on the works listed above in notes 16–17.

have. In this case, there is no assumption. We have the reduced texts. The only assumption made is that stories were told before they were reported—that performance preceded report.

The story texts of the Older Testament range from a verse or two to fifty or sixty verses. Some of these texts read well in church; but the synagogues of ancient Israel came long after the stories. A few of these texts could well have been used at the festivals of ancient Israel; they are relatively few however. Most are not suitable for festival use. The settings were almost certainly not simple; they range across the gamut from entertainment to theology. Two claims can be made. First, these reported stories were used to compile the extensive narrative documents that are part of the present biblical text. Second, it is a reasonable assumption that these reported stories served as the bases from which continued storytelling was launched in ancient Israel.

Biblical narratives are often familiar texts, sacred texts, treasured texts. It is difficult to look at these texts differently, yet difference may not mean loss and the beneficial implications may be considerable.

In a classic study, Erich Auerbach comments that Hebrew narrative is 'fraught with background'.[22] For example, Auerbach points out that the sacrifice of Isaac (Gen 22) starts without any divine journey or divine council. Yet, as we are well aware, Israelite narrative knows of both: in Genesis 17, God journeys (God appears to Abraham and goes up from him); in 1 Kings 22, we are privy to the proceedings of the divine council. But not in the text of Genesis 22.

Auerbach's comparison of the Older Testament with Homer is an important starting point. Comments from his conclusion to the chapter on 'Odysseus' Scar' are worth repeating.

> The two styles, in their opposition, represent basic types: on the one hand [that is, Homer] fully externalized description, uniform illumination, uninterrupted connection . . . all events in the foreground, displaying unmistakable meanings . . . on the other hand [that is, the OT], certain parts brought into high relief, others left obscure, abruptness, suggestive influence of the

---

22. E Auerbach, *Mimesis: The Representation of Reality in Western Literature* (Princeton, NJ: Princeton Univ. Press, 1953; original, 1946), 12.

> unexpressed, 'background' quality, multiplicity of meanings and the need for interpretation . . . [23]

Auerbach's reading of the Older Testament is marked by orthodoxy and piety. In his view, the sole concern of the biblical stories is with moral, religious, and psychological phenomena. Furthermore:

> Their religious intent involves an absolute claim to historical truth . . . The Biblical narrator was obliged to write exactly what his belief in the truth of the tradition . . . demanded of him . . . his freedom in creative or representative imagination was severely limited; his activity was perforce reduced to composing an effective version of the pious tradition.[24]

A different experience of the biblical text denies this limiting of the biblical narrator to the composition of an effective version of the pious tradition. This is a far cry from Robert Alter's 'historicized prose fiction'.[25] For all that, Auerbach's 'fraught with background' has caught something characteristic of Hebrew narrative text. What is the significance of this characteristic within the texts? Is it possible that Genesis 22, for example, is a reported story or a story base? It has all the makings of a most powerful story, but as the text stands the story takes about four minutes to tell. It is a brilliantly shaped literary text; it need not reproduce the performance of storytelling.

Would it spoil this story if, in its telling, a storyteller mentioned God's coming down to speak to Abraham? Would it spoil this story if a storyteller allowed a glimpse into the proceedings of the divine council so that an audience might be more informed as to God's purpose? Would it spoil the story to introduce Sarah (cf Genesis 21)? Would it spoil the poignancy of the dialogue of father and son about the victim, as 'the two of them walked on together' (vv 7–8), if a little bit of storytelling attention was given to the strained silence that might have preceded Isaac's question or if Abraham was allowed to give his son some inkling of what was at stake? The text ignores Isaac. What if

---

23. *Mimesis*, 23.
24. *Mimesis*, 14.
25. R Alter, *The Art of Biblical Narrative* (New York: Basic Books, 1981), 24. The term itself is taken from Herbert Schneidau's *Sacred Discontent*.

the issue of Isaac's return with his father was raised by the storyteller? In the text it is a gap. In all the gaps and the silences, we have to ask how this brief text functioned. It is a brilliant literary text. Is it a brilliantly reported story, a base for equally brilliant storytelling?

Social conditions
Economist Maynard Keynes is reputed to have said that people who claimed they had no need of economic theory were simply in the grip of an older theory. It tends to be the same with assumptions. Older assumptions do not easily release their grip. We cannot avoid assumptions about how an ancient society functioned, what went on in a society where literacy was highly restricted, what sort of a literary industry gave rise to our Bible texts. We make those assumptions best if we project off knowledge of similar societies rather than re-trojecting our own prejudices. All this makes Niditch's book immensely valuable.[26] At the same time, in biblical studies we have to square our assumptions with the biblical text. The hypotheses and social conditions we assume need to be the sort that would bring about the texts we actually possess. Wise generalisations are of no use to us if they do not shed light on the texts we look at in their detail. The modern recovery of antiquity is extremely important, but hypotheses have to be measured against the texts they supposedly produced.

If modern study is not totally wrong—and it may be—there is an intensity of editing in the priestly documents and the deuteronomistic texts. We know about parties and factions in the ancient world. We do not know the details of how these swirled in and out of royal courts or sacred temples or established families (for example: we can trace three generations of Shaphans in Jerusalem, from Secretary Shaphan ben Azaliah ben Meshullam [2 Kgs 22:3] to Governor Gedaliah ben Ahikam ben Shaphan [2 Kgs 25:22; Jer 39:14; 40:5, 9, 11; 41:2]). The intensity of factional partisans need not correlate with their influence in society. I recall the words of an American candidate for presidential nomination: 'I am not bound by the party platform; I have not even read it.' I doubt that such a disavowal did much to stop

---

26. Particularly chapter 3 ('New Ways of Thinking about Orality and Literacy: Israelite Evidence') and chapter 4 ('Logistics of Literacy: Archives and Libraries, Education, and Writing Material').

infighting over the platform. Were similar passions at work in priestly and deuteronomistic circles? The texts suggest it. Where were such circles and their texts housed? Were they institutionally based? We do not know. We have only the texts and their characteristics that we must account for.

Examples

Leaving the Pentateuch aside, when we start scrutinising texts using the 'reported story' concept as a lens for reading, examples are legion. The crossing of the Jordan text (Joshua 3-4) makes much more sense as a base story that has been annotated with liturgical options instead of an unconvincing weaving of incomplete traditions. The text of the fall of Jericho (Josh 6:3-20) lacks plausibility as present text or a combination of sources. It makes sense as a script suitable for storytelling or liturgy, either suspenseful and silent (Alfred Hitchcock) or showy and noisy (Cecil B de Mille).[27] To pull a couple of texts out of Judges, Jephthah's is a story that might be told of a hero empowered by the spirit (Judg 11:29) or of a warrior who made a stupid vow and stubbornly stuck to it (Judg 11:30-31). These are options for a storyteller. Samson's too is a cycle that offers a storyteller multiple options. Samson 'shall begin to deliver Israel' (Judg 13:5). Which will get the emphasis: the beginner or the deliverer? Samson is scarcely a hero figure.[28] With Delilah, for example: three times he is deceived, three times he has lied. Smart. The fourth time he has to know that he will be deceived; this time, he tells the truth. Not smart. No theological nobility either; savage selfishness instead: 'So that with this one act of revenge I may pay back the Philistines for my two eyes' (Judg 16:28). What a contrast with David facing the Philistine (1 Sam 17:45-47).

David and the Philistine champion offers a good example of the storyteller's need either to choose or to demonstrate remarkable mental agility (1 Sam 16:14-18:30). There is a choice between David the armor-bearer, acting out of lofty theological faith (17:36-37, 45-

---

27. See the treatment of both passages in *Unfolding the Deuteronomistic History*, 112-17 and 119-23.
28. Gerhard von Rad comments: 'The oddest figure amongst the judges is Samson: the reader will indeed find it absolutely impossible to understand him as judge over Israel' (*Old Testament Theology*, [2 volumes; Edinburgh: Oliver and Boyd, 1962-65] 1.333).

47), or David the shepherd-boy, acting out of raw ambition (17:26). The present text hints at combining the two. A skilled storyteller might be able to do it, but it would demand no little agility. A storyteller's development of the text base is needed for the story of David and Saul in the cave (1 Sam 24). The present text has David emerge from the cave, waving the corner of Saul's cloak, while three thousand of Saul's finest look on. A storyteller could easily have David discuss the situation with his men in the cave, slip away through a gully behind the cave, and call to Saul from concealment in a section of forest higher up the hill. The text does not. The text also has David's moral stance in the cave come a verse or two too late (24:4–7). It is an option for the storyteller, not a plot development in the text. The chapter is not the telling of a story but its report, the base for storytelling. The narrative of how David rose to power in Israel is a composition of some twenty-five to thirty-five stories, brilliantly woven together and provided with the necessary narrative thread. Almost all of them are candidates for a storyteller's enhancement. Almost all of them, some more evidently and others less so, are candidates for reported story status—are too short or too multiplex to be anything but bases for storytelling.

The stories of 2 Samuel 11–20 are renowned for the issues they raise and the gaps they leave.[29] These chapters may have served their purpose as literary texts. They are also wonderful bases for storytelling. In the case of Bathsheba and David, for example, a storyteller might choose to note whether Bathsheba's washing was unduly revealing or not and whether it mattered. The text is silent (2 Sam 11:2). A storyteller might reflect on Bathsheba's feelings going to or returning from David's palace. The text is silent (11:4). A storyteller might have spent time on why she sent the dangerous message, 'I am pregnant', and what David's options might have been. The text is silent (11:5–6). And so many more. When Absalom's revolt is announced, David takes flight from Jerusalem without a word of counsel. What became of the claim for the impregnable city that 'even the blind and lame will turn you back' (2 Sam 5:6)? The text is silent. Hushai's runners hid in a well at Bahurim (2 Sam 17:15–20). Details of why it was risky for them to be seen and how Absalom's people knew to search the house

---

29. M Sternberg's treatment of gaps is classic (cf chapter 6 of *The Poetics of Biblical Narrative* [Bloomington: Indiana University Press, 1985], especially190–222).

at Bahurim are not given. A servant girl has been introduced as an apparently regular courier (17:17); the present text leaves no time for any such repeated activity.

Rehoboam's loss of the north invites development (1 Kgs 12:1–20). Were the young counselors greedy? Were the old wise? How was God's will at work? A choice is forced on the storyteller: was Jeroboam called to Shechem before (v 3) or after (v 20) the political split? In 1 Kings 21, a storyteller might have focused on the responsibility of either Ahab or Jezebel, or might have combined the two more thoroughly. The text leaves the options open (vv 1–16) and includes multiple traditions in vv 17–29. 2 Kings 3 mingles water and war, victory and retreat, two kings or three. A storyteller faced choices or development. In 2 Kings 13, King Joash is buried in v 13 and visits the dying Elisha in v 14; the regnal formula for Joash is given at 13:12 and repeated at 14:15. There is storytelling material in between, not necessarily edifying. The text presents it; a storyteller could have chosen how to handle it.

Multiplying examples will simply take us through most of the storytelling texts of the biblical tradition. The brevity of the texts and the nature of the texts combine to make a powerful case for the movement from oral to written to oral—the reported story recapitulates the oral performance, can be integrated into one of Israel's longer narrative compositions, and can serve as base for future retellings of the tradition.

Conclusion

These observations on the reported story have a radical impact on our understanding of the nature of biblical text. They impose caution on critical analysis of the text. They enhance access to the literary qualities of the present text. They give scope to creativity and flexibility in the interpreters of old and of today.

Access to the present text is not constrained by the need to find everything within the text itself. When the text recapitulates a story or is a base for a future story, the freedom left to the ancient storyteller is also there for today's interpreter. The control exercised by the text is not abolished but is altered. The written text is no longer the whole story, but it captures the nature of the story. If it offers options, like the storytellers of old we too know what they are. The option has always been there for us to accept or to reject. The choice may now be widened.

The literary quality of the text is not diminished by recognition of its status as reported story. A high tradition of storytelling leads to a high tradition of reporting and serves to foster equally high standards in the future. Many of our narrative texts are respected as highly polished works. We have no reason to believe that those who created the written text of reported stories did not take a pride in their literary achievement. Gaps left in the text need not be filled by the storytellers, ancient or modern; if we leave them unfilled, we know that we leave them because of the value of the gap. Shades of meaning in the choice of vocabulary are shades of meaning that any worthwhile storyteller would take over into the story. Insights into character preserved by the text are insights to be developed in the storytelling. And so on.

Texts that preserve options and retain contradictory traditions are responsibly respectful of the traditions of ancient Israel. It is one of the wonders of the Israelite scriptures that they offer so rich a palette of contrasting views. Whether it is creation, exodus, wandering, conquest, monarchy, or divine providence confronted with human suffering, Israel's contrasting views are preserved in its scriptures. Even in the traditional self-description of God, tension is maintained: 'forgiving iniquity and transgression and sin' (Exod 34:7a); 'by no means clearing the guilty, but visiting the iniquity of the parents upon the children' (Exod 34:7b). Israel offered choice to its theologians and to its storytellers. Today the biblical texts still offer us choices.

The Storyteller's Role: Reported Story and Biblical Text

(original: *CBQ* 64, 2002)

The three great narrative works of the Older Testament are the Pentateuch, the Deuteronomistic History (within Deuteronomy—Kings), and the Chronicler's History.[1] All three draw on earlier traditions and, within them, larger or smaller story units are visible. Among others, three factors in particular impact on the understanding of these great narrative works or their component elements. All three are well known to us; their implications are not always fully integrated into the way such narrative text is discussed and understood.

The three factors needing to be considered here are:

i. Limited distribution of the works, resulting from the need for copying by hand
ii. Limited literacy of the people, restricting use to specific circles
iii. Limited length of the smaller story units, requiring reflection on the function of such texts.

---

1. See M Noth, *The Deuteronomistic History*, JSOTSup 15; second edition (Sheffield: JSOT, 1981/91) German original, 1943, 13-15. My own experience is particularly based on the Pentateuch and the Deuteronomistic History. See Antony F Campbell, *Of Prophets and Kings: A Late Ninth-Century Document (1 Samuel 1—2 Kings 10*_CBQMS 17; (Washington, DC: Catholic Biblical Association of America, 1986); Antony F. Campbell and Mark A. O'Brien, *Sources of the Pentateuch: Texts, Introductions, Annotations* (Minneapolis: Fortress, 1993); idem, *Unfolding the Deuteronomistic History: Origins, Upgrades, Present Text* (Minneapolis: Fortress, 2000); and Antony F Campbell, *1 Samuel*, FOTL 7 (Grand Rapids: Eerdmans, in press) and *2 Samuel*, FOTL 8 (Grand Rapids: Eerdmans, forthcoming). I am leaving aside here shorter stories in their own right, such as Ruth, Esther, Tobit, and Judith. These—and similar pieces—deserve a separate investigation.

With the invention of printing, only a few centuries ago, it became possible to produce books for a relatively wide readership. Computers and the web are extending this possibility. Such possibilities did not exist in a pre-printing world. Distribution was limited to those relatively few who by position or wealth had access to particular manuscripts. The issue of literacy in ancient Israel is still disputed. Few, however, would disagree that—even more than in our world today—ease of use of sophisticated documents would have been restricted to relatively few, mainly among the elite.[2] These two factors alone bring up the issue of the function of Israel's great narrative works. The third factor, limited length, may take the matter to a further stage. The great narratives—Pentateuch, Deuteronomistic History, and Chronicler's History—are in large part composed of smaller story units. It is the brevity of these smaller components (to be discussed more fully below) that is of particular interest for understanding the function of such texts and, correlatively, the role of the storyteller in interpreting them.

It is these smaller story components of the great narratives that are the focus of this article. Concern with the great narratives themselves is a separate issue; at the moment, there is serious discussion about their composition and associated issues; there is not much point in discussing nature and message until the basics are better understood and agreed on. There may also be extensive narrative units within the big three: for example, the Yahwist Narrative and the Priestly Document in the Pentateuch or the Prophetic Record and the stories of David, whether on the rise or in power, for the Deuteronomistic History. The concern here is not with these extensive narrative units but with the smaller, usually independent, story units which often constitute much of the composition of these longer narratives.

The discussion will move in three stages. First, to get the idea itself clear as an approach to text. Then, to show in detail how the approach

---

2. Valuable background to this whole area of oral and written traditions, the levels and extent of literacy, the role of written documents, and so on, is provided by Susan Niditch, *Oral World and Written Word: Ancient Israelite Literature* (Library of Ancient Israel; Louisville: Westminster John Knox, 1996). For reflections on the scribal class in antiquity, see Philip R Davies, *Scribes and Schools: The Canonization of the Hebrew Scriptures*, Library of Ancient Israel (Louisville: Westminster John Knox, 1998), 15–30. Similar comments are appropriate in relation to storytellers.

is helpful in resolving some otherwise difficult problems in certain texts and to offer some further examples without the same degree of detail. Finally, to assess the implications of this understanding for the scholarly interpretation of texts.

Reported story: The idea

The independent smaller story units often range in extent from between ten verses or so (for example, Gen 12:10–20) to some forty verses or so (for example, 1 Sam 25:2–42). When we take into account the three factors mentioned—limited distribution, limited literacy, limited length—we need to interrogate these texts as to their nature and their function. A number of questions might be asked; my basic question is simple. Do these texts function as the record of the actual performance of stories in ancient Israel or do they serve some other function? The evidence all points to 'some other function'.

To anticipate subsequent discussion, that 'other function' may be to provide a record of what a particular story contains by way of tradition. This is not the same as a record of the performance or telling of a story. It is a record of what a story is about. Such a record of what a story is about is an abbreviation of the telling of a story; it is shorter than the performance. Such a record offers a base for future storytelling, or for whatever use may be made of story tradition. Such a record—the independent smaller story units—can be termed a 'reported story'.[3] It is the report of what a story is; it is not the telling of a story. For the telling of a story, the storyteller is required; reported

---

3. I first used the term 'reported story' some years ago in 'The Reported Story: Midway Between Oral Performance and Literary Art', in *Semeia* 46 (1989): 77–85. The idea preceded the term; the first reference to the idea that I am now aware of comes from Jay Wilcoxen, discussing three forms of ritual in Josh 6 and commenting, 'On any single occasion, however, only one of the forms must have been selected' ('Narrative Structure and Cult Legend: A Study of Joshua 1–6', in *Transitions in Biblical Scholarshi*, JC Rylaarsdam (ed) (Chicago: University of Chicago Press, 1968), 43–70, see 53; see also his 'Narrative', in *Old Testament Form Criticism*, JH Hayes (ed) (San Antonio: Trinity University Press, 1974), 57–98, especially, 'Gunkel may have missed the point of the brevity of the present texts. The individual stories are not brief because ancient narrations were brief, but because these texts only present basic plots which in any actual narration would be expanded and elaborated according to the skill of the storyteller and the occasion of his performance.' (65).

story and storyteller go hand in hand. Where distribution is limited, the impact of a story tradition has to be mediated to the many by a few. The reported story is a base for those few. Where literacy is limited, the telling of a story is mediated to those who cannot easily read by those who can. The reported story is a base for such storytelling. Where the length of a text is limited, the telling of a story will necessarily be expanded beyond the text on which it is based. The reported story reflects precisely that.

The limited length of the independent smaller story units in biblical narrative will be discussed below. We may anticipate one detail. The slow reading aloud of some ten verses of biblical narrative occupies about three minutes. The record of an hour's storytelling, therefore, would require something in the order of two hundred verses of text. When we reflect on this, it is clear that the great narratives, such as the Pentateuch or the Deuteronomistic History, needed the abbreviation of the story traditions from which they were composed. If we assume the practice of storytelling in ancient Israel and if we assume that the telling of stories lasted more than a few minutes, we are faced with the undeniable fact that many of Israel's stories had to be abbreviated in order to take their place in the great narrative compositions of ancient Israel.

Of course, such abbreviation could be envisaged as a relatively rare procedure, used when longer narratives were to be composed. The practiced skill of the narrators makes such a one-off procedure unlikely. The presence in the texts of variants and the like that are better explained as recording possibilities that need actualisation by a storyteller is a powerful argument against any one-off procedure. Such abbreviated records would have preserved Israel's traditions for storytelling. Such abbreviated records would have preserved Israel's traditions for other purposes as well, such as support for or opposition to policies, practices, personalities, and so on.[4]

---

4. That the written texts might have served for reading aloud at festivals or similar gatherings is a possibility invited by either ancient or modern practice. Yehoshua Gitay, for example, points to the case of Jeremiah's sayings read aloud by Baruch and other early examples ('Deutero-Isaiah: Oral or Written?', in *JBL* 99 (1980): 185–97, 192–94); Niditch refers to the examples of Josiah, Jeremiah, and Nehemiah (*Oral World and Written Word*, 102–6).Closer reflection is disconcerting. We know little of what was involved in the celebration of ancient Israel's festivals. Of course we have the classic child's question (*Kinderfrage*)

Such abbreviated records would have served as a base for future storytelling, recording the core content of what a story was about and recording variant traditions and variant, even contradictory, views about what was expressed in the tradition. The role of the storyteller is taken for granted in such abbreviated records. Decisions have to be made as to which variant will be told, which view presented, or the extent to which such differences will be put forward in the telling of the story. This task belongs to the storyteller. Those who wanted to use the traditions for purposes other than immediate storytelling would have needed to value and protect these differences or to evaluate them just as a storyteller might be expected to have done.

What will be argued here is that it often is very helpful to recognise that we may be dealing with abbreviated texts in some form or other that need expansion, if they are to be treated as individual stories. That expansion is the actualisation of the text's potential by turning the text into the oral performance or telling of the story. The function of the texts, then, is to serve as a record of the stories' core and potential as well as a base from which the stories can be told. The record of the story and the role of the storyteller are correlatives.

The description I have used for 'reported story' in *1 Samuel* (FOTL 7) may helpfully pinpoint what is meant.

As a genre, reported story is used of narrative texts that stand in only an indirect relationship to the performance of storytelling. Instead, they look in two directions: rearward, back to the storytelling tradition that they report; forward, to the stories to be told in the future.

The rearward glance is the report of storytelling tradition. We know the texts we have and the high quality of their literary style; it is tribute to the quality of ancient Israel's storytelling. Those who told the stories told them well; those who reported the stories reported them well. The plot structure is there. The gems of dialogue are there. The details that go to make a good story are there. There is enough stuff there to hold a report together. The trimmings that any good

---

found in Exod 12:26; 13:14; Deut 6:20; Josh 4:6, 21. The recital such questions evoke is credal in quality; it is not to be confused with storytelling. A few of the biblical story texts could have been used at such festivals; however, they are relatively few. Most of the stories are scarcely suitable for festival use. Synagogues came on the scene too late to be of help.

storyteller can generate are not there. Variant versions are there, even if only briefly noted. A storyteller may choose to use one; no good storyteller would actualise conflicting ones. Contradictory traditions are sometimes noted. Good storytellers knew how to handle them. Fundamentally, a good report preserved whatever possibilities the tradition contained. The aim of a reported story is to recapitulate the story—not to retell it.

The reported story also looks forward as a base for the storyteller whose task is to retell the story. Choices may be made from that base: which variants to tell, which details to include. A good storyteller knows, on any given occasion, which details to provide and which to withhold, which gaps to fill and which to leave as gaps. A good storyteller knows when to extend a story and when to shorten it. The base may contain several variants; the good storyteller will only actualise one and will know which is the right one to actualise for the particular audience. It is not a matter of being bound to a text but bound to a story—to the opportunities that a text offered and limited for the telling of a story. To be more nuanced for later generations: canonically, it is a matter of being bound to a text; aesthetically, it may be a matter of being bound to a story, which in its own appropriate fashion is duly bound to the text.

The reported story preserves a past tradition, rehearsed in the telling of the story, and prepares for a future rehearsal of the tradition, in the retelling of the story. There is a structured move from the oral into the written with a view to returning to the oral. We have no certainty that such reported stories functioned as bases for storytelling; it is an assumption, based on respectable grounds. The description given is fully compatible with the processes described in the field studies reported by Culley and Long.[5]

How Israel's traditions, preserved in some instances as reported stories, can be woven into Israel's longer narratives is adequately illustrated in 1 Samuel. Clearly, it is possible for a longer report to be condensed for the sake of an extended narrative. Clearly, it is equally possible for a terse report to be expanded during its incorporation into another narrative. We cannot identify where such possibilities

---

5. Robert C Culley, *Studies in the Structure of Hebrew Narrative* (Philadelphia: Fortress, 1976) especially 4–20; Burke O Long, 'Recent Field Studies in Oral Literature and Their Bearing on OT Criticism', in *VT* 26 (1976): 187–98.

may have been actualised. What we can affirm is this: some texts bear characteristics that point to the reporting of stories rather than the performing of stories. Such characteristics do not affect any canonical aspects of a text, which are unchanged. Instead, they point to the possibility of a text's addressing both readers and also storytellers—which can change matters quite significantly.

Reported story: The evidence

The basic issue confronting us is not whether the idea of a reported story makes sense but whether such a practice existed in ancient Israel and may be visible in some of our biblical texts. Of the three factors noted at the beginning, only the brevity of the texts needs further discussion. Limited distribution is obvious, given the invention of printing a couple of thousand years later—although what we know as history may not always permeate our imaginings. Limited literacy is also clear, not simply in terms of the issues of literacy in an ancient agrarian society but also in terms of ease of access to sophisticated documents in most societies. Our familiarity with biblical texts may mean that we have to be shocked into realising the significance of their brevity.

This section will, therefore, move in three stages: first, some reflection on the brevity of many narrative texts in the Older Testament; second, detailed analyses of some texts to show the need for the storyteller's role in expanding the biblical text we have; and third, some further examples, without the same detailed analysis.

It is important to be clear from the outset that there is no intention to demonstrate that all biblical narrative consisted of reported stories. It did not. It has already been noted that biblical stories vary considerably in length. This variation may reflect the complexity of some stories or their suitability for abbreviation. It may also reflect fascination with the task of rendering stories in reduced written form. Some stories can be easily reported; others seduce the reporter into at least a partial telling of the story. What is argued here is that some of the shorter biblical story texts can be understood as reported stories that leave a significant role for the storyteller.[6] The attribution of a

---

6. This view is not unprecedented in scholarship; its implications have not so far been systematically explored. So, for example, Susan Niditch comments,

role to the storyteller resolves significant problems in these texts. It may be important to extend this understanding to texts where it is not so evidently demonstrable.

'We also think it entirely possible that the telling of pan-Israelite stories was aided by notes or some sort of written texts' *(Oral World and Written Word*, 122). Stephanie Dalley points to the possibility of something similar in some Sumerian and Akkadian literature. 'We should probably understand some of the abrupt changes of theme as bare skeletons which were fleshed out in practice by skilled narrators' (*Myths from Mesopotamia: Creation, the Flood, Gilgamesh and Others* [Oxford: Oxford University Press, 1989], xvi). Alexander Rofé waxed justifiably indignant over Gunkel's paternalism. He comments, 'The oral stage must have been longer, much longer, than the version we have now in scripture . . . [Whoever] reduced these narratives to writing took the pains, and had the skill, to condense them' ('The Classification of the Prophetical Stories', in *JBL* 89 [1970]: 427–40, 432–33). Even Erich Auerbach's famed comparison of Genesis with Homer, concluding that Hebrew narrative was 'fraught with background', in my judgment identifies factors that can point to the reported story. For example: 'The two styles, in their opposition, represent basic types: on the one hand [that is, Homer] fully externalised description, uniform illumination, uninterrupted connection . . . all events in the foreground, displaying unmistakable meanings . . . ; on the other hand [that is, the OT], certain parts brought into high relief, others left obscure, abruptness, suggestive influence of the unexpressed, 'background' quality, multiplicity of meanings and the need for interpretation . . . ' (*Mimesis: The Representation of Reality in Western Literature* [Princeton, NJ: Princeton University Press, 1953; original, 1946], 23). Auerbach's description of the Older Testament style reflects exactly what is said here of the reported story.
This assumes a quite different culture from the illiterate singers of Yugoslavia central to Albert B Lord's *The Singer of Tales* (New York: Atheneum, 1971; original edition, 1960). In their performances, rather than telling stories, the singers created poems with markedly formulaic characteristics. Their illiteracy is not a key difference. Rather it is a matter of, first, formulaic poem versus story and, second, the manner of acquisition of new material. A new song was acquired by listening to a full performance of the song (even if read to the illiterate singer), not by extrapolating from an abbreviated report, oral or written (assumed above as a possibility). However, 'identical' performances related to themes and outlines rather than to words; repeat performances were not verbatim repetitions. There is an aspect of Lord's treatment of 'theme' that may reinforce our reflections here. The theme for Yugoslav oral poets, akin to Robert Alter's 'type-scene', can be grasped when heard and then given particular expression by the individual singer (cf Lord's *The Singer of Tales*, 68–98). Making due allowance for the difference between creating formulaic narrative poems and telling prose stories, note Lord's 'he [the singer] builds his performance . . . on the stable skeleton of narrative' (Lord's *The Singer of Tales*, 99). The oral and written techniques discussed by Lord (for example, Lord's *The Singer of Tales*, 129) are not our issues here.

Brevity: the brevity of the texts we have
The limited length of the smaller story units in our biblical narrative texts can be addressed by going back to Hermann Gunkel, the pioneer of the academic study of biblical storytelling. Gunkel's observations in the Introduction to his classic commentary on Genesis are addressed primarily to the issues of the stories told.[7] Beyond noting that the writing down of stories is a later stage in development and making the revealing comment that written versions are likely to be longer than oral versions ('for the eye can take in larger units in reading than the ear in hearing'),[8] there is no reflection on the relationship between biblical text and oral performance. Gunkel is concerned with oral storytelling, the storytellers, and the audience.

For Gunkel, the telling of stories, in the earliest stages, lasted scarcely fifteen minute.[9] The cultural prejudice underpinning this perception is blatant and unsustainable today. According to Gunkel, the brevity of these earliest stories reflected the art of the storytellers and the capacity of their audience; neither the earliest storytellers nor their hearers were able to cope with longer stories. After fifteen minutes or so, the audience's capacity to listen was exhausted; for Gunkel, the ancient Israelites are to be compared with 'our children' ('so wie unsere Kinder').[10]

Perhaps the cultural prejudice was overwhelming or Gunkel's mind was elsewhere, because unfortunately there is no reflection on the correlation of this view of ancient storytelling and the biblical text of these stories. The stories Gunkel was discussing are of the ten-verse range. While the 'scarcely a quarter hour' allowed ancient audiences is untenably short, the biblical texts are shorter still. On

---

7. Hermann Gunkel, *Genesis*, third edition (Göttingen: Vandenhoeck & Ruprecht, 1910).
8. Gunkel, *Genesis*, XXXIV. 'So ist es zu größeren Gestaltungen gekommen. Begünstigt ward dieses Anschwellen der Sagen besonders dadurch, daß man begann die Sagen niederzuschreiben; nun ist aber das Geschriebene seiner Natur nach weitläufiger als das Gesprochene; denn das Auge vermag beim Lesen größere Einheiten aufzufassen, als das Ohr beim Hören.'
9. 'Die kaum ein Viertelstündchen ausfüllen' (XXXIV). In the first edition (1901), Gunkel allowed for 'not much over half an hour' (from the translation of the Introduction, WH Carruth, [New York: Schocken, 1901] ,47). This was changed to a quarter hour in the second edition (1902), as noted by Jay A Wilcoxen ('Narrative', 64).
10. *Genesis*, XXXIV.

average, ten verses of biblical Hebrew take some three minutes to read aloud slowly. The implication is unavoidable: even imagining the most unacceptable constraints of storytelling, our written texts must have been expanded in the oral telling of their stories. This appears to stand as an incontestable datum.

Story texts in need of the storyteller: detailed analyses
It will be helpful to look more closely at some story texts that seem to demand expansion. As a rule, normal biblical storytelling does not contradict itself, does not run different scenarios for the same story, and does not locate key elements of a plot in the wrong place. Some of the story passages in our narrative texts do one or other of these things, raising the questions: what is their function? what sort of texts are they? We will take a couple from each category for closer analysis.

Contradicts itself
For an Israel that had never had the institution of monarchy, the establishment of a king was a powerfully significant experience. It needed explanation; it evoked theological evaluation. 1 Samuel 9:1–10:16 portrays kingship as God's gift, given Israel for defense against external foes. 'He [the king-to-be] shall save my people from the hand of the Philistines; for I have seen the suffering of my people' (9:16). On the other hand, 1 Sam 7:1–8:22 portrays a situation where kingship was unnecessary for external defense—Samuel provided that by interceding with God—but became necessary for internal justice. Samuel had made his sons judges over Israel and his sons took bribes and perverted justice (cf 1 Sam 8:1–3). So 1 Samuel 8:1–22 portrays kingship originating in God's order, responding to Israel's request flowing from the need for internal justice. 'Listen to their voice and set a king over them' (8:22).

The negative theological evaluation of kingship is also expressed within 1 Sam 8:1–22. The elders' request for monarchy is judged to be apostasy: 'they have rejected me from being king over them' (8:7). The result is high tension: in ordering Samuel to set a king over them God is, according to the text, ordering apostasy. This is not God's normal practice; the embarrassing ambivalence is well known. Recent commentaries are revealing: kingship is not welcomed but indulged, sanctioned in 'a backhanded way' (McCarter); God's generosity despite

Israel's 'sinful request' (Klein); God's grudging grant, characterised as 'permitted-but-disapproved' (Brueggemann).[11] Israel has rejected God in asking for a king (8:7–8); God commands the granting of a king (8:22).

Technically speaking, the traditions of 1 Samuel 8 are formulated as accounts; however, the potential for storytelling and expansion is there. A less troubling text is achieved if the role of the storyteller is respected and the negative theological evaluation is regarded as an inbuilt option that the storyteller will take into account. A storyteller might emphasise God's instruction, omitting the characterisation as rejection, or might emphasise the rejection involved in the request, omitting the divine command to grant it, or might present both, reflecting on the implications. The dilemma can be approached in various ways. Recognising options for the storyteller is one of them.

Similarly, the conclusion to 1 Samuel 15 contains an inbuilt contradiction. Saul, who has disobeyed, begs for forgiveness and for Samuel to return with him; Samuel refuses. 'I will not return with you' (15:26). A little later, Saul repeats his request and this time Samuel accedes to it. 'So Samuel turned back after Saul' (15:31). The difficulty is compounded by the presence of v 29, insisting that God does not change God's mind. Once the role of the storyteller is allowed for and the preservation of variant traditions is taken into account, the text becomes intelligible as a reported story. Expanding the abbreviated text, a storyteller could omit the scene with Samuel's **cloak and proceed from Saul's request (v 25) to Samuel's granting it (v 31)**. Or a storyteller might emphasise the rejection and omit Samuel's return and his slaughter of Agag. Or the storyteller might develop the understanding that forgiveness of Saul's sin does not revoke the rejection of his kingship. The text holds together both Samuel's refusal and his return.

Runs different scenarios for the same story
The manner of David's emergence on the public scene in Israel attracted the interest that might be expected. Two quite different scenarios have been preserved, both being combined in the MT and

---

11. P Kyle McCarter, Jr, *I Samuel*, AB 8 (Garden City: Doubleday, 1980), 162; Ralph W Klein, *1 Samuel*, WBC 10 (Waco: Word, 1983), 79; Walter Brueggemann, *First and Second Samuel* (Interpretation; Louisville: John Knox, 1990), 63, 66.

only one preserved in the LXX.[12] In one presentation, David is the faith-filled armor-bearer: 'The LORD, who saved me from the paw of the lion and from the paw of the bear will save me from the hand of this Philistine' (1 Sam 17:37). In the other presentation, David is the ambitious achiever (even adventurer, mover-and-shaker) who saw his chance and seized it: 'What shall be done for the man who kills this Philistine' (1 Sam 17:26). In the first case, David is one whose destiny was thrust on him and who loyally fulfilled it; in the second, David is one blessed with luck and ambitious enough to take advantage of it.

The presentation of David the ambitious achiever is a good example of a reported story because it is incomplete. The key segments are given; the intervening details are left to the storyteller's imagination. First, there is David's arrival on the scene, with the Philistine's challenge and David's inquiries (17:12–30); second, after the killing, there is David's encounter with Saul and then Jonathan (17:55–18:5); third, there is the denial of Saul's daughter Merab to David and the increasing enmity between David and Saul (18:17–19, 29b–30). The killing of the Philistine is swiftly dealt with (17:48b, 50); a couple of other details are noted. For the most part, the shape to be given the story is left to the storyteller.

The present MT text hints at ways of combining the two presentations (cf 17:15, 16, 31). A skilled storyteller might do so, pointing to the complexity of all human motivation and reflecting how faith need not exclude ambition or how ambition can fire faith. The text juxtaposes the two presentations without interpretation. Alternatively, a storyteller might have told the story with emphasis on the ambitious David who made the best of an unexpected opportunity or on the faith-filled David who stepped into the gap left by the dispirited Saul. The present text preserves both traditions and entrusts their appropriate actualisation to the storyteller.

The story of Jonathan's final determination of Saul's attitude toward David is reported in 1 Samuel 20; in the event of Saul's hostility, Jonathan must get a message to David without betraying David's whereabouts. David considers Saul's hostility to be definitive; Jonathan believes that is not the case. So David is to hide in the countryside and Jonathan

---

12. There is wide-ranging discussion around these texts; no consensus has yet emerged. For details, see Campbell, *1 Samuel*; for a visual presentation of the texts, see Campbell and O'Brien, *Unfolding the Deuteronomistic History*, 258–65.

is to explore the situation and get word to David. If Saul is hostile, Jonathan must be careful not to give away David's hiding place. As it stands, the text holds three possibilities: a sign to David, a message for David, a meeting with David—a sign given David by the shooting of arrows (20:18–22, 36–37); a message given David solely by the shout to the servant (20:38); a farewell meeting after the servant has been dismissed (20:40–42). The story could well be told actualising only one option for getting the message across, the shout (v 38), the sign (vv 18–22), or the meeting (vv 40–42). Or two options might be actualised: after the shout or the sign, the servant is dismissed and the pair meet. Or all three options are actualised: the sign is followed by the shout and eventually the meeting. The text retains all three options but leaves their actualisation to the storyteller. Naturally, as the event unfolds the best of plans may be abandoned—for example, if a sign is not seen or a shout not heard, or under the emotional pressure for one last meeting and farewell. The text, however, does not report an event but reports a story and leaves the choices and explanations to the storyteller.

Locates key elements of a plot in the wrong place
Denied Merab, David married Saul's daughter Michal. The story of David's escape, let down from a window during the night, is a classic that pits David's wife against her father, Saul (1 Sam 19:11–17). There is great potential for the exchange in which Michal convinces David that she knows her father better then he does. There is also great potential in the exchanges between Michal and her father's soldiers, fobbing them off while David gets clear away. The text includes the motif of a 'dummy in the bed' as proof that poor David was indeed sick.

 Two elements reveal the text as a reported story, rather than the account of an anecdote's performance. First, there is the report of Saul's putting David's house under surveillance with the intention of killing him in the morning (19:11). Nothing in the text accounts for Saul's change of mind and his seeking David during the night. Learning that David had fled would account for the change of mind; it is incompatible with seeking David at the house. Second, and more significant for our purposes, is the placement of the motif of the dummy in the bed. The function of the dummy is to convince Saul's soldiers that David is sick in bed and cannot be brought to Saul. In the present text, the motif of the dummy is left until too late, after Saul's order 'Bring him up to me in the bed that I may kill him' (19:15). At that point, Saul's decision has been made and no time is to be gained. But time is gained for David to get farther out of reach of possible pursuit if the dummy is introduced into the story between the first and second part of v 15. Saul sends his soldiers 'to see David' (v 15a) and they are shown the dummy in the bed and are convinced that David is indeed sick and in bed. The soldiers report to Saul what they have seen and are ordered, 'Bring him up to me in the bed' (v 15b). But the text does not do that. It retards appeal to the dummy until v 16—too late to be of any use.

It makes eminently good sense to read the text as a reported story, offering two ways in which the story might be presented, one relying entirely on Michal's rhetorical skills, the other appealing to the dummy to reinforce her case (so Josephus AJ 6.217–18, with the added graphic detail of a liver quivering to simulate a fever-racked patient). Either option is possible; the sequence in the present text is not. The text offers options to the storyteller and relies on the storyteller to choose appropriately.

A final example can be taken from the well-known story of Saul's vulnerability while easing nature in a desert cave (Heb, 1 Sam 24:2–23; NRSV, 24:1–22). Saul entered a cave to respond to a call of nature while David and his men were lurking in the recesses of the cave. The troops saw this as David's God-given chance to kill Saul (24:5a; NRSV, 24:4a). Instead, David stealthily cut off a corner of Saul's cloak. After David has taken not Saul's life but the corner of his cloak, and only after this, David is smitten with remorse and rebukes his men for their proposal, insisting on Saul's inviolability as the LORD's anointed. David 'did not permit them to attack Saul' (24:8a; NRSV, 24:7a). Clearly, two traditions are intermingled: first, sparing the king without further complication; second, resisting the urging to kill the king.

What prevents the text from being a simple unfolding of a plot combining both elements is that the protest against an attack on Saul comes after David has cut off a corner of Saul's cloak. Ordinarily, we would expect protest against violence to the royal person to come first, then the corner of the cloak to be cut off instead as a symbol of the power to kill that was not exercised. The text does not do this. While the ordinary is not necessarily the golden rule of storytelling, in this case the protest is out of place (it comes a couple of verses too late) and David's remorse over the corner of Saul's cloak does not fit with what follows where David waves it in proud token of his sparing the LORD's anointed. This is not a story of the sacredness of the royal person but of sparing the royal life; the issue is whether to kill or not to kill. David's belated protest, 'the LORD forbid that I should do this thing to my lord . . . to raise my hand against him' (v 7; NRSV, v 6) clearly reflects more than snipping a corner of the royal cloak. The proposal to kill Saul may be an option for the storyteller to exploit; it is not a plot development in the text. As in so many cases, recognition of the possibility of a reported story may be a preferable alternative to emending or reordering the text.

Various options are open: a storyteller could have David demonstrate that he had been in a position to kill Saul, without involving any incitement from David's men; or the incitement from David's men could have been made explicit, with David's rebuke to them preceding his sparing Saul's life (while cutting a corner from Saul's cloak as evidence of his respect for the king's life); or his men might have been portrayed seeking authorisation to kill Saul themselves, a permission David refused. Possibilities are open; the text holds them all. A competent storyteller will choose among them and tell the story appropriately.

Story texts in need of the storyteller: further examples
From Joshua
The text of the Jordan crossing (Joshua 3–4) is more appropriately treated as a base story that has been annotated with liturgical options and the like instead of an unconvincing weaving of incomplete traditions. The text of the fall of Jericho (Josh 6:3–20) lacks plausibility as present text or a combination of sources. It makes sense as a base script with inbuilt options, suitable for storytelling or liturgy, either suspenseful and silent (Alfred Hitchcock) or showy and noisy (Cecil B de Mille).[13]

---

13. See the treatment of both passages in Campbell and O'Brien, *Unfolding the Deuteronomistic History*, 112–17 and 119–23.

From Judges

Jephthah's story might be told of a hero empowered by the spirit (Judg 11:29) or of a warrior who made an unfortunate vow and stubbornly stuck to it (Judg 11:30–31). These are options for a storyteller. After being gifted with the spirit, a vow is unnecessary; the gift of the spirit is demeaned by a foolish vow. Samson's too is a cycle that offers a storyteller multiple options. Samson 'shall begin to deliver Israel' (Judg 13:5). Which will get the emphasis: the beginner or the deliverer? Samson is scarcely a hero figure.[14] With Delilah, for example: three times he is deceived and betrayed; but no matter, for three times he has lied. Smart. The proverbial fourth time of course, he was deceived and betrayed again; but this time it did matter, for he had told the truth. Not smart at all. No theological nobility either; savage selfishness instead—'So that with this one act of revenge I may pay back the Philistines for my two eyes' (Judg 16:28). What a contrast with David facing the Philistine (1 Sam 17:45–47).

From First Samuel

A storyteller's development of the text base is needed for the story of David and Saul in the cave (1 Samuel 24). We have already seen the inbuilt options related to the earlier stage within the cave. A storyteller is badly needed to actualise the scene outside the cave and make some choices. The present text has David emerge from the cave, do obeisance and hold an exchange of speeches with Saul, waving the corner of Saul's cloak as evidence of his loyalty to the king—while all the time three thousand of Saul's picked warriors are presumably present (cf 24:3; NRSV, 24:2). Saul then asks the 'night-time' question: 'Is this your voice, my son David?' (24:17; NRSV, 24:16; cf 1 Sam 26:17). A storyteller could easily have Saul keep his troops at bay with a royal gesture or have David slip away through a gully behind the cave and call to Saul unseen from the safety of a section of forest higher up the hill. The text does neither. A storyteller could follow Robert Alter's option and have Saul blinded with tears.[15] The text, however, does not; it places the tears after the question and ignores the troops.

---

14. Gerhard von Rad comments: 'The oddest figure amongst the judges is Samson: the reader will indeed find it absolutely impossible to understand him as judge over Israel' (*Old Testament Theology,* 2 volumes [Edinburgh: Oliver and Boyd, 1962–65] 1.333).
15. *The David Story* (New York: Norton, 1999), 150–51.

From Second Samuel
The stories of 2 Samuel 11–20 are renowned for the issues they raise and the gaps they leave.[16] These chapters may have served their purpose as literary texts. They are also wonderful bases for multiple storytelling. In the case of Bathsheba and David, for example, a storyteller might choose to note whether Bathsheba's washing was unduly revealing or not and whether it mattered. The text is silent (2 Sam 11:2). A storyteller might reflect on Bathsheba's feelings going to or returning from David's palace. The text is silent (11:4). A storyteller might have spent time on why she sent the dangerous message, 'I am pregnant', and what David's options might have been. The text is silent (11:5–6). And so many more. When Absalom's revolt is announced, David takes flight from Jerusalem without a word of counsel. What became of the claim for the impregnable city that 'even the blind and lame will turn you back' (2 Sam 5:6)? The text is silent. Hushai's runners hid in a well at Bahurim (2 Sam 17:15–20). Details of why it was risky for them to be seen and how Absalom's people knew to search the house at Bahurim are not given. A servant girl has been introduced as an apparently regular courier (17:17); the present text leaves no time for any such repeated activity.

From First Kings
Rehoboam's loss of the north invites development (1 Kgs 12:1–20). Were the young counselors greedy? Were the old wise? How was God's will at work? A choice is forced on the storyteller: was Jeroboam called to Shechem before (v 3) or after (v 20) the political split? In the Naboth story (1 Kings 21), a storyteller might have focused on the responsibility of either Ahab or Jezebel, or might have combined the two more thoroughly. The text leaves these options open in vv 1–16 and includes multiple traditions in vv 17–29.

From Second Kings
The strange and complex text of 2 Kings 3 mingles water and war, victory and retreat, two kings or three. A storyteller faced choices or development. In 2 Kings 13, King Joash is buried in v 13 and visits the dying Elisha in v 14; the concluding regnal formula for Joash is

---

16. M Sternberg's treatment of gaps is classic (cf chapter 6 of *The Poetics of Biblical Narrative* [Bloomington: Indiana University Press, 1985], especially 190–222).

given at 13:12 and repeated at 14:15. There is storytelling material in between, some of it far from edifying. The king of Israel not only defeated Judah—a case of fratricidal strife; he also broke down a couple of hundred yards of the defensive wall of Jerusalem and plundered the treasures of the temple of the Lord (2 Kgs 14:12–14). The text presents the material; a storyteller could have chosen how to handle it.

Multiplying examples would take us through most of the storytelling texts of the biblical tradition. The brevity of the texts and the nature of the texts combine to make a powerful case for the movement from oral to written to oral—the reported story recapitulates the oral performance, can be integrated into one of Israel's longer narrative compositions, and can serve as base for future retellings of the tradition. Israel's longer narrative compositions exist. Storytelling does not stop because of such creations. A culture that had a place for the reported story or its equivalent may have existed too. A role may have been assumed for the storyteller.

Reported story: The implications

The implications of the reported story for critical analysis of the smaller story units of the biblical text are highly beneficial. By relegating to the storyteller the task of smoothing out minor issues in the text or of selecting between competing traditions within the text, critical analysis can give its attention to more major issues in relation to the text. Once the storyteller's role has been recognised and revalued, the intolerable fragmentation of texts through a series of editorial refinements can be avoided. For the most part, the difficulties involved can be entrusted to the good sense of the skilled storyteller.

This understanding of much narrative text also allows for due respect to be paid to the skills and intelligence of ancient editors. Observation of editorial activity in major parts of the biblical text points to a high level of skill and intelligence on the part of ancient editors. Editors, as well as storytellers, can add alternatives or even contrary views to the abbreviated texts either because they see a need for the preservation of such views or on the understanding that storytellers will be quite capable of handling them appropriately.

In its turn, this has implications for postmodern interpretation of the text. Reported stories can be expected to have come from a number of different hands or people. Their integration into more extensive compositions need not involve their being rewritten; any interpretation needs to respect the differences of their origins. Interpretation of the final text should not be such as to devalue the process by which the text has come into being. Equally, the process of growth should not be envisaged in ways that devalue the final text.

The implications of the reported story for aesthetic appreciation leave the situation unchanged. Where beauty has been found in specific narrative passages, it remains there. The actual performance of biblical storytelling has never been accessible to the post-biblical observer. We may assume that where stories were skillfully and artfully reported, similarly stories will have been skillfully and artfully told. The aesthetics of text may be better appreciated when it is taken for granted that fractious tensions in a reported story may be addressed by the teller of the story.

The implications for the canonical authority of biblical narrative should be noted. The text accepted by the Jewish and Christian communities remains the biblical text. The pluralism that has been openly avowed in the biblical text is open to potential expansion—that is, the recognition of variant versions allows for greater clarity in understanding. In one form or another, this pluralism has always been there. The idea of the reported story and the revaluing of the role of the storyteller enhance the text without diminishing its value.

Women Storytellers in Ancient Israel

(original: *ABR* 48, 2000)

Something of a paradigm shift has been in the making for a while in biblical studies. A future shape has yet to jell. The old historical-critical analysis has not been generating new life for a long time.¹ Other approaches have not so far struck lasting root. The interaction of developmental (cf diachronic) reading and interpretational (cf synchronic) reading is under way, but far from any agreed integration. A resolution of tensions between critical and literary approaches is still on the far horizon. The factors involved in any shift are complex; among them, the often competing needs of faith communities, universities, and so many competent individuals. One element in the total equation is surely scholarly assumptions about the nature of much biblical narrative text.

Assumptions are unavoidable. We live with them all the time. Like automatic routines, they help simplify life and eliminate the overburden of decisions to be faced at every turn. Like routines, assumptions can be dangerous; they can trap us in ruts we do not even realise. Those we are least aware of can be the most dangerous. Assumptions must be re-examined regularly; the outgrown need to be replaced.²

---

1. Herbert Hahn's comment was made over half a century ago: 'The conclusion seems to be unavoidable that the higher criticism has long since passed the age of constructive achievement' (*The Old Testament in Modern Research* [Philadelphia: Fortress, 1966; original, 1954], 41).
2. One of the great values of Susan Niditch's recent book, *Oral World and Written Word: Ancient Israelite Literature* (Louisville: Westminster John Knox, 1996) is that it seeks to bring to the surface some of our unconscious assumptions about literature and ancient Israel. Undoubtedly, some will feel that assumptions of little importance have been caricatured. Yet even caricature serves to challenge; and given what we know today of ancient Israel, it is time to reexamine and

This note is about an assumption current in biblical studies that needs reexamination and replacement. The assumption concerns the gender of tellers of stories in ancient Israel. There are three texts that are good evidence for the assumption that storytellers in ancient Israel included women as a matter of course.

Storytellers in ancient Israel
There are stories in the Bible; it is assumed there were storytellers. We know almost nothing about them. Their belonging to something akin to a medieval guild has been thought probable, but there is a paucity of evidence for it.³ Until now, most people considered it a safe assumption that storytellers in ancient Israel were normally men. Three little texts in out of the way places suggest that it is not a safe assumption any longer. Eighty-year-old Barzillai lists the pleasures of court life as food, drink, and 'the voice of singing men and singing women' (2 Sam 19:35, MT v 36). Among the royal pleasures, Qohelet lists 'singers, both men and women' (Qoh 2:8). According to the Chronicler, King Josiah rated a mention in the laments of 'all the singing men and singing women' following his death (2 Chron 35:25). The same pair of words is used in all three texts: *sharim wesharot*. They are not to be confused with the markedly different terms used for the male and female temple singers (*mesharerim wemesharerot*).

It is an assumption we make that these palace singers were among the storytellers of Israel, whether their stories were told or sung. It is not unlikely. In that case, we have evidence for the existence of Israel's storytellers and for their being both men and women. Presumably the palace performers were at the top of their profession; presumably then other practitioners existed elsewhere in Israelite society.⁴ One clear example in the biblical text would be the 'wise woman' hired by Joab in 2 Samuel 14. For the job envisaged, she needs to be unknown

---

challenge assumptions.
A recent study building on Niditch's work is Raymond F Person, Jr, 'The Ancient Israelite Scribe as Performer', in *JBL* 117 (1998): 601–9.
3. See, for example, Cyrus H Gordon, *Before the Bible* (London: Collins, 1962), 37–38; see also Gunkel, *Genesis*, third edition xxxi. For a survey of wisdom and women across the ancient Near East, see *The Sage in Israel and the Ancient Near East*, edited by JG Gammie and LG Perdue (Winona Lake: Eisenbraun's, 1990).
4. Note two lines of uncertain meaning in Judg 5:10–11, 'Tell of it . . . to the sound of musicians at the watering places, there they repeat the triumphs of the Lord'.

to David and a skilled storyteller. In the narrative, when the king intervenes suspecting Joab's influence, she switches flawlessly into a polished piece of political flattery. A professional storyteller would fit the bill perfectly. There may be several reasons for using a woman in the role, but the parallel is with the king and his son; the part could have been played by a man.

The gender of the storyteller need not impact on the gender bias of the storytelling. Storytellers earned their living by satisfying their patrons. In a male-dominated society, that might not have left much place for reflection on the lot of most women.

Child Sacrifice and God Wrestling: Genesis 22 and 32

Original: Adapted from *Genesis Revisited: A New Reading–Beyond Sources* [in preparation])

The two most outrageous stories in the Bible have to be what Christians call the sacrifice of Isaac (in Jewish tradition: the binding of Isaac) and Jacob's wrestling with God all night at the Jabbok. In a recent novel, a son asks his father, 'Daddy, if God ordered it would you sacrifice me?' The father replied, 'No. For the first time in my life I would disobey God'. The son and his father were talking about historic time, this life, here and now. The son asked his question in historic time. Of course the father could only say, 'I would not obey'. In historic time or historic mode, hallucination is always possible; in mythic mode, there is no question of hallucination. The stories of sacrifice and wrestling must not be understood in historic mode. They can only make sense in mythic mode.[1] The participants were the same in both. Not Abraham and Isaac in one or Jacob and the figure at the ford in the other. The participants were God and Israel in both.

In Gerhard von Rad's words about the Jabbok wrestling text: 'It contains experiences of faith that extend from the most ancient period down to the time of the narrator; there is charged to it something of the results of the entire divine history into which Israel was drawn.'[2]

---

1. What on earth do we mean by terms like 'mythic mode'? Myth is one of those ideas that is hard to discuss in less than a book or two. What I am driving at here with 'mythic mode' is a concern that focuses on matters of primal importance. Because they are primal, they cannot be restricted to individuals and cannot be restricted to concrete times and places. Stories illustrating them (myths) have to involve individuals and localities but what is characteristic of a myth—in the sense I am using it here—is the telling of a story that gets at the core of things and that goes beyond the individuals involved. Faith in God and God's commitment are primal. How these play out in human life is explored in stories that belong in mythic mode.
2. Gerhard von Rad, *Genesis*, ET: (Philadelphia, PN: revised edition Westminster,

To understand the mythic, we need to put our resistance to the historic stories aside.³ So Jacob is wrestling an uncertain figure: a man at the start of the story, Yahweh at its end. The wrestling lasted all night, as Jacob's had lasted all his life. Finally, God pulled a move that only God could pull: he dislocated Jacob's hip. Jacob is done for, finished as a wrestler. Only his upper body is not directly affected. Jacob has his hold. All he can do is hold on. Then God speaks: 'Let me go.' Jacob's strained and sweaty face begins a smile. God is obliged to go. While Jacob holds on, God cannot go. So God blesses Jacob: 'Your name is Israel.' Jacob has got what he needs; he can let God go. He can smile as the sun rose upon him, limping because of his hip, smiling because he had hung on. He had prevailed.

The story begins with 'a man' and it ends with 'a God', the God of Israel. In historic mode, identification would be needed; participants do not trade identities so easily. In mythic mode, it can go on without problem. Shunning the daylight cannot be Yahweh; naming Jacob Israel can only be Yahweh. In historic mode, impossible; in mythic mode wholly possible.

The message for Israel at all times and for Jacob about to confront Esau and the four hundred, is clear: when everything seems lost, hang on to trust in God and all will be well. So Jacob does and everything is not lost but all is well.

For Abraham, the father, and Isaac, the only son, the story is quite different but its meaning is the same. There is no wrestling match and Abraham has no hold on God and God does not ask to be released at the coming of the day. For all that, the message is the same and the

---

1972), 325,

3. Gunkel was seriously embarrassed by the wrestling text. In Gunkel's view, it had nothing to do with the Jacob-Esau traditions; the God was certainly not Yahweh; the link to the present text was merely the name Penuel (Hermann Gunkel, *Genesis*. ET (Macon, GA: Mercer University Press, 1997). Von Rad sticks to the age of the passage and its role in the present text: 'It was in motion for centuries until it finally crystallised in the final form which it now possesses.' (*Genesis*, 319). Accepting literary unity, Westermann indicates where his own concern is focused: 'What is contested is what has been added subsequently and when, and hence the meaning and purpose of the text as a whole. ... One concludes that the remaining verses, 23–26a, 27, 30, 31a, 32 give a narrative that is self-contained and comprehensible.' (Claus Westermann, *Genesis 12–36*. ET [Minneapolis, MN: Augsburg, 1985], 514). Observation of his commentary suggests that the 'self-contained and comprehensible' is what he deals with.

meaning to be taken to heart by all Israel is the same. There is no place for hallucination in mythic mode; there is always place for delusion in faith. Up against God, in mythic mode, Abraham has one weapon, a weapon far better than a wrestler's hold but a weapon potentially white-anted by delusion or doubt. Abraham's weapon: faith in God's commitment, 'God will provide'. Once mooted, the idea gets massive weight (v 14).

As the story unfolds, God orders Abraham, 'Take your son, your only son Isaac, whom you love and . . . offer him there as a burnt offering' (Gen 22:2. The Hebrew allows a slightly different emphasis holding the proper name till last, 'Take your son, your only son whom you love, Isaac and . . . offer him there as a burnt offering'.) Abraham has his knife in one hand and the other on Isaac. He has no wrestling hold on God. He has also his faith in a commitment God made to him, 'I will make of you a great nation' (Gen 12:2). Without Isaac, this commitment is broken. In historic mode, perhaps not; in mythic mode, certainly. As Abraham looks at God and looks at the knife, he must also look at his faith in God's commitment. As the two look at each other, God and ancestor, which will blink first? Abraham reaches for the knife, Isaac looks into the faith-crazed eyes of his father—and God blinks. The voice is just in time: 'Do not lay your hand on the boy.' God's commitment trumps God's command. We have no reflection on Abraham's experience as he weighed his faith in God's commitment against the reality of God's command.

For Israel, it is its existence that is put on the line; nothing less will do. For God, it is God's commitment to Israel that is put on the line. If Israel holds to its faith in God's commitment, God has no option; God must be faithful to that commitment. Storytellers had no option in illustrating this. Isaac's life had to be on the line; there was no other way of putting Israel's existence on the line. Yes, in the story it is a test of Abraham's faith, in reality of Israel's faith. But it is God's commitment that is being tested. In mythic mode, of course, one cannot test God's commitment; the promise has been made, the commitment is there. In historic mode, the commitment must be trusted in order to be experienced—whatever form the exercise of that commitment takes.

The story of the wrestling at the Jabbok, with 'a man' who in the course of the narrative morphs into the God of Israel, provides the pointer to how both outrageous stories are to be interpreted. In the Jabbok story, the God-figure has to be gone at break of day and so must ask: 'Let me go.' Jacob has God at a disadvantage. Crippled, Jacob can still say: 'I will not let you go.' So God gives Jacob what he needs. In the case of Abraham, there is no wrestling and no fear of daybreak. But God is at a disadvantage. He has made a promise, a commitment, to Abraham and, in mythic mode, what he has said he cannot unsay. In faith, Abraham can only obey. But if Abraham obeys, God cannot carry out God's promise. In the equivalent of a poker game between the two of them, God has to blink first. Otherwise God will be shamed as one who makes a commitment and does not carry it out. So Abraham has God at a disadvantage.

As far as I know, we have no situations in early Israel that fit with the interpretation being suggested—basically: when all else fails, trust God's commitment. Later in Israel's story, the issue looks very different.[4] Up against Assyria or Babylonia, what can Israel do except trust God's commitment. Later passages in Isaiah, for example, speak splendidly of a future. Regrettably, the following centuries do not bear them out. Trust in God's commitment is fine, but we have no idea what it might look like (= Jesus Christ for Christians).

In the story, all Abraham could do was trust in his faith and believe God would blink first. In the other story, all Jacob could do was hang on and wait for God to blink (i.e., ask to be let go). Faced by the overwhelming power of Assyria or Babylonia, little Israel had not much choice: trust in its faith in the nature of God, trust in its faith in the promise and commitment of God.

In looking at these texts, what we have is two outrageous stories that express what is quintessentially Israel's destiny: to hold to faith, to hold to God when all else seems lost. When there is nothing else Abraham can do, he can refuse to lose faith in God's commitment. When there is nothing else Jacob can do, he can refuse to let go. When there is nothing else Israel can do, it can hold to the faith that God will provide, it can hold on to God and never let go.

---

4. In his critical analysis of the Jabbok text, Westermann occasionally uses age to determine additions. The perils of such a procedure are obvious (*Genesis 12–36*, 514).

Preparatory Issues in Approaching Biblical Text
(Original: *The Blackwell Companion to the Hebrew Bible*)

Interpretation does not happen in a void. Interpretation emerges out of a context and speaks into a context. Interpreters are not disembodied voices. There is an interplay of interests at work, whether social or emotional, cultural or national, academic, financial, or religious. It is tempting to focus exclusively on the insights and achievements of individuals; these are usually accessible in their publications. We need to be aware of the existence of wider influences and interests that surge around individual scholars and shape something of their work.

This contribution to *A Companion to the Old Testament* aims at providing those interested with a basic understanding of some of the insights and practices at work in modern scholarship. Fundamentally, this means coming to grips with preparatory questions that may be relevant for modern biblical study and recognising elements important for the exploration of a biblical text. There is no such beast as 'modern biblical scholarship'; there is a multitude of biblical scholars. Observations about what is done must, therefore, remain tentatively sketchy; not everyone will recognise themselves. On the other hand, what is written here may initiate people into what this practitioner believes are among the central preparatory tasks of biblical interpretation.

This contribution is not a history of modern biblical interpretation. That has been done in German (Kraus, 1969). Something similar has been done in English (Hahn, 1966). John Rogerson has gone into detail for the 19th century in Germany and England (Rogerson, 1984). A study of the Hebrew Bible and its modern interpreters has appeared in the SBL centennial trilogy (Knight and Tucker, editors, 1985). Significant figures and movements have left their mark on modern biblical interpretation; their concerns cannot be ignored. Here, however, respectful mention of our forebears will be subordinated to the attempt to prepare for the task that they have left to us: interpreting the biblical text.

The key element of biblical interpretation in recent centuries can be summed up in the adjective 'critical'. 'Historical-critical' is misleading; it can suggest a concern with history that is not necessarily central. Understood as the opposite of 'ahistorical', 'historical' describes a state of intellectual awareness; in this acceptation, 'historical-critical' is an acceptable descriptor. 'Method' is misleading; it can suggest predetermined steps that follow each other in logical sequence instead of the verification of insight and intuition. 'Critical' is the element that separates moderns from their predecessors. The interpreters of the past were often great scholars and brilliant minds. But at a certain point in the intellectual history of western Europe a critical spirit emerged and decisively influenced the way that texts have been read ever since. It is this critical spirit that we need to identify and see at work in the task of interpretation.

Some maps of the United States trace a continental divide or watershed from Montana to New Mexico. Mountains obviously mess this up—for example, the Appalachians in the northeast or the San Gabriels in the southwest. The messiness is helpful for the use of watershed as a literary metaphor. For there is a watershed between the process of a text's coming into being, its growth and development, and the task of interpreting the text that has come into being, that exists. But it is messy. There is no hermetic partition keeping the two aspects apart; they tend to impact on one another. Where biblical text is concerned, most of the issues discussed in this chapter explore aspects of the development of a text, its coming into being. The modern issues relating to the task of interpreting the already existing text are treated in chapter 2.

Beneath the watershed separating development from interpretation lies the massive issue of the nature of the text involved. The issue can be considered from the point of view of the origins of the text: from above or from below—directly divine (few), directly human (few), somewhere in between (most). Considered reflection reveals that origins do not determine nature. Both divine and human texts can claim to impose thought or to invite to it. The nature of the biblical text can only be determined by observation of the text itself. A signpost pointing in a single direction is helpful to the traveler, if the direction is the right one. Several signposts pointing in different directions to the same destination may also be helpful, but not immediately; perhaps they invite to reflection and further exploration. Many readers will find that the Bible often offers conflicting signposts (that is, competing YHWH faith claims), from extensive issues—such as creation, flood, deliverance at the sea, sojourn in the desert, conquest of the land, emergence of monarchy, and even divine providence—to matters that can be compassed in a verse or two. The biblical text tends not to adjudicate, but to amalgamate. In such cases, readers are invited to thought; the signposts point in differing directions. The decision about what is predominantly the nature of biblical text and how it functions is one that needs to be remade out of the experience of the text by each generation of its readers. Any other way risks dogmatism or superstition. These considerations should not deflect attention from the complementary roles of the biblical text: to arouse feeling, fire imagination, and fuel faith.

It may also be helpful to realise that we approach texts in much the same way as we approach people. Mutual communication requires us to sort out languages and accents; the influence of cultural origins may be important; at some stage we become aware of whether someone has their act together or can, for example, be subject to unexpected emotions; over time, we come to know something of people's early history and later influences. We have people we meet for the first time, where we learn as much of this as we need to for the present; we have old friends, where much of this is well-known to us. Reading a biblical text can involve similar processes, both when we are reading it for the first time and when it is an old favorite.

It is also helpful to be aware of the difference between our meeting people and doctors, psychiatrists, therapists—health professionals—meeting patients. We listen attentively; they listen attentively too, but differently. They pay attention to things we might not think of: skin color, tension, breathing, energies, conflicts, posture and body language, etc. We are meeting somebody; they are not only meeting somebody but they are also making a diagnosis, correlating symptoms with possible conditions. The enjoyment of friends is not a time for the exercise of professional expertise. Professionals approach a patient differently. The difference between *reading* a text and *studying* a text has a lot in common with the difference between meeting a person and meeting a patient.

What we discuss below are aspects of biblical text that experience has shown—in shifting contexts—to be of lasting value for modern study.

The developmental insights and questions of modern study

Text boundaries
Boundaries are important, whether we are talking about acquaintances, friends, or professionals—to say nothing of real estate. Boundaries are also important for texts. Since Aristotle, we have known that a text has a beginning, a middle, and an end. Not all the texts we are called upon to study will form such rounded wholes.

The boundaries of a text—where a passage begins and ends—are not always easily determined. A student needs to be aware of the issue; more may not be readily possible. Hebrew usually repeats subjects and objects sparingly. Prefixes and suffixes, often translated by pronouns etc in a language like English, can sustain meaning for longish passages of text. Independent passages do not normally begin with a prefix or suffix; subjects and objects are named within such passages. As a rule of thumb, this can be useful; beyond it, a student is often left to reflection and intuition.

Where a text is considered to begin or end may radically alter its interpretation. Often, all that can be asked of an interpreter is awareness of the issue.

Text criticism
With the wealth of texts available to us today, text criticism—i.e., among differing textual witnesses, determining which to rely on in a given passage—is best left to professionals (cf Tov, 1992).

The reevaluation of subjectivity has correctly crept up on the text critic. Modern discoveries have tended away from simplicity: 'the Scriptures were pluriform . . . until at least 70 CE probably until 100, and quite possibly as late as 135 or beyond. Thus we must revise our imaginations and our explanations . . . we can see now more clearly that there were multiple literary editions of many of the biblical books' (Ulrich, 1994, 92).

In Genesis 1:26, the Hebrew text has 'over the cattle, and over all the earth'; the Syriac text has 'over the cattle, and over all the wild animals of the earth.' Comparison with vv 24 and 25 leads many moderns to the view that the Syriac is correct; the Greek and Latin, however, follow the Hebrew. In 1 Samuel 1:18, the Hebrew text has 'and the woman went her way and she ate and she no longer had her [sad] face'; the Greek text has 'and the woman went her way and entered her lodging and she ate with her husband and drank and her face was no longer fallen.' Explanations are possible; certainty is not. In Isaiah 2:12, the Hebrew text has 'against all that is lifted up and low'; the Greek text has 'against all that is high and towering, and they shall be brought low'. Translations follow the Hebrew, or emend the Hebrew, or follow the Greek; unanimity is not to be had.

Origin criticism
This section should be headed 'source criticism'; why origin criticism can be explained a little later. The basic insight from which this approach began was that some biblical passages were made up of material from more than one origin. In 1753, Jean Astruc entitled his book: *Conjectures about the sources which it appears Moses used in the composition of the book of Genesis*. For those who worry about Darwinism, it helps to note Darwin's dates: 1809–82. Critical analysis of the Bible began from the Bible; it was on the scene before Darwin boarded the Beagle (cf Roberts, 1999). While we can trace the beginnings of this insight back at least to Richard Simon in 1678, the name most deservedly associated with its application is that of Julius Wellhausen (1844–1918). His insight and clarity of expression have left their mark indelibly on modern biblical studies.

Wellhausen was not alone. While for many his name stands as symbolic of critical analysis of the Older Testament, he came toward the end of a long period of passionate engagement with such studies, above all at German universities. Figures such as Herder (1744–1803), Eichhorn (1752–1827), De Wette (1780–1849), Ewald (1803–75), and Vatke (1806–82) are only a few of those who preceded him. Many were to follow, with shifting emphases; among the Germans, there are scholars like Gunkel, Greßmann, Alt, Noth, von Rad, Fohrer. There are others of eminence in other countries; overall, it would be invidious to single out names. For many, the analytical study of biblical origins brought conflict with traditional church teachings or traditional church people. Wellhausen himself wrote to the government minister responsible asking to be transferred from his chair in theology, because he did not consider he was adequately fulfilling his practical task of preparing theology students for their future. While the fact of diverse origins is taken for granted today, the best way of understanding the shape of such origins is vigorously debated. Academics and church people have come to terms with the diversity of origins in biblical text. It may not be unfair to say that many adherents, whether in academic or church circles, have not yet come to terms with how these understandings can be fully used to fire imagination and fuel faith.

Once upon a time, this aspect of biblical study was designated 'literary criticism', following the German term *Literarkritik*. With the application of literary study, properly so called, to the realm of biblical literature, 'literary criticism' in English at least could only be used for the study of the literary qualities of a text. The old 'literary criticism' came to be referred to generally as 'source criticism'. This would be perfectly suitable, if it were not for the drawback of confusion with pentateuchal sources (for example, J, E, and P). What is now termed 'source criticism' should have a far wider range than the comparatively narrow concern for pentateuchal sources. Source criticism is concerned to ask about the origin of material in a biblical passage. If we think of it as 'origin criticism', we will understand the term 'source' correctly.

Once the insight has been gained, the question has to be asked: what is the origin of this material? As no less a critic than Martin Noth has argued, the fact that a source division is possible does not mean that it is necessary. The practice of some source criticism, especially in the Pentateuch, has given rise to obsessive fragmentation of texts as well as conditioned refusal to see the obvious. The observation of origins is largely about differences and duplication. Not all duplication and not all differences, however, go back to different origins. So the focus has to be sharpened to differences that cause difficulty and duplication that causes difficulty. When such difficulties arise, the issue of origins needs to be raised and the question has to be asked.

Examples from the Pentateuch, the Deuteronomistic History, and the prophets will shed light on what is meant. The issue here is not primarily how questions are best answered; rather, the issue is primarily what in the text requires that such questions be asked?

In the early chapters of Genesis, two sets of details are found about the flood. One set involves a forty-day block of time—with seven pairs of clean animals and a sacrifice and only one pair of unclean animals, and the floodwaters come from a rainstorm. The other set involves a one hundred and fifty-day block of time—with one pair of all animals and no sacrifice, and with floodwaters that come from above and below. However these signals are accounted for, there are difficulties that need to be considered. Later in Genesis, two stories are told about Hagar. In Genesis 16, harshly treated she takes the initiative and is a survivor; she leaves her brutal mistress and is found at a well on her way home. In Genesis 21, she is deprived of initiative and expects her child to die. Harmonisation is possible; the biblical text does it with Genesis 16:9. But difficulties are there and need to be considered. Difficulties need to be considered regarding Jacob the deceiving rat of Genesis 27 and Jacob the model son of Genesis 28:1–9. Different origins may be helpful in making sense of the difficulties.

In Exodus 13–14, there is the traditionally significant account of Israel's deliverance at the Reed Sea. At the gesture of Moses' hand, the waters are parted to left and right, Israel marches across, followed by the Egyptians who are then swamped. But also, in the same text, there is reference to the pillar of cloud moving from in front of Israel to take up station between Israel and the Egyptians all night (14:19-20*; * = 'parts only'), to God's wind blowing the water away all night (14:21*), and finally to God from the pillar of cloud causing panic among the Egyptians at the end of the night so that they retreated across the dry seabed and were swamped by the returning waters (14:27*)—assuming that God's 'all-night' wind stopped with the dawn. Since the Israelites were told to turn back and camp by the sea (14:2), they had already gone past it. Crossing the sea was not the problem; escaping the Egyptian pursuit was. The text has difficulties; they need consideration. Exodus 15:1–18 adds to the complexity. Different origins may need to be taken into account.

In the Deuteronomistic History, similar difficulties can be encountered and appeal to different origins may be involved in a solution. In 1 Samuel 7–12, for example, chapters 7–8 have the prophet Samuel subdue the Philistines for a generation and agree to setting up a king for Israel (cf 7:13; 8:22) before chapter 9 gives God the initiative of bringing Saul to Samuel to be anointed by Samuel as ruler and to save Israel from the Philistines, since Israel's cry has reached God (cf 9:15-17). Furthermore, Saul is acclaimed king in 10:24 and made king again in 11:15. Harmonisation is attempted in 1 Samuel 12, but not very successfully. According to 8:1–5, the request for a king resulted from the unjust behavior of Samuel's sons; in chapter 11, the crowning of Saul as king followed his stunning victory over the Ammonite Nahash. According to 12:12, it was the threat posed by Nahash that triggered the demand for a king. Some modern harmonisations have done better, but Noth's comment remains: 'it was not without obvious effort and contrivance that Dtr supplemented the old account which dealt favorably with the institution of the monarchy by adding long passages reflecting his disapproval of the institution' (Noth, 1991, 83–84). Appeal to different origins may help interpret a difficult text. Other examples may be found in 1 Samuel 17–18 and 1 Kings 8 (see Campbell and O'Brien, 2000).

In the prophets, assessment of the origin of material often comes under the rubric of 'editing history' (see below). However, there are cases where the assumed combination of prophetic collections of sayings is not unlike the combination of traditions assumed for the Pentateuch. A case in point may be found in Isaiah 5–10. Isaiah 6 witnesses to Isaiah's call (or at least a commission to the prophet). Isaiah 7:1 – 8:15 follows with traditions relating to the Syro-Ephraimite war, including the famous Immanuel oracle. With Isaiah 8:16–22, Isaiah's activity appears to have reached closure. Finally, Isaiah 9:1–7 (NRSV) has a strong prophecy of salvation for those now in gloom and darkness. In short, all the components of a prophetic collection are encompassed: commission, ministry, closure, and future hope.

Surrounding this collection, however, there may be another. Isaiah 5:1–7 is the Song of the Vineyard. It ends with the powerful poetry of v 7:

> he expected justice (*mishpat*),
>   but saw bloodshed (*mispakh*);
> righteousness (*tsedaqah*),
>   but heard a cry (*tse'aqah*)!

A series of 'woe' sayings (in the NRSV: 'Ah, you') follow (5:8–24), illustrating the absence of justice and righteousness and exemplifying the bloodshed and outrage. There are seven sayings in the series, but the seventh is in 10:1–4. After the joyous ending of 9:7 comes a series of sayings against Israel, each ending with a refrain: 'For all this his anger has not turned away; his hand is stretched out still.' The refrain occurs in 9:12, 17, 21; 10:4, but also in 5:25. That a collection should be put together exemplifying and illustrating a poem as powerful as the Song of the Vineyard is not surprising. That the series of woe sayings and the series with the refrain should both be represented on either side of the apparent collection in Isaiah 6:1–9:7 is surprising. These are difficulties that need explanation. A difference of origins may contribute to better understanding.

The issue of origins in the Pentateuch is a special case. Over more than a couple of centuries of analytical study, it was observed that relatively coherent texts could be built up from extensive passages attributed to a Yahwist (using the personal name of Israel's God, YHWH), or to an Elohist (using the common noun for God, *elohim*), or to a Priestly writer (initially using the common noun for God, *elohim*). To these was added the book of Deuteronomy, thus giving four so-called sources, J, E, P, D. Debate raged over the nature of these texts, their relationship to the law codes (Ex 20:22–23:33; Lev 1–16 and 17–26; Deut 12–26), the order and dating of their composition, and the manner of their combination to form the present text. Further subdivisions and variants were proposed; various ways of combination or supplementation were put forward. When consensus seemed achieved, consensus fell apart (cf Campbell and O'Brien, 1993). Since the collapse of consensus, there is agreement that the Pentateuch is made up of materials of widely differing origins; there is agreement on precious little else. For the present, a fresh consensus seems unlikely.

Form criticism
Form criticism may be the most elusive of the creatures in the garden of Older Testament scholarship. The association of form with setting promised histories of Israel's literature, and its religion; such promises were not fulfilled. The psalms would seem an ideal field for form-critical research. Assured results have been meager: a distinction

between individual and communal, between psalms of complaint and lament and psalms of praise and thanksgiving, and royal psalms; the leftovers are left over. After Westermann, we have grown familiar with the form-critical structure of the prophetic oracle: accusation, messenger formula, and announcement (Westermann, 1967). The most rigorous attempt to put form-critical study on a thoroughly scientific basis had the unexpected effect of making clear that this is not a fruitful way to go (Richter, 1971). For all its elusiveness, form criticism embodies one of the central gains of modern biblical study.

Form criticism is based on the insight that significant features of certain works of literature derive from something quintessential to those works, often associated with the social settings that generated the literature. Form criticism appeals to a modern concern for the whole, the gestalt. It seeks to answer the question, 'What sort of text are we dealing with?' and to address the issue of the interrelationship of the parts within the whole.

Viewed generally, form criticism is as automatic as breathing; it is something we do regularly, for example, when we distinguish reporting from comment from humor from advertising in our newspapers. Few of us, confronted with 'Dear Sir or Madam' and 'My darling beloved', would hesitate as to which was the business letter and which the love letter. From another point of view, it may not be easy to distinguish convincingly between a story being told and a report being given of what happened. In theory, reports follow the sequence of events and stories move through plot from the creation of tension to its resolution. In practice, such distinctions may not be easy to make. Is the text about Samuel's beginnings (1 Sam 1) a story or a report? Does it matter? The text about the first couple in the garden (Gen 2–3) is one thing if it is a story and another if it is a report. As a rule, report is un-interpreted; story begins the task of interpretation—or may have been created to address what needs interpretation.

From one standpoint, form criticism is a liberation from the obsession with history. The so-called 'historical books' (that is, Joshua, Judges, Samuel, Kings) may well be more theological than historical, more concerned with the meaning of Israel's destiny than with reporting its past. To ask the question 'What is the literary form of this text?' is to open the way to what may be a more adequate understanding of a text's meaning.

What robs form criticism of the capacity for tidy classification is an essential quality of literature and art: there needs to be a fundamental model of expectation in relation to which the individual work can situate itself. It was the hope of form criticism to be able to work back toward the understanding of such matrixes. It is the sorrow of form criticism that we are usually left contemplating the individual achievement, without the matrix. Nevertheless, despite the uncertainty of the answers, the form-critical questions are essential for the interpreter.

The first question is: what is the literary form of this text? The answer may be simplistically easy. Apodictic law is quite different from casuistic law. A psalm of praise is quite different from a psalm of lament. The answer may not be easy at all, relying on the observation and intuition of the interpreter. The second question is more complex: what are the basic components of this text and how do they relate to each other? It is relatively easy to talk about features in a text; it is more challenging to talk about their interrelationship. If a passage is only a part of a larger text, then we need to ask what sort of a part it is, how it relates to its context, and what is the literary form of the larger text it belongs to? Similarly, we can address this question to the larger blocks forming a text or to the elements that go to forming one of the blocks. The third question is: how does the interrelationship of the text's components function to communicate its meaning?

Two trends particularly militate against the successful application of form criticism. One is the security given by a focus on detail; outreach to the whole is dangerous. The other is the difficulty of putting persuasive words on the perceptions that underlie an intuitive conviction. Up till now, there has been no adequate codification of the body of experience and observation that takes form criticism beyond the relatively obvious and easy. It may be that no such codification is possible; the equivalent to a diagnostic manual may never be achieved. Just as anxieties about air quality should not stop us breathing, anxieties about form-critical uncertainty should not stop us from attempting to articulate what is intuitively assumed.

Some examples will help. Early in Genesis, it is relatively simple to realise that Genesis 2–3 (the garden) and Genesis 4 (Cain and Abel) are stories and that Genesis 5 and 10–11 are genealogies. It takes closer observation to notice the differences between Priestly and Yahwist (10:8–30) genealogies. The different origins of the material in the flood text (Gen 6:5–9:17) have been noted above; the structural interrelationships of the present text are noteworthy. The decision to destroy is first made in God's heart (6:5–8), then communicated to Noah (6:9–22); after the flood, the decision never again to destroy is first made in God's heart (8:21–22) and then communicated to Noah (9:1–17). The significance of this second decision is theologically huge: despite human sinfulness, God's commitment is unshakable.

The sacrifice of Isaac (Gen 22; in Jewish tradition, the binding of Isaac) is a story; it begins with the announcement of a test and the whole hangs on its outcome. The story form reaches its conclusion in v 14, with the naming 'The Lord will provide', closed off with Abraham's return to Beer-sheba in v 19. It is possible to see the highly enigmatic story as one of basic trust—'The Lord will provide'. The angel's second intervention (vv 15–18) has a different focus (blessing) and a different interpretation (obedience, v 18b). The variant has been skillfully introduced between vv 14 and 19.

In the Deuteronomistic History, the text on the loss of the ark is instructive (1 Samuel 4). The structure is simple. There is a battle report; Israel lost (vv 1b–2). There is an inquiry into the loss and a decision to bring the ark from Shiloh (vv 3-9). There is a second battle report; Israel lost more heavily and lost the ark (vv 10–11). Appended to this are two anecdotes, emphasising the significance of the loss: Eli died when he heard of it (vv 12–18); his daughter-in-law, dying in labor, gave her child a name meaning 'the glory has departed from Israel' (vv 19–22). The form-critical question is whether all this is a matter of report or a matter of storytelling.

If it is a matter of report, then the question of the elders in v 3 is reported because the elders asked it before anything else happened. If it is a story, then the storyteller has the question asked knowing full well what the outcome is going to be in vv 10–11. The question is: 'Why has the Lord put us to rout today before the Philistines?' (v 3a). In a report of what happened, one might surmise that the elders answered their question with the thought that they may have lost because they did not have the ark with them. In a story, where vv 10–11 are known as the outcome, the answer to the elders' question has to be to the effect that it was the Lord's will to do so. The absence of the names of any military leaders and the emphasis on Philistines, Israel, and elders may be a pointer to a story rather than a report. The reaction credited to the Philistines (vv 6–9) heightens the likelihood of the text being a story; it heightens the tension. If it is a report, the potential is there for theological reflection to be distilled from the event; if it is a story, the process of theological distilling has been begun. Israel's storytellers were often theologians.

In 1 Kings 4:1–19, there is an account of Solomon's officials and those responsible for the provisions of his court. The text is regarded as deriving from authentic records of the royal court. In Numbers 2, there is an account of the marching order of Israel for the journey from Sinai to the promised land. The slightest familiarity with the tortuous terrain of the Sinai peninsula dismisses its authenticity as a record; it can then be recognised as a programmatic document, with interest for the priorities of the tribes. These are form-critical decisions. They are made in the light of our knowledge today, building on what we know of the Bible and the Ancient Near East.

In 2 Kings 6:8–24, there is a fascinating text about Elisha supplying intelligence to the king of Israel, the Aramean king getting upset about it, and Elisha blinding the commandos sent to arrest him, leading them through the city of Samaria, and providing them with a banquet before sending them home. Plausibility is not the issue. As a report, it would tell of a remarkable event—whether fact or fiction. As a story, the interpretation of the event has been begun: prophetic knowledge is praised, Aramean folly laughed at, and the power of God's prophet celebrated. Report or story? Asking the question is sometimes easier than ascertaining the answer.

In the book of the prophet Amos, form-critical observation of Amos 1–2 and 7–9 shows how strongly patterned both collections are and how different they are from each other and from Amos 3–6. Both collections, however, portray Israel's situation as beyond appeal, beyond intercession. Close observation of form-critical aspects of a small passage such as Amos 3:3–8 is also revealing. In vv 3–6, questions are asked, each assuming a statement or state of affairs. 'Do two walk together unless they have made an appointment?' In v 8, however, two statements are made, each followed by a question. Clearly, v 8 is the formal climax of the passage.

Verses 3–5 constitute a five-line series, each line containing one example and each beginning with the Hebrew interrogative particle (*ha-*). The examples are drawn from natural observation; if the effect can be observed, then the cause may be assumed. Verse 6 consists of two lines, each beginning with the Hebrew 'if'. A literal translation is:

> If a trumpet is blown in the city, surely (Heb 'and') the people are afraid?
> If disaster befalls a city, surely (Heb and) the LORD has done it?

The first is a natural observation; given the cause, the effect follows—when the alarm is sounded, people are afraid. The second is a theological observation, a faith claim; if an effect can be observed (destruction), then the cause (the LORD) may be assumed. The final pair of lines in v 8 builds on all this. The cause is stated: 'the lion has roared . . . the LORD God has spoken'; the effect necessarily follows: 'who will not fear? . . . who can but prophesy?' A further step is needed to articulate the full interpretation of the passage, but the use of form in the service of meaning is clear.

Tradition history
The insight that lies behind the traditio-historical question is the realisation that often aspects of tradition can be identified—whether by language, faith, concern, or other particulars—so that a text can be situated within the sweep of Israel's traditions, highlighting the earlier contributions it draws on and the contribution of its own that it makes. It is also often considered possible to trace the earlier forms of texts or their smaller original units, so that the process of composition and the contributions made along the way can be identified hypothetically. Such 'tradition history' has occasionally been used for large-scale presentations of Israel's literature within the history of its growth. Sometimes a distinction has been attempted between oral and written tradition; it is complex and difficult at best—and dubious where it seeks to blend orality with antiquity and antiquity with God. The capacity to trace Israel's traditions, allowed us by Israel's reverence for its past, permits us precious access to the unfolding of Israel's thinking. The intensive pursuit of such insights can have wide ramifications (for example, von Rad, Noth); in other situations, the observations remain within a more restricted realm.

Examples may be taken from the Pentateuch, the Deuteronomistic History, and the prophets. The scope is wide; the examples only a tiny fraction of the totality available. So, for example, it is possible that Genesis 17:1–2 echoes an older tradition of God's commitment to Abraham, earlier expressed in Genesis 12:1–3 (or equivalent). The promise that through Abraham blessing will be mediated to all the families of the earth is expressed in identical terms in Genesis 12:3b and 28:14, in slightly different terms in Genesis 18:18b, and with a further difference again in the deuteronomistic passages Genesis 22:18 and 26:4b. The implication of tracing this tradition through these five occurrences is the possibility of its theological claim having existed in Israel at least from the Yahwist to the Deuteronomist (perhaps beyond; cf Isa 19:24–25 and Gal 3:8).

In 1 Kings 8, in Solomon's prayer of dedication (vv 14–21), there is a strong appeal to God's promise to David in 2 Samuel 7. It is a good example of how two texts, presumably of interest to the same deuteronomistic circles, can formulate the same tradition with notable differences. For all its reverence for the past, there are places where Israel's theologians appear remarkably free of any obsession with verbal accuracy.

At the end of the Deuteronomistic History (in 2 Kgs 25:27–30), there is a notice of King Jehoiachin, the last reigning survivor of David's line, being released into a form of house arrest at the Babylonian court. The passage can be read as echoing favorable actions of God in Israel's past; it can also be read as echoing the fate of Mephibosheth and the end of Saul's line (2 Sam 9:1–13; also 2 Sam 19:28 and 21:7). Whatever the implications of the passage, it plays on the traditions of Israel (cf Granowski, 1992).

In Hosea 12, we find a wide range of references to Jacob, among them: trying to supplant his brother in the womb, wrestling with God, the encounter with God at Bethel, his service in Syria for a wife and his shepherding there. Much of the pentateuchal tradition associated with the patriarch Jacob can here be the subject of discussion in the 8th century prophet (cf de Pury, 1989).

Editing history

The insight that leads to asking questions about editing is the realisation that Israel's editors often allowed their interventions to be visible—inviting reflection. In English, the terms 'redaction criticism' and 'redaction history' are widely used. These reflect transpositions of the German 'Redaktion' and the French 'rédaction', both terms that refer to matters in English called 'editorial'. The English word is preferred here, not on chauvinistic grounds, but to avoid potential mystification arising from the use of foreign terms. 'Editing' is appropriate to the partial or total reworking of a text; it can be operative at any stage in a document's history, from early to middle to late—but it presumes the existence of a text. Editors can piece together components to form extensive documents (so the editors termed R^{JE} and R^{JEP} in the Pentateuch or the editors of prophetic collections and prophetic books); naturally, they can also do smaller editing jobs. Some study of a text's editing history (as for its tradition history) might be described in terms of intertextuality. There is scope for overlap between origin criticism and editing history.

From the Pentateuch, for example, Exodus 19:3b–9a is of a different origin from its surroundings; it could owe its place in the text to editorial activity. The difference of origin is evident. 19:5 already has a covenant in view, before the one that lies well ahead in the present text. In v 9a, the passage has its own preparations for God's self-disclosure. Two aspects may have attracted an editor's attention. It is an unusual covenantal text, in that the outcome is explicitly conditional: 'if you obey my voice and keep my covenant'. On the other hand, at stake is more than bare relationship. Israel does not become simply God's people, but God's 'treasured possession', 'a priestly kingdom and a holy nation'. The last two are unheard of elsewhere in the Hebrew Bible; the first is rare (cf Deut 7:6; 14:2; 26:18). The passage does not appear to belong in one of the pentateuchal sources; an editor may well have felt the need to preserve the tradition.

In the Deuteronomistic History, 1 Kings 9:6–9 offers an example. In vv 3–5, God has answered Solomon's prayer, consecrated the temple Solomon has built, and has put there for all time God's name and God's eyes and heart. Solomon's dynastic rule over Israel is assured, on condition of Solomon's fidelity (v 4). All this is expressed in second person *singular* address to Solomon. With the exile of Judah in 587, the Davidic/Solomonic dynastic rule came to an effective end; with the Babylonian sack of Jerusalem, God's consecrated temple was destroyed. So in vv 6–9, God's words are expanded in a second person *plural* address that has to include the people and that deals with the possibility of infidelity and apostasy. The tension is acute and difficult. One solution is to see vv 6–9 as an editorial expansion, bringing an earlier theology into line with a later reality. Similar editorial comments on this issue are to be found in 1 Kings 11:32–33*, 39.

Toward the end of the Deuteronomistic History, King Josiah and Judah made a covenant before YHWH. Details of the participants are given in 2 Kings 23:2. The final statement is: 'all the people joined in the covenant' (23:3). A few verses earlier, these same people are written off as hopeless apostates who have incurred God's unquenchable wrath (see 22:16–17). The context does not allow for repentance; editorial adjustment is an appealing possibility. If the hypothesis of a Josianic Deuteronomistic History is envisaged, Josiah's death and the abandonment of his reform required an extensive editorial undertaking, bringing a different vision to bear on seven books of biblical text (see Campbell and O'Brien, 2000).

Among the prophets, Amos has a couple of chapters in which God's judgment is pronounced over Israel's neighbors and, finally, over Israel itself (Amos 1–2). The pronouncements are structured on a remarkable pattern. There is an introduction ('Thus says the LORD'), a proverbial opening ('for three . . . and for four'), a denial of appeal ('I will not cause it to return'), a reference to the crime, a reference to the punishment, and in all but three cases a concluding phrase ('says the LORD'). There are eight such sayings: against Damascus, Gaza, Tyre, Edom, Ammon, Moab, Judah, and Israel. In seven of them, the crime is a matter of social justice, usually related to excessive violence in war. In the case of Judah, however, the crime is in a totally different sphere: 'they have rejected the law of the LORD, and have not kept his statutes, but they have been led astray by the same lies after which their ancestors walked' (2:4). Of course, prophets are entitled to an exception or two. On the other hand, the combination of factors may suggest later editorial activity here.

While with Amos we might note 3:7, passed over earlier. Its interruption of the tight sequence of vv 3–6 and v 8 creates a difficulty. Its reference to the prophets as God's servants suggests deuteronomistic origin. The combination of the two makes an editorial comment from deuteronomistic circles a distinct possibility.

Conclusion

How recent and how radical the discovery of the Ancient Near East has been regularly comes as a surprise. The staples of early exploration were languages and archaeology.

Among the major languages, Egyptian was deciphered in 1822 (thanks to the Rosetta Stone, a tri-lingual inscription we owe to Napoleon's troops in 1799). Of the Mesopotamian languages, Sumerian was not translated until 1907; the translation of Assyrian and Babylonian was recognised by 1857 (thanks to the Behistun inscription, again a tri–lingual carved on a mighty rock-face). Fledgling studies of Hittite civilisation culminated in excavations at Boghazköy, begun in 1907; decipherment of the language had to wait for the discovery of the bi-lingual Karatepe inscription in 1947. The discovery of Ugarit (also known by its modern name of Ras Shamra) began in 1928; decipherment of the language, in an alphabetic cuneiform script, was agreed on by 1932.

Archaeology is a recent science, especially when distinguished from the adult version of a glorified treasure hunt. Excavation in Mesopotamia led the way, but did not begin until 1843 (Khorsabad, 1843; Nimrud, 1845; Warka, 1850; Ur and Eridu, begun in 1854–55). In 1871, Schliemann began digging at Hissarlik in western Turkey and found Homer's city of Troy. In 1877, de Sarzec, a French consul, began digging at Telloh and found the Sumerian civilisation. In 1899, Sir Arthur Evans began digging at Knossos in Crete and discovered the Minoan civilisation. Where Palestine is concerned, tunneling began in Jerusalem in 1864–67, the Palestine Exploration Fund was founded in 1865, and in 1890 Sir Flinders Petrie undertook the first stratigraphical excavation in Palestine at Tell Hesi (cf generally, Daniel, 1968).

There are many more; others take up the story. In recent years, much has been learned; in the years ahead, we may assume there will be much more to learn.

What was said early in this essay may be recalled: the approaches discussed here are related to insights and questions about the nature of Older Testament text and its development; they are not methods, to be applied in much the same way that sausage-making processes are applied to minced meat and the rest.

As insights, these approaches have been validated over a long period of time. The phenomena discussed are to be found in some biblical texts, not in all. Not all are equally important for understanding a text where they might be found. As questions, they need to be asked of texts. Not all interpreters will give the same answers. Not all interpreters will give their answers the same significance. Nevertheless, the awareness flowing from these insights and questions will in varying ways shape part of the context within which any interpretation of biblical text proceeds.

Further Reading

Method and 'how to' books are often problematic. Some leave nothing out and cover too many good things; others leave too much out and do not cover enough good things. The inexperienced risk being confused, misled, or overwhelmed; the experienced, who ought not need them, can find them insightful and stimulating. Rather like reading the Bible, it is matter of knowing what to make one's own and what to leave alone; an experienced guide can be most helpful. If that caution can be taken to heart, the English-language books listed below may be useful in varying ways.

Barton, J. *Reading the Old Testament: Method in Biblical Study* (London: Darton Longman and Todd, 1984).

Hayes, J and C Holladay. *Biblical Exegesis: A Beginner's Handbook* (Atlanta: John Knox, 1982).

Haynes, S and S McKenzie (editors). *To Each Its Own Meaning: An Introduction to Biblical Criticisms and Their Application* (Louisville: Westminster/John Knox, 1993).

Kaiser, O and W Kümmel. *Exegetical Method: A Student's Handbook* (New York: Seabury, German copyright: 1963; translator's copyright: 1967).

Morgan, R with J Barton. *Biblical Interpretation* (Oxford: Oxford University Press, 1988).

Steck, OH. *Old Testament Exegesis: A Guide to the Methodology*, translated from the thirteenth German edition by JD Nogalski, second edition, SBLRBS 39 (Atlanta: Scholars Press, 1998). German versions have been in use for over twenty-five years.

Stuart, D. *Old Testament Exegesis: A Primer for Students and Pastors*, second edition (Philadelphia: Westminster, 1984).

The series of booklets, *Guides to Biblical Scholarship*, with an Old Testament series and a New Testament series, published by Fortress Press.

Relevant Bibliography

Campbell, A and M O'Brien. *Sources of the Pentateuch: Texts, Introductions, Annotations* (Minneapolis: Fortress, 1993).

———, *Unfolding the Deuteronomistic History: Origins, Upgrades, Present Text* (Minneapolis: Fortress, 2000).

Daniel, G. *The First Civilizations: The Archaeology of their Origins* (London: Thames and Hudson, 1968).

Granowski, J. 'Jehoiachin at the King's Table: A Reading of the Ending of the Second Book of Kings', in *Reading Between Texts: Intertextuality and the Hebrew Bible*, edited by DN Fewell (Louisville: Westminster/John Knox, 1992), 173-90.

Hahn, H. *The Old Testament in Modern Research* (Philadelphia: Fortress, 1966).

Knight, D and G Tucker, (editors). *The Hebrew Bible and Its Modern Interpreters.* The Bible and Its Modern Interpreters (Philadelphia: Fortress, 1985).

Kraus, H. *Geschichte der historisch-kritischen Erforschung des Alten Testaments.* second edition (Neukirchen: Neukirchener Verlag, 1969).

Noth, M. *The Deuteronomistic History.* JSOTSup 15, second edition (Sheffield: JSOT, 1991. German original, 1943).

Pury, A de. 'La tradition patriarchale en Genèse 12-35', in *Le Pentateuque en question: Les origines et la composition des cinq premiers livres de la Bible à la lumière des recherches récentes*, edited by A de Pury MDB (Geneva: Labor et Fides, 1989), 259-70.

Richter, W. *Exegese als Literaturwissenschaft: Entwurf einer alttestamentlichen Literaturtheorie und Methodologie* (Göttingen: Vandenhoeck & Ruprecht, 1971).

Roberts, M. 'Not Literalist After All: A Response to Paul Badham', in *Expository Times,* 111 (1999): 17-18.

Rogerson, J. *Old Testament Criticism in the Nineteenth Century: 'England and Germany* (London: SPCK, 1984).

Tov, E. *Textual Criticism of the Hebrew Bible* (Minneapolis: Fortress, 1992).

Ulrich, E. 'The Bible in the Making: The Scriptures at Qumran', in *The Community of the Renewed Covenant: The Notre Dame Symposium on the Dead Sea Scrolls*, edited by E Ulrich and J VanderKam (Notre Dame: University of Notre Dame, 1994), 77-93.

Westermann, C. *Basic Forms of Prophetic Speech* (Philadelphia: Westminster, 1967).

Associated books:
Campbell, A. *Genesis Revisited* (in preparation)

Form Criticism (OT)

The Emergence of the Form-critical and Traditio-historical Approaches

(Original: *Hebrew Bible / Old Testament: The History of Its Interpretation*)

Bibliography

Sources

Greßmann, Hugo. *Mose und seine Zeit*. FRLANT 18 (Göttingen: Vandenhoeck & Ruprecht, 1913).

———. 'Die literarische Analyse Deuterojesajas', in *ZAW*, 34 (1914): 254–97.

———. 'Die Aufgaben der alttestamentlichen Forschung', in *ZAW*, 42 (1924): 1–33.

———. Contributions to *Die Schriften des Alten Testaments in Auswahl*. Göttingen: Vandenhoeck & Ruprecht, first edition 1910–14; second revised edition, 1920–25.

Gunkel, Hermann. 'Die Grundprobleme der israelitischen Literaturgeschichte', first published in *Deutsche Literaturzeitung*, xxvii, 1906; then in *Reden und Aufsätze*, 29–38. It was intended as a brief report on the fundamental positions of Gunkel's piece on Israelite Literature in *Kultur der Gegenwart* 1/7 (1906): 51–102, now available in a 1925 printing (see below). ET: 'Fundamental Problems of Hebrew Literary History', 57–68 in *What Remains of the Old Testament and Other Essays* (London: Allen & Unwin, 1928).

———. *Genesis*. HAT. third edition (Göttingen: Vandenhoeck & Ruprecht, 1910). ET: (Macon, GA: Mercer University Press, 1997).

———. *Reden und Aufsätze* (Göttingen: Vandenhoeck & Ruprecht, 1913).

———. German title unavailable. First printed in *Die Deutsche Rundschau*, xli, 1914. ET: 'What is Left of the Old Testament?',

13–55 in *What Remains of the Old Testament and Other Essays* (London: Allen & Unwin, 1928).

———. 'Jakob', in *Preussische Jahrbücher* 176 [1919]. ET: 42–67 in *Water for a Thirsty Land: Israelite Literature and Religion* (Minneapolis, MN: Fortress, 2001).

———. *Das Märchen im Alten Testament* (Göttingen: Vandenhoeck & Ruprecht, 1921); reprinted, (Frankfurt: Athenaum, 1987). ET: *The Folktale in the Old Testament*. Almond.(Sheffield: Sheffield Academic, 1987).

———. *Die israelitische Literatur* (*Kultur der Gegenwart*, volume 1/7, first printing 1906, second printing 1925; reprinted, 1963)

———. *Die Psalmen*. HAT (Göttingen: Vandenhoeck & Ruprecht, 1929).

———. *Einleitung in die Psalmen: Die Gattungen der religiosen Lyrik Israels* (completed by J Begrich). HAT (Göttingen: Vandenhoeck & Ruprecht, 1933); reprinted, 1966. ET: *Introduction to Psalms* (Macon, GA: Mercer University Press, 1998).

Kittel, Rudolf. 'Die Zukunft der alttestamentlichen Wissenschaft', in *ZAW,* 39 (1921): 84–99.

Studies

Alt, Albrecht. 'The Origins of Israelite Law', 81–132 in *Essays on Old Testament History and Religion* (Oxford: Blackwell, 1966); German original, 1934.

Campbell, Antony F. 'Form Criticism's Future', 15–31 in *The Changing Face of Form Criticism for the Twenty-First Century*, edited by Marvin Sweeney and Ehud Ben-Zvi (Grand Rapids, MI: Eerdmans, 2003).

Hardmeier, Christof. *Texttheorie und biblische Exegese: Zur rhetorischen Funktion der Trauermetaphorik in der Prophetie* (Munich: Kaiser, 1978).

Hempel, Johannes. *Die althebräische Literatur* (Wildpark-Potsdam: Akademische Verlagsgesellschaft Athenaion, 1930).

Hyatt, J Philip. 'Were There an Ancient Historical Credo in Israel and an Independent Sinai Tradition?', 152–70 in *Translating & Understanding the Old Testament*, edited by HT Frank and WL Reed (Nashville, TN: Abingdon, 1970).

Klatt, Werner. *Hermann Gunkel: Zu seiner Theologie der Religionsgeschichte und zur Entstehung der formgeschichtlichen Methode.* FRLANT (Göttingen: Vandenhoeck & Ruprecht, 1969).

Knierim, Rolf. 'Old Testament Form Criticism Reconsidered', in *Interpretation,* 27 (1973): 435-68.

———. Editor, *Forms of the Old Testament Literature* (Grand Rapids, MI: Eerdmans, 1981–).

———. 'Criticism of Literary Features, Form, Tradition, and Redaction', 123–65 in *The Hebrew Bible and Its Modern Interpreters*, edited by DA Knight and GM Tucker (Philadelphia, PA: Fortress, 1985).

———. *Text and Concept in Leviticus 1:1-9: A Case in Exegetical Method.* FAT 2 (Tübingen: Mohr, 1992).

Koch, Klaus. *The Growth of the Biblical Tradition* (New York, NY: Scribner, 1969); German original, second edition, 1967.

Mowinckel, Sigmund, *Psalmenstudium I-VI.* 2 volumes (Amsterdam: Schippers, 1961); Norwegian original, 1921-24.

———. *The Psalms in Israel's Worship.* 2 volumes (Oxford: Blackwells, 1962); Norwegian original, 1951.

Muilenburg, James. 'Form Criticism and Beyond', in *JBL,* 88 (1969): 1–18.

Noth, Martin. *A History of Pentateuchal Traditions* (Englewood Cliffs, NJ: Prentice-Hall, 1972); German original, 1948.

Rad, Gerhard, von. 'The Form-Critical Problem of the Hexateuch', 1–78 in *The Problem of the Hexateuch, and Other Essays* (New York, NY: McGraw-Hill, 1966). Reprinted: 'The Form-Critical Problem of the Hexateuch', 1–58 and 243–49 notes) in *From Genesis to Chronicles: Explorations in Old Testament Theology* (Minneapolis, MN: Fortress, 2005). German original: BWANT 78, 1938; reprinted, *Ges Stud*, Volume 1, 1958.

———. *Genesis*, OTL (Philadelphia, PA: Westminster, 1961); German original, 1956.

———. 'Gerhard von Rad über Gerhard von Rad', 659–61 in *Probleme biblischer Theologie* (Munich: Kaiser, 1971).

Richter, Wolfgang. 'Beobachtungen zur theologischen Systembildung in der alttestmentlichen Literatur anhand des "kleinen geschichtlichen Credo"', 175–212 in *Wahrheit und Verkündigung*, volume 1 (Munich: Ferdinand Schöningh, 1967).

Sweeney, Marvin A. 'Form Criticism', 58–89, in *To Each Its Own Meaning: An Introduction to Biblical Criticisms and Their Application* (revised and expanded), edited by SL McKenzie and SR Haynes (Louisville, KY: Westminster John Knox, 1999).

Sweeney, Marvin A, and Ehud Ben-Zvi (editors). *The Changing Face of Form Criticism for the Twenty-First Century* (Grand Rapids, MI: Eerdmans, 2003).

Westermann, Claus. *Basic Forms of Prophetic Speech* (Philadelphia, PA: Westminster, 1967); German original, 1960.

———. *The Praise of God in the Psalms.* (Richmond, VI: John Knox, 1965); German original, 1961.

———. *Praise and Lament in the Psalms* (Atlanta, GA: John Knox, 1981); German original, 1977.

Wolff, Hans Walter. 'Gesprach mit GERHARD VON RAD', 648–58 in *Probleme biblischer Theologie* (Munich: Kaiser, 1971).

Before we examine the emergence of what is now called form criticism (German: *Formgeschichte*; 'criticism' in English and 'history' in German—not an insignificant difference), a preliminary observation may be important. As a general rule, reflection on movements in human awareness (correlatively, religious awareness) is usually more appropriate a century or two after the movements have ended rather than a mere century or so after they have begun. In the present case, however, it may be necessary to hazard some preliminary thoughts related to moves in the world of Older Testament study over the last century or so.

Primary among these moves may be the beginnings of a slow, almost imperceptible transition, consisting in a movement *from* what was traditionally faith in a God who, in the biblical text, spoke through people so that one might speak of the biblical text as God's word (with varying levels of complexity or transparency) associated with a corresponding movement *toward* a possible emergence of faith in a God who, in the biblical text, was spoken of by people, articulating their experience of their God, so that one might speak of the biblical text as word of God's people (again with varying levels of complexity or transparency). Traditionally, God 'owns' this process of articulation. Through it, God's word becomes heard.

To put this in slightly different language: a move in religious awareness may have been stirring for a century or so, and may be likely to extend for at least another century or so, that among other things involves a transition *from* seeing the biblical text as in some way being God's vehicle for proclaiming to people *toward* seeing the biblical text as in some way being people's vehicle for proclaiming God. Couched in simpler terms, it is not so much the biblical text emanating from God but God emanating from the biblical text; not so much the word that God proclaims as the word that proclaims God. In the bluntest and simplest of terms, these moves might be characterised as a highly sophisticated and complex modulation away from the potentially naïve notion of 'a God speaking' in the direction of 'a God spoken of'.[1]

The catch phrases are simple; the reality, in any of its detail and in the development of its implications, is massively complex. The process as a whole is subtle in the extreme and highly uneven; far advanced in some pockets, while in others it is far from begun. The parallel moves toward an increasingly widespread secularisation in the Western world have probably been associated with the process. To say so is simple; to look at any aspects of detail is similarly of massive complexity.

Alongside this but more recently, the world of Old Testament scholarship has experienced the deterioration of the Documentary Hypothesis as a sure foundation for the understanding of the Pentateuch. No consensus has yet formed as to what might eventually take its place. At this point, it is important to go back to the beginnings of both form criticism and tradition history, to explore what they emerged from, what their defects were, and what insights of value they embodied. That means looking at the early twentieth century before biblical scholarship ventures too far into the twenty-first century.

From an observation point some one hundred years later, the unavoidable question that must inevitably be addressed is: what captured the attention of figures such as Gunkel Gressmann, and von Rad (and so many others) that led in their research and writing to form criticism? The question leads less to a catalogue of *what* they did

---

1. These concerns are adumbrated in Gunkell's 'What Is Left of the Old Testament', 13–56 of *What Remains* (1928): 13–56.

(we have their works) but rather more to an enquiry into *why* they did it and *how* they envisioned the task.

Certain questions emerge from within the texts themselves; for example, the reliability of the text (text criticism), the issue of the unity of the text, its sources, etc. (source criticism), and so on. From this point of view, form criticism is a somewhat nebulous approach to the interpretation of text, involving a concern for the recognition and classification of literary types in various texts. It is not a new set of methodical steps to be taken in the task of interpreting a text. It does not respond to questions such as the texts themselves pose directly.

As we shall see, form criticism emerged from a combination of at least two factors: first, frustration with current practice; second, the perception of possibilities opening up for the interpretation of biblical text, despite conservative resistance. 'Current practice' in pentateuchal studies at the start of the twentieth century was dominated by literary or source criticism (German: *Literarkritik*; not to be confused with the criticism appropriate to literary study). The discomfort felt with it presaged more than a mere shift in academic disciplines.[2]

Hermann Gunkel

Hermann Gunkel is the acknowledged pioneer of the form-critical approach to Older Testament text. Within the complexity of human motivation, a major factor motivating the approach he advocated was dissatisfaction not with the achievements but with the limitations of source criticism (*Literarkritik,* above all in the Pentateuch). Legitimating that dissatisfaction, and prophetic for what was to come, is the realisation that those limitations of the then *Literarkritik* have in no small measure contributed to today's current unease with the Documentary Hypothesis.

From early in the piece, it would appear that the motivation driving Gunkel included a desire to give their full worth to biblical texts and not to stop short at the dryly technical.

---

2. I am greatly indebted to Claremont's emeritus professor Rolf P Knierim for long conversations about form criticism and its beginnings. At Heidelberg, he was *Assistent* with Westermann in 1958/59 and with von Rad in 59/60–62/63. *Assistent* in German universities was an academic post, roughly equivalent to the US assistant professor.

> The beauty of the legendary stories (*Sagen*) in Genesis has always been the delight of sensitive readers. It is not a matter of chance that artists have so gladly taken the subjects of their paintings from Genesis. Scholars have been much more backward in showing themselves touched by the beauty of these stories, probably often on personal grounds but often because aesthetic dispositions did not seem to them compatible with the seriousness of scholarship.[3]

Academic acceptability, compatibility with the seriousness of scholarship, was clearly an issue.

In 1906, between the second and third editions of Gunkel's *Genesis* commentary, biblical form criticism first emerged as an essential element of biblical interpretation with his observation that 'the prime task of a history of Israelite literature must consequently be to determine the genres represented in the Old Testament'.[4] In his summary of his extensive and more discursive text, he mentions briefly some of the main genres, with a first division into prose and poetry. Within prose: narrative, myth, folktale, saga (*Sage*, better: legendary story), novella, spiritual legend (*Legende*), and lastly historical narrative; within poetry: wisdom saying, prophetic saying, and lyric poem (both secular and spiritual). Secular lyrics

---

3. '*Die Schönheit der Sagen der Genesis ist von jeher das Entzücken feinfühliger Leser gewesen; nicht zufällig ist es, dass die Maler die Stoffe für ihre Bilder so gern aus der Genesis genommen haben. Viel seltener haben die Gelehrten sich von der Schönheit dieser Erzählungen berührt gezeigt, vielfach wol aus persönlichen Gründen, vielfach wol deshalb, weil ihnen ästhetische Stimmungen mit dem Ernst der Wissenschaft nicht vereinbar schienen*' (*Genesis*, [first edition], xvii). '*vielfach wol aus persönlichen Gründen*': Gunkel dropped this from later editions; perhaps he felt it inappropriate to intimate that colleagues may have been aesthetically challenged. The importance of going beyond disparate details to grapple with the whole echoes throughout Gunkel's 'Ziele und Methoden' (11–29 of *Reden und Aufsätze*), along with concern for ensuring exegetical technicity (*Nüchternheit*).
4. 'Grundprobleme der israelitischen Literaturgeschichte', 31 in *Reden und Aufsätze* (ET: 59). See Gunkel's *Die israelitische Literatur* (first printed in 1906 in *Kultur der Gegenwart*, volume 1/7; widely available in the second printing, 1925), 2 [54]; summarized in Gunkel's 'Grundprobleme der israelitischen Literaturgeschichte'. A 1919 comment puts Gunkel's position in perspective: 'The lengthy task of separating the documentary sources of this book [Genesis] pushed all the other problems connected with Genesis into the background' ('Jakob', 42).

include: dirge, love song, ridiculing song, drinking song, wedding song, victory song, and royal song. Spiritual lyrics include: hymn, thanksgiving song, complaint song (individual and community), and eschatological song. Prophetic writings include numerous genres: narrative of vision, prophetic word, and discourse (including threat or promise, invective, exhortation, and many others).[5]

What Gunkel does in this paper is provide a programme for further work in Older Testament.[6] In 1901, Gunkel himself had begun with the assertion of the presence in Genesis of legendary stories (*Sagen*; recent ET, 'legends') , rather than history; in 1921 his *Märchen* appeared; in 1929 his *Die Psalmen*, followed posthumously in 1933 by his *Einleitung in die Psalmen* (completed by J. BEGRICH). Unshackled from the tyranny of history as dominant literary genre, he pointed to a future in terms of valuing the beauty and meaning of Old Testament texts; he pointed to a past in terms of the oral world in which such traditions had flourished; and he pointed to the need for levels of classification and systematisation so that research could proceed on a scholarly basis. More than that he could not do; further development had to be left to those who followed.

What brings form criticism formally into the academic realm is the assertion: 'Most of these types (*Gattungen*) have long been recognised, and it is the task of Literary History to study them systematically and scientifically. Each type (*Gattung*) must be studied in order to show the materials (*Stoffe*) with which it deals and the forms (*Formen*) that it necessarily assumes.'[7] The work is not done, but it is called for. We note that content and form are both involved; form is not independent of content.

The impetus toward these form-critical and traditio-historical approaches appears to have been rooted in Gunkel's recognition of the limited appeal of pentateuchal source criticism (*Literarkritik*) to non-specialist Bible readers and the value of an aesthetic approach, which was where he believed his own particular skills predominated. In 1910, the year of the third edition of his Genesis commentary, he wrote to his publisher in connection with a more popular Genesis edition in *Schriften des Alten Testaments* regarding non-specialist readers

---

5. 'Grundprobleme der israelitischen Literaturgeschichte', 31–32 (ET: 59-60).
6. See his comment in *Einleitung in die Psalmen*, 20 (ET: 14).
7. Gunkel 'Problems of Hebrew Literary History', 60 (*Reden und Aufsätze*, 32).

> the way to the content (*Inhalt*, understood as involving the totality of what is there [subject, topic, plot, beauty, style, rhetoric, etc.]) lies through pleasure in the aesthetic form. It is quite different with source criticism (*Literarkritik*) ...
> Now it is my particular gift to have a feeling for the aesthetic, and to bring it to the fore.[8]

More than a decade earlier, he had written to the same publisher, 'in the commentary, I will lay full worth on the unfortunately much neglected interpretation of content (*Sacherklärung*), while in my view up till now source criticism (*Literarkritik*) has been one-sidedly in the foreground.'[9] We need to notice Gunkel's insistence on 'full worth'; the biblical text is not to be sold short because of academic timidity.

As any reader of his Genesis commentary will know, Gunkel was no slouch when it came to the contemporary practice of source criticism (*Literarkritik*). In the German original, seven fonts are used to reflect the source analysis of the biblical text. (Unfortunately, this immediate visual effect has not been reproduced in the English translation, opting to omit Gunkel's own translation.) Gunkel speaks highly and with pride of the achievements of such source criticism.

> An amazing expenditure of industry, of discernment, of brilliant powers of comprehension has been applied to this work. The result is a product of which future generations may be proud. It is currently possible in many cases to determine the source documents to the verse, in a few cases to the word, although, of course, much will always remain uncertain. The final decisive turn in the history of Genesis criticism was the work of WELLHAUSEN, who taught us in his masterpiece *Prolegomena zur Geschichte Israels* to determine the sources of Genesis chronologically and to locate them in the total course of the history of Israel's religion.[10]

As the 1910 Introduction to *Genesis* makes clear (his 'final position' on such matters—his words), Gunkel's primary interest was in

---

8. Klatt, *Hermann Gunkel*, 118.
9. Klatt, *Hermann Gunkel*, 117.
10. Gunkel, *Genesis*, LXXXI (ET: lxx).

legendary story (*Sage*), not history (*Geschichte*). For Gunkel, such legendary story was from circles unaccustomed to writing, discussed personal and private matters, and was by nature poetry, seeking to gladden, elevate, inspire, and touch. (In terms of German intellectual history, the echoes of Herder, Goethe, etc are clear.) History, on the other hand, presumed the practice of writing, had as its subject great public events, and was by nature prose, seeking to instruct concerning actual events.[11] It was important to Gunkel that such legend be seen as respectable. The burden of contemporary church society weighed on the scholar: 'The evangelical church and its commissioned representatives would do well not to be closed—as has so often been the case to this point—to this awareness that Genesis contains legends (*Sagen*), but to recognise that only this awareness makes a historical understanding of Genesis possible.'[12]

A brief detour is appropriate here.
Biblical narrative is usually about the presentation of the past. History, in Gunkel's sense, has its preoccupation with *the past*, as to what actually happened. Literature has its preoccupation with *the presentation*, allowing an intellectual distancing from what actually happened. Two examples will help. First, the question in the biblical text: 'Why has the LORD put us to rout today' (1 Sam 4:3). Why is it in the text? History answers: because of the past—the question was asked. Literature answers: because of the presentation—the question is theologically significant (and the answer is withheld until 2 Sam 6). Second, in the biblical text David has Uriah murdered not Bathsheba (2 Sam 11–12). Why is it in the text? History: because that is what happened. Why did David do it?—good question! Literature: because it has significance in the presentation of the episode. What does the narrator mean by telling it?—good question! Gunkel's identification of Genesis texts as 'legendary stories' (*Sagen*) opened the way to the presentation: what is the significance of telling what is told? The presentation can be explored in ways that the past cannot.

---

11. Gunkel, *Genesis*, IX–XIII (ET: viii–xi).
12. Gunkel, *Genesis*, XII–XIII (ET: xi). As late as 1964, the issue of what might be thought shocking still surfaced frequently in Koch (*Growth of the Biblical Tradition*).

End of detour.

Legend (*Sage*) took various forms, largely determined by content. There were ethnological legends, giving reasons for the status of peoples; etymological ones, offering the beginnings of linguistics, cultic ones, explaining the institution of worship; geological ones, explaining the origins of a locality; and more besides, left undescribed.[13] Gunkel's underlying concern is clear. It is the question, 'What is the nature of these texts, what sort of texts are these?' This question is central to the form-critical approach. For Gunkel, of course, the focus was on the *typical* narrative (genre) of a distant past considerably removed from the *individual* stories (form) found in the present biblical text.

Latent here are tensions that will bedevil form-critical scholarship in generations to come. There is the tension between genre and form: genre, the typical narrative often discussed in relation to the past; form, the individual story found in the present text. There is tension as regards the role played by content in the characterisation of a genre. Further tension lurks in Gunkel's prejudiced portrayal of the 'poverty' of both narrator and audience in past generations and his recognition of the 'extraordinary feats' and 'artistic power' of those responsible for the present text. Finally, there is the practice of highlighting what are isolated elements from the past while needing to reckon with complete texts in the present. Any exposition of the past narratives, beyond the isolated elements, is necessarily speculative and subjective. The traditio-historical approach has its first stirrings with Gunkel's affirmation of transmission from these traces of the past to the texts of the present.

Above all else, Gunkel insisted on the recognition of what much of the Genesis text was not; it was not history (in Gunkel's time: what actually happened). By this simple assertion, Gunkel grounded the query: then, what sort of a text is this? The need for form criticism emerged. Similarly, he sought to trace the transmission of material from a distant past to a present text. Although it may prove dubious, the space for tradition history was created.

The noting of categories among the legendary stories was a bare beginning. Some two decades later, classification burgeoned with the publication of Gunkel's *Die Psalmen* (1929), followed posthumously by his *Einleitung in die Psalmen* (1933). Preceding *Die Psalmen* was,

---

13. Gunkel, *Genesis*, XXI–XXV (ET: xviii–xxi).

of course, Gunkel's early study of Israelite literature.[14] It is important to note that, even at this stage, Gunkel's emphasis is on genres. Of its essence, the genre (*Gattung*) lies behind the present text; the genre is the typical that, in each case, finds expression in the individual form of the present text. A major aspect of Gunkel's interest, at least overtly, was with the (often ancient) past from which the present text had developed. By its nature, source criticism (*Literarkritik*) engaged with the present text. By his predilection, Gunkel turned to the aesthetic that he claimed to find predominantly in the freedom of the past. This involvement with the ancient past necessarily brought into play the subjective and the speculative. The tension, as noted above, has long bedeviled form-critical scholarship.

Gunkel's 1921 study of *Märchen* (accepted English equivalent for Older Testament: folktale) in the Older Testament is less a study of the folktale genre and more concerned with the occurrences of folkloristic qualities in passages of the Older Testament. The comment in his Introduction is to be noted: 'The elevated and rigorous spirit of biblical religion tolerated the folktale as such at almost no point and this near total eradication from the holy tradition is one of the great acts of biblical religion. It is, however, quite a different matter whether the people of whom the Bible speaks still preserved such stories.'[15] Rather than a systematic study of the genre, the book's aim is 'to collate the material which comes into consideration for the folktale scholar in the Old Testament'.[16] At the same time, a wide range of content categories emerges. Gunkel's principal aim would appear to be to distance much of the Bible's storytelling from confusion with a concern for history.

The Psalms commentary opens with Gunkel's lament that some of the most reliable and scholarly psalms commentaries of the time were not always able to overcome a certain aridity (*Trockenheit*) and stolidity (*Unempfänglichkeit*). As he summed it up: 'Criticism and linguistics are to the fore in this area; the religious and the poetic take a back seat.'[17] The confusion of genre and form remained: 'one

---

14. *Die israelitische Literatur*.
15. *Folktale in the Old Testament*, 33 (1987 German reprint, 23).
16. *Folktale in the Old Testament*, 35 (1987 German reprint, 24).
17. '*Kritik und Sprachwissenschaft stand auf diesem Gebiet im Vordergrunde, Religion aber und Dichtung traten zurück*' (Gunkel, *Psalmen*, V).

of the most important tasks of genre research (*Gattungsforschung*) is to recognise the language of form (*Formensprache*).[18] His dearest wish would be that the dam might finally break which held so many contemporaries back from a recognition of the forms (*Erkenntnis der Formen*) and therefore from genre research (*Gattungsforschung*).[19]

The Introduction to his psalms commentary makes clear Gunkel's conviction of the absolute necessity of genre research for understanding the psalms ('*genre research* in the Psalms is nonnegotiable [*nicht eine Liebhaberei*] . . . *the foundational work* without which there can be no certainty in the remainder').[20] That needs to be coupled with his strenuous repudiation of accusations of undue subjectivity. He lays down three criteria for genre research where psalms are concerned: (1) SETTING: belonging to a typical *occasion in the worship service*, or at least deriving from one; (2) CONTENT: indicating a common treasury of *thoughts and moods/emotions*; (3) LANGUAGE: a common 'language related to the form'.[21] The interplay of form and content is unavoidable. Form is indubitably related to the particularity of individual text, but it is not closely defined; the potential for the confusion of genre and form is not eliminated. The reality of the new directions being taken may be judged by Gunkel's reference to the conspiracy of silent refusal on the part of representatives of the older school.[22] Comparison with his predecessors shows clearly how Gunkel's classification of the psalms has stood the test of time.

W Baumgartner's insight in his centenary address is central; he notes the quotation 'Research is as much about art as science' and adds that, for Gunkel, 'art' included instinct or intuition, sensitivity or feeling, as well as imagination.[23]

---

18. '*So ist es eine der wichtigsten Aufgaben der Gattungsforschung, diese 'Formensprache' zu erkennen*' (Gunkel, *Psalmen*, IX).
19. '*Von Herzen möchte ich wünschen, daß der Damm, der so manche der Mitlebenden von der Erkenntnis der Formen and darum auch von der Gattungsforschung ferngehalten hat, jetzt endlich zerrisse!*' (Gunkel, *Psalmen*, IX).
20. *Einleitung in die Psalmen*, 8 (ET: 5).
21. *Einleitung in die Psalmen*, 22-23 (ET: 15-16).
22. *Einleitung in die Psalmen*, 21 (ET: 15), evidenced by Kittel in 1921 (see below).
23. '"*Forschung ist ebensoviel Kunst wie Wissen*". *Und Kunst schloss für ihn das Mitwirken von Instinkt, Gefühl, Phantasie ein*' (see now *Genesis* [from the sixth German printing], 14*).

After a century or so, reflection is regrettably restricted to people's publications and the relatively rare reminiscence. We know Gunkel was a man of powerful personal influence with a remarkable gift for friendship; alas, print seldom catches these qualities. Prescinding from his commentaries on Genesis and Psalms, as well as his treatment of folktale in the OT—where the broader ideas are put to the detailed test—Gunkel's legacy revolves around two pillars: first, a programme for form-critical research (laid out in 1906 and reprinted in 1925); second, a further focus to OT research beyond the pentateuchal source criticism of the time. The future will see that focus sometimes relaxed, sometimes exaggerated. Whatever its fate, thanks to Gunkel, it is an integral part of the task of biblical interpretation.

Gunkel's legacy was not in terms of an advance in method, if method is understood as a procedure or process to attain a purpose, as so many steps to be taken to achieve a goal. On the other hand, if method is understood in more general terms, as a body of skills or techniques flowing from insight, then the form-critical approach would come under the term. First and foremost was the question: what sort of a text is this? Beyond the tyranny of history (so often assumed as genre automatically, frequently unawares), the extensive list of genres showed the need for this question. The question needed to be asked about whether pointers were available to the oral background of the text. The question was there to be asked whether patterns within a genre might serve as pointers to the meaning of a particular text. These observations and questions led beyond the scope of pentateuchal source criticism (*Literarkritik*). A significant shift, a sea change, had occurred in the understanding of the discipline of biblical exegesis.

Hugo Gressmann

Rudolf Kittel's address to the first congress of German orientalists (*Deutsche Orientalistentag*) in Leipzig in 1921 is a most helpful context in which to set form criticism itself and to understand the contribution of Hugo Gressmann.[24]

Kittel's topic was the future of Old Testament scholarship. The timing is important to note. It is between Gunkel's commentary on

---

24. 'Zukunft der alttestamentlichen Wissenschaft', 84–99.

Genesis and his commentary on Psalms as well as his *Introduction to the Psalms*. It is several years after Gressmann's form-critical work on the Moses material (*Mose-Sagen*) and his lengthy article analysing Second Isaiah form-critically. With Kittel, the old guard is making a stand.

There is much to be said about this address but perhaps these telling figures are enough: mention is made of Wellhausen's name some twenty times; there is no mention at all of Gunkel's name nor that of Gressmann and others—not a word (perhaps because they were among the living [cf 84], but it could scarcely be that alone). For Kittel, and those of similar cast of mind, the recent contribution of the comparative religion school (*religionsgeschichtliche Schule*) and the genre research people (ästhetisch-folkloristische Schule) might be conceded—but without apparent emphasis or enthusiasm. The significance and achievements of genre research are not mentioned; on the other hand, the limitation of literary history is emphasised. According to Kittel, what is needed is the intellectual history of Israel (*die Geistesgeschichte Israels*); life before literature. For Kittel, then, it is life (the setting) that leads to understanding the literature; for Gunkel, on the other hand, it is the genre of the literature that leads to the setting in life. For Kittel, the essential source-critical work had been done—regarding the Hexateuch, the historical books, and the prophets. Nevertheless, three directions would mark the near future for Kittel, and source criticism was one of them—*Literarkritik*, associated above all with the name of Wellhausen.[25]

The decision to launch a new series of the figurehead journal, *Zeitschrift für die alttestamentliche Wissenschaft,* sent a highly symbolic and contrary signal: a stage had been achieved at which fresh directions were required to build on the new foundations that had been laid. In an article celebrating this signal, Gressman, the new editor, referred to the past as the period of source criticism (*Literarkritik*); new vistas were opened up for present and future generations by what he termed the Near Eastern period—in which, following the source–critical period and now in the Near Eastern context, OT scholarship might look for fresh understandings (*neue Erkenntnisse*).[26]

---

25. 'Zukunft der alttestamentlichen Wissenschaft', 90–91.
26. 'Aufgaben der alttestamentlichen Forschung', *ZAW* 42 (1924): 1–33.

After highlighting the unquestionable achievements of source-critical work, as well as a number of associated failings, Gressman concludes: 'What we need in our scholarship are not more but rather less source-critical studies'.[27] Source-critical work is essential; it cannot be neglected. However, it should not be overrated; it is an aid to scholarship (*Hilfswissenschaft*, a loaded term), not its end.[28]

As Gressmann perceived the present and future, source criticism (*Literarkritik*) designated the past, while remaining an essential subsidiary. It had been replaced by a period to be designated by the context of the ancient Near East. Emphasis had moved from concern with language to concern with culture. Israel had become a part of the ancient Near East—with confidence that the Older Testament and its religion would not lose but could only benefit from this.[29] What was needed was the spiritual story of the ancient Near East—not of Israel alone, but of Israel as part of its surrounding world.

Looking to the present and future, Gressmann emphasised the importance of developments in areas including text criticism (with cautions), metre, grammar, syntax, lexicography, geography, and history. Source criticism (*Literarkritik*) escaped mention; perhaps because the needed advances in source criticism had been achieved and further progress was not needed. Conflict may not be explicit; but it is clear. Kittel subsumed genre research and associated material under the themes of aesthetics and folklore (*ästhetisch-folkloristische Schule*). When he comes to the area, Gressmann comments: 'Genre research has nothing whatever to do with folklore and only a little to do with aesthetics.'[30] The conflict is clear.

The tasks of genre research are spelled out: to investigate narrative and history, song and prophecy, law and wisdom for their nature or essence (*Wesen*), their setting, form, content, mood (*Stimmung*), and history.[31] Reduced to a single question: what sort of a text is this?

Gressmann was coming out of substantial experience in the form-critical arena. Already in 1913, he had published a full study

---

27. 'Wir brauchen darum in unserer Wissenschaft nicht mehr, sondern weniger literarkritische Untersuchungen' ('Aufgaben', 8).
28. 'Aufgaben der alttestamentlichen Forschung', 4.
29. 'Aufgaben der alttestamentlichen Forschung', 8–10.
30. 'Die Gattungsgeschichte hat mit der Folkloristik gar nichts und mit der Äesthetik nur wenig zu tun' ('Aufgaben', 26).
31. 'Aufgaben der alttestamentlichen Forschung', 26.

of the legendary Moses stories (*Mose-Sagen*), discussing the songs, individual stories (with the possibilities of their oral background), the collections, and the cycles.[32] In 1914, his major study of Second Isaiah had appeared, with a panoply of form-critical observations.[33] In these years, he was lead editor and a contributor to *Die Schriften des Alten Testaments in Auswahl*.[34]

It is not necessary here to go into Gressmann's use of form criticism, whether in the Moses material, Second Isaiah, or elsewhere. It is enough to see that he evaluated the form-critical approach as a new way into biblical interpretation, situated within the ancient Near Eastern context. The past (source–criticism) had taken giant steps; the future lay open to be explored, employing new understandings and new insights.

What appears clear is that the early advocates of genre research/ form criticism saw in it the potential for a new way of generating meaning from the biblical text, a way that had previously been blocked by a culturally constrained scholarship with valid but now subsidiary concerns. Form criticism was an escape into wholeness. It was not so much a stage along the path toward interpretation of the text as an opening to a wider and deeper understanding of the task of interpretation.

At the end of this quarter-of-a-century or so, two activities were on the scene as absolutely necessary to any biblical interpretation: source–criticism and form–criticism (however the latter is named). Much more will emerge; these two remain. The issue of the unity or composite nature of a text must be assessed. This is the task of source criticism; but the task of interpreting a text cannot stop there. Each unit, whether of the text itself or within the text itself, must be assessed for its identity and its meaning. This is the task of form–criticism. Small wonder forward-looking scholars embraced it.

Romanticism, as a major movement of the human spirit, sought beauty, truth, and meaning. Idealism placed its emphasis on logic, thought, and critical analysis. Both streams are essential to the fullness of human flowering. Neither can be neglected without cost.

---

32. *Mose und seine Zeit*.
33. 'Analyse Deuterojesajas'.
34. For his personal contribution, see especially 'Die älteste Geschichtsschreibung und Prophetie Israels', in *Schriften des Alten Testaments in Auswahl*, 2. Abteilung, 1. Band.

The initial moves of the form-critical approach, spearheaded by scholars such as Gunkel and Gressmann, was to break free of the constraints of the past and seek out ways in which the human genius could be given a fuller role in the appreciation of biblical text. What others did for art and architecture, music and literature, these scholars did for biblical interpretation, emphasising appropriate procedures such as close observation, accurate identification, and painstaking classification.

The New Testament

Discussion of the emergence of form criticism in the New Testament would be out of place in this series on the Hebrew Bible/Old Testament. It is enough to note that three of the pioneers studied with Gunkel in Berlin: Martin Dibelius, Karl Ludwig Schmidt, and Rudolf Bultmann.[35]

Johannes Hempel

In 1930 (still within the Weimar Republic and before the publication of Gunkel's *Einleitung in die Psalmen*), Johannes Hempel sketching the history of biblical criticism in Europe wrote:

> The heritage of HERDER, whose recognition of the aesthetic values of Israelite literature remained with EICHHORN and later REUSS but otherwise almost immediately had little influence ('*sonst aber zunächst unmittelbar nur wenig nachwirkt*'), should not be lost. Alongside the scholarly task (*Wissenschaft*) of essentially analytic research into the literary composition of individual books and groups of books came, programmatically formulated at its sharpest by Herman Gunkel, the scholarly study (*Wissenschaft*) of Israelite literary history—which can never survive without the results of analysis but which sought to bind these results into a new unity . . .[36]

It is clear that in Hempel's book the careful identification of literary

---

35. Campbell, 'Form Criticism's Future', 17.
36. *Althebräische Literatur*, 5.

forms goes hand in hand with the exploration of the meaning of each text and the issues of religious values—insight into a rich life ('*in ein reiches Leben hineinsehen*').[37]

Albrecht Alt

GW Anderson, a careful and distinguished scholar, writes: 'The work of Albrecht Alt [1853–1956] must be reckoned among the most far-reaching and fruitful influences in European Old Testament scholarship in the twentieth century.'[38] It is therefore informative and confirming to find Alt sketching much the same picture of the emergence of the form–critical approach as has been presented here. Reflecting on the need for scholarly research to look at the origins of Israelite law, he remarks:

> Work carried out in other branches of Old Testament literature, and in particular those of lyric poetry and epic narrative, has shown that the most appropriate method of research into the pre-literary origins of the material embedded in written works is the study of their formal characteristics as related to the circumstances in which they were produced (*Gattungs-* or *Formgeschichte*).[39]

As Alt saw it, source-critical work seemed in the main complete; a further step was needed. He writes of 'reliable methods'; I find 'responsible scholarship' preferable language. Academic respectability appears to have been a bone of contention. Is 'method' a largely unconscious code or shorthand for 'methodical'? If so, it may be misleading but acceptable. Method can be repeated, as in the scientific validation of a procedure or experiment. Responsible scholarship can be observed and absorbed; it cannot be replicated like so many steps in a procedure.

---

37. *Althebräische Literatur*, 30.
38. *Essays on Old Testament*, biographical note.
39. 'Origins of Israelite Law', 86–87. In a footnote, he comments that 'H Gunkel, who introduced the investigation of stylistic forms (*Gattungsgeschichte*) to the study of the Old Testament, has left only a brief discussion of the forms of Israelite legal material . . .'

In this regard, Alt writes:

> Considerable use has been made of the method in these fields. It depends on the observation that in each individual literary form . . . the ideas it contains are always connected with certain fixed forms of expression. . . The inseparable connection between form and content goes back behind the written records to the period of popular oral composition and tradition, where each form of expression was appropriate to some particular circumstance among the regularly recurring events and necessities of life.[40]

Rather than 'the method' used 'in these fields', what is described here is a matter of observation combined with intuition. The observation: the presence of certain fixed forms of expression. The intuition: a hypothesis to explain how this presence might be accounted for.

Alt was a careful and meticulous scholar, with the capacity to fascinate others. Two elements are present in his famous essay, 'The Origins of Israelite Law', that will be evident in later scholarship. One is the conviction that Israel's present can only be understood from consideration of its oral past, embedded in the secular of the ancient Near East (casuistic law). The emphasis on the past will recur in the work of Martin Noth. The other is the emphasis on what is peculiarly and religiously Israelite—the place of YHWH in apodictic law. This emphasis on the distinctive in Israel will recur equally powerfully in the work of Gerhard von Rad.[41]

Sigmund Mowinckel

Chronologically, we have run ahead of ourselves. It is time to backtrack a little. Sigmund Mowinckel studied with Gunkel in

---

40. 'Origins of Israelite Law', 87.
41. Alongside the work of Noth and von Rad, mention must also be made of Claus Westermann. Three works stand out: *The Praise of God in the Psalms* (ET, 1965; orig., 1961); *Basic Forms of Prophetic Speech* (ET, 1967; original, 1960); and the later *Praise and Lament in the Psalms* (ET, 1981; original, 1977). Of *Basic Forms*, the translator writes: 'a clear example of how the form-critical method may be thoroughly and consistently applied to the study of prophecy' (9). *Mutatis mutandis*, the comment holds good for all three works.)

Giessen (1911/12). He then returned to Oslo, becoming an associate professor in 1922; a full professorship was not available until 1933. His *Psalmenstudien I–VI* date to 1921–24. Leaving aside the sorcery issue, his primary interest in psalms was not so much in their classification as in their role in organised worship, with a setting for many in a seldom noticed enthronement-of-YHWH aspect of the Succoth harvest festival. While his work—which clearly assumed form criticism (more extensively developed in *The Psalms in Israel's Worship*), acknowledging Gunkel of course and seeking to go beyond him—attracted the eager attention of the myth and ritual school, uncertainty about hypothetical aspects of festivals relegated much of it to a position outside the mainstream development of form criticism.

Gerhard von Rad

To return now to the course of events in Germany, a brief resumé is in order. Gunkel used as a key to further understanding of the biblical text the perception that often what in the Genesis text appeared to be history was better classed as legendary story (*Sage*). His close observation of the text led him to identify different types of legendary stories and to classify them, with attention to their mood, language, and setting. In theory, such legendary stories extended into a distant oral and poetic past. In his publications, this aspect is not to the fore in his interpretation.

For Gressmann, this further understanding of the biblical text led, among other things, to an insistence on situating the biblical text within its context in the ancient Near East. Israel had become a part of the ancient Near East and the OT and its religion could only benefit from this.

For Alt, the key to a further understanding of the text was provided by the study of the formal characteristics of written works correlated with the circumstances in which they were produced, that is *Gattungs-* or *Formgeschichte*. 'The inseparable connection between form and content goes behind the written records to the period of popular oral composition and tradition' (see above). In the specific instance, painstaking observation of syntax and content led to the identification of casuistic law with its secular and Canaanite associations and of apodictic law with its religious and Israelite associations.

In OT circles in post-war Germany (the war of 1939–45), von Rad was a major figure and a prominent promoter of form criticism. His *pre-war* assessment of the OT scene, however, was blunt; dissatisfaction with the resistance of past approaches to a further understanding of the text was evident. The need was felt for something more. Referring to the analysis of source documents, he wrote of:

> signs that the road has come to a dead end . . . It may be said without exaggeration that scholars, especially the younger ones, are weary of research in hexateuchal studies . . . Indeed even those who are fully prepared to recognise that it was both necessary and important to traverse these paths [of source analysis] cannot ignore the profoundly disintegrating effect that has been one result of this method in hexateuchal criticism.

He noted that, on almost all sides, the final form of the text was considered 'barely worthy of discussion', to be moved away from as rapidly as possible.[42]

A decade or so later, the pain was still evident in the foreword to the first edition of his *Genesis* (1949): 'Precisely this commentary may make one perceive that source analysis is not the final conclusion of wisdom.'[43] A decade later still, Koch could write: 'For centuries the dogma that the Bible is the Word of God has been understood in far too rigid a sense. A form–critical approach permits us to discover afresh the vitality of God's word.'[44] The tension between church and academe was still felt. Form–criticism was seen as moving beyond the tension.

---

42. The German text of von Rad's 1938 monograph is widely available in volume 1 of his *Gesammelte Studien* (noting the original pagination). The classic English translation by Trueman Dicken is in *Problem of the Hexateuch* (1966), reprinted in KC Hansen's *From Genesis to Chronicles*, 1 (2005). For convenience, the last three are referenced here. Ges Stud, 1.9 / Problem of the Hexateuch, 1 / From Genesis to Chronicles, 1.
43. *Genesis* (Philadelphia: Westminster, 1961), 11] von Rad, of course, followed the sequence of the final canonical text in his Genesis commentary. Even Gunkel, at the start of the century, had privileged source criticism over canon, treating P first in each section and then J.
44. *Growth of the Biblical Tradition*, 13.

Von Rad was enthusiastic for form criticism and generated great enthusiasm in its favour. Looked at from some distance, it would appear to have been less a matter of steps in an interpretative procedure and more an openness to suppositions about an ancient faith and life.

Von Rad's major pre–war monograph is rightly entitled *The Form–Critical Problem of the Hexateuch*, because it is a study of the form of the Hexateuch. It seeks out small units, sees them taking shape in larger forms (Exodus, Balaam, Settlement), and traces their shaping into the final form of the Hexateuch. Gunkel in Genesis and Psalms sought to focus on *shapes* (genres); von Rad goes beyond shapes to their combination in the *shaping* of Israel's faith. Alas, the books are also form-critical in another, less laudatory sense. The adjective 'form–critical' is used a number of times to bolster procedures that can hardly be defended as form-critical. This is possibly no more than a pointer to a trend, but nevertheless the pointer is there.

The monograph was widely influential. It is brilliant: insightful, imaginative, and strikingly comprehensive. Unfortunately, in the light of today's knowledge, it is wrong. Assumptions that now we would not dream of making are made so *Ges Stud*, 1.58 / *Problem of the Hexateuch*, 64 / *From Genesis to Chronicles*, 48 confidently so many years ago. What was so persuasive at the time seems so ingenuous now.

Beyond letters on a page, von Rad reached out, not to some distant oral past, but to the faith of the ancient people expressed in the final OT text. His *Form–Critical Problem of the Hexateuch* was an imaginative masterpiece, with many significant insights. However, many of its assumptions that allowed for an attractive portrayal of salvation history (*Heilsgeschichte*)—with its inbuilt tension between faith and fact—could not be sustained over time. The starting point in the ancient credo was reversed by Richter (but not till almost three decades later); the credo was not at the beginning of a process of faith, but emerged as the end result of that process.[45] From Noth to Finkelstein, via Mendenhall and Gottwald, the settlement tradition (*Landnahme*) could not play the validating role claimed for it by von Rad ('the historical truth that Yahweh had continued to care for Israel

---

45. 'Beobachtungen zur theologischen Systembildung', 210–12; see also the studies noted by Hyatt, 'Ancient Historical Credo' (the Sinai issue is far from resolved).

on the basis established in the Settlement').[46] Among other things, today's knowledge of the books of Joshua and Samuel does not allow for that.

Insight and imagination can be risky and von Rad was aware of it—'with all the certainty that is ever attainable in such matters'.[47] Little of worth does not run risks. As is so often the case with human civilisations, faith and history can be at odds. 'Salvation history' (*Heilsgeschichte*) has an inbuilt ambiguity that can allow for illusion. Faith is not grounded in knowledge, but knowledge can sometimes remove the ground from under aspects of faith.

Form–criticism was to the fore in many studies in the mid-twentieth century. Whether explicitly or implicitly, the dominant question may be claimed to have been: what sort of a text are we dealing with? The approaches to an answer involved issues of form and genre, patterns of structure and language, settings whether social or literary, and so on. For many, it might be said that form criticism was the flag under which they sailed for the open sea of fuller and livelier OT interpretation.

In 1943, *Divino Afflante Spiritu* ('Inspired by the Divine Spirit'), an encyclical letter of Pope Pius XII (believed ghost-written by Cardinal Bea), with its 'discovering and expounding the genuine meaning' of biblical text, was widely regarded as official acceptance of Roman Catholic involvement in critical biblical scholarship.

The wave of form-critical studies may have been an endorsement of imaginative promise that was not matched by the satisfaction of procedural progress. In time, the absence of procedural progress gave rise to doubt; what was felt to be real was too often found to be beyond professional reach. The language of form criticism lost much of its appeal.

In all of this, von Rad was an influential figure. Yet in his brief reflection on his scholarly life, form criticism is not mentioned.[48] In Wolff's respectful comments on von Rad's life and role, form criticism is not mentioned.[49] For both men, clearly, form criticism was not a

---

46. *Ges Stud*, 1.79 / *Problem of the Hexateuch*, 72 / *From Genesis to Chronicles*, 53.
47. *Ges Stud*, 1.58 / *Problem of the Hexateuch*, 64 / *From Genesis to Chronicles*, 48.
48. This is the brief 1964 reflection in which he describes his professional vocation as 'lesen zu lernen und lesen zu lehren'—to learn to read and to teach to read.
49. Both may be found in *Probleme biblischer Theologie*, 648–61.

new method, an essential discovery to be excited about and proud of. It was an attitude of mind, a readiness to interpret text, that should be taken for granted. Gunkel and Gressmann felt the need to fight for it, especially in terms of academic acceptability; later OT scholars could take it for granted.

Martin Noth

Leaving aside the now discarded amphictyony proposal and the still unresolved issues associated with Israel's twelve-tribe system, Martin Noth's legacy to OT studies stands unquestionably among the foremost. Those familiar with his work in Pentateuch or Deuteronomistic History and abundantly elsewhere know him for a thorough and discerning scholar, gifted with insight and imaginative power, marshalling a wealth of knowledge, and endowed with the moderation and mature judgment essential to groundbreaking scholarship.

Early in the twentieth century, present certainly in Gunkel and reaching back perhaps to Herder or beyond, we have observed a wistfulness and yearning for the distant oral past—a 'lionisation' of the oral.[50] Hints in the text were allowed to form the basis for major hypotheses, all too often built on the sand of scholarly speculation. Noth did little of this in his work on the Deuteronomistic History. He did rather too much of it in his *History of Pentateuchal Traditions*. Too many of Noth's insights there are richly imaginative but regrettably speculative.

In his *History of Pentateuchal Traditions*, Noth rightly insisted that the Pentateuch had as its theme 'all Israel', even if the emergence of that reality (all Israel) lay beyond the scope of his book.[51] In its final sections, Noth was painfully aware of the negative impact of his conclusion on the inflexibility of much traditional belief. He goes out of his way, therefore, to emphasise the pre-state solidity of Israel's twelve-tribe system and the early entry of various tribes into the arable land of Canaan. Significant elements in the process for Noth were 'the sacral covenant league' (252, associated with the amphictyony

---

50. See *Changing Face of Form Criticism*, 2–3.
51. Pages 43, 259. The difficulty of accounting for 'the emergence of that reality' remains today.

and the ark) and 'the divine guidance into the possession of the arable land of Palestine' (253). At the end of the twentieth century, both these elements were shrouded in uncertainty, on biblical and archaeological grounds. Any reflections (even if advanced with Noth's remarkable prudence), which took these for granted, to say nothing of other elements, could only be viewed as overshadowed by speculation and hypothesis. For Noth, the creative stage of the pentateuchal traditions lay 'between the time of the occupation of the land and the beginning of the formation of the state'.[52] A more complicated alternative might extend this period until considerably later. There has been no substantial follow-up to NOTH in this area. One might say that tradition history ground to a halt with the failure of this major effort.

History is both important and elusive. The pursuit of traditions into Israel's past can be suspect of indulgence in speculation. In theory, transmission history—understood as attention to the history of particular literary types—may appear to have a firmer base in existing text.[53] In practice, this is often far from the case. Both approaches are desirable; regrettably, neither is trouble-free. The 'remarkable terminological confusion' noted by Knierim may well have reflected the confusion as to what was genuinely possible.[54]

Klaus Koch

In 1954, Rad asked Klaus Koch to write 'a small guide to form criticism for our students'.[55] Regretfully, as a guide for students Koch's

---

52. *History of Pentateuchal Traditions*, 45. It is not surprising that, in the English-speaking world at least, Noth's *History of Pentateuchal Traditions* has been highly valued for its presentation of a once widely accepted consensus regarding pentateuchal source division (JEDP) and largely ignored with regard to the core of the book, its thesis on the themes leading up to the Pentateuch.
53. See *Growth of the Biblical Tradition*, 53.
54. 'Criticism of Literary Features', 147. Noth's own recognition, formulated late in his life (*1. Könige 1–16*, 246), that 'a literary–critical possibility is not a literary critical necessity'— what can be envisioned need not have been done—provides an insight that contributes to the uncertainty.
55. *Growth of the Biblical Tradition*, ix. The English main title of Koch's book (*Growth of the Biblical Tradition*) reflects more accurately the contents of the book; the German title does not (*Was ist Formgeschichte*, What is Form Criticism?— reduced in the English publication to a sub-title, *The Form-Critical Method*).

book has to be judged a hindrance rather than a help. It opens with the question: 'What is form criticism?'⁵⁶ Alas, the question is never directly answered. After a brief discussion of literary forms, the closest Koch came to an answer to his question is too general to be genuinely helpful, at least to the beginner:

> historical research has proved that the Bible is not a unit with a single literary form. Indeed the book [the Bible] contains a most remarkable assortment of literature . . . The use of words, the style and construction follow correspondingly varied principles and all these must be considered before a text can be accurately interpreted. This is form criticism.⁵⁷

The value of the form–critical approach is discussed and illustrated by a number of studies. Unfortunately, the approach itself is not analyzed, abstracted from the illustrative studies, and described for the benefit of students and others. The elements of the approach can be dug out; they are not laid out. The end product tends as a result to challenge or worse to mystify—not helpful to students. The discussions can be illuminating to the advanced; they may not help the beginner with the question, 'What is form criticism?' and what is involved with it?

There can be no doubt that, in the mid–years of the twentieth century, form criticism generated great interest and excitement, which waned with the waning of the century. Writing in 1963, Koch could say: 'So much has been written under the name of form criticism that the reader sometimes feels that this field of exegesis should be kept within some sort of bounds . . . Many exegetes tread with caution.'⁵⁸ We are left with the questions: What caused the excitement? What caused the caution? What caused the waning of it all? He added: 'Many readers will ask . . . What with literary criticism (*Literarkritik*) and its emphasis on accuracy, and the more attractive aspects of the 'positivist' tendency of the last century, haven't we enough?'.⁵⁹ From

---

56. *Growth of the Biblical Tradition* 3.
57. *Growth of the Biblical Tradition*, 6.
58. *Growth of the Biblical Tradition*, ix.
59. *Growth of the Biblical Tradition* x.

the beginning of the century, we have heard dissatisfied voices with the clear answer: No, we haven't enough; we need something more.

Five years later, introducing the English edition of his book, Koch wrote that 'form–criticism is an attempt to discover the principles underlying the language of the Bible'.[60] Honesty even more than modesty demands that this claim be characterised as grandiose. The emphasis shifts slightly when Koch's discussion moves beyond the sentence to 'the larger unit of the *literary type* of speech, which has a definite sociological function. This applies not only to the human word, but also to the Word of God as it is found in the Bible. Thus we come to the underlying purpose of this book: to try to discover what lies behind the speech of God in the Bible.'[61]

Dissatisfaction with past approaches was not the whole story. Dissatisfaction with the understanding of 'what lies behind the speech of God in the Bible' may have been part of it. What was the 'something more' that was wanted and why has interest in it waned?

Koch spoke of the 'many problems of method'.[62] It would seem that the promise of method (offering a degree of certainty regarding outcome) outweighed the caution suggested by the 'many problems'. As the century progressed, awareness of unresolved problems predominated, coupled with inadequate generalities about method.

What form criticism did, beginning with Gunkel, was pay close attention in the biblical text to more emphatically human aspects of structure and pattern, of language, content, and mood, of social and literary setting. This led to the identification of literary types and their classification. It went further in the exploration of text. All this called for imagination and insight on the part of the interpreter, as well as meticulous scholarship. Furthermore, all this drew attention to the human qualities evident in the biblical text. Form criticism may often have functioned as a label legitimating the moves to scrutinise the text in new and different ways, rethinking 'what lies behind the speech of God in the Bible', the Word of God.

---

60. *Growth of the Biblical Tradition*, xiii.
61. *Growth of the Biblical Tradition*, xiii.
62. *Growth of the Biblical Tradition* ix.

Rolf Knierim

In the latter part of the twentieth century, the standard-bearer for form criticism in North America was Rolf Knierim. Almost three-quarters of the way into the century, the complexity inherent in any theoretical consideration of the interpretation of literature, including biblical literature of course, was explored through a form-critical lens by Knierim with insight and depth in 'Old Testament Form Criticism Reconsidered'—including the potential shake-up that form criticism must face.[63] A few selections will highlight form criticism, its core, its fragility, and its outreach.

> *Core*
> Concentrating on the texts of the biblical literature as literary entities, form criticism has attempted to interpret these individual entities by discovering the matrices to which they owe their existence and which they reflect. And since a matrix is assumed to be typical in nature, individual texts emerging from it can be explained as specifications of a distinct typicality . . . The linguistic types underlying the individual texts are genres that arise out of a typical societal or life setting (435).
>
> *Fragility*
> We are no longer so clear as to what exactly a genre is. More pointedly: It is doubtful whether this has ever been clear (436).
>
> *Outreach*
> The centrality of this problem [genre] is indicated by its high visibility in different fields of research such as literature, folklore, myth and symbol, phenomenology of religion, linguistics and, most vocally, structuralism. (438).

---

63. Following this 1973 article, reference is appropriate to Christof Hardmeier, *Texttheorie und biblische Exegese*, especially 258–69 (1978); more recently, for the interpretation of the Hebrew Bible as ancient literature, Knierim 'Criticism of Literary Features' (1985) and, for the interpenetration of methodology and exegesis Knierim, *Text and Concept* (1992).

> Recent progress in the methods for interpretation of language and literature does shed new light on the problems which form criticism has faced with its own texts (467).[64]

At the end of the century, Knierim's legacy is a multi-volume series, Forms of the Old Testament Literature. The project, complementing Koch, began with a small group—editors Knierim and Tucker, with seven other leading scholars—who met annually envisaging a one-volume encyclopedia covering the form-critical work already done on each book of the OT. The plan had to be changed when it was clear that there was not enough form-critical work on the books of the OT to make it viable. The change ended up with the present series.

As a small group, meeting annually, working together on a single volume, focus could be maintained with an agreed coherence as to how form-critical issues were to be presented. The change to a multi-volume series involved greater variety and greater authorial freedom; focus and coherence was maintained by the structure required of each volume in the series.

The analytical structure of each unit of text guaranteed the close observation of a text, essential to form criticism. Such an analysis could easily deteriorate into a list of contents, but ideally it was intended to be based on form (what sort of a text does this sub-unit constitute?) and relationship (how do the parts relate to form a whole?). This observation of the text must, clearly, concentrate on the present text, reversing the earlier priority given to orality; only then might study move to anything earlier.

Beyond observation is the question of identity. What sort of a text is the whole that forms this unit? If observation was central to the analysis of structure and its discussion, identification was the task of the 'genre' section. Along with that goes 'setting'. The final section, 'intention/meaning of the text', looked at how one scholar (the modern author) saw the meaning best derived from this particular form–critical unit. The aspect of classification was left to the listing of genres, and their descriptions, at the end of each volume.

As the twentieth century ended, the series was a work in progress, with Knierim and Sweeney as editors and seventeen volumes

---

64. 'Form Criticism Reconsidered' (1973), paragraphs 435, 436, 438, 467.

completed of twenty-seven planned. An enlightening and detailed study by Marvin Sweeney (1999), with model interpretation of Genesis 15, closed out the century.[65] What the twenty-first century will make of form criticism lies ahead.

Conclusion

The Bible is a foundational religious text and such texts are almost always deeply intertwined and enmeshed with their culture. Interpretation never wholly escapes the cultural.

The cultural has many manifestations. Among them, clearly, are academy, church, and social structure. Apart from factors of personal identity—faith, heritage, experience, and so on—constraints will come from academy (perhaps eminence or career), church (perhaps respect or esteem), and social structure (perhaps influence or standing) that may have their influence on a scholar's interpretation of biblical text.

Gunkel resisted the dominant acceptance of history as automatic literary genre in Genesis, bringing observation, identification, and classification to bear against it. In full agreement, Gressmann further resisted constraining the Bible to a single local culture, instead studying it within the wider ancient Near Eastern context. In the two studies discussed here, von Rad and Noth reached back into the past of the literature; subsequent study, however, has found the convictions that were central to both works to be speculative (often faith-based) and untenable. Knierim focused on observation, identification, and classification in relation to the patterns of the present text and 'let the chips fall where they may' (a Knierim mantra).

Scientific method and procedure are essential for progress in many areas of knowledge. These do not and cannot replace sensitivity, intuition, and flair, backed up by meticulous observation, extensive knowledge, and careful scholarship. Top physicists know this; modern biblical scholars need to be comfortable with it.

A significant conclusion coming from this brief survey of the major players in the emergence of the form-critical and tradition–historical approaches to the interpretation of OT text in the twentieth century is clear beyond doubt. Form criticism is not and never was

---

65. 'Form Criticism'.

a method, in the sense of a tool in the biblical interpreter's kit, in the exegete's tool box, along with transmission history, redaction history, and the like—which in turn are themselves not tools but insights and approaches that may, on occasion, be valuable for unfolding and further interpreting a text. Professionals have a variety of tools available to them; well-trained workers only use the few that apply to the job in hand. The traditional approaches to biblical interpretation (or methods for interpreting biblical texts) are questions to be asked of a text, certainly not a sequence to be slavishly followed. The form-critical question, 'What sort of a text is this?'—with associated decisions—helps determine what tools to use. The claim, all too frequently made, that form criticism is a method, implying a series of methodical steps to be taken in order to unlock the interpretation of a text, can place an unfair burden on form criticism by creating unreal expectations that cannot be fulfilled.

Also emerging from this brief survey is clear evidence of tension between social and religious attitudes of the time and the new approaches and their consequences for biblical interpretation. It is evident with Gunkel, less explicit in Gressmann, present in von Rad's remark about his own commentary, and still there as late as Koch's book in the 1960s. It is important for those outside the German university system to be aware of the procedure for appointment to prestigious academic posts. Candidates did not, at the time, submit their applications for such posts; they were invited to apply. The relevant authorities within a university prepared the triad (or terna), the ranked list of three names of those considered suitable to be invited. This triad was then submitted to the appropriate government authority responsible for the university. The invitation to the favoured candidate was issued by this government authority. Social, ecclesiastical, and political influence make themselves felt in almost any system. The conjunction of university and government in the process of invitation means that such influence cannot be underestimated and should not be discounted. Form criticism may have on occasion functioned as a legitimation for an activity as academic that might have been frowned upon in certain circles. The subtle shift in religious attitudes, touched on at the start of this chapter, presumably played its role.

Above all, OT form criticism was (and should be) the outcome of an attitude of mind on the part of the interpreter. It was an attitude that allowed and allows for openness to the nature of any given text. It was an attitude of mind that embraced the reality of patterns in human expression and of settings in human living and that hoped/aspired/yearned to reach these in ancient Israel through attention to the structures and language of OT text. What sort of a text is this? What meaningfully can be said about it? What flows from it that contributes to meaning? This is the stuff of form criticism.

Biblical study cannot be restricted to a central focus on the analysis of composite text (*Literarkritik*) or on the history of ideas in the past (*Geistesgeschichte*), and not even to a central focus on the history of the past itself (*Geschichte*); it will always examine literature for its insights, its beauty, its religious value, and its witness to the power of thought or the play of illusion and imagination. Assuring this has been, at its best, the achievement of OT form criticism in the twentieth century.

At the end of the twentieth century, OT form criticism needed:
- first, to be reintegrated into the task of biblical interpretation;
- second, to recover its role in assessing the nature of a text and its function;
- third, alongside these, to confront issues common to all biblical interpretation and, indeed, common to any interpretation of literature.[66]

Among such issues were: awareness of literary genre in all its complexity; the equal complexity of the concept of setting or matrix; the interplay of structure and content in the understanding of genre; the potential interaction of both typical and individual in literature.[67] The future will not lack for work.

---

66. See Knierim 'Form Criticism Reconsidered' (1973), reinforced by his 'Criticism of Literary Features' (1985).
67. This last issue is shared by Muilenburg early in his 'Form Criticism and Beyond', especially 5.

Form-Criticism's Future

(original: *The Changing Face of Form Criticism for the Twenty-First Century*)

Form criticism had a meteoric rise in the early part of the twentieth century and fell from favour toward its end. For some, the future of form criticism is not an issue: it has none. But if form criticism embodies an essential insight, it will continue. If it is to continue in the reflective and thinking world of academic scholarship, the attraction that triggered its rise, the flaws that caused its fall, and the aspects that assure its future all need to be analysed. So this article will have three parts: the past—the rise and fall of form criticism; the essentials—form-criticism's insight; the future—form-criticism's changing face.

To read the pioneers of form criticism is to be left with little doubt that their enthusiasm for the new approach was fueled in part by their aversion to the excesses of source–critical (in those days, literary-critical) research and in part, too, by a less explicit resistance to claims for the historicity of the Bible's earlier traditions.[1] There is both an irony and a rightness in the recognition that it has been the excesses

---

1. See Hugo Greßmann's comment on *Literarkritik*: 'In our field we need not more but less literary-critical research. Literary criticism (*Literarkritik*) has generally exhausted the tasks which it had to and was able to do' ('Die Aufgaben der alttestamentlichen Forschung', in *ZAW* 42 (1924): 1–33, see 8).
   Both concerns come together in Klaus Koch's comment in the context of historicity. 'It [the study of the transmission of a tradition] is of particular significance for the early history of Israel, that is, before 1000 BC. It was naive of the literary critics ... to translate as they did the accounts of the early history of Israel ... directly into events. First of all it is essential to make a form-critical assessment of the changes which the pre-literary traditions will have undergone' (*The Growth of the Biblical Tradition: The Form-Critical Method* [New York: Scribner's, 1969; original German, *Was ist Formgeschichte? Neue Wege der Bibelexegese*], 54).

of both source-critical and form–critical claims coupled with the demands of interests in other areas that relegated so-called historical criticism to the backburner of biblical publication.

Highly competent and intelligent scholars, at the top of their field, do not usually embrace the new solely out of aversion to the old. An insight and a value is seen in the new that lead to its embrace. If form criticism, which once was new, is to regain a place in the panoply of the interpretative arts, it needs to be refocused on the lasting insight and value that once contributed to firing enthusiasm for it. Two elements embody this insight and give it its value: concern for the nature of a text and for its shape or structure. If the incrustations can be scraped away, the good stuff may still be there. A couple of the areas of incrustation are certainly the passion for the preliterary past of stories and the condescension—at times almost contempt—felt on occasion for the storytellers, audiences, and even the later writers of ancient Israel.

In this present time, we have two choices: either to go back or to go beyond. The move beyond has been well under way for some time. A fresh grasp of form criticism may help it find its place in that move. We cannot go back. It would be as if scientists decided quantum mechanics was just too complicated and uncertain and it would be surer to go back to Newtonian physics or, better still, to flat earth theory. After all, flat earth theory is quite accurate within a radius of ten to fifteen miles. The only difficulty with flat earth theory is that it is wrong—shown so by observation, such as global travel. An uncertain literalist could go back to the biblical text as a unity with a single author; it works all right for a while. The only difficulty is that it is wrong—shown so by observation, such as a couple of centuries of scholarship or any close reading today.

So insight has to go forward. It will help to recognise that much twentieth-century biblical research was burdened with holdovers from the nineteenth century: an obsession with the recovery and reconstruction of history, a conviction about progressive stages of development, and an often constipated view of religion. Form criticism contributed its share to this malaise. The literary forms would reveal origins and show progressive stages of development. The settings in life of the forms would be of value in the historical reconstruction of ancient Israel's institutions and literature. An understanding of form would give genuine insight into the religious feeling and life of Israel.

The past: the rise and fall of form criticism

The beginnings of the modern phenomenon of biblical form criticism go back to the figure of Hermann Gunkel and a relatively small group of those stimulated by him. For the Newer Testament, the names and dates are Martin Dibelius (1919), Karl Ludwig Schmidt (1919), and Rudolf Bultmann (1921)—all three sat at Gunkel's feet in Berlin (1894-1907); but that is another story and it will not be told here. For the Older Testament, Gunkel's form-critical insights began with his commentary on Genesis (1901), were developed in his commentary on the Psalms (1929), and culminated in his Introduction to the Psalms (published posthumously in 1933).[2] Work on the psalms was taken further by his pupil, Sigmund Mowinckel;[3] the implications for law, prophecy, and wisdom followed in due course. For narrative text, Gunkel's close friend Hugo Greßmann moved beyond Genesis, first with a commentary on most of Samuel—Kings (also Amos and Hosea) and then with his study on the figure of Moses (reflecting Exodus and Numbers).[4]

---

2. Hermann Gunkel, *Genesis*, eighth edition (Göttingen: Vandenhoeck & Ruprecht, 1969; 1st ed., 1901); idem, *Die Psalmen*, fifth edition (Göttingen: Vandenhoeck & Ruprecht, 1968; 4th edition and Gunkel's first, 1929); idem, *Einleitung in die Psalmen*, completed by J Begrich; second edition (Göttingen: Vandenhoeck & Ruprecht, 1966; first edition, 1933). The mention of these three books is, of course, far from exhaustive of Gunkel's output.
3. Sigmund Mowinckel, *The Psalms in Israel's Worship*, 2 volumes (Oxford: Blackwell, 1962); Norwegian original, 1951. Mowinckel acknowledges his debt to Gunkel, his teacher in Giessen; his own move beyond Gunkel began with the *Psalmenstudien I–VI* (1921–24). For a summary overview of OT form criticism, see John Barton, *ABD* 2.838–41; for form criticism and narrative, see Jay A Wilcoxen, 'Narrative', in *Old Testament Form Criticism*, edited by JH Hayes (San Antonio: Trinity University Press, 1974), 57–98. For background to Gunkel's life and scholarship, see the tribute by Walter Baumgartner, *Congress Volume, Bonn, 1962*, VTSup 9 (Leiden: Brill, 1963), 1–18, reprinted in Gunkel's *Genesis*, sixth and later editions as well as Werner Klatt, *Hermann Gunkel: Zu seiner Theologie der Religionsgeschichte und zur Entstehung der formgeschichtlichen Methode*, FRLANT 100 (Göttingen: Vandenhoeck & Ruprecht, 1969).
4. Hugo Greßmann, *Die Schriften des Alten Testaments in Auswahl neu übersetzt und für die Gegenwart erklärt von Hermann Gunkel, W. Staerk, Paul Volz, Hugo Greßmann, Hans Schmidt und M. Haller*, 2. Abteilung, 1. Band: *Die älteste Geschichtsschreibung und Prophetie Israels (von Samuel bis Amos und Hosea)* second revised edition (Gottingen: Vandenhoeck & Ruprecht, 1921; first edition, 1910), XII-XVII, 1–220, 240–323, for 1 Samuel 1—2 Kings 14; idem, *Mose und*

The early pages of Gunkel's introduction to Genesis witness to a need for freedom from the oppressive weight of the concern for history. For example: 'The Evangelical Church . . . would do well not to oppose—as has so often happened—this recognition that Genesis contains stories.'[5] From the outset, the establishment was uneasy about him; senior figures at Göttingen had not wanted his habilitation.[6] He would hardly have been unaware.[7] Also significant for form criticism's later demise is the recognition that Gunkel's focus of attention was on the original story in its oral transmission phase.[8] The tyranny of history was probably lurking in the surrounds.[9] For Gunkel, the stories were not history; yet they were surely understood as history by those who told them.[10] Stories were oral; history was written.[11] History deals with major public events; story treats the personal and private.[12] History has to be susceptible of being traced

---

seine Zeit (Göttingen: Vandenhoeck & Ruprecht, 1913).

5. 'Die evangelische Kirche und ihre berufenen Vertreter würden gut tun, gegen diese Erkenntnis, daß die Genesis Sagen enthält, sich nicht—wie es bisher so vielfach geschehen ist—zu sperren' (*Genesis*, XII–XIII). Gunkel goes on: unless this is recognized, a historical understanding of Genesis is impossible.
6. Cf Klatt, *Hermann Gunkel*, 16–17.
7. To be noted, in this context, is his 1891 move from Göttingen to Halle and with it from NT to OT, as well as the subsequent goings-on in Berlin (cf Klatt, *Hermann Gunkel*, 40–45).
8. *Genesis*, XXXII–III.
9. A phrase like 'the tyranny of history' must be understood with exactitude when speaking of a scholar as passionately concerned for history as was Gunkel (cf Klatt, *Hermann Gunkel,* 24–27). 'Historical' is a descriptor that goes hand in hand with modern scholarship; 'historical' may describe a state of intellectual awareness required in most modern scholarship. But as every modern knows, meaning is more than history; the interest of the historical is not restricted to its history alone. When the search for history denies value to whatever does not contribute to historical reconstruction of events, the obsession with history has denied worth and meaning to all that does not serve this purpose—and is rightly called tyranny. Too frequently in biblical study, the often blithely unquestioned assumption that traditions have meaning insofar as they provide access to the events that happened is a subtle mask for the denial of worth to whatever is not of value for such reconstruction. This I call 'the tyranny of history'. Stories have value; faith has worth.
10. Gunkel goes to considerable length in arguing against the historicality of these Genesis stories (cf *Genesis*, VIII–XIII). Note also XXX.
11. *Genesis*, VIII.
12. *Genesis*, IX.

back to eyewitnesses; not so with story.¹³ The clearest indication that we are dealing with story, however, is the presence of things we find unworthy of belief.¹⁴ Of its nature, history is prose; of its nature, story is poetry.¹⁵

There are signs of the times. Greßmann was sometimes rather more publicly venturesome than Gunkel. In approaching his work on Samuel—Kings, what he takes for granted today has heads shaking with surprise, sadness, or outrage. For example: i) story is easily distinguished from history (story: distant past and out of touch with reality—its heroes, the leading figures of the distant past; history: the present or the recent past and in touch with reality—its heroes, the leading figures in the State); ii) competent scholars will eliminate 'clumsy' additions (*ungeschickte Zusätze*) and recognise the 'mutilation' (*Verstümmelung*) of traditions; iii) story claims belief but does not earn it; history presents what actually was (*was wirklich gewesen ist*).¹⁶ The literary types—story, idyll, history, legend, märchen, etc—are not described with appropriate precision by Greßmann; to today's practiced eye, his discussion seems highly subjective.

'After Gunkel's death there was a period of relative inactivity in the field of form criticism.'¹⁷ For Gunkel, the move to the distant and mostly non-Israelite oral past may have been liberating, despite its highly hypothetical quality and deep uncertainty; it offered an opening to literary appreciation that the cold precision of contemporary literary-critical analysis did not allow for. But, added to the fragmentary activity of the analysts and Gunkel's frequent comparison of the naivety of ancient Israel with that of his generation's children, the focus away from the present text into a surmised past accessible to a sensitive few did not generate enough value to find favour with those focused on the present reality of what was possessed in the final text.¹⁸

---

13. *Genesis*, X–XI.
14. *Genesis*, X–XI.
15. *Genesis*, XII–XIII.
16. Greßmann, *Schriften*, II/1, XII–XIV.
17. Koch, *Growth*, 72, n 2.
18. The 'sensitive few' reflects Gunkel's comments on 'Formensprache' (the appropriateness of language to form) as demanding aesthetic study ('ästhetische Betrachtung') on the part of the researcher and his appeal to Goethe's dictum that raw material or subject matter ('Stoff') was available to all, that artistic worth or substance ('Gehalt') was only accessible to the initiated, and that shape or

Both Gunkel and Greßmann exhibit what is, for me, a disturbing focus on history as the primary value within their texts. It may be ironic, but I believe it accurate to situate their emphasis on historical value within the need they felt to devalue the historical aspect of early story traditions. The need to differentiate meant that, in their introductory material at least, the attention given to text that was believed to be of historical worth appears to distract from the value of the earlier 'story' traditions, whose focus is quite different. Thought and faith go unmentioned. It may not be an exaggeration to say that both scholars felt the need to loosen the grip (the stranglehold ?) of history on the earlier traditions of the Bible. Intrinsic to form criticism is a focus on text before event.

For the Older Testament, form criticism's second wave is typified by the publications of Martin Noth and Gerhard von Rad. Both had been associated with Albrecht Alt at Leipzig, who was not one of the circle personally associated with Gunkel. For Alt, however, Gunkel was the 'founder of form–critical research in OT scholarship', and Alt's famous essay on the origins of Israelite law was seen by him as filling out an aspect of Gunkel's program.[19] Alt's interests were transmitted to Noth and von Rad; clearly, these scholars were attracted by something of lasting value they saw in Gunkel's perception of Israelite literature. Von Rad's form–critical interest is best evidenced in his concern with the forces shaping the Hexateuch.[20] Noth was led particularly to his study of the remote origins of the Pentateuch.[21]

Von Rad credited the shape and structure of the present Hexateuch (Genesis to Joshua) to remote origins in the short historical credo and the themes of Israel's early worship (cf Deut 6:20–25; 26:5–9; Josh 24:2–13). Initially well-received, this understanding was doomed to dissatisfaction once it could be shown that the short credos

---

pattern or form ('Form') was a mystery to most—'die Form ist ein Geheimnis den meisten' (*Einleitung*, 23).

19. 'Der Begründer der gattungsgeschichtlichen Forschung in der alttestamentlichen Wissenschaft' (Alt, 'Die Ursprünge des israelitischen Rechts', *Kleine Schriften*, volume I [Munich: Beck, 1959], 278–332, see 285, n. 1).
20. 'Das formgeschichtliche Problem des Hexateuch' (TB 8; *GS* [Munich: Kaiser, 1965; original, 1938], 9–86). ET: 1–78 in *The Problem of the Hexateuch and Other Essays* (London: SCM, 1984).
21. *Überlieferungsgeschichte des Pentateuch* (Stuttgart: Kohlhammer, 1948); ET by BW Anderson, *A History of Pentateuchal Traditions*).

came late in the process, more as summaries than the original core from which the process began. For Greßmann and von Rad source criticism's work (*Literarkritik*) was largely done; for Noth, it was a lively and continuing debate into which he sought to introduce a new view or two. Nevertheless, in the context of his tradition–historical study, the source-critical results for the Pentateuch are relegated to 'Prolegomena'.[22] From von Rad's form-critical work, Noth presumed the originating role of the 'basic themes' in the ritual confessions of Israel's worship. He was aware that it would frequently 'be impossible to go beyond probabilities or even possibilities . . . [when moving] . . . into the dark and impenetrable area of the preliterary oral tradition'; the 'creative stage' of the history of the Pentateuch was 'the preliterary history of the formation and the growth of the tradition'.[23] The abandonment of von Rad's proposal and the murky uncertainty of Noth's deterred the bulk of scholarship from following in their footsteps.

The task of systematising OT form criticism was taken up by two of von Rad's former students, operating in different directions. Klaus Koch, asked by von Rad to write 'a small guide to form criticism for our students', ended up with 'a full-length book', intended 'as a guide for students, as an introduction to form–critical research'.[24] Rolf Knierim set out, with co-editor Gene Tucker and a team of colleagues, to gather together the results of form-critical study of the OT in a single volume.[25]

Instead of providing a springboard into future form-critical activity, Koch's book in hindsight has had the function rather of being its gravestone. The claims on the future were too big for the present to bear. For a book that was to be a guide for students, there are far-reaching claims—'A form-critical approach permits us to discover afresh the vitality of God's Word' (13); 'The study of literary types . . . is the groundwork without which nothing can be

---

22. *History of Pentateuchal Traditions*, 5–41 (cf in particular 5–7).
23. *History of Pentateuchal Traditions*, 3 and 44 (German, 4 and 47).
24. Koch, *Growth,* ix. The title of the original German is revealing: *Was ist Formgeschichte? Neue Wege der Bibelexegese* (What is Form Criticism? New Paths in Biblical Exegesis). The title and even the subtitle of the English translation are more muted.
25. Known as the Old Testament Form–Criticism project and headquartered at the Institute for Antiquity and Christianity, at the then Claremont Graduate School.

maintained with certainty' (66)—and there are serious lacunae. An 'Index of Biblical Literary Types and Their Elements' is provided (231–33), but it is no more than an index of references to these. Few literary types are described with any degree of precision; guidelines for the identification and description of such types are not given. The troubling aspects of early form-critical research are not addressed. The major advantages of a form-critical approach are claimed rather than articulated. There is little differentiation offered between studies giving helpful evaluation and those moving instead toward unhelpful fragmentation and overly hypothetical outcomes. Such silences suggest that learning was from apprenticeship to a master and not from the guidance of a handbook. The book is a valuable pointer to the possibilities of the form-critical approach; it is not, as one might expect from an introduction intended to benefit students, the summary of a mature field of study. Harsh reality set bounds to the book. As Koch notes in his introduction, on many points convincing results were far from being achieved; many parts of the Bible had not yet been studied from a form-critical point of view. Of necessity, he was limited to 'a few examples, choosing only the focal points'.[26] The limits suggest an approach to research that had an early flowering and stunted subsequent growth. In other words, there was much work to be done; in the decades ahead, few were interested in doing it.

The concern of Gunkel and Greßmann for a story's growth from an ancient oral past to its incorporation into the biblical text is systematised by Koch as 'the history of the transmission of tradition'. Research is needed 'because many biblical passages have been passed down either orally or in writing over a long period of time and have therefore been much modified before reaching their final shape'.[27] At the least, a caution against subjectivity is needed here; it is not given.

The Knierim-Tucker project ran into the dual problem of the inadequacy of the form-critical coverage of the OT and the inadequacy of some of the form-critical work done.[28] A new focus was needed.

---

26. Koch, *Growth*, ix.
27. Koch, *Growth*, 39.
28. 'The original plan of the project was to record critically all the relevant results of previous form–critical studies concerning the texts in question' (Rolf Knierim and Gene M Tucker, editors, in Roland E Murphy, *Wisdom Literature: Job, Proverbs, Ruth, Canticles, Ecclesiastes, and Esther*, FOTL 13 [Grand Rapids: Eerdmans, 1981], x—and subsequent Forewords.) The plan had to be expanded.

The project was reorganised, but across the discipline of OT studies, the form-critical impulse was running into the sand.

Multiple factors were involved in form criticism's fall from favour. The remove to the distant and mostly non-Israelite oral past may have been liberating in certain areas; for many later, it failed to satisfy. Furthermore, the hopes raised produced too little in the way of secure results or the approach itself produced too much in the way of festivals and liturgies.²⁹ Above all, as noted, the focus away from the present text into a surmised past accessible to a scholarly few was too burdened with subjectivity to survive in a generation focused on the present reality of what was possessed in the final text.

I had considered this article to be basically finished when I came across a passage of Gunkel's that I think of as the 'smoking gun'. It goes a long way to explaining his attraction to form–criticism and, I believe, it also sheds light on form criticism's later fall from favour. In 1910, in a letter to his publisher, Gunkel wrote: '[For the non-specialist] the way to the substance (*Inhalt*) lies through pleasure in the aesthetic form. It is quite different with source criticism (*Literarkritik*) . . . Now it is my particular gift to have a feeling for the aesthetic and to bring it to the fore.'³⁰ Gunkel turned to form–criticism because, for him, the current source criticism lacked any meaningful attraction. A later

---

29. 'Apparently, once the search for a cultic 'situation in life' of Old Testament narrative had got under way, there was no portion of the literature which could escape such an interpretation' (Herbert F Hahn, *The Old Testament in Modern Research* expanded edition; [Philadelphia: Fortress, 1966; original, 1954], 142–43). Note Hahn's later comment on the repeated discovery of cultic liturgies in the prophetic books: 'Frequently, these studies showed greater zeal than judgment' (Herbert F Hahn, *The Old Testament*, 146). On the fragility of the concept of setting, see Burke O Long, 'Recent Field Studies in Oral Literature and the Question of *Sitz im Leben*', in *Semeia* 5 (1976): 35–49. Long writes: 'The attempt to suggest settings or setting for a biblical genre on the basis of written texts should be made. Without this, the link between literature and life is lost. But such recontructions ought to be treated with much more than usual reserve and joined with a good deal more serious sociological research . . . I cannot conceive of an anthropologist reconstructing the typical occasion for a literary piece on the basis of its *literary* features alone. If he were to do so, he would be more often wrong, totally wrong, than right' (44).
30. 'Der Weg zum Inhalt geht ihm [the layperson] durch die Freude an der ästhetischen Form. Ganz anders ist es mit der Literarkritik. ... Nun ist es meine besondere Art, das Ästhetische nachzuempfinden u. darzustellen' (from Klatt, *Hermann Gunkel*, 118).

generation turned away from form criticism because, for many, it had been refined to the point of losing all meaningful attraction.

If my judgment is right, the source criticism of Gunkel's day denied worth to the present text because it was thought to be all too often a mechanical composite without the possibility of literary merit. So Gunkel was forced to retreat to the pre-literary oral stage. The discovery some modern scholars have yet to appropriate fully is that the composers responsible for the present text were knowledgeable, skillful, and presumably aesthetically aware. So today we can contemplate the present text and, without scholarly embarrassment, find it aesthetically pleasing.

In the language of recent psychology and spirituality, the approach to text needs to appeal to the whole person, not just to the head or intellect. Gunkel experienced the intellectual analysis of source criticism (*Literarkritik*) as cold and alienating. He looked for something more attractive in a form-critical approach to the whole. As the form-critical approach became fragmented into analytical demands that could not be met and hypothetical claims that could not be substantiated, later scholarship found it unappealing and in turn became alienated from it. Central to the attraction of the original impulse was the focus on the whole. This focus on the whole remains at the core of form-critical insight.

The essentials: Form criticism's insight

The essential insight of form criticism, the attraction that led to its wide acceptance by first-rate scholars, can—I think—be summed up in these terms: whatever is regarded as individual text, whether shorter or longer, needs to be treated as a whole and each individual whole will be affected by the influence of the typical. Two issues are thus central to the task of interpreting literature. One is ascertaining the nature of the particular work of literature under interpretation. The other is coming to grips with the particular work as a whole in order to see how its parts relate to the whole and communicate its message.

The first of these relates to the typical; the second to the individual. The first asks the question: what is typical of this text that situates it within a particular class of texts? The second asks the question: what is it about the way this text is shaped and structured that communicates its meaning?

It is important to eliminate two misunderstandings. First, the decision about the literary type (genre) is not an understanding imposed on the text; it is a decision that emerges out of the understanding of the text. Second, the question of the shape and structure of the text is to be asked of the passage in the present biblical text; it is not asked of some remote uncertain original form putatively assumed from the past.

The meaning of text emerges from the text as a whole, not substantively from the fragments that can be found in it. If biblical interpretation is to find meaning, it must focus on a text as entity: what we believe a text said and says. It is of the nature of form criticism to name the whole; that is what it means to declare the literary genre of a text. It is of the nature of form criticism to study how the parts of a text interrelate to form a whole and to give it meaning. The more advanced and specialised academic biblical study becomes, the greater the need at the right times to pull back and view the whole. The enormous contribution of form criticism to future biblical studies may be in requiring and legitimating this view of the whole.

Literary genre or type
 (= the typical, a matrix for the text [German: *Gattung*])
Naming something is of the essence of knowledge. Form criticism, in its concern for literary genre, is all about naming.

It may help to say what a literary genre—or literary type, if a monosyllable is preferred—is not, before moving on to what it is.

> i. It is not a license to launch out into uncertain surmises about a distant past.
> ii. It is not an invitation to indulge in subjective speculation about how a text might have come to be what it is.
> iii. It is not a key to unlock the secrets of a text's understanding.

A literary genre, or literary type, is:
> i. A tag that an interpreter can put on a text after its secrets have been explored.
> ii. A name that helps situate a text within a general class so that it can be more easily understood.

iii. A summary of observations about a given text validating an initial intuition as to its nature.

It may be important, for example, to be able to name stirring legends as such, or well-loved stories, or the report of treasured memories; it may be important to be able to say with good reason that certain texts are not to be mistaken for history or for reflective theological pieces.

Literary form or structure
   (= the text itself, in all its individuality [German: *Form*])
The term literary form should not be an optional alternative for those who find literary genre rather too difficult to pronounce; often used interchangeably, genre and form are not the same. 'Form' is a good English word for the shape or structure of something. To avoid confusion in this context, the German *Form* can be best rendered by the English 'structure'.[31]

The meaning of a text can only emerge from the study of its shape or structure. There are many ways in which the results of such study can be reported. What is important is that the reporting renders accessible to the reader the decisions about the text on which its interpretation is based. Whether the structure is represented diagrammatically (for example, a tabular structure analysis) with comment or whether it is expressed in an undiagrammed discussion of the text is unimportant. What matters is that the decisions about the text taken by the interpreter and the reasons for them are accessible to the reader. The shape or structure is, of course, that of an individual text. It is this constellation of its components that allows each text to makes its own individual communication.

In order to regain its usefulness, modern form criticism had to shuck off the attention given to earliest origins and focus on the actual rather than the hypothetical.[32] The refocusing of form criticism,

---

31. So, for example, John Barton in his dictionary article on 'Form–Criticism: Old Testament': the German *Form* properly so called 'is the structure or shape of an individual passage or unit'; the German *Gattung* is used for 'a general class or genre' (*ABD* 2.839). See also GM Tucker, 'Form Criticism, OT', in *IDBSup*, 342.
32. The past is not easily dispensed with. John Barton, while claiming form criticism as 'an indispensable tool for the historical study of the OT', asserts that its focus is 'on preliterary stages of the text's growth' (*ABD* 2.839). Once upon a time, it was; it should no longer be.

after some seven decades on the biblical scene, can be typified by the statement of purpose in the editors' foreword to the first volume published in the FOTL series. 'If the results of form criticism are to be verifiable and generally intelligible, then the determination of typical forms and genres, their settings and functions, has to take place through the analysis of the forms in and of the texts themselves . . . In contrast to most traditional form-critical work, the interpretation of the texts accepts the fundamental premise that we possess all texts basically at their latest written stages . . .'[33] Appropriately stripped down, devoid of the folly and pretension of some of the aspects that attended its beginnings, form–criticism must take its place as an essential element in the art of interpretation.

The future: form criticism's changing face

Two questions, then, are central to what needs to flourish again as form–criticism redivivus, embodying the direction of the changing face of form criticism.[34] The first: what is the nature of this text, its literary genre or type? The second: what is the shape or structure of this text, its basic components and their relationship to each other? Both questions are in the service of the fundamental task of textual interpretation: the expression of a text's meaning.

Literary genre or type
    (= the typical, a matrix for the text)
At one level, form criticism is as automatic as breathing and anxieties about air quality should not keep us from breathing. Sometimes form criticism is simplistically easy; sometimes it is not. When it is not easy is precisely when it is usually important.

---

33. Knierim and Tucker, Editors' Foreword in Murphy, *Wisdom Literature* (FOTL 13), x. This concern with the present text can be overlooked if it is not realised that the move from 'larger literary corpora' to 'any prior discernible stages' is a move that remains at the level of the present text. It is not a move from the text to its past; it is a move from larger units (for example, an entire biblical book) to the smaller constitutive units.
34. It may be symbolized by the renewed and expanded FOTL project; it should not be restricted to it. For some of the complexities that can beset OT form-critical theory, see Rolf Knierim, 'Old Testament Form Criticism Reconsidered', in *Interpretation* 27 (1973): 435–67.

Martin Buss has compared form criticism with learning the rules of a language, bringing into awareness considerations which are known subconsciously.[35] It is always important that we are able to name what we observe. In many cases, it probably will not be necessary to go much beyond the list of genres noted below. Specialists in particular areas will know where the need is felt for further work. My own area is narrative and there is a potential misunderstanding that makes the naming of literary genres a major concern. Without adequate reflection, it is frequently taken for granted that the focus of OT narrative traditions is history. The naming of the matrix is essential. It brings to full awareness what may be only latent. It situates the individual text within the broader horizon of expression arising out of human experience.

Historicity is often a complex and delicate matter; it is only muddled by those who insist on treating it as simple. It is certainly not an exclusively form-critical issue. For example, reports can be accurate or erroneous; stories can be factual or fictional; and so on. A variety of elements comes into play. Form-critical clarity might contribute to the greater clarity needed amid complexity.

A variety of literary genres or types have been identified in biblical text over the years. It is unlikely—perhaps even undesirable—that a manual of stylistic diagnosis will be produced listing and describing achieved results for all the biblical genres. Room needs to be left for individual assessment of texts and recognition given to the reality that individual interpreters will understand the same genres in different ways, no matter how carefully they are defined. Interpretation is an art, not a science. In key areas, I believe basic agreement already exists about the understanding of certain genres.

    i. In narrative, story is distinguished from account, report, or notice, as well as from legend and märchen and the like. Story moves from tension to its resolution, via plot; account, report, and notice do not. Legend and märchen etc have their own specific characteristics and are rare enough not to worry most of us much.

    ii. In prophecy, judgment is distinguished from

---

35. Martin J Buss, 'The Study of Forms', in *Old Testament Form Criticism*, edited by JH Hayes (San Antonio: Trinity University Press, 1974), 1–56, see 2–3.

salvation, Israel from the nations, and the nation from the individual. Since Westermann's *Basic Forms,* a prophetic judgment speech is associated with the combination of an accusation and an announcement, often linked by the messenger formula or equivalent.[36]

iii. In psalms, lament and complaint are distinguished from thanksgiving or praise, individual from communal, and we are aware of royal psalms and others.

iv. In law, apodictic is distinguished from casuistic and most of us are aware that there are priestly genres such as ritual and instruction.

v. In wisdom literature, there are certain literary genres that are accepted and that it is probably unhelpful to look at more closely here.

Something like this may be enough for the form criticism we cannot not do.

Gunkel took for granted that the storytellers of ancient Israel regarded their traditions as historical; for Gunkel himself, it was obvious that the early ones were not.[37] The passion for history in biblical study does not die easily. No less a figure than Claus Westermann claimed recently (1970s/1994) that in a work of history (such as the Deuteronomistic History) the primary function is expected to be the presentation of history as it unfolded (*so wie sie verlaufen ist*). Westermann complains that the portrayal of the Deuteronomistic Historian as an interpreter of the past does not preserve posterity's access to what happened in Israel's history (*was in der Geschichte Israels geschehen ist*).[38] Gunkel may write off ancient Israel's early storytellers; the poor things just were not advanced enough to distinguish clearly between fiction and fact (*Dichtung und Wirklichkeit*).[39] Westermann may yearn for posterity to know just what happened in ancient Israel. There is a genuine need to know

---

36. Cf Claus Westermann, *Grundformen prophetischer Rede* (Munich: Kaiser, 1960); ET: *Basic Forms of Prophetic Speech.*
37. *Genesis,* XXX; see above, n 7.
38. Claus Westermann, *Die Geschichtsbücher des Alten Testaments: Gab es ein Deuteronomistisches Geschichtswerk?* (Gütersloh: Kaiser, 1994), 28–29.
39. 'Die Sage stammt aus Zeiten und Kreisen, die noch nicht die geistige Kraft haben, Dichtung und Wirklichkeit deutlich zu unterschieden' (*Genesis,* XXX).

how we tell when we are dealing with imaginative storytelling and when with historical reporting.

No modern observer, aware of 'historical' novels and 'historical' films, should fail to see the difficulty. A report is easily enough distinguished from a story in terms of literary type; in a nutshell, story has plot and report does not. Whether a particular piece of biblical narrative has been composed as report or story is often not at all easy to distinguish. A good example of the importance of the issue at stake is 1 Sam 4 on the loss of the ark. Israel's elders are said to have asked: 'Why has the Lord put us to rout today before the Philistines?' (1 Sam 4:3). If the text is a report of what happened, then the question is in the text because the elders asked it. The probable answer to it can be implied from their proposal: 'Let us bring the ark . . . from Shiloh' (4:4). It does not matter that the reporter knows what is going to happen soon; the reporter is retailing what occurred on the day of the first defeat—the question was asked. If the text is a story about what happened, then the question is in the text because the storyteller wanted it there. On the other hand, because the storyteller knew the second battle would result in a disastrous defeat and the ark would be lost, it becomes legitimate to ask why the elders' question was told in the story. If this is a story, the answer can no longer be simply that the elders asked it. The storyteller knows that the absence of the ark was not the cause of the first defeat. The question, then, is fraught with much deeper meaning. A preliminary answer is offered in a dying mother's naming of her son: 'the glory has departed from Israel' (4:21–22). The following narrative will resolve the ambiguity of 4:22, with its active and passive verbs. The active voice gets the nod; God has chosen to go—and later to return.

It is important to recognise that what is reported provides the raw material for interpretation. In the telling of a story, interpretation has often been begun.

Interpretative comments such as 'God tested Abraham' (Gen 22:1) or 'the Lord raised up a deliverer for the Israelites' (Judg 3:9) do not establish the distinction between report and story. Test and deliverance can be reported. The comments do hint at how the text could be used to rehearse the tradition as story. The tension of the plot is given. What sort of a test will it be and will Abraham pass it? How will deliverance be brought about in Israel after so many years' oppression? The Bible's framing of the deliverer stories in Judges 3–8 (Ehud, Deborah/Barak/Jael, Gideon) is an example of how Israel's experience articulated in tradition can be transformed into a theology.

Form-critical assessments need to be made for every text we deal with. When the literary genre or type is obvious, the task is easy. When the literary type is far from obvious, and the task is far from easy, responsible interpreters will need to identify as explicitly as possible the elements that bear on any decision. Honesty should keep form criticism in business.

Literary form or structure
      (= the text itself, in all its individuality)
Matrixes are all very well, but the biblical texts are the only certain realities we have. It may be important to know the class or type to which a text belongs. It is equally or more important to know what the communication is that this text, of this particular class or type, is articulating. Texts do not fall into types according to the whims of authors or classifiers. Texts adopt types because there is something typical in what the text is to communicate. The communication of a particular text may be typical (for example, history, report, prophecy of judgment, song of praise), but as a particular text it will have its own particular communication to make (for example, this history, this report, this prophecy of judgment, this song of praise, etc). Discussion of the shape or structure of a text is a sure route to its particular communication.

That most biblical texts will have had some sort of oral past is nowadays largely taken for granted, as is the recognition that any precision in reconstructing aspects of that past is usually out of reach.

To use 'method' as a noun with reference to the art of interpretation comes close to a crime—at least if method is understood as a systematic procedure following prescribed steps to achieve a preordained end. The aspects of biblical study which precede the interpretation of a text—text criticism, source criticism, form criticism, tradition history, editing history, etc—are best described as approaches. They begin with insight and intuition that have to be tested and validated or verified methodically—and for that careful, reflective, and systematic study is needed. Not all approaches apply to every text. Not all interpreters will assess various approaches in the same way.

Woodenly understood, method can muzzle. Texts control; they do not muzzle.

Nevertheless, it can be helpful to have some principles of guidance when approaching a text. In my practice, awareness of certain steps is often helpful in beginning to unpack the approach to a text. The steps for an interpreter will vary from text to text and from interpreter to interpreter, but the following is a useful initial checklist.

   i. Boundaries: what is the extent of the passage, its beginning and end.
  ii. Blocks: what are the component elements of the passage and their relationships.
 iii. Relationships: how are the blocks structured within a passage, so that the parts form a whole?
  iv. External elements: if required by a particular text, assess the nature and extent of any imported components (earlier tradition or later editing).
   v. Explore the possibilities of the passage for meaning, in its time and now.

The boundaries accepted for a text can often determine its meaning. Beyond simple measures, such as not having pronouns or suffixes referring across boundaries and not having verbs dependent on a subject beyond a boundary, much has to be left to the interpreter's intuition. Interpreters and readers need to be aware of the issues; often, not much more can be asked. Blocks are important. How do texts begin and end? How much is contained between beginning and end? Relationships are even more important. Is there development? Is there contrast? Are there thematic moves? Imported components, whether earlier elements that have been incorporated or additions made later, can often be identified by aspects of language or ideology, or by the fact that they do not quite fit, and so on. The point is not to dismiss what has been identified as external, but to see what meaning is given by its use or insertion. The issue of meaning is where text and reader need to be rubbed together until fire is generated. Texts often do not yield up meaning easily. All the issues of extent, components, relationships, everything that is part of shape and structure goes into the making of meaning. Few texts worth interpreting will be restricted to a single meaning. Few attempts at articulating meaning will be convincing if they do not pay appropriate attention to the signals of the text. It is in seeking to grasp the shape and structure of a text that these signals are best noticed.[40]

Interpretation needs to know what sort of a text is being interpreted. Interpretation needs to know the shape and structure of the text being interpreted. Modern form criticism is concerned with precisely these two areas of knowledge. It has a future—if its past is allowed a decent burial.

---

40. It is appropriate that the last question should be left to the last footnote. The question: where is the diachronic dimension in all this? If, out of the shape and structure of the text, diachronic or growth issues force themselves on an interpreter, they need to be investigated with all the insights available to scholarship. Such investigation is part of the task of interpretation. I would be slow to see it is as intrinsic to form criticism.

Structure Analysis and the Art of Exegesis (1 Samuel 16:14–18:30)

(original: *Problems in Biblical Theology*)

The Holy Grail of biblical interpretation should be the meaning of a text: the best insight the interpreter can offer, after all the acumen of scholarship has been brought to bear, as to what the text is doing or saying.[1] Like the Grail itself, meaning proves elusive to those who engage in its quest. It is easy to make archaeological, geographical, and historical comments or to note critical and linguistic issues. It is quite another question to lay bare one's conviction as to a text's meaning. The process tends to lay bare the interpreter's being.[2]

Gerhard von Rad noted long ago that, although we have a vast panoply of exegetical weaponry to bring to bear upon the biblical text, when exegetes ask what, with all its details, the text is saying they generally find themselves alone. 'It would be a great mistake to regard this establishment of the meaning of a text, which is the final stage and crown of exposition, as something simple, a thing

---

1. I appreciate Frederick W Locke's comment in a study of the Grail legend: 'Only when the ultimate significance of the Grail has been uncovered will the complexity of the work yield, revealing that center of unity which is at the heart of every artistic creation' (*The Quest for the Holy Grail: A Literary Study of a Thirteenth-Century French Romance* [Stanford: Stanford University Press, 1960], 12).
2. It is not appropriate to go into the many discussions of what is meant by 'meaning'. Our context should make clear that it is not paraphrase or description of the text; it is not a mass of facts about the text, even facts grammatical and syntactical. Meaning is the interpretative experience emerging out of the encounter between the reader and the text. Meaning can be spoken of as a function of the text: what the text says or does. Or it can be spoken of as a function of the reader: what is said or done to the reader by the text. It is necessarily the outcome of the conjunction of both forces, reader and text and their worlds, involving the baggage that both bring to the encounter.

which dawns as it were automatically on the expositor's mind'.[3] The meaning of a text should be the Holy Grail of exegesis, which is the art of interpretation.

Rolf Knierim, the jubilarian we celebrate in this volume, is a first-rate teacher, with remarkable gifts for uncovering the meaning of a text. It is a common phenomenon that graduate students regard their senior professors as great teachers and revered figures. Knierim's remarkable talents as a teacher, however, are well known to his friends and associates; by any standard, Rolf Knierim is an extremely good teacher.

One of the tools that Knierim uses most powerfully to introduce students to a text, to involve them in it and enthrall them with it, is what he calls 'structure analysis'. As used by him, structure analysis is peculiar to Knierim and the Forms of Old Testament Literature project which he initiated with Gene Tucker. Apparently similar analyses are frequently used; often they have not been crafted along the specific guidelines which are critical to Knierim's understanding of the art. On occasion, in such cases, we may have little more than glorified tables of contents. Structure analysis is a key to Knierim's approach to texts and their interpretation.

It is a source of regret that Knierim has never written up a descriptive analysis of his approach with a full unfolding of its theoretical underpinnings. This festschrift provides the occasion for a poor substitute: an analysis of the approach by a former student. In doing so, we are not straying too far from the central focus of this volume, for it is the way that his structure analyses take Knierim into the text that allows him to bring rich theological lode out of it.

The reason for offering this analysis is not simply to honor the jubilarian. Rather Knierim's concept of a structure analysis has an important role to play in the methodology of interpretation. It is a starting point for getting into a text; it is a summary point for verifying and validating an interpretation. Life is short and academics are busy people; we often do not have the time to take a text apart with painstakingly meticulous care before we tell a class or an audience what is all about. I cannot speak for all those who have been schooled in the art of structure analysis, but for myself I know that if I deal with

---

3. G von Rad, *Old Testament Theology*, volume 2 (New York: Harper & Row, 1965) 416.

a text which I have not subjected to structure analysis I am selling the text short and working at a predominantly superficial level. Similarly, when I have put an enormous amount of time and effort into the study of a text, if I have not pulled it together in a structure analysis, then I have not yet put the final crown on the text's interpretation.

As starting point, the methodological contribution of Knierim's structure analysis is to provide a relatively neutral way into the text. While this may seem so basic as to be banal, it is not. In most manuals of exegesis, for example, the first step to be taken is text–criticism. Without having established a text, any task of interpretation would be premature. But no text criticism can take place without some idea of the nature of the text under study, what might make sense in such a text and what can be expected of such a text. The expectations in a legal text are not identical with those in a narrative text.

As summary point, the methodological contribution of Knierim's structure analysis is to check that every element of the text has been accounted for. For an interpretation to claim adequacy and validity, it must at least account for the majority of elements and signals in the text it interprets. It is relatively easy to produce a fine-sounding interpretation of a text, if we discreetly ignore those parts of the text which do not fit our understanding. Of course, none of us reading this would do such a thing, but we may notice it occasionally in the work of others. A structure analysis does not allow us to do this unawares. It forces us to name the form or function of every element in the text, within its context. By obliging us to write out the verse numbers in sequence down the right-hand side of the page, it brings to our attention aspects we may have too conveniently overlooked.

Basics of the approach

Structure analysis, as advocated by Rolf Knierim, focuses directly on the text. First of all, it has to be identified: as text, where does it start and where does it end? Second, what are the major building blocks of its construction: does it have an introduction, a conclusion, and what are the principal constituents of the body of the text? Third, how do these building blocks relate to each other within the text to shape its meaning?

The primary difference between a Knierim structure analysis and a table of contents is that the former normally focuses on form and the latter on content. This focus does not take us prematurely into the form-critical arena. Its concern is not yet with the form of the text as a whole, but rather with the form of the elements which make up that whole. Some examples may help.

- Introduction is a statement about form
    Persons, places, and times are matters of content
- Exhortation is a statement about form
    Importance of keeping the law is a statement about content
- Motivation is a statement about form
    Promise of prosperity and peace is a statement about content
- Prohibition is a statement about form
    Against lying and stealing is a statement about content
- Conclusion is a statement about form
    Death of the king is a statement about content

Not everything can be expressed in the language of form and often form needs to be specified with content. The issue is one of focus and priority; the focus is on form and form gets priority. 'Promise of prosperity and peace' can be a statement of form; this verse is in the form of a promise. Where the promise of prosperity and peace is understood to reinforce an exhortation to live wisely and well, it is primarily a motivation; its content is a promise. On occasion content is the most concise label available for recording a formal observation in a structure analysis. It should seldom be content for its own sake.

Interrelatedness—how the building blocks relate to each other to shape the text's meaning—is an essential element of analysis. Aristotle's remark in the *Poetics* is still valid: all works of literature have a beginning, a middle, and an end. What functions as introduction and what contribution does it make to the shape of the text? What does the end bring into focus and what aspects of the text does it leave aside?[4] How does the middle move to enable the beginning to

---

4. For example, in the sacrifice of Isaac the first ending (Gen 22:14, 19) focuses on God's providing and leaves aside issues of sacrifice; it focuses on Abraham's return to Beersheba and leaves aside the fate of Isaac as well as any implications

reach an end, a lack to be satisfied, an imbalance to be brought into balance?

These building blocks in a text can be described by a variety of metaphors. The reality is not a matter of scientific analysis but of intuitive perception. 'Focus' is an optical metaphor; 'conceptualisation' takes it into a more abstract level. Both seek to grasp the structure of a text by how it may be seen and understood. 'Act' and 'scene' are dramatic metaphors. They correlate major blocks with subordinate ones, as acts in a play are subdivided into scenes. 'Take' is a similar metaphor from cinema or television. A take is an uninterrupted piece of photography; it therefore has some sort of inherent unity. Whatever metaphors are used for description, the aim is to visualise and name how the parts of the text fit together to form a whole.

One way of envisaging this task is to think of it as recapturing the outline that was in the author's mind. A storyteller, for example, has to have a sense of where a story will begin, how it will unfold, and where it will end. The main actions will be grouped in clusters, for ease of memory. The details can be left to the imagination of the moment, as the telling proceeds. While this approach is appealing, it is methodologically dangerous. It must be true that storytellers organised their material in their minds, so that the bold outline was clear and the details could take care of themselves in due course. Methodologically, however, we must remain aware that we do not have access to the storyteller's mind, only to the storyteller's text. Our concern has to be for the structure in the text, not the structure outlined in the storyteller's mind. Similarly, our concern has to be for the meaning in the storyteller's text, not the meaning in the storyteller's mind. What is out of reach is out of reach—the storyteller. What is within our reach is the text in all the manifold complexity of its signals.

The phrase quoted earlier (n 1 above)—'that center of unity which is at the heart of every artistic creation'—can be understood with 'creation' interpreted as process or as product. As process, the center of unity would be the driving purpose that was in the author's mind. It is better understood as product, where the artistic creation is the text and the center of unity is to be found in the text itself.

---

for the life of Abraham.

Practical illustration

As a process, structure analysis will vary with different texts having different requirements and different interpreters having different skills. Rather than attempt an abstract and global presentation of the concept—difficult to do and difficult to follow—it may help more to use a specific text as a practical illustration. Given that structure analysis follows a concentric rather than a linear approach, a certain amount of repetition is inevitable. On balance, it should not be harmful.

The first temptation of anyone beginning the process of structure analysis is to list in sequence the component elements of the text. This is precisely what a table of contents does; it is precisely what a structure analysis should not do.

Invariably, in narrative, the constitutive blocks of a text are grouped in twos or threes rather than sixes or sevens. Beginning, middle, and end is a threesome. The folkloric triad is a threesome; it is somehow natural for things to come in threes. Hence the French proverb: 'Jamais deux sans trois'—never two without a third. Proverbs remind us that three can be expanded into four; 'Three things are too wonderful for me; four I do not understand' (Prov 30:18). When our assessment of a text stretches to five blocks, we may begin to suspect that a higher grouping or a different grouping has escaped our notice. A number beyond four is not impossible, simply suspect. Two of course is not only the natural binary division of left and right, front and back, raw and cooked; it is also the primary structure of Hebrew poetry—the division of a line into two versets, or sometimes three. The first verset will often be expressed in general terms, while the second verset is more concrete and more specific.[5] A similar movement is often visible in Hebrew narrative; a general statement, for example, is followed by its unfolding in concrete detail. Narrative movement may often be structured in pairs: a command is followed by the report of compliance; acts are followed by their consequences, and so on.

Once this tendency toward groupings of two and three has been recognised, attention to the focus of interest in the movement of a text will frequently reveal groupings and structure within a superficially purely sequential text. In such ways, meaning emerges

---

5. See, for example, Robert Alter, *The Art of Biblical Poetry* (New York: Basic Books, 1985).

from unordered fact. It is not a matter of imposing an order on a text; it is a matter of reflecting whether there is such an order in a text. There is no hard and fast commitment to twos and threes, simply a predilection for them.[6]

The process of structural discovery
There is no hard and fast procedure for creating a structure analysis. One of the beauties of the beast is its freedom from mechanical method. Others might proceed in other ways. In my experience, the following steps are usually central.

> Establishing the limits of the unit constituting a text.
> Establishing the limits of the major blocks within the text.
> Analyzing the elements and their relationship within each block.
> Analyzing the relationships of the blocks to the whole.
> Establishing an initial hypothesis as to the meaning of the text .

As noted, an abstract description is difficult to give and difficult to follow. I will use the story of David's single combat with the Philistine as a practical illustration of what structure analysis involves and offers.[7]

Establishing the limits of the unit constituting a text
The first task in analysing a text is to discover where it begins and where it ends. Often an instinctive form–critical judgment will operate here.

---

6. No one has ever said that seven and eight are not significant numbers, so potential factors for order. The body of Amos 1–2 in the present text is structured around a sequence of eight, to be understood as seven plus one: Damascus, Gaza, Tyre, Edom, Ammon, Moab, Judah, and Israel. If Judah is omitted as a later addition, we have a sequence of seven. If Tyre and Edom are also regarded as secondary, the original sequence is reduced to five. A prophetic collection, of course, need not be bound by the same conventions as narrative.
7. The text refers to David's opponent throughout as 'the Philistine'. It mentions the name Goliath twice only (17:4, 23); in v 23, in particular, the proper name seems intrusive in the text. Hence my preference for conforming to the text and referring to the Philistine.

Beginning and end may not be identifiable without knowing what 'it' is. What 'it' is, of course, is always a form-critical judgment. 'It' is the text to be analysed. Its beginning and end may depend on the sort of text it is. Often the decision about beginning and end can be made on basically syntactical grounds; at other times, matters of theme and content, even narrative plot or literary form may have a role to play. The question is: What is the text? What is its extent?

The story of David and the Philistine is a good example of the subtleties involved. If we think of the text simply as a battle story, the battle story begins in 1 Samuel 17:1. The Philistine champion is introduced in 17:4–7; David is introduced in 17:12–15. The battle story ends with 17:52–54, the pursuit of the fleeing foe and the taking of plunder.

Two oddities may attract our attention however. First, the Philistine has been shouting his challenge morning and evening for forty days (v 16). It is, therefore, very odd that all Israel should be reported to have fled from him in fear when they saw him (v 24). Such fearful flight can hardly have happened twice a day for forty days or have erupted only on the first and fortieth day. Second, when David is summoned by Saul, there are no introductions, no questions asked about David's identity; David speaks up and addresses Saul (v 32). Only later, in a segment that is situated outside the frame of the battle story, as Saul sees David going out against the Philistine, does Saul ask Abner, 'Whose son is this young man?' (v 55). Abner does not know.

Another segment associated with this identification scene (17:55–58) has Jonathan form an instant friendship with David, solemnise it with a covenant, and celebrate it in an exchange of garments—and David is so successful that he is given an army command (18:1–5). The focus has moved from the little group on the battlefield to a far wider view of space and time.

Finally, in yet another segment, David is said to be playing the lyre for Saul, troubled by an evil spirit; it is noted as common practice, 'as he did day by day' (18:10). There is no introduction to this practice in chapter 18. This might not matter, except that there is an introduction to it in chapter 16. Possibly the story may have to be extended back to at least 16:14.

It is possible that it may have to be extended forward too. In the battle story, as the Philistine's challenge is discussed, the Israelite troops assure David that 'The king will greatly enrich the man who kills him, and will give him his daughter and make his family free in Israel' (17:25). There is no talk subsequently of David's family being made free, but twice the issue of David's marriage to a daughter of Saul's is taken up and developed (18:17–19, 20–29).

Tentatively, it is worth considering that the limits of the text may extend from 16:14 to 18:30.

Our primary focus is less the clarification of the story of David and the Philistine than the clarification of the process of structure analysis. My concern is with a holistic interpretation of the text and the contribution of structure analysis to this task. The discussion, in commentaries and elsewhere, of the issues and details of 1 Samuel 16:14 – 18:30 cannot be debated in the space available to us. Almost all are well known; it is a text where few stones have been left unturned. What is significant is the context the interpreter creates within which these details are understood. The valuable collection of studies and discussion by D Barthélemy, DW Gooding, J Lust, and E Tov points to the difficulties of finding agreement across differing interests.[8] Room remains for more insight into the text, more options for understanding, more possibilities for meaning.

In this paper, my interest is in exploring a structure analysis of the text, while assuming intelligent compilers and giving weight to the involvement of tradition and the creative liberty of the ancient storyteller. Of course, if the substantial compilation of the text were demonstrably late, the proposals advanced here might require nuancing in the light of our understanding of the circles responsible. The need to shape scripture and preserve tradition might take precedence over the creative activity of storytellers. Discussing all the options would, again, extend this paper unreasonably .

Establishing the limits of the major blocks within the text
The second task in analysing a text is to discover where the major constitutive blocks within it begin and end. As part of a text there

---

8. D Barthélemy, DW Gooding, J Lust, and E Tov, *The Story of David and Goliath: Textual and Literary Criticism*, OBO 73 (Fribourg, Suisse: Editions Universitaires, 1986). A unitary view is defended by Gooding against traditional analyses (especially 55–86). See also R Polzin, *A Literary Study of the Deuteronomic History*, part 2, *Samuel and the Deuteronomist* (San Francisco: Harper & Row, 1989) 152–81.

may be framing blocks such as introduction, body of the text, and conclusion. Such framing structures may seem simple, but they are often significant. Within the body of the text, there will be the blocks which are the load-bearing pillars of the text's center. The task of identifying these requires attention to the movement of the text through plot or its equivalent and to the syntactical signals embedded in the text for our guidance.

Movement through the text will vary according to the nature of the text. In a series of laws, each law might be a single block or several laws together might constitute a block. In a narrative text, the blocks are likely to correspond with aspects of the plot or its equivalent. They may be large or as small as a single sentence; they are unlikely to be numerous. Syntactical links seldom extend across major blocks. So a block will begin with its own subject and verb; pronouns and pronominal suffixes will find their antecedents within their own block. The syntactical signals can be varied; the message they send is that a new block begins or ends here.

We might look, for example, at the blocks in 1 Samuel 16:14 to 18:30. Something new is signalled in 16:14: the spirit of the LORD has departed from Saul and he is tormented by an evil spirit from the LORD.[9] Saul's need for attention is identified by his servants, a remedy is proposed, David is hired as lyre-player to soothe Saul, and Saul's need is satisfied. The block is 16:14–23. Within the block, it is noted that David became Saul's armor–bearer. There is no reference back to 16:1–13 that might require its association with this text. The thematic link is from 16:1–13 to 16:14–23 and what follows, not the reverse. 16:1–13 has potential to illuminate the following text; but it remains in the background, it is not spelled out.

With 17:1, a new block clearly begins. The principals are new: the Philistines on one side, Saul and the Israelites on the other. The location is new: Ephes-dammim and Elah. The topic is new: battle.

---

9. Those who do not have access to the Hebrew text must always remember that English conjunctions such as and, but, if, then, when, and others usually represent the one principal Hebrew conjunction 'w^e-.' Translation depends on context. In the NRSV, 16:14 begins with 'Now'; 16:15 begins with 'And'. Both times, the Hebrew has the same conjunction 'w^e-': the context, however, is different. In narrative prose, almost every Hebrew sentence begins with this conjunction 'w^e-'. Conclusion: when working with a translation, conjunctions cannot be relied on for structure analysis unless they have been checked against the Hebrew.

So far, so good. Determining where this block ends is more difficult. There is a temptation to close it at 17:11, because of the evident new beginning in v 12. Against this, vv 1–11 have set the scene for a battle between Israel and the Philistines and the battle has hardly been begun, much less brought to a narrative conclusion. So 17:12 probably begins a sub-block rather than a major block. Once this is agreed, the major block must extend to 17:54 where the battle story is brought to a conclusion. The block is 17:1–54.

The next block is larger than it appears at first sight. It might first seem to be constituted by 17:55–58. But the Hebrew of 18:1 begins: 'When he had finished speaking to Saul . . .' Although David is mentioned later in the sentence, this 'he' depends on 17:58 for the identification of its subject. The next move seems to be to extend the block to 18:5. Here again 18:6 begins: 'As they were coming home . . .' This syntactical link exists at the level of the present text. An earlier independent text might have begun: 'When David returned . . .'; but the present text does not begin that way. While 17:55–18:9 might look to be the appropriate block in the present text, the opening of 18:10—'The next day'—ties it into what precedes, as well as the thematic association with jealousy. The block, at the level of the present text, has to be 17:55–18:11. It comprises Saul's becoming aware of David's identity, the friendship with Jonathan, Saul's heir, and the emergence of Saul's jealousy toward David.

The timelines in this block are complicated. The first part overlaps with the battle story; Saul's first question is put to Abner as David goes out against the Philistine (17:55). In the middle, the report surveys enough time for sustained success to be established on David's part (18:5). The issue of Saul's jealousy brings us back to the return from battle and the day following that return.

The next block is 18:12–16. It stands out for its shift in focus, standing outside the detailed narrative as comment. It makes statements and then substantiates them. It deals with the major players: Saul, David, and all Israel and Judah.

The remaining text, 18:17–30, comprises two episodes about Saul's daughters being offered to David in marriage. At first sight they appear syntactically independent, one a short notice about Merab and the other an anecdote about Michal. In the present text, however, they are linked by the second's reference back to the first: 'Therefore Saul said to David a second time' (v 21). Once viewed as a block, the thematic unity is clear: Saul used the promise of his daughters in marriage as a snare to have David killed. Saul's attempts to kill David continue in the subsequent narrative and become increasingly direct. They drive David first from Saul's court, then from Saul's kingdom. What focuses these two stories as a block is the issue of the marriage to Saul's daughters. What closes off this final block is the narrative irony of v 30. Using his daughters as bait, Saul has twice tried to create a situation in which the Philistines kill David. Saul fails. This narrative ends on the note that as often as the Philistines came out to battle, David had more success than Saul's followers. Saul tried to have the Philistines kill David. David turned out to be extremely good at killing Philistines. David succeeds.

It is time for a rudimentary structure analysis:

I. Introduction of David to court of Saul
II. Story of battle
III. Introduction of David to court of Saul
IV. Saul's jealousy toward David

Such an analysis may be expressed in a triple structure, but the dual introduction of David to Saul's court remains.

I. Prelude to battle: introduction of David to court of Saul
II. Story of battle
III. Aftermath of battle

    A. Introduction of David to court of Saul
    B. Saul's jealousy toward David

The shape of a narrative is stirring here, but the repeated 'introduction of David to court of Saul' is a clear signal that the present text is not straightforward. An examination of the interrelationships within the blocks may be the best procedure to discover where the meaning of this text lies.

Analyzing the elements and their relationship within each block
1 Samuel 16:14–23. The movement of the text is straightforward: a problem exists which needs to be remedied. Saul is tormented by an

evil spirit. Music is recommended and a musician is sought. David, a skillful player of the lyre, is identified and summoned to Saul's service.

On its own, the passage is complete. It exhibits the classic movement of story: from an imbalance which needs to be corrected to the establishment of equilibrium. Certain elements point further. The evil spirit which torments Saul is 'from the LORD'; worse still, the spirit of the LORD is said to have departed from Saul. Something is amiss in the kingdom. Secondly, as has been widely noted, the description of David, unnamed, goes beyond the requirements of a lyre-player. Six pairs of words describe six courtly attributes: musically skilled, sufficiently well-off, militarily trained, able speaker, good presence, and divinely favoured (the LORD with him). Such qualities seem more in keeping with the court of David than with Saul's. Finally, David is not only to be Saul's musician; he is also given the role of Saul's armor-bearer.

In brief, the structural elements are:

I. Need: description of Saul's plight	v 14
II. Remedy: proposal to seek a lyre-player	vv 15-16
III. Outcome: successful—David enters Saul's service	vv 17-23

1 Sam 17:1–54. Here the elements are more complex. The block opens with an introduction which sets the scene for battle between the Philistines and Israel. Specifically a challenge is issued to settle the battle by single combat. Saul has been established as king over Israel because of his demonstrated ability to deliver Israel in time of trouble.[10] Such is the role of a king. This should be Saul's moment. But the spirit of the LORD has departed from Saul (16:14). The future movement of the narrative has to be uncertain.

Instead of proceeding with Israel's response to the Philistine challenge, the narrative turns to the figure of David. It situates him within his family in Bethlehem, refers to the three eldest sons at the war, and through the device of paying a visit to them brings David on to the scene in time to hear the challenge to single combat. All Israel flees and the soldiers begin to discuss what might be in it for

---

10. Cf 1 Sam 11. In 1 Sam 9:16, Saul's anointing is specifically with a view to saving Israel from the Philistines. On tradition–historical grounds, I would prefer not to appeal to 9:16 here.

the Israelite who kills the Philistine. The response is almost that of standard folktale: half of the kingdom and the hand of the king's daughter in marriage. The victor is assured of great wealth, the hand of the king's daughter, and honoured status for his family. David is instantly interested and verifies the possibility. His eldest brother comes on the scene for a brief and bitter exchange. David leaves him to continue questioning as before. Finally he comes before Saul.

It is clear that David is to play a dramatic role in this story. On the level of literary unity, this flashback to the ancestral home in Bethlehem might serve to give a sense of local colour and a trace of the human touch to the man so soon to be Israel's hero. The narrative is aware that David was in service at the court of Saul, but it makes the flashback possible by having David return home regularly. We might object that Saul's armour-bearer should be by the king's side in preparation for a major battle with the Philistines. We might also recognise that a gifted storyteller would probably have little difficulty in making such an absence plausible.

A gifted storyteller may make plausible what appears to be a difficult text. This assertion rests on a basic assumption: that often the biblical text may not be the end-product of a narrator's art—a polished gem or the verbatim mirror of a performance—but the basis from which a narrator's performance began. There is not space to develop this here.[11] However, there is a serious question as to 'whether all our biblical texts are the final product of literary output or whether some of them are intended as the starting point from which literary output is produced'.[12] If the question is answered affirmatively, then we must take into account the potential a storyteller might develop from a text that at first sight seems difficult or disjointed.[13]

The flashback has its problems however. The Philistine is portrayed uttering his challenge twice a day for forty days (17:16). David is chatting with his brothers when the Philistine repeats his challenge. The narrative continues: 'All the Israelites, when they saw

---

11. See AF Campbell, 'The Reported Story: Midway between Oral Performance and Literary Art', in *Semeia* 46 (1989): 77–85 and AF Campbell and MA O'Brien, *Sources of the Pentateuch: Texts, Introductions, Annotations* (Minneapolis: Fortress, 1993), 203–11.
12. *Sources of the Pentateuch*, 208.
13. For example, see the treatment of Gen 37:21–35 in *Sources of the Pentateuch*, 231–35.

the man, fled from him and were very much afraid' (17:24). This is odd behaviour in response to a ceremonial challenge which has been being proclaimed twice daily for forty days. Had the Israelites advanced toward the Philistine lines and fled in panic for forty days, morning and evening? It would tax a storyteller's skills to make this plausible. An isolated panic by the Israelites would be just as hard to portray as credible. There is a difficulty here.

There is also a difficulty in deciding whether the next section, within this block, begins with 17:31 or 32. With the focus on David's words, v 31 could be taken as a conclusion: David has got what he wants, an audience with the king. David's words to Saul then burst into the narrative baldly and bluntly. To avoid this, v 31 could be seen as the introduction to David's audience with Saul. While this is satisfactory for the context of chapter 17 alone, we have begun our text at 16:14. David is Saul's armour-bearer and could be expected to report to his king once this critical challenge has occurred. Verse 31 has to be the conclusion to the portrayal of David's ambition and David's speech has to begin baldly and bluntly.

Despite this, it is odd that Saul, who has sent for David, has nothing to say to him. Instead it is David who initiates the conversation. His words to Saul refer directly back either to 17:11, where 'Saul and all Israel . . . were dismayed and greatly afraid' or to 17:24, where 'All the Israelites . . . were very much afraid.' Summoned to the royal presence (v 31), it would have been arrogant and presumptuous of David to assume Saul's fear. In the present text, Saul's fear is mentioned in v 11, when David was not present to witness it. It is not mentioned in v 24, when David was present, perhaps because David while on the battlefield was not in Saul's presence.

We might want to argue that Saul's fear is not central, since the Hebrew text in 17:32 does not refer to Saul specifically—'Let no one's heart fail because of him'. The Greek, however, has specific reference to 'the heart of my lord'. Even with the more discreet and diplomatic Hebrew version, Saul cannot be taken out of the picture. As king, it is his role here to show courage and exercise command. The initiative given to David in the story is an initiative that belongs to Saul, that Saul should have taken. Saul's silence after he has sent for David (v 31) is odd. A skilled storyteller would have little difficulty using it to highlight the king's fear. At this point in the story the focus is on the contrast between Saul and David.

David is eager to fight the Philistine; Saul is reluctant to let him. Saul's reluctance is not spelled out beyond David's inexperience (youth). Within the context of contrast between the two figures, Saul is paralysed by un-kingly fear. Within the context of the Philistine challenge, Saul may be rightly unwilling to risk the fate of all Israel on the fighting skills of an untested David. The text is silent. No better warrior is named. David protests that it is the LORD who will give him victory. Saul concedes: 'Go, and may the LORD be with you' (v 37).

David's trust in God is brought out in the next two episodes. It is implicit in the symbolism of his refusing the offer of Saul's armour. It is explicit in the speeches exchanged with the Philistines. It is common to tie the rejection of Saul's armor to David's small size, being a boy. Three sources contribute to this image of David: his description as Jesse's eighth and youngest son (16:11-12); the comment by Saul that he is no match for the Philistine (17:33); and the Philistine's disdain (17:42).[14] While there are different traditions at work here, none specify the size of the youngest son or his absence of military training. The inexperience of the recent recruit and his good looks and lack of impressive equipment can account for all three occurrences.

This 'small boy' interpretation is in stark contrast with David's self-description in vv 34-35—fast enough to overtake a marauding predator, strong enough to kill it, and with reflexes good enough to grab it by the jaw. In earlier text, Saul is described as a head and shoulders taller than any soldier in Israel (1 Sam 10:23). In the present text, David has been appointed Saul's armour-bearer. The rejection of Saul's armour is best read symbolically, in conjunction with the exchange of speeches. In rejecting the armour, David turns aside from 'the sword and spear' that are not the Lord's instruments (v 47). In the exchange of speeches, David emphasises that his trust is explicitly in the LORD.

---

14. The NRSV prejudices the interpretation in translating one and the same Hebrew root in v 33 by 'just a boy' for David and by 'from his youth' for the Philistine. In v 42, it reverts to 'only a youth.' The qualifiers 'just' and 'only' are from the interpretation; they are not specified by the text. The precise meaning of the Hebrew *na'ar* is determined by its context. It can be used of an infant (1 Sam 1:22), a young soldier (2 Sam 2:12-17), or a royal overseer (1 Kgs 11:28)—see AF Campbell, *The Study Companion to Old Testament Literature* (Collegeville: Liturgical Press, 1989/92), 209. The plain meaning in this context is that David is now what the Philistine was at the start of his military career: a young and untried soldier.

For a storyteller who wants to exploit it, there is irony here. A big man in Saul's armour has no chance against the giant Philistine. A fast, light–armed slinger, with good reflexes, is militarily Israel's best chance against the big champion. David is the perfect pick.[15] As the speeches are exchanged, David has a stick in his hand and the Philistine focuses on it in his contempt (v 43). Presumably, the sling in the other hand is behind David's back. The longer the speeches go on, the closer David can get while the Philistine's shield is still on his shield-bearer's arm (v 41). The closer David gets, the surer his shot will be. All he needs is cool nerves and good luck—and that is where trust in the LORD comes in.

This discussion has taken us a long way from the structural concerns that are central to this paper. It is necessary as an attempt to free the text from the numerous presuppositions that beset it. It is time to move on.

With the preliminaries to battle out of the way, the narrative moves swiftly to the single combat itself. The two antagonists move toward each other and, with a single shot from his sling, David drops his opponent to the ground. The death of the Philistine raises a difficulty, however. According to v 50, David killed his man with the slingstone; quite explicitly, the Philistine is dead and there is no sword in David's hand. According to v 51, to the contrary, David killed his man with the Philistine's own sword; just as explicitly, David drew the Philistine's sword and killed him with it, and then he cut off the Philistine's head. It is not easy to reconcile these two views of the final act of combat.

The final act of the battle story, of course, is the pursuit and plunder. David is reported to have brought the Philistine's head to Jerusalem, at that time a Jebusite city not under Israelite control. Maybe this is an anachronism read back into the text. More likely the meaning is symbolic. The note that David brought the Philistine's

---

15. For some readers, the issue here can be confused by the American usage of slingshot for 'a forked stick with an elastic band attached for shooting small stones' (Webster's). In British usage, these are called catapults (Oxford). Confusion with the ancient catapult, used as a siege weapon against walled towns, would be most misleading. The sling—which was 'whirled round to discharge its missile by centrifugal force' (Webster's)—was as much a military weapon in ancient Israel as the sword and spear. It was accurate (Judg 20:16); it was standard military equipment subject to normal procurement (2 Chron 26:14).

head to Jerusalem serves as a reminder that it was the Philistine's head that brought David to Jerusalem. David's triumph over this Philistine champion is at the cost of Saul's royal destiny. This deed is symptomatic of David's destiny which will bring him to the throne over all Israel in Jerusalem.

Structurally, what we have seen might be expressed as follows.

I. Introduction	vv 1–23
A. The battle scene	vv 1–3
B. The Philistine and his challenge	vv 4–11
C. David and the challenge	vv 12–23
II. Complication: David's response to the challenge	vv 24–40
A. Before the soldiers: what profit is there for David?	vv 24–31
B. Before the king: what David can do with faith	vv 32–40
III. Resolution: the single combat	vv 41–54
A. Preliminaries: exchange of speeches	vv 41–47
B. Climax: combat and death of the Philistine	vv 48–51a
C. Conclusion: pursuit and plunder	vv 51b–54

This analysis, however, rides roughshod over a number of signals in the text. An adequate interpretation should be able to account for the signals in the text within a coherent horizon, all things being equal. The clearest mark of inadequate interpretation is that it leaves significant signals unheeded.

In this case, the signals are:

i. The triple uneasiness engendered by David's movement to and from court and home (v 15), by the twice daily challenge over forty days (v 16), and by the panicked flight of all the Israelites as late in the piece as the fortieth day (v 24).
ii. A certain ambiguity in the portrayal of David. Before all the soldiers, he appears inspired by ambition (vv 25–31). Before the king, he appears inspired by faith in God (vv 32–40). Situated between these two portrayals is Saul's summoning of David and David's initiative in the conversation. While we have seen that a

competent storyteller could well blend these into a harmonious narrative, we note that the text itself does not achieve this harmony.

iii. There is a dual portrayal of the Philistine's death, killed once by the sling-stone and killed once by his own sword (vv 50–51).

1 Samuel 17:55–18:11. As we have noted already, this block comprises Saul's becoming aware of David's identity, the friendship with Jonathan, David's reputation as a commander, and the emergence of Saul's jealousy toward David; the timelines are complicated.

Abner, the army commander, appears as a new figure in the narrative.[16] The question Saul puts to him is puzzling. Its literal meaning is: whose son is this young man? Yet recently in the narrative Saul was talking to David and did not ask the question (17:31–39); earlier in the narrative David found favour in Saul's sight and was engaged as armour-bearer and lyre-player, by royal command sent to his father Jesse (16:19–22). When David is finally brought before Saul (17:57–58), the information that Saul elicits is information that in the narrative he has known since David's arrival at the court or that at least he might have asked before permitting David to accept the Philistine's challenge. The literal meaning is difficult. The question remains open whether a different understanding can throw light on the question.[17]

The next section within the block does not shed light directly on the point of Saul's question. A deep and committed friendship between David and Jonathan is reported. It could have been triggered by the appearance on the scene of this newcomer; it could equally have been triggered by the heroic achievement of the recently appointed armor-bearer. Saul's action in keeping David at court (18:2) could report the engagement of a newcomer; it could equally report the termination of David's freedom to go back and forth to his father's house (cf

---

16. Abner is first named in the summary of Saul's household, 1 Sam 14:50-51. After his role here, he reappears at Saul's side in 1 Sam 20:25 and 26:5, 7, 14-15. Later he leads the house of Saul against David, until his apparent peace mission ends in his assassination by Joab.
17. We remember that the literal meaning of David's taking the Philistine's head to the foreign city of Jerusalem made no sense. On a symbolic level, it could be a pointer to the significance of this victory—it began David's move to kingship over Israel in Jerusalem.

17:15).[18] Even the transfer of Jonathan's gear to David is open to two interpretations: either Jonathan's equipping the newly arrived slinger or the sign of his new friendship for the young armour-bearer. A storyteller could clarify these ambiguities. The text does not.

The report of David's success (18:5) extends well beyond the record of Jonathan's friendship offered to David. David is given a command, which meets with the approval of Saul's troops. A considerable period of time is in view. The exercise of command, the gaining of success, and the winning of the soldiers' approval are all part of David's establishing of a reputation, once taken into Saul's court.

The final section in this block returns to the time period associated with the Philistine battle. The song of the women greeting the returning warriors angers Saul and provokes Saul's jealousy. A whole new horizon is suddenly created by Saul's angry rhetoric: 'What more can he have but the kingdom?' (18:8).

The jealousy which started by stirring within Saul's mind is promptly brought on to the stage of the external world. The evil spirit from God which has so far tormented and disempowered Saul now moves him to the folly of destroying Israel's deliverer. Twice Saul seeks to spear David; twice David eludes him.

The structure of the block in its literal sense is as follows.

```
    I.  Introduction of David to Saul: identity         17:55–58
   II.  Incorporation of David into Saul's court         18:1–6a
    A.  Jonathan's devotion to David                     v 1
    B.  Saul's engagement of David                       v 2
    C.  Jonathan's demonstration of friendship           vv 3–4
  III.  Establishment of David's reputation as a
        commander                                        v 5
   IV.  Conclusion: onset of Saul's jealousy             vv 6–11
    A.  In Saul's mind                                   vv 6–9
    B.  In Saul's action                                 vv 10–11
```

1 Samuel 18:12–16. This is a fascinating block of text. It opens with theological interpretation of the situation, it moves to narrative report, and it concludes with comments on each of the three players in the contest for royal power in Israel. First, Saul's fear of David

---

18. See Polzin, *Samuel and the Deuteronomist*, 171-76.

is noted and theologically interpreted: because the LORD was with David but had departed from Saul. Then the text notes Saul's action as a result of his fear: he removes David from the court and gives him a senior command. Saul has made two errors. He has removed the source of his own healing. He has put David in a position where he will enhance his reputation and transform Saul's fears for his kingdom into political reality.

The final three verses of the block sum up the situation. David is successful, because the LORD is with him. Saul is fearful, because of David's success. All Israel and Judah love David, because of his military leadership. The issue of military leadership is repeated in almost identical language in 2 Samuel 5:2.[19] The narrative is clear that the kingship is on the line.

The structural representation is as follows.

I.	Theological comment on the situation	v 12
II.	Report of consequent action	v 13
	A. Taken by Saul	v 13a
	B. Achieved by David	v 13b
III.	Summary comment	vv 14–16
	A. Concerning David	v 14
	B. Concerning Saul	v 15
	C. Concerning all Israel and Judah	v 16

1 Samuel 18:17-30. The final block takes up the issue of marriage to the king's daughter, which was part of the reward the soldiers assured David would come with victory. As a conclusion to this narrative, the royal marriage is no longer the victor's reward. Saul wants David dead and is willing to use his daughters as bait in the process.

Merab is first offered as a wife, not for the past victory but on condition of future valour. The initiative is Saul's. His thought is simple—let the Philistines kill David for me: 'I will not raise a hand against him; let the Philistines deal with him' (18:17). In due course, Merab is given to another.

---

19. It is 'went out and came in before them' (*qal*) in 1 Sam 18:16. It is 'led out and brought in Israel' (*hiphil*) in 2 Sam 5:2. Unfortunately, the NRSV does not catch this echo as effectively as it might.

The second time, Michal makes it easy for Saul. She falls in love with David. This time the story is more complex and Saul negotiates through intermediaries. This time Saul is also trickier. He asks for a marriage present that ought give the Philistines every opportunity to kill David for him—he asks for one hundred Philistine foreskins. David delivers. The marriage occurs. Saul's fear turns to hostility. David's success increases.

The structural representation can be briefly noted.

    I. First attempt to eliminate David: Merab   vv 17–19
    II. Second attempt to eliminate David: Michal vv 20–29
    III. Conclusion: David's success increases   v 30

Analysing the relationships of the blocks to the whole
The task that lies before us at this stage is the most challenging in the process of interpretation. Now that the blocks have been established and their components analysed, the data is available to determine the overall shape of the text. It is now time to put the pieces together. We are rather like someone doing a jigsaw puzzle. The box has been emptied, the pieces have been counted and sorted according to the major components of the picture where they might belong; then the picture has to be assembled.

    Earlier, we established a broad preliminary structure.

    I. Prelude to battle: introduction of David to court of Saul
    II. Story of battle
    III. Aftermath of battle
      A. Introduction of David to court of Saul
      B. Saul's jealousy toward David

The study of the elements within each block has not changed this basic perception. The difficulty of the double introduction of David into Saul's court remains. Rather than being lessened, the difficulty has increased because further signs of duality have emerged in the course of closer study.

    To recapitulate, the difficulties are:

a) David's going back and forth appears to harmonise two introductory sections (17:15).

b) The Philistine's repetition of his challenge twice a day for forty days seems a similar harmonisation (17:16).
c) Israel's flight and panic after forty days appears forced (17:24).
d) Ambiguity in the portrayal of David before and after his meeting with Saul (17:25–30, 32–37).
e) Saul's silence after sending for David (17:31–32).
f) Duality in the report of the Philistine's death (17:50–51).
g) Saul's sudden and belated interest in David's identity (17:55–58).

In analysing the relationship of the blocks in this narrative to the whole narrative, these difficulties pose a primary question. Can we find the most satisfactory meaning in relating the blocks to each other in a single narrative sequence? Or can we find meaning more satisfactorily in some other way of relating these blocks?

Since part of the problem is the existence of two introductions of David to the court of Saul, an obvious solution is to eliminate the first one from the story. If the text begins with 17:1, the difficulty may be thought to disappear. Unfortunately it does not. First, Saul's interest in David's identity, at the moment when David is on his way out to meet the Philistine, remains odd; it would seem appropriate when they spoke together earlier in the story. Second, the other pointers to duality, noted above as c, d, e, and f, remain as obstacles to a single narrative sequence. If the forty days is set aside as a later harmonisation, the Philistine's challenge and Israel's fear are still reported as two pairs of events, first in 17:10–11 and then in 17:23–24—although vv 23–24 might be seen as a repetition meant to bring the flashback up-to-date with the main story. The other difficulties remain: the ambiguous portrayal of David, Saul's silence, and the manner of the Philistine's death. Furthermore, if 16:14–23 is not part of the narrative, the context for Saul's fear about the loss of his kingdom is changed (18:8, 14–16). With 16:14–23, Saul's kingdom is at risk because the spirit of the LORD has departed from him (16:14).

Another approach offered is to eliminate the second introduction. Effectively, this is what Robert Polzin does. For him, Saul's question to David—'Whose son are you, young man?'—is not about identity but about loyalty. 'Saul's question carries with it a threat of coercion, for Saul thereby asks David formally to renounce Jesse's paternity in favor of his own ... The king recognises how necessary it is that David give his full allegiance to him by renouncing Jesse's paternal hold over him . . . As for David, his straightforward answer carries with it a refusal to respond as Saul would have wished, and the chapter ends on a note of defiance that will necessitate Saul's immediate and coercive reaction . . .'[20] So there is no longer a second introduction of David; instead there is the issue of loyalty and permanence at Saul's court.

Unfortunately, this interpretation flies in the face of the plain sense of the words. Of course a polite reply can communicate veiled defiance—but hardly here. Can all of the weight of Saul's demand for exclusive loyalty be expressed in so ambiguous a form? How is it to be projected back to make sense of the earlier question to Abner—is Abner being asked where David's loyalties lie? Hebrew has adequate words for dealing with matters of choice and loyalty. They are absent here. In order to achieve sequential coherence in the narrative, the exchange is being asked to mean what it does not say. Texts can do that; in this text, in my judgment, it is not plausible.

How, then, can a meaningful relationship be established between the component blocks of 1 Sam 16:14–18:30? The earlier references to duality point to the simple solution of two or more traditions. Nevertheless, the same question remains: can a meaningful relationship be established between the component traditions of 1 Sam 16:14–18:30? The appeal to sources or traditions does not answer the question of the meaningfulness we can discern in the present text.

If a single sequential narrative seems to be excluded, there is another option to be considered. Earlier, we discussed the possibility that at least some of our biblical texts are best understood as 'the basis

---

20. Polzin, *Samuel and the Deuteronomist*, 175. I admire Polzin's passion for the present text and I have learned much from him. Here, however, I have to differ. Polzin celebrates the quality of repetition as a central characteristic in this story (163–64). But such signals are set in the text to generate meaning and the meaningfulness of much of this repetition needs to be made clear. Similarly the artfulness of segments of the narrative, indicated by Polzin (164–67), is to be expected of good storytelling. What needs to be shown is how these various gems of the narrator's art combine to form an artful whole.

DW Gooding takes another tack, seeing the text focusing on the identity of David's father so that his family may be free in Israel (cf 17:25; *Story of David and Goliath,* 60). In our context, this still creates difficulty for a unitary text. Saul is given Jesse's name before he is given David's (16:18). Apart from this, Gooding's view remains problematic since the family is honored through David alone, without reference to Jesse—if these attempts on David's life are to be considered honors. Note that the reward was not promised by Saul but talked about by the soldiers.

from which a narrator's performance began' (above). If so, a biblical text might well offer a gifted storyteller more than one way of telling a story. Where two or more stories were traditional, the text—as the basis for a narrator's performance—might well include key aspects of both stories, or tell one in its entirety and include key aspects of the other. In my judgment, this possibility makes eminent sense in the case of 1 Sam 16:14–18:30.

Before presenting the structure analysis which attempts to summarise these observations, one aspect needs to be emphasised. Anyone familiar with the differences between the Greek and Hebrew manuscripts in this text will be aware that the division within the following structure does not correspond completely with the difference in the text traditions. The structure has been driven by the present Masoretic text of the Hebrew Bible; it has not been driven by concern for the earlier textual versions. By and large, the main story mirrors the text common to both Hebrew and Greek text traditions; the variant sections reflect material that is found in the Hebrew but not in the Greek. However, the structure below includes in the main story the following verses that are not part of the text common to both traditions, i.e. that are not found in the Greek: 17:41, 48b; 18:6a*, 10–11, 12b, as well as 17:50 (noted as a variant). On the other hand, the structure includes in the variant story 18:20–29a which is part of the text common to both Greek and Hebrew traditions (except for 18:21b). In the present text, the marriage stories in 18:17–30 are associated with the variant story through the assurance given David of the gift of the king's daughter for the man who kills this Philistine (17:25–26). Saul's realisation in 18:28 that the Lord is with David, a main-story theme, is too commonplace to carry weight against the marriage interest.

What this structure analysis identifies are the relationships discernible within the present biblical text. How these relate to the sources which may have been used to compile the present text is a question for source criticism (see below). It is part of the exegetical process. But it should be subordinate to the interpretation of the present text as a whole. What this structure analysis makes surprisingly clear is that the present text is more than and different from the sum of its component parts. The usual process of exegesis, beginning with text criticism and source criticism, will miss this reality by the simple fact of the process. To this degree, the process is prejudicial. Structure analysis, as process, is a relatively neutral way into the text. The structure of the text, then, unfolds as follows.

I. **Main story:** opening	16:14–17:11
A. Introduction: coming of David to the court of Saul	16:14–23
1. Need: Saul's plight	14
2. Remedy: lyre-player	15–16
3. Outcome: David's entry into Saul's service	17–23
B. Story of battle	17:1–54*
1. Introduction: the battle scene	1–3
2. Challenge and single combat	4–51*
a. The challenge	4–40*
1) Challenge from the Philistine	4–10
2) Response from Israel	11–40*
a) From Saul and all Israel: fear	11
IA. Variant story: opening	*12–31*
A. David and the Philistine challenge	*12–23*
B. David's response to the challenge	*24–30*
C. Saul summons David	*31*
II. **Main story:** continuation—	32–54
b) From David: courage	32–40
b. The single combat	41–51a
1) Pre-battle speeches	41–47
2) Battle proper	48–51
a) The approach	48
b) Victory to David by the sling	49
c) Death of the Philistine	50–51
(1) Version 1: no sword	50
(2) Version 2: Philistine's sword	51a
3. Conclusion: pursuit and plunder	51b–54
IIA. Variant story: coming of David to the court of Saul	*17:55–18:5*
A. Introduction of David to Saul	*17:55–58*
B. Incorporation of David into Saul's circle	*18:1–5*
1. Jonathan's devotion to David	*1*
2. David's entry into Saul's service	*2*
3. Jonathan's demonstration of friendship	*3–4*

C. Reputation of David as a commander	5
III. **Main story:** conclusion	6–16
A. Onset of Saul's jealousy	6–13
1. Influenced by the song of the women	6–9
2. Influenced by an evil spirit	10–11
3. Influenced by fear	12–13
B. Concluding summary comment	14–16
1. Concerning David	14
2. Concerning Saul	15
3. Concerning all Israel and Judah	16
IIIA. *Variant story: conclusion*	*17–30*
A. First attempt to eliminate David: Merab	*17–19*
B. Second attempt to eliminate David: Michal	*20–29*
C. Conclusion: David's success increases	*30*

This is not a normal structure analysis by Knierim's standards. I am not sure whether he would approve the paralleling of I-II-III by IA-IIA-IIIA. Normal structure analyses flow in a smooth consecutive sequence; but this is not a normal text. I did not envisage such a structure when I began this article. My only justification is the claim that this structure was forced on me by the text—to my surprise.

The roman numerals I-II-III and IA-IIA-IIIA do not represent the narrative flow within the text as a whole; rather they indicate the major blocks of each story in the text. This is particularly clear for the heading 'II. Main story: continuation—' which, within its own story, comes between two contiguous verses portraying the responses from Israel to the Philistine's challenge (17:11 and 32). The narrative sequence within each story is begun at the levels of A-B-C. Note, for example, 'A. Introduction' and 'B. Story of battle' under the overarching heading 'I. Main story: opening'.[21]

This is a good example of the difference between 'a text' and 'the text'. Where we have a coherent unified narrative, to the best of our knowledge of the ancient Israelite conventions, we have 'a text'—for example, the main story here. When, as here, the coherent unified narrative has been augmented by enhancements or variant versions etc that disrupt the unity and flow of that narrative, we do not have

---

21. I am grateful to Keith Eades for drawing my attention to this aspect of the analysis.

'a text'. We have 'the text'—the present biblical text. Here, 'the text' is structured at the level I-II-III and IA-IIA-IIIA. The levels A-B-C and beyond structure what is either 'a text' (the main story) or key elements of 'a text' (the variant story). It is a mistake to assume that 'the text' always constitutes 'a text'—at least in the sense used here.[22]

The roman numerals I-II-III and IA-IIA-IIIA do not represent the narrative flow within the text as a whole; rather they indicate the major blocks of each story in the text. This is particularly clear for the heading 'II. Main story: continuation'—which, within its own story, comes between two contiguous verses portraying the responses from Israel to the Philistine's challenge (17:11 and 32). The narrative sequence within each story is begun at the levels of A-B-C. Note, for example, 'A. Introduction' and 'B. Story of battle' under the overarching heading 'I. Main story: opening'.

This is a good example of the difference between 'a text' and 'the text'. Where we have a coherent unified narrative, to the best of our knowledge of the ancient Israelite conventions, we have 'a text'—for example, the main story here. When, as here, the coherent unified narrative has been augmented by enhancements or variant versions etc that disrupt the unity and flow of that narrative, we do not have 'a text'. We have 'the text'—the present biblical text. Here, 'the text' is structured at the level I-II-III and IA-IIA-IIIA. The levels A-B-C and beyond structure what is either 'a text' (the main story) or key elements of 'a text' (the variant story). It is a mistake to assume that 'the text' always constitutes 'a text'—at least in the sense used here. [automatic footnote number] A couple of points need noting. First, the structure analysis presents the component elements of the text in their relation to each other and to the whole so that what we might call the text's skeletal structure emerges which interpretation must clothe with the flesh of meaning. The analysis has not been represented in comprehensive detail or with full attention to aspects of form. Nevertheless, the skeletal structure is clear.

The main story has its three parts: introduction, story of battle, and conclusion. The elements within these are clear. For the introduction: need, remedy, and outcome; for the story of battle: the

---

22. For further discussion of the concepts of 'a text' and 'the text', see AF Campbell, 'Past History and Present Text: The Clash of Classical and Post-critical Approaches to Biblical Text', in *AusBR* 39 (1991) 1-18.

battle scene, challenge and single combat, and pursuit and plunder; for the conclusion: onset of Saul's jealousy and summary comment. Within each of these, the component elements are identified where appropriate.

The variant story is incorporated at three nodal points. The main story has David come to the court of Saul as lyre-player and armour-bearer. The first variant has David come to the battle from his father's farm, hear the Philistine's challenge, and explore the possibilities that it opens for David. The second variant offers a different view of how David came to the court of Saul: his introduction to Saul after killing the Philistine, his incorporation into Saul's circle, and the establishment of his reputation as a commander. The third variant offers two accounts of Saul's attempt to eliminate David using his daughters as bait.

As presented, there is not a continuity between these three blocks of text. There is a gap between David's response to the challenge (vv 24–30) and his introduction to Saul (v 55). We may assume that a storyteller would have no difficulty filling such a gap. What we do not know is whether the storyteller would choose to have David summoned to Saul. The inquiry about David's identity suggests not, so that David would have been depicted moving against the Philistine without a commission from Saul. In this scenario, 17:31 becomes a bridging verse without structural significance. There is a second gap between the establishment of David's reputation as a successful commander and the attempts by Saul to have him killed. Again, we may assume such a gap is easily filled by a storyteller.

It is worth noting how small observations control the analysis of structure. The pursuit and plunder (17:51b–54) is not the conclusion to the single combat. It returns to the wider perspective of the battle scene, with all the Philistines and the Israelites. The reputation of David as a commander (18:5) is not part of his incorporation into Saul's circle. Its purview is far wider in terms of time and people involved. Accurate structure analysis, like responsible interpretation, is built on close observation of the text in its form and content, its grammar and syntax, and its interrelatedness.

Second, the text manifests both unity and duality. Any claim to the meaning of the text must account both for its unity and its duality.

Establishing an initial hypothesis as to the meaning of the text
What is the basic conceptualisation that underpins the text? What meaning for the text can we generate which makes best sense of the features revealed by the structure analysis?

How do we account for the unity and duality which is so striking a feature of this text? In my judgment, this is best done by seeing this text not as the final product of literary output but as a starting point from which literary output is produced. The text is not conceptualised as a performed or polished story. It is rather the basis from which a storyteller's performance might begin. The justification for this view is the presence in the text of two story-lines, one relatively complete, the other with significant gaps. While both stories reflect the same event, they deal with it quite differently. The event which powers the two stories is David's single combat with a Philistine champion.

The two stories could have been preserved separately; this happens elsewhere in the Davidic traditions. Duality would reign. The interweaving of the two indicates a desire to retain both traditions and a concern for their unity. The concern for unity makes good sense if the story of David's fight with the Philistine was widely seen as the charismatic point of departure for his rise to being Israel's king. The unity of the event must be maintained, while differing views of how it took place are preserved. In one view, David's charisma is fuelled by faith, within the context of God's activity; in the other, it is driven by the coincidence of opportunity and ambition.

The main story opens with David coming to Saul's court to soothe the troubled king, because the spirit of the LORD has departed from Saul. It concludes with Saul's jealousy and fear for his kingdom and with the narrator's summary comment which points to David's ultimate leadership over all Israel and Judah. A glance at the structure analysis shows that the response to the Philistine challenge is twofold.

    a) From Saul and all Israel: fear   v 11
    b) From David: courage   v 32

In the present text, these are separated by the variant story's introduction. In the main story, the verses stand side by side. In the main story, Saul and David stood side by side—the king and his armour–bearer. In the main story, Saul's unkingly cowardice and David's kingly courage stand in stark contrast. The contrast is pursued in what follows. The Philistine is portrayed sharing Saul's view of David—to Saul's shame, narratively speaking. The contrast reaches its peak in the summary comment: the dispirited Saul is in awe of the successful David, who is admired as leader by all Israel and Judah.

This main story lays out in microcosm the path by which the much more extensive Story of David's Rise leads David to kingship over Israel and Judah.[23] David, who trusts in the LORD (17:37), succeeds in all his undertakings because the LORD is with him (16:18 and 18:14).

The variant story is set in a different context. The youngest son comes from the family farm to visit his three eldest brothers who are in service with Saul's army. He hears the Philistine's challenge and is assured that fame and fortune will go to the soldier who kills the challenger. When he has slain the Philistine with a well-placed stone from his sling, he is summoned before Saul. He is rewarded with a place at court, the friendship of the crown prince, and a significant military command. Finally, the variant story takes up the theme of marriage to the king's daughter, an assurance given earlier by the soldiers (17:25). However, the promise of marriage has become Saul's attempt to eliminate David, now seen as a rival. A hero to the end, David triumphs over the snares set by Saul and Saul is confirmed in fear.

The variant story takes David's path to the throne and tells of its beginning in a folktale in which the youngest son seized the opportunity to distinguish himself, win a place at court and the hand of the king's daughter in marriage. The note of Saul's hostility and fear allows the folktale to lead into the well-known traditions of the struggle between Saul and David for power in Israel.

The text, as we have it, offers a storyteller the option of telling one version or the other or, perhaps, of combining elements from both. For example, a flashback technique could be used to combine the opening of the main story (16:14–17:11) with the start of the variant story (17:12–23). The storyteller has two versions to choose from for the Philistine's death. If v 50 is selected, perhaps for theological reasons, part of the plundering will need to include the severing of the giant's head, with a view to either v 54 or v 57. Similarly, the storyteller has

---

23. See AF Campbell, 'From Philistine to Throne (1 Sam 16:14–18:16)', in *AusBR* 34 (1986) 35-41.

three motifs to choose from in depicting the onset of Saul's jealousy; a choice might be made, or all three might be exploited. The same can be said of the offers of Merab and Michal in marriage.

On the other hand, we may assume that a storyteller would not select contradictory elements from the text. If the main story's account of David's coming to the court of Saul is used (16:14–23), the variant version would have to be omitted (17:55–18:5). David's ambition in the variant story (17:25–30) would not sit well alongside the portrayal of David's faith in the main story (17:32–37).

It may seem that we are requiring too much of an ancient storyteller, apparently asked to be aware of the results of modern analytic exegesis. It is my assumption that Israel's storytellers were familiar with their repertoire and recognised automatically what we moderns have to labor to discover. We come to the text as a unity and laboriously discover its duality. They, on the other hand, were familiar with both storytelling traditions; presumably, they would have had little difficulty identifying their respective traits.

Conclusion

The process of structure analysis, as we have explored it in this example, has been principally at the preliminary level. The analysis has served as a relatively neutral tool to open up the text for interpretation. The text has merely been opened up. It is now ready for exploration with all the tools and insights that modern exegesis brings to the interpretative process.

Text-critical study can now be done aware of the function of each part of the text within the whole. In some cases, this is can be highly significant for text-critical decisions.[24]

Source-critical (or literary critical) study can examine not only the identification of main and variant stories in the analysis, but it will go further to examine the textual traditions and their relevance for understanding the sources of this text. As we pointed out above, the analysis of the present text does not correspond one hundred percent with the division into textual traditions. The text is more than its

---

24. In this area, for this text, see particularly the work of Barthélemy, Gooding, Lust, and Tov in *The Story of David and Goliath*. The close association between text and source/literary criticism recurs through the final reflections (121–54).

component sources. Study of the interplay of sources and final text can illuminate the text's meaning and its possible functions for a storyteller.

Form-critical study can assess the present text as compilation and go beyond to study the traditions which have been incorporated into it or are associated with it. Attention to the bridging verses, in conjunction with redaction-criticism, may sharpen our focus on the nature of the compiled text.

Tradition-history can situate the text in its place in Israel's literature. Where does the material come from? What are its links to traditions not included in this text? What is the correlation between the main story and the Story of David's Rise? Where does the variant story fit in the Davidic traditions? What other associations can be traced?

Redaction-criticism may be concerned for the bridging verses, in particular 17:15, 16, 31. Is there any evidence that enables us to know whether they were part of the original compilation or were added later? The implications of this question are important for understanding the nature of the compilation. Equally, redaction criticism will be sensitive to the possibility of later theological touches or observations, such as 18:5 or 12b for example.

As these areas are being explored, the initial hypothesis as to the meaning of the text is constantly challenged or confirmed. Space does not allow a detailed presentation here; an outline will have to do.

In my judgment, the horizon most appropriate for finding meaning in this text is not that of a unified narrative composition. The nature of the materials found in the text suggests a focus on the unity of the combat story as a significant event, coupled with the expression of two different optics for viewing this event.

The central focus of the text is David's emergence into public prominence through his victory over the Philistine challenger at a climactic point in the Israel-Philistine conflict.

The main story associates David's prominence from the outset with the issue of kingship (16:14; 18:9). This story is set within a major theological interpretation of political developments. Its opening statement is that the spirit of the Lord has departed from Saul. Its central image is less the triumphant slinger and the prostrate Philistine than the dispirited and fearful Saul compared with the courageous and spirited David. The point of the story is that David came to power in Israel because he stepped into the vacuum left by Saul's failure of nerve in the critical area of Israel's survival against the Philistines. David's success is theologically interpreted as the LORD's being with him when Israel was bereft of royal deliverance. It depicts in microcosm what is painted with a broad brush in the Story of David's Rise. This is a story of royal failure and divine favour.

Right or wrong, this is a tendentious interpretation of the process that brought David to power. It was not shared throughout Israel (cf the views of Shimei ben Gera, 2 Sam 16:5–8). Perhaps that is why the variant story is also preserved, with its key elements incorporated into the text.

In the variant story, the central issue is still David's rise to prominence. However God's guidance and even Saul's failure are pushed firmly into the background. David seizes opportunity when it is offered. David comes on the scene in time to hear the Philistine's challenge. He realises that an agile slinger is more than a match for the lumbering infantryman. He sees his chance and grasps it. Without the comment in 17:11 and perhaps with no report of David's coming into Saul's presence, the king's paralysed fear is swallowed up in the general statement that all the Israelites were very much afraid (17:24). In the text we have identified as the variant story, the LORD's favour is left unmentioned until 18:28.[25] This is a story of singular chance swiftly seized.

Prophetic circles will later claim that David's rise to power was triggered by their prophetic anointing (16:1–13).[26] The two traditions in 1 Sam 16:14–18:30 have as their common focus that David's prominence in Israel began with his victory over a Philistine champion. The main story, associating the combat with the Story of David's Rise, depicts a flawed and abandoned Saul and a divinely favoured David. It is highly compatible with the prophetic view in 16:1–13. Far less compatible with the prophetic claim is the variant story, with its portrayal of an ambitious young man seizing on a

---

25. In the separation according to textual traditions, 18:28 belongs with the main story, leaving the variant story fully secular.
26. See, for example, AF Campbell, *Of Prophets and Kings: A Late Ninth-Century Document (1 Samuel 1–2 Kings 10)* (CBQMS 17; Washington, DC: Catholic Biblical Association of America, 1986).

window of opportunity, although it too could be used to begin a different version of David's rise to power. Israel kept both these traditions alive, while remembering that both bore on one and the same moment of human experience.

Finally, when all this work has been done, the structure analysis can be revisited. After playing its initial role as a starting point, and providing a framework and control point during subsequent study, it can play its final role as a summary point. If we fill out the analysis for ourselves in detail, single element by single element, we will know whether we have found a coherent horizon within which all the signals of the text can be situated, interpreted, and given meaning. If successful, we will have good grounds to claim that we have found 'that center of unity which is at the heart of every artistic creation'. The complexity of the work will have yielded up an adequate and responsible meaning.

Associated books:
Campbell, A.F. *1 Samuel:* (FOTL, Eerdmans)
Campbell, A.F. *2 Samuel:* (FOTL, Eerdmans)

Nature of the Bible

Creationism! Utterly Unbiblical

(Original: *Eureka Street* 7, 1997)

As a Bible person, it maddens me to read claims that creationism takes the Bible literally. It does not. There are numerous portrayals of creation in the Bible and there are radical differences between them. Three of the combat variety are noted by way of allusion and reference. They portray a picture of creation by combat between the God of Israel and the forces of chaos. They portray a picture of creation that should send shivers down a creationist's spine. No wonder these portrayals do not get a mention. Two others are lengthier, more direct, and better known to us. In fact we are so familiar with them, in Genesis 1 and 2, that we often do not notice how widely they differ from each other.

We may look at three images of God's role in creation within the biblical texts. There are others, for example Psalm 104:5–9 or Psalm 136:4–9, or with a more lateral approach as in Proverbs 8:22–31. The nature of the creative process often may not be addressed. The big three images of the creator God, however, are:

1. The mighty fighter
2. The cooperative artist
3. The majestic proclaimer

Of these three, the mighty fighter is present in two psalms, in several places in Job, and twice in Isaiah; a God who is portrayed as mightily victorious against the awesome forces of chaos. The cooperative artist is the God of Genesis 2: as artist, labouring to shape all the beasts and birds out of the (friable) ground; as cooperative, bringing them to the man and talking about their names—and perhaps their suitability as partners. The majestic proclaimer is, of course, the God of Genesis 1 who has only to speak for it to be done and who has a strong liturgical sense, leaving the seventh day empty so that it might be hallowed for the sabbath.

What comes out of this clearly is that Israel believed in a creator God—that should be beyond doubt. Secondly, Israel used its belief in creation in a variety of ways for maximum theological effect. Belief in God as creator was a resource for life and prayer—not for freezing into the formulations of dogma.

I do not begrudge scientists their complaint that creationists distort, misunderstand, and misapply science in the presentation of their creationist views. It is the right of scientists to defend their bailiwick. What I object to intensely is any claim by creationists or on behalf of creationists that their view emerges from a literal understanding of the Bible. That is my bailiwick and I will defend it. Creationism as a literal understanding of the Bible is bunk.

Literalism can be a bit of a red herring. I take the Bible as literally as it wants to be taken—but it is not always easy to determine how literally it wants to be taken.

For example, it could be a savage distortion of meaning for a passage of lyrical poetry to be taken literally. (Quotations and verse numbering are from the *New Revised Standard Version*.)

> How beautiful you are, my love . . .
> Your eyes are doves . . .
> Your hair is like a flock of goats . . .
> Your teeth are like a flock of shorn ewes . . .
> Your lips are like a crimson thread . . .
> Your cheeks are like halves of a pomegranate . . .
> Your neck is like the tower of David,
>   built in courses;
> on it hang a thousand bucklers,
>   all of them shields of warriors.
> Your two breasts are like two fawns . . .
> (Song of Songs 4:1–5).

Pity help the lover if this description of his beloved were to be taken literally. It disclaims any literal interpretation; it is entirely metaphor and simile.

Literalism can be a red herring in creation issues. In Genesis 1, for example, the days of creation are almost certainly to be understood literally as twenty-four hour days, with evening and morning. The account culminates in sabbath, and sabbath was a twenty-four hour day. The issue for Genesis 1 is not the nature of the day, but whether the text is best understood as an inspired description of what actually happened. Decisions about literal meaning can be difficult, but when the biblical text gives us multiple and clearly conflicting images about a topic such as creation, we know for certain that we are not being told what happened. That will surprise no one seriously familiar with biblical texts.

If creationists are one day proved to be right in their views, I will be surprised but I would submit to the evidence. The only thing that I am certain of is this: creationism is not supported by the biblical text. The biblical text itself is the best evidence for that.

Creation in Psalms 74 and 89

Psalm 74 is a community lament, with an appeal to God's creative power in the middle of it. God is a mighty fighter who deals summarily with the opposition forces:

> You divided the sea by your might;
>   you broke the heads of the dragons in the waters.
> You crushed the heads of Leviathan;
>   you gave him as food for the creatures of the wilderness
>   (vv 13–14).

Leviathan and the sea and the dragons are all figures of chaos in the mythology known to us from the ancient Near East. Under different guises or names, they will recur in the texts of Job and Isaiah. There should be no doubt of the power and universality of the creator God in Psalm 74:

> Yours is the day, yours also the night;
>   you established the luminaries and the sun.
> You have fixed all the bounds of the earth;
>   you made summer and winter (vv 16–17).

Why does Israel appeal to a God of raw power in this psalm? Because 'the enemy has destroyed everything in the sanctuary' (v 3). 'How long, O God, is the foe to scoff? Is the enemy to revile your name forever?' (v 10). Under such circumstances, what the singer of psalms wants from God is power, raw power, the sort of power that can shatter God's foes and encourage God's friends, the power displayed in shattering the forces of chaos at creation.

Psalm 89 is in essence another community lament. It begins with a portrayal of God, 'feared in the council of the holy ones, great and awesome above all that are around him' (v 7). So it hymns God's power in creation:

> You rule the raging of the sea;
>   when its waves rise, you still them.
> You crushed Rahab like a carcass;
>   you scattered your enemies with your mighty arm.
> The heavens are yours, the earth also is yours;
>   the world and all that is in it—you have founded them.
> The north and the south—you created them;
>   Tabor and Hermon joyously praise your name (vv 9–12).

Here we meet the sea again and the new figure of Rahab, along with the enemies of God. At this point, the evocation of divine power does not emerge out of the powerlessness of Israel; that finds expression toward the end of the psalm. It emerges out of the psalmist's desire to find words and images to express the unique supremacy of Israel's God. Yet it is not divorced from Israel's need of God's supremacy and power.

Creation in Job 7, 9, and 26

Several times in the book, Job appeals to the image of the creator God. The image is that of the raw irresistible power of the mighty fighter.

> Am I the Sea, or the Dragon
>   that you set a guard over me? (7:12)
> God will not turn back his anger;
>   the helpers of Rahab bowed beneath him.
> How then can I answer him,
>   choosing my words with him? (9:13–14)
> By his power he stilled the Sea;

> by his understanding he struck down Rahab.
> By his wind the heavens were made fair;
>   his hand pierced the fleeing serpent.
> These are indeed by the outskirts of his ways;
>   and how small a whisper do we hear of him!
>   But the thunder of his power who can understand?
> (26:12–14)

In these passages, we meet Sea, the dragon (in Hebrew, Tannin), Rahab, and 'the fleeing serpent'—all figures in the combat myths of creation.

Job is no stranger to the most sublime literary language of creation. See, for example, either the immediately preceding verses here (26:6–11) or the magnificent imagery of Job 38–41, in God's discourse from the whirlwind.

Why then does Job use this combat creation language and imagery? Because, in his conflict with his friends, Job paints an image of a God of irresistible and aggressive power. Job is livid with anger against this God:

> What are human beings, that you make so much of them,
>   that you set your mind on them,
> visit them every morning,
>   test them every moment?
> Will you not look away from me for a while,
>   let me alone until I swallow my spittle?
> If I sin, what do I do to you, you watcher of humanity?
>   Why have you made me your target?
>   Why have I become a burden to you?
> Why do you not pardon my transgression
>   and take away my iniquity? (7:17–21)

At this point in his journey, Job feels attacked by God; and he resents it. The helpless state of the creature confronting the creator God is what Job feels and what Job would like to be freed from: 'How then can I answer him, choosing my words with him?' (9:14). Job's plea to God: 'Withdraw your hand far from me, and do not let dread of you terrify me' (13:21).

The book of Job draws on the language of creation by combat and the image of God as mighty fighter in order to convey Job's frustration at his inability to meet God on even terms, as one prince to another (cf 31:37).

Creation in Isaiah 27 and 51

Isaiah 51 reflects the agony of exiles who long to return home. The agony finds words in poetry that is both plea and promise.

> Awake, awake, put on strength,
>   O arm of the Lord!
> Awake, as in days of old,
>   the generations of long ago!
> Was it not you who cut Rahab in pieces,
>   who pierced the dragon?
> Was it not you who dried up the sea,
>   the waters of the great deep;
> who made the depths of the sea a way
>   for the redeemed to cross over?
> So the ransomed of the Lord shall return,
>   and come to Zion with singing . . . (51:9–11).

Here again, we meet Rahab, the dragon (Tannin), and the sea (and the deep that was covered by darkness in Gen 1:2). Almost like a modern film-maker, Isaiah blends the image of the sea, dried up in creation, into the image of the sea divided at the exodus. So creation blends into salvation. The power of the God who subdued Rahab and the dragon is the power at God's disposal for the salvation and return of those in exile—the return to Zion with singing.

Isaiah draws on this imagery of awesome power because of the exiles' need to have faith in a God who has the capacity to bring them home.

Elsewhere in the book of Isaiah, the prophecy points to a future time when God will restore order to creation. The passage, Isaiah 24:20–27:1, begins by pointing to the future when God 'will punish the host of heaven' (24:20) and 'the moon will be abashed, and the sun ashamed' (24:23). The passage ends with imagery that is by now familiar:

> On that day the LORD with his cruel and great and strong sword will punish Leviathan the fleeing serpent, Leviathan the twisting serpent, and he will kill the dragon that is in the sea (27:1).

Before we moderns are too easily dismissive of primitive mythology, we need to be aware that these combat images occur in some of the most sophisticated literature of our Bible: Isaiah, Job, and Psalms. The power of God is celebrated as creator, magnificently superior to the forces of chaos: the dragon, the serpent, the sea; Leviathan, Rahab, Tannin—the enemies of God. This is creation faith used for maximum theological effect.

Creation in Genesis 2

Actually, the text we are looking at is Gen 2:4b–25. 'Genesis 2' is a comfortable shorthand; and 'Genesis 1' will be a similar shorthand for Gen 1:1–2:4a. Genesis 2 is the text of the cooperative artist, we might almost say 'artisan'. The God of Genesis 2 is a working God:

> Then the LORD God formed man from the dust of the ground . . . (2:7).

Similarly, in pursuit of a partner for the man:

> Out of the ground the LORD God formed every animal of the field and every bird of the air, and brought them to the man to see what he would call them; and whatever the man called every living creature, that was its name (2:19).

'Every animal' and 'every bird' would have used up a lot of 'ground' and surely left a weary God. Yet it is the God of Genesis 1 who will rest on the seventh day from all the work that he had done—who hardly 'worked' at all (cf Gen 2:2).

A lot of people forget the major differences between this account of creation and the account in Genesis 1. In Genesis 1, of course, everything is created, including the earth and its vegetation, birds and beasts, man and woman. Yet in Genesis 2, these are created again—vegetation, birds and beasts, the man and the woman. The order is strikingly different. In Genesis 1, man and woman are created together and are created last (1:26–27). In Genesis 2, man and woman are created separately, with the man created at the beginning of the account and his incompleteness brought to partnered completion in the creation of the woman at the end of the account (cf 2:7 and 22). Not only is the order different, but the images of the beginning are as different as night and day. Genesis 1 begins in the dark and the wet: 'darkness covered the face of the deep, while a wind from God swept over the face of the waters' (1:2). Genesis 2 begins in barren dryness, with no plant and no herb and no water, 'for the Lord God had not caused it to rain upon the earth, and there was no one to till the ground' (2:5). Notice the assumption that we humans would till the ground, long before there is any talk of sin. The initial situation is barren and dry; it is evocative of the searing light of the desert sun.

What do we make of a text like this? The cooperative labouring God is not one of the staple figures of Israelite theology. It may be that the biblical narrative is portraying Israel's (and our) distancing from intimacy with God. This is the God whose nearness allowed the first humans to hear 'the sound of the Lord God walking in the garden at the time of the evening breeze' (3:8). A story of increasing distance between creature and Creator needs to start with a creation story of intimacy and cooperation.

Creation in Genesis 1

And so we come to the text so beloved of those who talk about creationism. Into the darkness of the formless void and the windswept deep, God by the sheer power of proclamation launches brilliantly symbolic light (1:3). There are many activities of God in the chapter: God sees, God separates, God calls, God makes, God commands the waters and the earth, God creates, and God blesses. Above all, God says.

This is the account of the majestic proclaimer. At every stage, there is the basic proclamation, 'And God said'. No matter how many activities God performs—separating, making, commanding, creating, blessing—the overarching statement is always: 'And God said'. There is no question here of God forming anything from the ground. The earth is commanded to bring forth vegetation (v 11) and living creatures of every kind (v 24—although in v 25 God makes the animals). There is no question of God bringing his creation to the man and talking with him about it and its names. God created humankind in God's image and likeness. That is the closest we come in this account to intimacy. The God of Genesis 1 is a majestic and distant proclaimer.

What can never be overlooked is that all the activity of creation is fitted into six days, thanks to a couple of activities on the third and sixth days. So the seventh day is empty and God is able to hallow it as the sabbath day. It is a great pity that we have no English word to convey the identity of 'resting' and 'sabbath'. Twice our English translations note that 'God rested' on the seventh day (2:2 and 3). The Hebrew word that is translated 'rested' is from the verb *shabat* and can be heard to say: 'And God sabbathed'.

Here Israel's scriptures open with a statement that the God of all creation, the Lord of heaven and earth, the God responsible for all that we can see and touch, this God is a God who sabbathed on the seventh day. And only Israel in all the earth observed sabbath. Israel might be defeated and overwhelmed by the mightier political powers of its day, but Israel encountered its God in its sabbath. Everything that Israel saw—from the light and sky to the earth and sea, the plants and trees, the sun and moon and stars, the birds and beasts—everything reminded Israel of the God who created by majestic proclamation and then sabbathed, rested on the seventh day. And only Israel in all the earth observed sabbath. It is a faith statement of the highest order. Deuteronomy says: 'What other great nation has a god so near to it as the LORD our God is whenever we call to him?' (Deut 4:7). Genesis 1 says: what other great nation has a God who has created the heavens and the earth and who sabbaths as we alone do? In an unstable and insecure world of exile, Genesis 1 stood as a faith statement affirming stability and security in the power of God.

Conclusion

It is a sad day for us when we allow ourselves to be persuaded to abandon all this theological wealth and believe that when we take the Bible literally we find so insipid a message as creationism.

The Bible's Basic Role
(original: paper read at MCD Centenary Conference
and ACBA 2003; published *2 Samuel*, Afterword)

The Bible has many roles to play in support of the life of faith and in fanning the flame of spirit.

For some, the well-supported avowal that 1–2 Samuel is not the best authenticated near-contemporary record of aspects of the history of Israel comes as a matter of relief and liberation; for others, such distancing from history is a cause for sorrow. For some, the realisation that 1–2 Samuel contains optional variants and conflicting, on occasion contradictory, traditions comes as no surprise; for others, the fact that it is not a reliable source of information, to be trusted once academically sifted, comes with a feeling of great loss.

Text-based biblical scholarship is primarily concerned with the interpretation of text, an activity which is fundamentally different from the recovery of event. Form criticism of its nature is text-based. Within the subtlety of text, as opposed to the potential simplicity of event, we are obliged to recognise, as inherent in human effort, the presence of advocacy and opposition, of insight and inadequacy, of partisanship and prejudice, which divine concurrence—however understood—has not excluded. For some, this recognition is a source of relief; for others, it is a source of pain.

It may help to put these two books of Samuel in context, so that the Bible as a whole speaks for itself. The Bible may not be a mine of information and instruction; instead, as text, it may be an invitation to reflection and response.

Beyond this, it is important—if we are to take the Bible's account of itself seriously—that we become aware of the full justification of our own interest in the Bible and our study of it. Form criticism has always taken the Bible seriously; as form critics, academically we must justify that seriousness. For all of its brevity, that is the purpose of this Afterword. (An earlier version of these reflections appeared in *ABR* 50 [2002]: 1–9; see also Campbell, *Authority of Scripture*).

It will help to list from the outset two triads that, for many, sum up their main reasons for turning to the Bible.

• For a spiritual approach: usually reading rather than study—looking primarily to spirituality, prayer, preaching, etc.

>—To arouse feeling
>—To fuel faith
>—To fire imagination

• For a critical approach: usually study rather than reading—also available for the service of spirituality, prayer, preaching, etc.

>—To explore the incarnational, a God almost concealed in the human
>—To probe the foundational, the base of our faith-identity
>—To risk the interpretational, the challenge of self-discovery

The first triad deserves more space than can be allotted here; it is better to prescind. The second needs our closer exploration. Somewhere in the middle of these, there is also the well-informed and highly knowledgeable reading that is not necessarily critical; it can be most important to the life of faith and to bringing the fire of spirit to a blaze.

The base for any initial discussion here is well-known, whether we speak of it as the options offered in the Bible, the multiplicity of vantage points available, the complementarity of views expressed, or the contradictions presented. What concerns us is the conclusion drawn from these observations. Is the basic role of the biblical text to provide something (for example, information), impose something (for example, ideas), witness to something (for example, God's action), or invite to something (for example, reflection)? Experience of the text leads me to the last, to invitation.

The implications are there for those who read or pray the Bible, for those who teach in relation to the Bible, and for those who are leaders in communities of biblical faith. The elaboration of these implications will not be undertaken here. Of course, there is challenge, encouragement, energising, etc—another story.

A saying that I have not heard contested or queried over the years sharpens the issue. It is not an axiom; it is a matter of observation.

> We do not believe something because we can quote it from the Bible; we quote something from the Bible because we believe it.

This confronts us with two questions: i) By what process and for what reasons do we come to believe something of relevance to our faith, if it is not on the authority of the Bible? ii) Why then do we quote from the Bible in support of what we believe? What need is operative in us?

I find the metaphor of signposts useful. Signposts may be vital to travelers on a journey. A signpost pointing in a single direction is helpful, if the direction is the right one. Several signposts, pointing in different directions to the same destination, invite reflection. They may be misleading, having been tampered with by vandals for example; but maybe not. Several routes can lead to the same goal; sometimes, the longest way round (in distance) is the shortest way there (in time or effort). Further exploration may be needed; reflection is invited. Many readers will find that the Bible often offers conflicting signposts (that is, competing YHWH faith claims), from extensive texts—about creation, flood, deliverance at the sea, sojourn in the desert, occupation of the land, emergence of monarchy, and even divine providence—to matters that can be compassed in a verse or two. In such cases, readers are invited to reflection; the signposts point in differing directions. The biblical text tends not to adjudicate, but to amalgamate.

The decision about what is predominantly the nature of biblical text and how it functions is one that needs to be remade out of the experience of the text by each generation of its readers. Any other way risks dogmatism or superstition. Each generation must study its Bible. These considerations should not deflect attention from the complementary roles of the biblical text: to arouse feeling, fire imagination, and fuel faith. The task here is to explore the biblical text and reflect on its signposts.

Biblical text

Creation

The Bible offers us manifold allusions to creation, whether lengthy descriptions or shorter references. Psalm 104 moves magnificently from the earth on its foundations and the deep as its cover to the ocean with ships sailing on it and Leviathan sporting in it. Proverbs 8 has a marvelous image of creation, with wisdom's primacy over everything else, 'the first of God's acts of long ago' (v 22) through to rejoicing in the world and delighting in the human race (v 31). Job 38, opening God's discourse out of the whirlwind, has a wonderful series of questions about the laying of the foundation of the earth, the shutting in of the sea with doors, the origins of morning and the dwelling of light, the storehouses of the snow and the channels for the rain. Genesis 2 has the forming of a man and God's search for human completeness, achieved in the forming of a woman. Genesis 1 has the creation of our visible world, majestically segmented into days, finding its completeness in the hallowing of the seventh day, the creator God's observance of later Israel's sabbath.

Alongside these, in the sophistication of Isaiah, Job, and Psalms, we have allusions to creation by combat and the dismembering of the primeval sea monsters—with Rahab cut in pieces in Isaiah 51:9; with the dragon (Tannin), Rahab, the Sea, and the serpent (Nahash) all featuring in various parts of Job (for example, 7:12; 9:13–14; 26:12–14); with Leviathan being crushed in Ps 74:14 and Rahab crushed in Ps 89:10. When, in its times of distress, Israel needed a God with grunt, the awesome power of the conqueror in creation was available.

In all of these, God creates. Nothing else is common. We have witness to faith in God as creator. As to the 'how' of creation, we are invited to reflection.

Flood

We know well that there are at least two traditions of the Flood. They are interwoven because both end with God's solemn commitment never to destroy sinful humankind again (Gen 8:21–22; 9:1–17). Arranged differently, one would subvert the other.

In one set of traditions, the flood is portrayed in forty-day blocks, comes from a great rainstorm, and with the preservation of seven pairs of clean animals as well as one pair of each of the unclean has surplus enough for a great sacrifice. In another set of traditions, the flood is portrayed in 150-day blocks, comes from the bursting forth of the fountains of the great deep and the opening of the windows of the heavens, and with the preservation of only one pair of all animals fortunately does not end in a sacrifice.

We may be comforted by faith in a God who will not destroy or reject us because of innate human evil. If we wish to know more detail, we are invited to reflection.

Sea

The deliverance at the Sea (Exod 13:17–14:31), whether Red Sea or Reed Sea, is one of the great images in Israel's experience of salvation worked by God (cf Deut 11:1–7; Josh 2:10; 4:23; 24:6; Ps 106:7–12, 22; 136:13–15).

The classic image is clear: at the gesture of Moses' hand, the waters were parted to left and right, Israel marched across, followed by the Egyptians who were then swamped. But also, in the same text, there is a tradition of deliverance but no crossing. The pillar of cloud moves from in front of Israel to take up station between Israel and the Egyptians all night (14:19–20*); God's wind drives the sea back all night (14:21*); at the end of the night, near dawn, from the pillar of cloud God causes panic among the Egyptians so that they retreat across the dry seabed and are swamped by the returning waters (14:24, 25b, 27*), assuming that God's 'all-night' wind stopped with the dawn. Since, at the start of it all, the Israelites were told to turn back and camp by the sea (14:2), they had already gone past it. Crossing the sea was not the problem; escaping the Egyptian pursuit was. (Note: the asterisk [*] indicates 'only relevant portions' of the verse or text given.)

Israel believed they had been delivered. As to how, at best reflection is invited. To quote from Campbell and O'Brien:

> The maintenance of duality within this carefully combined text can only be understood as witness to the conviction in ancient Israel that Israel's history did not declare God to Israel without interpretation. Rather Israel's theologians and people of faith read and interpreted their experience of history and declared God from it. The unity achieved in the text attests a faith that

the passage from Egypt to the wilderness, from slavery to freedom, a passage symbolic of Israel's emergence from the womb of history, was a moment of such significance to Israel it needed to be focused in the uniqueness of a single story, in which Israel expressed their confession of deliverance by the God who was the source and center of their being. (*Sources of the Pentateuch*, 256)

Israel's authors were professing and celebrating faith; they were not reporting details of fact, not informing the people of the present of precisely what had occurred in the past. Deliverance is reported; as to the processes, reflection is invited.

Wilderness
In the pentateuchal texts of Israel's sojourn in the wilderness, it—the wilderness—is the classic location for Israel's rejection of their God. If we forget for a moment Israel's longing for the fleshpots of Egypt and their fill of bread (Exod 16:3), along with the fish, the cucumbers, the melons, the leeks, the onions, and the garlic (Num 11:5), we can hear God's angry complaint to Moses, 'How long will this people despise me? And how long will they refuse to believe in me, in spite of all the signs that I have done among them? I will strike them with pestilence and disinherit them, and I will make of you a nation greater and mightier than they' (Num 14:11–12), followed by God's characterisation of the people who 'have tested me these ten times and have not obeyed my voice' (Num 14:22).

For Jeremiah and Hosea, the wilderness is a time and place for honeymoon fidelity. For Jeremiah: 'I remember the devotion of your youth, your love as a bride, how you followed me in the wilderness, in a land not sown' (2:2). For Hosea: 'I will now allure her, and bring her into the wilderness, and speak tenderly to her . . . There she shall respond as in the days of her youth, as at the time when she came out of the land of Egypt' (NRSV, 2:14–15).

Infidelity and fidelity are marvellously mingled. If we seek for understanding, we are invited to reflect.

Occupation
Israel's occupation of its land is as complex an issue as any in the biblical tradition. For our purposes, we can set aside recent scholarly

reconstructions involving infiltration, peasant revolt, social upheaval, and all that sort of thing; what we need is already in the biblical portrayal. Three traditions dominate the picture; two are enough for us here. In one, Israel wages a military campaign, with God's help. Kings and their soldiers are handed over to the Israelites (cf Josh 6:2; 8:1–2; 10:1, 16–27; 24:11). In the other, the work is entirely God's, with Israel having little more role than that of being there—that is, the stories of the Jordan crossing, the capture of Jericho, and the failed attack on Ai. The capture of Jericho is a good example. To march around a besieged city once a day for six days and finally seven times on the seventh day may be brilliant psychological warfare, unnerving the defenders. But a shout, no matter how fierce, does not cause the walls to collapse. Only God can do that.

If we want to look back to Israel's occupation of the land and reflect on its meaning for Israel's life in the land, we cannot go beyond speculation as to what took place. There is an invitation to thought; there is no imposition.

Monarchy

At least three traditions are preserved about the origins of monarchy in Israel. One reflects Israel's need for defense against its external enemies. Another reflects Israel's need for internal justice. A third regards the request for a king as apostasy, the rejection of God. (For details, see Campbell and O'Brien, *Unfolding the Deuteronomistic History*, 217–19, 230–49.)

Should we want to think about it, we are not told what to think. We are invited to reflection.

Providence

In much of the wisdom literature, providence and God's relationship to goodness and wickedness is clear. Psalm 1 puts it well: 'Happy are those . . . [whose] delight is in the law of the LORD . . . In all that they do, they prosper. The wicked are not so . . . the way of the wicked will perish.'

Job's verdict is equally clear: What rubbish! 'Have you not asked those who travel the roads, and do you not accept their testimony, that the wicked are spared in the day of calamity, and are rescued in the day of wrath?' (Job 21:29–30).

Conclusions

In all of this, it seems clear that the biblical text does not impose thought on us from outside. It invites us inside ourselves and calls us to reflection. I have nothing against thought and reflection, but I am not alone in needing something more to account for my particular passion for the Older Testament.

Three areas at least catch something of what fires that passion and excites my critical interest in the Bible. They can named the incarnational, the foundational, and the interpretational (as noted rather densely in the Introduction to *1 Samuel*).

The **incarnational** is important to me (it may well be different for others). For me, it is not restricted to God's becoming one of us, but expanded to reflect our experience of God as unobtrusive and intangible, almost concealed from us in the ordinariness of life. It speaks of God who is not distant from us, but deeply involved with us. The imagery is intense: 'as the bridegroom rejoices over the bride, so shall your God rejoice over you' (Isa 62:5); 'as the loincloth clings to one's loins, so I made the whole house Israel and the whole house Judah cling to me, says the LORD' (Jer 13:11). At first sight, God as unobtrusive and intangible, the ordinariness of God, may not seem evidently applicable to the Bible. Many long to escape the ambiguity and uncertainty of so much human living and the Bible often seems to offer a way into the certainty and clarity of the divine. Closer acquaintance with it calls us back to explore, be reconciled with, perhaps rejoice in the incarnational (involvement-in-the-human) uncertainty and ambiguity we find in the Bible as well as in ourselves—an invitation to compassion.

The **foundational** is for me at the base of faith identity. It arises where we quest for what is of ultimate concern to us in our lives. We need to know about the wellsprings in our past that are vital to our present. We yearn for foundations that rest in bedrock. We may need to examine the nature and the quality of the foundations on which major aspects of our faith-identity are built—just as people buying a house run checks on foundations and structural soundness, plumbing, roofing, and wiring, etc., or financial institutions contemplating takeovers run due diligence checks. In such a situation, adherents of biblical faith need to explore the Bible.

The **interpretational** relates to that risky activity of exploring our present beings, of self-discovery, when we need to make meaning for ourselves of our living, when we need to interpret our lives to ourselves. For many, the exploration of the Bible—probing in the foundations of faith and even discovering there roots and something of the incarnational—is an indispensable aid in interpreting life.

To simplify, the attraction exciting much critical engagement with the Bible can be spelled out in terms of three activities: being at home with God, being at home with one's faith, and being at home with oneself.

Incarnational
The God I experience in my faith is a God who engages with the human rather than bypassing it, a God experienced as unobtrusive and intangible, almost concealed from us in the ordinariness of life. I would be suspicious if the God of the Bible were much different.

It is true, of course, that Exodus 14 has the Sea parted to left and right; but the same chapter records wholly other actions by God. It is true that the Jordan is portrayed as parted and the walls of Jericho as collapsed; it is equally true that factors in the text point to the role of liturgy. It is true that the text has the ark dispense death in the Philistine cities, at Beth-shemesh, and on the way to Jerusalem; theology is not unlikely. The issue is not whether Older Testament traditions can be demythologised, whether by the text or by its interpreters. The issue is not whether some of the Newer Testament miracles can be conveniently explained. The reality is that these play a relatively small part in the traditions of either Testament, as do wonders and miracles today. The God of the Bible was scarcely more demonstrably evident in the life of the community than is God today. I am grateful.

I do not want neon lights, but the soft uncertain illumination that filters through so much of human living and allows for the occasional insight.

I believe I am a modern well-informed and questioning human being, with a pleasantly broad critical streak. I have a very strong religious faith; I have very deep doubts. I do not find the fact of doubt to be in conflict with the act of faith. What I look for in biblical texts is not in conflict with what I learn from recent science. I do not look for modern science in biblical texts; I do not look for insights into the meaning of life in recent science.

When I look into biblical texts, I can find faith and doubt there. I can find prayer and politics there. The faith I find there is occasionally expressed in terms I would today describe as grossly unscientific. What I find in the wide range of biblical texts is a struggle to find meaning in human existence. That struggle is not denied; it is not always successful. It is there. Recent science does not for me deny the struggle for meaning; it does not resolve it either. The struggle is there. Biblical text that neither denies nor always resolves the struggle for meaning is for me text that is deeply steeped in the mystery of human experience. It is incarnational and I am at home with that. On occasion, biblical text can offer meaning that I do not find helpful; on occasion, it can offer meaning that helps me in making sense of my life, meaning that I can build on and enlarge—and I am at home with that.

Foundational

Once upon a time, it was said that a career in the church was the bolthole for the fool of the family. I would be disappointed and uncomfortable to find too many of the family fools among the pillars of the Bible.

I would not want the core documents of my faith to be substantially the work of those who might be characterised as credulous, gullible, and unsophisticated. Fortunately for me, the evidence suggests quite the opposite.

As should be clear from these commentaries on 1–2 Samuel—and as is equally evident for me in close study of the Pentateuch and the Deuteronomistic History—those responsible for our biblical text, whether in its beginnings, in the process of its development, or in its final form, were highly intelligent, highly skilled, and insightful thinkers and theologians.

Interpretational

There can be joy in encountering text that challenges one's understanding of life and self. Jeremiah puts it well:

> They have forsaken me, the fountain of living water
> and dug out cisterns for themselves,
> cracked cisterns that can hold no water (Jer 2:13).

We need the challenge of living water; all too easily we can lapse into making cisterns for ourselves that can hold no water—cannot generate life and cannot sustain it or nourish it.

For me, that 'fountain of living water' involves awareness of what is named 'spirit' and acceptance of 'commitment to faith in God'. The idea of God is not, I hope, the product of need, the preserver of privilege, the opiate that anesthetises by holding out a hope beyond injustice and oppression. Commitment to faith in God is at bottom a giving weight and worth to the whisper of spirit at the deep core of human life. Yearning for the spirit has been an issue across all human history: whether to seek it, spurn it, or ignore it. Often, the options are fundamental and basic, involving the meaning or absurdity of life lived at depth. For some, Christian faith may be chosen because it gives most meaning (for example, acceptance of God's reality). Again, of the absurdities on offer, Christian faith may be the least absurd (for example, acceptance of God's love). For such faith, the reality of God, incarnation, eucharist, and resurrection are too vital to be lost in the turmoil of church politics or institutional change. (I speak of 'Christian faith' because it is the faith I know and live; I dare not speak of the 'meaning or absurdity' of other faiths that I do not know from within.)

Spirit can impact on us in many ways. It may be extraordinary, erupting into our lives powerfully, overwhelming us. We may have to be careful; it can be risky. It may be very ordinary, quietly and unobtrusively present. We may have to be attentive; it can be elusive. A biblical example of the extraordinary might be Elijah's great wind, or earthquake, or fire (1 Kgs 19:11–12a); since the Lord was not in these—but could have been—another example nearby is Elijah's long-distance run in front of Ahab, halfway across Israel (1 Kgs 18:46). In our lives, it could be a passionate love affair, at its best, or the cataclysmic encounter with nature or great art. The prime biblical example of the ordinary is surely Elijah's 'sound of sheer silence' (1 Kgs 19:12b). In our lives, there is the stillness of intimacy, the quiet of contemplation, the wonder of fidelity—and so much more.

The awareness of spirit is often coupled with an awareness of ourselves and our world as insufficient—inexplicable to the best of our understanding. The discoveries and theories of science are fascinating and illuminating. They open avenues to new universes of the mind. They do not diminish our sense that we and our universe are insufficient. So we seek a cause that is sufficient; the sense of spirit validates our search. The outcome of the search is not factual and certain knowledge; it is chosen belief—commitment to a point of view, while recognising that it might not be right. CS Lewis's biographer refers to the whole European philosophical tradition since Plato attempting to account for 'our sense that we do not belong in this world, that we are pilgrims and strangers here, homesick for another place where one day we shall be truly ourselves' (Wilson, *Lewis*, x). We might never use such language—for we do indeed belong in this world as well as beyond it—but is that 'sense' (what Karl Rahner calls the transcendental experience of God) romantic rot or does it touch on ultimate truth? Awareness of spirit leans toward the latter. At the core of it all is a mystery that says Yes—a mystery whom we name God.

Postscript

Responses are now possible to the two questions raised at the beginning.

To the first: why do we believe something that is of relevance to biblical faith, if not on the authority of the Bible?

We believe it because it has its proper place within the **interpretation** of ourselves, our lives, and our world that we have shaped—from our experience of ourselves and the various levels of community within which we have been shaped—based on an insight into ourselves and our world to which we are committed and which gives meaning to our lives.

To the second: why do we quote from the Bible in support of what we believe, if it is not the authority for our belief?

We quote from the Bible because of **foundations**. It is important to us that our faith-identity and our present belief are in substantial conformity with some aspect of the experience we find articulated within the Bible, in substantial conformity with some aspect of our foundations.

Works cited: listing with appropriate details

Campbell, Antony F. *The Authority of Scripture: Canon as Invitation.* Occasional Paper No 37. (Claremont, Calif: Institute for Antiquity and Christianity, Claremont Graduate School, 1996).

———. 'Invitation or … ?: The Bible's Role', in *Australian Biblical Review* 50 (2002): 1–9.

Campbell, Antony F, and Mark A O'Brien. *Sources of the Pentateuch: Texts, Introductions, Annotations* (Minneapolis: Fortress, 1993).

———. *Unfolding the Deuteronomistic History: Origins, Upgrades, Present Text.* (Minneapolis: Fortress, 2000).

Wilson, AN. *C.S. Lewis: A Biography* (London: Collins, 1990; paperback, Flamingo, 1991).

Word of God or Word of God's People: The Bible's View

(original: adapted from the Epilogue of *Experiencing Scripture*)

Abstract

There is no question that the Bible is the Sacred Scripture of the Jewish faith and the Christian faith. There is the question Why? An obvious answer would begin that the Older Testament is concerned with the origins of the Jewish people, of much of their law, and wise reflections on their lives, besides being the Word of God. The faith of Christian people embraces that and goes on in the Newer Testament to the life, death, and resurrection of Jesus Christ—the story of it in the Gospels and reflection on the meaning of it in much of the rest of the Newer Testament.[1] Is that the whole story or is there more to it? 'The word of the Lord' or 'the word of God' (*debar yhwh*) has a lot to do with it, but there is an enormous amount of thinking that has to go into that. There is also the fact that verses of the Bible often differ from or contradict one another (my mantra: the Bible often amalgamates, it seldom adjudicates). That involves the invitation 'Go think' and that invitation can be offered by our God or by the wise among God's people. What does that say about the nature of at least substantial parts of our Bible?

---

1. For reflection on the terms Older and Newer Testament see the box on 2 of AF Campbell, *Making Sense of the Bible: Difficult Texts and Modern Faith* (New York/Mahwah, NJ: Paulist, 2010). While no terminology is fully satisfactory, Older and Newer indicates sensitivity to Jewish sensibilities and may not pose insuperable problems to many NT scholars.

Introduction

The most significant factor contributing to the weighty significance of the Bible is probably the phrase 'the word of the Lord' or 'the word of God' (*debar yhwh*) in its various equivalents in Hebrew and in translations. Church councils, church authorities, preachers, teachers, and so many others contribute to our understanding of the phrase, from literal to highly metaphoric. Leuven professor Msgr Raymond Collins in that most orthodox of reference works, *The New Jerome Biblical Commentary*, in his article on Inspiration, writes: 'This traditional formula [the word of God], apparently simple, is extremely complex and polyvalent.'[2]

It is valuable for each of us to be aware of the influences bearing on our understanding of the phrase. What weight do I give to the current voices of my Church tradition? What weight do I give to theological voices within my Church tradition, or to authoritative voices within my life experience—teachers, preachers, voices among my family and friends?

Not all of us need to grapple with this issue. Many of us do not enter these lists. For those of us who do, we do because we must. Throughout my academic life, as one who writes about Bible and teaches it, I have had to grapple with this issue. I am torn and I comfort myself that to be torn in such matters is to be human. I also give thanks for those like Richard Dawkins and Christopher Hitchens who pour scorn on the worst of faith's aberrations. My experience of the biblical text for years has been: it tends to amalgamate rather than adjudicate. When I need to push beyond that, as I need to now, in recent years I have realised that it is not a matter of reading a better theologian or finding a better book. How the Bible is to be understood we will learn from the Bible itself, not from anyone else. Not for example from someone writing *about* the Bible (not 2 Tim 3:16, which, while leaning in this direction, is not particularly helpful anyway); the issue for me is what the Bible itself is doing. In recent years that issue—that we learn from the Bible itself—has been paramount for me. 'Amalgamate rather than adjudicate' has taken concrete form in certain specific texts. Pondering these led to 'Go Think', the epilogue of my *Experiencing*

---

2. Raymond F Collins, 1033 in RE Brown, JA Fitzmyer, and RE Murphy (eds), *The New Jerome Biblical Commentary* (Englewood Cliffs, NJ: Prentice Hall, 1990).

Scripture. Further reflection leads to this article. But first, a couple of issues are basic.

Why bother believing in God? Because we are here and while we can easily enough reach the Big Bang we cannot so easily reach the Beginning which is somewhere beyond it. Either we are here as the result of an extraordinary fluke (as far as we know for now) or we are here as the result of an extraordinary God.[3] My experience of life draws me to the whisper of an extraordinary God. If we believe in God, the word of God matters.

Why bother believing in Jesus Christ? Because he was here and the only reason for not accepting that is that what it involves can be very difficult to believe. The early Church accepted the fact of his existence and believed the faith claim that he was Son of Mary and Son of God. Extremely difficult to believe but they did and so can we. Were they more gullible and superstitious than we are? Quite possibly. Certainly less scientifically minded. But they knew a ruddy mystery when they saw one. They saw this one and accepted it, while hassling over the language to be used in relation to it. To my mind, of the early witnesses we have, the Gospel of John, around the end of the 1st century, understood the meaning of Jesus Christ better than any of the others. If we want to understand God the Creator, we need to understand Jesus the Christ ('Whoever has seen me has seen the Father', John 14:9). What we know of the Father we have observed from the Son.

It is theologically fascinating that Jesus lived a very ordinary life, despite the miracles. He did not have political power, as king or emperor. He was not blessed with wealth, as were some of the great of the time. He was not at the pinnacle of academic wisdom, in one of the academies of the time. He was a citizen of the powerless province of Judea. He disturbed Jews and Romans and died on a Roman cross—a common enough death for troublemakers in those days. Christians believe he rose from the dead, in what is technically called the Resurrection.

The understanding of Jesus' life can be greatly bedevilled by association with human sin. The reality of human sin is massive enough, God knows, but dragging the incarnation of Jesus into it

---

3. See my *The Whisper of Spirit: A Believable God Today* (Grand Rapids, MI: Eerdmans, 2008), especially 157.

is not helpful (for example Paul on atonement in Romans or Paul on reconciliation in 2 Corinthians). The primary objection to this I know through John Duns Scotus (c 1265 – 1308) who saw the incarnation of Jesus as far too important to be dependent on human sin. As I understand Scotus, he made the enormous faith claim that God brought the world and humanity into existence so that in Jesus God could become part of the human race, one of us. In Johannine terms, 'God so loved the world'. A big ask in faith, but anything less is unworthy.

Argument

With the issue of faith out of the way (for me at least), we can turn to looking at aspects of what the Bible actually does.

Creation

In the Older Testament, at least, there are multiple texts about creation, some extensive and others mere references. Here, it will be enough to look at three of those that are extensive: Genesis One, Psalm 104, and Proverbs 8. The first reflects a systematiser (one possessed by the need for regularity and system), the second a naturalist, and the third a poet. What matters though is that all three are quite different; they have next to nothing in common. Second Timothy offers us inspired scripture as 'useful for teaching, for reproof, for correction, and for training in righteousness'. We will need to include more categories if we are to involve creation. The passages mentioned are of little value for teaching; they differ too markedly. The only teaching could be: God brought all of this into existence.

Genesis One is regarded by many as THE biblical doctrine of creation. Of course it cannot be, with the existence of others portraying creation quite differently. Depending on interpretations (was the chaos there or did God create it?), Genesis One begins before creation and proceeds methodically and systematically day by day, element by element, until all is created by the sixth day leaving the seventh open for sabbath.

Psalm 104, on the other hand, begins and ends with praise of God. It opens its reflections on creation with God setting the earth on its foundations, the waters covering the whole show until their retreat to the boundary set by God. Then springs flow down to the valleys, the birds and the beasts profit from it, grass grows for the cattle and plants for the people, there is night for the predators and day for the workers, there is the wonder of it all and its relationship with God. It is about as far distant from Genesis One as it is possible to imagine.

Proverbs 8:22–31 is as different again. Wisdom was established long before creation of the earth was begun. The process of creation is not that of Genesis One or Psalm 104. First, those things that Wisdom preceded: depths, springs, mountains, earth and fields and clods of soil. Then the process of creation with Wisdom accompanying God: the heavens, a circle traced on the face of the deep, the skies above, and the limits of the sea, and finally the foundations of the earth. Wisdom was there rejoicing. This is a totally different imaginative picture from that of Genesis One or Psalm 104.

There is so much more, including all the combat aspects, with God slaying sea monsters and so on, found in highly sophisticated contexts like Isaiah, Job, and Psalms. What do these texts have to do with us? What is the nature of the Bible which provides such texts for us?

Flood

Within Genesis 6:4–9:17 there are two traditions of the Flood.[4] They are combined of course because both end with God's commitment never to do it again. Following one another would be absurd. When seeking out what the Bible is doing, it is important to be aware that, although these two traditions are not contradictory, they are quite different.

Without bothering with details, one story has a forty day flood and the other has a flood for one hundred and fifty days. One story uses the personal name for God, *yhwh*, and the other the common noun for God, *elohim*. One story has two classes of animals, clean and unclean, with seven pairs of clean animals (to allow for a final sacrifice) and one pair of unclean and the other has only clean animals, with one pair of each (no sacrifice)—the description of the pairs differs, in one story 'the male and its mate' and in the other 'male and female'. In one story the flood waters come from a great rain storm and in the other the waters are cosmic, coming from the opening of the windows of the heavens above and the opening of the fountains of the great deeps

---

4. For the texts of the two and full details, see most recently my *Making Sense of the Bible*, 53–75.

below. The two stories are radically different; their radical message is much the same. The presentation of the mythological event assumed is radically different.

The message is radical enough in both: at the beginning, God will destroy evil; at the end, God will not destroy evil. There is no change in humankind. Both use a story of an event as the vehicle of the message. While the message is the same, the event as used is not. What is the nature of the Bible that does this to us?

Plagues in Egypt

In the account of Israel's time in Egypt, the stories are told of a series of ten plagues that force Pharaoh's hand to let Israel go. There are two patterns within the traditions of the plagues.[5] In one form, Aaron and also the Egyptian magicians are involved. In the other, neither Aaron nor the magicians are mentioned, but there is greater emphasis on Pharaoh who authorises Israel's departure and with the stopping of the plague Pharaoh's heart is hardened and the authorisation for Israel to leave is revoked.

Given the two patterns, we cannot know what was believed to have happened in Egypt. We are left to think about it.

Deliverance from Egypt

There are in fact two accounts of Israel's deliverance at the Sea.[6] The interpretation has for many been determined by Cecil B de Mille, aided and abetted by many Holy Saturday liturgies with their emphasis on the triumphant passage through the sea. They do not notice that it says of the Egyptian group (NRSV, army) and the Israelite group (NRSV, army) that 'one did not come near the other all night' (Exod 14:20). The text also says 'the LORD drove the sea back by a strong east wind all night' (14:21), a statement that is hardly compatible with the division of the sea to either side only while the Israelites crossed. Two traditions are skilfully blended into one text.

Once alerted to the two traditions, they are easily enough identified. One is associated with Moses's hand as God's instrument

---

5. For details, see AF Campbell and MA O'Brien, *Rethinking the Pentateuch: Prolegomena to the Theology of Ancient Israel* (Louisville, KY: Westminster John Knox, 2005), 68–71.
6. For text and details, see AF Campbell and MA O'Brien, *Sources of the Pentateuch; Texts, Introductions, Annotations* (Minneapolis, MN: Fortress, 1993), 238–54.

in the dividing of the sea. The other is associated with the strong east wind as God's instrument in the driving back of the sea all night. In the first tradition, the Israelites march into the divided sea pursued by the Egyptians who are swallowed up when the sea closes over again. In the second tradition, the pillar of cloud or fire moved behind the Israelites and kept Israelites and Egyptians apart all night and then at the end of the night the east wind which had driven the sea back all night stopped and at the same time the Lord in the pillar panicked the Egyptians who fled across the dry sea bed into the path of the returning sea. When the Israelites woke up (unsaid), they saw 'the Egyptians dead on the seashore' (14:30). Two traditions in one of which the Egyptians followed the Israelites in hot pursuit between two walls of water and in the other the Egyptians fled in panic in the early morning and were overwhelmed by the returning sea, while the Israelites were apparently unaware of their departure.

With two conflicting traditions, we have little possibility of learning what we did not know—how did it happen.

One of the aspects that is easily overlooked is that crossing the Sea was not the problem. The problem was escaping the Egyptians. According to the biblical text, God told the Israelites 'to turn back' and camp on the Egyptian side of the Sea (Exod 14:1). *Turning back* implies that Israel *had gone beyond* the Sea, presumably by going around it (quite clearly it is not the Red Sea; it is too close to Egypt for that—despite both having the same name in Hebrew). According to this text, the point of the exercise was for God to get glory and for the Egyptians to know, in God's words, that 'I am the Lord' (Exod 14:4). For Israel, getting past the Sea was not the point; escaping the Egyptians was. That Israel escaped the Egyptians we know. The details of the event are unknown to us.

What follows the deliverance at the sea is even more surprising. As part of the song that celebrates the deliverance, Israel moves directly to Canaan. They pass by Philistia, Edom, Moab, and up to Canaan. According to this tradition, it was all God's doing:

> You brought them in and planted them on the mountain of your own possession,
> the place, O Lord, that you made your abode,
> the sanctuary , O Lord, that your hands have established (Exod 15:17).

It may be powerfully mythological; it is in the same vein as what precedes, the celebration of the deliverance at the sea.

The far better known tradition that follows the deliverance at the sea has Moses take Israel across the desert to Sinai, with the giving of the Law and the construction of the sanctuary there, and the trajectory up through Kadesh Barnea, through Edom and Moab, until, with Moses dead on the heights of Mt Pisgah, Israel stands on the brink of Canaan. With conflicting traditions, we cannot be informed of what we do not know.

The origins of kingship

In the secular realm, the origins of monarchy (= central government) are reported in ways that reflect different traditions. In four chapters of 1 Samuel, four traditions are given for the origins of Israel's monarchy. None agree with the others; the case is clear: wise reflection is needed.

In 1 Samuel 7, the prophet Samuel does everything that is needed. There is no need for a king. In 1 Samuel 8, the prophet's sons had been appointed judges over Israel by the prophet—we understand neither Samuel's power to do this nor anything about the office to which he purportedly appointed them—and they 'did not follow in his ways, but turned aside after gain; they took bribes and perverted justice' (1 Sam 8:3). The people therefore demanded a king to provide the justice that was not forthcoming from Samuel's sons and a king was granted by God, with a warning—a warning taken up negatively in a later revision. In 1 Samuel 9, without any demand from the people, God instructs Samuel to anoint Saul king-to-be for the purpose of defence against the Philistines (1 Sam 9:16; 10:1). Finally, in 1 Samuel 10:17–27, Samuel accepts the king designated by lot, but not before he has categorised the choice of a king as apostasy ('you have rejected your God . . . and you have said "No!" but set a king over us.' [1 Sam 10:19])—a view prepared for in a revision of 1 Samuel 8.[7]

So in the short space of four chapters, we are presented with four views on the origin of kingship in Israel: 1) quite unnecessary if the

---

7. Details in my *1 Samuel*. FOTL 7 (Grand Rapids, MI: Eerdmans, 2003), 87–118. Commentators struggle to bring these texts into some sort of cohesion, with God acting unwillingly—a characterisation most unlike the God of the rest of the Older Testament.

prophet is doing his job; 2) demanded on grounds of internal justice; 3) spontaneously given by God on grounds of external defence; 4) achieved after being categorised by Samuel as apostasy. What is the nature of these texts?

The diversity of prophecy
The pattern of amalgamating rather than adjudicating is common throughout the Older Testament, with issues of a verse or two more common than the more extensive cases. But there are still a couple of very extensive cases we need to be aware of. We frequently forget the presence in ancient Israel of two quite different groups of prophets, both claiming to speak God's word and each at odds with the other. Apart from the less direct 1 Kings 13, two passages in particular highlight this, 1 Kings 22 (Zedekiah to Micaiah: 'Which way did the spirit of the Lord pass from me to speak to you?' 1 Kgs 22:24) and Jeremiah 28 ('the prophet Jeremiah said to the prophet Hananiah, "Listen, Hananiah, the Lord has not sent you, and you made this people trust in a lie"' Jer 28:15). Robert Carroll acknowledges the issue. 'When the divine word may be a lie, prophecy itself becomes an activity in which true and false are indistinguishable.'[8] His brief appeal to the 'redactional framework' to resolve the difficulty will be unsatisfactory to many; more developed reflection on the theme might be more satisfactory. Thought and reflection are badly needed in ancient Israel and today.

Divine providence: wisdom literature and the book of Job
The chapters of 1 Samuel from 7–12 may seem an unusual and rather special case, and the diversity among the prophets seldom comes to the fore, but we should also be aware of the example of the whole of the Wisdom literature which is flatly contradicted by the book of Job. It may seem improper to have argued the case earlier for the smaller over the larger and then end up with the biggest of them all. But the issue of evil befalling the innocent has been with us for a very long time and we are no wiser now than we were then. Revisiting the issue will do no harm.

The Wisdom literature's case is adequately expressed in Psalm One. 'The Lord watches over the way of the righteous, but the way of

---

8. Robert P Carroll, *Jeremiah* (London: SCM, 1986), 548.

the wicked will perish' (Ps 1:6). The contrary is expressed by Job: 'the wicked are spared in the day of calamity, and are rescued in the day of wrath' (Job 21:30). My concern here is not to argue the case for one side or the other. My concern is simply that with two such contrasting witnesses in the biblical text we are invited to undertake some very serious and sustained thinking.

Conclusion

My apologies to readers who find what I am about to say inelegant and unsophisticated. There are times when the very basics must be said, so that those of us who believe we know them are nevertheless confronted with them. In very basic terms, if the inspiring God wanted to have us informed about some matters we do not know, one tradition would be enough. Two traditions expressing the same would mean that one was superfluous. Any knowledge of communication theory will include awareness of the importance of superfluity. On the other hand, two traditions expressing what is contradictory or quite different are seriously troublesome. The trouble is resolved if instead of informing us of what we do not know such passages are understood to invite us to reflection, bluntly are inviting us to 'Go Think'.

It is important for us to be aware of the exact limits of what we have done, the results of which are incontrovertible. We have taken a sample of narrative passages where information is provided twice, in more or less parallel fashion, and where the information is either contradictory or differs significantly. Examples from the Pentateuch relate to Israel's distant past; the issue of kingship relates to Israel's relatively recent past; the issue involving Providence is definitely an issue of Israel's present.

From these observations, two questions arise. First, does what is obviously true of two differing passages remain possibly true where there is only one such passage? Second, does what is true in the realm of narrative hold true in other literary realms?

While responses to these two questions are necessarily speculative, they are not devoid of importance. Where the first is concerned, is the same judgement that is obligatory *in the case of two conflicting passages* possible *in the case of only one passage*, without the probative force of a second conflicting passage? What is obligatory is for us to think and reflect, above all in the shaping of our individuality which is after all a major part of why we're here Where the second is concerned, it is far from clear why what is true in the realm of narrative should not hold true in other realms. Where law is concerned, the law of the jubilee return (Lev 25) is clearly project to be thought about rather than legal prescription that was observed. Regarding prophecy, Isaiah's desperate longing for peace in the book's twice repeated statement—'They will not hurt or destroy on all my holy mountain' (Isa 11:9 and 65:25) and alas they have done nothing else but hurt and destroy ever since—is not a statement of the future but an invitation to thought. Ezekiel's statements about the future of Judah (Ezek 47–48) are not a statement of what will be but an invitation to thought about what might be. Overall it would seem that what is true of the passages we have looked at in the body of this article may be equally true of much of the Bible.

Why do we quote biblical passages? For a multitude of reasons, surely, but among them the reality that what we quote supports what for the moment our thought and reflection—or more nefarious causes—have led us to believe. Believers in God should have no problem associating God with that thought and reflection, if not with those nefarious causes.

When it comes down to it, it is possible that a substantial part of our Bible is given to us as an invitation to thought and reflection. Such an invitation can come to us from an authoring Creator or an inspired creature. It is not the issue of authorship that matters; what matters is the function of the scripture.[9] Is it the nature of the biblical scripture to inform us, instruct us, command us and so on—all matters that pertain only to God if regarded as unconditionally enforceable? Or is the nature of the biblical scripture to invite us to thought and reflection—an invitation that can come from Creator or creature? In some cases, we can claim this statement of the Bible's nature as certain; it invites to reflection. In many cases, we can claim

---

9. Many are attracted to the description of scripture as the word of God in the words of God's people. This contains the same sort of trap that is found in many glib solutions to complex problems. The trap here lies in the meaning of 'the word of God'. Until that is clarified, the description remains no more than glib and clever.

The Pentateuch: Guard's Van or Engine?
(Original: paper read at MCD Centenary Conference, and ACBA)

Current biblical studies face the question whether the Pentateuch (Genesis–Deuteronomy) records traditions powering the beginning of Israel's story or traditions brought together at the end of Israel's story and powered by that story. In a railway metaphor, engine or guard's van (US: caboose).

Genesis 1–11 holds the texts for creation, garden, Cain, flood, and Babel. Reflections on humanity, these can come from any period, early or late.

The ancestral stories (Abraham, Isaac, Jacob, and also Joseph) fall into a different category altogether. Legendary is clear; early is unlikely.

The material associated with the Exodus is problematic. The introductory couple of chapters are at best unsatisfactory. The presence of duality (above all, two sets of plague narratives) is clear. What took place at the Reed Sea is evidently unclear; one tradition has Israel cross the Sea, while another tradition has Israel remain all night on the same side of the Sea. Above all, 'all Israel' is reported as present in the tradition; most modern scholarship believes that 'all Israel' did not exist early.

The traditions of Sinai are equally problematic; above all, the great tent sanctuary sets out from Sinai in Numbers 10:12–28 and is never heard of again, not on the journey, not in Canaan (the name occurs in Canaan, but for a quite different reality). As we have noted for the exodus traditions, 'all Israel' is reported in the Sinai tradition; as before, most modern scholarship believes that 'all Israel' did not exist early.

Engine or guard's van? The NT provides an analogy, with the infancy narratives coming into being after the gospels.

What we will do in the next fifteen to twenty minutes is look at these blocks briefly under the microscope—or better as the question of engine or guard's van?

Genesis 1–11 as reflective studies on human nature in relationship with God are far more open to interpretation than they were as inadequate historical reports relating to a distant past. There are a couple of points that are largely overlooked in the Garden story and similarly in the Flood story. We can touch on these briefly.

The two points for the Garden story are the need, all too often completely overlooked, to insist on the presence of act and consequence in Genesis 3:7 and of crime and punishment in Genesis 3:14–19 and on the radical differences between the two. Act and consequence (Gen 3:7) does not involve God; crime and punishment (Gen 3:14–19) directly involves God, uses singular address, and for the man and woman has no reference to descendants or subsequent generations.

The snake said: you will not die; your eyes will be opened; you will be like God. The act: they ate. The consequence: they did not die; their eyes were opened; they were not like God. They were created free; they abused their freedom. Beyond their creation, God is not further involved.

The two points for the Flood story are straightforward. First, the sinfulness related to the flood is not narrated before or after. Second, the decision attributed to God never to destroy again—the inclination of the human heart is evil from youth . . . I will never again destroy every living creature as I have done (Gen 8:21)—that decision authorises without restriction or condition the continued existence of a human race that is far from perfect. This conviction is reinforced in the slightly differently nuanced priestly traditions. In life after the flood, murder is foreseen and capital punishment required (Gen 9:6). With this less-than-perfect humanity, the text's 'never again' is emphatic (Gen 9:11), attributed to the priestly covenant.

When we come to the ancestral traditions, Hermann Gunkel was clearly right back at the start of the last century (third edition 1910); they are legendary stories (*Sagen*); 'sagas', for the last hundred years, has been sheer anglo-saxon chicken–heartedness.

For the Abraham traditions, we have three locations: Mamre, in the north–east of Judah's Negeb; Beer-sheba in the south-west of

Judah's Negeb; finally, 'between Kadesh and Shur' in the deep south of Judah's Negeb. Beyond that, we may say that the stories related to Abraham and Sarah are fragmented and disjointed, with a complexity we will not go into here.

For the Isaac traditions, we have two locations. In Genesis, as is well–known, around Beer-sheba in the south-west of Judah's Negeb. In the eighth century prophet Amos, Isaac occurs twice as the eponymous ancestor of a group in the north. 'The high places of Isaac' are in parallel with 'the sanctuaries of Israel' (Amos 7:9). 'The house of Isaac' is in parallel with 'Israel' (Amos 7:16). The northern origin is unexplained. It can be simply said: the traditions about Isaac and Rebekah are minimal. The presence of Rebekah to achieve a family unity and, to some extent, purity of blood–line is important and late.

In the Jacob traditions, we have a largely coherent and sustained narrative, with the exception of the material on Bethel. Unfortunately, nothing major in that coherent and sustained narrative can be reliably dated before the seventh century and significant elements are considerably later. Jacob is best understood as a legendary figure.

When we come to the Joseph traditions, the picture is clear and troubling. Clear because nothing, but nothing, is early. Troubling because the Joseph story is the bridge between the Israel of the ancestors and the Israel of Egypt and the Exodus. For the Germans, at present, the ancestral traditions and the exodus traditions are *competing* views of the origins of Israel. For me, they are *complementary* rather than competing. Either way, their combination is neither early nor original.

The two-chapter introduction to the exodus traditions (Exod 1–2) is lamentably and obviously inadequate (see *Rethinking*). There is a duality running through the exodus traditions themselves, particularly evident in the dual structures for the plague stories (Childs and *Rethinking*) and for the deliverance at the Sea (crossing and no crossing).

Finally, we come to the wilderness and Sinai. Before embarking on these traditions, I should point out that Wellhausen at the end of the nineteenth century pointed to other Older Testament texts that disagree with the Sinai traditions allowing Wellhausen to argue that they were late. Similarly, in the next century, Gerhard von Rad argued that the Sinai traditions were latecomers, preceded and followed as they were by Kadesh traditions. Both great scholars, Wellhausen and von Rad, were cheerfully ignored.

Exodus 15, of course, generally regarded as very early, has Israel move directly from the Sea to Canaan, without any detour into the south of the Sinai peninsula. Some maps have long recorded this route as an alternative (for example, Aharoni and Avi-Jonah, Carta/Macmillan).

The exodus traditions after the deliverance at the Sea comprise three sets of traditions: the wilderness stories; the gift of the law (Exod 19–24) which nobody attributes to priestly sources; and the presence of God to Israel assured by the text sanctuary (Exod 25–Num 10) which nobody attributes to non–priestly sources.

The wilderness stories are not a problem. They deal with survival in a death-threatening situation: the provision of water, the provision of food, the overcoming of enemies.

One of the great problems affecting the traditions associated with Mount Sinai itself is that there are two great blocks of tradition (the gift of the law; the assurance of presence) and only one itinerary leading to Sinai and no itinerary leading away from Sinai afterwards. The extremely elaborate and portable tent sanctuary and the massive organisation of Israel in association with the sanctuary are never heard of again, not on the journey to Canaan and not in the traditions within Canaan.

What is meant by 'itinerary' should be clear. The simplest form would be: 'and Israel left X and moved to Z'.

The two great blocks of tradition need attention. The first, Exodus 19–24, is frequently referred to as the establishment of the covenant. It is certainly not. At the beginning, a few short verses (19:3–6) presuppose a covenant (v 5a, 'if you obey my voice and keep my covenant') and describe the consequences that flow from its being kept. There is nothing to suggest that the covenant presupposed is in any way identified with what is to follow. There is nothing to suggest that the covenant presupposed is intended to provide a conditional interpretation for what is to come. I am in full agreement with Ernst Kutsch (*Verheißung und Gesetz*) that covenant in the Older Testament is basically unconditional promise, expressing what God will do, or law, expressing what Israel will do. The covenantal verses at the end of the block (Exod 24:3–8) are totally inappropriate to a desert situation. What is central to Exodus 19–24 is the gift of the law to Israel. Where this law is concerned, no follow-up is needed in the journey ahead.

The second block of tradition is massive (Exod 25–Num 10, including the book of Leviticus). Even leaving Leviticus aside, the energy involved in the production, first of the sanctuary in Exodus 25–40 and then of the organisation of the twelve tribes of Israel around this sanctuary, for camping and travelling, is enormous. The total absence of this sanctuary and this organisation in what follows is evidence beyond a shadow of a doubt that this text has been produced independently of any account of Israel's journey from the Sea to Canaan.

The potential significance of this massive block of tradition has been insightfully illuminated by Sarah Hart in a forthcoming DTheol. thesis at the MCD.[1] Her presentation to this conference tomorrow will deal with aspects of her proposal. I find that it makes eminent sense of an otherwise very troubling block of text.

Apart from the many issues of detail, one phenomenon sticks out like a sore thumb in all these texts, from Egypt on: 'all Israel' is present throughout. Martin Noth, in his *History of Pentateuchal Traditions*, emphasises this. Noth sidesteps the issue by asserting correctly that it cannot be dealt with in his book. But his assumption that it took place before Israel's entry into Canaan is untenable, in the light both of biblical text and archaeological excavation. This 'all-Israel' understanding is, however, taken for granted in the Ahijah–Jeroboam story of the division of the kingdom (1 Kgs 11:26–40) The Sinai traditions cannot have been compiled early, before the emergence of Israel as a force to be reckoned with in Canaan.

To review: I believe the Pentateuch is indeed the guard's van. Thank God, the infancy narratives have blazed the trail for an understanding of this understanding. The implication for ongoing revelation is clear: the fact of our understanding ourselves and our situation better reveals to us something of who we are. As a consequence, it is inevitably a revelation to us of something of who God is. So it is for us; so it was for Israel. When, late in the piece, Israel came to an understanding of itself as one people, to whom God was deeply committed, Israel rummaged among the traditions of its beginnings to express something of the reality that it had come to be.

I believe this understanding of revelation to be helpful and

---

1. Now the University of Divinity.

potentially fruitful and this understanding of the early story of Israel to reflect accurately the data of the biblical text. If you are interested, buy the book, *Making Sense of the Bible*. If you are not interested, buy the book and get interested fast.

The book goes beyond the Pentateuch, finishing with a chapter on the first half of the book of Joshua and another on the treatment of David in the books of Samuel. My talk, however, had better finish right here.

Martin Noth and the Deuteronomistic History
(original: *The History of Israel's Traditions*)

My topic is 'Noth and the Deuteronomistic History,' and my instructions from my handlers were to stay close to Noth, which I am happy to do. In a short paper, it would be unwise to do anything else. Fifty years ago, in the middle of the bleak horror of World War II, Martin Noth presented the Deuteronomistic History to the world of biblical scholarship.[1] It met with wide but not total acceptance; it has been with us ever since. An architectural metaphor will help to structure discussion, so I invite you to think of it as 'the house that Noth built'. Over recent years, people have been sounding out its structures, suggesting substantial rebuilding or extensive redecorating. To some, the house seems to totter. The question is: can it still stand? To begin to answer that, we have to look closely at the foundations on which Noth built.

The concept of a Pentateuch gives a structuring unity to the early traditions of Israel. The picture sketching the known human world leads into the origins of what was to become the people of Israel; in the generation that is spanned by the birth and death of Moses, Israel is constituted as a people, brought out of Egypt into independence, and shaped as the people of God before being set on the journey to a promised land. The tradition of Israel had bequeathed to these texts a recognised unity as the Torah.

To the contrary, the following books bore a nomenclature which pointed away from unity toward diversity; they were placed among the prophets, later specified as the Former Prophets. The immense variety of traditions in Joshua, Judges, Samuel, and Kings lacked any sort of conceptual unifying focus, such as the idea of Pentateuch/Torah gave to the earlier traditions.

---

1. Martin Noth, *The Deuteronomistic History* (JSOTSup 15, second edition (Sheffield: JSOT, 1991); German original, 1943.

Noth's original design

When Noth came to his task, the source-critical foundations had long been laid and were generally accepted, that is the identification of what elements in the text were 'Deuteronomistic'. Noth's interest was not in the separate elements but in the whole. The question he set out to answer was: 'do we in fact have here a comprehensive framework indicating a large literary unit which has adopted much traditional material?'[2]

The first foundational evidence for the 'whole' that Noth sought to build was the structural organisation. 'In particular, at all the important points in the course of the history, Dtr brings forward the leading personages with a speech, long or short, which looks forward and backward in an attempt to interpret the course of events, and draws the relevant practical conclusions about what people should do.'[3] Noth identifies seven of these passages—either speeches or summaries: Joshua 1, Joshua 12, Joshua 23, Judges 2:11ff, 1 Samuel 12, 1 Kings 8, 2 Kings 17:7ff.

The second piece of foundational evidence alleged is an extension of this organisational claim. From close source-critical study of the junction between Joshua and Judges Noth argues against separate, individual, biblical books in favor of a direct transition from Joshua 23 to the period of the judges. The other transitions are considered 'smooth and clear.'[4] Against the division into books, the structural divisions in the deuteronomistic text are marked for Noth by Joshua 23, 1 Samuel 12, and 1 Kings 8.[5]

The third piece of foundational evidence—and in many ways the key claim—is the contrast between the remarkable diversity of the old traditional material and the coherent uniformity of the deuteronomistic parts. 'The unity of the latter is the more obvious because it stands in contrast to the diversity of the older material.'[6]

The fourth and final piece of foundational evidence built on by Noth is the recognition that the key date of 480 years from exodus to temple (1 Kgs 6:1) emerges from a calculation based on the figures

---

2. Noth, *Deuteronomistic History*, 15; German, 3.
3. Noth, *Deuteronomistic History*, 18; German, 5.
4. Noth, *Deuteronomistic History*, 20–24; German, 6–10.
5. Noth, *Deuteronomistic History*, 24; German, 10.
6. Noth, *Deuteronomistic History*, 25; German, 10.

that are given explicitly in the Deuteronomistic History, with a little fiddling of the facts at the end of the careers of Joshua and Samuel. All this confirms the understanding of the history as a self-contained unit.⁷

Noth's conclusion:'Dtr. was not merely an editor but ['nicht nur . . . sondern'] the author of a history which brought together material from highly varied traditions and arranged it according to a carefully conceived plan'.⁸ It is worth noting that much of subsequent scholarship revolves around the tension between editor and author, already embedded here by Noth in his description of the Deuteronomistic History.

Certain positions that were considered and rejected by Noth have been picked up and developed in subsequent studies. First, Noth did not allow for compiled sources available to Dtr, beyond the collection of the settlement traditions and the combination of the extended writings on Saul and David.⁹ Second, Noth insisted on the unity of the Deuteronomistic History. There were subsequent additions in the same style that do not take away from the unity of the original. This original should not be dated so early that obviously later passages—for example, substantial parts of Solomon's prayer in 1 Kings 8—must be attributed to a second deuteronomistic author.¹⁰ For Noth, therefore, an exilic date preempts the need for an exilic edition.

The vision of this structured, unified, coherent literary whole that so impressed Noth over against the diversity of the older traditions can best be seen in an overview of the text. The deuteronomistic contributions are in italics; the older traditions are in roman; the major later additions are noted in square brackets.¹¹

---

7. Noth, *Deuteronomistic History*, 34–44; German, 18–27. The rightness of this observation is not changed by the fact that different judgments about what belonged in the Deuteronomistic History can lead in other ways to the same figure of 480 years—the figures needed remain exclusive to the Deuteronomistic History (see W Richter, *Die Bearbeitungen des 'Retterbuches' in der deuteronomischen Epoche* BBB 21 [Bonn: Hanstein, 1964], 132–41; G Sauer, 'Die chronologischen Angaben in den Büchern Deut. bis 2. Kön.', in *TZ* 24 [1968]: 1–14).
8. Noth, *Deuteronomistic History*, 26; German, 11.
9. Noth, *Deuteronomistic History*, 25; German, 10.
10. Noth, *Deuteronomistic History*, 20; German, 6.
11. This overview cannot pretend to be a complete identification of the text of Noth's Deuteronomistic History. For that, readers must consult Noth.

Overview

Deuteronomy 1–4 provides the introduction, a speech by Moses presenting the final great act of his life—with some additions in chapter 4. Deuteronomy 4:44–30:20 is already existing tradition—the deuteronomic lawcode (chapters 12–26), with its own introduction and conclusion—presented as the law by which Israel was to live in the land (12:1). *The original core of Deuteronomy 31* and 34* forms an account of the commissioning of Joshua, the writing of the law, and the death of Moses.*

Joshua 1 is a speech to Joshua preparing for the conquest [vv 7–9 are secondary]. Joshua 2–11 is the old tradition on the conquest of the land. *Noth attributes Joshua 12 to Dtr.* [In Noth's view, Josh 13–22 did not originally belong in the Deuteronomistic History and Josh 24 was also added later.] *Joshua 23 is a speech of Joshua looking back over the conquest and forward to life in the land.*

Judges 2:6–16, 18–19 is a theological introduction to the period of the judges. [In Noth's view, Judg 1:1–2:5 and 2:20–3:6 did not belong in the Deuteronomistic History.] The period of the judges was worked up from the stories of the tribal heroes and a list of the minor judges. After Judges 3–9, *Judges 10.6–16 is a midway interpretation, after the abortive kingship of Abimelech.* The minor judges and the Jephthah story follow. [In Noth's view, Judg 13:2–16:31 were possibly a later addition, and Judg 17–21 certainly so.] *1 Samuel 7 concludes the period of the judges with an act of deliverance by Samuel.*

1 Samuel 8:1–22; 10:17–27a; 12:1–25 were arranged around older material, especially 1 Samuel 9:1–10:16 and 11:1–15, *to provide a suitably nuanced introduction to the monarchy. Samuel's speech in 12:1–25 looks back over the period of the judges and forward to life under the kings.*

Stories of Saul and David, above all the Story of David's Rise (1 Sam 16:14–2 Sam 5:12), bring the narrative up to the arrival of the ark in Jerusalem (2 Sam 6) and the promise to David of a dynasty (2 Sam 7). *Since 2 Samuel 7 already looked back over David's rise to power and forward to his successors, all Dtr had to add was a focus on the building of the temple in Jerusalem (2 Sam 7:1b, 11a, 12b–13a, 22–24).* The old material continues with 2 Sam. 8 and the Succession Narrative (2 Sam. 9–20; 1 Kgs 1–2). [In Noth's view, 2 Sam 21–24 were added later.] 1 Kings 3–7 chronicles Solomon's reign and, above all, the construction of the temple. *1 Kings 8, as Solomon's prayer at the dedication of the temple, looks back to the promise in 2 Samuel 7 and forward to the future history of Israel.*

1 Kings 9:1-9 is a warning to Solomon of the need to keep the deuteronomic law. There is a brief account of Solomon's reign and wisdom. *1 Kings 11:1-13 reports Solomon's apostasy and the Lord's anger.* There is then an account of both the northern and southern kingdoms, incorporating a considerable variety of traditions. *Dtr contributed the framework of chronological notices and judgments on each of the kings and also a number of observations.* This account begins with the division of the united kingdom into north and south, prophesied by Ahijah (1 Kgs 11:26–40) and realised in history under Jeroboam (1 Kgs 12). *A theological interpretation of the fall of the northern kingdom is given in 2 Kings 17:7–20, 32–34a.* Older material continues the account of the southern kingdom. *2 Kings 21:1-18 prepares for the failure of Josiah's reform and the fall of the southern kingdom.* The finding of the deuteronomic law was already recounted in 2 Kings 22:3–23:3, and the consequent reform under Josiah in 2 Kings 23:4–15, 19–20a. *2 Kings 23:16–18, 21–27 comments on the reform of Josiah, and the reason for its failure is attributed to the sin of Manasseh. 2 Kings 25:1-26 was adapted from Jeremiah 39–41:2 Kings 25:27–30, the favour shown to Jehoiachin in Babylon, concludes the Deuteronomistic History.*

The conceptual vision which unifies and structures the whole can be seen in the following analysis.

The Deuteronomistic History　　　　　　Deuteronomy—2 Kings
  I. The preamble: the law of God for life
     in the promised land　　　　　　　　Deuteronomy
  II. The history of Israel's life in the land,
     in the light of this law　　　　　　　Joshua—Kings
    A. Under Joshua: an account of the
       conquest of the whole land　　　　Joshua 1–12:23
    B. *Reflection: transition of generations*　Judges 2:7–10
    C. Life in the land: a history continued　Judges—Kings
       1. Under the judges　　　　　　　Judges 2:11–1 Samuel 7
      2. *Reflection: transition of institutions*　1 Samuel 8–12
       3. Under the kings　　　　　　　　1 Samuel 13–2 Kings 25
        a. Up to the building of the
          temple　　　　　　　　　　　1 Samuel 13–1 Kings 8
        b. After the building of the temple　1 Kings 9 – 2 Kings 25

This quasi-diagrammatic structure may help to concretise Noth's contribution to the understanding of these texts as a Deuteronomistic History. For Dtr, the guidance of God—pointing Israel toward life lived richly in the promised land—was expressed in Moses' final words to Israel in the book of Deuteronomy. Suitably introduced, Deuteronomy sits at the head of the history, as the guidebook for Israel's living within the land. The whole history is placed under this book of law.

However, a prerequisite for living within the land is first possessing the land. So a collection of stories and non-story material was taken from tradition and framed by speeches of Joshua. With the death of Joshua and his generation, a watershed was visible within the people of Israel. To one side were those 'who had seen all the great work that the LORD had done for Israel' (Judg 2:7); on the other were those 'who did not know the LORD or the work that he had done for Israel' (Judg 2:10), and who would live out their lives within the land until Israel was exiled from it. In the view of Dtr, the inability to communicate across the watershed of this generation gap led to the repeatedly recurring experience that the Israelites 'did what was evil in the sight of the LORD . . . abandoned the LORD, the God of their ancestors . . . followed other gods' (Judg 2:11-12).

Within the land, according to Dtr, the history of this people divided around a second watershed that was located in the politico-institutional life of Israel; it was the establishment of the monarchy. On the far side of this watershed was life under the judges. Again, a collection of traditions was available for this; all Dtr needed to do in order to shape tradition to his understanding was to provide an introduction, a midway reflection, and a conclusion. Otherwise, with some framing touches, the tradition spoke for itself.

On the near side of the watershed lay the extensive traditions of life under the kings. Before entering into this critical and, in his view, fatal stage in Israel's history, Dtr provided a further reflection on the transition of institutions—from judgeship to monarchy. The prophetic texts on the emergence of Saul as king in Israel were edited and interwoven with traditions more suited to the deuteronomistic judgment on the kings. For Noth, 1 Samuel 12 was the great deuteronomistic utterance on the question of kings, drawing together and balancing the threads in the earlier tapestry of traditions.

Given the centrality of the Jerusalem temple in deuteronomistic theology, it is not surprising that the construction of the temple emerged as the watershed in this phase of Israel's history. The period of the monarchy leading up to and including the building of the temple was drawn almost exclusively from the already extensive Davidic and Solomonic traditions. According to Noth, much of 1 Kings 8 brought to expression what was critical for Dtr at this stage in Israel's history.

With the temple built, Dtr could judge the kings of Israel and Judah by two criteria: where they worshipped and how they worshipped. Were they faithful to Jerusalem as the place of worship prescribed in Deuteronomy? Were they faithful to the integrity of worship prescribed in Deuteronomy? Dtr laid down the criteria in 1 Kings 9:1–9; in 1 Kings 11:1–13 Dtr spelled out the implications of the first major failure under these criteria. The downfall is traced first to the northern kingdom's fall and finally to the fall of Judah. According to Noth, in 2 Kings 17:7–20 Dtr provided an extensive interpretation of the fall of the north, his last substantial contribution to the history.

Noth envisaged a five-stage structure in this carefully conceived plan. First the Mosaic period, ending in the transition to Joshua. Second the period of conquest, ending with Joshua 23. Third the period of the judges, ending with 1 Samuel 12 and the transition to monarchy. Fourth the period of the first three kings, ending not with 1 Kings 8 and the consecration of the temple but with 1 Kings 9 and 11 and the prophet Ahijah of Shiloh. Finally, the period of decline and fall under the kings of Israel and Judah.

In the first two periods, under Moses and Joshua, there is fidelity. In the third period, under the judges, there is instability. In the fourth period, under Saul, David, and Solomon, there is an ascendant movement toward the capture of Jerusalem and the building of the temple there, dropping suddenly and sharply at the end with the infidelity of the aged Solomon and its condemnation by Ahijah. From there on, in the fifth period—despite glimmers of light with Hezekiah and Josiah—the movement is steadily downward to destruction.

For Noth, Dtr's concern was to teach the authentic meaning of the history of Israel from the conquest to the exile. 'The meaning which he discovered was that God was recognisably at work in this history, continuously meeting the accelerating moral decline with warning and punishments and, finally, when these proved fruitless, with total annihilation.'[12] The echoes of Joshua 23, 1 Samuel 12, and 2 Kings 17 are unmistakable.

The house after Noth

What we have been examining is 'the house that Noth built'—its foundations, its structure, and the purpose that it served. The house was left untouched for a couple of decades. Then slowly admirers succumbed to the urge to be developers and improvers.

Where 'the house that Noth built' is concerned, what happened next can be best described in terms of restorers, rebuilders, and redecorators.

Restorers
The restorers sanded back deuteronomistic surfaces and claimed to find old structures beneath. I will single out the work of Wolfgang Richter in Judges, Kyle McCarter in Samuel, and myself in Samuel–Kings.

Noth himself was well aware that his Dtr used prefabricated materials in his building. They were extensive. They included the deuteronomic law code (Deut. 4:44–30:20); the old collection of stories on the conquest (Joshua 2–11); the stories of the tribal heroes and the list of the lesser judges (for Judges 3–12); finally, there were extensive traditions—about fifty chapters—from the time of Saul and David.[13] These are prefabricated structures, with the exception of the Judges material.

In 1–2 Kings Dtr was dealing less with structures than with raw materials. For Solomon, Noth appeals to 'the book of the acts of Solomon' (1 Kgs 11:41) and, after Solomon, to the Chronicles of the Kings of Israel and the Chronicle of the Kings of Judah. Besides these, Noth's Dtr drew on an extensive collection of prophetic narratives. The totals are of the order of twenty-six verses from the Chronicles of the Kings of Israel, 133 verses from the Chronicles of the Kings of Judah, and twenty-three chapters or so from the prophetic narratives.

All told, of the approximately 156 chapters in Noth's Deuteronomistic History, he attributed more than two-thirds to prefabricated

---

12. Noth, *Deuteronomistic History*, 134; German, 100.
13. These traditions are 1 Sam 1–4; 4–7; 9:1–10:16; 10:27b–11:15; 13–15; 16:1–13; 1 Sam 16:14–2 Sam 5:25; 2 Sam 6 – 7; 9–20; 1 Kgs 1–2.

sources.[14] No wonder that Noth comments: 'In general, then, Dtr. gave his narrative very markedly the character of a traditional work, the intention was to be a compilation and explanation of the extant traditions concerning the history of his people.'[15]

In the book of Judges, Wolfgang Richter isolated shifts in thought and language that identified an earlier collection of stories which served as a source for Dtr. Before being taken over by Dtr and given a deuteronomistic preface (Judg 2:11ff), the deliverer stories had already been held together by an interpretative framework and even given a model paradigm in the Othniel story (Judg 3:7–11). Richter's work is no threat to 'the house that Noth built.' It makes Judges 3–9 a source, just as Joshua 2–11 was in Noth's eyes. It allows Dtr to plead diminished responsibility to any charge of cyclic theology. The cyclic theology comes from the source; it is not Dtr's creation.

As part of the outcome of two massive and painstaking studies, Richter isolated shifts in thought and language within the redactional material of the book of Judges.[16] The most easily identifiable and repeatable aspect of Richter's complex observations is that, in the early part of Judges, the typical deuteronomistic language and thought—especially the term 'judge'—is found in Judges 2:6–11, 14–16, 18–19, but is not found in Judges 3:7–11 or in the framework surrounding the deliverance stories of Ehud, Deborah/Barak, and Gideon. The framework speaks of Israel's doing evil but does not name what that evil is; in the framework, the deliverers are not termed judges.[17] Judges

---

14. If anything, this is an underestimate. The core of Deuteronomy (twenty-six chapters), Joshua (ten), Samuel (fifty), and the prophetic narratives in Kings (twenty-three) adds up to 109 chapters. This total does not include the deliverer stories in Judges, or the Book of the acts of Solomon, or the Chronicles of the Kings of Israel and Judah. I have left these as not being 'prefabricated sources'—a description that may be legitimately given to the individual prophetic narratives. The 156 is made up as follows: Deut, 34; Josh, 13; Judg, 11; 1 Sam, 31; 2 Sal, 20; 1 Kgs, 22; 2 Kgs, 25.
15. Noth, *Deuteronomistic History*, 133; German, 100.
16. See above, fn 7, and *Traditionsgeschichtliche Untersuchungen zum Richterbuch*, BBB18: second edition (Bonn: Peter Hanstein, 1966). On record is Noth's approval for the first part of Richter's work, in a review in *VT*, 15 (1965): 126–28. In his final paragraph Noth has an ominous comment: the author writes in a style that is fairly difficult even for a German and above all for the foreigners who really ought to read the book.
17. Deborah's activity at the start (Judg 4:4b) is not that of a deliverer-judge; this

3:7–11 does not itself constitute a story; rather it is a combination of the elements that make up the framework around the following stories. However, it moves a step in the direction of the deuteronomistic material in Judges 2:6–11, 14–16, 18–19 when it names the evil (v 7) and refers to the deliverer 'judging Israel' (v 10). The language of v 7 and the ideas of vv 9–10 are not quite those of Judges 2:6–11, 14–16, 18–19. For example, the LORD raises up a deliverer who delivers Israel (v 9); Othniel, called the deliverer, is assigned the activity of judging (v 10) but is not given the title of judge.

In Richter's view, therefore, Dtr took over from tradition a narrative in which three stories of deliverers were contrasted with the abysmal episode of Israel's first attempt at monarchy under King Abimelech. A framework surrounded the three different stories of deliverance, pointing out that Israel's peril was punishment for evil, that the deliverer was given when Israel cried to the LORD, and that deliverance was followed by rest for the deliverer's lifetime. The attempt at institutionalised monarchy, on the other hand, was a disaster. Dtr's contribution was to express the message of the framework formally in a preface, clarifying the nature of the evil in deuteronomistic terms and characterising the deliverers as judges. Thus what might have been seen as a series of significant episodes is transformed into a major period in Israel's history, extending from the generation after Joshua to the generation of Samuel.

In the books of Samuel, P Kyle McCarter, argues for 'a prophetic history of the origin of the monarchy that was intended to present the advent of kingship in Israel as a concession to a wanton demand of the people. Beyond this purely negative purpose, however, the history was written to set forth according to a prophetic perspective the essential elements of the new system by which Israel would be governed.'[18] Its trace is to be found right across 1–2 Samuel, although the concentration is in 1 Samuel 1–16.[19] The criteria for its identification are not formally discussed, but they include form-critical considerations and issues of theme and content. McCarter

---

comes in the course of the story.
18. P Kyle McCarter, Jr, *I Samuel*, AB 8 (Garden City: Doubleday, 1980), 21.
19. In 2 Sam, McCarter attributes to prophetic redaction 2 Sam 7:9a, 15b, 20–21; 11:2–12:24; and 24:10–14, 16a, 17–19 (see *II Samuel*, AB 9 [Garden City: Doubleday, 1984], 8).

includes in it predeuteronomistic texts in 1 Samuel 8; 10:17–25; and 12. The prophetic history is of northern origin, from the late eighth century.

A comment by Noth is significant here: 'As in the occupation story, the existence of this traditional material [in Samuel] absolved Dtr. from the need to organise and construct the narrative himself.'[20] McCarter's claim that part of the organisation had been done by a northern prophetic redaction would pose no threat to 'the house that Noth built'.

This comment of Noth's interests me, because I think it suggests that Noth himself—like his Dtr—paid less attention to Samuel than to Kings. I believe that the prophetic texts in Kings cannot be adequately handled unless they are associated with those in Samuel. This will be evident in what follows.

According to Noth, there were

> some narrative cycles, each of which accumulated around one prophetic figure and was handed down in the circle of *homines religiosi*. Much space is given to the Elijah and Elisha cycle which is made up of originally independent episodes and a short series of anecdotes, *welded together into a more or less unified continuous narrative before Dtr's time*. Dtr incorporated it into his history splitting it up into parts.[21]

Noth speaks in similar terms of the Isaiah cycle, the story of Ahijah of Shiloh, of Micaiah ben Imlah, and a further cycle of stories of the prophets' interventions in the succession of Israelite kings and dynasties.[22] Most noteworthy is that Noth relates these cycles of prophetic narratives exclusively to the books of Kings.

In view of later developments, it is significant that Noth paid almost no attention to the prophetic materials in the books of Samuel. As

---

20. Noth, *Deuteronomistic History*, 86; German, 62,
21. Noth, *Deuteronomistic History*, 107; German, 78–79 (emphasis mine).
22. Noth, *Deuteronomistic History*, 107–9; German, 78–80. Noth continues: '1 Kings *11, *12, *14 and 1 Kings (20) 22 and 2 Kings 9–10 would have belonged to this cycle; but it cannot be proved since these sections are not specifically linked with each other and they have in common only the subject and the idea of the word of the prophet and of its effect' (109; German, 80).

Noth saw it, for telling the stories of David and Saul Dtr 'had access to a comprehensive and coherent narrative tradition'.[23] Its components included: the old Saul traditions (1 Sam 9:1–10:16; 10:27b–11:15; 13–14; with 1 Sam 15 added later and 16:1–13 added last); the story of the rise of David (1 Sam 16:14–2 Sam 5:25); and the story of the succession to David ([1 Sam 4:1b–7.1] 2 Sam 6–7; 9–20; 1 Kgs 1–2). The degree to which Noth saw this Saul–David material as a source that did not need further attention is emphasised by his comment quoted above that Dtr was absolved from the need to organise and construct the narrative.

It is important to see what Noth made of these prophetic traditions. There is a revealing comment at the beginning of his treatment: 'The prophets, "men of God", appear chiefly as *opponents* to the kings and surely Dtr meant them to be understood in this way'.[24] The role of prophets like Samuel (who anointed King Saul and King David), Ahijah (who designated King Jeroboam), and Elisha's disciple (who anointed King Jehu) does not fit at all well with this comment. It puts intolerable strain on Noth's 'chiefly' (*vorzugsweise*).

Since Noth, the literature exploring this prophetic activity in Samuel has been extensive. In A Jepsen's work, overshadowed by Noth's, the equivalent of Dtr's contribution is designated a prophetic ('nebiistische') redaction.[25] Afterwards, several German dissertations—Nübel, 1959; Mildenberger, 1962; Macholz, 1966; Schüpphaus, 1967—concluded to the presence of a level of prophetic redaction in the text of 1–2 Samuel.[26] Along with these, the 1970 Yale dissertation by Bruce C Birch may be singled out.[27]

---

23. Noth, *Deuteronomistic History*, 91; German, 66,
24. Noth, *Deuteronomistic History*, 107; German, 78. Emphasis mine.
25. Alfred Jepsen, *Die Quellen des Königsbuches*, second edition (Halle: Niemeyer, 1956); first edition 1953.
26. HU Nübel, *Davids Aufstieg in der Frühe israelitischer Geschichtsschreibung* (Bonn: Rheinische Friedrich-Wilhelms-Universität, 1959); F Mildenberger, *Die vordeuteronomistische Saul-Davidüberlieferung*, unpubl diss; Eberhard-Karls-Universität, Tübingen, 1962; GC Macholz, *Untersuchungen zur Geschichte der Samuel-Überlieferungen*, unpubl diss; Heidelberg, 1966; J Schüpphaus, *Richter- und Prophetengeschichten als Glieder der Geschichtsdarstellung der Richter-und Königszeit* (Bonn: Rheinische Friedrich-Wilhelms-Universität, 1967).
27. Bruce C Birch, *The Rise of the Israelite Monarchy: The Growth and Development of 1 Samuel 7–15*, SBLDS 27 (Missoula, MT: Scholars Press, 1976).

In the books of Samuel and Kings, I have argued in Part I *Of Prophets and Kings* that three sets of signals in the text indicate a predeuteronomistic interrelatedness that needs to be accounted for.[28] First, the similarities between the prophetic anointing texts for Saul, David, and Jehu; only these three of all Israel's kings are so anointed by prophets. Second, the similarities between the prophetic texts designating or dismissing kings, especially Jeroboam, Ahab, and Jehu; despite later expansions, the similarities are strong. Jehu is the figure common to both series. Third, there are interrelationships and a wider context to be considered. These signals need to be explained. My claim is that a continuous and coherent predeuteronomistic narrative can be identified, extending from 1 Samuel 1 to 2 Kings 10, which I call the Prophetic Record and which makes a claim for prophetic authority over kings in Israel, consequently legitimating Jehu's coup and his campaign against the worship of Baal. Its date: late ninth century.

The Prophetic Record does not constitute a threat to 'the house that Noth built'; it merely extends into Kings what Noth saw as already structured in Samuel and it gives a tighter focus and unity to that structure. McCarter and I have a lot in common; we differ in our basic criteria and on the issue whether kingship as wanton popular demand came within the early prophetic perspective—I think not.[29] On a predeuteronomistic date, we agree.

Some additional remarks may perhaps be permitted here. The northern use of so-called southern documents is a lot easier to understand when it is recognised that the material is used to legitimate the power of northern kings. These prophets claim that they, God's prophets, were God's instruments in the designation of Saul, the rejection of Saul, and the designation of David. What they had given in God's name, they were entitled in God's name to take away; indeed they claimed to take away the substance of the Davidic kingdom and

---

28. Antony F Campbell, *Of Prophets and Kings: A Late Ninth-Century Document (1 Samuel 1—2 Kings 10)*, CBQMS 17 (Washington DC: Catholic Biblical Association of America, 1986), see especially Tables I, II, and III, 23, 39, and 63 respectively. The only change I would make since 1986 is to omit 1 Kings 1* from the Prophetic Record. The text moves from 2 Sam 8:15 to 1 Kgs 2:1a, 10, 12—or equivalent.
29. In his presentation to the Noth Symposium, McCarter indicated that he no longer considered this popular demand material as part of a prophetic history.

transfer it with the legitimacy of divine election to Jeroboam and the north (1 Kgs 11.37, 38b). What they had done in the first place to Saul they did now to Solomon. The interest for northern circles is evident.

It is worth noting that the hypothesis of a Prophetic Record is not in the least dependent on the analysis of the patterns in regnal formulas. The only connection between them is that the odd distribution of the patterns happens to coincide with the end of the Prophetic Record. So the Prophetic Record can make sense of the distribution of the regnal formulas; the regnal formulas do not contribute anything to the Prophetic Record. The Prophetic Record is dependent on the signals set by the texts schematised in Tables I, II, and III in *Of Prophets and Kings*.

The similarity between the texts in these Tables I, II, and III is not so rigid as to demand an individual author. The growth of ideas and texts within a like-minded group would make satisfactory sense of the signals. The followers of Elisha are prime candidates for such a group. The role of a disciple of Elisha in anointing Jehu is scarcely an invention; for better or worse, invention would surely attach the anointing directly to Elisha himself. It is most plausibly seen as a fragment of historical memory within the group of Elisha's followers.

There is no mention of something like a Prophetic Record in the sources identified by the Deuteronomists. The sources that the Deuteronomists specify are cited in reference to information that is not recorded in the history—now 'the rest of the acts' of X are they not written in source Y? The Prophetic Record is preserved in its entirety in the Deuteronomistic History; there is no need to identify a source for 'the rest'.

Rebuilders

Frank Cross launched the campaign to rebuild 'the house that Noth built.'[30] Cross strongly endorsed Noth's description of the primary Deuteronomist as a creative author and historian and fully agreed with the sharp distinction between the Tetrateuch and the Deuteronomistic History.[31] In opting for a Josianic first edition, Cross

---

30. *Canaanite Myth and Hebrew Epic: Essays in the History of the Religion of Israel* (Cambridge: Harvard University Press, 1973), 274–89 (first published as 'The Structure of the Deuteronomic History', 9–24 in *Perspectives in Jewish Learning*, volume III [Chicago: Spertus College of Judaica Press, 1967]).
31. Cross, *Canaanite Myth and Hebrew Epic*, 289.

was opposing a strongly held conviction of Noth's. The basis of the argument, at least at first, was intuitive and thematic. Cross claimed two themes for the Josianic history: God's commitment to David and Jerusalem; the destructive influence of the sin of Jeroboam. The subtheme of the exilic edition was the unforgivable sins of Manasseh.

The material attributed to this exilic edition by Cross is limited. A few spots in Deuteronomy, five verses in Joshua 23, one verse in 1 Samuel 12, a handful of verses in 1 Kings, and a few more, as well as the final chapters, in 2 Kings.[32]

Decisive evidence is hard to come by. For example and by way of anticipation, Cross claims the expression 'to this day' as a very strong argument; Noth relegates it to Dtr's sources or to secondary additions—no occurrence is attributed to Dtr. Cross appeals to the theme of God's unconditional promise to the house of David. For Noth, the promise has been rendered conditional; for Cross, the conditional material is secondary.

A Josianic history not only runs counter to Noth's vigorous opposition. It also reverses the understanding of the basic Deuteronomistic History. It is no longer, with Noth, an account of the definitive downfall of Israel. It becomes, with Cross, 'a propaganda work of the Josianic reformation . . . in David and in his son Josiah is salvation'.[33] For all that the creativity and integrity is held intact, this is a major rebuilding project. Ironically, its success or failure depends on numerous other factors, not least evidence to be uncovered in the redecorating proposal to be looked at next.

In the light of later developments, it is valuable to consider what Noth overlooked—at least in the judgment of later critics. Since Noth opted for an exilic date, he had no problem incorporating evidently exilic material. The question is how did he treat the texts that were later claimed as evidence for a Josianic Deuteronomist? For this, it is appropriate to compare Noth with Cross, contrasting the founder of the Deuteronomistic History with the founder of its Josianic edition.

Cross, as mentioned, cites from earlier scholarship as a very strong argument for a pre-exilic Deuteronomistic History the presence of

---

32. Specifically Deut 4:27–31; 28:36–37, 63–68; 29:27; 30:1–10 (11–20); Josh 23:11–13, 15–16; 1 Sam 12:25; 1 Kgs 2:4; 3.14 (?); 6:11–13; 8:25b, 46–53; 9:4–9; 2 Kgs 17:19; 20:17–18; 21:2–15; 22:15–20; 23:25b–27; 23:26 – 25:30.
33. Cross, *Canaanite Myth and Hebrew Epic*, 284.

the phrase 'to this day,' which in context presumes the existence of the Judean state. According to Cross, it occurs 'not merely in the sources but also in portions by the Deuteronomistic author'.[34] Cross singles out 2 Kings 8:22 and 16:6, but adds also 1 Kings 8:8; 9:21; 10:12; 12:19; 2 Kings 10:27; 14:7, 17:23. However, for Noth none of these occurrences is attributed to the Deuteronomistic Historian; they either belong to his sources or are secondary. They create no problem for Noth's exilic history.[35] The problem they create is for others wondering how best to read these signals. If one agrees with Noth's judgment on the nature of these texts, they are certainly not evidence for a Josianic edition; they are no bar to one either. Certainly, it is almost impossible to argue their attribution to the Deuteronomistic Historian on grounds of language or ideology.

For Cross, the strongest arguments are thematic. The two themes of the first edition of the Deuteronomistic History are: 1) the destructive weight of the sin of the house of Jeroboam; 2) the commitment of God to David and Jerusalem. 'These themes must stem from a very specific setting having a specific social function'—a Josianic edition of the Deuteronomistic History.[36] Clearly these themes in themselves will

---

34. Cross, *Canaanite Myth and Hebrew Epic*, 275.
35. According to Noth, both 2 Kgs 8.22 and 16.6 were taken from the Chronicles of the Kings of Judah (*Deuteronomistic History*, 106 and 104 respectively; German, 77-78 and 76). Noth claims that 1 Kgs 8:7-8 'were evidently added, but prior to Dtr.' (*Deuteronomistic History*, 96, fn 1; German, 70, fn 2—although among Noth's reasons for this claim appears to be the presence of 'to this day' in v 8). 1 Kgs 9:21 was from 'the Book of the Acts of Solomon' (cf 1 Kgs 11:41); Noth explicitly refers to 'the official tradition in 9:20-22' ('und abweichend von der amtlichen Überlieferung in 9:20-22' [*Überlieferungsgeschichtliche Studien*, 69]). The translation in *The Deuteronomistic History* (94) is misleading—'letting Solomon levy forced labour from the whole of Israel (9:20-22)' is not from 9:20-22, of course, but from 5:13-18 (NRSV; = 5:27-32 in Hebrew and German). It contradicts the 'official tradition' in 9:20-22. 1 Kgs 10:11-12 is attributed to the Book of the Acts of Solomon (*Deuteronomistic History*, 92, 94, 97; German, 67, 68, 71), 1 Kgs 12:19 was written before the end of the northern kingdom (ibid., p. 108; German, p. 79), 2 Kgs 10.27 belonged to a prophetic story (2 Kgs 9:1 - 10:27, *Deuteronomistic History*, 108-9; German, 80), 2 Kgs 14:7 is attributed to the Chronicles of the Kings of Judah (*Deuteronomistic History*,104; German, 76), 2 Kgs 17:21-23 is a later addition (*Deuteronomistic History*, 115, fn 2; German, 85, fn 4). As a general statement about the northern exile, v 23 could have been written by either a Josianic or an exilic historian.
36. Cross, *Canaanite Myth and Hebrew Epic*, 279.

not nail down specific dates: the destruction of the northern kingdom can be a theme earlier or later than Josiah, as well as Josianic; the hope put in the figure of David is capable of being sustained after Josiah. The interest, therefore, lies in the way specific texts are handled.

Cross considers the neglect of the theme of God's promise to the house of David to be 'a serious failure in Noth's study,' the more so as it appears that 'the Deuteronomist never really repudiated this promise'.[37] The key texts are 1 Kings 2:3–4; 9:5–7; 2 Kings 24:2. For Cross, 1 Kings 9:6–9 is secondary, 'in direct conflict with 2 Samuel 7:18-29 and the Deuteronomistic theme to be discussed below'; 2 Kings 20:17–19 is 'an obvious addition.'[38]

Neither Noth nor Cross discuss 1 Kings 2:3–4; it is deuteronomistic for Noth, while for Cross v 4 belongs to the second edition. However, v 4 is the second of two *lema'an* clauses following one another without an intervening main clause; in all other cases, each *lema'an* clause is attached to its own main clause.[39] This supports Cross, strongly suggesting that v 4 is an addition, attaching a conditional aspect to the promise made David in 2 Samuel 7.

Noth claims 1 Kings 9:1–9 for Dtr, with the comment that only an erroneous early dating for the deuteronomistic redaction would cause it to be considered post-deuteronomistic.[40] Cross claims 9:4–9 for his exilic edition, because it conflicts with 2 Samuel 7:18–29 and the theme of Cross's Josianic edition.[41] Against Cross, v 3 as the original theophany is unsatisfactory; the simple declaratory statement is too terse to be plausible. Against Noth, the change at v 6 from singular to plural—you (plural) and your children (plural)—has to be taken into account. It suggests that vv 6–9 are added with the exile in view, while vv 4–5 merely prepare for the loss of the northern kingdom after Solomon.[42]

On 2 Kings 24:2, Noth claims vv 1–2a* as from the Chronicles of the Kings of Judah and does not say a word about the rest.

---

37. Cross, *Canaanite Myth and Hebrew Epic,* 277 and 276 respectively.
38. Cross, *Canaanite Myth and Hebrew Epic,* 276, fn 11.
39. See, for example, Deut 8:1, 2, 3; 17:19, 20; Josh 1:7, 8.
40. Noth, *Deuteronomistic History,* 96, fn 7; German, 70, fn 8.
41. Cross, *Canaanite Myth and Hebrew Epic,* 276, fn 11.
42. See, for example, the discussion by Richard D Nelson, *The Double Redaction of the Deuteronomistic History,* JSOTSup 18 (Sheffield: JSOT, 1981), 73–76, 103–5, and Mark A O'Brien, *The Deuteronomistic History Hypothesis: A Reassessment,* OBO 92 (Freiburg, Schweiz: Universitätsverlag, 1989), 159–60.

1 Kings 11:39 is an important text for Cross, 'a striking promise'.[43] It enables the Davidic covenant of 2 Samuel 7 to be kept intact. Noth eliminates any hint of promise, since at best only v 39a is to be attributed to Dtr: 'For this reason I will punish the descendants of David.' Verse 39b is an addition; perhaps the whole of vv 38b*–39 is to be considered an addition (from: 'And I give Israel to you'); it is lacking in the Greek).[44]

It is hard to avoid the conclusion that arguments like these are vulnerable to the tactic we might jestingly call 'secondary pingpong' or 'redactional roulette', in which Rule One requires that the opposition's key texts be relegated to the status of secondary additions, and Rule Two requires that Rule One be always applied. Clearly there are contexts in which secondary additions can be convincingly identified. But that is not always the case. In some of the contexts just mentioned, it is evidently not the case. We might conclude: many of the key texts here will not be immune to secondary ping-pong; the overall decision results from a basically intuitive survey of the signals, under the influence of exegetical observations.

Redecorators
With an article in the von Rad Festschrift, between the first and second publications of Cross's study, Rudolf Smend opened a campaign to redecorate 'the house that Noth built'. His article was followed by a monograph from Walter Dietrich (on Kings, 1972) and two from Timo Veijola (on Samuel, 1975 and 1977).[45]

Smend began with Joshua 1:7–9, a text that Noth agreed was a secondary addition to the Deuteronomistic History. However, Smend identified thought and language that could be found elsewhere,

---

43. Cross, *Canaanite Myth and Hebrew Epic*, 283.
44. Noth, *Deuteronomistic History*, 99, fn 2; German, 72, fn 9.
45. Rudolf Smend, 'Das Gesetz und die Völker: Ein Beitrag zur deuteronomistischen Redaktionsgeschichte,' in *Probleme biblischer Theologie*, edited by HW Wolff (München: Kaiser, 1971), 494–509; Walter Dietrich, *Prophetie und Geschichte: Eine redaktionsgeschichtliche Untersuchung zum deuteronomistischen Geschichtswerk*, FRLANT 108 (Göttingen: Vandenhoeck & Ruprecht, 1972); Timo Veijola, *Die ewige Dynastie: David und die Entstehung seiner Dynastie nach der deuteronomistischen Darstellung*, AASF B 193 (Helsinki: Suomalainen Tiedeakatemia, 1975) and *Das Königtum in der Beurteilung der deuteronomistischen Historiographie: Eine redaktionsgeschichtliche Untersuchung*, AASF B 198; (Helsinki: Suomalainen Tiedeakatemia, 1977).

especially in Joshua 23 and also in other passages again considered secondary by Noth in Judges 1-2. Identifying a common level of redaction here, which he called 'nomistic', Smend suggested a reorganisation of the deuteronomistic book of Joshua. Joshua 23 goes out; the bulk of Joshua 13-21 goes in, as does Joshua 24. The new redactor, responsible for a carefully planned rereading of the deuteronomistic text is designated DtrN.

In the material studied, Smend attributes to DtrN Joshua 1:7-9; 13:(1bb) 2-6; 23:1-16; and Judges 1:1-2.9; 2:17, 20-21, 23. Contrary to Noth, Smend includes Joshua 13:1-21:45 and Joshua 24 in the original Deuteronomistic History.

Dietrich introduced a new figure, DtrP. Dietrich's work is a careful study of the deuteronomistically influenced prophetic passages in 1-2 Kings. Working through the prophetic threats and texts, with an analysis of the language used, Dietrich gave the Smend school's picture of the Deuteronomistic History its classic form: DtrG (now DtrH) after 587, DtrP between 580-60, and DtrN about 560. Some key texts in 1 Kings 8 and 9 and 2 Kings 17 go to these later redactions.[46]

The details of Dietrich's attributions are: *

To DtrP, 1 Kings 11:29-31, 33a, 34a, 35ab*, 37a*b; 12:15; 14:7-11; 15:29; 16:1-4, 12; 21:18a*, 19b, 20b*-24, 27-29; 22:38; and 2 Kings 9:7-10a; 10:17; 17:21-23; 21.10-4; 22:16-17, 18-20; 24:2.
To DtrN, 1 Kings 2:4; 8:14-26, 28-30a, 53-61; 9:1-9; 11:32, 33b, 34b, 35b*, 36, 37a*, 38ab*; 14:8b-9a; 15:30; 16:13; and 2 Kings 8:19; 9:36b-37 (?); 10:10, 30-31a; 13:4-6, 23; 14:15-16, 26-27; 15:12; 17:12-19; 18:6-7a, 12; 21:4, 7b-9, 15-16, 25-26; 22:17a*, 19b (?); 23:26-27; 24:3-4, 20a; 25:22-30.

. The asterisk (*) is used here in place of the Greek letters alpha, beta, gamma of earlier days. Apart from verse fragments, the asterisk was also used when citing longer passages to mean 'not all of it, but excepting the exceptions'. Here it follows a letter to mean 'not all of it'. So 'a' means the first part of the verse, but not all of it; 'b*' means the second part of the verse, but not all of it. Readers scrutinizing the Hebrew will easily identify what Dietrich and Veijola were attributing to their DtrP or DtrN.

---

46. Specifically, 1 Kgs 8:14-26, 28-30a, 53-61; 9:1-9; and 2 Kgs 17:12-19 (DtrN), 21-23 (DtrP).

Beyond this, Dietrich identified prophetic traditions, assumed as original, that were incorporated by DtrP into the Deuteronomistic History. The prophetic traditions are given in roman; redactional seaming is noted in italics within parentheses.

The texts are: 2 Samuel 12:1-14 *(11:27b and 12:15a; also 12:7b, 8ab*, 9a** [from 'to do'] *b*, 10ab*)*; 1 Kings 13:1-32 *(13:2b*, 32b, 33b-34a; also 2 Kings 23:15*, 16b, 19b)*; 1 Kings 14:1-18* *(14:13b)*; 1 Kings 16:34; 1 Kings 17:2-24 *(17:2-4, 5a, 8-9, 14aa*; 18:1-2a)*; 1 Kings 20; 1 Kings 22:1-38 *('Ahab' and 22.38)*; 2 Kings 1 *(1:17a*b)*; 2 Kings 14:25; 2 Kings 18:17-20:19.

The major contribution made by Dietrich lies in focusing on the deuteronomistic interest in the prophetic materials incorporated into the history and its theological implications. Theoretically, there is minimal conflict here with Noth; Dietrich's conflict is with McCarter and myself as to whether much of his DtrP is better allocated to predeuteronomistic prophetic sources. This conflict highlights the lacuna in *Prophetie und Geschichte*—a study of prophecy and history which does not treat the books of Samuel.[47]

Veijola's two monographs fill the Samuel lacuna. He ventures into territory where Noth feared to tread and finds extensive traces of deuteronomistic contribution. As a pioneer, we can be grateful to Veijola that practically every possibility has been explored for us. The corresponding risk, of course, is that what is possible or desirable sometimes becomes distanced from what is demonstrable. Particularly helpful is the identification of levels of deuteronomistic editing in what Noth had already claimed for Dtr. This is an important gain. One of its results: 1 Samuel 12 goes to DtrN.

The details of Veijola's attributions are:[48]

To DtrG (now often termed DtrH), 1 Samuel 2:27-36; 4:4b, 11b, 17b*, 19a*, 21b, 22a; 7:2-15, 17; 8:1-5, 22b; 9:16b; 10:1b LXX, 16b, 17, 19b-27a; 11:12-14; 13:1; 14:3, 18, 47-52; 20:12-17, 42b; 22:18b*;

---

47. I hasten to add that Dietrich moved into selected Samuel texts in a 1987 monograph, *David, Saul und die Propheten: Das Verhältnis von Religion und Politik nach den prophetischen Überlieferungen vom frühesten Königtum in Israel*, BWANT 122 (Stuttgart: W Kohlhammer, 1987). Within the Smend school, however, he had been preceded by Timo Veijola's more extensive coverage.

48. Developed from W Dietrich, 'David in Überlieferung und Geschichte', in *VF*, 22 (1977): 49.

23:16–18; 24:18–19 (20a) 20b–23a; 25:21–22, 23b, 24b–26, 28–34, *39a; 2 Samuel 3:9–10, 17–19, 28–29, 38–39; 4:2b–4; 5:1–2, 4–5, 11, 12a, 17a; 6:*21; 7:8b, 11b, 13, 16, 18–21, 25–29; 8:1a, 14b–15; 9:1, *7, *10, 11b, 13a*; (14:9); 15:25–26; 16:11–12; 19:22–23, 29; 21:2b, 7; 24:1, 19b, 23b, 25b*; 1 Kings 1:*30, 35–37, 46–48; 2:1–2, 4a*b, 5–11, 15b*, 24, 26b, 27, 31b–33, 35b, 37b, 42–45.

To DtrP, 1 Samuel 3:11–14; 15:1–16:13 (?); 22:19; 28:17–19a*; 2 Samuel 12:*7b–10, 13–14; 24:3–4a, 10–14, 15a*, 17, 21b*, 25b*.

To DtrN, 1 Samuel 8:6–22a; 12:1–25; 13:13–14; 2 Samuel 5:12b; 7.1b, 6, 11a, 22–24; 22:1, 22–25, 51; 1 Kings 2:3, 4a*.

Interim conclusion

It is highly ironic that one of the major implications of the Smend redecorating proposal is to confirm the rightness of the Cross rebuilding proposal. Early in this paper, we noted the unmistakable echoes of Joshua 23, 1 Samuel 12, and 2 Kings 17 in Noth's view of an exilic history in which the ultimate outcome of God's work was to meet accelerating moral decline with warning and punishment and, finally, total annihilation. With such a message, such a text must be exilic. But once the three great minatory pillars have been removed and clearly identified with later redactional levels,[49] the likelihood of a Josianic Deuteronomistic History suddenly gains weight and momentum. It is highly ironic, but there it is.

There has been a considerable number of studies that support the Josianic edition. I single out among early studies Richard Nelson, who was converted from opponent to supporter in mid-thesis,[50] and more recently Gottfried Vanoni, whose 1985 article on 2 Kings 23:25–25:30 is regarded by many as bringing the case for a Josianic Deuteronomistic History to a successful close.[51] In these, the detailed issues are discussed far beyond the irony highlighted in the preceding paragraph.

---

49. Rather than removed, 2 Kgs 17 has been seriously weakened, with the attribution of vv 12–19 to DtrN and vv 21–23 to DtrP.
50. Richard D Nelson, *The Double Redaction of the Deuteronomistic History*, JSOTSup 18 (Sheffield, JSOT, 1981) in which the reference to the mid-thesis change of heart has been omitted. The original ThD thesis was presented in 1973.
51. Gottfried Vanoni, 'Beobachtungen zur deuteronomistischen Terminologie in 2 Kön 23,25–25,30,' 357-62 in *Das Deuteronomium: Entstehung, Gestalt und Botschaft*, edited by N Lohfink BETL 68 (Leuven: University Press, 1985).

The impact of the Smend approach on the Cross approach is, however, twofold. The identification of DtrP and DtrN with much that is negative in the Deuteronomistic History generates an openness toward a Josianic edition of the history. On the other hand, the identification of DtrP and DtrN points to the weaknesses and oversimplification of a two-edition hypothesis. The observations of both groups must be taken into account. Attempts to do this have so far been regrettably sporadic.

Space and focus force me to leave aside huge masses of scholarship.[52] It is appropriate to focus on the two schools with a wide following—Cross and Smend; it is immensely regrettable to have to leave so many others untouched. Three that make far-reaching claims about the Deuteronomistic History cannot be left without some mention.

Brian Peckham's *Composition of the Deuteronomistic History* is a fundamental reworking of the Pentateuch and the Deuteronomistic History from the ground up.[53] There are some fine observations about

---

52. Regular reviews of the literature are, of course, available in *Theologische Rundschau*. Selective mention may be made of: RE Friedman, 'From Egypt to Egypt: Dtr^1 and Dtr^2; in *Traditions in Transformation: Turning Points in Biblical Faith* (edited by B Halpern and JD Levenson) (Winona Lake: Eisenbrauns, 1981), 167-92; AR Green, 'Regnal Formulas in the Hebrew and Greek Texts of the Books of Kings; *JNES* 42 (1983), pp. 167-80; J. Van Seters, 'Historiography in the Books of Samuel', chapter 8 of *In Search of History* (New Haven: Yale University Press, 1983), 249-91; N Lohfink, 'Zur neueren Diskussion über 2 Kön 22-23', in *Das Deuteronomium: Entstehung, Gestalt und Botschaft*, (edited by N Lohfink) BETL 68 (Leuven: University Press, 1985), 24-48; M Weinfeld, 'The Emergence of the Deuteronomic Movement: The Historical Antecedents', in *Das Deuteronomium: Entstehung, Gestalt und Botschaft* (edited by N Lohfink) BETL 68 (Leuven: University Press, 1985), 76-98; A Lemaire, 'Vers L'histoire de la Rédaction des Livres des Rois', in *ZAW*, 98 (1986): 221-36; N Lohfink, 'The Cult Reform of Josiah of Judah: 2 Kings 22-23 as a Source for the History of Israelite Religion', in *Ancient Israelite Religion* (edited by PD Miller *et al* (Philadelphia: Fortress, 1987), 459-75; B Halpern and DS Vanderhooft, 'The Editions of Kings in the 7th-6th Centuries B.C.E', in *HUCA*, 62 (1991): 179-244; HM Niemann, *Herrschaft, Königtum und Staat: Skizzen zur soziokulturellen Entwicklung im monarchischen Israel*, Forschungen zum Alten Testament 6 (Tübingen: Mohr, 1993); E Talstra, *Solomon's Prayer: Synchrony and Diachrony in the Composition of I Kings 8,14-61*, Contributions to Biblical Exegesis and Theology 3 (Kampen, Netherlands: Kok Pharos, 1993).
53. J Brian Peckham, *The Composition of the Deuteronomistic History*, HSM 35 (Atlanta: Scholars Press, 1985). In my experience, it is helpful to identify

potential early text forms. The enterprise as a whole fails, because almost all the problem texts from Genesis to 2 Kings are tipped unresolved into his Dtr² level.

Iain Provan's *Hezekiah and the Books of Kings* proposes a pre-exilic deuteronomistic history, beginning with an early form of the books of Samuel and ending with Hezekiah (2 Kings 18 – 19); its composition is dated early in Josiah's reign.[54] In an exilic edition, the books of Deuteronomy, Joshua, and Judges were added, as well as redactional activity in Samuel and Kings. The primary observations are based on a shift in the understanding of the high places and a shift in the nature of the references to David. The proposal for the beginning in Samuel, with Deuteronomy–Judges as secondary, is acknowledged by Provan to be brief and tentative; handled within a dozen pages, it is not broadly based. A thorough evaluation cannot be done here.

Steven McKenzie's *The Trouble with Kings* proposes a Josianic Deuteronomistic History, with a diminished Dtr², and subsequent additions that do not constitute redactional levels.[55] In what is a comprehensive and eirenic study, drawing inspiration from John Van Seters, McKenzie nevertheless puts himself offside with Noth, Cross, and the Smend school. With Noth, because he argues for a Josianic history. With Cross, because he reduces Dtr2 to 2 Kings 21:8–15 (16) and 23:26 – 25:26. With the Smend school, because he denies any redactional coherence in the later additions. Regrettably, as with Provan, this cannot be the place for a thorough evaluation.[56]

Peckham's text from his listings of chapter and verse (figures 1-7) before reading the corresponding chapter of his monograph.

54. Iain W Provan, *Hezekiah and the Books of Kings: A Contribution to the Debate about the Composition of the Deuteronomistic History*, BZAW 172 (Berlin: de Gruyter, 1988). Provan is one of those who argues with regard to the judgment formulas that 'the minor variations by themselves . . . can easily be understood in terms of a single author' (54). This may be correct but it seriously misses the point. The point is why these finely nuanced differences of expression are distributed across the text with a remarkable and determined regularity. They are not random variations. There is a patterned regularity. It is this patterned regularity that needs explanation, whether it is from one author or several.
55. Steven L McKenzie, *The Trouble with Kings: The Composition of the Book of Kings in the Deuteronomistic History*, VTSup 42 (Leiden: Brill, 1991).
56. McKenzie remarks that 'There is no evidence for any kind of earlier running history, prophetic or otherwise beneath Dtr's composition in the book of Kings' (147–48). In this, he disavows his 1985 article, wisely in my view ('The Prophetic History and the Redaction of Kings', in *HAR*, 9 [1985]: 203-220). In his treatment

The house now: disaster or comfortable renovation
Despite myriad studies, it is surprising how little has been done to compare or integrate the insights of both Cross and Smend schools. Our needs are, first, a treatment of the shape and form of the supposed original Deuteronomistic History and, second, a thorough and careful scrutiny of the characteristics of language and thought identifying the later deuteronomistic levels. Has 'the house that Noth built' shifted off its foundations to the point where it is in danger of collapse?

Mark O'Brien's *The Deuteronomistic History Hypothesis: A Reassessment* is a serious move toward answering these questions.[57] There is room only to note the insight O'Brien offers into the overarching structure and driving forces of a Josianic Deuteronomistic History and to outline the three discernible focuses of later redaction. Three factors are isolated: fidelity to the God of Israel, fidelity to Jerusalem, and fidelity to proper leadership. Proper leadership is dependent on God's word and God's prophets. Stage One: Moses, the prophet par excellence, hands on authority to Joshua and all is well. Stage Two: No one takes up the leadership from Joshua; a new phase is begun and all is not well. God raises up Judges, but there is not a stable leadership. The last judge is Samuel the prophet and as prophet Samuel presides over the transition to Israel's monarchy. Stage Three: The prophetic power over the monarchy is shown in Samuel's dismissal of Saul (1 Sam 13–15) and anointing of David, in David's consultation with Nathan regarding his temple proposal, and in the interventions of subsequent prophets to designate or dismiss kings. The collapse after Solomon is authorised by the prophet Ahijah, who transfers not only power but also legitimacy and divine promise to Jeroboam. There are the further prophetic roles of Elijah, of the disciple of Elisha, and of Isaiah. Deuteronomistic texts mark the key transitions.[58]

---

of the prophetic confrontation with northern kings—especially Jeroboam, Ahab, and Jehu—while McKenzie has taken potshots at outposts of my positions he has not, in my respectful judgment, come to grips with my case for a predeuteronomistic core in these texts. Despite the potshots, I believe my analysis stands up extremely well and continues to offer a valid hypothesis.

57. Mark A O'Brien, *The Deuteronomistic History Hypothesis: A Reassessment*, OBO 92 (Freiburg, Schweiz: Universitätsverlag, 1989).
58. The key deuteronomistic texts are the introduction to the period of the judges

The relentless downhill slide is momentarily halted with Hezekiah: a reforming king rescued from the Assyrians after consulting a prophet, Isaiah. Finally, the upturn comes when the word of God is brought to Josiah and confirmed by a prophet, Huldah. Josiah's reform and restoration is in conformity with this word of God, purging the wrongs of Manasseh.[59] The new era, returning to the ideal, is ushered in with a formal covenant (2 Kgs 23:1-3*), a cleansing of temple, city, and land (23:4-12*), and a proper celebration of the passover, such as had not occurred under the kings or under the judges (23:21-23). On this high note, the Josianic history ends.

According to O'Brien, there are three discernible stages of redaction in the continuing development of the Deuteronomistic History. The first, from 2 Kgs 23:28 to 2 Kgs 25:21 (without 2 Kgs 24:2-4, 13-14, 20a), takes the narrative down to the exile; with its limited scope and its uniformity, it might well be the work of one person. The next two stages are more extensive and their boundaries more fluid, with some overlapping of terminology and theology. A degree of variation within each stage cautions against attributing these to individual redactors; 'stage of redaction' is the preferred term.[60] Three elements characterise the second stage of redaction: a focus on the sin of Manasseh and also on the evil ways of kings, emphasis on the prophet-king relationship, and insistence on the schema of prophecy and fulfillment.[61] The third stage is also marked by three characteristics: the use of nomistic (law-oriented) language, a shift of responsibility from monarchy to people, and a different perception of

---

(Josh 24:29-31 and Judg 2:10 along with Judg 2:11ff), and the introduction to the period of the kings (1 Sam 8:1 - 11:15*). At three key points in the history of Israel under the prophets and kings, prophetic consultation is of critical significance: i) Nathan, following the coming of the ark to Jerusalem; ii) Isaiah, following the Assyrian threat to Jerusalem; iii) Huldah, following the discovery of the law book. These are the three good kings: David, Hezekiah, and Josiah.

59. Manasseh: rebuilt the high places (2 Kgs 21:3), erected altars for Baal (v 3), made an Asherah (v 3), worshiped all the host of heaven (v 3), built altars for the host of heaven in the two courts of the temple (v 5), set a carved image of Asherah in the temple (v 7). Josiah: bring out the vessels made for Baal (2 Kgs 23:4), for Asherah (v 4), and for all the host of heaven (v 4), pulled down the two altars that Manasseh had made in the two courts of the temple (v 12), and brought out the (image of) Asherah from the temple (v 6).
60. O'Brien, *Reassessment*, 272.
61. O'Brien, *Reassessment*, 273-80.

the role of the prophets who become preachers of the law.[62] The seven prayers of 1 Kings 8:29b–54, along with some other additions, may well be later still.[63]

The picture offered is one of considerable fluidity after the primary composition of a Josianic Deuteronomistic History, but with certain points of focus emerging, identifiable both by the thematic concerns and the language used to express them.

Deuteronomistic language

I do not want to conclude without a word on deuteronomistic language. Moshe Weinfeld is right: identification has to be based not on words alone but on words, or better phrases, in the service of thought. The only sure foundation for claiming deuteronomistic attribution is language shaped exclusively in the service of deuteronomistic ideology.[64] As anyone knows who has looked for it, it exists. All else has to be correlated with this foundation or run the risk of being built on sand. Nothing wrong with sand—but it is risky to build on. It is not that the Deuteronomists cannot express ideas in ordinary language. It is simply that the primary criterion we have to differentiate their utterance from that of ordinary folk is when the utterance consists of or is associated with 'those recurrent phrases that express the essence of the theology of Deuteronomy'.

A cautionary comment is also in order. Noth asserts that solutions to the Pentateuch must be built on the whole Pentateuch and not on sections, such as Genesis. It is equally true, and probably just as fruitless, to insist that solutions to the Deuteronomistic History must be built on Deuteronomy through Second Kings. Partial studies cannot generate definitive results.[65]

Conclusion

It is right that this Noth Symposium has been organised. Gratitude is

---

62. O'Brien, *Reassessment*, 280–83.
63. O'Brien, *Reassessment*, 283–87.
64. M Weinfeld, *Deuteronomy and the Deuteronomic School* (Oxford: Clarendon Press, 1972); ses 1–3 and 320–65. 'Only those recurrent phrases that express the essence of the theology of Deuteronomy can be considered "deuteronomic"' (3).
65. Fortress Press has contracted with Mark O'Brien and myself to present the mass of observations involved in the growth of the Deuteronomistic History in a visually accessible form, under the title *Sources and the Deuteronomistic History*, as a companion volume to our *Sources of the Pentateuch*.

in order to Steven McKenzie and Patrick Graham. The contribution made by Martin Noth is magnificent: the trees of individual books are now seen within the context of the single unified wood where they belong.

There is no longer a single Deuteronomistic History. In its place there is a concerted Deuteronomistic industry. The primary edition was probably Josianic; any Hezekianic forerunners are yet to be thoroughly explored and accepted. Overtaken by events, it was updated and reworked. In the reworking, certain major shifts of focus can be identified, with corresponding characteristics of thought and language.

We who now live and work in 'the house that Noth built' need to learn how to see it and use it as a whole. We need to be aware of the past structures built into it and recognise the contributions made by rebuilders and redecorators since Noth.

Recently, after a warm review of Mark O'Brien's *Reassessment*, Richard Nelson heaved a great sigh in print: 'Nostalgia has no place in scholarship, but perhaps the time has come for us to reread Noth with an open mind'—even after fifty years, Noth's Deuteronomistic History in a form something like that he proposed still 'explains so much so well that it deserves a fair and sympathetic hearing'.[66]

Perhaps we cannot reoccupy the Deuteronomistic History as Noth built the house. But we can do something similar: we can live in the house we now have without closing our eyes in ignorance of its past. The architectural metaphor may help.

Our clan, of course, has lived on the same site for generations. Guests have visited and died here. The ghosts of prophets past and even kings are said to walk the occasional corridor. Our forebears may have laid the foundations for this imposing structure back in Hezekiah's time. There are traces of an old building visible, a cornice here and a beam there. The most notable feature we inherited was the idea of a great staircase. As father said with a twinkle: they were very concerned then about going up to the high places.

Our grandparents' generation built most of the present structure, very splendid and grand, reflecting all the optimism and hope of the good times under Josiah. After the bubble burst and the national collapse came, we grandchildren realised that parts of the old structure

---

66. R Nelson, *Biblica* 71 (1990), 567.

were unrealistic and insecure and needed careful restoration, shoring up and reshaping. Our children have helped since, redecorating here and there, now and then. We turned over the conservatory and the library for archival storage, theology in the conservatory and prophetic art in the library. The more appropriate bits have been put on display around the house. If you keep the family history in mind, it can be a richly evocative house to live in.

In short, the house that Noth built has not been left untouched, but it can be lived in now more comfortably than before.

We are badly in need of metaphors for reading the present biblical text. We have not yet, it seems, found our way to a comfortable and responsible post-critical reading of that complex entity which is our biblical text. We badly need to escape from the redactional fragmentation of much past study. The instincts and literary insights of a print media culture that treats all text as literary text proves to be a blind alley, offering an escape that is ultimately illusory. We need metaphors that allow for the appropriate display of traditions, their touching-up occasionally, and their interactive association. The architectural metaphor of the building is, I believe, a good one. The art gallery with its exhibition halls is another metaphor that is helpful. One other that I have found valuable in reflecting on the Deuteronomistic History is a version of the family album—the metaphor of the collages of memories, snapshots, and treasures that are preserved and presented in some form of extended famil0s the album away for a month or so—along with the memorabilia case containing all the leftovers and unused bits—and rearranges parts of it. Then we all gather to look at it and talk over the rearrangement and explore once again where we have come from and who we are.

Studying the Deuteronomistic History, we may not be able to reconstruct the past documents with enough accuracy to win full consensus. However, we can read the signals that point to the forces which powered the shaping of our text. We are not concerned with the vestiges of an author, but we listen for the voices of a text.

The Deuteronomistic History
as identified by Martin Noth

This identification of the Deuteronomistic History (DH) presents the text described by Martin Noth in his study *The Deuteronomistic*

History (JSOTSup 15, second edition (Sheffield: JSOT, 1991); German original, 1943. The presentation follows the chronological sequence in this sense that the text assumed as original is aligned with the left margin, the deuteronomistic material is indented from the left margin and italicised, and the principal texts considered by Noth as subsequent additions are aligned with the right margin and also italicised.

DEUTERONOMY

Deuteronomy 4:44–30:20 already existed as the deuteronomic law code (chapters 12–26) with its own introduction and conclusion.

31:1, 2, 7–9a*, (10, 11a*b, 12b–13), 24–26a is from Dtr
34:1a**a, 4–6 is from Dtr

> *Most of the verses omitted from chapter 31 are considered to be later additions, as are chapters 32; 33; and 34:10-12. 34:1b*–3 is an explanatory addition; 34:1a*, 7–9 is from P.*

JOSHUA

1:1–6, 10–18 are from Dtr Subsequent addition: 1:7–9
Joshua 2–11 already existed as a collection of stories on the conquest.
In Joshua 2–11, Noth attributes the following to Dtr:
2:10b
3:2–3, 4b, 6, 7, 8, and the word 'priests' in 3:13, 14, 15, 17
4:12, 14, 24, and the word 'priests' in 4:3, 9, 10, 18
5:4, 6, 7
6:4a*b, 6, 8, 9a, 12b, 13a, 16a* (the priests), 26, cf 1 Kings 16:34
8:1a, 30–35
9:9b*, 10, 27b*
10:25
11:15, 20b, 23
14:6a*b-15a—these may belong after 11:21–23a
12
Joshua 13–22, according to Noth, did not originally belong in DH, but was added shortly after its conclusion.

The material is very similar to the work of Dtr; within it, 21:1–42 and 22:7–34 are secondary additions.

23
Joshua 24, for Noth, is an independent passage, probably unknown to Dtr, which was later reworked in deuteronomistic style and added to DH.

JUDGES

Judges 1:1–2:5, for Noth, does not belong to DH.
2:6–11, 14–16, 18–19 are from Dtr. Subsequent additions: 2:12–13, 20–3:6
Judges 3–12 was worked up by Dtr from two complexes of tradition: stories of the tribal heroes and a list of the lesser judges.
    In Judges 3–12, Noth attributes the following to Dtr:
    3:7–11—Othniel
    3:12–15a, 30b—Ehud
    4:1a, 2–3a, 4b; 5:31b—Deborah & Barak
    6:1, 6b–10; 8:27b–28, 30–35—Gideon
    10:6–16
    13:1 is from Dtr.
    13:2–16:31, according to Noth, was possibly added later to DH; note the absence of Samson in the list of judges in 1 Samuel 12:9–11.
    Judges 17–21 is widely recognised as a subsequent addition.

1–2 SAMUEL

For the portrayal of the end of the period of the Judges, in which Samuel is the last Judge, and the establishment of kingship in Israel, Dtr had several blocks of old tradition available:
1 Samuel 1:1–4:1a—prophetic traditions
1 Samuel 4:1b–7:1—ark narrative (first part)
1 Samuel 9:1–10:16; 10:27b–11:15—old account of Saul's kingship.
    In 1 Samuel 1–12, Noth attributes the following to Dtr:
    2:25b, 34–35 (Note: *2:27–33* is a pre-deuteronomistic addition)
    7:2–17
    8:1–22

10:17–27a
  12:1–25
For the portrayal of the period of Saul and David, Dtr had the extensive Saul-David traditions available. For example:
Saul—1 Samuel 13–15; 16:1–13
David—1 Samuel 16:14– 2 Samuel 5:25
2 Samuel 6–7
2 Samuel 8:1–14*, 15–18
2 Samuel 9–20 and 1 Kings 1–2

> *In 1 Samuel 13–2 Samuel 20, Noth attributes the following to Dtr:*
> *1 Samuel 13:1*
> *2 Samuel 2:10a, 11* (Note: 2 Sam 3:2–6a is a pre deuteronomistic addition*)*
> *2 Samuel 5:4–5* (Note: 2 Sam 5:13–16 is a pre-deuteronomistic addition)
> *2 Samuel 7:1b, 7a*, 11a, 12b–13a, 22–24*
> *2 Samuel 8:1aa, 14b*
> *Subsequent addition: 2 Samuel 2:1–24*

1–2 KINGS

1 Kings 2:2, 3–4, 27b are Dtr's final insertions in the David traditions.*

For the portrayal of the period of Solomon after 1 Kings 1–2, Dtr drew on traditions of a different kind, building from various disparate and as yet unconnected elements. The main source appears to have been 'the book of the acts of Solomon' (1 Kgs 11:41).

> *In this material in 1 Kings, Noth attributes the following to Dtr:*
> *3:3, 14, 15ba*
> *4:1–5:8*   (NRSV, *4:1–28*)   Based on official records
> *5:15–32*   (NRSV, *5:1–18*)
> *6:1, 19b*
> *7:47–51*
> *8:1b–2a*, 4b, 9, 14–66*
> *9:1-9, 10, 14*
> *11:1–13, 29a*, 36b*, 38-39a, 41–43*

For the portrayal of the final period of the history, Dtr drew on the Chronicles of the Kings of Israel or Judah. From this, Dtr derived particularly the framework of the presentation, as a history not of individual kings but of the monarchy as a whole in Israel and Judah.

Apart from the framework, Noth assumes that Dtr derived the following material from these Chronicles.

From the Chronicles of the Kings of Israel:
    Usurpations
        1 Kings 15:27–28; 16:9–12, 15–18, 21–22
        2 Kings 15:10, 14, 16, 25, 30a
    Changes of royal residence
        1 Kings 12:25; 16:24
    Other
        1 Kings 16:31, 34; 22:39*
        2 Kings 14:25; 15:19–20, 29

From the Chronicles of the Kings of Judah:
    Mainly plundering of the temple
        1 Kings 14:25–28; 15:12–13, 16–22
        2 Kings 12:5–17, 18–19; 14:7, 8–14, 22; 15:35b; 16:5–6, 7–18;
        18:4b, 13–16; 23:4–15, 19, 20a; 24:10–16
    Usurpations, etc.
        2 Kings 11:1–20; 12:21–22; 14:5, 19–21; 15:5; 21:23–24; 23:29–30, 33–35; 24:17
    Other
        1 Kings 22:48–50
        2 Kings 8:20–22; 17:3–6, 24, 29–31; 18:9–11; 24:1–2a*, 7

Noth assumes that Dtr also drew widely on prophetic narratives:
    1 Kings 11:29ab*-31, 36a*b, 37; 12:1–20, 26-31; 14:1-18—Ahijah of Shiloh
    1 Kings 12:32–13:32—prophetic legend about Bethel
    1 Kings 17–19; 21—Elijah
    1 Kings 20:1–43—prophetic anecdotes
    1 Kings 22:1–37—Micaiah ben Imlah
    2 Kings 1:2-17a*; 2; 3:4–8:15; 13:14-21—Elijah and Elisha
    2 Kings 9:1–10:27—anointing of Jehu
    2 Kings 18:17–20:19—Isaiah narratives
    2 Kings 22:3–23:3—finding of deuteronomic law

Apart in general from the framing passages for each king, Noth attributes the following to Dtr:

1 Kings
13:33–34
14:14–16, 19–20, 21*, 22–24
15:15, 29–30
16:1–4
21:21–22, 24–26 Subsequent additions: 21:20, 23
22:38–40, 43, 47

2 Kings
1:1   (cf, 3:5)
8:28–29   (cf, 9:15a, 16b)
9:8b–10a
10:28–33
13:3–7, 22–25
14:6, 26–27
15:12, 37 (cf, 10:30, also deuteronomistic)
16:3–4
17:7–20, 32–34a Subsequent addition: 17:34b–40
21:1–18
23:16–18, 21–27
24:19–20
25:1–26 (using material from Jeremiah 39–41), 27–30 (from Dtr's own knowledge)

Rethinking Revelation:
The Priority of the Present Over the Past
(original: not located)

Abstract

In most circles it has long been taken for granted that the composition of priestly material (P) in the Pentateuch dates to around the time of Israel's exile. With the more recent disintegration of the claim for a Yahwist (J), the trend in biblical circles is to see that the composition of non-priestly material in Genesis 1–11 could well have come from about the same time. It is difficult to date the composition of most ancestral texts much earlier than the book of Deuteronomy, around the late seventh century (see A Campbell and M O'Brien, *Rethinking the Pentateuch*, especially 22, Table 1). Close examination of two texts, Genesis 6:5–9:17 (the Flood) and Exodus 25–Numbers 10 (the Sinai sanctuary), allows the argument to be made that such texts do not portray how it was thought to have been back then, long ago, but rather how God is to be understood in the authors' day, the time of composition. The experience of their present determines how texts were written for ancient Israel. The experience of the present determines which texts are read by us today. Where revelation is concerned, because the practice of selective reading has existed for a long time, we change nothing in what we *do*. On the other hand, it may be necessary for much to change in what we *say* and *think*.

Preamble

With the exception of some solidly conservative biblical scholarship, the assumption is widely accepted that the present text of the Pentateuch in its final form came together in post-exilic Israel. If most of the priestly writing (P) is situated around the time of Israel's exile (587–538), it is clear enough that the final form of the Pentateuch has to be later. It should also be clear that the final form of the Pentateuch was not compiled in terms of the age of the texts concerned, but in terms of the chronology of their contents. The first chapter of Genesis, as text, is assumed to have been composed in the sixth century; its contents require its being at the beginning.

Much of the book of Deuteronomy is generally dated to the seventh century, around the time of Judah's King Josiah. Deuteronomy probably provides the earliest datable evidence for the traditions of Israel's Pentateuch. It can be argued on solid grounds that, in the Pentateuch, for the most part, neither priestly (P) nor non-priestly (JE) material is attested earlier than Deuteronomy. In the light of this, our understanding of revelation may need rethinking. The purpose of this paper is to explore the implications for our understanding of revelation confronted with the spreading acceptance in biblical circles that little of Genesis–Numbers is significantly earlier than the period around Israel's exile.

The initial moves toward this view have been in place for some time. This paper explores a fraction of one possibility where these implications are concerned. Discussion of Genesis 1–11 is restricted to the Flood text; discussion of other texts is restricted to the Sinai sanctuary. The paper falls into four parts: (1) a brief summary of the theme; then the biblical core, (2) the Flood and (3) the Sinai sanctuary; finally, (4) a fuller discussion of the revolution in our understanding of revelation.

Preview

What is meant by 'rethinking revelation'? Once upon a time, by revelation we meant *what came from the past*, from the *word of God*. Instead of this, the rethinking is to suggest that revelation for us means primarily *what comes from the present*, from a *multiplicity of influences*.

Despite appearances, many of the influences that impact on our reading of the Bible as we articulate our thinking about God do not come to us from the Bible itself but come to us from our reflection on circumstances now. The legitimation for naming this revelation: it is how the Bible was written. Such reflection, of course, takes into account the influence of the traditions that have shaped us.

We shape our understanding of Jesus quite differently, in dependence on the documents of that time. Our present may shape our reading of those documents; it does not diminish their role.

To return to the issue of our understanding of God and rethinking revelation. Israel's theologians pondered their present, reflected on their God, and produced their scriptures. We today ponder our present, reflect on our understanding of God, and then we select and read our Scripture in the light of this understanding.

The Flood text (Gen 6:5–9:17)
Beyond serious doubt, there are two relatively complete accounts of the Flood in Genesis 6:5–9:17. Naturally, we can smooth out passages here and there; the compilers who put the combined text together were competent operators. The reality of two relatively complete accounts, however, cannot be avoided. Given that two names are used for God, YHWH (personal name) and ELOHIM (common noun), one in each account, it is simple to designate the two as the YHWH-account and the ELOHIM-account. The high quality of their theology is remarkable; as remarkable is the theological difference between them.

To summarise swiftly, the principal differences between the two are: the names for God; the blocks of time; the nature and number of the animals; the origins of the floodwaters.

> In the YHWH-account, (1) the blocks of time are counted mainly as seven days and forty days; (2) the animals are both clean and unclean, seven clean and two unclean (probably pairs), and are described as 'the male and its mate'; (3) the origin of the floodwaters is from above ('the rain').
>
> In the ELOHIM-account, (1) the blocks of time are counted mainly as one hundred and fifty days; (2) the

animals are undifferentiated as to ritual cleanliness ('two of every kind'), and are described as 'male and female'; (3) the origin of the floodwaters is both from above ('the windows of the heavens') and from below ('the fountains of the great deep').

In discussing the biblical Flood text, two points need highlighting here. First, the two accounts are notably different in their theological accentuation. Second, the theology derives from present knowledge not past revelation.

The YHWH-account begins with a real shocker. 'The LORD saw that the wickedness of humankind was great in the earth and that every inclination of the thoughts of their hearts was only evil continually' (Gen 6:5). Even after all the horrors of the last century or so, we could hardly put it more bluntly and brutally. That the wickedness of humankind has been great is beyond dispute; history leaves no doubt. The 'only evil continually' may be considered harsh, but is certainly true where large blocks of human activity have been concerned. God is not portrayed as angry, but as 'sorry' and 'grieved'. So God concludes: I am sorry that I made them; I will wipe out humans and everything else that lives. In the YHWH-account, it is only at this point, almost a postscript, that Noah gets a mention as finding favour in God's sight (6:8).

To the contrary, the ELOHIM-account opens with a couple of verses about Noah, as blameless and righteous and walking with God. It even mentions his sons (Gen 6:9–10). Then comes the judgement on the world, but—surprisingly—humans do not rate a mention. Instead of singling out humankind, the focus is on 'the earth' as corrupt and filled with violence, because 'all flesh' (which, of course, includes humankind) had corrupted its ways on the earth. Only then does the narrator have God tell Noah that there is going to be a flood to destroy 'all flesh'. (The phrase 'all flesh' is peculiar to this ELOHIM-account of the Flood, occurring eleven times between Gen 6:12 and 9:17; it occurs nowhere else in Genesis.) In this ELOHIM-account, God's opening speech ends with the covenant to be made with Noah (6:18), and the intention of preserving in the ark Noah's wife and children and the whole animal world.

These initial passages are avenues leading to two very different theologies—not accounts of past events but present theologies. In the first, the emphasis is entirely on the human race, seen as thoroughly evil. Noah is mentioned, late in the passage, as 'finding favour in the sight of the LORD'. In the text we have, nothing is said, about any ark or any lifesaving; we can assume something was there in the original YHWH-account. In the second, Noah's goodness is to the fore, the human race is lost sight of in the generic 'all flesh', and a covenant and the ark are explicit lifesavers.

What must not be lost to sight in all this is that the evil of humankind and the corruption of all flesh *are not narrated*. They are assumed as evident; adequate evidence is not narrated. We will return to this.

In any telling of a flood story, the middle is relatively predictable. The floodwaters arrive; all aboard. The ark floats; the rest drown. The floodwaters subside; all ashore.

It is the ending of the Flood story that is a real surprise and that as biblical texts go is a brilliant piece of the most profound theology. Both stories are surprising.

The conclusion of the YHWH-account comes first. God is portrayed alone ('said in his heart') and God is portrayed completely changing God's mind. For the same reason that God sent the flood in the first place (because of human wickedness), for that same reason (because of human wickedness), God will never do it again. The reason is given in almost the same words as it was at the beginning: 'for the inclination of the human heart is evil from youth' (8:21). It was a little harsher at the beginning (6:5): 'every inclination', 'only evil', and 'continually', a trace worse than 'from youth'. So, at the end, the verdict is softened a little; but the softening is slight. More surprising even than God's change of mind is the reality that in the narrative there is absolutely no evidence to support God's verdict. Noah and his family are just off the ark. All they have done is offer a sacrifice and its odour was pleasing to God. The evidence that 'the inclination of the human heart is evil from youth' (8:21) does not come from the story. As one possibility, it can come from Israel's experience of human living over the centuries. If so, the narrative is not about how things were back then, but about how things have always been, *from* the beginning until now.

The conclusion of the ELOHIM-account comes next (9:1–17) and is just as surprising. God talks to Noah and his sons. Under the new dispensation, the world they are to repeople will have 'fear and dread' resting on every animal (9:2) and, at the human level, murder and capital punishment (9:6). The surprise: with this less-than-perfect world, God is portrayed making an unconditional and everlasting covenant never again to destroy the earth with a flood (9:8–17).

The combined text, putting the two accounts together, helps to lessen God's unpredictability. The human wickedness of 6:5 and 8:21 is combined with the change of divine dispensation for the world. Unquestionably, God is portrayed having come to terms with a less-than-perfect world. Human existence is not threatened by divine holiness. This is not a reflection on 'back then'; it is a faith claim for 'right now'.

The necessary combination of the two accounts has been very competently done. The horror of human evil is to the fore. The goodness of Noah is emphasised. The announcement of the Flood ends with the promise of salvation. In the YHWH-account, however, what happens at the end is not prepared for in any way—and cannot be. It is a total reversal on the part of God. In the ELOHIM-account, the ark, the covenant, and those in it prepare us to a limited degree for what is to follow. It is not to be a total reversal on the part of God, but a change in God's planning. The combined account does not shrink from the horror of human reality. The combined account emphasises that life will go on.

Here, in a double tradition, the All-holy is committed to the continued existence of the unholy—committed to humankind, to Israel, to us. It is the most profound theology, a theology of the human relationship with God. God is committed to us, unholy though we are. We are loved, sinners though we are. Right from the beginnings!

From the point of view of rethinking revelation, it is important to emphasise that in the biblical text there is absolutely no evidence to support God's verdict, at the end of the flood, that 'the inclination of the human heart is evil from youth' (8:21). This implies that despite the elimination of human life portrayed in the Flood and the affirmation of Noah's righteousness, there has been no change whatsoever in the behaviour of the human race. Noah and his family are just off the ark. All they have done is offer a sacrifice; its odour was pleasing to God. The evidence that 'the inclination of the human heart is evil from youth' (8:21) does not come from the story. As one possibility, it can come from Israel's experience of human living over the centuries.

What in the Bible's past came 'from Israel's experience of human living over the centuries', *in our present context* comes from our experience of human living in our own centuries.

The Sanctuary at Sinai (Exod 25 – Num 10)

Israel's exodus from Egypt is easy enough to trace in the biblical text. There are two accounts of the call of Moses, two accounts of the plagues, two accounts of the Passover on the eve of Israel's departure, and two accounts of Israel's deliverance from the pursuing Egyptians at the Sea. Once past the Sea, a *single song* takes Israel all the way to Canaan (Exod 15). After Exodus 15, a *single itinerary* takes Israel to Mount Sinai; it is a priestly itinerary and would generally be regarded as relatively late. So, two accounts: (1) Israel gets into Canaan in Exodus 15; (2) on a different trajectory, Israel does not get into Canaan until the book of Joshua.

Following the second trajectory, we have Israel at Mount Sinai. Between the first two verses of chapter 19 and the last four verses of chapter 24, there are some five chapters of what we may term the 'Sinai capsule'. There is the theophany in chapter 19, the ten commandments in the first part of chapter 20, then some three chapters of the Covenant Code (20:22–23:32), and finally a covenantal ceremony and meal occupying most of chapter 24. We will not deal with this 'Sinai capsule' here. The reason is simple, if shocking. There is only one itinerary leading from the Sea to Sinai and it is in priestly language which is not the language of the 'Sinai capsule'. The narrative in the present biblical text does not get the Israel of the 'Sinai capsule' to Mount Sinai.

After Israel arrived at Mount Sinai in Exodus 19:1–2, passing over the 'Sinai capsule', we find in Exodus 24:15–18 that Moses went up on the mountain, the glory of the LORD covered the mountain for six days, and on the seventh day God called to Moses from the cloud and Moses entered the cloud and remained there for the next forty days. On the mountain, during those forty days, God gave Moses detailed instructions for the building of a sanctuary so that God may dwell in Israel's midst (25:8; 29:45). Once Moses has come down from the mountain, this sanctuary is built according to God's instructions, and is filled with God's glory (40:34).

The instructions given by God on the mountain are extremely detailed. First, there are the instructions for the sanctuary's equipment:

ark of the covenant, table for the bread, lampstand, the tabernacle itself with its frame and curtains; there is also the altar, the court of the tabernacle, and the oil for the lamp. Second, there are instructions for the sacral vestments, ephod, breastplate, etc. Third are the instructions for the ordination of the priests. Following this, there are instructions for the daily offerings, for the altar of incense, the half-shekel sanctuary tax, the bronze basin, and the anointing oil and incense. Finally, the two principal workers are named, Bezalel and Oholiab.

Two features need to be noticed about this sanctuary, commanded by God on Mount Sinai.

• First, the sanctuary is portable. The ark of the covenant is made with rings and poles by which it is to be carried (25:14), so too the table (25:28), the altar (27:7), and the incense altar (30:4); the tent covering of the tabernacle is to be made of curtain units so constructed that it can be assembled to form one whole (26:11); the supporting framework is made of multiple units to be assembled according to the plan shown on the mountain (26:15–30). Other details need not detain us here.

• Second, the sanctuary is to be God's dwelling among the people of Israel (at the beginning of the instructions, 25:8; almost at their end, 29:45–46).

We need to have an idea of the detail specified to realise how important all this was to somebody. When Moses comes down from the mountain, six chapters are consecrated to the carrying out of the instructions in exquisite detail (Exod 35–40). The tabernacle is satisfactorily erected. 'The cloud covered the tent of meeting, and the glory of the LORD filled the tabernacle' (Exod 40:34).

Next follows the book of Leviticus, twenty-seven chapters regulating many aspects of Israel's moral, ritual, and sacrificial life before God in minute detail. Then comes the book of Numbers, with the first ten chapters devoted, among other things, to laying out in great detail instructions for the disposition of the camp and for the positions in the march away from Sinai. The camping order: Israel's tribes were to camp with the sanctuary in their middle. The marching order: Israel's tribes were allocated positions for the march with three tribes in the lead, three bringing up the rear, and two groups of three on either side, with the sanctuary in the centre.

Once again, two features need to be noticed:

- Probably at least three groups are involved in the composition of all this. The reason for emphasising this plurality is simple: if a number of groups were involved in this large complex of text, then a number of groups believed the whole enterprise to be important. Which leads to the second feature needing notice.
- Amazingly, this portable sanctuary, with its surrounding camp and protective order of march, leaves Mount Sinai and does not arrive at any definitive destination, not even the end of the first day. The detailed description of *departure* (Num 10:12–28) is nowhere followed by an equivalent description of *arrival*.

Because it goes against the grain for us to have Israel going no further than Sinai, even if only in this late tradition, it may help to add a detail or two. The departure, specified as 'for the first time' (10:13), takes place according to the planned order of march (10:14–27). At the end, it is noted simply: 'and they journeyed' (10:28; NRSV, 'when they set out'). In the centre of the march is the sanctuary. The tabernacle was taken down and carried by the Gershonites and the Merarites. The 'holy things' (we presume basically what belonged in the tabernacle) were carried by the Kohathites. The tabernacle was set up 'before their arrival' (10:21; literally, 'against their coming' [JPS]). The difficulty is glaring: they never arrive anywhere. They don't come. This whole massive sanctuary complex, to which some seventeen or so chapters have been devoted, goes *absolutely nowhere*. It starts splendidly; but the detailed description of *departure* (Num 10:12–28) is nowhere matched by any equivalent description of an *arrival*.

Conclusion

Regarding the Flood, a basic issue to be observed is *what is not narrated*, either at the beginning or at the end; namely, there is no narrative adequate to justify the charge of human wickedness.

At the beginning: in my judgement, the Flood text begins at 5:1, with verses 1–2 giving a succinct account of creation (differing slightly from Genesis One) and a ten-generation genealogy taking us down to Noah. No violence. If someone were to point to the earlier chapters with Adam and Eve, Cain, and Lamech, my reply would be simple. I do not believe that the disobedience in the Garden, the killing of Abel, and the intensification of violence associated with Lamech can possibly be considered adequate justification for the two statements:

(1) that 'the wickedness of humankind was great in the earth', and that 'every inclination of the thoughts of their hearts was only evil continually' (Gen 6:5); and (2) that 'the earth was corrupt in God's sight, and the earth was filled with violence' (6:11).

At the end: there can be no question whatsoever that the narrative does not allow the slightest space for evidence to justify the statement that 'the inclination of the human heart is evil from youth' (8:21). The only humans on hand at the time are Noah and his family, Noah who has 'found favour in the sight of the LORD' (6:8) and who has been described as 'righteous' and 'blameless', walking with God (6:9).

Conclusion: the wickedness of humankind does not emerge from the narrative but is part of the narrator's present experience—as it is of ours. It is not a question of having been bad eggs in the distant past; it is the issue of being rotten eggs right up to now.

For the Sinai sanctuary, a basic issue is this: the sanctuary, so painstakingly described at Sinai, in the narrative *never moved* beyond the confines of the desert; furthermore, ancient Israel may well have known that no such sanctuary had ever arrived in Canaan. So why was so extensive a block of text consecrated to it. At least three reasons are possible: (1) it portrayed God as able to dwell in Israel's midst, independently of the Jerusalem temple; (2) it portrayed God as able to journey with Israel, guiding and controlling Israel's moves; (3) it portrayed God's presence in Israel's midst outside the land of Canaan.

The exiles of ancient Israel needed to believe that God could still dwell in their midst when the temple in Jerusalem was a smouldering ruin. The exiles of ancient Israel needed to believe that God could still journey with them, wherever that journey led and they needed to believe that God would guide and control their journey. The exiles of ancient Israel, exiled beyond their land, needed to believe that God could be present in their midst outside the land of Canaan. The priestly theologians who held firmly to these beliefs created an understanding of Sinai that took account of their present experience.

Does this stretch our imaginative faculties too far? The facts are there in the text of Exodus and Numbers; the sanctuary is lovingly detailed and goes absolutely nowhere.

Two parallels in the biblical text are well-known.

Leviticus 25 is devoted to the prescriptions, given by God to Moses, expressly at Mount Sinai, for the sabbath and jubilee years. We have no evidence that any such practice of the jubilee ever happened in ancient Israel, no expression of concern about failure to comply with it. It is a visionary idealisation, an imagined ideal, a theology expressed in law.

Ezekiel 48 has a geographical listing of the portions of territory allocated to each of the twelve tribes in Israel, north and south of the sanctuary. Nothing of the kind ever existed in ancient Israel. It is a visionary idealisation, a theology expressed in terms of a geographical vision.

Because the Sinai sanctuary goes nowhere in the text that prepares so carefully for it to go somewhere (right there is the signal to switch mindsets to *symbol*) and because such a sanctuary was not known in ancient Israel, I believe it too is a visionary idealisation, a theology expressed in terms of a sanctuary–centred vision.

The conclusion from all this: revelation does not come out of the past; its roots are in the present. The wickedness of humankind was not a revelation from the past; it was recognised in the present. God's capacity to journey in the midst of God's people was not a revelation from the past, but a reshaping of Israel's understanding of their God brought about by the needs of their present.

Briefly: for the biblical writers, their present shaped the way they understood their God and therefore how they *wrote* Scripture; for us, our present shapes the way we understand our God and therefore how we *read* Scripture.

To conclude: in terms of what we have been *doing* in our lives and our understanding of God, I am not at all sure that this rethinking of revelation changes anything much at all. I have no doubt that it changes enormously what we *say* and *think* about what we perceive ourselves doing. As such it is important because it requires us to be honest in our self-awareness.

We have always chosen what we appeal to from the Bible in proclaiming our understanding of God. Academics speak of 'a canon within the canon'. Whether such a view meets with appropriate approval as academic practice, in our day-to-day living it is unquestionably there.

When I say that this rethinking of revolution may not change much of what we do, I am claiming that the awareness of our present determines and has always determined what we select from Scripture and so shapes our understanding of God. What needs to be *said* then is that *this puts revelation for us in our present*.

The Reported Story: Midway Between Oral Performance and Literary Art

(original: *Semeia* 46, 1989)

Abstract

This paper sets out to argue the beginnings of a case for the possibility that some of the Old Testament narrative texts contain neither the record of the oral telling of a story, nor the skilled fashioning of a story as a work of literary art, but, instead, provide the report of a story. Such a reported story would contains the basic elements of character and plot as well as key details, but would pass over much that could be easily supplied from the storyteller's imagination. Beyond the theoretical possibility, the case has to be argued for the existence of such reported stories in the Old Testament text. To escape the subjectivity of intuitive judgment, argument is based particularly on the absence of elements necessary to the proper unfolding of the plot, elements which are significant but easily supplied or developed. Examples discussed are 1 Samuel 18:20–27; 19:11–17; 22:6–19; 2 Samuel 3:12–16. The possible recording, in such reports, of variant ways of telling the same basic story is also noted. Examples discussed are 1 Samuel 19:1–7; 20:1–42; 24:1–22 (*RSV*). A particularly evident setting for the reported story would be a major written narrative composed of a considerable number of stories which needed to be condensed from their full oral potential (for example, the Story of David's Rise). Another setting would be as aide-mémoire for other storytellers. The intention of the reported story, as literary genre, would be to communicate the gist of a story so that it might be recalled or retold.

This paper emerges from a combination of three factors: intuition, commonsense logic, and everyday observation. The intuition is simply a storyteller's conviction, after working with the text of 1–2 Samuel for a while, that no storytellers worth their salt would be able to tell some of the stories the way they are in the text.[1] In exciting areas, they are too bare, too bald; they cry out for embellishment. Commonsense logic says that as well as the simple telling of a story and the skilled fashioning of a story as a work of literary art, there is also the possibility of reporting what a story is about. Everyday observation makes it clear that the report of a story, telling what it is about, has its place in our narrative conventions—people do it. But the question of literary competence arises and our ability to know the conventions of another culture.[2] We may recognise a phenomenon in our own culture or in another, which then opens the possibility that such a phenomenon existed in the culture of the Old Testament; it is a further step to demonstrate that it did.

A reported story—the outcome of reporting what a story is about—would provide the basic elements from which the full narrative of a story can be developed, but would fall short of actually telling the story. The basic elements include characters and plot, key details which impart colour or significance, and memorable lines or exchanges. In the telling of a story, all these must be introduced and unfolded in the appropriate sequence demanded by the plot.[3] In the

---

1. By my observation, while the assumption is never explicit, a narrative text is usually treated as though either it reproduced the oral version of a story, or was composed as the written version of a story. P Kyle McCarter, for example, speaks of 1 Sam 19:11–17 as 'a fast-paced and entertaining story' (1980a: 326). Once the conviction that the text actually is a complete story has been recognised as an assumption, McCarter's comment may be rendered with much more accuracy: the report outlines briefly and sketchily a story with evident potential for entertainment.

    JP Fokkelman, discussing the division into scenes, writes that the scene 'regularly coincides with an independent story, and I suspect that it reflects the phase of the original, oral recounting' (9). How much is implied here depends on the weight given to 'reflects'; it appears to bring the original text, now a scene, into close association with the original, oral recounting.

    An important survey of recent anthropological literature on oral storytelling is provided by Burke O Long.
2. See, for example, the discussion in John Barton (11–16, 26–29).
3. The extreme example is provided by the analysis of the sequence of functions in fairy tales, by V Propp. See also the comments of T Todorov (116–19).

report of a story, the sequence is less significant; the obvious or the ordinary can be left out, since they can be supplied easily from the storyteller's imagination.

The argument for the existence of reported stories in Old Testament narrative texts must proceed in two stages. It is necessary, firstly, to establish the likelihood that there is such a thing as the reported story in Old Testament narrative. After that, there is the second stage of assessing which texts should be assigned to this category. The purpose of this paper is to argue for the strong likelihood that there are reported stories in the Old Testament text, and to point to some of the implications of this for literary critical exegesis. The subsequent task of making the inventory of such stories lies beyond the present scope.

The intuitive criteria of 'too bare, too bald, cries out for embellishment' are subjective and assume a fair knowledge of the Old Testament's narrative conventions. A surer argument for the existence of the reported story is the recognition that there are texts in the Old Testament in which elements required for the appropriate sequential unfolding of the plot are absent. The gist of the story is communicated and the possibility is there for fuller development, but the sequence in the text is incomplete, being marked by evident gaps. These gaps can easily be filled in with a little exercise of imagination; but until they have been filled in, the story has not been told—it has merely been reported.

An excellent example of what is meant is the dummy-in-the-bed story, involving the stratagem by which Michal saved David's life (1 Sam 19:11-17). A central feature, imparting colour to the story, is the delaying tactic which made it possible for David to escape from Saul and certain death: 'Michal took an image and laid it on the bed and put a pillow of goats' hair at its head, and covered it with the clothes' (v 13). The sole purpose of the dummy is to gain time for David to get clear of the city, once his absence has been noted by the guards Saul has posted. Yet, at the appropriate place in the sequence of the story, the dummy is completely neglected: 'And when Saul sent messengers to take David, she said, "He is sick"' (v 11). If the storyteller had intended to portray Michal as able to put off Saul's minions with the simple affirmation that David was sick, there would have been no need for the elaborate description of the dummy. When the dummy is finally mentioned, in v 16, it is too late for delay; once the soldiers enter the room to seize the bed, it is solely a matter of discovery. The time for the use of the dummy was when the soldiers first arrived: they are being held off, they are being stalled, they are simply permitted a glimpse of the sick man in his bed before being sent back to King Saul. Instead, there is no dialogue at all between Michal and the soldiers, just her statement, 'He is sick'; yet the scene cries out for some clever exchanges, building up the tension, pitting the quick-witted woman against her father's soldiery. The decisive criterion is that the very logic of the central feature of the story demands its expansion at this point.[4] There is a gap, and it has been left unfilled. The elements for filling it are provided, but are not exploited. The story is not so much told as reported.

Once this observation has been made, a number of other features in the text may be noted which cry out for embellishment; they enhance the likelihood that 1 Samuel 19:11–17 is indeed a reported story. No explanation is given why Saul was ready to wait until morning (v 11a). Michal's opening line to David is brief beyond belief: 'If you do not save your life tonight, tomorrow you will be killed' (v 11b). If distilled succinctness were the essence of the art, this would be brilliant—but is that its aim here?[5] Would a storyteller pass up the opportunity to

---

4. HW Hertzberg, in dealing with this passage, has allowed his imagination to fill in the details which are not in the text, but would obviously be supplied by a storyteller. So he can say: 'Her deception of the messengers with the help of the teraphim and the readiness of the messengers, indeed of Saul himself, to be deceived, is narrated with furious joy and put to the discredit of the first king' (167). A more careful reading of the text reveals that the 'deception of the messengers with the help of the teraphim' is in the unnarrated scene between v 14 and v 15; the readiness to be deceived and the furious joy might all have been part of a telling of the story, but they have to be read into the text we have. Josephus has his version of the unnarrated scene: 'and she showed them the bed all covered up, and by the quivering of the liver which shook the bedclothes convinced them that what lay there was David gasping for breath' (*Jewish Antiquities*, VI, 217). LXX may have resolved the difficulty very subtly. Its 'And they said' in place of 'and she said' (v 14b) implies that the soldiers sent word back to Saul, which allows for the possibility that they have been deceived by the dummy (cf HJ Stoebe, 358).
5. Succinctness can be characteristic of Old Testament storytelling (for example. Genesis 4; 22), but it need not be (for example. 2 Samuel 11–12). In this case, it has to be decided whether it is due to literary art or literary genre. Robert Alter is rightly attentive to the elements of urgent compactness in the story, but does not advert to the implications of the failure to exploit the story's central and most

have Saul's daughter tell David a few things about the character of her father? 'So Michal let David down through the window' (v 12a)—no details at all. No indication is given whether it was morning when Saul's messengers came (v 14), or, if they came during the night, why their change of plan. When the messengers come again, there is no dialogue at all, nor any indication that Michal was taken by them to Saul (v 16). Finally, Michal's concluding line to her father is as brief as was her opening line to her husband.[6] These features, taken together with the central failure to exploit the device of the dummy, constitute a reasonable case for considering this text a reported story.

A few other cases of stories, within the larger context of the Story of David's Rise, may be noted briefly which have similar gaps in their narrative sequence. In the story of David's bride–price for Michal (18:20–27), the MT refers to a deadline (v 26b), which has not been mentioned earlier. While there are other explanations, the possibility of a reported story is worth considering; the text is certainly susceptible of considerable expansion.[7] In the story of the slaughter at Nob (22:6–19), Saul's complaint of conspiracy against him, including Jonathan and David (v 8), calls for a previous exposition. While the facts are provided in earlier stories, neither in those nor in this one is it said how Saul came to know of them; it is hardly covered by v 6. Clearly, information has been given to Saul from somewhere. Beyond this, the transition to v 9 is abrupt; no mention is made of the forces at Doeg's disposal in the slaughter (vv 18–19), which can hardly have been presented as an individual effort. There are traditio-historical complications in this material. But there is also the possibility that much of it is in the form of a reported story. Finally, we may note the episode of the return of Michal to David (2 Sam 3:12–16). Evidently the agent in Michal's return is Abner; the condition (v 13b) demands evidence of Abner's goodwill and his power to deliver what he promises. Yet in vv 14–16a, Abner is completely in the background, only to reappear again in v 16b. Again, the reported story makes good sense, without the need for literary critical solutions.[8]

---

      colorful feature—the dummy in the bed (119–20).
6. For further reflections on what is left unsaid here, see Stoebe (360–61).
7. For other explanations, see McCarter (1980a: 316), Stoebe (353).
8. See the discussion in McCarter (1984: 114–15). Alter notes: 'The remarkable suggestiveness of the Bible's artistic economy could scarcely be better illustrated'

Before turning to a second aspect, we should look at the setting in which the need for such reported stories would have arisen. Storytellers, surely, learned their art and enriched their repertoire by listening to stories being told—the oral performance. The compiler of the Story of David's Rise, however, was more than an accomplished storyteller with an extensive repertoire. Depending on how one views it, the Story of David's Rise is either brilliant propaganda or a brilliant reflection on human experience and the working of the divine will. What is significant is that its subject matter is an extensive collection of stories, some thirty of them or more. It is mainly through the organisation and arrangement of these stories that the impact of the Story of David's Rise is made. If all of these were to be told in full, one would certainly have a very lengthy text. It is essential for the Story of David's Rise that some of the component stories be reported, rather than told at length. The setting of a narrative which expounds an understanding of history, distilled from a number of stories, is exactly what one would expect to give rise to the literary genre of the reported story. A further extension of this setting would be the composition of what might be termed an aide-mémoire for other storytellers. The intention of a reported story is to communicate the gist of a story, so that it can be recalled or retold. This is quite different from telling or writing a story for edification, education, or entertainment.

There is a second phenomenon which, strictly speaking, is unrelated to the question of the reported story, but which makes particularly good sense in connection with it: the appearance within a narrative text of indications of variant versions of basically the same story. While these apparent expansions might be considered as simple contamination from the other versions, in the hypothesis of a reported story they make eminent sense as reminders of other themes which can be introduced or of other ways in which a story can be told.[9]

For example, in 1 Samuel 20, there is quite a long story about the carefully prearranged code by which Jonathan is to alert David,

---

(122). It may well be that the literary genre of reported story is sometimes responsible for such artistic economy.

9. Note the comment by Long: 'If we assume that oral literature lay behind a given text, and recognise that a performer may produce two or more distinct versions of a piece on different occasions, then such differences might persist in the written document...' (194).

should Saul turn out to be hostile toward him. We need to note, from the outset, that the story is really only concerned with the eventuality of Saul's hostility (cf v 10). If Saul were well disposed, Jonathan could come out and meet with David without any precautions. The precautions are necessary only in the event that Saul is ill-disposed and that, therefore, Jonathan is likely to be followed by Saul's men in order to discover David's hiding place. The code is carefully prearranged. The only problem with the story is that the code is not observed. After carefully arranging for a secret code (vv 20–22), Jonathan adds a different code (v 38), and he and David openly meet and embrace anyway, making any secret code quite unnecessary (vv 41–42). In the traditional understanding, either one is confronted with an example of quite confused story telling, or there has been serious contamination of the story from other versions.

Once 1 Samuel 20 is looked at as a report of a story, with due note taken of a couple of optional variations, a very different picture emerges. I would like to propose that one basic story is being reported, with brief notes indicating two possible variations on the theme. Basic to all three is the presumption that Saul is hostile to David, and so will have Jonathan followed in an attempt to discover David's whereabouts and kill him. The stories and the planning of their action are based on this contingency. The first optional variation is noted in vv 20–22. The sign is basically visual; the arrows are to be shot to the side of David's hiding place, presumably either falling short of it or landing beyond it. The words do not add any specific content; they merely specify the code and emphasise the assumed visual message: if the arrows fall short of you, come back, all is well; if the arrows fall beyond you, be off.[10]

The second optional variation is noted within vv 36b–39. In this version, after the agreed code has been employed (v 37b), a clever piece of stage business transforms the audible aspect of the sign into an actual and direct message: 'Hurry, make haste, stay not' (v 38). It is apparently shouted to the boy (literally: 'after the boy'); it is in fact destined for David.[11] While it can be presented as Jonathan's

---

10. In this version, the concern of v 10 has been forgotten. If Saul were favorably disposed toward David, there would be no need for concealment or signals.
11. There is one assumption made in the conflation of the stories. Verse 36a belongs to the version to be discussed in a moment. The present participle here, 'which I

inventiveness, in fact it renders the earlier code unnecessary. The two are not mutually exclusive, but do offer a basis for two ways of telling the story.

All that is left is to determine the sense of the basic story, without either of these optional variations. Jonathan goes out in the morning with his young attendant. If there is to be neither visual nor audible sign with the arrows, what is the purpose of the lad's accompanying Jonathan? I suggest that the attendant was included in order to create the impression that Jonathan was simply going out for some archery practice, thus defusing any anxieties Saul's men might have had about his going off alone. And so Jonathan got away into the country, and once well clear of the city he sent the boy back (v 40). He was then free to meet David and confirm the danger that threatened David's life. If anyone should be doubtful about the plausibility of this basic version of the story, I will take the liberty of appealing to Josephus for support, according to whose version David went off with the lad, 'seemingly for exercise'—that is, for archery practice (*Jewish Antiquities* VI, 239).

So, I would submit, there were three possible variants of this story in circulation: one where the attendant functioned simply to allay the suspicion of Saul's watchmen; another in which the security was so tight that only a primarily visual signal could be given, in proximity to a known hiding place (cf 19:3; 20:19); the third in which a clever ruse was adopted where an order shouted at the attendant was in fact a concealed message, directed to David. 1 Samuel 20 need not, then, be the outcome of incompetent redaction, nor the result of contamination by inattentive copyists; rather, it may be a careful report of a story, including reminders of the possible variants. In an oral performance, a storyteller might choose whichever version was most appropriate to the audience, the mood, or the time available.[12]

---

shoot', may well reflect a continuous process as Jonathan walks into the country. In v 36b, it is assumed that they have reached the appointed tryst, in David's vicinity. The textual variations between multiple arrows, three arrows, and one arrow may reflect the influence of the different versions of the story.

12. McCarter's treatment is along classical lines: 'vv 11–17 interrupt the flow of our narrative and seem to have been inserted, along with vv 23, 40–42, by the hand that joined the history of David's rise to the subsequent material'—probably the Josianic historian (1980a: 344). The intention was to show that the survival of Saul's house was the direct consequence of David's loyalty to Jonathan. McCarter passes over the variation in v 38 in silence. Presumably, it is felt to lie within the

A couple of other stories, within the Story of David's Rise, which show similar possibilities may be mentioned briefly. Firstly, in 1 Samuel 19:1-7, v 3a presumes a conversation that is secretly overheard ('I will go out and stand beside my father in the field where you are'), while in vv 3b and 7 the conversation is to be reported to David. Contamination from the story of 1 Samuel 20 is possible. But it makes good sense to see the motif in v 3a as a deliberate indication of a variant version of the story, in which the conversation takes place near David's pre-arranged hiding place and so is overheard rather than reported later. Secondly, 1 Samuel 24 provides traces of considerable complexity. There is a marked awkwardness in vv 4-7 (RSV) //. There is a most admirable admonition against harming Saul (vv 6-7, RSV), but it comes after David had had his chance to do so, that is, when he snipped off the skirt of Saul's robe (v 4b, RSV). The difficulty is most simply resolved by recognising indications of two versions: one in which Saul strayed into a cave where David and his men were, and in which David resisted the incitement to kill his enemy; the other in which the motif of cutting off a piece of Saul's cloak was introduced, so as to attach the cave story to vv 8-22 (RSV) and fashion a story parallel to that of chapter 26. The second version is indicated by the insertion of vv 4b-5 (RSV) in the middle of the story of Saul in the cave, between the incitement from David's men and David's reply. A further awkwardness supports the suggestion of combined motifs. As the story stands in chapter 24, there is an inherent improbability in David's emerging from the cave, waving a piece of Saul's robe in his hand, while apparently three thousand of Saul's chosen troops stand passively looking at the man who is the object of their expedition. The need to establish a safe distance and the security of night is emphasised in chapter 26, but neglected

---

legitimate license of the storyteller.

More important is the question of the transmission of material like vv 11-17 and 40-42. It is not likely that either passage would be handed down independently of the main story, especially if a period of several centuries is envisaged. It is more probable that they were handed down as a variant versions of the story. In fact, only vv 40-42 have a bearing on the plot of the story, since they render the system of signals patently unnecessary. The question then is whether they have been added by a later redactor whose interest in David's loyalty to Jonathan overrode any concern for the story's plot, or whether they have been added as a pointer to a variant version of the story with a marked change in the plot.

here. It is compounded by the tension between the portrayal of Saul looking back toward the worshipful David in 24:8 (RSV) and the use of the recognition of the voice motif in 24:16 (RSV, cf 26:17).[13] Skilled telling of this version of the story would be required to cope with these anomalies plausibly. This aspect may point to the presence of a reported story here.

The central interest of the proposal made in this paper is not so much to point out the possible ways in which variants of a story might have been represented, but rather to draw attention to the literary genre of the reported story, which may be present in a number of our texts. The idea of a reported story obliges us to reflect on the limited nature of the knowledge we have about the oral performance of Old Testament stories. It is probable that in relatively few cases do we have what might be called a transcription of the oral performance of a story. And the cases where whole stories are clearly works of literary art are not overwhelmingly numerous. The reported story may account for a considerable number of our texts.

In my understanding, such reports appear to pass over lightly what might easily be left to the storyteller's imagination or memory. On the other hand, they may dwell in some detail on key aspects of the story. We need to be aware of this distinction, in order to have a better grasp of the skills of Israelite storytelling. Those parts of the story which are passed over in matter-of-fact fashion may reveal nothing of the way the Israelites told their stories; those parts which are dwelt on in more loving detail, on the other hand, may give a clearer notion of how a skilled Hebrew storyteller functioned.

---

13. Alter comments: 'Perhaps he asks this out of sheer amazement at what he has just heard, or because he is too far off to make out David's face clearly, or because his eyes are blinded with tears, which would be an apt emblem of the condition of moral blindness that has prevented him from seeing David as he really is' (37). While this may be a legitimate approach to the text as we have it now, when it is viewed in conjunction with the other factors—the accompanying soldiery and the unevenness in the cave scene—it has to be taken seriously as evidence of the nature of the text.

Works cited: listing with appropriate details

Alter, Robert. *The Art of Biblical Narrative* (New York: Basic Books, 1981).

Barton, John. *Reading the Old Testament: Method in Biblical Study* (London: Darton, Longman and Todd, 1984).

Fokkelman, JP. *Narrative Art and Poetry in the Books of Samuel*, volume 1 (Assen: Van Gorcum, 1981).

Hertzberg, HW. *I & II Samuel* (Philadelphia: Westminster, 1964).

Long, Burke O. 'Recent Field Studies in Oral Literature and Their Bearing on OT Criticism', in *VT,* 26 (1976): 187–98.

McCarter, P Kyle Jr. *I Samuel.* AB 8 (Garden City: Doubleday, 1980).

———, 'The Apology of David', in *JBL,* 99 (1980): 489–504.

———, *II Samuel*, AB 9 (Garden City: Doubleday, 1984).

Propp, V. *Morphology of the Folktale*, second edition (Austin: University of Texas, 1968).

Rendtorff, Rolf. 'Beobachtungen zur altisraelitischen Geschichtsschreibung anhand der Geschichte vom Aufstieg Davids', in *Probleme biblischer Theologie: Gerhard von Rad zum 70. Geburtstag.* Ed. H.W. Wolff (Munich: Chr. Kaiser, 1971).

Stoebe, HJ. *Das erste Buch Samuelis,* KAT 8/1 (Gütersloh: Gerd Mohn, 1973).

Todorov, T. *The Poetics of Prose* (Ithaca, NY: Cornell University, 1977).

Past History and Present Text: The Clash of Classical and Post-Critical Approaches to Biblical Text

(original: *ABR* 39, 1991)

This paper is concerned with the current clash of academic approaches to the biblical text, specifically that of the Older Testament. These clashing approaches could be designated critical and literary, or classical and post-modern, but perhaps classical and post-critical catches the issue best. The new concerns—once structuralist, then canonical, now predominantly literary—are with the present text. Both enchantment and disenchantment seem to have had their role to play.

Enchantment with the biblical text as literary text is as old as the Bible's origins. The endeavour to bring this enchantment to fruition in compelling interpretation has, over recent decades, been fraught with difficulties. There is a new and welcome move afoot with more determinedly professional literary scholarship being brought to bear upon biblical interpretation. This move is still in its infancy. In a number of published examples it is problematic; the theoretical coherence with critical study is far from fully worked out. In this paper, I will be sticking to my last and offering the contribution of a reflective practitioner, which I believe I am, rather than that of a literary theoretician, which I am not. Theory has to keep in touch with the realities of the biblical text. It is these realities I seek to explore here.

Disenchantment has played its role in the recent emergence of a series of new approaches to the biblical text. Perhaps the compounding increase in the complexity of knowledge and skills demanded of the scholarly exegete has effectively stolen the Bible from its ordinary readers. Certainly, the inadequacy of the exclusively critical approach has made itself felt. It is forcefully expressed by a colleague in ascetical/mystical theology:

> It is now clear to everybody that the historical-critical approach, however valuable, is woefully insufficient. It alone will not put us in touch with the underlying mystery; it alone will not bring us to those eternal realities towards which the Scriptures point; it alone will not enrich our lives with mysticism.[1]

The key here is the phrase, 'it alone'. The historical-critical approach is valuable and often indispensable; but it is not the be-all and end-all of exegesis or biblical study. The question remains: once critical study has robbed us of our first innocence, is there a literary innocence which may be legitimately regained?

Naturally, individual studies vary. Among the examples of recent approaches there is reason to question whether in their essential functioning some have returned to a pre-critical position, or whether we are witnessing a further development in the sequence of critical disciplines (that is, text, source, form, tradition, and redaction criticism), or whether again some are signalling a genuinely post-critical phase in the study of the biblical text. Significant shifts have occurred. The cultural mindset which dominated the disciplines of biblical interpretation had its roots in the early nineteenth century and in developments in the classical and historical disciplines. Literary approaches to the task of biblical interpretation, with their roots in the late twentieth century, are having a significant impact on this formerly dominant cultural mindset. Some shifts can be sketched, without attempting to be exhaustive.

Significants Shifts

1. Shift in attitude towards the aim of interpretation
Once upon a time, it was said that the aim of critical interpretation was 'to determine what the writer intended to say and the first readers could and must have understood'.[2] Nowadays, I would prefer to say that it is to determine the meaning of the text—in other words, what the text says.[3]

---

1. William Johnston, *The Wounded Stag* (London: Fount Paperbacks, 1985), 25.
2. Quoted from Kümmel with regard to Schleiermacher by Edgar Krentz, *The Historical-Critical Method*, Guides to Biblical Scholarship (Philadelphia: Fortress, 1975), 24.
3. Should this sound too bland, it may be balanced by the insight given paradoxical

Ideological issues aside, experience has taught that this change of language brings with it a change of mental focus. 'Intention of the author' is open to the intentional fallacy, to be corrected by attention to the text. 'Intention of the text', the terminology of the FOTL project, is still an invitation to personify the text, again to be corrected by attention to the text itself.[4] Language which focuses initially and primarily on the text forces a more direct attention to the source of meaning in the phenomena of the text.[5] This is not to deny or decry the place of the author, but to insist on the focus of our attention. With Paul Ricoeur, I cannot conceive of a text without an author, but the author is known only through the text and our attention must therefore be directed to the text without distraction.[6]

2. Shift in attitude toward the aim of historical-critical scholarship
Once upon a time, the aim of historical-critical scholarship was the recovery of history: the history of Israel itself, the history of Israelite literature, the history of Israel's literary forms, the history of Israel's theology. Nowadays, while all these are important, the primary aim should be moving toward interpreting the text with historical consciousness and critical awareness. 'Historical-critical' refers less

---

formulation by Paul Beauchamp: 'Expliquer un text est, a toujours été, dire ce qu'il ne dit pas'—to exegete a text is, and has always been, to say what it does not say! (*Création et séparation: étude exégétique du chapitre premier de la Genèse* [Bibliothèque de Sciences religieuses; np (Aubier Montaigne/ Editions du Cerf/ Delachaux & Niestlé/Desclée De Brouwer, 1969], 15). Failure to see the paradox is not license for criticism or parody.

4. FOTL: the series, The Forms of the Old Testament Literature, published by Eerdmans, Grand Rapids.
5. I gratefully acknowledge that my conversion to this language is due to the sustained efforts of Stephen Prickett.
6. 'L'intention de l'auteur n'est pas son vécu psychologique, son expérience, ni l'expérience de la communauté à jamais insaisissable car déjà structurée par son discours. L'auteur est précisément celui que dénonce ou annonce le texte, par rétro-référence à celui qui l'a écrit ... pour ma part, je ne concevrais pas ce que pourrait être un texte sans auteur, un texte qui n'aurait été écrit par personne ... ce qu'il importe de découvrir, c'est que la notion d'auteur n'est pas une notion psychologique, mais précisément une grandeur herméneutique, une fonction du texte lui-même' (P Ricoeur, 'Esquisse de Conclusion', in R Barthes, *et al*, *Exégèse et herméneutique* [Paris: Editions du Seuil, 1971), 292–93. See also my *The Ark Narrative (1 Sam 4-6; 2 Sam 6): A Form-critical and Traditio-Historical Study*, SLBDS 16 (Missoula: Scholars Press, 1975), 195–97

to the goal of study and more to the attitudes of the practitioner. A baneful over-emphasis on history is tending to yield place to an appropriate concern for faith and theology or other issues.

A substantial contributory factor to this shift is the recognition that many of our scriptural texts are themselves concerned primarily not with the facts but with the meaning and the proclamation that can be woven from them. Redaction criticism points to this for the gospels. In the Older Testament, the duality of evidently contrasting accounts for both creation and flood, for exodus from Egypt and entry into Canaan, for the occupation of the land and the emergence of statehood—to mention only these—point in the same direction. They point to the narrative biblical texts as texts of faith, written from a stance of faith with a view to promoting faith.[7]

3. Shift in attitude toward the interpreter

Once upon a time, the emphasis was on the ideal of 'impartial and objective research'.[8] Nowadays, we are likely to prefer language about informed and responsible research as the ideal. Many factors have given subjectivity a better press than was formerly the case.

4. Shift in attitude toward the redactor

Once upon a time, the redactor was an ever-available and definitive explanation for any perceived clumsiness or incoherence in the text. Nowadays, redactors are coming to be recognised as consummately careful people and compilers or preservers with authorial status.[9]

---

7. See AF Campbell, 'Old Testament Narrative as Theology', in *Pacifica* 4 (1991): 165–80.
8. See Krentz, again with regard to Schleiermacher (*Historical-Critical Method*, 24).
9. See Shemaryahu Talmon's description of the Tannaitic fifth-century scribe: 'a man of many parts, a comprehensive literate who could be author, editor, transmitter, scribe or copyist when performing different aspects of his profession' ('The Textual Study of the Bible—A New Outlook', in *Qumran and the History of the Biblical Text*, edited by FM Cross and S Talmon [Cambridge: Harvard University Press, 1975], 336; see also 381). In this context, we may note Robert Polzin's comment—rightly inveighing against the tendency to brush redactors aside as clumsy and therefore a self-sufficient explanation for incoherence in the text: 'Is the narrative hand "crude"—what critics usually mean when they write *redactional*—or "careful"—what I mean when I write *authorial*?' (*Samuel and the Deuteronomist* [San Francisco: Harper & Row, 1989], 57). The phenomenon he pillories is only slowly fading from the exegetical scene.

5. Shift in attitude toward the text
Once upon a time, it might have been taken for granted that a composite text was not available as a whole for interpretation, since it was no more than the sum of its sources. Nowadays, with the change in attitude toward compilers and redactors, there is a demand for the final text to be interpreted in its own right.

Alongside these aspects, there is the question of the root cause for the resistance by much of traditional scholarship to approaches based primarily on the present text. If it is more than mere curmudgeonly dislike for change, it is important to know what is at stake. One area in particular is significant here: the question whether compilation and redaction allow the present text to be claimed as a text in all cases and invariably.[10]

We are so accustomed to the world of the printed book and the computerised recovery of information, it is immensely difficult to conceptualise a world in which books were written but not printed. In such circumstances, what use were written texts put to and what was their audience? How much was for private reading and how much for public? Did written texts accurately reflect their oral performance, or were oral performances based on texts, yet developing and expanding far beyond them? Without files or footnotes, how were valuable items to be preserved, which might not fit particularly well with a given text? Or how were dissenting views recorded and recovered? On all this vast area of the storage, recovery, and disseminating of information in ancient Israel we know very little. Yet it is significant for understanding the texts and the purposes they served.

6. When the text is not always a text
A useful working definition of a text is given by Harald Weinrich:

---

10. Polzin expresses this trenchantly in a criticism of the present writer. 'As I suggested in the Introduction, a relevant matter in this regard may be a scholar's view of the final text: does it appear so incoherent, ideologically speaking (because of the complicated process that the scholar believes lies behind its historical composition and because of the supposed crudity of its redactors), that any full-blown account of it as "narrative functioning as a vehicle for theology"... would be an unsatisfying and embarrassing exercise?' (*Samuel and the Deuteronomist*, fn 15, 237). In the particular instance, Polzin unjustifiably overlooks the limits imposed by the length of a journal article; the wider application of the comment is nevertheless valid.

'A text is a meaningful (that is, coherent and consistent) sequence of language signs between two evident breaks in communication.'[11] The correlation with Zellig Harris's definition of an utterance is worth noting: 'any stretch of talk, by one person, before and after which there is silence on the part of that person.'[12] The increasing number of literary studies which assume or argue for the literary unity of the biblical text raises the issue of whether the biblical text is, in fact, always a text.[13]

We often use the term 'biblical text' to designate a sequence of words on a manuscript or page. When we pay attention to an understanding of 'a text' such as Weinrich's—a meaningful (that is, coherent and consistent) sequence of language signs between two evident breaks in communication—we have to ask whether discussion of the 'present text' may often involve a confusion of the two senses of text and whether this has serious consequences.

The question becomes acute when we take note of an observation associated by Weinrich with his definition of text. He remarks: 'Even arbitrarily juxtaposed pieces constitute in this sense evident (quasi-metalinguistic) breaks in communication.'[14] Is it possible that on occasion the juxtaposition of material by redactors or transmitters constitutes such a break in the sequence of communication that we are no longer correct in referring to the juxtaposed pieces as a text (in the strict sense)? If such a possibility exists, must we conclude that an indispensable step in all interpretation is to ascertain the existence

---

11. 'Ein Text is eine sinnvolle (d.h. kohärente und konsistente) Abfolge sprachlicher Zeichen zwischen zwei auffälligen Kommunikationsunterbrechungen' (Harald Weinrich, *Tempus: Besprochene und erzählte Welt*, third edition (Stuttgart: Kohlhammer, 1977); first edition 1964, 11.
12. ZS Harris, quoted in John Lyons, *Introduction to Theoretical Linguistics* (Cambridge: Cambridge University Press, 1968), 172.
13. In normal usage, phrases such as 'the text', 'the biblical text', 'the present text' certainly denote words on a page and also automatically include the notion of a text in the strict sense. In this paper, I shall retain this common usage. 'A text', with the indefinite article, is adequate in most circumstances to denote a text in the strict sense of the term; the qualification can be added explicitly when needed. In these terms, the issue under consideration is whether it is justifiable to assume automatically that 'the biblical text' is always 'a text' in the strict sense.
14. 'Auch willkürlich angelegte Schnitte schaffen in diesem Sinne (quasi-metasprachliche) auffällige Kommunikationsunterbrechungen' (Weinrich, *Tempus*, 11).

and limits of the text as a text, technically understood, which is to be interpreted?

A critical element in this regard is the explication given by Weinrich for the qualification 'meaningful': that is, coherent and consistent. Coherence and consistency are relative terms. In using them, we claim a 'competence' to determine what is coherent or consistent in a given piece of literature or in the literature of a given culture.[15] If we were totally out of touch with the canons and conventions of ancient Israelite literature, we would not be able to understand the Hebrew scriptures. But insofar as we do not have any explicit and exhaustive description of these canons and conventions, we need always to proceed with caution, basing assertions on careful analysis of comparable passages.

In my observation of the Bible, I believe we encounter texts which may be better understood and given meaning better by interpretations which do not assume their unity, the assumption that they constitute a text. Certain aspects of this phenomenon need exploration and clarification. The issue might be said to be basically which of the three 'C's' is dominant in any given text: communication, conservation, and contradiction or modification (change).

- Communication, plain and simple, usually leads to a unified text.
- Conservation may interrupt such a text to point to another and different text or tradition. I think, for example, of the tree of life in Genesis 2–3 or the special collection of Davidic traditions in 2 Samuel 21–24.

---

15. A brief treatment of the issues is given by John Barton, *Reading the Old Testament: Method in Biblical Study* (London: Darton Longman and Todd, 1984), 11–16. A good example of what is meant is provided by a note of Polzin's: 'Fokkelman's remarks on the apparent incoherence between and within chapters 16 and 17 [of 1 Samuel] are, in my opinion, unsatisfactory because they assert that *in this particular case* the Bible's "consistency requirements" are different from ours (*Narrative Art*, volume 2, 144ff.). There is no doubt that in many respects ancient and modern consistency requirements are different; the question here, however, is whether the type of "inconsistency" represented, say, by the known-to-Saul David of chapters 16:14-23 and 17:32-39 and the supposedly not-known-to-Saul David of 17:55-58 is an example of one of these differences. I maintain that such a supposed inconsistency as this would have been as obviously unacceptable to an ancient Israelite as it is to us' (*Samuel and the Deuteronomist*, fn 19, 258–59). The only source for Polzin's conviction is his experience of the consistency requirements of the Bible in other texts.

- Contradiction or modification may seek to express a viewpoint which is diametrically opposed to that of the coherent literary text, and may do so at the cost of substantial incoherence without sufficient integration to form a literary text.[16]

So a methodological step must be the inquiry whether a text is straightforward communication, or contains a dominant element of conservation, or is strongly marked by the expression of contradiction or modification. In the latter cases, the question has to be carefully investigated whether the text can be understood in such a way as to constitute a text in the strict sense.[17]

At this point, it is appropriate to move to three texts which can function as useful exemplars of the three different possibilities of communication, conservation, and contradiction or modification. In the first, in my judgement, a unified text has been created through composition (communication); in the second, two versions of a story have been preserved in combination, without achieving a unified text (conservation); in the third, different opinions have been given expression in a careful composition (contradiction/modification).

1 Samuel 1–7

A debate has existed, at least since Wellhausen in 1878, over the relationship of chapters 1 – 3 and chapters 4 – 6 in 1 Samuel. More recently, in a difference of opinion between myself and PD Miller and JJM Roberts, it has focused on whether a substantial part of 1 Samuel 2 belonged to the Ark Narrative or not.[18] Put in this way, the question is argued as one of authorial identity. I believe, however, that it is fundamentally a present-text question.

There is neither space nor reason for going over the arguments in detail here; they are all available.[19] The issue is a theologically

---

16. Over and above these, of course, there is M Noth's concept of the 'enrichment' of texts in the Pentateuch or elsewhere. Also significant is my concept of the reported story (see 'The Reported Story: Midway between Oral Performance and Literary Art', in *Semeia*, 46 [1989]: 77–85).
17. This is the aspect which is so frequently omitted, as Polzin, for example, rightly complains.
18. Campbell, against the inclusion, *The Ark Narrative,* above, note 5; Miller and Roberts, for the inclusion, *The Hand of the Lord: A Reassessment of the 'Ark Narrative' of 1 Samuel* (Baltimore: Johns Hopkins University Press, 1977).
19. See my discussion in 'Yahweh and the Ark: A Case Study in Narrative', in *JBL*, 98

significant one. Does Israel's narrative present its God as one who punishes the nation as a whole for the cultic and sexual sins of two priests and the alleged failure of their aged father to discipline them effectively? Or is there no causal connection between the loss of the ark and the sins of the Shiloh priests, so that the causes need to be looked for elsewhere?

For Miller and Roberts, for example, it is the former. The early part of the narrative (1 Sam 2:12-17, 22-25, 27-36) 'both describes the sin and announces the consequent punishment. This part of the narrative provides the motivation for all that follows. It gives an explanation for what would otherwise be an utterly inexplicable event—the defeat of Israel and the seeming defeat of Yahweh at Ebenezer'.[20]

My primary argument is that the text in 1 Samuel 2 does not sustain this interpretation. The narrative looks forward to a time of dishonour for the family of Eli, when they are replaced by another priestly family in the service of the king, a punishment normally understood to reflect Solomon's banishment of Abiathar in favour of the family of Zadok.[21] Specifically, the death of Eli's sons, Hophni and Phinehas, on the same day is to be a sign for Eli of this punishment. A sign is not to be confused with what it signifies.[22]

In my view, unless one takes for granted that chronological sequence is to be equated with causal sequence, a careful reading of the text of chapter 2 indicates that it is not predicting chapter 4 as the punishment of the Elide sins, and a careful reading of chapter 4 shows no sign of any attempt to explain the at-first-sight inexplicable defeats by reference to these sins and their punishment.

This is not a matter of genetic pre-texting, with an exclusive interest in sources and no interest in the present text. It is a question of giving serious attention to the meaning of the present text. In

---

(1979): 31-43.
20. Miller and Roberts, *Hand of the Lord*, 61-62.
21. See M Tsevat, 'Studies in the Book of Samuel', in *HUCA*, 32 (1961): 191-216.
22. The key text is: 'See, a time is coming when I will cut off your strength and the strength of your ancestor's family, so that no one in your family will live to old age. Then in distress you will look with greedy eye on all the prosperity that shall be bestowed upon Israel; and no one in your family shall ever live to old age' (1 Sam 2:31-32). This is more than the loss of two sons in a single day. There is no suggestion that the loss of the ark precipitated a period of prosperity in Israel; the reference is surely to the monarchy.

a critical reading of the text, it is possible to account for this lack of causal sequence by seeing the text as a composition of separate traditions. In a post-critical reading of the text, it is possible to be aware of this difference in origin and still interpret the movement of the text as a whole.[23]

While Wellhausen's comment that it is beyond doubt that chapters 1–3 were written with chapter 4 in mind would need a lot of nuancing today, it does acknowledge the presence of links between the texts and the direction of those links.[24] I have no difficulty in accepting that 1 Samuel 1–3 and 4–6 form a single text. The critical issue is how this is to be understood. In my judgement, both blocks of text prepare for the emergence of the monarchy, but in quite different ways.

1 Samuel 1–3 prepares the way for Samuel to step on to the stage of Israel's history as the prophet who would preside over the establishment of the monarchy in Israel. In my understanding, this aspect derives from the Prophetic Record.[25] The anti-Elide traditions were used as a foil to the presentation of Samuel; with a little help from the Deuteronomists, they also prepare the way for the new institution of monarchy by discrediting the old way of things. 1 Samuel 4–6, on the other hand, prepares the way for the emergence of the monarchy quite differently. The message of these chapters is entirely focussed on the ark, as the manifestation of God's power and purpose. In the withdrawal of the ark from the mainstream of Israel's life of worship, the way is left clear for new developments to occur. In the return of the ark to David's Jerusalem, under God's control of course, the seal of God's approval is placed on the newly established institution.

So I believe it is perfectly legitimate to speak of a text here. It is not a single sequence of sin and punishment. It is not a single text penned by one author; it is a composite text arranged by one author. It draws on the richness of Israel's traditions to portray the move toward the monarchy.

---

23. For my attempt to do this, see the *New Jerome Biblical Commentary;* contrast a different approach by Robert Polzin, for whom it is clear that chapter 4 is fulfilment of the prophecies in chapters 2 and 3 in all their dimensions (*Samuel and the Deuteronomist*, 60).
24. J Wellhausen, *Die Composition des Hexateuchs und der historischen Bücher des Alten Testaments*, fourth edition (Berlin: de Gruyter, 1963), 238.
25. For the Prophetic Record, see AF Campbell, *Of Prophets and Kings: A Late Ninth-Century Document (1 Samuel 1–2 Kings 10*, CBQMS 17 (Washington DC: Catholic Biblical Association of America, 1986).

1 Samuel 16–18

This is the well-known story of David and Goliath. Robert Polzin comments that it 'offers a serious challenge to anyone intent upon illustrating the narrative coherence of the present text'.[26] While admiring the courage of Polzin's effort with this text, I do not believe that he adequately spells out the full extent of the challenge, so I will endeavour to sketch it briefly here.

In 16:1–13, David, the youngest of Jesse's eight sons, is anointed by Samuel as Saul's replacement. As we know well, nothing more is heard of this anointing in the rest of the stories. In 16:14–23, Saul is in need of a lyre player to soothe his troubled spirits and David is summoned, enters Saul's service and becomes his armour-bearer as well as his lyre player. In chapter 17, we have the famous story of David's combat with the Philistine, Goliath. There are divergent text traditions in the Greek and Hebrew.[27] After the initial setting of the two armies in place, the giant Philistine champion comes forth to make his challenge to Israel: risk all in one-to-one combat with me! The reaction to the challenge is in v 11:

> When Saul and all Israel heard these words of the
> Philistine, they were dismayed and greatly afraid.

The Greek version continues with what is now v 32 in the present text. David, Saul's armour-bearer, speaks up from beside his king:

> Let no one's heart fail because of him; your servant will
> go and fight with this Philistine.

The sharp contrast between the dispirited Saul and inspired David is clear.

In the present text, however, v 11 is followed by v 12 which form-critically resembles a new narrative beginning. David is presented as Jesse's son, one of eight. This repeats information already given in 16:1–13. More significantly, it is a usual way to start an Israelite story.

---

26. R Polzin, *Samuel and the Deuteronomist*, 161.
27. In chapters 17–18, the shorter version common to Hebrew and Greek traditions is: 17:1–11, 32–40, 42–48a, 49, 51–54; 18:6a*b–9; 12a, 13–16, 20–21a, 22–29a; beyond this, the Hebrew alone has: 17:12–31, 41, 48b, 50; 17:55–18:6a*; 18:10–11, 12b, 17–19, 21b, 29b–30.

As a beginning, it would seem to be unaware of David's earlier role in the narrative. In v 15, however, it says that 'David went back and forth from Saul to feed his father's sheep at Bethlehem', indicating an awareness of David's place with Saul. It also notes in v 16 that the Philistine took his stand for forty days, morning and evening. This reflects an awareness of the earlier part of the David and Goliath story.

The story then takes its own independent way. Jesse despatches David to the camp with provisions for his brothers and a gift for their commander. The location of the Israelite camp is specified, as in v 2. The Philistine champion is brought on to the scene, introduced no more definitely than in v 4, and repeats his challenge, speaking 'the same words as before'.[28] The text adds:

> All the Israelites, when they saw the man, fled from him
> and were very much afraid (v 24).

We must wonder whether this flight and fear by all Israel was repeated morning and evening for forty days.

The story continues with the exchanges between David and the soldiery. Royal reward is promised for the one who will defeat this Philistine.

> The king will greatly enrich the man who kills him, and
> will give him his daughter and make his family free in
> Israel (v 25).

Form-critically, this is almost fairy-tale stuff: the youngest son, fresh from the farm, offered half of the kingdom and the hand of the king's daughter in marriage. David is portrayed taking up this theme and emphasising the issue of the reward to be gained. Finally the matter reaches Saul's ears and David is brought before the king. At this point, the two story-lines have converged, although for a while there is no more talk of reward.

---

28. *RSV* and *NRSV* have 'a champion' in v 4 and 'the champion' in v 23. The difference in translation reflects the present text rather than the Hebrew; that is, the definite article is used in v 23 because it is the second occurrence in the present text, not because of any change in the Hebrew from v 4.

At this point, it is time to pause and take stock. At first sight, we have two stories here: two introductions of David, of the battling armies, of the Philistine challenger. Is it possible to make sense of the present text? We could appeal to the flashback technique, as legitimate in story as in film.[29] The narrative has brought the story to the point where King Saul quails before the menace to Israel's survival posed by the giant Philistine; David is about to face the menace and meet the challenge. But before we are allowed to hear David's response, then, the narrative takes us back to the origins of this brave man. So we see him coming from the farm to the camp, ready to be where he is now, brought by his bravery to Saul's side.

For Polzin, the opening description of the battle scene is expository (vv 1–11), with the exposition followed by the description of what happens at the battle scene when David actually arrives (vv 19–24). 'These two narrative sides of the battle scene are related to each other as exposition to story proper.' They are bracketed around the narrative introduction of David into the story (vv 12–18).[30]

The difficulty with this approach is that David has already been introduced into the story when he was brought to Saul's court and made his armour-bearer and lyre player. Even if David shuttled between his home and the court, a second introduction is not needed. The strongest argument against any harmonisation of the two passages is the continuation of the two stories, with noted differences at several key moments, and with fundamentally quite different themes. Harmonisation, as the key to understanding the text, founders on the repetition both of the killing and the question, 'Whose son are you?'

There is the moment of the killing. It is repetitive and different in the two versions. The version found in the Greek has David do the killing with a sword, after felling the Philistine with a slingstone.

> When the Philistine drew nearer to meet David, David put his hand in his bag, took out a stone, slung it, and struck the Philistine on his forehead; and the stone sank into his forehead, and he fell face down on the ground. Then David ran and stood over the Philistine; he grasped his sword, drew it out of its sheath, and killed him; then he cut his head off with it (vv 48a, 49, 51 [*NRSV*]).

---

29. David evokes his past when referring to his experience as a shepherd (17:34–36).
30. Polzin, *Samuel and the Deuteronomist*, 164–65.

The Hebrew verses which are absent from the Greek have David do the killing with sling and stone, there was no sword in David's hand.

> David ran quickly toward the battle line to meet the Philistine. And David prevailed over the Philistine with a sling and a stone, striking down the Philistine and killing him; there was no sword in David's hand (vv 48b, 50 [NRSV]).

While the two versions can be harmonised, there is a clear difference in the presentation. If it were simply a matter of repetitive and full detail, v 51 need only have read: And David ran and stood over him and took his sword and cut off his head. There would have been no need to repeat 'and he killed him'.

To clinch the matter, the two stories continue their separate ways, pursuing quite different plots.

i. The story of David, the armour-bearer and lyre player, after contrasting the dispirited Saul and the inspired David, follows this contrast through with the song of the women and the success of David, the jealousy of Saul, and the commitment of all Israel and Judah to David (18:6a*–9, 12a, 13–16).

ii. The story of David, fresh from the farm and eager for a reward from the king, continues with Saul's inquiries about David's identity ('Whose son are you?') and taking David into his service,[31] the friendship between David and Jonathan, Saul's offer of the hand of his eldest daughter Merab to David, and finally his failure to honour the offer, provoking enmity between the two men (17:55–18:6a*, 18:10–11, 12b, 17–19 [21b], 29b–30).[32]

---

31. Polzin recognises the difficulty here fully and frankly. He makes a valiant attempt to construe Saul's 'Whose son are you young man?' (17:58a) as asking David 'formally to renounce Jesse's paternity in favor of his own' and to read as 'a note of defiance' David's reply, 'I am the son of your servant Jesse the Bethlehemite' (v 58b). Despite the ingenuity and insight, it just does not carry conviction (see Polzin, *Samuel and the Deuteronomist*, 175).

32. For a fuller presentation of my interpretation of these stories, see my 'From Philistine to Throne', in *AusBR* 34 (1986): 35–41 and my *Study Companion to Old Testament Literature* (now Michael Glazier Books; Collegeville: Liturgical Press, 1989), 206–13. Extensive treatment of the text traditions is given in D. Barthélemy, DW Gooding, J Lust, and E Tov, *The Story of David and Goliath: Textual and Literary Criticism*, OBO 73 (Fribourg, Switzerland: Éditions

My point in going into this degree of detail about a well-known story is to raise as clearly as possible the question: can this be a text? In my judgement, this text cannot be 'a text'. Attempts to unify its beginning by appeal to a flashback or differentiation between exposition and narration fail to do justice to the two clear and distinct story-lines which are present. Does this then force us to adopt the position that its interpretation, as present text, would be an unsatisfying and embarrassing exercise? This may depend on how we understand the possibilities for interpretation of the text.

We have to reflect on the phenomena in the text and decide what kind of understanding will do the text most justice. There is no question of a covert appeal to the supposed crudity or clumsiness of redactors. If we do not have 'a text' here, we have the very skilled preservation of two texts, woven into a single narrative presentation. In my understanding, the phenomena of the text are best interpreted as an attempt to preserve two different stories, respecting their integrity and their difference. It is not to be understood as a attempt to compress and unify two stories into one. The differences have been maintained far too cleverly for that and could have been stamped out so very easily.

What the compilation has achieved here is to offer us two different visions of David's first moves to prominence and power. There is uncertain ambiguity in so much of the Story of David's Rise. Was it simply that God was with the David whom Samuel anointed? Or was there truth in Shimei ben Gera's taunts, 'Murderer! Scoundrel! Man of blood' (2 Sam 16:7-8). These two stories, at the beginning, leave avenues open to both views. David, the (anointed) armour-bearer and lyre player, is portrayed as the man who had God with him all the way to the throne. David, fresh from the farm and eager for a reward from the king, is more open to a portrayal as Shimei's ambitious and grasping scoundrel.

If the combined stories do not constitute 'a text', the outstanding question remains: why the interweaving here into a sequential text? It would have been perfectly possible to juxtapose them, as elsewhere in the Pentateuch or the Story of David's Rise (for example, 1 Samuel 24 and 26). On reflection, however, we can see the pitfalls involved in launching the royal career twice. Further, the difficulties encountered

---

Universitaires, 1986).

in interpreting the present text would be hugely multiplied if the two stories were told separately. Combined into a sequential text, all the details are available to a story-teller who then has the freedom to shape them as best befits the story to be told.[33]

One of the interesting aspects of this David and Goliath story is that there appears to be an attempt to harmonise the two stories in the text itself. 1 Samuel 17:15 portrays David moving back and forth between his father's flock and Saul's court. 17:16 creates space for this by claiming that Goliath proclaimed his challenge morning and evening for forty days.[34]

Has such harmonisation succeeded? In my judgment, it has not. Close inspection shows that it fails.[35] But does that leave open a second way of reading the text in which we prescind from close inspection, a reading in which the unity of the text is foregrounded? We know that most unsuspecting readers of the flood story, the story of the deliverance at the sea, and the story of David and Goliath read these foregrounding the unity and leaving the issues of discontinuity unnoticed in the background. Once the critical perception of the nature of the text has been achieved, is there anything which disqualifies such a reading? I tend to think not. Such a reading is panoramic rather than close-up; it foregrounds unity rather than foregrounding diversity.

A panoramic reading can be greatly assisted by judiciously delimiting the text considered. If the David and Goliath story is begun at 1 Samuel 17:1 instead of 16:14, the tension with the David who is already in Saul's service is lessened. If the story is stopped at 17:54, the problem of Saul's ignorance of David's identity is avoided. For many purposes surely this is a legitimate procedure.

---

33. See my 'Reported Story', above, note 16.
34. Such a forty day span would fit comfortably into the narrative horizon of the more legendary story as long as the motif of the flight of the troops was handled carefully—'All the Israelites . . . fled from him' lacks verisimilitude if repeated twice a day for forty days.
35. In fact, these two verses create considerable difficulties for close reading. Nevertheless it could be argued that since a modern scholar (for example, Polzin) believes the unity of the text can be sustained, the ancient compiler might have thought the same. While perfectly possible, if that were the case it may also be possible that both ancient and modern were wrong in their judgement.

1 Samuel 7–12
The complexity of these chapters is well-known, with the claim to original texts, and prophetic and deuteronomistic overlays. To simplify brutally:
- In 1 Samuel 7, God delivers Israel at Samuel's intercession by thundering mightily and throwing the Philistines into confusion (7:10).
- In 1 Samuel 8, the people demand a king in place of Samuel's sons, much to his displeasure, but he is instructed by God to set a king over them.
- In 1 Samuel 9:1–10:16, without any reference to this request, God acts to bring Saul before Samuel to be anointed king in order to deliver Israel from the Philistines—an action which is unnecessary in the light of thunderous divine power available through prophetic intercession.
- In 1 Samuel 10:17–27, despite having previously anointed him, Samuel uses oracular procedures such as the casting of lots to locate and identify Saul, in hiding, who is then acclaimed king.
- In 1 Samuel 11, a message reaches Saul, without any reference to his having been acclaimed king, and, empowered by the spirit, his military deliverance of a threatened town leads to his being crowned king at Gilgal.
- In 1 Samuel 12, most of this is pulled together, with an emphasis on Israel's sin and Samuel's continued prophetic intercession.

In a panoramic foregrounding of unity, much of the detailed disunity of these chapters can be overlooked. But is the pursuit of unity the best and richest way to derive meaning from them? Careful redaction has been at work with what result? Not a unified narrative by a long chalk. Nor is it an explicitly discursive text. Rather, we have the juxtaposition of differing traditions, with implicit possibility for the discerning of meaning between them.[36] There is conservation

---

36. Lyle M Eslinger comments: 'The existence of a text containing contradictory views should be assumed to present an examination of a controversy' (*Kingship of God in Crisis: A Close Reading of 1 Samuel 1–12* [Sheffield: Almond, 1985]. 38). Such an assumption seems to me thoroughly justifiable; Eslinger's scorn for a composite text stands in need of better justification than it gets. He manifests an appalling concept of historical critical interpretation (see 35).

of at least one viewpoint, juxtaposed with contradiction or major modification from other viewpoints, resulting in communication of the varying views in Israel about the emergence of the monarchy.

I think it fair to say that a text has been constituted by the careful and unconcealed juxtaposition of differing positions. Such an interpretation is justified in foregrounding the unity. The backgrounded diversity, not only between the blocks but above all within them, is immense and complex. I believe it is a fairer reading of the final text to recognise and respect the diversity, which has here been marshalled into line without being muted into unity.

Issues of meaning then and now

Turning to the question of meaning brings us within range of hermeneutic and literary theory. Without wishing to engage in the debates, there are certain elements worth a practitioner's while singling out.

The autonomy of a text is a gain since the days of Wimsatt and Beardsley which cannot be relinquished. As ED Hirsch notes, 'Self-evidently a text can mean anything it has been understood to mean. If an ancient text has been interpreted as a Christian allegory, that is unanswerable proof that it can be so interpreted.'[37] It is equally significant that we are able to distinguish between a critical construal of an ancient text and its anachronistic interpretation as a Christian allegory.

Our increasing awareness of the inevitability and value of subjectivity in all interpretation, as in so much else of human activity, prepares us to forgo the claim to *the* definitive interpretation of a text. Any interpretation I propose is my interpretation of the text, as informed and as responsible as I know how, as adequately and fully controlled by the text as I am able to make it. It is not humility but hermeneutic which renounces all claim to the definitive.

For the biblical believer, the autonomy of a text cannot be used universally to separate the interpreter's understanding of it from its origin as the word of God (however that might be spelled out). The

---

37. ED Hirsch, Jr, *The Aims of Interpretation* (Chicago: The University of Chicago Press, 1976). It is useful to remember Hirsch's distinctions between original meaning and anachronistic meaning, and between meaning and significance, and their various combinations.

historical or incarnational quality of God's word is essential to most Christian and Jewish belief. It is ultimately an issue of the nature of God's word: on the one hand, is it written in clear or in code; on the other, is it free of the trammels of human ambiguity or is it richly enmeshed in them? If association with an author and the distinction between meaning then and meaning now are totally written off, the scriptures risk becoming either code or divorced from human involvement with God. Must either of these things happen?

If interpretation is always *my* interpretation, then it may be my interpretation of what it is appropriate for a text to mean now and my interpretation of what, in my best judgement, is appropriate for a text to have meant then, in the time of its composition.[38] The limits of my or our knowledge about 'then' may often mean that this aspect of interpretation is more negative than positive. That is, it may more often permit us to exclude meanings which we have reasonable grounds to be sure do not apply, rather than giving us reasonable and positive grounds to affirm a particular meaning. It is meaning controlled by my informed and responsible reading of the text, in the light of what I am able to know of its time. It may not and need not be identical with the anachronistic meaning which an informed and responsible reading of the text suggests to me as appropriate for today.

Today, in a post-critical world, I believe there is room for both critical and creative readings of the biblical text, each in its proper settings. We may signal these with antithetical balance. A critical reading will need to be informed and responsible, with particular reference to the time and context of the composition of the text, but aware of today. A creative reading will need to be informed and responsible, with particular reference to the time and context of today, but aware of the nature of the biblical text—and so post-critical. Today, a pre-critical reading would not be informed or responsible.

Hirsch argues that the decision between original meaning and anachronistic meaning is ultimately an ethical one.[39] The Bible was written, it is said, for the building up of the Jewish and Christian communities. Is it unethical for it to be read responsibly for this same purpose today?

---

38. It is not my recovery of the author's meaning, but my interpretation of the text's meaning.
39. Hirsch, *Aims*, 77.

Can the Bible be read as any other book? As incarnate word, can it be read in any other way? Yet it cannot be regarded as any other book, for the Bible is foundational for the faith-communities of Judaism and Christianity and that can be said of no other book.

Associated books:
Campbell, AF. *God and Bible* (Paulist Press)
Campbell, *Making Sense of the Bible: Difficult Texts and Modern Faith* (Paulist Press)
Campbell, AF, *Of Prophets and Kings* (CBQMS)
Campbell, AF. *Experiencing Scripture* (ATF Press)
Campbell, AF. *Joshua to Chronicles* (WJKP)
Campbell AF and O'Brien, MA. *Sources of the Pentateuch* (Fortress Press)
Campbell and O'Brien. *Unfolding the Deuteronomistic History* (Fortress Press)
Campbell, AF and O'Brien MA. *Rethinking the Pentateuch* (WJKP)

Relationship to God

St Ignatius Loyola and God's Unconditional Love
(original: *The Way*, 43, 2004)

Introduction

How can we say God loves us? What does it mean to use that language? The fine tissue of the life of spirit needs constant attention and regular revising of its language to express what is sometimes so faintly felt, so easily swamped, and yet is at the core of human life. We need words that move us, words of wonder, words of wisdom. It can happen, though, that what sounds right at one moment may have implications that in the long term are not right. Love is one of those words that touches deeply. The need has been in us since the beginning: 'it is not good that the man should be alone' (Gen 2:18). Do we need the love of God? Does God need our love? What does it mean to say that God loves us?

Language of a loving God is commonplace in today's spirituality. One could be forgiven for wondering whether, sometimes at least, the language of an unconditionally loving God might be almost the equivalent of a useful code for refusal to believe in hell-fire and purgatorial punishment. On the other hand, acceptance of God's unconditional love is an invitation to us to rise above the oldest archaism of the human spirit. In my own words elsewhere:

> The invitation is to aspire to a level of spirit-filled existence that so far too few have managed to sustain for more than fleeting moments: a disclaimer of self-interest in divine order and a freedom to be loved and to love in the disorder of life's experience, to accept in faith God's unconditional love and faithfully respond to it.[1]

---

1. Antony F Campbell, *God First Loved Us: The Challenge of Accepting Unconditional*

Throughout our lives today, faith and experience may require that, as paradox in the mystery of the divine, we hold together both the powerlessness of a loving God—who rages, weeps, and rejoices with us—and the 'otherness' of God. Perhaps we have to hold together in one faith the God who is 'utterly other' (of whom we can hardly speak and had best be silent) and the God who has been and is 'here among us' (with whom we must engage). In an earlier day, God's love was seldom expressed in terms of unconditional love. The language of an unconditionally loving God is absent from the *Spiritual Exercises* of St Ignatius Loyola. Does its reality, nevertheless, have a place in his thought and prayer? Using his text, can we find it there for ourselves?

Ignatius Loyola came to the life of the spirit from the life of a soldier. Unconditional love might be wrapped in the mystic heights of courtly romance; he dreamed about it. She was the Infanta Catherina; he was not in her league. In due course, she married King John III of Portugal.[2] Fortunately for the future, Ignatius's daydreams moved beyond romantic imaginings and took a turn for the more spiritual. In those days, unconditional loyalty was something every soldier knew about; you died for it. Three of Ignatius's brothers died for it. Ignatius starts with loyalty and moves towards love.

The unconditional in the life of Loyola was the loyalty a knight owed his lord. Ignatius's first lord was Juan Velázquez, 'a noble in the finest traditions of old Spain',[3] but who died in disfavour. With the death of Velázquez, Ignatius transferred his services to the duke of Nájera and was facing the French on his behalf at Pamplona, capital of Navarre, when the cannon ball shattered his leg. Ignatius knew the loyalty of the soldier. As anyone at the time knew, it was a two-way loyalty. The soldier was expected to be loyal to his lord; the lord was expected to be loyal to his vassal. Brought up at court, enamoured of the Infanta, this was the air that Ignatius breathed. 'The ideal of chivalry articulated these ideas [of honour, loyalty, disinterested self-sacrifice] and softened the harshness of the military code which was its heart.'[4] These were the structures of Ignatius's world; veiled in these structures may be his understanding of the love of God.

Love (New York: Paulist, 2000), xi.
2. WW Meissner, *Ignatius of Loyola: The Psychology of a Saint* (New Haven: Yale University Press, 1992), 240–241.
3. Meissner, *Ignatius of Loyola*, 18, and n. 4.
4. J.M Roberts, *The Penguin History of Europe* (London: Penguin, 1996), 160.

With those pained by the martial imagery, we need to remember that somewhere around the turning of the nineteenth into the twentieth century the human emotional and intellectual attitude to the activity of war changed. Unfortunately, as we well know, Ignatius Loyola lived, experienced, and wrote several centuries before that.

A loving God

All language about God has to be analogical. We can only speak of God by analogy, by comparison with something else, applying the appropriate safeguards. Whatever faith claims may be made, we may often not have direct sense-experience of God. Language about God's love for us is necessarily analogical. When faith has made the leap to the existence of God (or from the end-point of an argument for the existence of God to the actual commitment of oneself to the acceptance of God), what does it mean to say God loves us?

For us human beings, at a first level at least, love implies extensive involvement of the senses: sight, touch, hearing, taste, and smell. Aspects and circumstances vary so much, but so often there is a glance, a kiss, holding, hugging, sexual play and bonding; there's a closeness physically and emotionally. There is so much more: understanding, intimacy, acceptance, commitment, and more. It is the sense experience that is lacking with God: no glance, no touch, no sound. In the context of faith, God's impact on us may be felt; it is our own sensory contact with God that is lacking. How do we talk of love where mutuality is so stretched, where the disparity is as wide as creator and creature?

Does God need us as we need God? Perhaps yes, but if so it shakes up a lot of classical theological understanding. If not, it puts an enormous weight on the analogy aspect of God's love. What might it mean to love someone and not need them? Acceptance, benevolence, commitment (the ABC of love) are all very well, but most of us need something more—something somewhere along the spectrum from affection to passion. Passion need not be excluded from the relationship. Not for us. Our being passionately in love with God may take many forms, but it is possible. St Teresa's 'though you damn me I will love you still' is as good an example as we get. Not for God either. I've heard those I'd trust—the wise and theologically well-informed—speak of our being passionately loved by God.

If we find all this passionate love a bit far away from where we are, it may help to go back to the opposite—the apparently cold logic of Ignatius's text. However, even if it is not the whole story, it does help to image our God as accepting of us, benevolent toward us, committed to us—where it is OK for us to be in the divine doghouse because we believe that, despite our flaws, our frailty, our failures, God is committed to us. Deeply displeased (there are other ways of putting that), but committed to us.

Put bluntly: it is tricky to say God loves us when the experience of the senses is out of the question, without prior belief in God. A possible balance lies in our awareness that Ignatius Loyola was a highly emotional man. His spiritual diary is awash with his tears. The emotion was felt; it was evidently there in the man, available to him in his reflection on his experience.

The Spiritual Exercises

Ignatius starts his 'contemplation for obtaining love' with the dry note that love is more a matter of works than words ('más en las obras que en las palabras'). He goes on to talk about mutual communication ('comunicación de las dos partes'). We need to push the idea of communication more widely than his examples of knowledge, honours, wealth, etc; we need to be alert to the 'mutual'. It is there for Ignatius in his repeated prayer: you, O God, have given to me, so I give to you.

We can broaden it massively; we can also feel the sheer terror of the prayer—at least in some of its words. For example, 'take and receive . . . all my memory'; not on your sweet nelly, dear Lord (but then I don't have to face Alzheimer's, at least I hope not, at least not yet). Unfolding the contemplation itself, before its prayer, Ignatius talks about remembering the benefits we have received from God (creation, salvation, special gifts); he talks about life and all the ways we can experience that in the environment (plants, animal kingdom, humanity); from there he moves out to the whole of creation, daring to speak of a working God as Genesis dared speak of a resting God, and ending up with God as the source of all goodness. He dares even to speak of a God who 'desea dárseme', who longs to give God's own self to me. That is love. The bulk of the contemplation is a take on the love of God that operates out of faith, that invites our senses to play on the objects of our sense-experience and tie these in faith into God.

Ignatius does not so much sidestep what it means to talk about God loving us; he comes at it from a particular angle. For Ignatius, as we have seen, love is grounded in deeds more than words and is a mutual communication between lover and beloved. Not surprisingly, therefore, the evidence of God's love for us is sketched in the facts, available to the eye of the believer, rather than in the weaving of words. We can see what we believe God does for us and around us; it is a further step in faith to attempt to find words for the emotions of God, to speak of God's love for us. It is interesting that the process of the *Spiritual Exercises* begins with God (Principle and Foundation, First Week), turns to Jesus Christ for his life, death, and resurrection (Weeks 2–4), and at the end of this introduces the Contemplation for Obtaining Love ('para alcanzar amor'). The implications require reflection.

The principle and foundation
The 'Principle and Foundation', at the beginning of the *Exercises*, is surprisingly loveless—devoid of any mention of the word. In the Gospel parable, Jesus suggests builders and warriors prudently count the costs before committing themselves (Luke 14:28–32). Ignatius asks for chivalrous commitment to Jesus' cause in the Two Standards meditation. From the start of the Exercises, with the Principle and Foundation, the process of counting the cost begins. Cost counting is a hard-headed business.

The opening statement is one that we could hardly make today. Ignatius says: man is created to praise, reverence, and serve God our Lord ('El hombre es criado para alabar, hacer reverencia y servir a Dios nuestro Señor'). The issue is not inclusive language; that is important, but it is easy. 'We are created . . .' The more significant change is massive and facing it is not easy. To be responsible today, we would have to preface this sentence with 'we believe': 'We believe that we are created . . .' There is a deep gulf between an age when an affirmation of faith could be made as a matter of fact, without any thought of faith, and an age when accuracy demands the avowal of faith. We might also wonder whether the absence of love from Ignatius's sentence reflects the gulf between the sixteenth century and now. Not so. In 1570, Mary Queen of Scots wrote to her three-year-old son that she hoped he would know that he had in her 'a loving mother that wishes you to learn in time to love know and fear God'.[5]

Gulf number two follows in Ignatius's next clause: and by this means to save his soul ('y mediante esto salvar su ánima'). Human salvation occupied the centre of Ignatius's universe. Salvation, as Ignatius understood it, no longer has that place today. For those who believe in a world without God, such salvation has no meaning. For many of those who believe in a world with God, there is nothing certain enough in today's world to warrant staking eternal salvation on it. For a chivalrous soldier in the sixteenth century, there was one thing certain enough to die for: loyalty to one's liege lord.

The first week
The 'first week' of the Ignatian *Spiritual Exercises* is taken up with what is today the immensely unpopular theme of sin: first, the angels, Adam and Eve, the single lost soul; then, my own sins and my own insignificance; finally, the horrors of hell-fire. For many a modern, such thoughts and imaginings are miles away from reality—and miles away from the idea of an unconditionally loving God. What they hold to is the utter seriousness of human life. In the light of Christian faith, we are not on this earth for the fun of it. Today, with global communications, we know enough of the horrors inflicted by humans or by nature not to take this life lightly. There are no easy answers, unless we stay with superficiality; at a level of depth, we face either absurdity or mystery.

The imagery of Ignatius is pretty brutal; it is the imagery of the time. Dr Johnson's observation that the knowledge that you are to be hanged wonderfully concentrates the mind may be true; it is certainly unduly blunt and, to many today, highly insensitive. But that was almost three centuries ago. Early in the last century, James Joyce, in *A Portrait of the Artist as a Young Man*, could have his hero say: 'God would not be God if He did not punish the transgressor.' For some today, God would not be God if God did. So we recognize in Ignatius the thought and language of his time. We cannot let it obscure for us the essential: if we believe there is a God, then nothing is more central in life.

---

5. Antonia Fraser, *Mary Queen of Scots* (London: Weidenfeld and Nicholson, 1969), 421.

Commitment to Christ

The 'second week' of the Ignatian *Spiritual Exercises* opens with a prayer of deliberate commitment to the cause of Christ. The imagery of chivalry is everywhere. The human king is there, at the pinnacle of earthly prestige. His offer is irresistible; the cause is unquestioned and the burdens will be shared by followers and king alike. Any soldier with the slightest sense of honour would sign up to the cause without hesitation.

The whole fabric of the world of chivalry is the background against which Ignatius portrays Christ's call for commitment. The irresistible offer is made. Those signing up are admired. The soldier with any sense of honour will set out to distinguish himself. Unspoken here, but utterly real, is the conviction that the follower's commitment to Christ is matched by Christ's commitment to the follower. As anyone at the time knew, loyalty was two-way: the soldier was expected to be loyal to the lord and the lord was expected to be loyal to the vassal. Christ's commitment could be counted on and taken for granted. Twentieth-century readers will be aware of the masculinity of much of this imagery from centuries long past.

What is wonderfully liberating about the text of the *Exercises* is that at certain key points Ignatius does not spell out his meaning in detail. It is left for readers to do it for themselves. So here. The 'cause of Christ' is put in broad general terms: to conquer the whole world and all the enemies, and so to enter into the glory of my Father ('conquistar todo el mundo y todos los enemigos, y así entrar en la gloria de mi Padre'). The nature of the 'conquest' is not spelled out; neither is 'the glory of my Father'. We are free to fill these out for ourselves. We are not bound to images of redemption; we can be free for images of salvation. 'The glory of my Father' can be our recognition of who we are, our recognition of the achievement involved in our becoming who we are, and our recognition of the value that is ours in the eyes of our God. At least, that is a good start.

In what follows in the *Exercises*, hell and redemption do have a part to play, even if restricted; this is sixteenth-century theology after all. But right at the beginning, we are free to make our choices. We can envisage a conquest that is free of negative overtones and that instead involves the overwhelming conviction of God's commitment to this 'whole world and all the enemies'—seeing a value in us that can so often be hidden from us in all the horrors of too much human life. In such an understanding, we are not so much redeemed from a power that holds us bound and must be conquered. Rather, we are saved, overwhelmed by the awareness of our right relationship with God that is truly called salvation. For Ignatius, the Trinity contemplate the human fate of hell and the human need for redemption and they decide on the Incarnation. Ignatius does not spell out a theology of this incarnation and redemption. For us, the incarnation—Christ's becoming 'God here among us'—can be the expression of God's commitment to us, of God's capacity to value and hold precious all that is human (cf Isa 43:4). Must God punish the transgressor? Isaiah does not seem to think so (cf Isa 43:25) and nor does Job (cf Job 7:20–21).

The life, death, and resurrection of Christ
Subsequent prayer in the *Spiritual Exercises*, with a few exceptions, is dedicated to contemplating the life, death, and resurrection of Christ. The commitment to Christ has been made. The leader is put under the microscope and studied in minute detail. The aim is to enhance the follower's commitment. The assumption of the leader's commitment is automatic.

In contemplating the events of Christ's Passion, the petition of the first contemplation in particular notes that it is 'for my sins' that Christ suffers ('porque por mis peccados va el Señor a la passión'). Quite rightly, this can be understood in terms of my need for redemption from sin. Interestingly though, in the second contemplation Ignatius shifts the focus from sin and speaks simply of the suffering Christ bore 'for me' ('tanta pena que Christo passó por mí'). Without claiming to know precisely what Ignatius might have meant by the shift, we are entitled to put our emphasis on the incarnation as God's great saving act, from which Christ's passion and death follow as the natural results of sharing our human life to the full. To put this sharply: Christ's incarnation need not be seen as the necessary prelude to his suffering and death by which we are redeemed; instead, Christ's incarnation itself—his becoming one of us—can be seen as the expression of God's commitment to humankind and Christ's suffering and death are then the inevitable consequence of his life, his values, and the way he lived them in that particular period of time.

This is 'suffering for my sins'. It is a sharing in human life that, in the 'sinfulness' of that life, can have violent and appalling consequences.

Psychologically, it makes good sense to have the process of the contemplation of Jesus' life precede the 'contemplation for obtaining love' (for comprehending love, see below). When we have absorbed through all the senses what human life and suffering meant to Jesus, how deeply Jesus must have found value in all the ordinariness and burden that is part and parcel of human living, at that point we are better prepared to accept the extraordinary faith-claim of God's love for us. As at the Transfiguration, so in the Resurrection appearances, some hint is given of the value God puts on human life. Against the background of the resurrection, it is appropriate to become increasingly aware of the love of God for us. What has gone before is not Christ's suffering in order to free us from sin. It is the fullness of salvation—the awareness of the value God sets on human life, the awareness of the love God has for us—that frees us to live abundantly.

The contemplation for comprehending love
It is against this background that we come to the 'contemplation for obtaining love'. The Spanish has 'para alcanzar amor'. I believe it is best understood as 'for comprehending love', becoming fully aware of, coming to grips with God's love, grasping or reaching an understanding of God's love for us—before turning to the immensity of our response. The title is suitably ambiguous; it has the advantage of making space for the dual focus of the contemplation as a whole. Primary is God's love for us; secondary is our response (against Ganss, for whom it is the other way around [n 117]). 'Obtaining love' is a traditional English rendering; it is loaded and too easily misunderstood. 'Obtaining' or 'attaining' or 'arousing' are all focused on the prayer we are to make; they do not take adequate account of the contemplation itself that Ignatius wrote, which in each part precedes the prayer. In his preamble, the inner recognition ('cognoscimiento interno') of God's goodness to us and love for us precedes the concern for our response. The prayer, repeated at the end of each part, is focused on our return of love to God, balanced by 'give me only your love and your grace' at the prayer's end. The rendering in Fr Caswall's hymn does justice to the core of the contemplation: 'I love thee, O thou Lord most high, / Because thou first hast loved me.' The contemplation itself, in its

core, focuses on God's love for us. We do not 'obtain' love; it has been given us. This contemplation does not invite us to 'obtain' God's love; it invites us to contemplate and realize the love of God that has been given us and continues to be given us, not as reward but as free gift—like the sun from above and the waters from a spring. We are entitled to speak in faith of the experience of God's commitment to us, God's love for us. In Ignatius's eyes, we may not be justified in calling that commitment and that love unconditional—although the sun and the spring are. The fate of the sinner, as portrayed by Ignatius, argues against the unconditional. In feudal eyes, treachery wiped out any obligation on the part of the liege lord. Such reality had to be present to Ignatius's mind.

In our own eyes today, we know that we cannot argue our way to the acceptance of love; we believe it, and rejoice. We do not argue to God's love for any of us, much less to God's unconditional love for all of us. We do not know that there is a God; we may believe. We do not know whether our God saves the few, saves the many, or saves the lot—all of us, including those we don't approve of. We choose, we believe, we may hope. From the beginning, Scripture can give us hope: 'Never again will I doom the earth because of man, *since the desires of man's heart are evil from the start*; nor will I ever again strike down all living beings, as I have done'[6]—God is committed to us in all of our frailty (cf Isa 54:9-10). We are able to love each other, despite knowing the flaws of those we love and who love us. Dare we deny that God, who knows our flaws far better than we do, is able to love us too? As with any love, we cannot argue our way to God's love for us. We can eliminate some of the obstacles and then hope for the leap of faith. The invitation is not to look on the miseries of Ignatius's world or ours; it is rather the invitation to look for the goodness of God within us and around us—to see ourselves as God would see us.

What Ignatius offers to God repeatedly in this prayer—take Lord and receive ('Tomad, Señor, y recibid')— is worth noting. It is basically everything: liberty, memory, understanding, will, possessions. If God took us up on this offer—taking it literally, of course—we would be in for a shock, left with life and little else. In the context of this prayer, we are entitled to reflect on just how much Ignatius must have experienced as God's giving and loving. For him: your love and

---

6. Gen 8:21, translation adapted from the *New American Bible* and emphasis added.

your grace ('vuestro amor y gracia'). For us, perhaps that may bear reformulation: your free gift of unconditional love. Even further: is the 'unconditional' quality of that love precisely what enables us to hear the invitation to accept and to respond?

Exercises in prayer are not studies in theology. The underlying theology may be visible; it is not explicitly addressed. Here, we may note that sin is present early in the piece without an explicit focus on God's love for the sinner. We may note that in the final reflection on God's love there is not an explicit focus on the sinfulness of those who are so loved. That the two are in the same little book suggests that Ignatius could hold them together. The invitation to Christian faith today may be to hold together explicitly both God's love and human sinfulness: we are loved, sinners though we are.

Conclusion

Once the 'Foundation' and associated prayer have enabled someone to establish the place of God in their life, the Second, Third, and Fourth weeks of the *Spiritual Exercises* take them into the life of Jesus Christ. At the end of this journeying, the person may be more ready to appreciate God's love for them that has been there from the outset— like the sun. Like the sun, God's love for us has not been offered as a reward to be earned but is presented as a given to be treasured. Like the sun, it is there.

God: Judge or Lover?
(original: *The Way* 30, 1990)

There is no more challenging theme in contemporary faith's struggle for understanding than that of God's unconditional love for us and its relation to issues of divine justice, anger, and punishment. Here we will focus on some of the issues connected with anger, God's anger and also ours.

Talk of divine anger often leads into complexity and confusion. Formulating a dilemma at its starkest helps focus the issue. If God is all-powerful, retaining absolute sovereignty over human freedom, then God has no cause for anger or grief, while humans seemingly have plenty of cause for anger against God. But if God is powerless, having granted human freedom, then God has plenty of cause for anger and grief, while humans have little or no cause for anger against God. The missing middle ground is where God has absolute sovereignty over human freedom and humans enjoy absolute freedom: a situation which certainly is recognised as deepest mystery and which needs to be recognized as most confusing in formulating any models for language about God—language must constantly take one or other stance.

Except perhaps in spirituality circles, talk of God's unconditional love can evoke negative reactions, ranging from a bored or irritable shrug to upset contestation. As a theological option, it is too soft! We have all heard comments like 'Have we wasted our time being good all these years?' or worse, 'Does that mean Hitler and Stalin are in heaven?' Beneath the superficiality of this initial response can lie something deeper, with grave issues at stake. If God's love is unconditional, is human life belittled and deprived of worth? Are we then no longer held responsible for our actions, our lives reduced to some sort of monstrous charade? Is the language of God's love deprived of serious meaning without a dose of the wrath of God?

There are enough issues involved to form a veritable jigsaw puzzle. We need to consider some of the elements which go to make up the puzzle, to look closely at some of the pieces, and finally to scrutinize the overall picture.

Some elements of the puzzle
Anger in God
Given what we know of our world, if we believe that God loves humanity as a whole and every human individual, it is hardly possible not to think of God as immensely angry and deeply grieved. As modern communications have given visual immediacy to so much of our world, our generation more than any other is confronted with the terrible reality of suffering. There is suffering which comes from the abuse of freedom, the savagery of human selfishness and greed. In such a context, how can God not be spoken of as furiously angered by suffering so brutally and callously inflicted on innocent victims— whom God holds precious, honoured, and loved (Isa 43:4). There is suffering which comes from the realm of nature: famine, disease, disaster. Faced with these, great or small, how can we speak of a loving God as other than grieving with us in our sorrow and our hurt.

Anger at God
Christian proclamation has always placed emphasis on the power of God, witness such liturgical address as, 'Almighty and everlasting God'. Confronted with human suffering and misery in its manifold forms, the conviction that God has the power to right all this leads naturally to anger at the God who has not righted it. Occasionally it is a diffuse anger at God for having created our world the way it is. More often, it is sharply and individually focused: why did God do this to me, why did God let this happen to me, where was God when I needed help?

Unconditional love and anger
Can we speak of God's anger while affirming God's unconditional love? Does language of God's anger suggest that the relationship of love has been broken? Does the language of God's unconditional love

project an image of an all-permissive all-condoning God—verging on the eminently wishy-washy?

Some of the pieces
The uses Israel makes of God's anger are quite remarkable. They extend far beyond the simple expression of anger. They repay close attention, although only a few can be touched on here.

God's anger and the world: the flood
Early in Israel's portrayal of the story of humankind, wickedness has become sufficiently widespread to drive God into destroying the human race in the flood. It is surely the most universally destructive display of the 'wrath of God'. Yet, surprisingly, there is no explicit mention of anger. Rather, the Yahwist speaks of God's sorrow and grief: 'the Lord was sorry that he had made man on the earth, and it grieved him to his heart' (Gen 6:5–7). The Priestly Writer has no reference to any emotion: 'I have determined to make an end of all flesh; for the earth is filled with violence through them' (Gen 6:13). So only grief and sorrow are explicit in what has all the potential for a very angry scene.

It is the outcome of the flood which is extraordinary. Both Yahwist (8:21–22) and Priestly Writer (9:1–17) conclude their accounts with God's commitment never again to act towards the human race in this destructive way. Even more remarkable is the fact that this commitment is given alongside acceptance of the flaws, frailty, and wickedness of a less-than-perfect world. In the Yahwist, it is bluntly explicit. Humankind is blotted out because 'every imagination of the thoughts of his heart was only evil continually' (6:5); it will never happen again, because God accepts that 'the imagination of man's heart is evil from his youth' (8:21). Human evil will no longer be the trigger for the divine destruction of humankind. Similarly, in the Priestly Writer after the flood, 'the fear of you and the dread of you' is on all the animal world, and murder is to be reckoned with in the human world (9:1–7)—it is clearly a second-best world. Yet it has God's guarantee that it will never again be destroyed by a flood (9:11).

The destructive action of God in the flood is narrated in order to express God's unconditional commitment to the existence of flawed and frail humankind.

God's anger and Israel: the desert generation

A similar phenomenon, where the anger of God is used to emphasize God's commitment, may be seen with regard to Israel itself. It is most remarkable that the Israelite narrator-theologians should twice have God threaten to annihilate Israel and start salvation history afresh with a new nation, descended this time from Moses. It happens once in the middle of the sojourn at Mount Sinai (Exod 32); it happens again in the middle of the journeying through the desert (Num 14).

The storytellers do not mince words. At Sinai, they have God say to Moses about Israel: 'Now therefore let me alone, that my wrath may burn hot against them and I may consume them; but of you I will make a great nation' (Exod 32:10); and in the desert: 'How long will this people despise me? . . . I will strike them with the pestilence and disinherit them, and I will make of you a nation greater and mightier than they' (Num 14:11-12). In this second case, Israel's alleged contempt for God is taken out of the category of occasional lapse and symbolized as a matter of permanent disposition: '(They) have put me to the proof these ten times and have not hearkened to my voice' (Num 14:22).

Each time Moses' intercession prevails (Exod 32:11-14; Num 14:13-25). Surely Israel has not retold these episodes as evidence of their own iniquity or of God's propensity to anger. Rather, these two critical episodes—one just after Sinai, the other just before the entry into the Promised Land—are used as witness to God's unshakable commitment to Israel, God's people.

God's anger and the prophets

The anger of God is not necessarily the first idea that comes to our minds in association with Israel's prophets. The school of thought which saw the prophets as God's messengers calling to repentance and reform, nobly spelling out the ideals of religious living, prevails in most people's minds over the image of the prophet as one who proclaimed the coming downfall of the nation, under the impact of divine anger. Yet this latter picture is closer to the reality of the pre-exilic prophets. Second Isaiah refers back to this anger before promising salvation for the future.

> For a brief moment I forsook you,
>   but with great compassion I will gather you.

> In overflowing wrath for a moment I hid my face from you,
>   but with everlasting love I will have compassion on you
>   (Isa 54:7–8).

The immense significance of this is that 'overflowing wrath' does not put an end to God's relationship with Israel. We speak often of the broken covenant; all too often we do not realize that the relationship to God remains unbroken, even unbreakable. We have only to listen to the one occasion on which a prophet clearly proclaims the relationship broken to realize just how rare it is. The prophet is Hosea and the proclamation is contained in the name of his third child, a name attributed directly to God.

> And the Lord said, 'Call his name Not-my-people,
>   for you are not my people and I am not your God.'
>   (Hos 1:9).

It is also vital to remember that this judgement is reversed in the very next verse: 'and in the place where it was said to them, "You are not my people", it shall be said to them, "Children of the living God" (Hos 1:10). In Amos's fifth and final vision, Israel is totally wiped out (Amos 9:1–4), but the visionary language does not have quite the disastrous impact of the direct speech of Hosea. In Isaiah and Ezekiel, while the imagery of devastation is almost total, some remnant is left to survive (cf Isa 6:9–13; Ezek 5:1–12). While there is anger and fury and fearful imagery, there is no declaration of irreparable rupture between God and Israel.

The scandal of God's anger in the Old Testament
The savagery of the expression given to God's anger in contexts like these can be felt as deeply scandalous. Yet we have to recall that it is language addressed to a people seen to be on the brink of disaster. The vividness and brutally shocking nature of the images and words can be understood as an attempt to break through the hardened shell of cynicism and apathy with which the people protected themselves from their prophets. We tend to think of religious apathy and scepticism as modern phenomena. The prophetic books make it abundantly clear that Israel's prophets were greeted in the same way by many.

For ourselves today, struggling with the fiery language of the prophets, there is need to recognize the inevitable tension between God's committed love and our human responsibility. We have been graced with God's love; we have been gifted with human freedom. Our acts have their consequences and God's love does not take those consequences away. The forces pilloried by Israel's pre-exilic prophets—lack of justice and loss of faith—were forces which destructively eroded Israel's national life from within. With people seized as slaves over debt or driven off their ancestral lands by vicious laws, injustice in society would have fast destroyed any sense of national cohesion, any social bonding that could give a conscript peasant army morale and the will to fight. Conscripts in any age do not fight to defend the lands which have been taken from them by an aristocratic elite. Similarly, religious infidelity would have eroded the beliefs which might have encouraged an army in the conviction that God was fighting for them. An Assyrian commander is portrayed undermining such faith with cruelly ironic propaganda: 'But if you say to me, "We rely on the Lord our God," is it not he whose high places and altars Hezekiah has removed' (2 Kg 18:22; for social justice in the same speech, see vv 31–32).

Israel was culpably involved in practices and processes which made the survival of its national independence in the tough political climate of the time so unlikely that its downfall was all but certain. Only a miracle, a massive change of attitude, might have prevented the collapse. The prophets pointed to the evils. They often spoke of God as the eventual destroyer. They were unable to pull off the miracle of national conversion. We cannot interrogate them on the specifics of their own theological understanding. We can only read between the lines of their texts—and the signals remain ambiguous. But we can say that often what they describe as God's wrath and anger is to be seen also as the evil effects and disastrous consequences of the misuse of human freedom and responsibility.[1]

The areas we have considered point to Israel's use of God's anger in remarkably subtle ways. With the flood, such anger allows expression to be given to God's unconditional commitment to humankind and the created world. With the desert generation, such anger allows the

---

1. For a fuller discussion of this aspect of prophetic theology, see chapter 13 of my *The Study Companion to Old Testament Literature* (Wilmington: Glazier, 1989).

communication of God's unshakable commitment to Israel. Both of these touch the issue of how anger relates to unconditional love. The language of the prophets, in particular, may have the effect for us of legitimating the use of highly human and analogical language in speaking of emotions and feelings in God. While it is not a matter of looking to Old or New Testament for clear teaching on issues of God's anger and grief, yet there is value in recognizing the considerable complexity of the use of God's anger in biblical expression. What is the most appropriate way for us to speak of God today?

God's anger and traditional theology
The issue of God's power is central to any talk of anger in relation to God, and God's power is inextricably bound to the question of human freedom. Karl Rahner expresses the traditional position with succinct clarity.

> The teaching of human freedom . . . and the teaching of an absolute sovereignty of God's freedom over human freedom cannot be resolved for us here and now into a higher synthesis. All the attempts to do this in Christian theology (in Augustine, Thomas, Calvin, Bañez, Molina) have been doomed to failure. One can only say that both teachings must be true and ultimately in their coexistence are nothing other than the highest way of expressing that an absolute God and a world distinct from him, yet real, can coexist because they actually do coexist.[2]

This is highest mystery. Before such mystery, we are compelled to remain tongue-tied and silent. The question has to be asked as to the theological grounds which require 'an absolute sovereignty of God's freedom over human freedom', granted God's gift of human freedom. But that query veers towards vast complexities of theological system–building, a detour we cannot take here. For us, the question remains whether, if tongue-tied and silent before such mystery, we must not also stammer, while aware of the inadequacy of our stammering.

---

2. Rahner, Karl: *Theological Investigations,* volume XXI *Science and Christian Faith* (London: Darton, Longman & Todd, 1988), 5.

The issue here is not to look at all the possible ways in which divine and human action might be imaged. The appeal to the analogy of 'the human relations of parent to child, lawgiver to subject, judge to judged' can be used to throw light on possible questions of principle.³ But it raises two dangers. One is the danger of trivializing and fatuity. Can analogies which point to lessons we can learn, or the good which can emerge from suffering, and the like, be mentioned credibly in contexts involving deep human suffering and anguish, whether on an individual or national scale? What happens to such analogies confronted with the unspeakable evil of the Holocaust? Here, surely, we can only speak of God's immense anger at the evil, of God's infinite grief for the victims; and we can only be silent as to why God was powerless to prevent such horror. The example of the book of Job cautions us against any attempt to encompass inexplicable evil in words. In this aspect of Job's case, both friends and Job failed; the answer does not lie in the dogmas of the friends, nor in Job's longing for adversarial debate with God. The second danger is the risk of trespassing on mystery. We have no analogies for an absolute sovereignty over human freedom which nevertheless leaves the human will absolutely free. Where this is claimed, it is sheerest mystery, far exceeding all attempt at explanation or clarification beyond simply setting the boundaries to understanding.

Some aspects of the picture—I: options for our language
Silence and mystery
If we believe that God has effectively retained absolute sovereignty over human freedom, there is little we can say about the 'why' for what happens in our world. If the ultimate control is God's, it should be apparent to us that we know next to nothing of the reasons governing the exercise of that control in its myriad specific instances. There is no point in language of God's anger or grief. Where there is absolute sovereignty, these words make little sense. Faith can correctly build up a picture of the parameters of this absolute sovereignty: benevolent creation, a deep and committed love, an ultimately right

---

3. See, for example, Mann, William E: 'God's Freedom, Human Freedom, and God's Responsibility for Sin', 182–210 in *Divine & Human Action: Essays in the Metaphysics of Theism*, edited by Thomas V Morris (Ithaca and London: Cornell University, 1988), especially 207–9.

outcome. Faith cannot enter into the details. There faith must be silent—mystery must be accepted with silence.

Words and inadequacy
At the same time, it is a human imperative to speak. The relationship with God is too important for faith to be reduced to silence in matters so central to existence. The very body-spirit reality of our human existence requires us to find words to express what is innermost to our being. If words are to be used, analogy is essential and the primary analogy has to be human relationships and human emotions—language of love and fidelity, of grief and anger, the language of Old and New Testament. The safeguard, both for human honesty and respect for the creator God, is constantly to be aware of the inadequacy of any language we may use. But speak we must, we can no other. Yet our speech will always be in human figures and we must always reckon with its inadequacy before the mystery and transcendence of God.

Some aspects of the picture—II: conclusions for our theological outlook
Anger in God
If we are to speak of God's love, we have to speak of God's anger and God's grief. How can the utterly horrendous happenings of human history, exemplified above all by the Holocaust, not be spoken of as causing immense divine anger? As we shift our gaze from crimes against humanity to those against communities, nations, or races, and then on to the violence visited on individuals in uncounted ways, how is it possible not to speak of God's anger. Where the actions are not those of sin and oppression but of frailty and failure, how can we not speak of God's grief at the folly of those whom we believe God so deeply loves?

Anger at God
With the amount of suffering and misery in our world, whether of national extent or individual intensity, it is hardly surprising that real anger is often felt towards God. How dare God have created such a world? Why does God not act to right such wrong? How dare God be powerless in such situations? Theologically appropriate or not, such anger is there. Emotions are not constrained by logic or theology, although they are related to our attitudes and basic beliefs. Where anger is felt towards God, it needs to be accepted, experienced, and

expressed; only then can it be dealt with helpfully. It may be only when acceptance is felt in the act itself of expressing fierce anger that unconditional love is experienced and known. But the danger of too blithe an acceptance of such anger is too facile an assumption of God's responsibility for what has gone amiss. That may be most unfair to God. It is also unfair to sufferers trapped in attitudes or basic beliefs which may not appropriately mirror God's reality.

In the silence of mystery, the place for anger at God is ambiguous. Where God is believed to be in absolute control, there is scope for anger; but where God is also believed to be absolutely loving, incapable of harming us, there is no reason for anger. In the inadequacy of words, where it makes no sense to speak of absolute sovereignty, it makes little sense to direct anger at God. If we do not attribute direct responsibility to God, why should we direct anger at God? It is logical enough to be angry with God for having brought into being a universe such as ours. But there again we must recognize the inadequacy of our words and the reality that we do not know if a better world could have been created with potential for fuller human life.

Where the powerlessness of God is assumed, the rug is largely pulled from under anger at God. It is hard to be angry with a God who grieves our pain. Where that anger is present, however, it must first be felt and handled creatively. After that is time enough to reflect on the theology underlying it all.

Unconditional love and anger
In all the complexity of theological reflection, a relatively simple choice has to be made between two fundamental metaphors we use of God. The choice really cannot be avoided and is immensely significant for a believer's attitudes towards God and life. The choice: whether God is thought of primarily as judge or as lover.

The Old Testament has been unjustly burdened with the God of wrath. The New Testament offers a mix of texts, although the balance tilts towards the image of lover. The core of faith, inspired by the parables, aided by the Johannine letters and abetted by Paul, has always opted for the primacy of the metaphor of lover. But the trappings of religious practice, in attitude and prayer and ritual, have all too often brought the metaphor of judge to the fore. It is a much needed grace in our threatened generation that the metaphor of God as lover has once again been given its due primacy.

Thought of as lover, God must be spoken of as angered and angry, for anger is the appropriate response to injustice inflicted on those who are loved. Thought of as lover, God must be spoken of as grieving and saddened, for grief and sadness are the appropriate response when those who are loved suffer or sin. Our human response to the same situations is one of sorrow and honest shame. Love does not prevent the pain and hurt when there has been betrayal; love offers forgiveness, the healing of hurt, and the deepened bonding of relationship. As Second Isaiah marvellously characterizes God:

> I, I am He who blots out your transgressions for my own sake,
> and I will not remember your sins (Isa 43:25).

The metaphor of God as lover does not take away human responsibility for the consequences of our choices. If we act stupidly or destructively, we are still loved but our own selves, our lives or the lives of others are destructively affected—now, and perhaps into eternity. The human seriousness of life is not diminished by the metaphor of God as lover. Indeed, as we allow the conviction of our being unconditionally loved by God to deepen, every instant of life becomes infinitely precious—to experience that love in all the depth of life while there is yet time. To be unconditionally loved by God is no license for lesser living or evil-doing, unless the shallowness of one's understanding of love is intolerably thin. There is no greater bond than love that knows no bounds.

Just as there is a place for the human response of shame and sorrow, so there is a place for anger and the fear of anger. We know the reality of anger between those who deeply love—and its value. We fear to anger those we love, partly because of the pain and hurt we cause them, partly too because we fear to erode and perhaps lose their love. We desire not to anger those who love us; how much stronger that desire when the lover is God.

In these reflections, we have not finished our puzzle and filled in the whole picture; not all options have been canvassed. But we have looked closely at some of the pieces and how they do or do not fit together. Confusion may be lessened and the expression of our faith enhanced by bringing the language we may and must use of God into sharp focus against that background of theological understanding where mystery remains. Responsible acceptance of God's unconditional love immeasurably deepens and enlivens our relationship with God. Recognition of what is left in uncomprehended silence keeps intact respect for the mystery of God.

The Growth of Joshua 1–12 and The Theology of Extermination

(Original: *Reading the Hebrew Bible for A New Millennium*)

'Growth-of-text' is certainly not flavor-of-the-month at the moment in exegetical circles. This article hews close to the contours of the present text, not attempting to go any further back into the history of the text than the pre–dtr level represented by Joshua 2. Joshua 1 provides the introduction to the deuteronomistic text of the book of Joshua.[1] It is a possibility worth considering that Joshua 2 provides the introduction to an earlier narrative version, with a significantly different presentation of the traditions. Identification of this possible narrative raises issues around the development of a theology of extermination.

What is argued here is a possibility that opens new avenues for understanding the text and theology of the book of Joshua. If exaggeration may be allowed to sharpen the point, the narrative begun in Joshua 2, with traces in chapters 3–4 and 6 and the substance of chapters 8–10, offers a presentation in which Joshua's Israel occupies much of the south by military or political action—with a little bit of help from God. Further developments change this presentation to one in which God's action gives the whole land to Joshua's Israel— with a little bit of help from them. This involves grafting the three sacral stories of Joshua 3–4, 6, and 7 into the narrative of the south and, simultaneously or separately, portraying a conquest of the north (within chapters 11–12). Later developments include the level of

---

1. V Fritz, in the new HAT commentary on Joshua, does not represent text earlier than the basic level of the Deuteronomistic History (*Das Buch Josua*, HAT I/7 [Tübingen: Mohr 1994]). This study explores the earlier 'Joshua 2' level, but does not investigate the prehistory of the texts that make up this level. For a professional monograph, grappling with the puzzling contradiction of dream and reality, see G Mitchell, *Together in the Land: A Reading of the Book of Joshua*, JSOTSup 134 (Sheffield: JSOT Press, 1993).

the Deuteronomistic History, the insistence on extermination of the locals, and the emphasis on the contribution and rights of the transjordan tribes (Reuben, Gad, and half Manasseh). Prehistory before the 'Joshua 2' level is not explored. A claim for definitive demonstration is not made. A claim is made for the possibility and legitimacy of this reading. What is explored are the avenues opened by such an understanding of the text.

Joshua 2 offers a picture that contrasts radically with the sacral context of the stories in chapters 3-7 in which God's action moves the world in ways that are wonderful to behold. In the narrative of Joshua 2, spies are sent out to view the land; quite unnecessary in a sacral context. The spies head for the Jericho brothel; a trifle out of place in a sacral context. The king demands the men and the prostitute, Rahab, lies to deflect his demand; unlikely in a sacral context. Rahab bargains with the men she has saved; the men fill in the fine print of the contract. Such bargaining ill befits the sacral. Finally the spies evade their pursuers for three days before returning to Joshua with assurances of success. This chapter has been dismissed as incompatible with the sacral stories to come.[2] It is worth while exploring whether it might be the other way around: the sacral stories are to be put on hold and the context of Joshua 2 retained.

My concern is to explore text, not to eliminate shameful theology and not to reconstruct events.[3] My intention is not to claim definitive interpretation but to point to possibilities.

---

2. J Van Seters: 'The story of Rahab ... Is Not the Beginning of the Earliest Conquest Account but a Later Addition and Fits Rather Awkwardly Within its Context' ('Joshua's Campaign of Canaan and Near Eastern Historiography', in *SJOT*, 4 (1990): 2/1-12, see 3. See also Van Seters, *In Search of History* (New Haven: Yale University Press, 1983), 325. For balance, see JK Hoffmeier, 'The Structure of Joshua 1-11 and the Annals of Thutmose III', in AR Millard *et al* (eds) *Faith, Tradition, and History: Old Testament Historiography in Its Near Eastern Context* (Winona Lake: Eisenbrauns, 1994), 165-79. More recently, Jacques Briend: Joshua 2 came into the narrative at a late date but before the deuteronomistic redaction ('Les sources de l'histoire deuteronomique: recherches sur Jos 1-12', in *Israël construit son histoire: l'historiographie deutéronomiste à la lumière des recherches récentes* (edited by A de Pury *et al* (Geneva: Labor et Fides, 1996), 343-74, see 357. Briend's analyses often nudge the possible beyond the necessary. He speaks, however, of 'une yahvisation du récit ancien' (351).
3. It would be unhelpful to discuss here issues of the emergence of Israel in Canaan. See now Diana Edelman (editor), 'Toward a Consensus on the Emergence of Israel in Canaan', in *SJOT* 5 (1991): 2/1-116.

What led me to push a little deeper into these unpleasant realms was an evening's discussion with Rolf Knierim. Knierim was waxing eloquent about that strand in the book of Deuteronomy that is insistent on the absolute purity of Israel. Did the passion that focused on the exclusive worship of YHWH, God of Israel, and on the temple in Jerusalem lead to a fanaticism that demanded the exclusion from Israel of all that did not meet a certain standard? It was only a question but the fact of asking it implied that certain parts of Deuteronomy could possibly be traced to an unacceptable fanaticism. Suddenly Knierim stopped in his tracks. 'What am I saying? I am a former student and colleague of Gerhard von Rad's; I am an admirer of Gerhard von Rad. For von Rad, Deuteronomy was the zenith of the Old Testament. Now I hear myself saying that Deuteronomy was the Old Testament's nadir.'

It is appropriate that this study should be part of a volume associated with the exegetical method and theological concerns of Rolf Knierim.

The pre–dtr 'Joshua 2' narrative
Joshua 2. Belonging in the 'Joshua 2' narrative from this chapter are probably: vv 1–9, 12–24.
An opening is needed, such as the innocuous 'After the death of Moses' (1:1). The narrative has the (whole) land in view and Joshua as the leader (cf 2:1). In the horizon of this chapter, and of this 'Joshua 2' narrative, the action is focused on Joshua and Israel rather than on YHWH. Rahab confesses, 'I know that the LORD has given you the land' (2:9) and the spies report to Joshua, 'truly the LORD has given all the land into our hands' (2:24); so the glory is given to the LORD. The action, however, is undertaken by Joshua and Israel. As in the case of Ehud, Jael, and Gideon (Judg 3; 4; and 7), while Israel's national deliverance may be attributed to the LORD, the acts are those of brave and courageous individuals. God is expected to go out with the armies; this is ancient Near Eastern narrative, not modern secular humanist atheism. All the more striking to realize that here, as in so many battle reports, it is Israel that is to the fore in the story, while it is YHWH who gives the victory.[4]

---

4. For wide biblical echoes that may be heard in the Rahab story, see T Frymer-Kensky, 'Reading Rahab', in M Cogan *et al* (editors), *Tehillah le-Moshe: Biblical*

In the narrative, the king of Jericho is involved, with a concern that extends beyond his own city to 'the land' (2:2). Rahab, described as a prostitute, is given the faith statement that 'the LORD has given you the land'; the context again extends beyond Jericho and the fear expressed is of Israel ('you') rather than of the LORD (2:9). As is well-known, Rahab's silence is obtained in a bargain that seems to envisage military capture and street-fighting rather than a collapse of the town's walls (2:17–21).

Later than the 'Joshua 2' narrative here may be: 2:10–11, attributed to dtr editing.
In v 10, Sihon and Og are mentioned together, probably an indication of later deuteronomistic origin.[5] In v 11b, a confession of God's nature is given that is almost identical with Deuteronomy 4:39, a secondary dtr text (cf also 1 Kgs 8:23). In the light of these signals, it is appropriate to attribute vv 10–11 to dtr editing. The reference to the Red Sea (2:10a) recurs in 4:23; the arguments for the secondary status of the crossing account may reinforce the secondary status of 2:10–11 here.

The impact of vv 10–11 is to heighten Rahab's confessional statement, bringing it into more explicit harmony with the preceding history and the sacral stories to come.

Joshua 3–4 Belonging to the 'Joshua 2' narrative from these chapters are probably: 3:1; 4:10b, 13.
As is well-known, there is nothing about these verses that is particularly appropriate to their context. That they would belong to the beginning and end of an account coherent with the military preparations undertaken in Joshua 2 is possible. Any coherence with Joshua 3–4 can only be obtained with difficulty. If a military story of crossing followed Joshua 2, as 4:10b and 4:13 suggest, it has been suppressed in favor of the present sacral version.[6]

---

and Judaic Studies in Honor of Moshe Greenberg (Winona Lake: Eisenbrauns, 1997), 57–68. Note also N Winther-Nielsen, *A Functional Discourse Grammar of Joshua: A Computer-assisted Rhetorical Structure Analysis* (Stockholm: Almqvist & Wiksell, 1995), especially 105–65. The detail of input does not generate a correlative outcome.

5. Cf Deut 1:4; 29:7; 31:4 apparently later dtr revision.
6. The prior element demanded by Briend for 'rose early in the morning' ('Sources',

Later than the 'Joshua 2' narrative here may be: 3:2–17; 4:1–10a, 11–12, 14–24, attributed to the sacral story of the Jordan crossing and subsequent editing.

The difficulties of these chapters are legion.[7] What is clear and beyond doubt is the sacral character of the narrative.[8] The ark of the covenant is central to the action; its movement initiates the people's (3:3), its arrival at the Jordan initiates the river's stoppage (3:13–16), its emergence from the Jordan allows the river's flow to resume (4:18). The people are sanctified for the occasion (3:5). Due distance, about a kilometre, is maintained between the people and the ark (3:4). Two sanctuary explanations are associated with the narrative (4:6–7 and 20-24); also two sanctuaries (in the middle of the Jordan, 4:9; where Israel camped, 4:8 and 19). Expansions within the text are possible. For example, 3:10 with its list of seven local nations and its repeated 'and Joshua said' might well be a later insertion (for this full list of seven, see also Deuteronomy 7:1 and Josh 24:11).

The exact nature of this text (3:2–17; 4:1–10a, 11–12, 14–24) may escape us.[9] Its original coherence with Joshua 2 is seriously doubtful. For its significance within the present text, see the discussion below, under the rubric of the 'sacral stories' expansion. Subsequent editing includes the Dtr (3:7–8; 4:14), the list of locals (3:10), and the reference to the trans–jordan tribes (4:12).

Joshua 5. None of the verses in this chapter calls for inclusion in the 'Joshua 2' narrative. In Noth's view, superseded to some extent by what is proposed here, the 'collector' who had shaped and introduced

---

356) is supplied by ch. 2.
7. The 'three days' (3:1) is scarcely one of these, despite Van Seters ('Joshua's Campaign', 3; *Search*, 325). Real time and storytelling time do not always coincide.
8. It has been argued that the idea of a liturgy here is absurd; how would the Jordan be stopped? Such an objection has never encountered Christians waving twigs and singing Palm Sunday songs. A ritual procession arriving at the unstoppable Jordan witnesses to the power of God who alone could and did once stop these waters at the appropriate moment. Ritual and symbol are not to be confused with rational discourse or the realistic rehearsal of significant events. What is to be evoked is more the significance and less the event.
9. For a fuller treatment, see AF Campbell, *The Study Companion to Old Testament Literature* (Collegeville: Liturgical Press, 1989/1992), 173–77. Once the military parts are eliminated, the remainder may be best understood as directions and variations for a liturgical celebration.

Joshua 2 could be identified in 5:1 (as also in 6:27; 9:3 – 4a*, 10:2, 5, 40–42; 11:1–2, 16–20). The mark of the collector was, above all, the drawing together of the individual stories into a broader picture. So, in 5:1, the mention of the kings of east and west witnessed to the extent intended for the portrayal of the conquest.[10] The traditions of Joshua 5—the circumcision after the wilderness sojourn (vv 2–9), the observance of passover and the end of the manna (vv 10–12), and Joshua's encounter with the 'commander of the army of the LORD' (vv 13–15)—belong at the point of transition between the wilderness and the land.[11] They have no specific association with the narrative prepared for in Joshua 2; while they belong where they are, they seem likely to reflect later concerns.

Joshua 6. Belonging to the 'Joshua 2' narrative from this chapter are probably: vv 1–2, 21–24a.
The story begins with the report of siege conditions (6:1); Jericho's 'king and soldiers' are to be handed over to Joshua by the LORD (6:2). What follows does not make any reference to the siege; the 'king and soldiers' are not heard of again. As the start to a story of military action, vv 1–2 are perfectly plausible. The tradition alluded to in Judges 1:23–25 is, of course, illustrative of how a town might have been taken. The Rahab story, with its 'crimson cord in the window' (2:21), evidently has a scenario in mind where a visual signal was significant for those outside the town. We would expect that v 2 was once followed by something equivalent to v 17 (perhaps with more detail, as in v 21).

The placement of Joshua's instructions for the ban between his command to shout (v 16) and the people's shout (v 20) is odd. As noted, if the ban were important to the story, it might be expected earlier. As it stands, the instructions seem more important for the story of Achan that follows. There is no such reason to exclude vv 21–24a. They report that the inhabitants of the city, animal and

---

10. M Noth, *Das Buch Josua*, HAT 7, second edition (Tübingen: Mohr, 1953) 12; also 29.
11. The command to Joshua to remove his sandals echoes the command to Moses (Exod 3:5); its focus is on the figure of Joshua rather than the future campaign (despite Van Seters, 'Joshua's Campaign', 9–11; cf Briend, 'Sources', 353). The drawn sword suggests a military context; the command does not offer one.

human, were put to the ban and the city burned. Joshua's orders to the two spies fit fully with the story of Joshua 2; there is no attempt to correlate the collapse of the town wall with the prostitute's house in chapter 2 and its window on the outer side of the wall (2:15; LXX lacks details but has the basics, cf vv 15 and 18 of LXX). These verses can belong with a story of military capture.

Later than the 'Joshua 2 narrative here may be: 6:3–20, 24b–27, attributed to the sacral story of the capture of Jericho and the integration of chapter 7, as well as some subsequent editing.
 There is good reason why this material should be seen as belonging in a sacral context and be excluded from any military narrative. There are plenty of soldiers in vv 3–20, but they are busier processing than besieging. The 'seven priests bearing seven trumpets' (vv 4, 6, 8 13) seem just as important. The ark of the covenant plays a central role. What makes this a sacral story, above all, is that it is not a story of military daring or skill, supported and brought to success by YHWH; it is a story of what is exclusively YHWH's action, orchestrated to coincide with Joshua's processions. As is well-known, there is a tension between the noisy circuits with a trumpet blast signalling the people's shout (cf vv 4–5, 20b) and the silent circuits with Joshua's command signaling the people's shout (cf vv 10, 20a).[12]

In particular, vv 17–19 stand out as intervening between Joshua's command and the people's shout. Verse 18 is pointing directly toward chapter 7. Verse 17 is necessary, if v 18 is to refer to 'the things devoted to destruction'. While the introduction of vv 17–18 (19) may seem clumsy, the interruption serves as a signal pointing to the subsequent introduction of the Achan episode. As to v 19, we have no reference to any treasuries earlier than those of the kings or the temple, starting with Solomon. At some point, it would seem that Joshua could not be thought to have done less than David (2 Sam 8:11).

The subsequent editing can be attributed to the Dtr. Verses 24b–27 begin with the same reference as v 19. The note on Rahab goes beyond v 23 to add that 'her family has lived in Israel ever since (v 25). The spies are referred to as 'messengers', distinguishing this material from the preceding stories. Joshua's curse (v 26) could have been recorded at any time and in any context. Its attribution is immaterial to the

---

12. For a fuller treatment, see Campbell, *Study Companion*, 177–81.

present concerns. Joshua's fame (v 27) fits better with 3:7-8 than with the horizon of Joshua 2.

Joshua 7–8. Belonging to the 'Joshua 2' narrative from these chapters are probably: 8:1–29 (with the exception of 'as before' in vv 5 and 6).
On close inspection, the story of Achan's breach of the ban, in Joshua 7, appears far closer to the other two sacral stories (the crossing of the Jordan and the capture of Jericho) than it does to the story it is associated with, the attack on Ai (Joshua 8:1–29).[13]

With the attack on Ai, the narrative moves the conquest out of the Jordan valley and up into the hill country, but still within the territory of Benjamin. As at the start of the 'military capture' of Jericho (6:1–2), king and army are to be handed over to Joshua. The ban is mentioned early (v 2), as might have been expected in the Jericho narrative. The ban carried out at Jericho included 'men and women, young and old, oxen, sheep, and donkeys' (6:21). For Ai, spoil and livestock are exempted (8:2, 27). There is no mention of Achan's folly. It is as if Jericho bore the initial symbolism of total ban, total dedication to Israel's God, and the subsequent experiences in the narrative could be relaxed once the high point had been established. Yet, ironically in view of what is to come, there was a flaw in the total ban: consciously, Rahab and her family were exempted from the ban. The man who let the house of Joseph into Bethel subsequently left the territory (Judg 1:26). The Gibeonites will later claim to have come from 'a far country' (9:6). They live in Israel's midst, by deceit. Rahab will live in Israel's midst, by the conscious commitment of the spies and of Israel.

In 8:3–9, the strategy is plotted and preparations executed; in vv 10–23, the successful carrying through of this strategy is narrated; finally, in vv 24–29, the fate of Ai and its inhabitants is reported. It is a story of battle, Joshua's battle, with some support from the LORD. As noted above, the strategy is twice referred back to chapter 7 ('as before' in 8: 5 and 6). Within chapter 7, the strategy is not discussed; within chapter 8, the references are not continued when the strategy is being implemented.

Several moments in the story of chapter 8 suggest that the attack on Ai is being told for the first time. In v 1, there is no hint that this

---

13. For Van Seters too, though with differences, Joshua 7 is an addition ('Joshua's Campaign', 4).

is a second battle. 'Go up now to Ai' in the NRSV's translation has no suggestion that they are going up for a second time; the Hebrew—which has no 'now'—is fully compatible with a first time. 'See, I have handed over to you the king of Ai . . .' has no 'this time' or anything equivalent to suggest that a defeat has just been experienced by Israel.

Later than the 'Joshua 2' narrative here may be: 7:1–26; the phrase 'as before' in 8:5 and 6; and 8:30–35—the first as a sacral story, the second as redactional, and the third as a late dtr passage.
Joshua 7:1–26 is not a story of battle. Apart from the reference to the few troops needed (7:3), a report of the so-called battle is found only in 7:4—they went up and they fled! The extent of the defeat is chronicled in v 5. The rest of the chapter focuses on the breach in the sacral ordinance of the ban. Chapter 7 is a story where the sacral is central. The fate of a people in battle is determined by one individual's breach of sacred regulations. The atmosphere is the same as in 1 Samuel 14. Verses 6–15 are taken up with the cause of the disaster. Verses 10–15 are devoted to a speech of the LORD. Verses 16–26 are taken up with the identification and punishment of Achan, 'the one who sinned against the LORD God of Israel' (v 20).

To have a sense of the direction that such a text is taking, it is worth noting where responsibility is located. Joshua's prayer begins: 'Ah, Lord GOD! Why have you brought this people across the Jordan at all' (v 7). His prayer concludes: 'Then what will you do for your great name?' (v 9). The protagonist in this portrayal is YHWH. This is not action where YHWH is supporting Joshua as leader of Israel; it is action where YHWH is taking the lead on behalf of Joshua and Israel.

Joshua 7:1 reads like a summary, anticipating the story. The breach of faith is not raised in the text until the LORD's speech; Achan is not identified until v 19; the anger of the LORD is first referred to at its end (v 26; it is only mentioned in Joshua at 7:1, 26; and 23:16). 'Breach of faith' is scarcely a dtr term (cf Deut 32:51 and Josh 7:1; 22:16, 20, 22, 31). Probably 7:1 derives from the editor who inserted the sacral stories into the 'Joshua 2' narrative, but only probably. The reference to transgression of YHWH's covenant in vv 11 and 15 is strongly mirrored in Joshua 23:16.

The phrase 'as before' in 8:5 and 6 is what would be expected when combining chapters 7 and 8. It is present in the strategic plotting, but not in the actual narrative of battle.

Josh 8:30–35 is attributed by Noth to his Deuteronomistic History; the passage may be even later.[14]

Joshua 9. Belonging to the 'Joshua 2' narrative from this chapter are probably: vv 3–9, 11–15a, 16–17, 22–23, 25*–27a.
Joshua 9:1–2 is not easily characterized. In much the same fashion as 7:1, it reads like a summary anticipating what is to come. The six-item list of locals is found here and Deuteronomy 20:17; Joshua 11:3; 12:8; and Judges 3:5 (also five secondary occurrences in Exod—3:8, 17; 23:23; 33:2; 34:11; the seven-item list, including the Girgashites, is found only at Deut 7:1; Josh 3:10; 24:11). The list itself can scarcely be determinative of the origins of the surrounding text. The text refers to kings; the list refers to local peoples. For this reason, the list is likely to be an insertion (cf Josh 9:1, 11:3; 12:8). Furthermore, 9:1–2 casts its net far wider than merely Gibeon. The wider context is not present when the narrative turns to 9:3. It is worth noting that the Hebrew construction (when they/he heard) is identical at the start of 9:1, 10:1, and 11:1; it is not the same in 9:3. Strange as it may seem, there is a reasonable probability that 9:1–2 has 11:1ff. in view. In that case, it is probably to be associated also with the list of kings in 12:7–24.

Like many of the older texts, the Gibeonite story has its own share of difficulties that need not be discussed here; they are not relevant to the present concern.[15]

Later than the 'Joshua 2' narrative here may be: 9:1–2, 10, 15b, 18–21, 24* 27b.
Verses 1–2 have already been discussed. Verse 10, with both Sihon and Og, is regarded as later dtr revision. The text associated with the 'leaders of the congregation' (vv 15b, 18-21) is almost certainly late; the term is late and almost exclusively priestly. In Joshua, Moses

---

14. M Noth, *The Deuteronomistic History*, second edition JSOTSup 15 (Sheffield: JSOT, 1991), 63–64. For M O'Brien, Joshua 8:30–35 is later than the DH (*The Deuteronomistic History Hypothesis: A Reassessment*, OBO 92 (Freiburg Schweiz: Universitätsverlag, 1989], 70, 79).
15. See John Gray, *Joshua, Judges and Ruth* (NCB; London: Nelson, 1967), 97–104; J Alberto Soggin, *Joshua*, OTL (London: SCM, 1972); French original, 1970, 109–14; RK Sutherland, 'Israelite Political Theories in Joshua 9', *JSOT*, 53 (1992): 65–74; and more recently, Briend, 'Sources', 344–47, 364–66. Soggin comments, 'the story of the ruse itself contains evident confusions' (111).

as God's servant is a favourite of late (dtr) editing; the substance of v 24 is likely to be late. The final clause of v 27b is to be attributed to the Deuteronomist.[16] The last reference to Gibeon/Gibeonites in the Deuteronomistic History is at 1 Kings 9:2; it is likely, therefore, that their role as 'hewers of wood and drawers of water' for the altar belongs in the original narrative, rather than being added later.

Joshua 10. Belonging to the 'Joshua 2' narrative from this chapter are probably: vv 1–27, 42–43.
The story of the Jerusalem coalition speaks of Ai, Jericho, and Gibeon (10:1–2); it is an appropriate continuation of these stories. The five kings and their towns are named: Jerusalem, Hebron, Jarmuth, Lachish, and Eglon (vv3 and 5). Joshua and the army are located in camp at Gilgal (vv 6–7, 9). The text appears to include variant versions for the storyteller. In 10:15, Joshua and all Israel return to the camp at Gilgal; all would appear to be over. In vv 16–21, the five kings are trapped and the pursuit is still in progress; when concluded, the people (or army) return to Joshua at Makkedah. By this account, the return to Gilgal is achieved in 10:43. The text presents an unpleasantly vivid account of how partisans deal with their prisoners.[17] At the same time, God's support is regularly evident and the associated miracles have entered into folklore (10:10–14).[18] However, what occurred is explicitly dissociated from anything 'before or since' (v 14).

A conclusion to this story is found in 10:42–43. It is appropriate to the coalition story. Joshua has vanquished five kings at one stroke (v 42); he and the army return to Gilgal, whence they had come (v 43; cf 10:6–7). The sequence of these verses brings out what has been the

---

16. See Noth, *Deuteronomistic History*, 64.
17. Noth attributes 10:25 to the Dtr, as an embellishment of the old story (*Deuteronomistic History*, 64). The action (v 24) requires some form of utterance to accompany it. The insertion of a single verse has to be suspect here. The pair of imperatives, 'be strong and courageous', appear in almost exclusively dtr contexts; however, here it is scarcely a commissioning. Sensitive comments on the pair are given in ch. 7 of Lori L. Rowlett, *Joshua and the Rhetoric of Violence: A New Historicist Analysis*, JSOTSup 226 (Sheffield: Sheffield Academic Press, 1996), 156–80.
18. See JH Walton, 'Joshua 10:12–15 and Mesopotamian Celestial Omen Texts', in AR Millard *et al* (eds) *Faith, Tradition, and History: Old Testament Historiography in Its Near Eastern Context* (Winona Lake: Eisenbrauns, 1994), 181–90; B Margalit, 'The day the sun did not stand still: a new look at Joshua x 8–15', in *VT*, 42 (1992): 466–91.

underlying tone of this narrative since Joshua 2: Joshua was successful, because the LORD God of Israel fought for Israel. The protagonist is Joshua; the supporting role is played by God.

Later than the 'Joshua 2' narrative here may be: 10:28–41, as an expansion of the dtr narrative.

The list-like quality of these verses is evident. They deal with six southern towns: Makkedah, Libnah, Lachish, Eglon, Hebron, and Debir. Three of these figured in the Jerusalem coalition. The kings of four are reported as killed. Only the king of Hebron is listed as killed with the five (v 23) and also in this campaign (v 37); the other two from the coalition, the kings of Lachish and Eglon, are not mentioned (cf vv 32, 35). An analysis of the language used shows that the concern for *herem* and extermination in these verses is denser and more marked than anywhere else.[19]

The language of *herem* is used for Makkedah (v 28), Eglon (v 35), Hebron (v 37), and Debir (v 39), as well as in the final summary (v 40). Apart from 2:10 (dtr), occurrences associated with the story of Achan (6:17, 18; 7:1, 11, 12, 13, 15), and secondary occurrences in chapter 11 (vv 11, 12, 20, 21), the *herem* language occurs only once in relation to Jericho (6:21), once for Ai (8:26), and once in relation to Ai and by implication Jericho (10:1). This puts 10:28-41 in a remarkably special category. Form-critically, it is a list not a story. Six towns are in the list; *herem* language is used for four of them. Even the four occurrences in chapter 11 bear no resemblance to this density. Note also that both Lachish and Libnah are brought within the ban (*herem*) by association with Eglon (v 35) and Debir (v 39) respectively. In this way, all six town are involved.

The language of extermination is even more intense. The phrase *hish<ir sarid* is often rendered 'left no one remaining.' It is used for four of the six towns (Makkedah, Libnah, Hebron, and Debir), for the army of Horam of Gezer (v 33), and in the final summary (v 40). It

---

19. The language is analysed in its 'stereotyped syntagms' in K Lawson Younger, Jr, 'The "Conquest" of the South (Jos 10:28–39)', in *BZ*, 39 (1995) 255-64. His comment that 'these syntagms function as broad sweeping statements of victory to create an image of complete conquest for ideological reasons. They overstate matters for emphasis and persuasion' (261) may be helpful and right. It does not change the fact that the language here is not found with similar stereotyped density elsewhere.

is absent for Lachish and Eglon, the two towns either side of Horam's defeat.[20] Once again, association with other towns (Libnah, directly v 32 and indirectly v 35) paints an all-embracing picture. Otherwise, this language is only used in Joshua for the battle report at Ai (8:22) and in secondary material at 11:8. The language of 'putting to the edge of the sword' is also packed densely into 10:28–41. It is used for all six of the towns (10:28, 30, 32, 35, 37, 39). Beyond these, it occurs once for Jericho (6:21) and once for the battle over Ai (8:24), and three times in chapter 11 (vv 11, 12, 14).

What these linguistic observations spell out is what a careful reader will have realised instinctively: the list of towns in 10:28–39 is quite different from the stories earlier in the book. What the language makes unpleasantly clear is the massive emphasis on total destruction in these verses, the emphasis on annihilation or extermination. Once this passage's marked difference in language density and emphasis is noted, it is perfectly possible for it to be seen as a separate development.[21]

In contrast with vv 42–43, vv 40–41 have a wide vision ('the whole land', with details), an emphasis on extermination and *herem*, and a concern for God's command. Verse 41 covers the extent of the southern campaign, from Kadesh-barnea to Gibeon; the pronoun 'them' binds it syntactically to v. 40. These two verses (vv 40–41) are the conclusion to the list in 10:28–39. Verses 42–43 constitute the conclusion to 10:1–27.

Joshua 11–12

It was at quite a late stage in the preparation of this paper that my suspicions were aroused whether any of Joshua 11–12 should be seen as original and so included in the 'Joshua 2' narrative. On closer inspection of the text, my suspicions were deepened and it seemed likely that none of the material from these two chapters belonged in the 'Joshua 2' narrative.

---

20. This pattern reinforces Younger's claim for a palistrophe or chiasm in these verses, emphasizing Gezer ('"Conquest" of the South', 260). R David provides a valuable analysis of the elements on 212–13 of 'Jos 10:28–39, témoin d'une conquête de la Palestine par le sud?', in *ScEs*, 42 (1990): 209–22.

21. The comment by Rowlett can be applied with particular force to these verses: 'Identity was being reasserted in the Joshua story, but it was done by adopting the violent ideology of the oppressors. The same ideology that had undermined their identity was now being used to exert their identity' (*Rhetoric of Violence*, 183).

Three pointers give rise to this suspicion. Pointer No 1 is the absence of any reference to Joshua's whereabouts. The LORD speaks to him (11:6) and Joshua and his army—last heard of at Gilgal (10:43, MT only; LXX not since 10:6–7, 9)—'suddenly' fall on the foe at Merom, far to the north in Galilee (v 7). Pointer No 2 is the vagueness of the introduction ('when Jabin heard', 11:1). Heard what? The NRSV adds an object, 'of this', where the Hebrew does not have it. In this, 11:1 parallels the secondary 9:1 (where again the NRSV has added an 'of this'); in 10:1, the object is mentioned, 'how Joshua had taken Ai'. Pointer No 3 is the preference given to the LORD as protagonist rather than Joshua. The case is not as clear as it is for the 'sacral stories'; hamstringing horses and burning chariots are good tactics. But before this, the LORD promises to give them 'slain' to Israel (v. 6, *halalim*); after it, 'the LORD handed them over to Israel' (v. 8). On balance, the victory is the LORD's, with a little bit of help from Joshua and Israel.

Any one of these pointers on its own might have been dismissed or explained away. Taken together, they give rise to grave suspicion. The fact that Jabin of Hazor/Canaan figures in the Deborah/Barak story (Judg 4:2, 23–24) may be significant but cannot be pursued here.

The conclusion to this account can be found in vv 16–19 and 23. 11:3 gives the same list of six local peoples as 9:1 and 12:8b (cf also Judg 3:5). The list of peoples sits uncomfortably with the appeal that is sent out to kings not peoples (cf 12:8b for similar discomfort). The emphasis and linguistic features that marked 10:28–41 recur in 11:8b–15—no survivors remain, they were struck down with the edge of the sword, the ban is in force. It is likely that 11:8b–15 belongs on the same level with 10:28–41.

11:20 has to be a separate note. God's hardening of hearts occurs only here and in Exodus (4:21; 9:12; 10:20, 27; 11:10; 14:4, 8, 17; but cf Isa 6:10).[22] The language of the ban recurs in the verse, as well as the theme of extermination; but the language of no survivors left remaining is not used. The use of *tehinna* here for 'mercy' or 'favor' has only one parallel and it is late (Ezra 9:8); otherwise the meaning is 'plea' or 'supplication'. All these signals point to the verse as a later

---

22. According to Noth's source division, 4:21 (supplementary) and 10:20, 27 (both supplementary) are found within J; 9:12 (plague of boils); 11:10 (supplementary); and 14:4, 8, 18 (Sea of Reeds) are found within P (cf AF Campbell and MA O'Brien, *Sources of the Pentateuch: Texts, Introductions, Annotations* [Minneapolis: Fortress, 1993]).

addition.

11:21–22, as a note on the Anakim, is one of those bits of tradition that it is difficult to identify with any precision; an association with the Joshua text is possible at almost any time. Concern with the Anakim, not to be confused with 'the descendants of the giants' (mentioned in 2 Sam 21:15-21), is restricted to the books of Deuteronomy and Joshua, often in association with the fear of foes 'stronger and taller than we' (Deut 1:28). There are pointers suggesting the verses may have been added along with 10:28-41 and 11:8b–15. First, there is the temporal note, 'at that time', found above in 11:10 and otherwise in the book of Joshua only in the equally secondary 5:1 and 6:26. The concern for utter destruction (herem) and those left remaining is also present (twice in v 22, with the positive and negative language reversed).

12:1–6 are concerned with the transjordan tribes (see below). 12:7–24 (with the exception of the later list in v 8b) shows an interest in kings and in the total conquest, including the kings of the northern coalition. The Dtr shows no interest in kings. The total conquest, including the north, betrays an interest beyond that of the 'Joshua 2' narrative. The list of kings is best associated with the expansions in 11:1–8a, 16–19, and 23.

The 'sacral stories' expansion
Under this rubric, we can treat the Jordan crossing, the Jericho capture, the Achan story, and the material just noted as an expansion beyond the 'Joshua 2' narrative (that is, Josh 11:1–8a, 16–19, 23; 12:7–8a, 9–24). The so-called 'expansion' need not have been made at the same time that the 'sacral stories' were inserted into the text. Nevertheless, it is convenient to deal with both groups together.

What the addition of this material does has already been noted: it moves the emphasis of the presentation from the action of Joshua's Israel to the action of Israel's God. The sacral stories emphasize God's action by achieving ends through means that are quite inadequate in the day-to-day world of military and political action. A flowing river is stopped by the presence of the ark, as the Sea of Reeds was parted by Moses' hand. City walls collapse at a simple shout. A battle is lost because one individual broke sacred rules, as Jonathan did in 1 Samuel 14.

In the understanding presented here, the sacral stories about crossing the Jordan and capturing Jericho have replaced the bulk of the stories of military crossing and capture. Traces of the older stories remain, allowing us to realise that they had been there. The presence of haste (4:10b) and the military (4:13) are there for the crossing; the king and his soldiers (6:2) are mentioned for Jericho. It would be surprising if these traces were left by oversight or negligence; Israel knew how to keep old traditions alive.

The traditions of the northern coalition (11:1–2, 4–8a, 16–19, 23) are not smoothly integrated into the 'Joshua 2' narrative. They could have been imported to complete the picture of national conquest. It is possible, but not necessary, that their inclusion occurred along with the introduction of the sacral stories.

The deuteronomistic text

What can be specifically identified as deuteronomistic contribution within Joshua 1–12 is remarkably little and focused primarily on Joshua's role as successor to Moses. Third person reporting of Moses' role as 'servant of the Lord' is restricted in its distribution and appears to be dtr at the earliest, often late dtr.[23] The keynote to the whole is spoken by God in the opening verses of the book: 'As I was with Moses, so I will be with you' (1:5). Neither here nor in the dtr conclusion (Josh 21:43–45: 22:6) is there any emphasis on the extermination of the local nations or any concern for their kings.[24]

Joshua's leadership role is underlined by the dtr addition in 3:7–8 and 4:14. 5:1 echoes the concern of 2:10. Joshua's role is echoed in his fame (6:27). A final emphasis is given with the addition of 'according to all that the LORD had spoken to Moses' in 11:23. The reference to the land being tranquil without war (*shaqtah mimilkhamah*) uses language akin to the pre-dtr framing material in Judges 3–9 and is unlikely to have originated with the Deuteronomist.[25]

---

23. The occurrences of 'Moses, the servant of the LORD' are Deut 34:5; Josh 1:1, 13, 15; 8:31, 33; 11:12; 12:6; 13:8; 14:7; 18:7; 22:2, 4, 5; 2 Kgs 18:12; 2 Chron 1:3; 24:6.
24. Noth attributes Josh 21:43–45 to an interpolation soon after the completion of the DH, because although 'so close to Dtr. in style that one could attribute it to Dtr. himself, except that, like the rest of the chapter, it comes after Josh. 11.23a*' (*Deuteronomistic History*, 66-67). A number of developments render this judgment no longer sustainable (cf O'Brien, *Reassessment*, 59, fn 41, 74–75).
25. The NRSV's 'the land had rest from war' here and in Judges is misleading; the dtr

To summarise the dtr contribution. Attributed to the Josianic Dtr are basically: 1:1–6, 10–11; 2:10–11; 3:7–8; 4:14; 6:19, 24b–25, 27; 9:10; and 11:23a*—omitting chapter 5 from consideration. The combination of Sihon and Og occurs in 2:10 and 9:10 (as well as in 12:1–6) and may be due to later dtr editing, as are 1:7–9 and three minor expansions within 2:11; 7:11, 15.

The 'extermination list' texts
What became clear in the study of the 'Joshua 2' narrative is the peculiar nature of the text in 10:28–41 and 11:8b–15. These two blocks of text, relating to the southern and northern conquest respectively, are treated here as later than the Deuteronomist because of the absence in the dtr texts of any emphasis on the extermination of the local nations.

In the 'Joshua 2' narrative, the ban was applied to Jericho (in full measure) and Ai (with mitigation) and was feared by Gibeon and the coalition of five. What the texts of 10:28–41 and 11:8b–15 do is to focus with intense density on this extermination and extend it beyond a couple of towns to the whole area of Israel's conquest. What is of interest is how a narrative that smacks of standard national boasting about land seizure has been turned into a thoroughgoing theology of extermination by those who must have known it was untrue. Who, when, and why? This will be taken up briefly below.

The transjordan tribes
Mention of the tribes of Reuben, Gad, and the half-tribe of Manasseh recurs often in the book of Joshua, but always located in the text at positions that suggest later additions. The texts are: 1:12–18; 4:12; 12:1–6; 13:8–32; 18:7; 22:7–9, 10–34. They seem to be late. The question raised is: what concern do they address? There would be relevance for returning exiles in quest of their 'rightful' lands. The issue cannot be pursued here.

Issues arising from this exploration

Two conclusions emerge from all this discussion. One has been flagged from the outset: the possibility is there that an earlier text can

---

'rest' is a different and specific term.

be pointed to without difficulty or distortion of the present text, a text that is coherent with Joshua 2 and that presents a picture of Israel under Joshua crossing the Jordan, capturing Jericho and Ai, cutting a deal with Gibeon, and defeating a Jerusalem-led coalition. Such a text might generate about the same level of outrage as the late ninth-century Mesha stele from Moab.

Such a possibility does not address the origins and issues of texts earlier than this 'Joshua 2' level; the texts now are there. Nor does it look at every possibility for later editing. What it claims is merely that such a 'Joshua 2' level text is possible. This is not claimed to be the definitive understanding of the book of Joshua. It is claimed to be a possible understanding of the book's growth.

A corollary of this view is the subsequent sacralisation of the Joshua account, leading to a far stronger role for God in the gift of the land to Israel. If we assume that the texts for the Jordan crossing, the Jericho capture, and the Achan episode derive from the Gilgal sanctuary, it may be possible that the sacralization of the narrative derives in some way from this sanctuary. Beyond that it is difficult to go.

The second conclusion relates to the issue of the extermination texts (10:28–41 and 11:8b–15). The limited extent of these has always been evident. It is heightened by the close study of the language involved. It is not impossible for these to have been old traditions; the distribution of the language, however, makes this unlikely.

The concern is clearly expressed in Deuteronomy (the ban: Deut 2:34; 3:6; 7:2, 26; 13:16, 18; 20:17; no survivors: Num 21:35; Deut 2:34; 3:3). Despite this, the concern with extermination is not given expression in the dtr framework that sets the tone for the book of Joshua (1:1–11; 21:43–45 and 22:6). It is possible, therefore, that it is later.

Whatever its date, it poses problems for the history of traditions. The later dtr revision in Joshua 23 insists that there were survivors and that Israel was not to worship their gods or intermarry with their women (23:7, 12). Furthermore, there are three passages early in the book of Judges, all potentially secondary, that seek to explain the presence of the surviving nations. According to Judges 2:1–5, the locals are to be Israel's adversaries and their gods a snare to Israel. According to Judges 2:20–23; 3:4, the locals were left as a test of Israel's fidelity; and, as far as 3:5-6 was concerned, Israel failed the test. According to Judges 3:1–3, the locals were left so that the inexperienced in Israel might be tested in war.

There are texts in Deuteronomy that speak of purging the evil 'from your midst' or 'from Israel' (Deut 13:6 [NRSV, 5]; 17:7, 12; 19:19; 21:21; 22:21, 22, 24; 24:7). There is no direct link in the language used in these texts with the extermination texts in Joshua. The mindset, however, is close. If there is evil within Israel, purge it. Similarly, if there are local peoples in the country, purge them. One is an evil within Israel that is to be put without; the other is viewed as an evil outside Israel that is to be kept out. The mindsets may be close; the language expressing them is not. Thematic association is possible; linguistic association is not.

Linguistic association emerges in Deuteronomy 13:13–19 (NRSV, 12–18), a passage related to Deuteronomy 13:6 (NRSV, 5). If the inhabitants of a town have been led astray by those saying, 'Let us go and worship other gods' (13:14, NRSV, 13; cf 13:3, 7–8, NRSV, 2, 6–7), they shall be put to the edge of the sword and the ban shall apply to them and to their goods. Missing is only the 'no survivors' language. The appalling nature of such a text has long been recognised.[26]

These texts are operating in a world that to many today is largely incomprehensible. Are the extermination texts in Joshua another attempt to come to terms with the locals by affirming that none survived? Joshua's generation alone is proclaimed as faithful to the LORD (Josh 24:31; Judg 2:7). Deut 7:1–4 makes clear the LORD's will for the locals: extermination. Therefore, despite texts to the contrary, Joshua's generation must have done it and it is to be recorded in the book of Joshua. Early or late, widespread or isolated, these texts pose problems for the history of traditions. Late and isolated looks more likely; even as such the origins of the theology of extermination remain obscure. Why, for God's sake, are the heights and depths so dangerously close?

---

26. The comment on Deuteronomy 21:18 is valid for both 21:18 and 13:13–19 (NRSV, 12–18): 'A Sage of the Talmud flatly declared that the conditions which would cause a court to decree the death penalty "never occurred and never will occur"'. See *The Torah: A Modern Commentary*, edited by W Gunther Plaut (New York: Union of American Hebrew Congregations, 1981), 1484; cf also 1431, 1435, 1489. 'The sole purpose of the warning is that it might be studied and that one might receive reward for such study' (*The Torah: A Modern Commentary*, 1435).

God, Anger, and The Old Testament
(Original: *Psychiatry and Religion*)

Apart from a detour in defence of Job last year, my contributions to these gatherings have been focused on the appropriateness of the language we use when speaking about God. In 1985, I entered a plea for the right of the human analogy to be given full value as a paradigm for language about God: in a nutshell, it is unlikely to be appropriate or helpful to speak of God's action upon a human person in ways that could not be applied to the action of another human person. In 1986, I appealed to the story of David and Goliath for support in the understanding of a God who, rather than replacing human weakness with divine power, enables full human potential to be realized—a God who empowers human beings to use their talents and prowess in courageous and full living.

The topic of anger is irresistible for a person committed, as I am, to the Old Testament. The God of wrath is an all-too-common stereotype for the God of the Old Testament; the Old Testament's witness to an unshakably committed God, one might say an unconditionally loving God, is frequently overlooked. There is, therefore, a strong temptation to come to the rescue of the worth of the Old Testament and the reputation of its God, pointing out that, in the Old Testament, while Israel is frequently depicted as having broken the covenant which bound it to God and God to it, God is never portrayed breaking off the relationship with Israel. Only once, in Hosea, is God's message proclaimed as definitive rupture: 'You are not my people and I am not your God' (Hos 1:9). It is followed in the very next verse by the affirmation of restoration:

> And in the place where it was said to them, 'You are not my people', it shall be said to them, 'Sons of the living God'. (Hos 1:10)

Israel believed that God's commitment could be counted on, strong words to the contrary notwithstanding. For example, in the book of Judges, after a period of repeated infidelity, the narrator has Israel beg for deliverance and can portray God replying:

> You have forsaken me and served other gods; therefore I will deliver you no more. Go and cry to the gods who you have chosen; let them deliver you in the time of your distress.

But Israel knew that this could not be God's final word, so the narrator-theologian has Israel repent and God deliver them (Judg 10:13–16). There is here a clear expression of faith in God's unshakable commitment.

I am convinced of the value of the Old Testament's witness to a deeply committed and trustworthy God, a God whose love is enduring, a God whose love is robust enough to survive the buffets of rebellion and rejection. As a result, for a long time my initial and instinctive reaction to the association of anger with the God of the Old Testament was to try and play down the anger aspect, countering it with emphasis on the texts that highlight God's love. Over recent years, I have come to realize that, if we believe in a loving God, we can scarcely avoid belief in an angry God. In fact, it would be quite intolerable to believe in a loving God without being able to use the language of a deeply angry God.

Belief in God's love for every human being—not only ourselves, but every individual on the face of the earth, in fact every person in the long history of humanity—belief in such love has to go hand in and with the language of God's powerful anger. Can one who loves be anything but angered and furiously outraged by the suffering inflicted on people by the wilful or institutional callousness of other human beings. When people died of starvation in Ethiopia or the Ukraine because governments for political reasons deliberately directed food supplies elsewhere, could a God who deeply loved those people be thought of or spoken of in any other way than as deeply angered? When people anywhere live in poverty and oppression because of the apathy, greed, or prejudice of others, can one think of God as genuinely loving these people without thinking of God as grieved and angered? It is agony to think of the innermost being of God confronted by the

Holocaust, the deliberate destruction of the Jews, God's chosen and beloved people. What commitment to human freedom could restrain God from action in such a situation? What fearful anger must have moved a loving God bound by such restraints? Or in the situations that are much closer to home, when someone acts coercively or selfishly toward another, we must speak of a loving God as grieved by the destructive behaviour of those who coerce and angered by the treatment meted out to those who are the victims of such violence, whether physical or more sophisticated.

It is important to give due place to this anger in God. Without it, the language of God's love has to be emptied of all emotional and passionate content—and the expression of passion in the Old Testament would have to be muted. Without it, what happens to us falls implicitly under the catch-all of divine providence and is understood to be willed or permitted by God to sufficient degree that it can leave God unmoved. If we shrink from using the language of God's anger, we run the twin risks of belittling God's love and burdening God with responsibility for all that befalls us.

Faith in the trustworthiness and lovingness of God, whether coming out of the Old Testament or the New, is immensely significant for an acceptance of the anger of God. We all know that the anger of a powerful figure inspires fear. Trust in a person's benevolence may make their anger tolerable; the certainty of a person's love makes it so much the easier to cope with their anger. When we have learned to trust God and to trust in God's love of us, it is easier to reflect on the anger of God—whether directed at others or directed at ourselves.

Most folklore about the Old Testament takes the primitive and angry behaviour of God for granted, without pausing to think about the nature of the sources. Some reflection, on the apparent manifestations of that behaviour in the Old Testament—even if very brief and incomplete—may be provocative of useful thought.

For example, God is believed to have commanded the extermination of Israel's enemies, every man, woman, and child. Sure enough, in 1 Samuel 15 there is a story in which Samuel gives God's command to Saul to go after the Amalekites:

> Now go and smite Amalek, and utterly destroy all that they have; do not spare them, but kill both man and

> woman, infant and suckling, ox and sheep, camel and ass (1 Sam 15:3).

Saul is reported to have done so, but with a couple of notable exceptions. He is in deep trouble with Samuel—and God—because he allowed himself to be persuaded to spare the best of the sheep and oxen, allegedly for sacrifice, and also because he spared the life of Agag, king of the Amalekites. Poor Agag, sole survivor of the Amalekites, did not last long. In holy fury, 'Samuel hewed Agag in pieces before the Lord in Gilgal' (15:33); a most unholy image—he chopped him up in church! My concern for the moment is simply to utter a caution against taking such a story too literally, either bemoaning the savagery of God or bewailing the fate of the late-lamented Amalekites. For fifteen chapters further on, the Amalekites are alive and well and plundering David's camp at Ziklag, taking captive the wives, sons, and daughters of David's six hundred men. When David struck back and caught them in the middle of a massive victory binge, despite David's being credited with wreaking most impressive havoc on the Amalekite forces, four hundred young toughs of the Amalekite camel corps are still around to escape (1 Sam 30:16–17). So much for the story about Saul!

Then there is the impression given in the book of Joshua that Joshua made a clean sweep of the country, killing everything that moved. As one verse sums it up:

> So Joshua defeated the whole land, the hill country and the Negeb and the lowland and the slopes, and all their kings; he left none remaining, but utterly destroyed all that breathed, as the Lord God of Israel commanded (Josh 10:40).

Joshua 11 concludes with Joshua having taken the whole land and given it for an inheritance to Israel according to their tribal allotments (11:23). Before we ponder this further example of apparently divine inhumanity, we need to take into account God's speech to Joshua in chapter 13 which asserts 'that there remains yet very much land to be possessed' (Josh 13:1), or Joshua's speech to all Israel in chapter 23 which warns against contact with the nations left in Israel's midst

(Josh 23:7, 12–13), or the traditions in Judges 1 which enumerate all the cities Israel could not capture and whose inhabitants Israel could not drive out, or the differing traditions in Judges 2 which give various explanations of God's purpose in leaving many of the local inhabitants in the land (Judg 2:1–5, 20–23; 3:1–2, 3–6). So much for Joshua's campaigns of extermination!

A further aspect, which I find more difficult to deal with, is the threat uttered by the prophets that God was going to destroy Israel. It was no idle rhetoric; it was fulfilled. In the disastrous defeats of 722 and 587, Israel lost its status as a free and independent people, never to regain it until modern times. Yet as I struggle with the thought that God brought this upon Israel, I am well aware that Israel's decline and fall was brought about by the economic, military, and political factors of a small nation caught up in the struggle of empires. I am also well aware that the evils for which the prophets pilloried their contemporaries—basically, religious infidelity and social injustice—these evils of their own would have significantly contributed to the downfall of the people. Religious infidelity would have struck at the heart of Israel's sense of unity and purpose, and therefore at their strength of will to resist an aggressor. Social injustice would have eroded the morale and the will to fight of Israel's peasant army; conscripted peasants do not fight to defend the land which unjust laws and avaricious landowners have taken from them. So the anger of God against Israel is not divorced from the factors which destroy a people from within.

We cannot explore and explain all of this in one brief paper. It may be enough to say that the stories mentioned, and many more, are expressions of theology rather than records of history. They may be dubious expressions of a quite admirable theology—'obedience is better than sacrifice' (1 Sam 15:22), the land and Israel's life in it is God's gift (Josh 2–11). Or they may be expressions of theologies that are downright bad. But as bad theology they are less difficult than the historical reality of destruction and extermination. For our present purpose, it is enough to caution that before giving the God of the Old Testament a bad press for wrath and ruthlessness, it is extremely important to look closely at the evidence being alleged for conviction.

So far we have looked at the need to be able to attribute anger to God, and conversely the misunderstandings which give rise to the image of the Old Testament's angry God. I would like to conclude by turning to the issue of our anger directed against God.

The book of Job provides a canonical example of the open expression of anger directed at God. The benefits are evident, bringing suppressed feelings to a plane where they can be dealt with and generating a healthier and less fear-ridden relationship with God. Surely that is to the good. Yet I would be uncomfortable if this anger at God were seen as an end in itself.

My concern is twofold. Given our lack of direct sense-based experience of God, the question of where anger at God comes from is significant. A theologically inadequate understanding of our world can generate anger at God by attributing to God happenings for which God should not be held responsible. A theologically inadequate understanding of God can also generate anger at God by creating expectations which God is powerless to meet.

An unsatisfactory understanding of the world, too immediately involving God in its day–to–day happenings, hardly needs much elaboration. The person who attributes failure in an exam or loss of a job to lack of prayer needs to be angry at an inadequate theology rather than at God. The person who blames catastrophe on a punishing God—'What did I do to deserve it?'—is more the victim of inadequate theology than of God's justice.

Of greater concern to me is the second aspect, the one involving an unsatisfactory understanding of God. Anger at God can result from attributing a responsibility and omnipotence to God which may be quite unfair. Addressing the first of these Psychiatry and Religion conferences, I argued: 'If God's action upon the human person is best spoken of in terms of the mind and heart, the inevitable question must be faced of divine omnipotence.' I went on to say: 'In terms of language and the outlook it expresses, the common tendency is to speak and think in terms of the omnipotence of the all-powerful God; due reflection may suggest that God's respect for other persons can render God almost infinitely powerless.' This was greeted by a gale of laughter!

Yet it is an idea I believe we have to take very seriously. If it is right, a lot of anger against God would be misplaced. It is my belief that theological reflection and everyday experience point to a God whose overwhelming love sets such value on human freedom and integrity that God will never do violence to our human freedom. In many situations, therefore, God is powerless.

As I have argued in the early part of this paper, this powerlessness on God's part may well be the context for us to use a language of God's anger and frustration. The reverse side of this reflection is that language of anger on our part, directed against God, may well be inappropriate. The things that happen to us through the exercise of free will are outside the area of God's responsibility—they point rather to God's frustration and powerlessness.

The free will can be our own. We beg God to achieve some goal for us, but we do not ourselves take the steps necessary for its achievement. Anger at God would be inappropriate. The free will can be that of others. Our world is shaped by the behaviour and decisions of so many people, individually and institutionally. Some of the most wounding experiences suffered by people I have known have been inflicted on them by the actions of others. A loving God suffers with such people, is powerless at act with violence against the aggressor. Anger at God would be inappropriate.

We have to account for the apparent powerlessness of God to act in many situations in our world which seem to cry out for divine intervention. In my understanding, love excludes coercion and the perfect love of God is therefore powerless to coerce. However we explain it, the powerlessness of God removes the grounds for much of the anger that is directed at God.

There is, of course, the further realm of things which happen to us, independently of anyone's freedom. Examples are the accidents of birth, health, death, etc. Should we hold God responsible for these and so make God the butt of our anger? In my theology, no more than indirectly. If I may conclude by quoting from my own discussion of the book of Job:

> There is suffering in human life and we do not know why it should be ... The denial of God does not alleviate the suffering one whit; all it eases is our inability to comprehend. Railing against God does nothing to help, unless it ventilates an anger that were better directed against the arbitrariness of misfortune.

Of course, we believe that it is God who created this universe in which we often experience either fortune or misfortune as arbitrary. So the problem remains at one remove—but the problem of evil will never simply go away. At least the recognition of the arbitrariness of misfortune places a distance between the responsibility of a loving God and our own experience of misery. It also leaves open the possibility that there is an overall value in the structure of our universe which is not visible in many of the individual situation we encounter. We have no guarantee that God created the best of all possible worlds, but we also have no way of knowing whether it was possible to create a better one (*The Study Companion to Old Testament Literature*, chapter 15, and fn 15).

Dei Verbum:
Literary Forms and Vatican II—
an Old Testament Perspective
(Original: *God's Word and the Church's Council*)

The invitation offered by the fiftieth anniversary of a Council document is a marvellous opportunity to look at the nature of an ecumenical council (such as Vatican II) and the nature of its documents. The nature of neither can be taken for granted. In days gone by, Council documents culminated in a series of propositions, each ending with 'anathema sit',—let any person holding this view be considered anathema, an outsider. Vatican II did not do this. At the earlier Councils, it was probably felt that the anathema would hold its force for all time. The passage of time would make clear that with the changing circumstances of Church and culture that was not the case. 'Anathema sit' might be best understood as 'we're really serious about this.' It is the responsibility of historians to determine how long that seriousness lasted. It is also the responsibility of historians to determine whether Council documents were a base from which the future might be developed or a culminating crown summing up the preceding developments or a stopgap while a process of theological reflection continued. Which was *Dei Verbum* and how does it look fifty years later?

John O'Malley is emphatic that the literary form of the documents from Vatican II is radically different from what preceded it, going back to the beginning with the Council of Nicaea.[1] Most of the documents of Vatican II sought to address the world; those of its predecessors addressed the Church. The code for the former would be 'pastoral'; for the latter, 'legislative and judicial'. The two must therefore be used quite differently. As a rule, in the 'legislative and judicial', the Council

---

1. John O'Malley, *What Happened at Vatican II* (Cambridge, MA: Harvard University Press), 11 and *passim*.

laid down the law for what was to be believed and condemned the errors opposed to that belief. The 'pastoral' quality of the Vatican II documents means that quite opposed positions can be found within the same document because quite opposed positions could be found within the same Church.

Dei Verbum provides as good an example of this as any. Early in the piece (1962), dissatisfaction with the initial schema for discussion was registered at sixty percent. In 1965, after four years of stubborn resistance from a group favouring tradition over scripture as the primary vehicle of revelation, the final vote was almost unanimous, 2344 in favour and six against. One side was not massively outvoted; the stubborn minority had not seen the light and caved in under pressure; instead, the text was such that both sides could vote for it. As one participant put it: 'We must not simply substitute the declaration of a different school of thought, but rather produce something acceptable to all'.[2] Congar clearly understood 'that Paul VI wanted to secure a large consensus of the Fathers and that that presupposed compromise.'[3] These Vatican II documents must be read very differently from their predecessors.

It is standard practice for Latin documents emerging from the Vatican to be known by their opening words. In this case, *Dei Verbum* (Word of God) can be misleading. The document is a Dogmatic Constitution on Divine Revelation, as it is correctly entitled. It is not exclusively concerned with the inspired word of scripture, as the title *Dei Verbum* might suggest. Its concern goes beyond the biblical word to touch on the many ways in which God is revealed to God's creatures, some dealt with in detail and some in a passing reference.

Close inspection makes clear that *Dei Verbum* intends to affirm an overall image of the past and encourage a sure march into the future. In its own words: 'Following in the footsteps of the councils of Trent and of First Vatican, this present Council wishes to set forth the authentic teaching about divine revelation and about how it is handed on' (*DV*, #1).[4] The document *Dei Filius* from Vatican I leaves

---

2. Dom Basil Butler, President of the English Benedictine Congregation, in Yves Congar, *My Journal of the Council* (Adelaide, SA; ATF Theology, 2012), 198.
3. Congar, *Journal*, xxii.
4. Translation throughout from Walter Abbott (editor), *The Documents of Vatican II: All Sixteen Official Texts Promulgated by the Ecumenical Council, 1963–1965,*

open the possibility of access to God by reason. Vatican II affirms it bluntly: 'God . . . can be known with certainty from created reality, by the light of human reason' (*DV*, #6). On the complex question of scripture and tradition, Trent's 'scripture and tradition' [et] is dealt with far more extensively by Vatican II (*DV*, ##7-10].

It is desirable that space should be given to the issue of scripture and tradition. It was a major sticking point at the time of the Reformation; Luther's 'sola Scriptura' [scripture alone] was a rallying cry of significance. A proposal at Vatican I affirmed that revealed truth was to be found *partly* in scripture and *partly* in tradition (*partim . . . partim*). The Council rejected this formulation, because the evidence for it was not there; instead it adopted the alternative more flexible, formulation 'scripture and tradition' [*et*].[5] I have seen a 'penny catechism' from the archdiocese of Sydney in the 1930s, that asked the question whether all revelation was to be found in scripture. In flat contradiction to Trent, it replied: certainly not; divine revelation was to be found partly in scripture and partly in tradition. Within the Roman Catholic Church of those days, Sydney was probably not alone in knowing what to do when it was a question of denying Protestantism or adhering to Trent. Let the Protestants lose.

That Trent's idea was right is clear; that its formulation was unsatisfactory is evident. Given the importance of the matter, it is small wonder that Vatican II devoted considerable effort on the issue. Anyone with ecclesial experience of ecumenism will be well aware that the Roman Catholic Church's approach to issues of divine revelation will often be different from that of other Churches. That difference can be summed up globally by the term 'tradition'. Exegetes (aka. biblical interpreters) may struggle with words, sentences, or passages; Churches more often grapple with matters of greater weight. Of course, tradition plays a role, along with scripture, in keeping faith alive and well—and moving in the right direction.

At this point it is time for a moment to take a look at the reality of an ecumenical council. It is not a wondrous gathering of mystical truthsayers who have the insight and intelligence to guide the Roman Catholic Church securely for the next century or two. It is

---

Translated from the Latin (London: Chapman, 1966).
5. Council of Trent, Decree concerning sacred books and traditions to be received; Denzinger-Schönmetzer. #1501).

a cross-section of the present-day Roman Catholic Church, with its conservative factions and its liberal factions, with its wise folk and its weirdos. The leadership will be tugged forward and backward. The future of the Church will be reflected in that tugging.

When a couple of thousand bishops, archbishops, and cardinals meet in a single place (St Peter's) for a relatively short period of time (four sessions) for a major ecumenical Council, it is a moment of massive significance for the whole of Western Christendom. The participants in such a gathering will reflect a wide range of people—as for believers, so for bishops—from astute front ends of thoroughbreds at one extreme of the range to the rear ends of hard-working draught horses at the other. An ecumenical council is not a gathering of learned theologians; it is not a gathering of naïve believers; it is not a gathering of specialist guides to lead the faithful toward the future. Far from it. A council is a mirror of the Church it represents. Its role is to reflect on where that Church is now and where it might best be going in living to the full the good news of Jesus Christ, of God's love for us in the ordinariness of our lives. It is a gathering of a couple of thousand leaders, reflecting a billion or so believers, including the learned and the naïve, the high-power administrators and the pastorally committed, the elite and the common-or-garden, the wise and the stupid. It is precisely the wide-ranging complexity of this variety that makes this gathering of such massive significance.

Vatican II was summoned by the much loved Pope John XXIII. The word primarily associated with both Pope and Council was *aggiornamento*. Modernisation, up-dating, bringing up to date are all accurate enough as translations go but a bit facile. It is not easy to catch the force of the image. It is not a matter of throwing open the doors and windows and letting daylight into the structure. The force of the image is day rather than light. Left untouched by the word is whether doors and windows are thrown open to invite 'day' into the structure or to invite the contents and people within the structure to move out into the 'day'. When revelation is under scrutiny, the issue then is whether the forces of day are to enter the structure and further burnish the understanding of revelation or whether the occupants of the structure are freed to move out into the day and inspect the revelation that is being understood out there. This may be very abstract imagistic language. What it points to is highly significant.

Where is revelation to be sought? Inside the bureaucracy of the Church or outside the bureaucracy among the believing faithful? The answer 'both' is easy; articulating what this answer means is not easy at all. It is this 'aggiornamento', this openness of the church to its surrounds, that is probably the high point and lasting contribution of Vatican II.

The dogmatic constitution on divine revelation, *Dei Verbum*, as its readers will gratefully acknowledge, casts its net wide, embracing whatever is of value to those who believe. So, for example, the document speaks early on of God buoying us up with the hope of salvation, with 'His promise of redemption' and it quotes Genesis 3:15 (*DV*, #3). A little later on, it insists that attention must be paid, among other things, to *literary genres* (*DV*, #12). In the reference to Genesis 3:15 as a promise of redemption and in the reference to the importance of literary genres for understanding the meaning of a text, *Dei Verbum* invokes two widely different approaches to the understanding of biblical text, approaches as different as the front and rear ends of a thoroughbred. For the historical-critical exegete, Genesis 3:15 has as its purpose 'to describe the phenomenon that enmity exists not merely in a determined situation but has grown to a continual state, something like an institution'.[6] Tradition, on the other hand, reaches back to Irenaeus (second century) for an understanding of the passage as a prophecy about Christ (seed of Mary) and the devil (seed of the serpent). Says Westermann, a relatively conservative modern exegete, 'there are two main reasons that do not allow such an interpretation'[7]—which we will pass over here.

Irenaeus was the second bishop of Lyons, in France, and was a major figure in the writings of the early Church; he lived a couple of hundred yards down the road from where, for four years, I lived and studied theology. It is said that Irenaeus first moved the interpretation of Genesis 3:15 from Eve's descendants and snakes to Jesus and Satan. This is a perfect example of what, since the term was coined in 1925, has been called *sensus plenior*. In the *New Jerome Biblical Commentary* (*NJBC*, #71.50) the *sensus plenior* is described as 'the deeper meaning intended by God but not clearly intended by the human author, that

---

6. Claus Westermann, *Genesis 1-11* (Minneapolis, MN: Augsburg, 1984); German original, 1974, 259.
7. Westermann, G*enesis 1–11*, 260.

is seen to exist in the words of Scripture when they are studied in the light of further revelation or of development in the understanding of revelation.' Its discussion peaked in the work of Fr Raymond Brown, SS;[8] interestingly, there has been almost no discussion of *sensus plenior* since 1970. Further comment in the *NJBC*, almost certainly from Ray Brown, goes on to say: 'the fact that advocacy of the SPlen [that is, *sensus plenior*] had its roots in distrust of excesses in patristic typology and allegory gave SPlen exegesis a more cerebral and cautionary aura. Reasonable homogeneity with the literal sense was insisted on, and the SPlen was seldom invoked even by strong supporters.' Two points can be underlined: (i) the *sensus plenior* was distinguished from the literal sense; (ii) reasonable homogeneity with the literal sense was insisted on.

There is a notion that recurs almost as a mantra in various formulations in a hugely important book on the Eucharist, *In Breaking of Bread:* 'The heritage of our belief is unsatisfactory, but that does not stop it from being revered.'[9] That applies precisely to what *Dei Verbum* has done in this case: it combines an unsatisfactory interpretation of Genesis 3:15 that is part of a past to be revered with an insistence a little later on the importance of attention to *literary genres*.[10]

This not an isolated example. The document, *Dei Verbum*, quietly insists on the reverence owed to tradition and equally quietly insists on the openness to the future owed to biblical studies.

The Council has done what it had to do and what has such massive significance. It has dressed the vine in such a way as to yield maximum fruit to the members of its Church, both learned exegetes and generalist believers. There are some, for example, who find the bridal language of late Isaiah ('with everlasting love I will have compassion on you,' Isa 54:8) a superb base for prayer; there are others for whom other passages echo spousal abuse ('double for all her sins,' Isa 40:2) and cause revulsion more than anything else. Both sorts of passages are in canonical scripture; both sorts of passages have meaning in the

---

8. Raymond Brown, *The Sensus Plenior of Sacred Scripture.* STD Dissertation. (Baltimore, MD: St Mary's University, 1955).
9. PJ FitzPatrick (a Catholic priest, in the department of philosophy at the University of Durham), *In Breaking Of Bread: The Eucharist and Ritual* (Cambridge: Cambridge University Press, 1993), 322.
10. Or 'literary forms'; original Latin, 'genera litteraria'.

right moments. Ecumenical councils must be careful not to exclude what may have meaning in the various right moments of our lives, whether in scripture, in theology, or in faith.

The full text of *Dei Verbum* on literary genres reads: 'In determining the intention of the sacred writers, attention must be paid, among other things, to *literary genres*.' With ancient texts, authors can only be reached through the text. So the phrase 'the intention of the sacred writers' is a convenient shorthand for the exact meaning of the text around the time of its composition. Scholars need to know this; often believers need not. There is often no one single reading of the text that alone is right and proper. There is the text to be read by scholars, the text to be read by preachers, the text to be read for prayer and reflection—and so many more. The danger of cross-pollination is real but avoidable. The beauty of a conciliar document is its ability to leave room for many such readings.

Form criticism, the primary discipline relating to the literary genres, was and is a scholarly means of getting at the appropriate academic meaning of a text. It asks the question that must be asked: what sort of a text is this? All too often that question has been answered glibly and wrongly: this text is history or this text is divine communication. In all cases, this text is to be proclaimed as the word of God. But as Msgr Raymond Collins has put it in the *NJBC*, 'This traditional formula, apparently simple, is extremely complex and polyvalent'.[11]

The polyvalence is evident. There are many words attested in Scripture that provoke reflection on the 'traditional formula' word of God. For example: there is the psalmist at prayer, marvelling at God's concern for us (Ps 8); there is David mourning for his Jonathan (2 Sam 1:25–26); there is a psalmist venting his rage most horribly (Ps 137:8–9); there is God's word, from a prophet wrapped in mystery, 'just as the Lord loves the people of Israel, though they turn to other gods' (Hos 3:1); there is God's contradictory word, powered by identical motivation (the evil inclination of the human heart) brought together by the mythmaker, 'I will blot out from the earth the human beings I have created . . . nor will I ever again destroy every living creature as I

---

11. Raymond Collins, 'Inspiration', 1023–33 (article #65) in *The New Jerome Biblical Commentary* (*NJBC*) edited by RE Brown, JA Fitzmyer, RE Murphy (Englewood Cliffs, NJ: Prentice Hall, 1990), #65:67.

have done.' (Gen 6:7; 8:21); there is God's word that must witness to a theologian at work, 'Let us make humankind in our image, according to our likeness' (Gen 1:26). 'Complex and polyvalent' is putting it mildly.

However there is more complexity and more polyvalence to deal with. Sayings such as 'thus says the LORD, "the word of the LORD" saying of the LORD' are common in the prophetic books, as might be expected. But there are also three prophetic stories (1 Kgs 13; 22; and Jer 28) that suggest the presence of thought in this area then and the need for it now. One prophet lies to another in the name of the LORD; acceptance of the lie brings the other prophet to his death (1 Kgs 13). In the divine council, one of the host of heaven proposes to be a lying spirit in the mouths of the royal prophets and God approves; it leads to the divinely willed death of Israel's king (1 Kgs 22). The conclusion of the scene is the statement: 'So you see, the LORD has put a lying spirit in the mouth of all these your prophets; the LORD has decreed disaster for you' (1 Kgs 22:23). Finally, at the start of a carefully structured story, the prophet Hananiah, in all the solemnity of the temple in the presence of priests and people, proclaims: 'Thus says the LORD of hosts, the God of Israel: I have broken the yoke of the king of Babylon' (Jer 28:2). At the end of the story, Jeremiah is given the last word: 'And the prophet Jeremiah said to the prophet Hananiah, 'Listen, Hananiah, the LORD has not sent you, and you made the people trust in a lie. Therefore, thus says the LORD: . . . Within this year you will be dead . . .' In that same year, in the seventh month, Hananiah died' (Jer 28:15–17).

The chilling conclusion is formulated by Robert Carroll: 'when the divine word may be a lie, prophecy itself becomes an activity in which true and false are indistinguishable'.[12] Carroll's concluding quote from ER Dodds (in the context of the Pythian oracle) may stifle criticism of Hananiah, but it does little to reassure: 'Anyone familiar with the history of modern spiritualism will realise what an amazing amount of virtual cheating can be done in perfectly good faith by convinced believers'.[13] Clearly, in the world of ancient Israel the complexity and polyvalence of the word of God was troublesome.

---

12. Robert Carroll, *Jeremiah*, OTL (London: SCM, 1986), 548
13. *Jeremiah*, 550.

For *Dei Verbum,* the phrase 'word of God' cannot be applied exclusively to the sacred scriptures; on occasion, it is given a wider meaning. 'Sacred tradition and sacred Scripture form one sacred deposit of the word of God, which is committed to the Church' (*DV,* #10). While such a statement may betray the origins of the document, it needs to be taken into account for understanding the final form. Reflection on the books of the Old Testament emphasises the *imperfect* and the *provisional.* 'These books, though they also contain some things which are incomplete and temporary, nevertheless show us true divine pedagogy' (*DV,* #15).

In all this, it is probably not unfair to smell some confusion. A wise course is to allow the future to sort out that confusion. That is precisely what *Dei Verbum* does when it turns to literary forms. But first, as noted earlier, an element bearing on that wisdom is worth noting. The commission responsible for *Dei Verbum* had been given a preliminary draft prepared by the Theological Commission, with a first chapter, 'Two Sources of Revelation' (that is, scripture and tradition). In due course, a vote was taken whether the draft should be returned for rewriting. Sixty percent voted to return it, falling short of the two-thirds majority required for this step. John XXIII pulled papal rank, sided with the sixty percent majority, and constituted a new joint commission to recast the text.[14] This accounts for the place of scripture and tradition early in the document, more in line with Trent's final text than the more polemical and inaccurate 'partly . . . partly' of an earlier version at Trent. Rather more important, this early vote in 1962 pointed to the need for delicacy on the part of the commission's authors who could only count on about sixty percent of the votes of their commission. Bold innovation was not to be the order of the day. The success of the approach adopted is indicated by the final vote of the full Council: 2334 for and six against.

The language of the document is: 'Those who search out the intention of the sacred writers must, among other things, have regard for "*literary forms*"... The interpreter must investigate what meaning the sacred writer intended to express and actually expressed in particular circumstances as he used contemporary literary forms in accordance with the situation of his own time and culture' (*DV,* #12).

---

14. Roderick MacKenzie, 'Introduction' to *Dei Verbum.* Pages 107–10 in *The Documents of Vatican II*, edited by Walter Abbott (London: Chapman, 1966).

There is a phrase here that is a quiet reminder that any Council document is a creature of its time and that also serves to banish any whiff of infallibility that might be about. The phrase, 'the intention of the sacred writers', was a helpful shorthand for invoking the historical-critical method and turning one's back on some of the fallacies of centuries past—which of course is precisely what *Dei Verbum* is doing. By now, any interpreter of text should know that the intention of a writer is mediated by the meaning of the writer's text. There is no other way of reaching an ancient writer's intention. What should be said is not 'the intention of the writer' but 'the meaning of the text'. A quibble of this kind is critical for interpreters of text; it is of no concern to ordinary people and of no concern to bishops, archbishops, and cardinals. The presence of the phrase is a valuable reminder that the document is a creature of its time.

Dei Verbum is emphatic on the role of the exegete: 'It is the task of exegetes to work according to these rules towards a better understanding and explanation of the meaning of sacred Scripture so that through preparatory study the judgment of the Church may mature' (*DV*, #12). Naturally enough for a council document, this task is performed within the church: 'All of what has been said about the way of interpreting Scripture is subject finally to the judgment of the church' (*DV*, #12). The portrayal of this may be more easily said—'it is clear, therefore, that sacred tradition, sacred Scripture and the teaching authority of the Church, in accord with God's most wise design, are so linked and joined together that one cannot stand without the others' (*DV*, #10)—than made tangible in the flow of church life.

There is an adage that applies in many professions: it is not so much what is said but what is not said that can be so very revealing. That is certainly the case with *Dei Verbum*. The insistence on the necessary place of literary forms in interpretation is not hedged around with prohibitions or cautions. The reality of literary forms is to be embraced by those searching out the meaning of God's communication. Naturally, since the communication is with the church, in order that 'the judgment of the Church may mature' (*DV*, #12), the church's oversight is present.

The choice of 'literary forms' as the shorthand for modern biblical studies is peculiarly apt. At the core of these literary forms is the discipline of form criticism. It came on the scene at the beginning of the twentieth century, with a view to supplementing source criticism (German: *Literarkritik*), which was considered by scholars such as Hermann Gunkel and Hugo Greßmann to have completed a necessary job.[15] About the time of *Dei Verbum*, form criticism was at its peak; that peak has passed and form criticism today is waning. It was hoped that scientifically describable literary forms could be identified and associated with specific settings (*Sitz im Leben*). That hope has been disappointed and replaced by an enhanced trust in intuition, validated by careful study. The question, however, has been raised and will not go away: what sort of a text is this? No longer can it be automatically assumed that that texts are either history or divine communication. *Dei Verbum*'s picture of the 'principal purpose to which the plan of the Old Covenant was directed' (*DV*, #15) may be challenging; the identification of smaller units may be more troubling yet. The question, 'what sort of a text is this?', must be asked, even if answering it is troublesome. The necessary follow-up to this question cannot be avoided; it must be answered. This follow-up question is: why has this text, in this form, been preserved in sacred scripture? One answer is the invitation to go think, the invitation to reflection on the matters involved, an invitation that can be offered by both creator and creature and that can be relevant down the ages. Other answers may be revealed as the future unfolds.

Dei Verbum has the comment that these books [Old Testament] 'contain some things which are incomplete and temporary' (*DV*, #15). The New Testament reflects the reality of a God who has embraced the weakness and fallibility of human life, 'true God and true man', in no way 'exempt and cut off from the divinely given but flawed world in which we live and die'.[16] Because we do not escape the vulnerability and incompleteness of the world in which we find ourselves and which we have been given, not escaped in the person of Jesus Christ, not escaped either in the words of sacred scripture, how then are troubling passages in scripture to be dealt with? The

---

15. For details, see Antony Campbell, 'The Emergence of the Form-critical and Traditio-historical Approaches', chapter 31 in volume III/2 of Magne Saebø (editor) *Hebrew Bible / Old Testament: The History of Its Interpretation* (Göttingen: Vandenhoeck & Ruprecht, forthcoming).
16. FitzPatrick, *Breaking of Bread*, 341.

Talmud, the authoritative body of Jewish tradition, comments on two passages in Deuteronomy that are rightly troublesome. Regarding the first (Deut 13), 'The destruction of a whole community because of idolatry (verses 13 ff) never occurred nor will it ever occur. The sole purpose of the warning is that it might be studied and that one might receive reward for such study';[17] regarding the second, according to which the wayward or defiant son will be stoned to death (Deut 21:18-21), commenting on a tradition that says this law was never operative, the Talmud records the following: 'If so, why was it written in the Torah? To study (more) and to obtain reward therefrom' .[18] Study, presumably, reached the conclusion that such a law was inappropriate, that such a view could not be held. We might reach similar conclusions. In relation to following another god (Deut 13:3), the use of common sense is commended: 'Is it really possible to "follow" God, who is described (Deut 9:3) as a "devouring fire"? Rather, you should follow His attributes: as He clothes the naked, so must you; as He visits the sick, comforts the mourners, and buries the dead, so must you.'[19]

Early on, I borrowed the terms 'complexity and polyvalence' from Msgr Collins; with them we are not at a great distance from the term 'mystery'. The final chapter of *Dei Verbum* takes us in this direction. The chapter opens with the affirmation that 'The Church has always venerated the divine Scriptures just as she venerates the body of the Lord, since from the table of both the word of God and of the body of Christ she unceasingly receives and offers to the faithful the bread of life, especially in the sacred liturgy' (DV, #21).

We might do well to see an invitation here to place our understanding of the role of God in the ownership of the scriptures in much the same category as our understanding of the eucharist. Over two or three thousand years, believers have associated the Bible with God in an intimate and sacred way. Various believing bodies and various believers have articulated this association between God and Bible in various ways. What may best embrace this variety is the concept of mystery.

---

17. Tosefta San 14:1.
18. San 71a.
19. Sotah 14a. The material above has been taken from Gunther Plaut, *The Torah: A Modern Commentary* (New York: Union of American Hebrew Congregations, 1981).

I have borrowed earlier from PJ FitzPatrick the notion that 'the heritage of our belief is unsatisfactory, but that does not stop it from being revered'.[20] This is said after careful study of medieval language around transubstantiation and equally careful study of recent attempts to replace it (courtesy of phenomenology). A summary of FitzPatrick's work may be drawn from his own words: 'What matters in eucharistic belief is what has always mattered, namely that the reality of what we receive is the Risen Lord; and what matters in the belief is not constricted by the categories of obsolete modes of thought, and not compromised by the incapacity of language to seize it.'[21]

To paraphrase for sacred scripture: 'What matters in belief regarding God's role in sacred scripture is what has always mattered, namely that the reality of what we have in scripture has God in some way ultimately responsible for it; and what matters in the belief is not constricted by the categories of obsolete modes of thought as to how that is to be understood, and God's role is not compromised by the incapacity of language to seize it.'

Dei Verbum, the document that began with Trent and the traditions that preceded it, that looked to the future with unfettered endorsement of literary forms, and that ended with the word of God and the body of Christ in the eucharist, is a document that has surely done well. Familiarity with the Council leaves no doubt that the battle raged on many fronts between the Curia and the Ecclesia, with the latter victorious while on the scene. The words of Paul VI at the United Nations, 'Jamais plus la guerre' ('no more war') can be taken to heart. The Curia should never again be at war with the Ecclesia. It may take a century or two to work out the balance, but the balance between centre and periphery is essential to the leadership of the Church.

---

20. *Breaking of Bread*, 322.
21. *Breaking of Bread*, 309.

The Good News and The Year for Priests

(Original: *The Summit* 37, 2010)

In this 'Year for Priests' it is particularly appropriate to reflect on the Good News of Jesus Christ, the unshakeable evidence of God's love for us, as experienced in the lives of ordinary people, ordained people and priestly people. Ordained priests, by vocation, are living witnesses to the 'Good News', possessed by that news, embodying that news in the totality of their lives. Priestly people, by commitment, take the Good News very seriously. Is witness to the Good News, kept vital and alive in the community, the core of priesthood from which all else flows? What is this Good News? What is the best use for this Year for Priests?

A former archbishop of Melbourne is reported to have said that the two major mysteries of Christianity are: 1) whether there is a God; 2) whether that God is benevolent toward us. The Good News of Jesus Christ is: 1) that there is a God; 2) that this God is indeed well-disposed toward us.

Christianity holds firmly to the belief that there is a God, one God yet Father, Son, and Holy Spirit (God: Creator, Saviour, and Sanctifier). We can take this belief for granted, but it is important that we do not forget it and that we do realise that—just as atheism is belief—this is indeed belief and is the core of the Good News.

Central to the Good News is that this God is well-disposed toward us. In the words John's gospel gives to Jesus: 'No one has greater love than this, to lay down one's life for one's friends' (John 15:13). To believe God is as deeply caring as that toward us is good news indeed.

In this age of the Hubble telescope and the unimaginable reach back in time of the vast arrays of the radio telescope, we take for granted that our own little world (the solar system) is about 4.5 billion years old. The numbers may be so vast as to be meaningless, but for the moment we reckon our universe at a little less than 15 billion years old (13.7, if we want to be precise). The vastness of the creator God of all this universe gives fresh meaning to traditional theological terms like mystery and transcendence. Richard Dawkins speaks scornfully of the complexity to be taken for granted regarding such a God. Perhaps Dawkins needs to give less scornful thought to the possible simplicity of such a God. Whatever the case, that such a God should love each of us lies almost beyond the realm of imagination. It is good news indeed.

The core belief of Christianity is that Jesus Christ is God's presence to the human race, not in the luxury of rulers or the rich (cf Matt 11:8; Luke 7:25) but in an ordinary life, ending in the ordinariness of a Roman cross, the gallows of the day. 'No one has greater love than this, to lay down one's life for one's friends.'

Mind you, we don't need Hubble telescopes and twentieth-century technology to have God's attitude toward us take our breath away. The Psalmist had none of our modern technology, but probably had a better vision of the night sky than city dwellers do today and could say: 'when I look at the heavens, the work of your fingers . . . what are human beings . . . that you care for them?' (Ps 8:3–5). That the God of all our universe should care for us, in the ordinariness of our lives, is good news indeed.

Jesus may have worked miracles in plenty and died a criminal's death on a cross—both out of the ordinary for the average life. Without penning a book or two to make the point, it should be obvious that Jesus was certainly not an ordinary person but, nevertheless, lived an ordinary life like any other ordinary person. He was not endowed with phenomenal wealth. His wisdom was not central to the fabled academies of those ancient times. Neither emperor nor governor, Jesus did not wield the political power of his day. He lived as an ordinary person. God's commitment to human living was not commitment to wealth, academic wisdom, or political power. Not excluding these, God's commitment was above all to ordinary human living. God's commitment was to ordinary human beings, us—good news indeed.

For centuries Christianity expressed its faith in this act of God in terms of God's love satisfying God's justice in the death of Jesus on the cross. For almost a thousand years, western theology has associated an understanding of this with the name of St Anselm. In the arcane and highly nuanced language of theologians, Anselm's theory of atonement can be seen as ingenious, acceptable. In the language of those who are not highly nuanced theologians, Anselm's theology can so easily be distorted that, in the words of the man who is now Pope Benedict XVI, 'its rigid logic can make the image of God appear in a sinister light'. Even worse, in Ratzinger's words again, 'Many devotional texts actually force one to think that Christian faith in the cross visualises a God whose unrelenting righteousness demanded a human sacrifice, the sacrifice of his own Son, and one turns away in horror from a righteousness whose sinister wrath makes the message of love incredible. This picture is as false as it is widespread.' False, widespread, and not good news at all!

At stake is the understanding of love. Love used of God must be transcendent love, love that transcends all that we know about love in order to be love that is truly God's. To have meaning for us, however, it cannot betray our human experience of love. The text of Job is not far off the mark. 'If I sin, what do I do to you, you watcher of humanity? . . . Why do you not pardon my transgression and take away my iniquity' (Job 7:20–21). The text of Isaiah has God saying much the same. 'I, I am He who blots out your transgressions *for my own sake*, and I will not remember your sins' (Isa 43:25; emphasis mine). That is closer to what I would call love. It points more clearly to what I would gladly call good news. The love we experience among humans is love for people who are flawed. That God's love for us should not be different in this respect is good news indeed.

The Roman Catholic liturgy of Holy Saturday still sings of the 'happy sin' ('felix culpa') that brought about the incarnation of Jesus Christ. It just might be that what is so traditional is also the most appalling theology. Should the incarnation as an expression of God's love for us be dependent on our sin! 'God's response to human sin' sounds more gracious. In the context of such theology, alas, without the sin there would have been no response—no Incarnation. Without freedom, there would have been no sin. Is it us in our freedom that God finds so lovable?

A momentous change is having its effect in Christian theology right now—in the centuries-slow movement of change in Christian thought. It is said that John Duns Scotus, 13th century theologian, sourced the incarnation to God's desire to be human. Another 13th century theologian, Thomas Aquinas, is said to have disagreed: only atonement for human sin could have motivated the incarnation. Today's thinking is creeping toward agreement with Scotus rather than with Aquinas. God so loved us that God wanted to become one of us—and so lived an ordinary human life and died an ordinary human death, before a quite extraordinary resurrection. For us ordinary humans, good news indeed.

This has been proclaimed a 'Year for Priests'. For many, there are two actions restricted exclusively to ordained priests: the consecration of the eucharist and the absolution of sin. It would be a shame if in a future Church the notion or reality of priesthood should be so restricted and so narrow.

In today's developed western Church, vocations to the ordained priesthood have fallen off hugely. Some attribute this to the attitudes of people (lack of generosity, resistance to celibacy, unreadiness for lifetime commitment, etc). Others attribute this to the attitudes of the Church (too uninspiring, too boring, too legalistic, too out of touch, etc). Others attribute it to the action of the Holy Spirit, in search of a more inclusive Church.

Pope Benedict XVI has said recently that the Church needs a change in mindset, particularly regarding laypeople. Archbishop Chaput of Denver has taken this up to insist that laypeople must no longer be viewed as 'collaborators' of the clergy but as 'co-responsible' for the Church's being and action. Much the same has been said by Cardinal Roger Mahony of Los Angeles.

An aspect of priesthood is surely leadership in witness among the Christian community to the good news of God's love for us. Leadership is essential in any organisation; but, as we all know, without membership, there is no organisation. To steal a phrase from St John, how leaders and members might interact in a future Church 'has not yet been revealed' (1 John 3:2). The Year For Priests is a good time to bring experience and thought to bear on this future. Church documents have given emphasis to the priesthood of the faithful resulting from baptism. Perhaps the time is coming when we will be able to give that even sharper focus. At this moment, today's Church faces a simple choice: empower the laity or die. Resurrection will follow, as surely as day follows night—a phoenix church. A focus on priesthood as essential witness to belief in the Good News offers a lens to view priesthood widely rather than narrowly. Cause to rejoice and be glad.

To absorb the Good News of God's love for us takes a lifetime at least. For the Church to absorb this proclamation of the Good News into its structures and its liturgies will probably take more than a lifetime; after all, God relies on us for the advance of humankind. But that the God of all our universe should be believed to love each one of us in the ordinariness of our lives is unbelievable good news, unbelievable but not beyond belief—we believe, we rejoice, and we have cause to be so deeply glad.

Qohelet the Wise
(Original: not located)

'Live your life and see the value in what you do.' Wise advice and a good mantra for human living. Simple, straightforward, and central to Qohelet (Eccl 2:24; 3:13; 5:17 [Heb.; NRSV 5:18]; cf 8:15). The Hebrew verbal root r-<-h is straightforward; it means 'to see'. The Hebrew adjective *tob* is straightforward; it means 'good'. The Hebrew noun *amal* is just as straightforward; it means 'toil'. In an agricultural society, most people work the land; working the land is toil. Toil is what most people do in an agricultural society. Today, in an industrial or post-industrial society, what most people do is called 'work'. Qohelet says 'Eat and drink and see the good in your toil'. Surely a modern rendering has to be: 'Live your life and see the value in what you do.'

Some modern translations are close to this; others are worse. Taking Eccl 2:24 as an example:

NRSV: eat and drink, and find enjoyment in their toil.
RSV: eat and drink, and find enjoyment in his toil.
NAB: eat and drink, and provide himself with good things by his labors.
NEB: eat and drink and enjoy himself in return for his labours.
NIV: eat and drink and find satisfaction in his work.
JB: eat and drink and to be content with his work.
NJB: there is no happiness except in eating and drinking, and in enjoying one's achievements
JPS: eat and drink and make his soul enjoy pleasure for his labour.
NJPS: eat and drink and afford himself enjoyment with his means.

My complaint is simple: why do all these translations betray Qohelet to greater or less degree? 'Find enjoyment' and its equivalents is good, but restrictive. Not all that is good is necessarily enjoyable. Why restrict Qohelet to enjoy when he does not make that move until 8:15? 'Be content with his work' is the sort of moralising we can do without. 'Provide himself with good things' is close to the familiar 'eat, drink, and be merry'. Poor Qohelet gets a bad name as a cynic. Put into context, Qohelet could be possibly surprising and is certainly wise.

He starts with great wealth and writes it off as vanity. He moves to great wisdom and writes that off too as vanity. His conclusion is the middle way: 'Eat and drink and see the value in what you do', in other words, live your life and value the worth of what you do.

Associated books:
Campbell, AF. *God First Loved Us* (Paulist Press)
Campbell, AF. *The Whisper of Spirit: A Believable God Today* (Eerdmans)
Frank Gil. *Have Life Abundantly: Grass Roots First* (ATF Press)

Reflections Around Frank Gil's
Have Life Abundantly: Grass Roots First
(Original: Interface Theology, Volume 1, Number 1, 2014)

The ultimate question for many may be: Have Life Abundantly—How? A burning question for some in today's increasingly secular world is certainly whether to believe in God and what sort of a Church, if any, is helpful to sustain that belief. Earlier this year (2014) ATF Press published a book by Frank Gil, *Have Life Abundantly: Grass Roots First*. According to the back cover, Frank Gil was a pseudonym for a widely-published priest; we can treat him as simply Frank Gil. What is of interest for today's 'burning question' is that Frank Gil abandons the idea of proving God's existence and seriously challenges two core aspects of the current Roman Church.

The first part of Gil's book is given to the question of how we know of the existence of God. Probably no one today believes in God because of proof. What you prove, you know. What is reasonable but cannot be proved, can be believed. In the first part of his book Frank Gil pictures four situations that can support people in their belief (associated with context, instinct, emotion, and reason). There is of course a huge debate at a philosophical level that looks at so much more. Gil is wise to leave it alone.

All the same, what Gil proposes is a view of Christianity that for many of us turns on its head the Christianity we have inherited (and maybe rejected). No more guilt and punishment, no more sacrifice and redemption. In their place, a God who loves, who has chosen to become one of the humans whom God loves—not to redeem them but out of love for them. If it sounds difficult to believe, it is—however, see below. Jesus Christ is more revealer than redeemer (note: not one or the other, but a massive shift of emphasis).

The second part of Gil's book looks at two aspects of what he sees to be centrally wrong with the structures of today's Roman Church. What Gil, quite rightly, does not do and where there is of course a huge need for further experience and some imaginative thinking is to sketch an outline of the sort of Church Roman Catholics may now need in order to sustain tomorrow's faith. Small wonder that Gil does not attempt to sketch such an outline. The needs to be satisfied have not yet emerged; beginnings are visible in smaller groups. When they do emerge more fully, they will be widely different in the varying regions of the world. The day of 'one size fits all' is long gone. Africa is not Asia, North America is not South America, and none of them is Europe. Gil is wise to refrain from the imagining that it must be left to others to do.

There is a saying that surfaces every now and then: 'faith is caught not taught.' The 'taught' bit may need some expanding; the 'caught' bit is pretty accurate. Gil is strong that it is not argument that generates faith; clearly, 'caught not taught.' What he offers are pictures of situations in which faith can be caught.

Second part of the book

In this article we may take up the second part of the book first and have a go at some of the imagining that Gil wisely leaves for others to develop. Two major problems are named by Gil as cancers in the core of the current Roman Church. They are clericalism and monarchism (for want of a better word). Clericalism is well-known, probably more widespread than generally thought, and more easily experienced than named (defined).

In terms of being 'more widespread than generally thought', clericalism extends to the non-clerics in the people of God as well as to the clerics. The clerical right to rule was claimed by the Council of Trent, reaffirmed in writing by Pope Pius X in 1906, and taken for granted in the behaviour of most Popes in recent times. The sole right granted to the people of God was to allow themselves to be led and like a docile flock to follow (language from Pius X in 1906).[1] Clericalism plays on the shadowy ambiguity of ruling and leading (on the part of the cleric) and compliance and conviction (on the part

---

1. The information here comes from the book *Predatory Priests, Silenced Victims: The Sexual Abuse Crisis and the Catholic Church*, edited by MG Frawley-O'Dea and V Goldner (Mahwah NJ: Analytic Press, 2007). See especially 147-62.

of the people of God). All too often, if compliance is given, it may be given grudgingly; conviction may be far away.

A contributing factor that has to be taken into account is the weight given to position in the clerical hierarchy and, in the case of priests, to ordination—claimed by some to bring about a change in the being of the person ordained (ontological change). Leadership is necessary; there can be little doubt of that. The issue is whether leadership is followed because of rank or sacrament rather than followed because of worth (on the part of the leader) and conviction (on the part of the follower). Esteem for rank (priest, bishop, and above) and sacrament (ordination) is naturally due to those in positions of rank in the hierarchy and naturally a due part of a person's self-esteem. Where such esteem seems out of place is where clericalism creeps in. Whether because of rank or sacrament, clerics can esteem themselves—and some people may esteem them—more highly than others might think appropriate. Both the contribution to self-esteem and to esteem inappropriately given by others are areas where clericalism can flourish. Leadership is like trust; it has to be earned. Where it is based principally on clerical status is where clericalism is to be feared.

Understood in this way, clericalism embraces popes, archbishops, bishops, priests—and beyond to the people of God. It is painfully widespread. It is a cancer that needs to be eradicated from the Roman Church before it kills it—therefore, soon.

Associated with clericalism is an issue that is central to a wider social concern—the issue of gender. A basic statement that needs to be made is: being female is no obstacle to occupying *any* position in the Church. The association of gender with clericalism may not be immediately evident. Exploring it needs more space than an article allows.

Taking a wholesale approach to clericalism, without plunging into detail, Frank Gil makes moves that are global and simple. He advocates that the grass roots take their share of the sacramental system of the Roman Church. As he is quick to point out, there is much that should remain unchanged in the life of a parish community. The major weekly Mass would retain its place as a central community eucharist, though with a focus on fulfilling needs that people have and avoiding what bores some stiff. The sense of belonging to a community and care for others would be there. But in the daily life of the people of God, small group eucharists are appropriate in many circumstances, circumstances where the nature of the gatherings is such that the presence of a cleric is not possible or inappropriate. These eucharists can heighten the sense of the spiritual and support the reality of faith—and of course community.

As Gil points out, the Council of Trent took its stand on two sacramental matters: the absolution of sin and the transformation of the bread and wine into the body and blood of Christ in the eucharist. These two were exclusively reserved to ordained clerics (priests). For the other sacraments, the issue is different. In moments of urgency, baptism can be performed by ordinary folk who are not even Catholic but want to do what the Church does. At the other end of life, it is unthinkable to restrict the sacramental act of care for the sick (anointing) to a cleric. There is no reason for the ordinary people of God to refrain from the anointing of the sick. Between these two (birth and death, baptism and anointing), it has long been Catholic teaching that marriage is brought about by the couple themselves; the couple perform the marriage. The Council of Trent declared that the presence of a priest was required for the *validity* of a marriage. In doing so, it was reacting against the phenomenon of clandestine marriage (no witnesses) where in later years a partner (alas, normally the man) would deny there had been any marriage at all.

The break-up of a marriage is often an extremely painful time. The complexity of Roman regulations around the sacrament of matrimony can involve much that is extremely painful. As a result of these factors, the encounter with the Church when a marriage community is dissolving can be alienating beyond belief. There is much to be said for handing over the legal issues at the beginning and ending of marriage to the State. The role of the Church would be to celebrate sacramentally the holiness of what has been achieved and to support the grieving over what has had to be dissolved.

That leaves two sacraments in the realm of bishops—confirmation and ordination. And it leaves two sacraments in the realm of priests—absolution and eucharist. Frank Gil's simple and global solution to clericalism: the people of God should take over their share of the sacramental system (not 'be given' but 'take over'—grass roots first, and the grass roots are the people of God and the leaders among the people of God. Pie in the sky? Perhaps, perhaps not). Under present conditions, that is sharing in three out of seven sacraments; under Gil's solution, that would be five out of seven. When the people of God share sacramental power with the clerics, that should help pull the rug from under much of clericalism. Gil just might be right.

Monarchism (terrible word) is not all that different a kettle of fish. It is primarily located with the pope, but there is a trickle-down effect on bishops and priests. My *Webster's New Collegiate Dictionary* (1976) has three descriptions of monarchy of which the third is the most useful here: 'a government having a hereditary chief of state with life tenure and powers varying from nominal to absolute.' Heredity has never been claimed for the Roman pope, life tenure has been the rule (mitigated by one abdication recently), and papal power is absolute rather than nominal. For the Roman papacy, two issues dominate: life tenure, absolute power. When we look around our world, major examples of these two factors are found only with dictators, despots, and tyrants. These are not good company for the papacy to be keeping. The association with God is effective as PR, but is unhelpful in day-to-day living.

Life tenure, coupled with election by the college of cardinals, is probably the major point on which the papacy differs from other forms of acceptable government. The issue of election will be taken up below. The issue of life tenure can be looked at here. Limited tenure opens the way to the pope's authority ultimately being under that of the Church. Theologians and the people of God need to determine whether that is a good thing. If it were, a ten-year term might be proposed, to be followed by an assessment reflecting as far as possible the view of the global Roman Church. The assessment might be limited to two possibilities: 1) renewal of the appointment for a further ten years; 2) dismissal or request for resignation, to be followed by a fresh election.

In such or similar circumstances, the absolutism of papal power would be modified by the moderating influence of the people of God. In such or similar circumstances, clericalism would be less of a problem.

Pope Francis has spoken out against cardinals as princes of the Church and courtiers of the king (my language, not his). If the role of pope as monarch is to go, the role of cardinals as courtiers to the monarch must go too.[2] Beyond papal election, what cardinals can do, archbishops can do; the only role that is exclusive to cardinals is the election of popes. Despite some advances, the college of cardinals is not truly reflective of the Church, the people of God. The dominance of Europe and also North America is rather too apparent. If the bishops of a region, as current leaders of the Church in that region, were to elect one or two people from that region—not necessarily bishops, but necessarily leaders—as electors of a pope, such an electoral college would represent the global Church more adequately. With such a system in place, the office of cardinal could cease to exist. The tenure of the pope would no longer be automatically for life. The appearance of the papacy as monarchy would be significantly diminished.

First part of the book
'Faith is caught not taught.' Gil outlines four situations that are eminently suitable for catching faith. At the same time, he emphasises that faith is unlikely to be the outcome of argument or proof. Charles Taylor, noted philosopher, has devoted over 800 pages exploring the secularity of our age.[3] Late in the book, he is remarkably even-handed regarding faith and humanism: 'It appears as a matter of who can respond most profoundly and convincingly to what are ultimately commonly felt dilemmas.'[4]

The acceptance of the core of Christian faith—that God became human—is radically challenging enough. It does not need to be entangled in issues of sin and guilt. The popular line, 'By your cross and resurrection, Lord Jesus, you have saved the world', leaves out the birth of Christ, chronologically prior and theologically prior to cross and resurrection (see Phil 2:6-7). Cross and resurrection lend themselves to theologies of atonement and sacrifice; birth does not.

---

2. It is of interest to note that in many countries ecclesiastics employ honorifics that reflect court dignities. For example, a cardinal is addressed as Your Eminence, an archbishop as Your Grace, a bishop as My Lord (in some regions: Your Excellency). In the USA, which avoids such courtly practices, cardinals are called Cardinal, archbishops Archbishop, bishops Bishop. The practice could well be extended more widely.
3. Charles Taylor, *A Secular Age* (Cambridge, MA: Belknap Press of Harvard University Press, 2007.
4. Taylor, *Secular Age*, 675.

Confronting the tension between Christian faith and humanism, people may ask the question: why did Jesus Christ die on the cross? An answer: in order to show God's esteem for human life by living a very ordinary life to the full, living by the principles that were his. In those Roman days, that meant crucifixion. And why that? Well, that raises the biggest, most unbelievable mystery of all: that God did this out of purest love for us. That is a challenge to our images of God and of ourselves. It is reason enough to water down if not to reject Christian faith. Equally, it is reason enough to explain Christ's cross as redeeming us from our sin (a need so close beneath the surface of so many then and now), something much more tangible than the challenging idea of love by God for us.

Death goes along with life; Jesus lived like us and died like us. The best available reason I know for the life, death, and resurrection of Jesus Christ is to show us two realities, two mysteries. First, the unbelievable value that God sets on an ordinary human life, by living one—the life of Jesus, son of God and son of Mary. Second, the commitment that God has to us ordinary humans, the love God has for us (see Psalm 8; 'what are human beings that you are mindful of them, mortals that you care for them?'). Nothing at all to do with sin or guilt. Nothing to do with atoning for sin. Nothing less than the love of God for us, sinners though we are. From the book of Genesis: 'As long as the earth endures, seedtime and harvest, cold and heat, summer and winter, day and night, shall not cease' (Gen 8:22). From the gospel: 'No one has greater love than this, to lay down one's life for one's friends' (John 15:13); we have to have a life before we can lay it down. If we want sacrifice, God's sacrifice was becoming human. What do we know of the Father? 'Whoever has seen me has seen the Father' (John 14:9); what we know of the Father, we have learned from Jesus—and Jesus loved. As said above, Jesus Christ as revealer rather than redeemer.

Personally, I am sometimes uneasy with the language of the 'love of God' for us. Given the horrors of so much human life—for example, the Holocaust or the Pol Pot regime; more recently, Taliban and jihadists, the horrors of Syria, Gaza, and so much of Africa, and much that is closer to home—language of God's love for those responsible can sometimes seem to me to be too facile, too far out of touch with the reality of human horror. Friends remind me that parents can love children who are destroyers of others' lives, drug addicts and drug dealers. The pain of the parents is unthinkable. The love of the parents for the children can be real (and for me touched by mystery). Can we deny the possibility of such love to God? For me, that is mystery. Frank Gil goes further, with more detail.[5] The mystery remains.

Viewed in the creeds of the early Church, Jesus is the son of God who became human and lived a remarkably ordinary life. Miracles to be sure, but none to benefit himself and none to bring certain conviction into the lives of his followers (Thomas, 'Let us go up and die with him' [John 11.16], but at the crucifixion only one was there, and it wasn't Peter and it wasn't Thomas).

The gospels offer the picture of a Jew's life in Palestine under Roman rule. Christ did not have it easy (as we don't). If he wanted to get from Galilee to Jerusalem, he walked. Christ had principles he lived by. These principles put him at odds with certain Jewish groups (scribes and pharisees, for example). His life, his principles, and the hopes of his followers made him a troublemaker in the eyes of the Romans. The Romans crucified their troublemakers. This one rose from the dead, suggesting a lasting value in human life.

A bit of a challenge to believe in—probably. An attractive view of God and human life—certainly.

If incarnation is the consequence of sin, incarnation would be conditional on sin (traditional: original sin). Incarnation, God's becoming human, is surely too important to be conditional on sin (Duns Scotus). The claim has been made that God brought the human race into existence in order to be one of that human race. To believe this is an enormous challenge. To believe anything less may dishonour both us and God. Love is one of life's great mysteries. But we humans can love. Adapting the song from 'Annie Get Your Gun', anything we can do God can do better. At least since Psalm 8 the mystery has been named. It remains a mystery. Christian faith accepts God's love, accepts the mystery. As a response to the mystery of human life, it is more attractive than atonement and sacrifice. It may be more of a challenge than liberal humanism, although that is open to doubt. It is, perhaps, easier to be caught.

While we're talking about what is 'more attractive', it is appropriate to mention the sexual abuse of children by people with status within

---

5. Gil, *Have Life Abundantly*, 59–61.

the Church, surely about as repulsive as it is possible to be. Pope Francis calls it 'leprosy infecting the Church'. Frank Gil, rightly in my judgement, ranks it secondary in his context, because it is not part of the *structure* of the Roman Church. Gil's reflections concern two cancers in the structure of the Church. The sexual abuse of children is not part of that structure. Alas, it is part of sin. Alas, in those countries where media coverage is widespread—and Australia can be proud to be one—it is utterly repulsive, so very far from attractive.

At the same time, it is important to recognize that a 'leprosy infecting the Church' is an understatement. Massively regrettable as it is, it must be admitted that it is a leprosy infecting the human race. Few institutions are free of it. Families are certainly not free of it. An article in *The Age* newspaper in Melbourne (29 JUL 13) reports that 'statistics from over 3500 incoming calls to the Adults Surviving Child Abuse helpline … show that 63 per cent of callers said they were abused by someone from their immediate family.' This is not a surprise to people close to the situation; many rate the percentage more highly. It is horrifying and how we deal with it is a massive problem we have yet to face.

What has been another occasion for my own surprise and horror comes from a recent book by retired lawyer Kieran Tapsell, *Potiphar's Wife*. Tapsell begins his book with a 'Chronology of Church Response to Clergy Sexual Abuse of Children'.[6] In 153 AC (= After Christ) the *Didache* prohibited adult men from sex with boys. In 1140, Gratian, the great figure in the history of canon law, supported the policy that clergy who rape young boys should be punished by the civil law. In 1866, under Pius IX, the soliciting of sex in the confessional was put under absolute secrecy because of the seal of the confessional. In the seven centuries before that Tapsell quotes numerous popes and Councils insisting that guilty priests be handed over to the secular authority for punishment. From the mid-eighteenth century, the same insistence is not repeated and secrecy replaced secular punishment. A 1922 document, *Crimen sollicitationis*, was concerned primarily with trials for allegations of seduction in the confessional—naturally a matter which, because of the confessional, would be overwhelmingly concerned for secrecy. It ordered that local proceedings were to

---

6. Kieran Tapsell, *Potiphar's Wife: The Vatican's Secret and Child Sexual Abuse* (Adelaide, SA: ATF Press, 2014), 9–48.

be subject to the secret of the Holy Office (various names, among them pontifical secrecy), the breach of which involved automatic excommunication that could only be lifted by the pope personally, an extremely severe penalty for any bishop. Much later, Paul VI declared that the excommunication was no longer automatic, but could still be imposed. The last four brief paragraphs of the document (§§71-74) define the 'foulest crime' (*crimen pessimum*) to include, among other things, a homosexual act by a cleric and sexual abuse of pre-adolescent children of either sex (firstly, same sex; later, either sex). Everything that had been laid down in the previous seventy paragraphs is valid for the *crimen pessimum*. 'Everything' includes the silence, the secrecy.

What I find puzzling and horrifying is that the central organs of a Church that had for centuries advocated handing over the guilty to the secular arm should in the last century or so forbid any involvement of the secular arm. I find it puzzling that the practice of the past should be so resolutely overthrown. I find this horrifying because it makes clear that protecting the reputation of the Church was given priority over the needs of victims. Much has changed in the understanding of paedophilia in the last fifty years. The overwhelming tsunami of accusations of child abuse could not have been foreseen a century ago. But for all that, the putting of Church respectability above the pastoral needs of victims is so contrary to all that the Church stands for as to be unthinkable.

What is utterly repulsive and reprehensible will keep many away from the Roman Catholic Church for a long time to come. There is hope that the 'whisper of spirit' will be drawing people toward togetherness with others, will be deepening awareness of spirit within us. There is hope that the sexual abuse of children will be eliminated from Church circles, whatever is done elsewhere. To my mind, there is likely to be a need for a global body that sustains the togetherness and supports the whisper of spirit in human hearts. What is present now in smaller groups needs to be shared in global awareness. The word we use for that global body is the Church. It will have the core faith in a God who became human because God is committed to us and loves us. It will have the correlative commitment to others for justice and fairness because we share God's commitment to them. The whisper of spirit is in each of us; it needs to be amplified and supported by what we call a Church. The smouldering in each of us needs to be fanned into flame. There is hope that such a Church would belong to its people and be sensitive to the people of God. There is hope that such a Church would be free of the clericalism and monarchism that Frank Gil pillories. There is hope.

Charles Taylor, in *A Secular Age*, pays considerable attention to the matter of ethics. In my judgement, the issue of religious faith is quite separate from issues of ethics. That is not to say that faith is devoid of ethics; that would be unbelievably stupid. People of religious faith will certainly be committed to their understanding of ethics. However it is also clear that people of faith will probably be committed to *different* understandings of ethics. Faith is not linked to any specific understanding of ethics. Faith is not necessarily prior to ethics; it is simply separate from ethics. When looking at what is attractive about a worldview with faith, a particular system of morals or ethics may invite someone's commitment. It may sit comfortably with the idea of religious faith; in matters of detail, there need not be any direct connection. Folk of faith don't have to be good folk. Their faith is only that God loves them. After that, it is God's problem.

This is not to say that the actions of the vast numbers of good priests doing good things, and the vast number of good people in the Christian Churches working respectfully and lovingly for the poor and going to great lengths to diminish suffering and lessen inequality is not immensely admirable—and attractive. Such actions may attract to faith. Faith's commitment to belief in a God who loves may be affected by attraction. It is an independent action.

Frank Gil writes wisely about the place of faith in God. He writes wisely about the potential shapes of a future Church. He leaves the details to those whose Church it will be. His emphasis is indeed wise: the 'grass roots' must grab what can be theirs; it would be unholy folly to wait to be given it.

Some Thoughts for a Theologically Fuller Eucharistic Prayer

(Original: Gil, *Have Life Abundantly*)

We thank you, loving God our Sustainer—our loving Creator, loving Saviour, and loving Sanctifier—we thank you that you are and that you have brought us into being.

We thank you, our loving God, for all of your creation. For our universe, so vast we see only the twinkling of its stars. Within our universe, we thank you for our own world that we can see and experience at closer hand, with its oceans, its mountains, the masses of its people, bringing home to us just how small we are—and yet how loved by you. And within this world, but completely unseen by us, we thank you for the mystery inside atoms and the wonder of the utterly small. Beyond all this, we marvel at the mystery of human beings, each one of us, and the mystery of the bonding that can be between us. And so we thank you, creator God, that you have given us life.

We thank you, our loving God, that you so loved us as to become one of us, that you, our God, became a human being in Jesus. We marvel in wonder at the love that led you to join us, as Jesus God. Jesus was a helpless infant as each of us was; Jesus became a child as each of us did; Jesus grew as we too grow; Jesus lived our life as we do, in all of its possibilities, its uncertainties, and all its limits. You see a value in our lives that we so often do not see so fully. In Jesus, you emptied yourself and did not fill the void with comfort, prestige, or power. Jesus committed himself to a life that took him to the cross and Jesus did not abandon that commitment, that life. You do not abandon us. We thank you.

We thank you, our loving God, that you so love us as to be present with us now as your Spirit in our midst. We do not touch or taste or see—we believe. Believing, we trust that you are with us wherever we are, whatever we are doing, whatever is being done to us. You are with us in joy and rejoicing; you are with us in sorrow and sadness; you are with us in so much that is simply ordinary—and you see into the ordinary with a love that is unfailing. By your love: heal what is hurt; straighten what is bent; warm what is frigid; water what is parched. We thank you for the living waters welling up within us; may we have life and have it abundantly.

And so, loving God, we give you thanks and we pray:

> Holy, holy, holy Lord, God of life and love, heaven and earth are full of your glory. Hosanna in the highest. Blessed are those who rejoice in the love of the Lord. Hosanna in the highest.

Blessed are you, loving God, that at a moment in human time, in the person of your Beloved, our Jesus God, you entered our human race. You, the vast and mysterious God, were born as we are born, fragile and utterly dependent, defenceless and utterly vulnerable.

Blessed are you, loving Jesus. You walked the paths of Palestine. You spoke of God in words of power, in words that moved and touched, that rang true. You had a knack for parables that stayed with people, teasing at their minds, tugging at their hearts. You put your arms around children, you cured lepers and healed the sick, and you steadied the uncertain.

You worked wonders often in the drabness of our world. You restored outsiders to community; you restored the troubled to peace; you gave sight to the blind, freedom to the crippled, and life to the dead. You gave health to the many with illnesses. You made wine, you multiplied bread, and you walked on the sea and calmed the storm.

Yet, when the time came and you arrived at Jerusalem for the festival, you did not take refuge in wonders. You suffered the agony of fear in advance, you suffered the indignity of capture and imprisonment, you experienced the majesty of justice in all its corruption, and like a common criminal you carried your cross and you died on it.

In this liturgy, we are grateful to remember your commitment to us, Jesus God, your love for us.

And so we turn and ask, loving God, may your Spirit come upon this bread and wine and let it become for us now what it was for Jesus and his followers in that final meal before he suffered.

For on the eve of his passion, at the time of the Jewish Passover, Jesus gathered in an upper room with his closest followers and shared a last supper.

> During the supper, he took some of the bread, blessed it, broke it, and passed it among them, saying: Take and eat, all of you; this is my body, which will be given up for you.
> At the end of the supper, he took the final ritual cup of wine.
> He blessed it and passed it among them, saying: Take and drink, all of you, this is the cup of my blood, the blood of the new and unending covenant; it will be shed for you and for everyone, for complete union with God. Do this in memory of me.

As we do this in memory of Jesus God, we remember that not only are we forgiven, but we are loved. So we join with the Church and say:

> When we eat this bread and drink this cup
> we proclaim your death Lord Jesus
> until you come in glory.

Loving God, as we have joined with your Church remembering the passion and death of Jesus God, the sign of your great love for us, may this bread and wine indeed be both the memorial and the presence of Jesus God and may all of us who share in it be filled with the life of your holy Spirit.

We ask you, loving God, to remember your Church throughout our world, those who are its leaders in various ways and at various levels and places, those whose faith is strengthened in your Church, those whose faith is troubled by your Church. Above all, we ask you, loving God, to remind us of all those you love: all those who have never heard of you; all those who are too familiar with what they hear; all those who reject you because of what they hear and see; and all those throughout our world who suffer powerlessness and oppression, symbolised for us in the biblical images of the widow, the orphan, and the stranger. May we remember them and be open to your invitation to be with them in what can only be a pale imitation of your love for them.

    We ask you, loving God, that we may live richly wherever we find ourselves. We realise and rejoice that we belong among the many—in fact, the all—whom you love. We believe ourselves honoured and precious in your sight, so we are proud and we give you thanks. May the pilgrimage of our lives culminate with you, with Mary the mother of Jesus, with Jesus' friends, and with that strange bunch who were his apostles. May we join with you, with all those the church has singled out as saints and role models, and with all of those whenever and wherever they may have been who have tried to live their lives as best they knew how, may we join in worship with all of them, directing our worship above all through Jesus Christ,

> For through him, and with him, and in him, in the unity of the Holy Spirit, all glory and honour is yours, all loving God, for ever and ever.

And a final reflection:
The core of the core: why did Jesus Christ die on the cross? To live a very ordinary life to the full, in those Roman days living by the principles that were his. And why that? Well, that raises the biggest, most unbelievable mystery of all—reason enough, firstly, to water down if not to reject Christian faith, and secondly reason enough to involve sin by us, so much more tangible than love by God for us. Death goes along with life; Jesus lived like us and died like us. The best available reason I know for the life, death, and resurrection of Jesus Christ: to show us two realities, two mysteries. First, the unbelievable value that God sets on an ordinary human life, by living one— the life of Jesus, son of God and son of Mary. Second, the commitment that God has to us ordinary humans, the love God has for us (see Psalm 8). Nothing at all to do with sin or guilt. Nothing to do with atoning for sin. Nothing less than the love of God for us, sinners though we are. From the gospel: 'No one has greater love than this, to lay down one's life for one's friends' (John 15:13); we have to have a life before we can lay it down. If we want sacrifice, God's sacrifice was becoming human. What do we know of the Father? 'Whoever has seen me has seen the Father' (John 14:9); what we know of the Father, we have learned from Jesus—and Jesus loved.

Index of Biblical References

Genesis
1–11	49, 314, 353, 354
1	277, 283, 285
1:1–2:4a	283
1:2	282, 284
1:3	284
1:11	285
1:24	165, 285
1:25	165, 285
1:26–26	284
1:26	165, 458
2–3	49, 170, 171, 383
2	277, 283, 284, 290
2:2	283, 285
2:3	285
2:4b–25	283
2:5	284
2:7	283, 284
2:18	399
2:19	283
2:22	284
3:7	314
3:8	284
3:14–19	314
3:15	455
4	171
4:22	368
5	171
6:4–9:17	305
6:5–9:17	172, 353, 355f
6:5–8	172
6:5–7	413
6:5	358, 362, 413
6:7	458
6:9–22	172
6:9	362
6:11	362
6:12	356
6:13	413
6:18	356
8:21–22	172, 290, 413
8:21	314, 357, 358, 362, 408n, 413, 458
9:1–17	172, 290, 357, 413
9:1–7	413
9:6	314
9:8–17	358
9:11	413
9:17	356
10–11	171
10:8–30	171
12:2	159
12:1–3	175
12:3b	175
12:10–20	135
16	167
16:9	167
17	126

17:1–2	175	11:10	436
18:8b	175	12:26	137n
21	167	13–14	167
22	126, 172	13:14	137n
22:2	159	13:17–14:31	291
22:14	172, 242n	14:1	307
22:15–18	172	14:2	167, 291
22:18b	172	14:4	307, 436
22:19	172, 242n	14:8	436
25–Numbers 10	353	14:17	436
25:21	86	14:19–20	167, 291
26:4b	175	14:20	306
27	167	14:21	167, 291, 306
28:1–9	167	14:24	291
28:14	175	14:25b	291
30:25–31:18	112	14:27	167, 291
30:25–34	112, 114	14:30	307
30:25	116	15	316, 359
30:32–34	112	15:1–18	167
30:32–33	112, 117	16:3	292
30:32	113, 116	19–24	316
30:33	117	19:1–2	359
30:35–42	112, 115	19:3–6	316
30:40	117	19:3b–9a	176
30:43	112	19:5	176
31:1–2	112, 114	19:5a	316
31:3–16	112, 116	19:9a	176
31:17–18	112, 114	20:22–23:33	169
37:21–35	252n	20:22–23:32	359
		23:23	432
Exodus		24	359
1–2	315	24:3–8	316
3:5	428n	24:15–18	359
3:8	432	25–Numbers 10	316, 317, 359
3:17	432	25–40	317
4:21	436	25:8	359
9:12	436	25:14	359
10:20	436	25:28	359
10:27	436	26:11	359

Index of Biblical References

26:15–30	359	6:20	137n
27:7	359	6:20–25	224
29:45–46	359	7:1–4	441
29:45	359	7:1	427, 432
32	414	7:2	440
33:2	432	7:6	176
34:11	432	7:26	440
34:7a	132	8:1	335n
34:7b	132	8:2	335n
40:34	359	8:3	335n
		9:3	462

Leviticus

		11:1–7	291
1–16	169	12–26	169, 322, 347
17–26	169	12:1	322
25	311, 362	13	462
		13:3	441

Numbers

		13:6	441
10:12–28	313, 361	13:7–8	441
10:13	361	13:13–19	441, 441n
10:14–27	361	13:13	462
10:28	361	13:14	441
11:5	292	13:16	440
14	414	13:18	440
14:11–12	292, 414	14:2	176
14:13–25	414	17:7	441
14:22	292, 414	17:12	441
21:35	440	17:19	335n
		17:20	335n

Deuteronomy

		19:19	441
1–4	322	20:17	434, 440
1:4	426n	21:18–21	462
1:28	437	21:18	441n
2:34	440	21:21	441
3:3	440	22:21	441
3:6	440	22:22	441
4	322	22:24	441
4:27–31	333n	24:7	441
4:44–30:20	322, 326, 347	26:18	176
4:7	285	26:5–9	224

28:36–37	333n	2–11	322, 326, 327, 347, 447
28:63–68	333n		
29:7	333n, 426n	2–6	337
30:1–10	333n	2:1–9	425
31	322	2:1	425
31:1	347	2:2	426
31:2	347	2:9	425, 426
31:4	426n	2:10–11	426, 439
31:7–9a	347	2:10	291, 426, 438, 439
31:10	347	2:10a	426
31:11a*b	347	2:10b	347
31:12b–13	347	2:11	439
31:24–26a	347	2:11b	426
32:51	431	2:12–24	425
34	322, 327n	2:15	429
34:1a*b*	347	2:17–21	426
34:4–6	347	2:21	428
34:5	438n	2:24	425
		3–7	424
Joshua		3–4	49n, 129, 147, 423, 426
1–12:23	323		
1	320, 322	3:1	426, 427n
1:1	425, 438n	3:2–17	427
1:1–11	440	3:2–3	347
1:1–6	347, 439	3:3	427
1:5	438	3:4	427
1:7–9	322, 336, 337	3:4b	347
1:7	335n	3:5	427, 432
1:8	335n	3:6	347
1:10–18	347	3:7–8	427, 438, 439
1:10–11	439	3:7	347
1:12–18	439	3:8	347
1:13	438n	3:10	427, 432
1:15	438n	3:13–16	427
1:23–25	428	3:13	347
2	423, 424, 425, 428, 429, 430, 432, 434, 436, 437, 439, 440	3:14	347
		3:15	347
		3:17	347

4:1–10a	427	6:10	429
4:3	347	6:12b	347
4:6–7	427	6:13	429
4:6	137n	6:13a	347
4:8	427	6:16	428
4:9	347, 427	6:16a	347
4:10	347	6:17–19	429
4:10b	426, 438	6:17–18	429
4:11–12	427	6:17	428, 429, 434
4:12	347, 439	6:18	429, 434
4:13	426, 438	6:19	429, 439
4:14–24	427	6:20	428
4:14	347, 427, 438, 439	6:20a	429
4:18	347, 427	6:20b	429
4:19	427	6:21–24a	428, 429
4:20–24	427	6:21	428, 430, 434
4:21	137n, 436n	6:24b–27	429
4:23	291, 426	6:24b–25	439
4:24	347	6:25	429
5	427f, 439	6:26	347, 429, 437
5:1	428, 437, 438	6:27	428, 438, 439
5:2–9	428	7–8	430
5:4	347	7	423, 429, 430, 431, 432
5:6	347	7:1–26	431
5:7	347	7:1	431, 432, 434
5:10–12	428	7:3	431
5:13–15	428	7:4	431
6	49n, 423, 428	7:6–15	431
6:1–2	428, 430	7:7	431
6:1	428	7:9	431
6:2	293, 428, 438	7:10–15	431
6:3–20	129, 147, 249	7:11	431, 434, 439
6:4–5	429	7:12	434
6:4	429	7:13	434
6:4a*b	347	7:15	431, 434, 439
6:6	347, 429	7:16–26	431
6:8	347, 429	7:19	431
6:9a	347		

7:20	431	10:a	49n,
7:26	431	10:1–27	433, 435
8–10	423	10:1–2	433
8	49n, 430, 432	10:1	293, 432, 434, 436
8:1–29	430	10:2	428
8:1–2	293	10:3	433
8:1a	347	10:5	428, 433
8:2	430	10:6–7	433, 434, 436
8:3–9	430	10:6	436
8:5	430, 431, 432	10:7	436
8:6	430, 431, 432	10:8	436
8:22	435	10:9	433, 436
8:24–29	430	10:10–14	433
8:24	435	10:14	433
8:26	434	10:15	49n, 433
8:27	430	10:16–27	293
8:30–35	347, 431, 432	10:16–21	433
8:31	438n	10:20	436n
8:33	438n	10:23	434
9	432	10:24	433
9:1–2	432, 433	10:25	49n, 347, 433
9:1	432, 436	10:27	436n
9:3–9	432	10:28–41	434, 435, 436, 437, 439, 440
9:3–4a*	428		
9:3	432	10:28–39	434n, 435
9:9b	347	10:28	434, 435
9:10	347, 432, 433, 439	10:30	435
9:11–15a	432	10:32	434, 435
9:12	436n	10:33	435
9:15b	432, 433	10:35	434, 435
9:16–17	432	10:37	434
9:18–21	432, 433	10:39	434, 435
9:22–23	432	10:40–42	428
9:24	433	10:40–41	435
9:24*	432	10:40	435, 446
9:25*–27a	432	10:41	435
9:27b	347, 342, 433	10:42–43	433, 434, 435
10	433	10:42	433

10:43	433, 434, 436	13:1	446
11–12	423, 435	13:1bb	337
11	446	13:1–21:45	337
11:1–8a	437	13:8–32	439
11:1–2	428, 438	13:8	438n
11:1	432, 436	14:4	436n
11:3	434, 436	14:6a*b–15a	347
11:4–8a	438	14:7	438n
11:6	436	14:8	436n
11:8	435	14:18	436n
11:8b–15	436, 437, 439, 440	18:7	439
11:10	436n	21:1–42	347
11:11	434, 435	21:15–21	437
11:12	434, 435, 438n	21:43–45	438, 440
11:14	435	22:2	438n
11:15	347	22:4	438n
11:16–20	428	22:5	438n
11:16–19	436, 437, 438	22:6	438, 440
11:20	434, 436	22:7–34	347
11:20b	347	22:7–9	439
11:21–23a	347	22:10–34	439
11:21–22	437	22:16	431
11:21	434	22:20	431
11:22	437	22:22	431
11:23	347, 436, 437, 438, 439, 446	22:31	431
		23	320, 322, 325, 326, 333, 337, 339, 348, 440, 446
11:23a*	438n, 439		
12	320, 322	23:1–6	337
12:1–6	437, 439	23:7	440, 447
12:6	438n	23:11–13	333n
12:7–24	432, 437	23:12–13	447
12:7–8a	437	23:12	440
12:8	432, 437	23:15–16	333n
12:8b	436	23:16	431
12:9–24	437	24	322, 337, 348
13–22	322, 347	24:1	427
13–21	337	24:2–13	224
13	327n, 446		

24:6	291	3:5–6	441
24:11	293, 432	3:5	436
24:29–31	342n	3:6	348
24:31	441	3:7–11	327, 328, 348
		3:12–15a	348
Judges		3:30b	348
1–2	337	4	425
1:1–2:9	337	4:1a	348
1:1–2:5	322, 348	4:2–3a	348
1	49n,	4:2	436
1:26	430	4:4b	327n, 348
2	447	4:23–24	436
2:1–5	441, 447	5:10–11	154n
2:6–16	320	5:31b	348
2:6–11	327, 328, 348	6:1	348
2:7–10	323	6:6b–10	348
2:7	324, 328, 441	7	425
2:9	328	8:27b–28	348
2:10	324, 328, 342n	8:30–35	348
2:11–1 Sam 7	323	9:1–5	87
2:11ff	320, 327, 342n	10:6–16	322, 348
2:11–12	324	11	327n
2:12–13	348	11:29	129, 148
2:14–16	327, 328, 348	11:30–31	129, 148
2:17	337	12:9–11	348
2:18–19	320, 327, 328, 348	13:1	348
2:20–3:6	320	13:2–16:31	322, 348
2:20–23	441, 447	13:5	129, 148
2:20–21	337	16:28	129, 148
2:20	348	17–21	322, 348
2:23	337	20:16	63, 255n
3–8	235	21	49n,
3–9	322, 327, 439		
3–12	326, 348	**1 Samuel**	
3	425	1–2 Kgs 10	330
3:1–3	441	1–16	328
3:1–2	447	1–12	348s
3:3–6	447	1–7	384
3:4	441	1–4	326n

1–3	384, 386	7:2–15	338
1:1–4:1a	348	7:13	168
1	170	7:17	338
1:18	165	8–12	323
1:22	67n, 78n, 254n	8:1–11:15*	342n
2	385, 386n	8	329, 393
2:12–17	385	8:1–22	142, 322, 348
2:22–25	385	8:1–3	142
2:25	91n	8:1–5	168, 338
2:25b	348	8:3	308
2:27–36	338, 385	8:6–22a	339
2:31–32	385n	8:7–8	143,
2:34–35	348	8:7	142
3	386n	8:22	142, 143, 168
3:11–14	339	8:22b	338
4–7	326n	9	168, 308
4–6	384, 386	9:1–10:16	50, 322, 326n, 330, 348, 393
4	172, 385, 386		
4:1b–7:1	330, 348	9:15–17	168
4:1b–2	172	9:16	251n, 308
4:3–9	172	9:16b	338
4:3	172, 194	10:1	308
4:3a	172	10:1b	338
4:4b	338	10:16b	338
4:6–9	173	10:17–27	308, 393
4:10–11	172	10:17–27a	322, 348
4:11b	338	10:17–25	329
4:12–18	172	10:17	338
4:17b	338	10:19	308
4:19a	338	10:19b–27a	338
4:21b	338	10:23	69n, 254
4:22a	338	10:24	168
4:19–22	172	10:27b–11:15	326n, 330, 348
7–12	49n, 167, 393	11	168, 251n, 393
7–8	167	11:1–15	322
7	308, 322, 393	11:12–14	338
7:1–8:22	142	11:15	168
7:2–17	348	11:28	254n

Reference	Pages
12	168, 320, 324, 325, 326, 329, 333, 339, 393
12:1–25	322, 339, 348
12:12	168
12:25	333n
13–2 Kgs 25	323
13–2 Kgs 8	323
13–2 Sam 20	349
13–14	330
13–15	326n, 342, 349
13:1	338, 349
13:13–14	339
14	431, 438
14:3	338
14:18	338
14:47–52	338
14:50–51	257n
15	67, 143, 330, 445
15:1–16:3	339
15:1–35	50
15:3	446
15:25	143
15:26	143
15:21	143
15:22	447
15:29	143
15:31	143
15:33	446
16–18	49n, 53, 63, 76n, 387f
16	246, 383n
16:1–13	63, 67, 248, 272, 326n, 330, 349, 387
16:1–11	389
16:2	388
16:11	387
16:11–12	254
16:12–18	389
16:12	387
16:14–2 Sam 5:25	326n, 330, 349
16:14–2 Sam 5:12	322
16:14–18:30	129, 239f, 247, 248, 262, 263, 272
16:14–18:16	63f, 71, 269n
16:14–17:11	264, 269
16:14–23	53, 64, 67, 77, 78n, 248, 250, 261, 263, 264, 270, 383n, 387
16:14	67, 78, 246, 247, 248, 251, 253, 261, 264, 271, 392
16:15–16	251, 264
16:15	248n, 388
16:16	388
16:17–23	251, 263
16:18	64n, 75n, 262n, 269
16:19–24	389
16:19–22	257
16:21	64n, 67
16:23	388n
16:24	388
16:25	388
16:32	387
16:48a	389
16:48b	390
16:49	389
16:50	390
16:51	389, 390
17–18	168, 387n

17	64, 67n, 92n, 383n, 387	17:19–24	77
		17:19	64, 76n
17:1–54	249, 251, 264	17:20b	65, 77n
17:1–23	256	17:21–31	64, 66
17:1–11	65, 67, 77n, 78n, 249, 387n	17:21b	66
		17:23–24	261
17:1–3	256, 264	17:23	64, 65, 76n, 77n, 92n, 245n
17:1	246, 248, 261, 392		
17:2	64, 76n	17:24–40	256
17:4–51	264	17:24–30	264, 267
17:4–11	256	17:24–31	256
17:4–10	264	17:24–25	64, 76n
17:4–7	246	17:24	246, 253, 256, 261, 272
17:4	65, 76n, 92n, 245n		
17:6	65	17:25–31	256
17:5	64	17:25–30	261, 270
17:9	68	17:25–26	263
17:10–11	261	17:25	66, 247, 262n, 269
17:10	69n	17:26	53, 67, 69n, 130, 144
17:11–40	264		
17:11	68, 77, 249, 253, 265, 266, 268, 272	17:29b–30	66
		17:30	66
		17:31–39	257
17:12–31	64, 67, 71n, 77, 264, 387n	17:31	53, 66n, 144, 253, 264, 267, 271
17:12–30	79n, 144	17:32–54	67n, 264
17:12–23	256, 264, 269	17:32–40	64, 65, 77n, 78, 256, 264, 387n
17:12–15	246		
17:12	53, 64, 76n, 77, 249	17:32–39	65, 77n, 383n
		17:32–37	261, 270
17:15–16	54, 66n	17:32	68, 77, 246, 253, 265, 266, 268
17:15	64, 76n, 144, 256, 258, 260, 271, 392		
		17:33–35	76n
		17:33	67n, 68, 78n, 254
17:16	64, 76n, 144, 246, 252, 256, 261, 271, 392	17:34–37	68
		17:34–35	75, 254
		17:36–37	129
17:17–19	66	17:36	69

17:37	68, 144, 254, 269	17:55–18:11	257f
17:37a	69	17:55–18:5	66, 144, 264, 270
17:40	67n, 79n	17:55–18:6aa	77n
17:41	387n	17:55–18:6a*	390
17:41–54	256	17:55–18:9	249
17:41–51a	264	17:55–18:11	249
17:41–47	256, 264	17:55–58	64, 77, 246, 249, 258, 261, 264
17:41	77n, 255, 263		
17:42–48a	65, 77n, 387n	17:55	65, 246, 249, 267
17:42	254	17:57–58	257
17:43–44	69	17:57	270
17:43	255	17:57b	65, 77n
17:45–47	129, 148	17:58	53, 249
17:47	79, 254	17:58a	390n
17:48–51	264	18	246
17:48–51a	256	18:1–6a	258
17:48	264	18:1–5	64, 71n, 246, 264
17:48a	70n	18:1	249, 258, 264
17:48b	70n, 77n, 144, 263, 387n	18:2	257, 258, 264
		18:3–4	258, 265
17:49	65, 70n, 77n, 264, 387n	18:5	65, 249, 258, 265, 267, 271
17:50–51	261, 264	18:6–16	265
17:50	65, 77, 144, 250, 263, 264, 269, 387n	18:6–13	265
		18:6–11	258
		18:6–9	258, 265
17:51–54	65, 70, 77n, 387n	18:6	65, 77n, 249
17:51	65, 77n, 250	18:6a	263
17:51b–54	267	18:6a*	66n
17:54	392	18:6a*b–9	387n
17:55–18:6a	387n	18:6a*–9	390
17:55	267	18:6–9	64
17:55–58	383n	18:6a*–9	65, 77n
17:61a	264, 264	18:8	70, 258, 261
17:51b–54	256	18:9	271
17:52–54	246	18:10–11	65, 66n, 77n, 258, 263, 265, 387, 390
17:54	249, 270		
17:54a	77n		

Index of Biblical References

18:10	246, 249	18:41	66
18:12–16	249, 258f	18:48b	66
18:12–13	265	18:50	66
18:12	259	18:55–58	66
18:12a	70, 77n, 387n, 390	19	65, 77n
18:12b	65, 66n, 77n, 263, 271, 387n, 390	19:1–7	365, 373
		19:3	371
		19:3a	373
18:13–16	70, 387n, 390	19:3b	373
18:13	77n, 259	19:4–7	373
18:13b	70, 259	19:4b–5	373
18:14–16	259, 261, 265	19:4b	373
18:14	70, 80n, 259, 265, 269	19:7	373
		19:8–22	373
18:14b	71n	19:9–10	65, 77n, 80n
18:15	70, 259, 265	19:11–17	80n, 145, 365, 366n, 367, 368, 373n
18:16	70, 259, 265		
18:16b	70		
18:17–30	249, 259f, 263, 265	19:11	145, 367
		19:11a	368
18:17–29	64	19:11b	368
18:17–19	65, 77n, 144, 247, 260, 265, 387n, 390	19:12a	369
		19:13	367
		19:14	368n, 369
18:17	259	19:14b	368
18:20–29	247, 260, 265	19:15	146, 368n
18:20–29a	263	19:15a	146
18:20–27	365, 369	19:15b	146
18:20–21a	387n	19:16	367, 369
18:21	249	19:40–42	373n
18:21b	65, 66n, 77n, 263	20	49n, 144, 370, 373
18:22–29a	387n	20:1–42	80n, 365
18:26b	369	20:10	371
18:28	263, 272	20:11–17	372n
18:29b–30	65, 66n, 77n, 144, 387n, 390	20:12–17	338
		20:18–22	145
18:30	247, 260, 265	20:19	372
18:31	66	20:20–22	371

20:23	372n	24:6	58, 147
20:25	257n	24:7	58, 147
20:36–37	145	24:8	58, 374
20:36a	371n	24:8a	146
20:36b–39	371	24:9–23	59
20:36b	372n	24:11–12	58
20:37b	371	24:12	59
20:38	145, 371, 372n	24:16	374
20:40–42	145, 372n	24:17	148
20:40	372	24:18–21	60
20:41–42	371	24:18–19	338
20:42b	338	24:20a	338
21:5	67n, 78n	24:20b–23a	338
22:6–23	88n	25:2–42	135
22:6–19	365, 369	25:21–22	338
22:8	369	25:23b	338
22:9	369	25:24b–26	338
22:18–19	369	25:26–31	60
22:18b	338	25:28–34	338
22:19	339	25:30–35	87
23	60	25:39a	338
23:1–14	80n	26	59, 60, 62, 373, 391
23:16–18	338		
23:17	60	26:1–2	60
23:19	60	26:5	257n
23:22	60	26:7	257n
23:24b–28	60	26:14–15	257n
24	59, 60, 62, 130, 373, 391	26:17	148
		26:19–20	89
24–26	53	26:19	91n
24:1–22	365	26:21–25	60
24:2–3	146	28:17–19a	339
24:3–8	57	30:16–17	446
24:3	148	31	327n
24:4–7	130	31:1–7	80n
24:5	58	31:2–12	88
24:5a	58, 146	31:12–13	88
24:5b	57		

2 Samuel

1:14–16	87	6	85n, 194, 322
1:25–26	457	6:1–11	85
2:1–24	349	6:2–23	85n
2:4–7	88	6:12–16:	
2:10a	349	17–20a	85
2:11	349	6:20–23	85
2:12–17	254n	6:21	339
2:12–16	67n, 78n	7	85, 175, 322, 323, 335, 336
2:18–23	80n	7:1b	322, 339, 349
3:2–6a	85n, 349	7:6	339
3:9–10	339	7:7a	349
3:12–16	365, 369	7:8b	339
3:13b	369	7:9a	328n
3:14–16a	369	7:11a	322, 339, 349
3:16b	369	7:11b	339
3:17–19	339	7:12b–13a	322, 349
3:28–30	339	7:13	339
3:32–30	80n	7:15b	328n
4:2b–4	339	7:16	339
4:5–12	80n	7:18–29	335
4:9–12	87	7:18–21	339
5	85	7:20–21	328n
5:1–3	85	7:22–24	322, 339, 349
5:1–2	339	7:25–29	339
5:2	259	8	85, 322
5:2a	68, 70	8:1a	339
5:2b	63	8:1a*	349
5:4–5	85, 339, 349	8:1–14*	349
5:6–10	85	8:11	429
5:6	130, 149	8:14b–15	339
5:11–25	85	8:14b	349
5:11	339	8:15–1 Kgs 2:1a	331n
5:12a	339	8:15–18	349
5:12b	339	8:16–18	85n
5:13–16	85n, 349	9	85
5:17a	335	9–20	80, 322, 326n, 330
6–7	326n, 330, 349		

9:1–20:22	85n	19:28	175
9:1–13	175	19:29	85n, 339
9:1	339	19:35	111, 154
9:7	339	19:36	111
9:10	339	20:22	90, 94
9:11b	339	21–24	83f, 85, 94, 322, 383
9:13a	339	21	84n, 87
10	85	21:1–14	84, 85, 86, 87, 91, 92
11–12	194, 368n	21:2b	339
11:2–12:24	328	21:7	175, 339
11:2	130, 149	21:8–22	92n
11:4	130, 149	21:12	88
11:5–6	130, 149	21:14	84n, 85n, 86, 94
11–20	92, 130, 149	21:14b	91
11:1	85	21:15ff	84n, 85n
11:27	80n	21:15–22	88f, 92
12:1–14	338	21:15–17	85
12:*7b–10	339	21:17	89, 92n
12:13–14	339	21:18–21	85
12:24	80n	21:21–31	90
12:29–31	85	21:22	88
13–20	xiii	21:24–25	90
14	154	22	84n, 85n
14:9	339	22:1–23:7	89
15ff	85n	22:1–51	85, 89
15:3–4	90	22:1	89, 339
15:25–26	91n, 339	22:2	85n, 91
16:5–13	84	22:22–25	339
16:5–8	272	22:51	94, 339
16:7–8	85n, 391	23:1–7	84n, 85, 90, 92n
16:10–12	91n	23:1	89, 90, 94
16:11–12	89, 339	23:4	90
17:14	80n	23:5	90
17:15–20	130, 149	23:8–39	84n, 85, 90, 92
17:17	131, 149	23:8ff	84n
18:2–4	89	24	49n, 84n, 85n, 87
18:3	92		
19:22–23	339		

24:1–25	84, 85, 86, 91, 92	2:27b	349
24:1	84n, 85n, 86n, 339	2:31b–33	339
		2:35b	339
24:1a	85n, 86, 87n, 91	2:27b	339
24:3–4a	339	2:42–45	339
24:10–14	85n, 328n, 339	3–7	322
24:10	91	3:3	349
24:15	92	3:14	333n, 349
24:15a	339	3:15ba	349
24:16a	328n	4:1–5:8	349
24:17–19	328n	4:1–19	173
24:17	91, 339	5:13–18	334n
24:19b	335	5:15–32	349
24:21b	339	6:1	320, 349
19:23b	335	6:11–13	333n
19:25b	335	6:19b	349
24:25	86, 91, 94	7:47–51	349
27:2	91	8	168, 175, 320, 321, 322, 325, 337
1 Kings			
1–2	80, 85n, 322, 326n, 330, 349	8:1b–2a*	349
		8:4b	349
1:30	339	8:7–8	334n
1:35–37	339	8:8	334
1:46–48	339	8:9	349
2:1–2	339	8:14–66	349
2:2*	349	8:14–26	337
2:3–4	335, 349	8:14–21	175
2:3	339	8:23	426
2:4	333n, 335, 337	8:25b	333n
2:4a*b	339	8:28–30a	337
2:4a	339	8:29b–54	343
2:5–11	339	8:46–53	333n
2:11	85	8:53–61	337
2:15b	339	9–2 Kgs 25	323
2:24	339	9	325, 337
2:26b	339	9:1–9	323, 325, 335, 337, 349
2:27	339		

9:2	433	11:38b	332
9:3–5	176	11:38b*–39	336
9:3	335	11:39	177, 336
9:4–9	333n, 335	11:39a	336
9:4–5	335	11:39b	336
9:4	176	11:41–43	349
9:5–7	335	11:41	326, 334n, 349
9:6–9	176, 335	12	323, 329n
9:6	335	12:1–20	131, 149, 350
9:10	349	12:3	131, 149
9:14	349	12:15	337
9:20–22	334n	12:19	334
9:21	334	12:20	131, 149
10:11–12	334n	12:25	350
10:12	334	12:26–31	350
11	325, 329n	12:32–13:32	350
11:1–13	323, 325, 349	13	309, 458
11:26–40	317, 323	13:1–32	338
11:28	67n, 78n	13:33–34	350
11:29–31	337	14	329n
11:29a	349	14:1–18	350
11:29ab*–31	350	14:1–8	338
11:32–33	177	14:7–11	337
11:32	337	14:8b–9a	337
11:33a	337	14:14–16	350
11:33b	337	14:19–21	350
11:34a	337	14:21*	350
11:34b	337	14:22–24	350
11:35a*	337	14:25–28	350
11:35b	337	15:12–13	350
11:36	337	15:15	350
11:36a*b	350	15:16–22	350
11:36b	349	15:27–28	350
11:37	332, 350	15:29	87, 337
11:37a	337	15:30	337
11:37a*b	337	16:1–4	337, 350
11:38–39a	349	16:9–12	350
11:38a*	337	16:12	337

16:13	337	**2 Kings**	
16:15–18	350	1	338
16:21–22	350	1:1	351
16:24	350	1:2–17a*	350
16:31	350	1:2	350
16:34	338, 347, 350	3	131, 149
17–19	350	3:4–8:15	350
17:2–24	338	3:5	351
18:46	297	6:8–24	173
19:11–12a	297	8:19	337
19:12b	297	8:20–22	350
20	329n, 338	8:22	334
20:1–43	350	8:28–29	351
21	131, 149, 350	9–10	329
21:1–16	131, 149	9:1–10:27	350
21:17–29	131, 149	9:7–10a	337
21:18a	337	9:8b–10a	351
21:19b	337	9:36b–37	337
21:20	351	10:1–7	87
21:20b	337	10:10	337
21:21–22	351	10:17	337
21:23	351s	10:27	334
21:24–26	351	10:28–33	351
21:24	337	10:30–31a	337
21:27–29	337	11:1–20	350
22	126, 309, 327n, 329n, 458	11:1	87
22:1–38	338	12:5–17	350
22:1–37	350	12:18–19	350
22:23	458	12:21–22	350
22:24	309	13	131, 149
22:38–40	351	13:3–7	351
22:38	337	13:4–6	337
22:39*	350	13:12	131, 149
22:43	351	13:13	131, 149
22:47	351	13:14–21	350
22:48–50	350	13:14	131, 149
		13:22–25	351
		13:23	337

14:5	350	18–19	341
14:6	351	18:4b	350
14:7	334, 350	18:6–7a	337
14:8–14	350	18:9–11	350
14:12–14	150	18:12	337, 438n
14:15–16	337	18:13–16	350
14:15	131, 149	18:17–20:19	228, 350
14:19–21	349	18:22	416
14:22	350	18:31–32	416
14:25	338, 350	20:17–19	335
14:26–27	337, 351	20:17–18	333n
15:5	350	21:1–18	323, 351
15:10	350	21:2–15	333n
15:12	337, 351	21:3	343n
15:14	350	21:4	337
15:16	350	21:5	343n
15:19–20	350	21:7b–9	337
15:25	350	21:7	343n
15:29	350	21:8–15	341
15:30a	350	21:16	341
15:35b	350	21:10–14	337
15:37	351	21:15–16	337
16:3–4	351	21:23–24	350
16:5–6	350	21:25–26	337
16:6	334	22:3–23:3	323, 350
16:7–18	350	22:3	128
17	326, 337, 339	22:15–20	333n
17:3–6	350	22:16–17	177, 337
17:7ff	320	22:17a	337
17:7–20	323, 325, 351	22:18–20	337
17:12–19	337	22:19b	337
17:19	333n	23:1–38	343
17:21–23	334n, 337	23:2	177
17:23	334	23:3	177
17:24	350	23:4–128	343
17:29–31	350	23:4–15	323, 350
17:32–34a	323, 351	23:4	343n
17:34b–40	351	23:6	343n

23:12	343n	33:13–19	86
23:16–18	323	35:25	111, 154
23:19–20a	323		
23:19	350	**Ezra**	
23:20a	350	8:23	86
23:21–27	323	9:8	437
23:21–23	343		
23:25b–27	333n	**Job**	
23:26–25:30	333n	1:1–2:13	27
23:26–25:26	341	1:1–2:10	31, 32, 43
23:26–27	337	1:1	13
23:28–25:21	343	1:8	13
23:29–30	350	1:9	26, 31, 32
23:33–35	350	1:11	32
24:1–2a*	335, 350	1:15–16	27
24:2–4	343	1:16–17	27
24:2	335, 337	1:17–18	27
24:3–4	337	1:19	27
24:7	350	1:20–22	3, 26
24:10–16	350	1:22	31, 32
24:13–14	343	2:7–8	33
24:17	350	2:10	3, 26, 31, 32
24:19–20	351	2:11–42:9	32, 43
24:20a	337, 343	2:11–13	27
25	327n	2:13	31, 33
25:1–26	323, 351	3–41	31
25:22–30	337	3	25
25:22	128	3:1–41:9	27
25:27–30	175, 323, 351	3:11	3
		3:20	3, 31, 34
1 Chronicles		3:23	34
1	49n,	4:7	40
5:20	86,	4:17	40
		5:8	40
2 Chronicles		5:17–18	15, 40
1:3	438n	7	280
24:6	438n	7:12	280, 290
26:14	63, 255n	7:16	34n

7:16a	35n	38	290
7:17–21	281	38:1–41:34	4, 5
7:20–21	406, 467	38:1–40:2	21, 28
8:3	40	38:1–39:30	6
8:4	41	38:1	5, 28, 29, 32n, 33n, 37
8:6	40, 41		
8:8	40	38:2	4, 6
8:20–21	41	38:4–28	17
9:4–19	2	38:4–7	19
9:12	29	38:4	21, 22
9:13–14	280, 290	38:5	21, 22
9:14	281	38:8–11	19
9:22	42	38:12–38	19
9:24	42	38:21	22
11:3	42	38:37–41	19
12:9	32n	38:39–39:30	17, 19
13:2	41	38:39–41	21
13:7	42	39:19–25	29
13:21	281	40:1–5	28
20:4–5	42	40:1	18, 32n, 33n, 37
21:29–30	293	40:2	24, 25, 32n
21:30	310	40:3–4	39
22:29–30	42	40:3	25, 32n, 33n
25:4	42	40:4	24, 25
25:6	42	40:6–41:34	6, 28
26:6–11	281	40:6–41:4	25
26:12–14	281, 290	40:6	32n, 33n, 37
26:14	29	40:8	6, 25
27:5–6	14	40:9	28
28	4, 25, 27	40:10–14	28
29–31	25	40:16	28
29:1–31:40	4	40:25–41:3	28
31	13	41:1–11	28
31:13	35	41:12	28
31:35–37	4	41:33	29
31:37	282	41:34	6
32–37	25	42:1–6	5, 6, 28,
38–41	25, 281	42:3	4, 6, 17, 39, 43

42:4	37	**Proverbs**	
42:5–6	34, 39	8	304
42:5	5, 6, 7, 29, 31, 34, 36, 39, 43	8:22–31	277, 305
		8:22	290
42:6	6, 7, 14n, 30, 32n, 34, 36, 39, 43	8:31	290
42:7	42	**Ecclesiastes**	
42:7–17	28	2:8	111, 154
42:7–9	4, 6, 7, 27, 33	2:24	471
42:7–8	14	3:13	471
42:7	5, 39,	5:17	471
42:8	5	8:15	471
42:10–17	7, 26		
42:10b–17	31, 32, 43	**Song of Songs**	
42:10	27	4:1–5	278
42:10b	32		
42:12	27	**Isaiah**	
		2:12	165
Psalms		5–10	168
1:6	309	5	22
8	457	5:1–7	168
51:3–5	90	5:7	168
74	279	5:8–24	168
74:3	279	5:25	169
74:7	279	6	168
74:9–12	279	6:1–9:7	169
74:13–14	279	6:9–13	415
74:14	290	6:10	436
74:16–17	279	7:1–8:15	168
89	279	8:16–22	168
89:10	290	9:1–7	168
104	304, 305	9:7	169
104:5–9	277	9:12	169
106:7–12	291	9:17	169
106:22	291	9:21	169
136:4–9	277	10:1–4	169
136:13–15	291	10:4	169
137:8–9	457	11:9	311

19:22	86	**Ezekiel**	
19:24–25	175	5:1–12	415
24:20–27:1	282	14:14	33
24:20	282	14:20	33
24:23	282	47–48	311
27	282		
27:1	283	**Hosea**	
40:2	456	1:9	443
43:4	406	1:10	415, 443
43:25	406, 421	2	22
51	282	3:1	457
51:9–11	282	12	175
54:7–8	415		
54:8	456	**Amos**	
62:5	294	1–2	173, 177, 245n
65:25	311	2:4	177
		3–6	173
Jeremiah		3:3–8	173
2:2	292	3:3–6	173, 177
5	22	3:3–5	173
7–12	309	3:7	177
13:11	294	3:8	173, 174, 177
23:11–17	95	7–9	22, 173
28	22, 309, 458	7:9	315
28:2	458	7:16	315
28:15–17	458	9:14	415
28:15	309		
36	51		
39–41	323, 351		
39:14	128		
40:5	128		
40:9	128		
40:11	128		
41:2	128		

Lightning Source UK Ltd.
Milton Keynes UK
UKHW010621070922
408462UK00002B/237